Depression: Clinical and Research Perspectives

Depression: Clinical and Research Perspectives

Editor: Dustin Layton

AMERICAN
MEDICAL PUBLISHERS
www.americanmedicalpublishers.com

AMERICAN
MEDICAL PUBLISHERS
www.americanmedicalpublishers.com

Cataloging-in-Publication Data

Depression : clinical and research perspectives / edited by Dustin Layton.
p. cm.
Includes bibliographical references and index.
ISBN 978-1-63927-438-3
1. Depression, Mental. 2. Psychology. 3. Psychiatry. 4. Psychotic depression.
5. Clinical psychology. I. Layton, Dustin.
RC537 .D47 2022
616.852 7--dc23

American Medical Publishers,
41 Flatbush Avenue,
1st Floor, New York,
NY 11217, USA

ISBN 978-1-63927-438-3 (Hardback)

Contents

Preface

Over the recent decade, advancements and applications have progressed exponentially. This has led to the increased interest in this field and projects are being conducted to enhance knowledge. The main objective of this book is to present some of the critical challenges and provide insights into possible solutions. This book will answer the varied questions that arise in the field and also provide an increased scope for furthering studies.

Depression is a condition that results in low mood and aversion to activity. It can be long term and short term. Depression can cause sadness, difficulty in thinking and concentration, a feeling of dejection and hopelessness. It also affects a person's behavior, thoughts, motivation, feelings, and sense of well-being. Some factors that cause depression are life events, gender identity and sexuality, medical treatment and substance-abused. The three major types of depression are bipolar disorder, major depressive disorder and persistent depressive disorder. Bipolar disorder is the condition in which a person experiences irregular states of depression and mania. The major depressive disorder is a condition with severe symptoms that disturb the daily life and affects a person's appetite, ability to enjoy life, sleep, work, etc. Depression can be treated with the help of psychotherapy and psychotropic medication, especially antidepressants. This book provides significant information of this condition to help develop a good understanding of depression and related disorders. It presents researches and studies performed by experts across the globe. This book is a vital tool for all researching and studying psychiatry.

I hope that this book, with its visionary approach, will be a valuable addition and will promote interest among readers. Each of the authors has provided their extraordinary competence in their specific fields by providing different perspectives as they come from diverse nations and regions. I thank them for their contributions.

Editor

1

The validity of Posttraumatic Stress Disorder Checklist for DSM-5 (PCL-5) as screening instrument with Kurdish and Arab displaced populations living in the Kurdistan region of Iraq

Hawkar Ibrahim[1,2,3*], Verena Ertl[1,2], Claudia Catani[1,2], Azad Ali Ismail[1,3] and Frank Neuner[1,2]

Abstract

Background: The Posttraumatic Stress Disorder Checklist (PCL) is a valid and reliable self-report measure for the assessment of Posttraumatic Stress Disorder (PTSD). Recently the PCL was updated according to the DSM-5 criteria for PTSD. So far only a few studies have examined the psychometric properties of the PCL-5, and all of these are restricted to populations living in industrialized countries. The aim of this study was to determine the psychometric properties and diagnostic utility of the PCL-5 as a screening instrument for war-affected displaced Kurdish and Arab populations. The specific goal was to determine a contextually valid cut-off score for a probable diagnosis of PTSD.

Methods: The PCL-5 was translated into Arabic and two Kurdish dialects. Trained interviewers administered these translations as assisted self-reports to 206 adults living in camps for displaced people in Iraq, together with depression and war-exposure instruments. Two weeks later, 98 randomly chosen subjects were reassessed by expert clinical psychologists. In the absence of a gold-standard instrument with proven validity in this context, the expert interviewers applied the PCL-5 items in the form of a clinical interview and used a DSM-5-algorithm to determine a diagnosis of PTSD. Receiver operator characteristics (ROC) were performed to determine a valid cutoff-score.

Results: The internal consistency of the PCL-5 was high (alpha = .85) and the instrument showed an adequate convergent validity. Using the cut-off score of 23, the PCL-5 achieved the optimal balance of sensitivity and specificity (area under the curve = .82, $p < .001$; sensitivity = .82, specificity = .70).

Conclusions: Given that the comparison of the two assessments included both a re-test interval and validation by different interviewers, our results indicate that the PCL-5 can be recommended as an assessment and screening instrument for Kurdish and Arab populations.

Keywords: PCL, PTSD, Validation, Arab spring, Displaced people

* Correspondence: hawkar@uni-bielefeld.de
[1]Department of Psychology, Clinical Psychology and Psychotherapy, Bielefeld University, Bielefeld, Germany
[2]vivo international, Konstanz, Germany
Full list of author information is available at the end of the article

Background

Current humanitarian crises are commonly related to civil wars or large-scale natural disasters. Such catastrophes threaten not only the safety and physical integrity of the affected populations, but also their mental health. A key challenge for an evidence-based response is the identification of cases with psychological distress who need assistance to avoid negative long-term outcomes [1]. One of the global hot spots of insurgencies and war is the Middle East region. Since the Arab Spring, which started as a revolutionary wave of demonstrations in the Arab world in 2010 in Egypt, Libya, Yemen, Bahrain, and finally Syria [2], the region has experienced a period of political instability and civil war. The civil war in Syria and Iraq forced many Syrians and Iraqis to flee, either within their own countries or to Lebanon, Jordan, Turkey, and the Kurdistan Region of Iraq (KRI) as well as to Europe [3, 4]. Although it is very likely that this crisis has had a significant impact on the mental health of the affected populations, studies addressing the effects on mental health arising from this disaster are still scarce. So far, only a few studies have systematically addressed the psychological consequences of the civil war and migration that followed the events of the Arab spring. Consistent with previous studies from other war regions, these investigations documented high rates of posttraumatic stress disorder (PTSD) [5–7]. Studies on mental health and violence in Arab and Kurdish populations have applied translated versions of standardized western instruments for the assessment of violence and trauma related disorders although the cut-off-score of these instruments have not been adjusted in the local context [8]. This procedure is critical, since, due to inevitable differences in subtle semantic nuances, the transference of a cutoff score across contexts and populations even with well-translated instruments may lead to considerable over- or underestimations of prevalence rates [9, 10].

In the past decades a range of assessment and screening tools for trauma and related symptoms, including self-report questionnaires and different types of interview methods have been developed (for reviews see [11, 12]). The PTSD Checklist (PCL) [13] is one of the most widely applied self-report measures for assessing PTSD in clinical and research settings. Recently the PCL was updated according to the new diagnostic criteria for PTSD in the Diagnostic and Statistical Manual of Mental Disorders, Fifth Edition (PTSD Checklist for DSM-5; PCL-5) [14]. The PCL-5 contains twenty items rated on a five-point Likert-type scale, with scores ranging from "Not at all" (0) to "Extremely" (4), resulting in a symptom severity score between 0 and 80. A preliminary version of the PCL-5 suggested a cut-off score of 33 for a diagnosis of PTSD, while validation studies recommended a variety of cutoff scores ranging between 28 and 37 [15–17] or following the DSM-5 diagnostic algorithm for PTSD with items that correspond to the DSM criteria. The findings of validation studies indicate that the optimal cut-off score depends on the context, the population as well as the gold-standard instrument applied in the validation studies.

The aim of this study is was estimate the psychometric properties and diagnostic utility of the PCL-5 as a screening instrument. This study sought to determine an appropriate cut-off score with the optimal balance of sensitivity and specificity for Arab and Kurdish populations affected by the Syrian and Iraqi civil wars. For several reasons, this task is far more challenging than the translation of a psychometric instrument for different European populations, and the established standards for such procedures can't be transferred to this population. The most obvious complication is that people living in the northern regions Syria and Iraq speak a variety of languages and it is often impossible to determine a main language spoken within this region. Even more, even single subjects living in these regions have difficulties to define their individual main, first or native language, since different languages may be spoken in different contexts. For example, many Kurdish rely on regional dialects for the communication within the families but have been educated in Arabic and refer to this language as soon as they talk to educated professionals or authorities. The individual skills in reading and writing Arab and Kurdish depend on ethnicity but also on the educational level and the specific community of origin. At the same time, different languages have been associated with specific war parties, and some individuals are reluctant to use a certain language as they feel reminded to confrontations with the enemy. Particularly in mixed populations such as in refugee camps and camps for internally displaced people in KRI it is impossible to predict the specific individual language skills and preferences of the single respondents. As a consequence, we refrained from determining a specific language for each population, but let each single respondent chose the individual preferred language for this specific context. Since a substantial proportion of the inhabitants are illiterate or lacks the skills to fill in a questionnaire, we trained local interviewers who were fluent in Arab and Kurdish to administer the Kurdish or Arab translations of the PCL in the form an assisted self-report. In absence of a valid gold-standard instrument available in Arabic or Kurdish, we used clinical interviews carried out by clinically experienced Master's or PhD-level psychologists from Koya University in KRI, who are fluent in Arabic and Kurdish, as a comparison. We hold that a clinical assessment carried out by experts who are familiar with the local culture and language, and also well educated in international perspectives in trauma research, would present a standard with the highest face-validity in this context. There was no alternative to this solution, since at the time of data acquisition there was no validated clinical interview schedule for the DSM-5 for PTSD in English.

Method

Participants

The participants were Iraqi IDP- and Syrian refugee couples who had fled to Arbat Camps in the Sulaymaniyah Governorate in the KRI as a result of the civil war and attacks by rebel armies. Data were collected in two waves and included a full study sample and a validation sub-sample. Participants in the full sample included 108 Iraqi and 98 Syrian displaced persons with diverse religious backgrounds and ethnicities. A random sub-sample consisting of 98 individuals (49 couples) was re-interviewed to determine the reliability and validity of this sub-sample (validation sample). Table 1 summarizes basic demographic characteristics of both samples.

Procedure

Local interviewers conducted the screening interviews, and the validation interviews were conducted by expert interviewers. Between December 2016 and January 2017, we recruited six local interviewers (three men and three women). The local interviewers were fluent in Kurdish and Arabic and they had at least a Bachelor's degree in psychology or social work. Each interviewer attended a one-week intensive theoretical and practical training course on the study instruments. Due to the absence of reliable census data from the refugee camps, we used a pragmatic sampling approach based on a random selection of individuals and households. The camp was sub-divided according to approximately equal household and population size. Local interviewers were assigned to the resulting zones and instructed to randomly select a sampling direction by spinning a pen from the zone center. The first household with one distance to another was selected and from each household, only main householder couples were interviewed.

Our study is part of a much more extensive and cross-national project, which aims to study psychosocial consequences of migration among Iraqi IDPs and Syrian refugees. In the current study, we interviewed displaced Iraqi and Syrian people. We began with a background questionnaire, followed by a war-related events checklist and Life Events Checklist for DSM-5 (LEC-5) [18]. Psychopathology was assessed using the PCL-5 and the depression section of the Hopkins symptom checklist [19]. Participants were fully informed about the procedures of the current study through a standardized informed consent, which included information about aims of our study, confidentiality, potential risks and discomforts, the right to withdraw without prejudice, benefits, and data protection. Verbal informed consent was given, and interviewers documented informed consent for each participant. The

Table 1 Sociodemographic information and traumatic experiences

	Full study sample	Validation sample
Interview language N (%)		
Kurdish	148(71.8)	57(58.16)
Arabic	58(28.2)	41(41.84)
Gender, N (%)		
Male	102 (49.5)	49 (50)
Female	104 (50.5)	49 (50)
Age, mean (SD)[a]	32.79 (10.11)	32.85(10.37)
Religion, N (%)		
Muslim – Sunni	154(74.8)	79(80.6)
Muslim – Shia	14(6.8)	3(3.1)
Yazidi	38(18.4)	16(16.3)
Ethnicity, N (%)		
Kurd	143(69.4)	70(71.4)
Arab	54(26.2)	28(28.6)
Other	9(4.4)	0(0)
Nationality, N (%)		
Iraqi	108(52.4)	47(48)
Syrian	98(47.6)	51(52)
Formal education, mean (SD)[a]	6.38(4.35)	6.02 (4.21)
Occupation, N (%)		
Household	117(56.8)	57(58.2)
Full-time work	24(11.6)	9(9.2)
Part-time work	50(24.3)	23(23.5)
Student	7(3.4)	3(3.1)
Unemployed	6(2.9)	5(5.1)
Receiving benefit	2(1.0)	1(1)
Having regular income, N (%)		
No	172(83.5)	82(83.7)
Yes	34(16.5)	16(16.3)
Number of children, mean (SD)	3.88 (2.97)	3.88(2.86)
Length of stay (or time period) in camp as a refugee, mean (SD)[a]	2.63(1.07)	2.68(.93)
Traumatic Experiences		
War-related event types experienced during displacement, mean (SD)[b]	4.28(1.88)	4.62(2.37)
War-related event types experienced life time, mean (SD)[c]	5.26(2.79)	5.87(3.30)
Traumatic event-types experienced, mean (SD)[d]	3.32 (2.67)	2.97(2.47)
Traumatic event-types witnessed, mean (SD)[e]	5.43(3.57)	3.32(2.50)

[a]in year. [b]score range: 0–11. [c]score range: 1–17. [d]score range: 0–15. [e]score range: 0–17

interviewers were matched in gender to the interviewees and they were asked about their readiness for re-interview by different interviewers. All participants (except three couples, who had moved to a new location) assented to a further interview. Two weeks later forty-nine couples between 18 and 67 years of age (48% Iraqi and 52% Syrian) were chosen randomly for re-interview by four expert clinical psychologists (two women and two men).

The expert interviewers had at least a Master's degree in clinical psychology and more than four years clinical experience with highly vulnerable populations including survivors of war, displacement, torture, genocide, and family and gender-based violence. All clinical psychologists were university lecturers at the department of clinical psychology at Koya University in the KRI, and they partially worked as psychotherapists at Koya university's outpatient clinic. This clinic offers psychological diagnostics as well as counseling and psychotherapy for individuals with different mental health problems in including trauma and PTSD.

About 15 days after the first interview, the expert interviewers conducted validation interviews based on the same instruments. However, the experts were instructed to ask the questions of the PCL in the form of a structured clinical interview. For every single PTSD symptom listed in the PCL5, the clinical experts asked about symptom's presence and it's occurrences over the past month. They were instructed to explore as much information as needed about the intensity, relevance, and frequency of each symptom to be able to judge the clinical significance of each symptom. We perceived that this procedure was the best approximation to culturally sensitive structured interviews that have been recognized as a standard gold for diagnosing PTSD.

Clinically significant symptoms were rated at least as "2 = Moderate". Expert diagnosis of PTSD was then determined using the DSM-5 algorithm, counting all symptoms rated 'two or more' as a present. The clinical psychologists were fluent in Kurdish and Arabic languages, and they were blind to the results of the screening interviews. The ethical review committees of Bielefeld University in Germany and Koya University in the KRI approved all study procedures.

Instruments

Sociodemographic information

The first part of the interview comprised a number of questions about basic demographic variables (e.g., gender, age, marital status, income, employment status, individual and household characteristics etc.) and information related to migration.

War-related event checklist

On the basis of previous war exposure scales, e.g. the Violence, War and Abduction Exposure Scale [9] as well as focus-group interviews with war-affected refugees and IDPs living in Iraq, we developed the War Exposure Scale (WES), a specific checklist to assess 13 typical war events before, during, and after migration, which reflected the Kurdish and Arab individuals' traumatic war-related experiences. The respondents were asked if they had ever experienced a specific type of event. The war exposure score was determined as the sum of "Yes" responses to specific event types.

Lifetime traumatic events

For assessing potential lifetime traumatic events, the Life Events Checklist for DSM-5 (LEC-5) [18] was used. The LEC-5 is a self-report measure that consists of 16 potential lifetime traumatic events (with one additional item for assessing any other extraordinarily stressful event that not captured in the first 16 items) in four response categories (1) direct experience. (2) witnessing the trauma. (3) learning that a traumatic event has happened to close family member or close friend. (4) experiencing a traumatic event as a part of the daily job or as a first responder (e.g., paramedic, and police). In the present study, only first 16 event items with the first two response categories "direct experienced" and "witnessed" were analyzed. Participants reported the presence of the events during their lifetime with "Yes" and "No" answers.

PTSD

The PTSD checklist for the DSM-5 (PCL-5) [14] was used to estimate the severity of PTSD symptoms as well as to establish the presence of a probable diagnosis of PTSD according to the DMS-5. Previous validation studies showed good psychometric properties for evaluating PTSD [15, 17, 20].

Depression

Depressive symptoms were recorded on the 15-item depression section (DHSCL) of the Hopkins Symptom Checklist [21]. The DHSCL is one of the most widely used tools for assessing depressive symptoms in cross cultural research [22]. Perceived severity of depressive symptoms in the week preceding the interview was recorded for each symptom on a 4-point Likert-type scale ranging from 1 to 4. The overall mean of the scale reflects depressive symptom level. The internal consistency of DHSCL in the validation sample as well as in full study sample was high ($\alpha = .87$ and $\alpha = .83$, respectively).

Instruments were developed and adapted following recommended procedures in transcultural research [23]. Instruments were translated following the guidelines of van Ommeren et al. (1999) [24]. These involve a translation, lexical back translation, blind back translation, as well as focus group discussions with a group of local bilingual experts and a group of study participants, to gain a semantically equivalent consensus translation. Using this procedure, all study instruments were translated into the Kurdish dialects Sorani and Kurmanji as well as into Arabic.

Data analysis

The statistical package for the social sciences (SPSS) version 24.0 was used for data analysis. Internal consistencies of the PCL-5 total score and its subscale scores were indicated by Cronbach's alpha. The stability and validity of the PCL-5 total symptoms score, and the subscale scores were calculated using the Pearson correlation coefficient. To determine the correspondence of the local and expert interviews in PTSD diagnosis, Cohen's kappa was used for different cut-off scores. Sensitivity and specificity coefficients were used to quantify the diagnostic utility of the PCL-5 [25]. Receiver operator characteristics (ROC) were performed to determine the optimum cutoff score by examining patterns of sensitivity and specificity compared to expert ratings. ROC is a graphical plot that visualizes the performance of a binary classifier (sensitivity on the y-axis and 1-specificity on the x-axis) and the area under the ROC curve quantifies the overall performance of a diagnostic test [26]. Examining the relationship between predictor variables of PTSD and PCL-5 score allowed us to investigate the convergent validity.

Results

Internal consistency

Cronbach's α coefficients calculated for the PCL-5 scores of the full study sample and the validation sample showed high alpha values (α = .85, α = .86 respectively). In the validation sample, Cronbach's α values for PCL-5 sub-scales (intrusion, avoidance, negative alterations in cognition and mood, and hyperarousal symptom clusters were α = .76, α = .88, α = .74, and α = .71, respectively.

Cutoff score

Receiver operating curves (ROC) analyses were carried out to determine the optimal cutoff score for the PCL-5 among the Kurdish and Arab populations. ROC is a commonly used method to visualize the sensitivity and specificity of a diagnostic test. ROC curves allow the identification of the best cut-off score for the test by determining the maximum of the area under the curve (AUC; [27]). As presented in Fig. 1 and in Table 2, the PCL-5 reached highest-level balanced sensitivity, specificity and Cohen's kappa values at cutoff score of 23.

Convergent validity

To evaluate the convergent validity of the PCL-5 in the context of this study, we examined the relationship between known predictor variables of PTSD (e.g., war-related and life events) and the PCL-5. Diverse types of traumatic events were significantly positively correlated with the PCL-5 sum score. Moreover, we found a significant positive correlation between symptoms of PTSD (PCL-5 total score) and depression (DHSCL score (Table 3).

Discussion

To evaluate the validity and diagnostic accuracy of the PCL-5 in the context of the civil war in Syria and Iraq, we calibrated the PCL-5 cut-off score to the assessment by experienced local clinicians. A ROC curve analyses determined the optimal cut-off score of 23 as marking the optimal balance of sensitivity and specificity. Consistent with previous research [16, 20, 28], we found a high internal consistency of the PCL-5 (alpha = .85). In addition, results showed convincing indications for the convergent validity of the PCL-5. Several types of traumatic events were positively correlated with PTSD symptoms, and this finding is in line with a large number of studies in post-conflict settings [29, 30].

Our findings are only partly consistent with previous validation studies of the PCL-5. The cutoff score in the present study is lower than the initially recommended value and it is lower than the empirically determined cut-off scores from previous validation studies, for instance; using CAPS as a gold standard instrument among military veterans, Bovin et al. (2016) [28] determined an optimal cut-off score of 31. Blevins et al., (2015) [16] evaluated the psychometric properties of the PCL-5 among undergraduate students who identified themselves as having experienced a "very stressful life event" and found that the PCL-5 achieved an appropriate sensitivity, with high specificity and efficiency at a cutoff cut-off score of 37. Similarly, Ashbaugh et al. (2016) [15] studied the psychometric properties of the English and French versions of the PCL-5 among undergraduate students and determined 31 as the optimal score, achieving a sensitivity of.85 and a specificity of.95. However, with the exception of the Bovin et al. (2016) study, these investigations are limited by the fact that other self-report measures were applied as standards.

Our results indicate that the PCL-5 and its contextually validated cut-off score has good psychometric properties as a screening instrument for identifying people with PTSD symptoms among Kurdish and Arab populations. However, it seems that the psychometric values obtained in our evaluation, in particular specificity and sensitivity are slightly lower than those reported in previous validation studies. In contrast to other validation studies we could not rely on a highly structured and reliable gold-standard instrument such as the CAPS, but applied interviews by local experts as standards. It is quite likely that this procedure ultimately reduced the reliability of the standard which, in turn, brought about lower sensitivity and specificity values. In our study, the validation interviews were

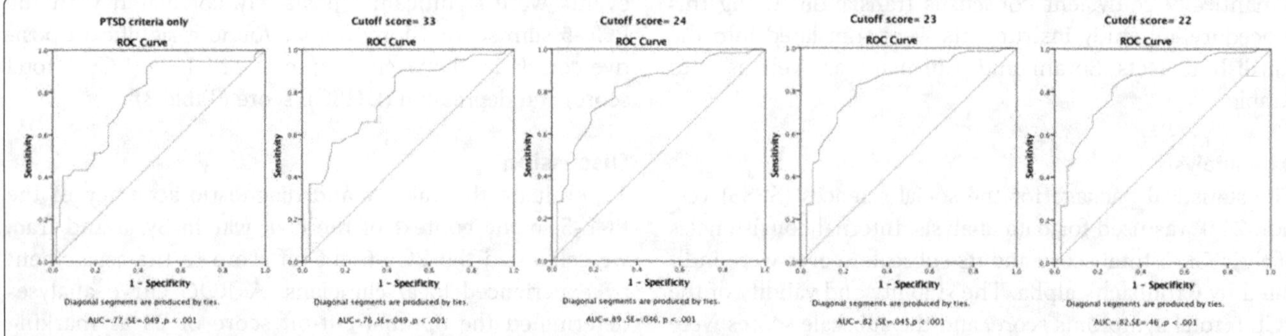

Fig. 1 Receiver operating characteristics curves (ROC curve) of the PCL-5 using different cutoff scores. AUCs shows under the curve

carried out by experts with a Kurdish and Arabic educational and cultural background, with experience in working in the challenging context of the war region. It is possible that this background has an impact on their evaluation of the thresholds for clinical significance of symptoms of psychological disorders, which may deviate from the standards of a psychiatrist or psychologist from a high-income country. This fact may have contributed to the determination of a lower threshold for clinical significance of a disorder. It is possible that in a challenging and threatening life-context and a hardly functional mental health system lower levels of symptoms lead to dysfunction than in a safe and less threatening environment. In this way, the lower cut-off value of the PSC-5 found in our study might depend on the context of a war-affected community.

The most striking difference is, however, that we determined a lower cut-off value for a potential PTSD diagnosis than in the original study. Several reasons might explain this finding. Possibly, the diagnosis arrived by the local experts in our study was more liberal than in the original validation study, since the decision about the clinical significance of each item did not depend on both, severity and frequency characteristics of each item (as requested in the CAPS that had been used as standard in previous studies) but on the estimation of the clinical importance of each item based on the frequency information as well as the judgement of the expert. Another explanation of this difference might be based on subtle semantic differences in wording that occurred in the translations and tended to result in a meaning that implied a more severe presentation of symptoms in the screening. While, based on the data, we can only speculate about the potential reasons we have to emphasize that, ultimately, any judgment of the clinical significance of a symptom depends on individual clinical expertise as a standard, for example in the validation of the CAPS itself. The involvement of clinical experts with other cultural backgrounds may lead to more discrepant but not necessarily to less valid findings. Future studies using different gold-standard evaluations in different cultures will have to show whether, in general, the recommended cut-off value is too low or if specific linguistic, cultural, or contextual factors contribute to the specific cut-off value in this population.

The results of our study are limited by the absence of a gold standard measure for diagnosing PTSD in Arab and Kurdish populations. While our procedure seems face-valid, it should be complemented by other possibilities, e.g. using standardized translations of established instruments, such as the CAPS-5, once validations of this instrument in English are available. Beyond a clinical interview and predictor variables, future studies should also test if the instrument predicts negative outcomes in mental health and general functioning, as an ultimate test of the performance of a mental health screening instrument. In addition, future studies evaluate should the factorial structure and measurement invariance of PCL-5 in larger samples across different nationalities, ethnic groups, and languages. Another limitation of our study is that we tested three

Table 2 Performance of the PTSD diagnose by expert interviewers in relative to local interviewers using PCL-5 sum score

Statistic	PTSD criteria only	Cutoff score = 33	Cutoff score = 22	Cutoff score = 23	Cutoff score = 24
Sensitivity	.486	.46	.73	.82	.65
Specificity	.833	.877	.76	.70	.81
ODP	.66	.71	.74	.73	.73
Kappa	.266	.41	.48	.48	.47
p value	.007	.000	.000	.000	.000
Prevalence (%)	37.75	41.83	65.30	64.28	62.24

PTSD criteria only = DSM-5 diagnostic algorithm for PTSD. *ODP* overall diagnostic power. Cutoff score of 33 is an initial cutoff score [14]

Table 3 Correlations between the PCL-5 and related constructs (Pearson's r)

Variables	PCL-5 sum score
War-related event types (during displacement)	.25**
War-related event types (life time)	.23**
Event types experienced	.27**
Event types witnessed	.29**
DHSCL- sum score	.65**

PCL-5 = Posttraumatic Stress Disorder Checklist for DSM-5. *DHSCL* Depression section of Hopkins Symptom Checklist
**. $P < 0.01$, two-tailed

translations of the PCL-5 simultaneously. Although we included almost 100 participants, our sample size was not large enough to allow the comparative evaluation of the single language versions. These limitations are an inevitable compromise reflecting the fact that multiple languages are present in a small region, and that even for single individuals, the preferred language is often not easy to determine. Many respondents spoke one language in their homes but another in the school and obtained different skills and a different vocabulary in the specific languages. Follow-up validation studies should include more distinct populations in other regions to determine the validity in specific populations.

Conclusions

The current study provided psychometric properties and the diagnostic utility of one of the most widely used screening measure for assessing PTSD as a screening instrument. Our study is the first validation study in the languages of the populations affected by one of the most severe current humanitarian crises. This study provides a potential foundation for further investigations into mental health and trauma in Arab and Kurdish refugee populations as well as a tool for the screening of affected individuals by local health services.

Abbreviations

DHSCL: Depression section of the Hopkins Symptom Checklist; KRI: Kurdistan Region of Iraq; PCL: Posttraumatic Stress Disorder Checklist; PTSD: Posttraumatic Stress Disorder

Acknowledgements

We acknowledge the financial support of the German Research Foundation (DFG) and the Open Access Publication Fund of Bielefeld University for the article processing charge. We would like to express our sincere thanks and appreciation to our research participants for their trust and for sharing their experiences with us. We thank our local research team (Hawara N. Karim, Chnar Z. Hamad, Sakar M. Ahmad, Sheraz I. Rashed, Shahen F. Mohammed, Sangar H. Abdulla, Haval I. Hussein, Dilshad H. Hussein, Tariq K. Hama and Nazhad H. Sultan) for their dedication and effort in this research project. We would also like to thank Arbat camp managers (Mr. Tariq A. Hamalaw, Ms. Pakhshan T. Fathullah and Mr. Payam S. Hama Sharif) for their facilitation and guidance.

Funding

This study was funded by Volkswagen Foundation. A part of this study was supported by a scholarship from the German Academic Exchange Service (DAAD) to the first author. The funders had no role in study design, data collection and analysis, decision to publish, and preparation of the manuscript.

Authors' contributions

All authors participated in the conception and design of the study. HI: he is a project manager, carried out the informal interviews and focus-group discussion with IDPs and refugees, trained the local interviewers, supervised data acquisition and performed the statistical analysis as well as the interpretation of data and wrote the manuscript draft. HI and AAL: are co-principal investigators and conducted the validation interviews with the male participants. VE and CC: are contributed to the statistical analysis and the interpretation of data. FN: he is the chief investigator for this study, supervised data analyses, participated in the interpretation of the data, and critically revised the manuscript for important intellectual content. All authors read and approved the final manuscript.

Consent for publication

Not applicable.

Competing interests

The authors declare that they have no competing interests.

Author details

[1]Department of Psychology, Clinical Psychology and Psychotherapy, Bielefeld University, Bielefeld, Germany. [2]vivo international, Konstanz, Germany. [3]Department of Clinical Psychology, Koya University, Koya, Kurdistan Region of Iraq, Iraq.

References

1. North CS, Pfefferbaum B. Mental health response to community disasters. JAMA. 2013;310:507.
2. Lynch M. The Arab uprising: the unfinished revolutions of the new Middle East. 1st ed. New York, NY: PublicAffairs; 2012.
3. UN Refugee Agency (UNHCR). Global Trends - Forced Displacement in 2015. Geneva: UNHCR Glob Trends 2015; 2015.
4. UN Refugee Agency (UNHCR). Mid-Year Trends 2016. Geneva: UNHCR; 2017.
5. Alpak G, Unal A, Bulbul F, Sagaltici E, Bez Y, Altindag A, et al. Post-traumatic stress disorder among Syrian refugees in Turkey: a cross-sectional study. Int J Psychiatry Clin Pract. 2015;19:45–50.
6. Ibrahim H, Hassan CQ. Post-traumatic stress disorder symptoms resulting from torture and other traumatic events among Syrian Kurdish refugees in Kurdistan region, Iraq. Front Psychol. Frontiers. 2017;8:241.
7. Nasıroğlu S, Çeri V. Posttraumatic stress and depression in Yazidi refugees. Neuropsychiatr Dis Treat Dove Press. 2016;12:2941–8.
8. Amawi N, Mollica RF, Lavelle J, Osman O, Nasir L. Overview of research on the mental health impact of violence in the Middle East in light of the Arab spring. J Nerv Ment Dis Lippincott Williams and Wilkins. 2014;202:625–9.
9. Ertl V, Pfeiffer A, Saile R, Schauer E, Elbert T, Neuner F. Validation of a mental health assessment in an African conflict population. Psychol Assess. 2010;22:318–24.
10. Rasmussen A, Verkuilen J, Ho E, Fan Y. Posttraumatic stress disorder among refugees: measurement invariance of Harvard trauma questionnaire scores across global regions and response patterns. Psychol Assess. 2015;27:1160–70.
11. Norris FH, Hamblen JL. Standardized self-report measures of civilian trauma and PTSD. In: Wilson JP, Keane TM, editors. Assess Psychol trauma PTSD. 2nd ed. New York, NY, US: Guilford Press; 2004. p. 63–102.
12. Orsillo SM. Measures for acute stress disorder and posttraumatic stress disorder. In: Antony MM, Orsillo SM, Roemer L, editors. Pract Guid to empirically based Meas anxiety. Boston, MA: Springer US; 2001. p. 255–307.
13. Weathers FW, Litz BT, Herman DS, Huska JA, Keane TM. Posttraumatic Stress Disorder Checklist. PTSD Checkl Reliab validity, diagnostic Util. San Antonio, TX: Paper presented at the 9th Annual Conference of the ISTSS; 1993.

14. Weathers FW, Litz BT, Keane TM, Palmieri PA, Marx BP, Schnurr PP. The PTSD Checklist for DSM-5 (PCL-5). National Center for PTSD. 2013; Scale available from the National Center for PTSD at www.ptsd.va.gov. Accessed 2 Aug 2017.
15. Ashbaugh AR, Houle-Johnson S, Herbert C, El-Hage W, Brunet A. Psychometric Validation of the English and French Versions of the Posttraumatic Stress Disorder Checklist for DSM-5 (PCL-5). PLoS One. 2016;11:e0161645. Mazza M, editor
16. Blevins CA, Weathers FW, Davis MT, Witte TK, Domino JL. The posttraumatic stress disorder checklist for DSM-5 (PCL-5): development and initial psychometric evaluation. J Trauma Stress. 2015;28:489–98.
17. Sveen J, Bondjers K, Willebrand M. Psychometric properties of the PTSD Checklist for DSM-5: a pilot study. Eur J Psychotraumatol. 2016;7:30165. Taylor & Francis
18. Weathers FW, Blake DD, Schnurr PP, Kaloupek DG, Marx BP, Keane T. The Life Events Checklist for DSM-5 (LEC-5). National Center for PTSD. 2013; Scale available from the National Center for PTSD at www.ptsd.va.gov
19. Derogatis LR, Lipman RS, Rickels K, Uhlenhuth EH, Covi L. The Hopkins symptom checklist (HSCL): a self-report symptom inventory. Behav Sci. 1974;19:1–15.
20. Wortmann JH, Jordan AH, Weathers FW, Resick PA, Dondanville KA, Hall-Clark B, et al. Psychometric analysis of the PTSD Checklist-5 (PCL-5) among treatment-seeking military service members. Psychol Assess. 2016;28:1392–403.
21. Hesbacher PT, Rickels K, Morris RJ, Newman H, Rosenfeld H. Psychiatric illness in family practice. J Clin Psychiatry. 1980;41:6–10.
22. Rask S, Castaneda AE, Koponen P, Sainio P, Stenholm S, Suvisaari J, et al. The association between mental health symptoms and mobility limitation among Russian, Somali and Kurdish migrants: a population based study. BMC Public Health. 2015;15:275.
23. Flaherty JA, Gaviria FM, Pathak D, Mitchell T, Wintrob R, Richman JA, et al. Developing instruments for cross-cultural psychiatric research. J Nerv Ment Dis. 1988;176:257–63.
24. van Ommeren M, Sharma B, Thapa S, Makaju R, Prasain D, Bhattarai R, et al. Preparing instruments for transcultural research: use of the translation monitoring form with Nepali-speaking Bhutanese refugees. In: Transcult psychiatry, vol. 36. thousand oaks, CA: Sage PublicationsSage CA; 1999. p. 285–301.
25. Mandrekar JN. Simple statistical measures for diagnostic accuracy assessment. J Thorac Oncol. John Wiley and Sons. N Y. 2010;5:763–4.
26. Akobeng AK. Understanding diagnostic tests 3: receiver operating characteristic curves. Acta Paediatr Blackwell Publishing Ltd. 2007;96:644–7.
27. Fan J, Upadhye S, Worster A. Understanding receiver operating characteristic (ROC) curves. CJEM. 2006;8:19–20. Cambridge University Press
28. Bovin MJ, Marx BP, Weathers FW, Gallagher MW, Rodriguez P, Schnurr PP, et al. Psychometric properties of the PTSD checklist for diagnostic and statistical manual of mental disorders–fifth edition (PCL-5) in veterans. Psychol Assess. 2016;28:1379–91.
29. Ayazi T, Lien L, Eide A, Swartz L, Hauff E. Association between exposure to traumatic events and anxiety disorders in a post-conflict setting: a cross-sectional community study in South Sudan. BMC Psychiatry. 2014;14:6.
30. Onyut LP, Neuner F, Ertl V, Schauer E, Odenwald M, Elbert T. Trauma, poverty and mental health among Somali and Rwandese refugees living in an African refugee settlement – an epidemiological study. Confl Health. 2009;3:6. BioMed Central

2

Genotype-dependent associations between serotonin transporter gene (*SLC6A4*) DNA methylation and late-life depression

Dilys Lam[1], Marie-Laure Ancelin[3], Karen Ritchie[3,4], Rosanne Freak-Poli[5], Richard Saffery[1,2] and Joanne Ryan[1,2,3,5*]

Abstract

Background: Disrupted serotonergic signaling is often a feature of depression and the role of the serotonin transporter gene (*SLC6A4*), responsible for serotonin re-uptake, has received much attention in this regard. Most studies have focused on the polymorphic *5-HTTLPR* upstream repeat, or DNA methylation at the promoter CpG island. Few studies have explored the influence of genetic variation across the gene on DNA methylation, and their combined association with depression risk. The aim of this study was to determine whether genetic variation in the *SLC6A4* gene influences promoter DNA methylation, and whether these are associated with depression status.

Method: The ESPRIT study involves a community-based population of older individuals (> 65 years of age). Major depressive disorder (MDD) was diagnosed according to DSM-IV (American Psychiatric Association, 1994) criteria, and severe depressive symptoms assessed by the Centre for Epidemiological Studies Depression (CES-D) Scale. Sequenom MassARRAY was used to measure *SLC6A4* methylation status ($n = 302$).

Results: Nominally significant associations were observed between *SLC6A4* genetic variants (*5-HTTLPR, rs140700, rs4251417, rs6354, rs25528, rs25531)* and DNA methylation at several CpG sites. In multivariate regression, DNA methylation was associated with depression status, but only in the presence of specific genotypes. In individuals homozygous for the short *5-HTTLPR* and *5-HTTLPR/r25531* alleles, lower methylation at two CpGs was associated with depression ($\beta = -0.44$ to $\beta = -0.31$; $p = 0.001$ to $p = 0.038$).

Conclusion: We present evidence for genotype-dependent associations between *SLC6A4* methylation and depression. Genetic variants may also play a role in influencing promoter methylation levels and its association with depression.

Keywords: Depression, DNA methylation, Epigenetics, Genetic variation, Serotonin transporter

Background

Serotonin deficiency was one of the earliest hypothesis of depression causality [1, 2]. This came from the discovery of a class of antidepressants, the selective serotonin re-uptake inhibitors (SSRIs), which block the reuptake of the neurotransmitter and therefore increasing its availability. SSRIs are thus commonly prescribed to treat depression, however the response rate remains relatively modest (around 50%) [3]. The serotonin transporter (5-HTT), encoded by the serotonin transporter gene (*SLC6A4*), is a principle regulator of serotonergic neurotransmission and the active target of SSRIs [4]. Thus, the role of *SLC6A4* and its (dys)regulation has been a major focus of depression research.

One feature of *SLC6A4* which has been the subject of much research, is the upstream gene-linked polymorphic region, *5-HTTLPR*. A 44 bp insertion/deletion variable number tandem repeat (VNTR), results in either short (S) or long (L) alleles. The S allele results in lower *SLC6A4* transcriptional levels and therefore reduced reuptake of serotonin [5, 6]. There is some evidence that *5-HTTLPR* genotype affects vulnerability to a broad range of behavioural disorders including depression [1]. However, these associations have not been consistently found [7], suggesting that other regulatory mechanisms and factors are likely to contribute to depression risk [8–10].

* Correspondence: joanne.ryan@monash.edu
[1]Cancer & Disease Epigenetics, Murdoch Children's Research Institute, Royal Children's Hospital, Parkville, VIC, Australia
[2]Department of Paediatrics, University of Melbourne, Parkville, VIC, Australia
Full list of author information is available at the end of the article

Approximately 1 kb downstream from *5-HTTLPR* lies another widely studied regulatory element, a CpG island that spans the upstream promoter of exon 1 and the transcriptional start site [11]. DNA methylation of this compact region of CpG sites has been associated with reduced expression [11]. Previous, generally small studies have investigated the association between depression and *SLC6A4* DNA methylation in peripheral tissues, but with conflicting findings [12–20]. It is now clear that genetic variation is an important regulator of DNA methylation across the genome [21], yet only a few studies have examined whether *5-HTTLPR* influences methylation and/or the association between methylation and depression [15, 16]. To date the effects of other *SLC6A4* genetic variants on DNA methylation and on the potential link between depression and methylation, have yet to be investigated.

Using data gathered as part of a large general population cohort study of older persons, this study firstly investigated whether *SLC6A4* genetic variation across the gene influences promoter DNA methylation and secondly, whether depression is associated with DNA methylation independently and/or in combination with genetic variation.

Methods

The ESPRIT study

Participants included in this study were part of the French ESPRIT study of neuropsychiatric disorders in an older population [22]. Eligible participants aged 65 years and older from the non-institutionalised general population were randomly recruited from electoral rolls within the Montpellier district. Recruited participants to ESPRIT provided written informed consent and were asked to undergo standardized health and psychiatric interviews, as well as extensive clinical assessments. Information was collected on the participants' lifestyle, health and medical use. The study protocol was approved by the Ethical Committee of University Hospital of Kremlin-Bicêtre, France.

Depression measures

Major depressive disorder (MDD) was diagnosed according to the Diagnostic and Statistical Manual of Mental Disorders-IV (DSM-IV) (American Psychiatric Association, 1994) criteria, using the Mini International Neuropsychiatric Interview (MINI, French version 5.00) [23]. Diagnoses were further reviewed and validated by a panel of psychiatrists and a psychologist with access to information from participants' health assessments. Severity of depressive symptoms was assessed by the Centre for Epidemiological Studies-Depression (CES-D) scale, a self-reporting questionnaire previously validated within the older population [24, 25]. A score of 16 or above is considered the threshold of depressive symptoms warranting further clinical investigation [25]. Thus, late-life depression was defined in this study as having a diagnosis of MDD or high levels of depressive symptoms (CES-D $\geq$ 16).

Genotyping

Blood samples were collected at recruitment following clinical assessment. In concordance with previous *SLC6A4* methylation association studies in blood [12–15, 17, 19, 20], genomic DNA was extracted from white blood cells using a standard procedure [26] and used for genotyping and methylation analysis. Along with *5-HTTLPR*, five single nucleotide polymorphisms (SNPs) (*rs140700, rs25528, rs4251417, rs6354, rs25531*) spanning the *SLC6A4* gene were also genotyped. These were chosen on the basis of allele frequencies and prior associations with depression [3, 26, 27]. Genotyping of *5-HTTLPR* was performed as previously described [26], and SNPs were genotyped by KBiosciences (UK), using the KBioscience Competitive Allele-Specific PCR SNP genotyping system (KASPar) [28]. *5-HTTLPR* can also be considered in combination with *rs25531*, a SNP that lies within the repeat region and has been reported to modify transcriptional activity of *5-HTTLPR* [27, 29]. *5-HTTLPR/rs25531* describes the triallelic polymorphism accounting for both *5-HTTLPR* and *rs25531* genotypes. χ^2-tests were used to calculate whether the distribution of genotype frequencies was in Hardy-Weinberg equilibrium (HWE).

SLC6A4 promoter methylation analysis

500 ng of genomic DNA was sodium bisulphite-converted using the EZ-96 DNA Methylation-Lightning MagPrep kit protocol (Zymo Research; Irvine, USA). The promoter-associated CpG island was targeted in our assay. This region is equivalent to amplicon 1 in a previous study [30]. A 335 bp region (UCSC Human Genome Browser GRCh/hg_38 build: chr17: 30235734–30,236,068) [31] was amplified in triplicate, to account for variation in the PCR step [32], and methylation of 11 CpG units, encompassing 20 CpG sites, were quantified using the SEQUENOM MassARRAY EpiTYPER platform (Additional file 1: Table S1) [32]. Raw methylation data was generated on 361 samples. Mean methylation values were calculated from replicates within 10% of the median value (Martino et al. 2013). Participants with < 50% of methylation data available ($n = 55$) and outliers (> 3 times the interquartile range (IQR)) ($n = 4$) were excluded from further analysis. Following these quality control steps (Additional file 1: Figure S1), methylation data was obtained for a sub-sample of 302 participants, with no significant difference in depression status, age, sex and key variables (Table 1) with the full ESPRIT cohort ($p > 0.05$ for all comparisons).

Table 1 Characteristics of study participants according to depression status

Characteristic[a]	No depression	Depression	*p*- value[g]
n	207	95	–
Age (Mean ± S.D.)	72.5 ± 5.2	74.6 ± 5.7	0.004
	Proportion (%)		
Female	55.1	68.4	0.028
Past major depressive disorder	25.3	38.6	0.062
High education level[b]	38.2	25.3	0.028
Living alone	20.9	43.2	< 0.001
Habitual alcohol drinkers (> 24 g/day)	19.2	20.4	0.81
Habitual smokers (≥10 pack years)	35.6	34.4	0.84
Functional impairment[c]	5.31	13.7	0.013
Ischemic disease[d]	10.6	22.1	0.008
Comorbidities[e]	12.1	29.5	< 0.001
Anxiety	15.9	29.5	0.044
Dementia	4.3	2.1	0.334
Impaired cognition (MMSE< 26)[f]	13.6	11.6	0.63
Antidepressants	3.38	12.6	0.002
Selective serotonin re-uptake inhibitor (SSRI)	2.90	6.3	0.158
Tricyclic antidepressant (TCA)	0.48	2.10	0.187
Other antidepressants	0.00	4.20	0.003
Benzodiazepines	4.83	9.47	0.123
Anxiolytics	7.73	16.8	0.017
Psychotropic drugs	4.83	11.6	0.032
Anticholinergics	4.83	7.37	0.374

[a]Not all participants with methylation data (n = 302) had information for each population characteristic listed, but missing data was < 2%, with exception of anxiety (20.5%) and past MDD (33%)
[b]Underwent post-secondary education of any type
[c]Unable to independently complete 2 items on both or either of the Instrumental Activities of Daily Living and Activities of Daily Living scales
[d]History of angina pectoris, myocardial infarction, stroke, cardiovascular surgery and/or arteritis
[e]Hypertension (resting blood pressure ≥ 160/95 mmHg), high cholesterol (total cholesterol ≥6.2 mmol/l), diabetes (fasting glucose ≥7.0 mmol/l), thyroid disease, asthma, or recent cancer diagnosed within the last 2 years
[f]MMSE: Mini-Mental State Examination
[g]Chi-squared tests used to assess *p*-value for all variables except age, where a t-test was used

Statistical analysis

Statistical analyses were performed using the statistical software package Stata 14.1 (StataCorp, College Station, Texas, USA). Univariate analysis (analysis of variance, t-tests, χ^2-tests) was performed to examine potential associations between genotype and DNA methylation, and between depression and DNA methylation. Additionally, these statistical tests were used to determine which population characteristics were associated with depression status (Table 1)and/ or DNA methylation levels independently. This step was performed to identify potential confounding factors of the association between DNA methylation and depression, which thus would be considered further in multivariate analysis. For associations between population characteristics and methylation, the significance threshold was set at a conservative level of $p < 0.15$, to ensure that no potential confounding variables were omitted. Characteristics associated with both depression and methylation were considered in subsequent multivariate regression analysis as covariates. This included age, sex, living alone, functional impairment, ischemic disease, anxiety, comorbidities. Multivariate linear regression models were used to model the association between DNA methylation (outcome variable) and depression (predictor variable), while adjusting for the potential confounding factors. Potential modifying effects of genetic variants on the association between depression and DNA methylation were also investigated through the inclusion of a multiplicative interaction term in the multivariate models. When potential modifying effects of a specific genetic variant were found (at $p < 0.15$), stratified analysis of methylation data across the genotype groups was performed. This involved t-tests to determine the association between depression status and DNA methylation, in each genotype group of the specific variant. Sensitivity analysis excluding antidepressant users ($n = 19$) was performed as antidepressants may potentially mask depression status and independently influence methylation levels [33]. Sensitivity analysis excluding participants with past depression ($n = 59$) was also performed. Correction for multiple testing was performed using the Benjamini-Hochberg false discovery rate (FDR) method (FDR = 0.05).

Results

Study population

In this study of 302 participants, depressed individuals (31.5%) were significantly more likely to be female, of older age, have a lower education level, live alone, be functionally impaired and have poorer health (ischemic pathologies and comorbidities), as compared to non-depressed participants. They were also more likely to be taking antidepressants. Characteristics of participants according to depression are shown in Table 1. All genotypes were in HWE ($p > 0.05$ for all polymorphisms). Of the six genetic variants and one combined variant examined, only *5-HTTLPR* was significantly associated with depression (Additional file 1: Table S2).

Association between promoter DNA methylation and SLC6A4 genetic variants

Overall, the methylation levels at the 335 bp promoter region were relatively low, apart from CpG 25.26 which had the highest and most variable distribution of methylation (Fig. 1). Potential associations were observed between specific genetic variants and DNA methylation, independent of depression status (Table 2). In particular, homozygous GG genotypes of *rs140700* ($p = 0.019$) and *rs25531* ($p = 0.007$) were significantly associated with higher methylation at CpG 16–20, while homozygous CC genotypes of *rs25528* ($p = 0.007$) and *rs6354* ($p = 0.023$) had significantly higher methylation at CpG 21. However, it should be noted that applying a FDR Benjamini-Hochberg correction for multiple testing of 11 CpG units and 6 polymorphisms (FDR = 0.05) abolished these associations.

Association between depression and methylation

In unadjusted analysis, no significant differences in methylation were noted between depressed and non-depressed participants at any individual CpG units or the mean methylation across the region ($p > 0.15$, except for CpG 3 with effect size $\Delta = 0.31\%$; 95% CI: 0.04; 0.67%, $p = 0.084$ comparing depressed with non-depressed individuals). These findings did not change after inclusion of potential confounders in regression models (as stated in methods), or in sensitivity analysis excluding antidepressant users ($n = 19$) or participants with past depression ($n = 59$).

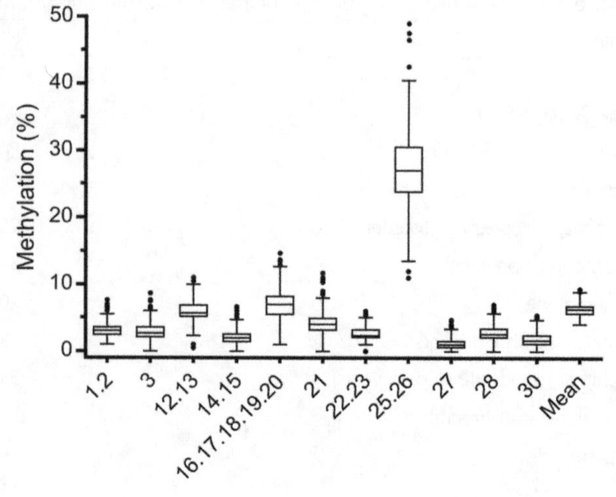

Fig. 1 Distribution of *SLC6A4* methylation levels at each CpG unit and mean methylation levels across the region studied for all study participants. The box denotes the interquartile range (IQR: 25–75% percentiles), the line shows the median and the whiskers are 1.5 x IQR below the 25% percentile or above the 75% percentile

Modification of the association between depression and methylation by SLC6A4 genotype

Five *SLC6A4* polymorphisms were found to potentially modify the association between depression and DNA methylation at multiple CpG units. *5-HTTLPR* and *5-HTTLPR/rs25531* polymorphisms significantly modified the depression-methylation associations at both CpG 21 (p-values for interaction term: *5-HTTLPR*, $p = 0.001$; *5-HTTLPR/rs25531*, $p = 0.006$) and CpG 25.26 (*5-HTTLPR*, $p = 0.064$; *5-HTTLPR/rs25531*, $p = 0.030$). In light of this, analysis was stratified by genotype, where clear differences in associations were observed.

Depression was significantly associated with lower methylation levels at CpG 21 and CpG 25.26, but only for individuals with the SS genotype of *5-HTTLPR* (SS, $\Delta = -1.60\%$; 95% CI: -2.54; -0.65%; $p = 0.001$, Fig. 2a and $\Delta = -4.31\%$; 95% CI: -7.14; -1.48%; $p = 0.004$, Fig. 2c respectively). In contrast, individuals with the LL genotype had highermethylation at CpG 21 (LL, $\Delta = 0.88\%$; 95% CI: 0.10; 1.65%; $p = 0.028$, Fig. 2a). Similar genotype dependent associations were likewise observed for *5-HTTLPR/rs25531* at CpG 21 (S'S', $\Delta = -1.10\%$; 95% CI: -2.01; -0.20; $p = 0.018$, Fig. 2b) and CpG 25.26 (S'S', $\Delta = -4.39\%$; 95% CI: -6.95; -1.84%; $p = 0.001$, Fig. 2d) and at CpG 21 for L'L' genotype ($\Delta = 1.18\%$; 95% CI: 0.21; 2.15; $p = 0.019$, Fig. 2b). These associations remained significant following multivariate adjustment for potential confounders, as shown in Table 3. Following correction for multiple testing (FDR = 0.05), associations between depression and methylation at CpGs 21 (*5-HTTLPR*, SS) and 25.26 (*5HTTLPR*, SS; *5HTTLPR/rs25531*, S'S') remained significant.

Table 2 Potential associations between *SLC6A4* DNA methylation and genotype

CpG unit	Genetic variant	Average methylation (%)			*p*-value[a]
		Major homozygote	Heterozygote	Minor homozygote	
3	*rs4251417*	GG (3.04)	GA (2.70)	AA (1.56)	0.12
14.15	*rs4251417*	GG (2.26)	GA (1.72)	AA (1.67)	0.095
16.17.18.19.20	*rs140700*	GG (7.14)	GA (5.73)	AA (4.92)	0.019
	rs6354	AA (7.29)	AC (6.43)	CC (6.03)	0.054
	rs25531	AA (7.06)	AG (5.74)	GG (8.44)	0.007
21	*rs25528*	AA (3.54)	AC (4.55)	CC (4.94)	0.007
	rs4251417	GG (4.03)	GA (3.17)	AA (3.06)	0.085
	rs6354	AA (3.53)	AC (4.30)	CC (4.94)	0.023
	5-HTTLPR	LL (3.85)	SL (4.03)	SS (4.55)	0.077

[a]*p*-values calculated by one-way ANOVAs and only those with $p < 0.15$ shown

Three other genotypes were also found to potentially modify the associations between depression and methylation: *rs140700* (mean methylation; *p*-values for interaction term = 0.083), *rs6354* (CpG 25.26; $p = 0.061$) and *rs4251417* (CpG 27, $p = 0.026$). Following stratification; mean methylation was significantly lower in depressed patients with heterozygote *rs140700* genotype (GA, $\Delta = -1.17\%$; 95% CI: -2.11; −0.24%; $p = 0.021$; Additional file 1: Figure S2A); CpG 25.26 had highermethylation in depression for heterozygote *rs6354* genotype (AC, $\Delta = 4.22\%$; 95% CI: 0.13; 8.32%; $p = 0.044$; Additional file 1: Figure S2B) and CpG 27 exhibited lowermethylation in depressed participants with homozygote *rs4251417* genotype (GG, $\Delta = -0.40\%$; 95% CI: -0.74; −0.062%; $p = 0.021$; Additional file 1: Figure S2C). However, none of these associations remained significant in multivariate linear regression models (data not shown).

The overall relationships between *SLC6A4* genetic variants, promoter methylation and depression are shown in Fig. 3.

Discussion

Our study investigated the relationship between *SLC6A4* promoter methylation and six polymorphisms (*5-HTTLPR, rs140700, rs42151417, rs6354, rs25528, rs25531*), plus a combined variant (*5-HTTLPR/rs25531*) independently and in the context of late-life depression. We found marginal

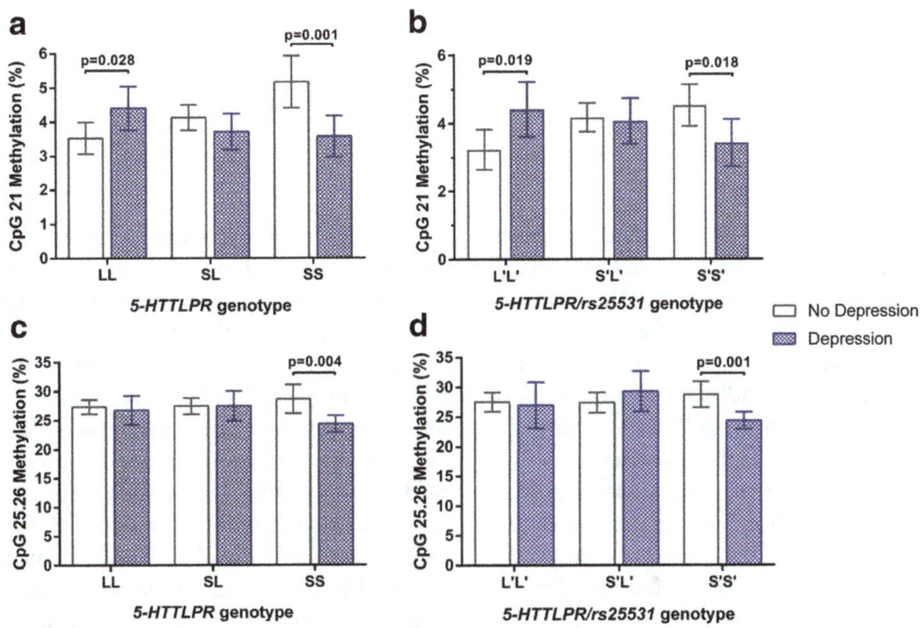

Fig. 2 DNA methylation at CpG units 21 and 25.26 according to depression status, stratified by serotonin transporter (*SLC6A4*) genotypes: *5-HTTLPR* and *5-HTTLPR/rs25531*. **a** CpG 21, *5-HTTLPR* ($n = 274$); (**b**) CpG 21, *5-HTTLPR/rs25531* ($n = 210$); (**c**) CpG 25.26, *5-HTTLPR* ($n = 234$); (**d**) CpG 25.26, *5-HTTLPR/rs25531* ($n = 182$). Data presented as mean methylation ±95% CI. T-tests were used to calculate *p*-values, with significant associations at $p < 0.05$ indicated in the figure

Table 3 Adjusted associations between depression and *SLC6A4* promoter methylation, stratified by *5-HTTLPR* or *5-HTTLPR/rs25531* genotype

CpG unit	Genotype	Variables	Unadjusted		Adjusted[a]	
			β(SE)	*p*-value	β(SE)	*p*-value
21	*5-HTTLPR* (LL)	Depression	0.24 (0.39)	0.026	0.28 (0.41)	0.016
		Female sex			− 0.092 (0.39)	0.39
		Age (yrs)			0.024 (0.036)	0.83
		Antidepressants			−0.15 (0.83)	0.18
	5-HTTLPR (SS)	Depression	−0.38 (0.52)	0.004	−0.44 (0.54)	0.001
		Female sex			−0.17 (0.58)	0.22
		Age (yrs)			−0.03 (0.068)	0.82
		Antidepressant			0.13 (0.96)	0.33
		Living alone			0.38 (0.69)	0.018
	5-HTTLPR/rs25531 (L'L')	Depression	0.33 (0.49)	0.019	0.36 (0.53)	0.019
		Female sex			0.074 (0.48)	0.60
		Age (yrs)			−0.005 (0.057)	0.97
		Antidepressant			−0.093 (1.3)	0.54
	5-HTTLPR/rs25531 (S'S')	Depression	−0.28 (0.49)	0.027	−0.30 (0.50)	0.023
		Female sex			−0.14 (0.49)	0.29
		Age (yrs)			−0.22 (0.59)	0.097
		Antidepressant			0.098 (0.87)	0.44
		Living alone			0.27 (0.60)	0.056
25.26	*5-HTTLPR* (SS)	Depression	−0.37 (1.58)	0.009	−0.31 (1.68)	0.038
		Sex			−0.26 (1.65)	0.068
		Age (yrs)			−0.076 (0.20)	0.60
		Antidepressant			−0.087 (3.06)	0.56
	5-HTTLPR/rs25531 (S'S')	Depression	−0.37 (1.53)	0.006	−0.31 (1.52)	0.020
		Sex			−0.19 (1.46)	0.13
		Age (yrs)			−0.26 (0.18)	0.046
		Antidepressant			−0.11 (2.71)	0.39

[a]Adjusted for age, sex and antidepressant use, plus confounding factors (see methods) which remained significant in the final models at $p < 0.15$

and nominally significant evidence that six genetic variants influenced site-specific methylation at four out of 11 CpG units. Whilst methylation was not independently associated with depression, specific genotypes were found to modify the association between depression and methylation at several CpG units. In particular, for individuals with the SS or S'S genotypes of *5-HTTLPR* and *5-HTTLPR/rs25531* respectively, depression was significantly associated with lowermethylation at CpG 21 and CpG 25.26. On the other hand, for individuals carrying the LL or L'L' genotypes, depression was nominally associated with higher methylation at CpG 21. These findings were not confounded by sex, age, antidepressant use, or other factors examined including living situation and comorbidities.

Differential *SLC6A4* methylation at the promoter CpG island has been correlated with risk factors and adversities related to depression. Associations has been observed between maternal depression and decreased infant *SLC6A4* promoter methylation [34]. In adults, increased methylation has been associated with childhood trauma [35] and stress (early life and recent) [30, 36]. An inverse correlation between *SLC6A4* mRNA levels and promoter methylation has been demonstrated [11]. Several studies support our findings, reporting no association between *SLC6A4* methylation in blood and depression in adults, in either Caucasian [12] or three Asian ($n = 108$; $n = 286$; $n = 100$) [14, 15, 17] populations, as well as in buccal mucosa from Caucasian adolescents ($n = 150$) [16] and EBV-transformed lymphoblasts ($n = 192$) [18]. In contrast, three studies found positive associations between peripheral *SLC6A4* methylation in blood and depression in Caucasian ($n = 57$) [13] and Asian adults ($n = 151$; $n = 84$) [19, 20], two of which had overlapping assay regions with our study [19, 20]. Interestingly, Shi et al. (2016) found significantly highermethylation at two CpG

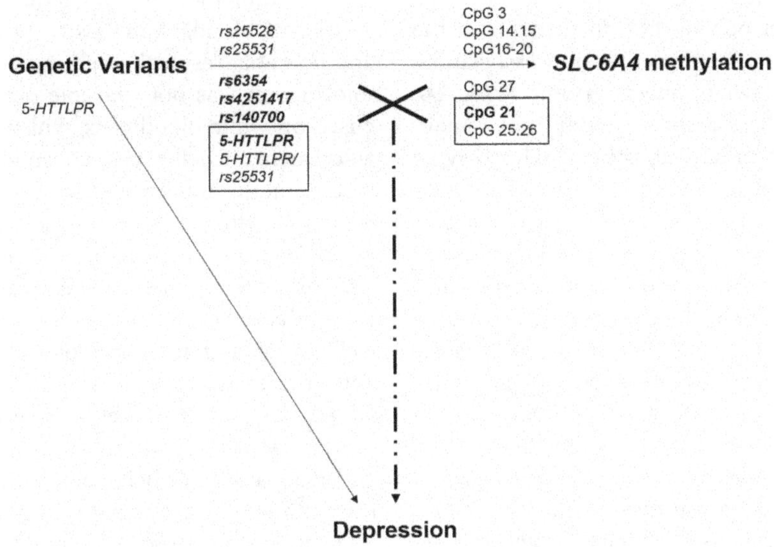

Fig. 3 Diagram of relationships between *SLC6A4* genetic variants, promoter methylation and depression. Solid lines indicate an association. The X denotes the interaction between genetic variants and *SLC6A4* methylation in association with depression (dot-dash line). Bolded genetic variants or DNA methylation sites in boxes were independently associated, but also interacted to influence depression risk. Interactions which remained significant following FDR correction are boxed

sites (Δ = 2.52 and 0.15) corresponding to CpG 25.26 in our study, which we failed to find, despite this unit having the highest level and variability of methylation.

It is increasingly clear that genetic variation plays a critical role in the regulation of DNA methylation [21]. Such loci, referred to as methylation quantitative trait loci (mQTLs), may also modify the association between DNA methylation risk of disease [37, 38]. Previous studies that have investigated the extent to which *SLC6A4* genotype can influence DNA methylation in the context of depression, have focused primarily on the *5-HTTLPR* polymorphism. Several reported no significant association with mean methylation [12, 16, 17], which is supported by our findings. However, we did observe a trend for an association between *5-HTTLPR* SS genotype and higherCpG 21 methylation ($p = 0.077$), which is in concordance with a study in post-stroke depression [15]. In addition, *rs25531*, which has been shown to modify the functionality of *5-HTTLPR* [27, 29] was also associated with site-specific methylation at CpG unit 16–20. Here we have shown for the first time that four other polymorphisms (*rs4251417, rs140700, rs6354* and *rs25528*) in *SLC6A4* may potentially regulate DNA methylation in the region.

Modifying effects of *5-HTTLPR* genotype on the association between *SLC6A4* methylation and several depression-related adversities, including childhood abuse [12] and stress [36], have been demonstrated previously. The few studies which have investigated this in the context of depression, have found that the S allele in combination with higher*SLC6A4* methylation increased the risk of depressive symptoms in adolescents [16] and adults following stroke [15]. This contrasts with our current study which observed lower methylation at CpG units 21 and 25.26 in depressed older individuals with the SS genotype. However, a recent study by Iga et al. (2016) (average age: 42.2–45.0 years) found that the L allele was associated with higherperipheral blood methylation in depressed patients [13]. More broadly, as an inverse correlation exists between *SLC6A4* methylation and mRNA levels [11], our finding of decreased methylation in depressed individuals is consistent with the observation of increased peripheral *SLC6A4* mRNA in un-medicated MDD patients [39–41].

The vast majority of epigenetic studies of *5-HTTLPR* did not consider *SL* genotype individually, which makes it hard to determine the real (in)consistency of data [8]. Similar to Iga et al., we found highermethylation at CpG 21 in depressed older individuals with the LL genotype, although this was only nominally significant in our study. Interestingly, previous findings also indicate that age can influence the association between *5-HTTLPR* and mental health [8].

Given the larger sample size, our findings further strengthen the evidence that *5-HTTLPR* plays a role in modifying the association of methylation with depression. We also found significant modifying effects from the triallelic *5-HTTLPR/rs25531* polymorphism. Whilst *5-HTTLPR/rs25531* modification effects have not been studied in relation to the CpG island, a recent study found that carriers of the S′ allele had lowermethylation at a neighboring Alu retrotransposon (AluJb) in association with stress [42], which is in a similar direction of effect found in our study.

This is also the first study to examine the potential modifying effects of other polymorphisms throughout the *SLC6A4* gene on the depression-methylation association. Here, we report modifying effects from *rs140700, rs4251417, rs6354,* but these associations did not remain significant following multivariate adjustment. This may be because of the relatively small sample size with these genotypes, in particular because there were too few minor homozygotes to include in the analysis, with the comparison instead been only between major homozygotes and heterozygotes. Therefore, a larger sample size able to capture the minor homozygote is needed to further investigate these associations. Overall, the effects of genotype and methylation may combine to exert another layer of regulation in modifying risk of depression. Further investigation is needed to examine the underlying mechanisms and its function in influencing depression risk.

Our study of 302 participants is larger than all previous studies investigating *SLC6A4* methylation and genetic variation in depression. However only subtle differences in DNA methylation levels have been observed in peripheral tissues in association with psychiatric disorders, suggesting that an even larger sample size may be required to fully reveal true associations. We were able to consider several polymorphisms throughout the gene in combination with promoter methylation in our study, and adjust for a wide variety of confounding factors including sex, age and antidepressant use. Our participants were from the general population, thus making our findings more generalisable, as opposed to studies focused only on depressed hospital patients. Late-life depression covers a range of mild to severe depressive symptoms [43], so the CES-D scale to assess depressive symptoms, together with the DSM-IV classification of MDD (American Psychiatric Association, 1994), has helped ensure non-depressed individuals in this study did not have significant levels of sub-clinical symptomatology. Whilst our results may be generalisable to the older population, it may not be the case for earlier onset depression and non-Caucasian populations. Contributors to the etiology of depression may vary by age of onset, with late-life depression more frequently comorbid with physical and psychiatric conditions such as cardiovascular disease and stroke [44]. Depressive symptoms are also more frequent amongst the oldest old, which may be explained by factors associated with aging, such as higher proportion of women and increased physical impairment [44]. This is consistent with our finding that depressed individuals are significantly more likely to be female, older and functionally impaired (Table 1). DNA methylation patterns have been reported to vary with age, sex and ethnicity [45, 46]. Specifically, global hypomethylation has been reported in females [46] and with increasing age [45]. Hence, decreases in *SLC6A4* methylation, as observed in this study, may be specifically associated with late-life depression.

Other limitations to our study are the cellular heterogeneity of blood, the cross-sectional design of this study and potential residual confounding from factors for which information was not available or collected. Our study focused on white blood cells, which contain a heterogenous assortment of cell types. Given the cell-type-specific nature of methylation, variation in cellular composition may lead to distinct methylation profiles between cell types, potentially confounding methylation-related analyses [47]. This may account for the lack of associations observed between depression and *SLC6A4* methylation in our study. Cellular heterogeneity cannot be controlled for in a candidate gene study such as ours. Epigenome-wide association studies, on the other hand, have the ability to computationally adjust for cellular heterogeneity [48], with the added advantage of being able to interrogate large proportions of the (epi)genome without an a priori hypothesis.

Finally, as an association study, we are unable to draw any conclusions about the functionality or causality of our findings. Using peripheral methylation to examine a brain-based disorder has its limitations, as methylation profiles can also be distinct across different tissues. A few studies have reported correlations between DNA methylation levels in blood and post-mortem brain tissue, although these are likely to be gene-specific [49, 50]. Changes in peripheral tissues, such as in inflammatory markers, have been observed in depression, therefore becoming increasingly recognised as a systemic disease [51, 52]. Further, both *SLC6A4* methylation and genetic variants have been correlated with brain structural changes, including the hippocampus and corpus callosum, in depressed individuals [12, 53–55]. As such, our study may provide support for *SLC6A4* methylation as a biomarker of depression, indicating that such a biomarker would need to consider *SLC6A4* methylation in combination with genetic variation.

Conclusion

Our study of late-life depression did not find any strong evidence for an independent association between *SLC6A4* promoter methylation and depression, however this may be modified by underlying genetic variants in the region. Further investigation is needed to examine the mechanisms behind such interactions, and replication in larger, independent and longitudinal studies are needed to help confirm these findings.

Abbreviations

CES-D: Centre for Epidemiological Studies Depression Scale; DSM-IV: Diagnostic and Statistical Manual of Mental Disorders-IV; HWE: Hardy-Weinberg equilibrium; IQR: Interquartile range; MDD: Major depressive disorder; MINI: Mini International Neuropsychiatric Interview; mQTL: Methylation quantitative trait loci; SNP: Single nucleotide polymorphism; SSRI: Selective serotonin re-uptake inhibitor; VNTR: Variable number tandem repeat

Acknowledgements
We thank all ESPRIT study participants, and Dr. Benjamin Ong for assistance with the Sequenom MassARRAY platform.

Funding
The ESPRIT project is financed by the regional government of Languedoc-Roussillon, the Agence Nationale de la Recherche Project 07 LVIE 004, and an unconditional grant from Norvartis. This work was also supported by the National Health and Medical Research Council, through a Senior Research Fellowship (APP1045161 to RS); the Murdoch Children's Research Institute (studentship to DL) and the Victorian Government's Operational Infrastructure Support Program. The funders had no role in the design and conduct of the study; in data collection, management, analysis or interpretation of the data and were not involved with the writing, preparation, review or approval of the manuscript.

Authors' contributions
MLA and KR lead the ESPRIT study and the collection of data. JR set up the study, DL processed all biological samples, generated the methylation data and performed all data analyses. JR and RS were involved in the interpretation of the data. DL drafted the manuscript and all authors were involved in its revision and gave final approval to the submitted manuscript.

Consent for publication
Not applicable.

Competing interests
Joanne Ryan is currently acting as an Associate Editor for BMC Psychiatry. All other authors declare that they have no competing interests.

Author details
[1]Cancer & Disease Epigenetics, Murdoch Children's Research Institute, Royal Children's Hospital, Parkville, VIC, Australia. [2]Department of Paediatrics, University of Melbourne, Parkville, VIC, Australia. [3]INSERM, Univ Montpellier, Neuropsychiatry: Epidemiological and Clinical Research, Montpellier, France. [4]Centre for Clinical Brain Sciences, University of Edinburgh, Edinburgh, UK. [5]Department of Epidemiology and Preventive Medicine, Monash University, Level 5, The Alfred Centre, 99 Commercial Road, Melbourne 3004, Australia.

References

1. Albert PR, Benkelfat C, Descarries L. The neurobiology of depression–revisiting the serotonin hypothesis. I. Cellular and molecular mechanisms. Philos Trans R Soc Lond Ser B Biol Sci. 2012;367(1601):2378–81.
2. Belmaker RH, Agam G. Major depressive disorder. N Engl J Med. 2008; 358(1):55–68.
3. Albert PR, Benkelfat C. The neurobiology of depression--revisiting the serotonin hypothesis. II. Genetic, epigenetic and clinical studies. Philos Trans R Soc Lond Ser B Biol Sci. 2013;368(1615):20120535.
4. Ramamoorthy S, Bauman AL, Moore KR, Han H, Yang-Feng T, Chang AS, Ganapathy V, Blakely RD. Antidepressant- and cocaine-sensitive human serotonin transporter: molecular cloning, expression, and chromosomal localization. Proc Natl Acad Sci U S A. 1993;90(6):2542–6.
5. Bradley SL, Dodelzon K, Sandhu HK, Philibert RA. Relationship of serotonin transporter gene polymorphisms and haplotypes to mRNA transcription. Am J Med Genet B Neuropsychiatr Genet. 2005;136B(1):58–61.
6. Lesch KP, Bengel D, Heils A, Sabol SZ, Greenberg BD, Petri S, Benjamin J, Muller CR, Hamer DH, Murphy DL. Association of anxiety-related traits with a polymorphism in the serotonin transporter gene regulatory region. Science. 1996;274(5292):1527–31.
7. Clarke H, Flint J, Attwood AS, Munafo MR. Association of the 5- HTTLPR genotype and unipolar depression: a meta-analysis. Psychol Med. 2010; 40(11):1767–78.
8. Ancelin ML, Ryan J. 5-HTTLPR x stress hypothesis: is the debate over? Mol Psychiatry. 2017. https://doi.org/10.1038/mp.2017.195. [Epub ahead of print].
9. Booij L, Wang D, Levesque ML, Tremblay RE, Szyf M. Looking beyond the DNA sequence: the relevance of DNA methylation processes for the stress-diathesis model of depression. Philos Trans R Soc Lond Ser B Biol Sci. 2013; 368(1615):20120251.
10. Booij L, Tremblay RE, Szyf M, Benkelfat C. Genetic and early environmental influences on the serotonin system: consequences for brain development and risk for psychopathology. J Psychiatry Neurosci. 2015;40(1):5–18.
11. Philibert R, Madan A, Andersen A, Cadoret R, Packer H, Sandhu H. Serotonin transporter mRNA levels are associated with the methylation of an upstream CpG island. Am J Med Genet B Neuropsychiatr Genet. 2007; 144B(1):101–5.
12. Booij L, Szyf M, Carballedo A, Frey EM, Morris D, Dymov S, Vaisheva F, Ly V, Fahey C, Meaney J, et al. DNA methylation of the serotonin transporter gene in peripheral cells and stress-related changes in hippocampal volume: a study in depressed patients and healthy controls. PLoS One. 2015;10(3):e0119061.
13. Iga J, Watanabe SY, Numata S, Umehara H, Nishi A, Kinoshita M, Inoshita M, Shimodera S, Fujita H, Ohmori T. Association study of polymorphism in the serotonin transporter gene promoter, methylation profiles, and expression in patients with major depressive disorder. Hum Psychopharmacol. 2016; 31(3):193–9.
14. Kang HJ, Kim JM, Stewart R, Kim SY, Bae KY, Kim SW, Shin IS, Shin MG, Yoon JS. Association of SLC6A4 methylation with early adversity, characteristics and outcomes in depression. Prog Neuro-Psychopharmacol Biol Psychiatry. 2013;44:23–8.
15. Kim JM, Stewart R, Kang HJ, Kim SW, Shin IS, Kim HR, Shin MG, Kim JT, Park MS, Cho KH, et al. A longitudinal study of SLC6A4 DNA promoter methylation and poststroke depression. J Psychiatr Res. 2013;47(9):1222–7.
16. Olsson CA, Foley DL, Parkinson-Bates M, Byrnes G, McKenzie M, Patton GC, Morley R, Anney RJ, Craig JM, Saffery R. Prospects for epigenetic research within cohort studies of psychological disorder: a pilot investigation of a peripheral cell marker of epigenetic risk for depression. Biol Psychol. 2010; 83(2):159–65.
17. Okada S, Morinobu S, Fuchikami M, Segawa M, Yokomaku K, Kataoka T, Okamoto Y, Yamawaki S, Inoue T, Kusumi I, et al. The potential of SLC6A4 gene methylation analysis for the diagnosis and treatment of major depression. J Psychiatr Res. 2014;53:47–53.
18. Philibert RA, Sandhu H, Hollenbeck N, Gunter T, Adams W, Madan A. The relationship of 5HTT (SLC6A4) methylation and genotype on mRNA expression and liability to major depression and alcohol dependence in subjects from the Iowa adoption studies. Am J Med Genet B Neuropsychiatr Genet. 2008;147B(5):543–9.
19. Shi M, Sun H, Xu Y, Wang Z, Cui H, Wang C, Liu W, An G, Hu J. Methylation status of the serotonin transporter promoter CpG Island is associated with major depressive disorder in Chinese Han population: a case-control study. J Nerv Ment Dis. 2016;205(8):641–6.
20. Zhao J, Goldberg J, Bremner JD, Vaccarino V. Association between promoter methylation of serotonin transporter gene and depressive symptoms: a monozygotic twin study. Psychosom Med. 2013;75(6):523–9.
21. Gaunt TR, Shihab HA, Hemani G, Min JL, Woodward G, Lyttleton O, Zheng J, Duggirala A, McArdle WL, Ho K, et al. Systematic identification of genetic influences on methylation across the human life course. Genome Biol. 2016;17:61.
22. Ritchie K, Artero S, Beluche I, Ancelin ML, Mann A, Dupuy AM, Malafosse A, Boulenger JP. Prevalence of DSM-IV psychiatric disorder in the French elderly population. Br J Psychiatry. 2004;184:147–52.
23. Association AP. Diagnostic and statistical manual of mental disorders. 5th ed; 2013.
24. Beekman AT, Deeg DJ, Van Limbeek J, Braam AW, De Vries MZ, Van Tilburg W. Criterion validity of the Center for Epidemiologic Studies Depression scale (CES-D): results from a community-based sample of older subjects in the Netherlands. Psychol Med. 1997;27(1):231–5.
25. Radloff LS. The CES-D scale: a self-report depression scale for research in the general population. Appl Psychol Meas. 1977;1:385:385–401.
26. Ritchie K, Jaussent I, Stewart R, Dupuy AM, Courtet P, Ancelin ML, Malafosse A. Association of adverse childhood environment and 5-HTTLPR genotype with late-life depression. J Clin Psychiatry. 2009;70(9):1281–8.
27. Wray NR, James MR, Gordon SD, Dumenil T, Ryan L, Coventry WL, Statham DJ, Pergadia ML, Madden PA, Heath AC, et al. Accurate, large-scale genotyping of 5HTTLPR and flanking single nucleotide polymorphisms in an association study of depression, anxiety, and personality measures. Biol Psychiatry. 2009;66(5):468–76.
28. Raitio M, Perälä A, Harinen R, Lampinen J. Validation of KASPar™ dual FRET based SNP genotyping assay. Thermo Fisher Scientific. 2012:1–5.

29. Wendland JR, Martin BJ, Kruse MR, Lesch KP, Murphy DL. Simultaneous genotyping of four functional loci of human SLC6A4, with a reappraisal of 5-HTTLPR and rs25531. Mol Psychiatry. 2006;11(3):224–6.
30. Duman EA, Canli T. Influence of life stress, 5-HTTLPR genotype, and SLC6A4 methylation on gene expression and stress response in healthy Caucasian males. Biol Mood Anxiety Disord. 2015;5:2.
31. Kent WJ, Sugnet CW, Furey TS, Roskin KM, Pringle TH, Zahler AM, Haussler D. The human genome browser at UCSC. Genome Res. 2002;12(6):996–1006.
32. Coolen MW, Statham AL, Gardiner-Garden M, Clark SJ. Genomic profiling of CpG methylation and allelic specificity using quantitative high-throughput mass spectrometry: critical evaluation and improvements. Nucleic Acids Res. 2007;35(18):e119.
33. Menke A, Binder EB. Epigenetic alterations in depression and antidepressant treatment. Dialogues Clin Neurosci. 2014;16(3):395–404.
34. Devlin AM, Brain U, Austin J, Oberlander TF. Prenatal exposure to maternal depressed mood and the MTHFR C677T variant affect SLC6A4 methylation in infants at birth. PLoS One. 2010;5(8):e12201.
35. Wang D, Szyf M, Benkelfat C, Provencal N, Turecki G, Caramaschi D, Cote SM, Vitaro F, Tremblay RE, Booij L. Peripheral SLC6A4 DNA methylation is associated with in vivo measures of human brain serotonin synthesis and childhood physical aggression. PLoS One. 2012;7(6):e39501.
36. Alexander N, Wankerl M, Hennig J, Miller R, Zankert S, Steudte-Schmiedgen S, Stalder T, Kirschbaum C. DNA methylation profiles within the serotonin transporter gene moderate the association of 5-HTTLPR and cortisol stress reactivity. Transl Psychiatry. 2014;4:e443.
37. Rakyan VK, Down TA, Balding DJ, Beck S. Epigenome-wide association studies for common human diseases. Nat Rev Genet. 2011;12(8):529–41.
38. Zhi D, Aslibekyan S, Irvin MR, Claas SA, Borecki IB, Ordovas JM, Absher DM, Arnett DK. SNPs located at CpG sites modulate genome-epigenome interaction. Epigenetics. 2013;8(8):802–6.
39. Belzeaux R, Azorin JM, Ibrahim EC. Monitoring candidate gene expression variations before, during and after a first major depressive episode in a 51-year-old man. BMC Psychiatry. 2014;14:73.
40. Iga J, Ueno S, Yamauchi K, Motoki I, Tayoshi S, Ohta K, Song H, Morita K, Rokutan K, Ohmori T. Serotonin transporter mRNA expression in peripheral leukocytes of patients with major depression before and after treatment with paroxetine. Neurosci Lett. 2005;389(1):12–6.
41. Tsao CW, Lin YS, Chen CC, Bai CH, Wu SR. Cytokines and serotonin transporter in patients with major depression. Prog Neuro-Psychopharmacol Biol Psychiatry. 2006;30(5):899–905.
42. Schneider I, Kugel H, Redlich R, Grotegerd D, Burger C, Burkner PC, Opel N, Dohm K, Zaremba D, Meinert S, et al. Association of Serotonin Transporter Gene AluJb methylation with major depression, amygdala responsiveness, 5-HTTLPR/rs25531 polymorphism, and stress. Neuropsychopharmacology. 2017;43(6):1308–16.
43. Fiske A, Wetherell JL, Gatz M. Depression in older adults. Annu Rev Clin Psychol. 2009;5:363–89.
44. Blazer DG. Depression in late life: review and commentary. J Gerontol A Biol Sci Med Sci. 2003;58(3):249–65.
45. Johnson AA, Akman K, Calimport SR, Wuttke D, Stolzing A, de Magalhaes JP. The role of DNA methylation in aging, rejuvenation, and age-related disease. Rejuvenation Res. 2012;15(5):483–94.
46. Zhang FF, Cardarelli R, Carroll J, Fulda KG, Kaur M, Gonzalez K, Vishwanatha JK, Santella RM, Morabia A. Significant differences in global genomic DNA methylation by gender and race/ethnicity in peripheral blood. Epigenetics. 2011;6(5):623–9.
47. Januar V, Saffery R, Ryan J. Epigenetics and depressive disorders: a review of current progress and future directions. Int J Epidemiol. 2015;44(4):1364–87.
48. Jaffe AE, Irizarry RA. Accounting for cellular heterogeneity is critical in epigenome-wide association studies. Genome Biol. 2014;15(2):R31.
49. Davies MN, Volta M, Pidsley R, Lunnon K, Dixit A, Lovestone S, Coarfa C, Harris RA, Milosavljevic A, Troakes C, et al. Functional annotation of the human brain methylome identifies tissue-specific epigenetic variation across brain and blood. Genome Biol. 2012;13(6):R43.
50. Horvath S, Zhang Y, Langfelder P, Kahn RS, Boks MP, van Eijk K, van den Berg LH, Ophoff RA. Aging effects on DNA methylation modules in human brain and blood tissue. Genome Biol. 2012;13(10):R97.
51. O'Donovan A, Hughes BM, Slavich GM, Lynch L, Cronin MT, O'Farrelly C, Malone KM. Clinical anxiety, cortisol and interleukin-6: evidence for specificity in emotion-biology relationships. Brain Behav Immun. 2010; 24(7):1074–7.
52. Thomson CA, McColl A, Cavanagh J, Graham GJ. Peripheral inflammation is associated with remote global gene expression changes in the brain. J Neuroinflammation. 2014;11:73.
53. Frodl T, Szyf M, Carballedo A, Ly V, Dymov S, Vaisheva F, Morris D, Fahey C, Meaney J, Gill M, et al. DNA methylation of the serotonin transporter gene (SLC6A4) is associated with brain function involved in processing emotional stimuli. J Psychiatry Neurosci. 2015;40(5):296–305.
54. Taylor WD, Steffens DC, Payne ME, MacFall JR, Marchuk DA, Svenson IK, Krishnan KR. Influence of serotonin transporter promoter region polymorphisms on hippocampal volumes in late-life depression. Arch Gen Psychiatry. 2005;62(5):537–44.
55. Won E, Choi S, Kang J, Kim A, Han KM, Chang HS, Tae WS, Son KR, Joe SH, Lee MS, et al. Association between reduced white matter integrity in the corpus callosum and serotonin transporter gene DNA methylation in medication-naive patients with major depressive disorder. Transl Psychiat. 2016;6

3

The relationship between marital satisfaction and depression in infertile couples: an actor–partner interdependence model approach

Saman Maroufizadeh[1], Mostafa Hosseini[1*], Abbas Rahimi Foroushani[1], Reza Omani-Samani[2] and Payam Amini[2]

Abstract

Background: Much evidence consistent with the Marital Discord Model of Depression (MDMD) suggests that marital discord is associated with depression, but no studies examine the relationship between marital satisfaction and depression at the dyadic level in infertile couples. This study examined the effect of actors' and partners' marital satisfaction on depressive symptoms in husband-wife dyads with infertility using an innovative dyadic analysis approach, the Actor–Partner Interdependence Model (APIM).

Methods: In this cross-sectional study, the sample comprised of 141 infertile couples in the evaluation phase of treatment. We collected data in a referral infertility center in Tehran, Iran between February and May 2017. Marital satisfaction and depression were measured using ENRICH marital satisfaction scale and Hospital Anxiety and Depression Scale, respectively, before starting the treatment. Dyadic analysis applying the APIM was used. In this study, actor effect is the impact of a person's marital satisfaction on his/her own depression. Partner effect is the impact of a person's marital satisfaction on his/her partner's depression.

Results: The APIM analysis revealed that both men and women's marital satisfaction excreted an actor effect on their own depression ($\beta = -0.412$, $P < 0.001$; $\beta = -0.263$, $P = 0.002$, respectively). Furthermore, men's marital satisfaction exerted a significant partner effect on their wives' depression symptoms ($\beta = -0.170$, $p = 0.047$). However, the wives' marital satisfaction was not related to their husbands' depressive symptoms ($\beta = -0.028$, $P = 0.735$).

Conclusions: The findings support that the MDMD is a valid theoretical model for the conceptualization of marital satisfaction and depressive symptoms among infertile couples and suggest that interventions to reduce depressive symptoms should include both men and women.

Keywords: Depression, Marital satisfaction, Infertility, Actor–partner interdependence model

Background

Infertility is medically defined as "the failure to achieve a clinical pregnancy after 12 months or more of regular unprotected sexual intercourse" [1]. It is a global public health concern affecting 9% of reproductive-aged couples worldwide [2] with negative psychological consequences. One of the most often-cited repercussions of infertility is depression disorder. For example, in two studies conducted by Maroufizadeh et al. [3] and Omani-Samani et al. [4] in Iran, the prevalences of depression were 33.0% and 30.5%, respectively, which are higher than what was reported in general population. Some of the demographic/fertility risk factors for depression in infertile couples include educational level, cause of infertility, duration of infertility, and having failure in previous infertility treatments [3–5]. One the other hand, infertility and its treatment has also a negative impact on a person's marital satisfaction, relationship satisfaction, and sextual functioning [6–8].

* Correspondence: mhossein110@yahoo.com
[1]Department of Epidemiology and Biostatistics, School of Public Health, Tehran University of Medical Sciences, Tehran, Iran
Full list of author information is available at the end of the article

Based on the Marital Discord Model of Depression (MDMD) [9], marital discord is an important risk factor for depressive symptoms in married couples. A growing body of evidence support the MDMD. For example, in a meta-analysis of 26 cross-sectional study, the effect size of marital satisfaction on depression was – 0.42 for women and – 0.37 for men [10]. In addition, longitudinal studies have found that marital dissatisfaction is associated with subsequent depressive disorder [11, 12]. On the other hand, marital satisfaction is strongly influenced by sexual functioning. Satisfying marital and sexual functioning protects against the development of psychological distress but is also a factor related to depression and anxiety [13, 14].

A fundamental assumption in behavioral and social science statistical methods is the independence of observations. Many of the phenomena studied in this context are dyadic in nature (e.g., research on man-woman dyads). The observations arising from such designs are not independent, but interdependent (i.e., the characteristics of one member of the dyad affects outcomes of the other member in the dyad) [15, 16]. In this case, conventional statistical methods are not proper for analyzing data; Instead, the methods that take into account the interdependence is required [16]. To address this issue, Kenny et al. [16] developed the Actor Partner Interdependence Model (APIM), the most frequently used analytical model of dyadic data. This model simultaneously estimates the effects of an individual's attributes on his/her own outcome variable (actor effect), as well as his/her partner's (partner effect).

Most studies examining the effect of marital satisfaction on depression in infertile couples use the conventional statistical methods. Although valuable, these studies fail to take into account the interdependency of couples' data, and consequently fail to show interpersonal relationships. In addition, since experience of infertility is a shared problem between members of a couple, examining the interpersonal relationship is especially relevant [17]. Due to these reasons, in the last few years, APIM framework has been used to examine many relationship processes, including the effect of depression on quality of life in Iranian infertile couples [18], and effects of spirituality and infertility-related stress on quality of life in Brazilian infertile couples [19]. The aim of the present study was twofold: (a) to examine whether there were differences in the levels of marital satisfaction and depression between men and women dyads with infertility, and (b) to apply the APIM framework to elucidate and differentiate actor and partner effects of marital satisfaction on depression in infertile couples.

Methods

Participants and procedure

This cross-sectional study was performed at the infertility treatment clinic of Royan Institute, Tehran, Iran. This clinic is one of the largest clinics for infertility treatment in Iran [20]. Infertile couples come to this center, not only from the capital of Iran but also from all around the country. The data were collected in the evaluation phase of treatment using the convenience sampling method between February and May 2017. Couples had to meet the following criteria to be eligible for the study: (1) married couple; (12) 18 years or older; (2) willingness to take part in the study; (3) experiencing fertility problems; and (4) ability to read, write, and comprehend Persian. Both husband and wife were asked to complete the measures with no discussion between them. In total, 141 infertile couples agreed to participate and filled out the instruments completely (response rate: 82.9%).

Measures

Marital satisfaction

Marital satisfaction was measured using the 10-Item ENRICH Marital Satisfaction Scale (EMS Scale). The EMS Scale is a 10-item self-report inventory that measures marital satisfaction [21]. Items are rated on a 5-point Likert scale, ranging from 1 (strongly disagree) to 5 (strongly agree). Total scores range from 10 to 50, with higher scores indicating greater marital satisfaction. In the current study, the Cronbach's alpha coefficients of EMS Scale for men and women were 0.752 and 0.790, respectively.

Depression

Depression symptoms was measured using the Hospital Anxiety and Depression Scale (HADS). The HADS is a frequently used 14-item self-report inventory composed of two 7-items subscales: anxiety (HADS-A) and depression (HADS-D) [22]. Items are rated on a 4-point Likert scale, ranging from 0 (no symptoms) to 3 (severe symptoms). Both subscales scores range from 0 to 21, with higher scores indicating greater levels of anxiety and depression. The Persian version of the HADS has shown satisfactory reliability and validity in infertile people [23] and has been used in many studies involving infertile people [3, 24]. In this study, we used only the HADS-D subscale. In the current study, the Cronbach's alpha coefficients of HADS-D subscale for men and women were 0.708 and 0.722, respectively.

Statistical analysis

Preliminary analyses

Comparison of demographics/fertility information, marital satisfaction and depression for husbands and wives were done using the McNemar test and paired t test. Pearson's correlation coefficient was used to determine the relationship among the study variables.

APIM analysis

In this study, we analyzed our data using the APIM approach. Figure 1 depicts the APIM framework of a husband-wife dyad in which there is two variables from each in the dyad: marital satisfaction and depression. This approach takes into account the interdependence of couples' data. Also, with APIM approach, both actor effects (e.g. how a person's level of marital satisfaction affects his or her own depression) as well as partner effects (e.g. how a person's level of marital satisfaction affects his or her partner's depression) can be examined simultaneously.

There are three methods to estimate the APIM parameters: the pooled regression modeling, multilevel modeling, and structural equation modeling (SEM). As recommended by Kenny et al. [16], SEM with distinguishable dyads is the simplest data analytic method for estimating the APIM.

The APIM analysis was done with Mplus software version 6.12 (Muthén & Muthén, Los Angeles, CA, USA), and preliminary analyses were done with IBM SPSS Statistics for Windows, Version 22.0 (IBM Crop., Armonk, NY, USA).

Results

Characteristics of the infertile couples

Table 1 shows the demographic and fertility characteristics of the infertile couples. The wives, on average, were 5.10 years younger than their husbands ($t_{(140)} = 12.88$, $P < 0.001$), but had a similar education level as their husbands ($\chi^2_{(1)} = 2.56$, $P = 0.109$). The mean duration of marriage and infertility were 7.37 ± 4.40 and 4.85 ± 3.76 years, respectively. Infertility was due to a male or female factor in 36.2 and 21.3% of dyads, respectively. In 19.1%, both male and female factors were observed, and 23.4% of couples had unexplained infertility. Of the couples, 27.7% had secondary infertility, 23.4% had history of abortion and 49.6% were treated for infertility for the first time.

Preliminary analyses

Means, SDs, and correlations for study variables are presented in Table 2. According to the paired t test, there were no significant differences between men and women on the depression ($t_{(140)} = 0.45$, $P = 0.653$) and marital satisfaction ($t_{(140)} = 0.09$, $P = 0.925$).

Within-dyad correlations revealed that wives' and husbands' scale scores were significantly correlated for depression ($r = 0.256$, $P = 0.002$) and marital satisfaction ($r = 0.423$, $P < 0.001$). Based on Pearson correlations, husbands' marital satisfaction was correlated with both their own depression ($r = -0.424$, $P < 0.001$) and their wives' depression ($r = -0.281$, $P < 0.001$). Wives' marital satisfaction were also correlated with both their own depression ($r = -0.335$, $P < 0.001$) and their husbands' depression ($r = -0.203$, $P = 0.016$).

APIM analysis

The APIM analysis indicated that the man's marital satisfaction as well as woman's marital satisfaction exhibited an actor effect on their own depression ($\beta = -0.412$, $P < 0.001$; $\beta = -0.263$, $P = 0.002$, respectively) (Table 3). With regard to partner effects, however, only the man's marital satisfaction had a partner effect on woman's depression ($\beta = -0.170$, $p = 0.047$). The partner effect of woman's marital satisfaction on man's depression was not significant ($\beta = -0.028$, $P = 0.735$).

Discussion

To the best of our knowledge, this study is the first of its kind to use the APIM approach to examine the intrapersonal and interpersonal influences of marital satisfaction on depression in a sample of infertile couples. Although the most of studies examining the relationship between marital satisfaction and depressive symptoms focused on the intrapersonal mechanisms (actor effects), there are growing calls to examine the interpersonal mechanisms (partner effects). Since infertility is also a shared problem between spouses, both men and women need to be

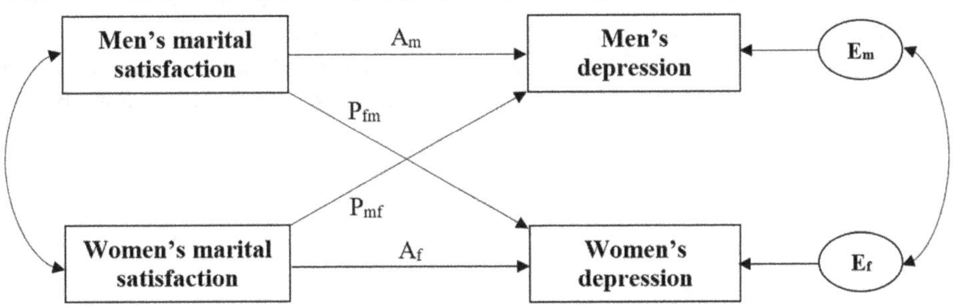

Fig. 1 Actor–Partner Interdependence Model of marital satisfaction and depression. Legend 1: A_m: actor effect of men's marital satisfaction on his own depression; A_f: actor effect of women's marital satisfaction on her own depression; P_{fm}: partner effect of men's marital satisfaction on women's depression; P_{mf}: partner effect of women's marital satisfaction on men's depression; E_m and E_f: residual errors on depression for men and women, respectively

Table 1 Demographic and fertility characteristics of the infertile couples (*n* = 141 couples)

	Men	Women	Test statistic	P
Age (years)	34.92 ± 6.35	29.82 ± 6.00	$t_{(140)} = 12.88$	< 0.001
Educational level			$X^2_{(1)} = 2.56$	0.109
Non-academic	96 (68.1)	85 (60.3)		
Academic	45 (31.9)	56 (39.7)		
Duration of marriage (years)	7.37 ± 4.40	–		
Duration of infertility (years)	4.85 ± 3.76	–		
Cause of infertility				
Male factor	51 (36.2)	–		
Female factor	30 (21.3)	–		
Both	27 (19.1)	–		
Unexplained	33 (23.4)	–		
Failure of previous treatment				
No (First treatment)	71 (50.4)	–		
Yes	70 (49.6)	–		
History of abortion				
No	108 (76.6)	–		
Yes	33 (23.4)	–		
Type of infertility				
Primary	102 (72.3)	–		
Secondary	39 (27.7)	–		

Values are given as "Mean ± SD" or "n (%)"

involved and considered as a dyad in the data analysis. According to within-dyad correlations, considerable correlations between wives' and husbands' scores were observed. These findings confirm that husbands and wives' scores were adequately related to be deemed statistically interdependent, and so APIM approach would be more appropriate than conventional statistical analyses.

In keeping with some previous studies [3, 25], we found that there was no significant difference between men and women in the depression level. However, in a two study conducted in Poland [26] and Pakistan [27], women had a higher level of depression than men. In this study, there was also no sex difference in the marital satisfaction, which is in line with Peterson et al. study [28]. In a study performed by Drosdzol and Skrzypulec [26], women had a worse marital satisfaction than their husbands. In addition, general population studies indicate that marital and psychological distress are more common among women than men [29].

Consistent with the MDMD, the current study showed the considerable actor effect of marital satisfaction on depression, which is also consistent with previous studies conducted in USA [30], China [31, 32], Brazil [33] and Israel [12]. However, in a study conducted among Chinese older couples, neither of the actor effects was significant [34].

The key finding of our study was the link between men's marital satisfaction and women's depression. In line with our expectation, we found that husband's lower marital satisfaction was associated with greater level of wives' depression. Contrary to our expectation, the present study does not confirm a strong partner effect of women's marital satisfaction on their husband's depression. In other words, regarding the partner effects, the

Table 2 Means, standard deviations, and correlations among study variables (*n* = 141 couples)

	Mean (SD)	1	2	3	4
1 Men marital satisfaction	39.31 (6.56)	1			
2 Men depression	4.94 (3.41)	−0.424***	1		
3 Women marital satisfaction	39.26 (6.70)	0.423***	−0.203*	1	
4 Women depression	5.09 (3.33)	−0.281***	0.256**	−0.335***	1

SD Standard Deviation
*P < 0.05; **P < 0.01; ***P < 0.001

Table 3 Actor and partner effects of marital satisfaction on depression in infertile couples ($n = 141$ couples)

	Men			Women		
	β (SE)	t	P	β (SE)	t	P
Actor's marital satisfaction	– 0.412 (0.078)	5.28	< 0.001	– 0.263 (0.084)	3.13	0.002
Partner's marital satisfaction	–0.028 (0.084)	0.34	0.735	–0.170 (0.085)	1.98	0.047

β: Standardized Coefficient; *SE* Standard Error

MDMD was partly supported asymmetrically among infertile couples. This type of asymmetrical pattern of partner effects has also been reported in several previous studies [34, 35]. However, contrary to our finding, Miller et al. [31] reported an opposite pattern of the partner effect in a sample of middle-aged Chinese couples.

The present research offers a number of important contributions to understanding the relationship between marital satisfaction and depression. Studies regarding this relationship tend to focus on individuals, despite the obviously dyadic nature of marital satisfaction. Many researches in this area also tend to focus on general population of adolescents and couples, most of whom have probably not yet become involved in long-term, committed marital relationships or have not yet experienced a shared health problem like infertility. The present study addresses these limitations, as it sought to test the MDMD in infertile married couples from a dyadic perspective. The findings of the present study have potentially important clinical implications. Probably one of the most key findings is the importance of taking a dyadic perspective on marital satisfaction and depression. Particularly, the study indicates that men's marital satisfaction is important to their wives' depression. Therapists working with infertile couples should be aware of these dyadic effects; thus, psychological interventions that target an enhancement of marital satisfaction and reduction of depression symptoms should treat the couple as a unit.

Our study had several limitations that should be considered when interpreting the findings. First, this study was conducted only in one center and therefore may not be generalizable. Second, the cross-sectional nature of the study design limits inferences about the causal relationships between marital satisfaction and depression. Longitudinal research is needed to better understand the relationship between marital satisfaction and depression symptoms, as these relationships can be multi-factorial and complex [36–38].

Conclusion

Despite the limitations, the study findings provide support for the MDMD among infertile couples.

Particularly, besides the actor (intrapersonal) effects for both male and female, there were partner (interpersonal) effects of male marital satisfaction on female depression symptoms. Based on these findings, interventions to reduce depressive symptoms in infertile couples should include both husbands and wives simultaneously.

Abbreviations

APIM: Actor–Partner Interdependence Model; EMS Scale: 10-Item ENRICH Marital Satisfaction Scale; HADS: Hospital Anxiety and Depression Scale; MDMD: Marital Discord Model of Depression; SEM: Structural Equation Modeling

Acknowledgements

The authors express their gratitude to the infertile couples who participated in this study and to the Royan Institute, Tehran, Iran for its kind cooperation in data collection.

Funding

This research did not receive any specific grant from any agency in the public, commercial, or not-for-profit sector.

Authors' contributions

SM and MH: Study design and conception, data analysis and interpretation, and manuscript writing; ARF: Study design and conception, manuscript editing; ROS: Study design and conception, data acquisition, data interpretation, and manuscript editing; PA: Study design and conception, data acquisition, and manuscript editing. All authors approved the final version of the manuscript for submission.

Consent for publication

Not applicable.

Competing interests

The authors declare that they have no competing interests.

Author details

[1]Department of Epidemiology and Biostatistics, School of Public Health, Tehran University of Medical Sciences, Tehran, Iran. [2]Department of Epidemiology and Reproductive Health, Reproductive Epidemiology Research Center, Royan Institute for Reproductive Biomedicine, ACECR, Tehran, Iran.

References

1. Zegers-Hochschild F, Adamson GD, de Mouzon J, Ishihara O, Mansour R, Nygren K, Sullivan E, Van der Poel S. The international committee for monitoring assisted reproductive technology (ICMART) and the world health organization (WHO) revised glossary on ART terminology, 2009. Hum Reprod. 2009;24(11):2683–7.
2. Boivin J, Bunting L, Collins JA, Nygren KG. International estimates of infertility prevalence and treatment-seeking: potential need and demand for infertility medical care. Hum Reprod. 2007;22(6):1506–12.
3. Maroufizadeh S, Ghaheri A, Almasi-Hashiani A, Mohammadi M, Navid B, Ezabadi Z, Samani RO. The prevalence of anxiety and depression among people with infertility referring to Royan Institute in Tehran, Iran: a cross-sectional questionnaire study. Middle East Fertil Soc J. 2018;23(2):103 6.

4. Omani-Samani R, Maroufizadeh S, Almasi-Hashiani A, Amini P. Prevalence of depression and its determinant factors among infertile patients in Iran based on the PHQ-9. Middle East Fertil Soc J. 2018. https://doi.org/10.1016/j.mefs.2018.03.002.
5. Maroufizadeh S, Karimi E, Vesali S, Omani Samani R. Anxiety and depression after failure of assisted reproductive treatment among patients experiencing infertility. Int J Gynaecol Obstet. 2015;130(3):253–6.
6. Omani-Samani R, Maroufizadeh S, Ghaheri A, Amini P, Navid B. Reliability and validity of the Kansas marital satisfaction scale (KMSS) in infertile people. Middle East Fertil Soc J. 2018;23(2):154–7.
7. Maroufizadeh S, Omani-Samani R, Almasi-Hashiani A, Navid B, Sobati B, Amini P. The relationship assessment scale (RAS) in infertile patients: a reliability and validity study. Middle East Fertil Soc J. 2018. https://doi.org/10.1016/j.mefs.2018.04.001.
8. Millheiser LS, Helmer AE, Quintero RB, Westphal LM, Milki AA, Lathi RB. Is infertility a risk factor for female sexual dysfunction? A case-control study. Fertil Steril. 2010;94(6):2022–5.
9. Beach SR, Sandeen E, O'Leary KD. Depression in marriage: a model for etiology and treatment. New York: Guilford Press; 1990.
10. Whisman MA. The association between depression and marital dissatisfaction. In: Beach SRH, editor. Marital and family processes in depression: A scientific foundation for clinical practice. Edn. Washington, DC: American Psychological Association; 2001. p. 3–24.
11. Du Rocher Schudlich TD, Papp LM, Cummings EM. Relations between spouses' depressive symptoms and marital conflict: a longitudinal investigation of the role of conflict resolution styles. J Fam Psychol. 2011; 25(4):531–40.
12. Dekel R, Vilchinsky N, Liberman G, Leibowitz M, Khaskia A, Mosseri M. Marital satisfaction and depression among couples following men's acute coronary syndrome: testing dyadic dynamics in a longitudinal design. Br J Health Psychol. 2014;19(2):347–62.
13. Trudel G, Goldfarb M. Marital and sexual functioning and dysfunctioning, depression and anxiety. Sexologies. 2010;19(3):137–42.
14. Faizal SA, Sidi H, Wahab S, Zin NM, Baharuddin N. Assessment of marital dissatisfaction and its association with sexual dysfunction and psychiatric morbidities among primary health attenders in Malaysia. Int Med J Malaysia. 2017;16(2):19–26.
15. Laursen B, Little TD, Card NA. Handbook of developmental research methods. New York: Guilford Press; 2012.
16. Kenny DA, Kashy DA, Cook WL. Dyadic Data Analysis. New York: Guilford Press; 2006.
17. Peterson BD, Newton CR, Rosen KH. Examining congruence between partners' perceived infertility-related stress and its relationship to marital adjustment and depression in infertile couples. Fam Process. 2003;42(1):59–70.
18. Maroufizadeh S, Hosseini M, Foroushani AR, Omani-Samani R, Amini P. The effect of depression on quality of life in infertile couples: an actor-partner interdependence model approach. Health Qual Life Outcomes. 2018;16(1):73.
19. Casu G, Ulivi G, Zaia V, MdC FM, Parente Barbosa C, Gremigni P. Spirituality, infertility-related stress, and quality of life in Brazilian infertile couples: analysis using the actor-partner interdependence mediation model. Res Nurs Health. 2018;41(2):156–65.
20. Abedini M, Ghaheri A, Omani Samani R. Assisted reproductive technology in Iran: the first national report on centers, 2011. Int J Fertil Steril. 2016;10(3):283–9.
21. Fowers BJ, Olson DH. ENRICH marital satisfaction scale: a brief research and clinical tool. J Fam Psychol. 1993;7(2):176–85.
22. Zigmond AS, Snaith RP. The hospital anxiety and depression scale. Acta Psychiatr Scand. 1983;67(6):361–70.
23. Amini P, Maroufizadeh S, Samani RO. Evaluating the factor structure, item analyses, and internal consistency of hospital anxiety and depression scale in Iranian infertile patients. Int J Reprod Biomed. 2017;15(5):287–96.
24. Omani Samani R, Maroufizadeh S, Navid B, Amini P. Locus of control, anxiety, and depression in infertile patients. Psychol Health Med. 2017; 22(1):44–50.
25. Kazandi M, Gunday O, Mermer TK, Erturk N, Ozkınay E. The status of depression and anxiety in infertile Turkish couples. Iran J Reprod Med. 2011; 9(2):99–104.
26. Drosdzol A, Skrzypulec V. Depression and anxiety among polish infertile couples–an evaluative prevalence study. J Psychosom Obstet Gynaecol. 2009;30(1):11–20.
27. Shahid S. Depression in infertile couples. J Coll Physicians Surg Pak. 2009; 19(6):395 6.
28. Peterson BD, Newton CR, Rosen KH, Skaggs G. Gender differences in how men and women who are referred for IVF cope with infertility stress. Hum Reprod. 2006;21(9):2443–9.
29. Goldfarb MR, Trudel G, Boyer R, Préville M. Marital relationship and psychological distress: its correlates and treatments. Sex Relation Ther. 2007; 22(1):109–26.
30. Beach SR, Katz J, Kim S, Brody GH. Prospective effects of marital satisfaction on depressive symptoms in established marriages: a dyadic model. J Soc Pers Relat. 2003;20(3):355–71.
31. Miller RB, Mason TM, Canlas JM, Wang D, Nelson DA, Hart CH. Marital satisfaction and depressive symptoms in China. J Fam Psychol. 2013;27(4): 677–82.
32. Cao H, Zhou N, Fang X, Fine M. Marital well-being and depression in Chinese marriage: going beyond satisfaction and ruling out critical confounders. J Fam Psychol. 2017;31(6):775–84.
33. Hollist CS, Miller RB, Falceto OG, Fernandes CLC. Marital satisfaction and depression: a replication of the marital discord model in a Latino sample. Fam Process. 2007;46(4):485–98.
34. Wang Q, Wang D, Li C, Miller RB. Marital satisfaction and depressive symptoms among Chinese older couples. Aging Ment Health. 2014;18(1):11–8.
35. Dehle C, Weiss RL. Sex differences in prospective associations between marital quality and depressed mood. J Marriage Fam. 1998;60(4):1002–11.
36. Musa R, Ramli R, Yazmie AWA, Khadijah MBS, Hayati MY, Midin M, Jaafar NRN, Das S, Sidi H, Ravindran A. A preliminary study of the psychological differences in infertile couples and their relation to the coping styles. Compr Psychiatry. 2014;55:S65–9.
37. Seen Heng Y, Sidi H, Nik Jaafar NR, Razali R, Ram H. Phases of female sexual response cycle among Malaysian women with infertility: a factor analysis study. Asia Pac Psychiatry. 2013;5(S1):50–4.
38. Yeoh SH, Razali R, Sidi H, Razi ZRM, Midin M, Jaafar NRN, Das S. The relationship between sexual functioning among couples undergoing infertility treatment: a pair of perfect gloves. Compr Psychiatry. 2014;55:S1–6.

4

The relationship between dispositional empathy, psychological distress, and posttraumatic stress responses among Japanese uniformed disaster workers

Masanori Nagamine[1*], Jun Shigemura[2], Toshimichi Fujiwara[3], Fumiko Waki[3], Masaaki Tanichi[2], Taku Saito[2], Hiroyuki Toda[2], Aihide Yoshino[2] and Kunio Shimizu[1]

Abstract

Background: Disaster workers suffer from psychological distress not only through the direct experience of traumatic situations but also through the indirect process of aiding disaster victims. This distress, called secondary traumatic stress, is linked to dispositional empathy, which is the tendency for individuals to imagine and experience the feelings and experiences of others. However, the association between secondary traumatic stress and dispositional empathy remains understudied.

Methods: To examine the relationship between dispositional empathy and mental health among disaster workers, we collected data from 227 Japan Ground Self-Defense Force personnel who engaged in international disaster relief activities in the Philippines following Typhoon Yolanda in 2013. The Impact of Event Scale-Revised and the Kessler Psychological Distress Scale were used to evaluate posttraumatic stress responses (PTSR) and general psychological distress (GPD), respectively. Dispositional empathy was evaluated through the Interpersonal Reactivity Index, which consists of four subscales: Perspective Taking, Fantasy, Empathic Concern, and Personal Distress. Hierarchial linear regression analyses were performed to identify the variables related to PTSR and GPD.

Results: High PTSR was significantly associated with high *Fantasy* (identification tendency, $\beta = 0.21$, $p < .01$), high *Personal Distress* (the self-oriented emotional disposition of empathy, $\beta = 0.18$, $p < .05$), and no experience of disaster relief activities ($\beta = 0.15$, $p < .05$). High GPD was associated with high *Personal Distress* ($\beta = 0.28$, $p < .001$), marital status (married, $\beta = 0.22$, $p < .01$), being female ($\beta = 0.18$, $p < .01$), medical unit ($\beta = 0.18$, $p < .05$), and no experience of disaster relief activities ($\beta = 0.13$, $p < .05$).

Conclusions: Among Japanese uniformed disaster workers, high PTSR was associated with two subtypes of dispositional empathy: the self-oriented emotional disposition of empathy and high identification tendency, whereas high GPD was associated with high identification tendency. Educational interventions that aim to mitigate these tendencies might be able to relieve the psychological distress of disaster workers.

Keywords: Disaster workers, Empathy, Interpersonal reactivity index, Identification, Secondary traumatic stress, Posttraumatic stress response, Psychological distress

* Correspondence: nagaminemasanori@gmail.com
[1]Division of Behavioral Science, National Defense Medical College Research Institute, 3-2 Namiki, Tokorozawa, Saitama 359-8513, Japan
Full list of author information is available at the end of the article

Background

On November 8, 2013, Typhoon Yolanda struck the Philippines and caused large-scale damage: 6300 individuals were killed, 28,688 were injured, and 1062 were missing [1]. The Japanese government responded to a humanitarian assistance request from the Filipino government and sent Japan Self-Defense Forces' personnel to the affected area. Disaster relief activities consisted of medical assistance, epidemic prevention, and transport of relief supplies [2], which continued until December 18, 2013.

Disasters result in mental health distress not only among survivors but also among disaster workers [3, 4]. These individuals have the burden of rescuing lives in disaster-stricken sites fraught with life-threatening danger. In addition to such direct traumatic stresses, disaster workers can also experience indirect psychological effects of aiding disaster victims, which is defined as secondary traumatic stress [5]. These psychological effects can result in various reactions, including depression and anxiety disorder, in addition to stress-related disorders, such as acute and post-traumatic stress disorder [6]. According to a recent meta-analysis, the pooled prevalence of posttraumatic stress disorder among rescue workers was 10% [7], indicating the magnitude of their work-related traumatic experience on worker's mental health. Countermeasures for work-related traumatic stress are crucial for disaster workers to prevent adverse mental health outcomes. Coping strategies to mitigate such impacts include sufficient training prior to missions [8–10], awareness of and pride in one's duties [11, 12], and humor [8, 13, 14]. Minimization of excessive empathy and identification with victims is also recommended to prevent traumatic stress [8, 15–17], which is supported by two empirical studies [15, 17].

Empathy is a multi-dimensional concept with emotional and cognitive components [18]. Davis defined empathy as the "reactions of one individual to the observed experiences of another" and developed the Interpersonal Reactivity Index (IRI), which is a multi-dimensional scale of empathic traits [19]. The IRI consists of four subscales: Perspective Taking (PT; the tendency to spontaneously adopt the psychological point of view of others), Fantasy (FS; the respondents' tendencies to transpose themselves imaginatively into the feelings and actions of fictitious characters in books, movies, and plays), Empathic Concern (EC; "other-oriented" feelings of sympathy and concern for unfortunate others), and Personal Distress (PD; "self-oriented" feelings of personal anxiety and unease in tense interpersonal settings). Although the construct of self-oriented negative feeling (e.g., PD) is not included in the narrowly defined empathy [20], IRI provides multifaceted information on aspects of dispositional empathy and thus, is one of the most widely used measures to evaluate empathy [21].

As to the relationships between empathy and secondary traumatic stress, Figley reported that individuals who have a great capacity to feel and express empathy tend to be more vulnerable to the traumatic stress in his studies of healthcare workers [22]. Klimecki and Singer suggest that the consequence of empathy take on two paths; one is an "other-oriented," or compassion that results in prosocial motivation or positive feelings, and the other is a "self-oriented" personal distress that results in withdrawal or the experience of negative feelings [23]. In disaster workers, the latter path might explain their development of post-traumatic stress responses. However, to the best of our knowledge, the relationship between the empathy and secondary traumatic stress has yet to be fully investigated. To expand the theoretical and professional knowledge regarding secondary traumatic stress in the field of traumatic stress, we examined the relationships between dispositional empathy (measured with the IRI) and mental health (posttraumatic stress and psychological distress) among Japan Ground Self-Defense Force (JGSDF) personnel who were deployed on a humanitarian mission in response to the disaster of Typhoon Yolanda in 2013.

Methods

Participants and procedure

This survey was conducted as part of the mandatory occupational health management of all JGSDF personnel who were engaged in the humanitarian mission after Typhoon Yolanda ($N = 283$). The self-report survey was administered immediately after they returned home using registered (i.e., non-anonymous) forms. Of all the personnel, only 227 participated and provided written consent (response rate: 80.2%).

Psychological evaluation

We assessed two outcome measures—posttraumatic stress responses (PTSR) and general psychological distress (GPD)—using the Japanese versions of the Impact of Events Scale-Revised (IES-R) [24] and the Kessler Psychological Distress Scale (K10) [25], respectively. The IES-R is a 22-item self-administered questionnaire (score range: 0–88) that is used to evaluate three domains of PTSR—intrusion, avoidance, and hyperarousal—following a traumatic event [26]. The K10 is a 10-item self-administered questionnaire (score range: 10–50) that was developed by Kessler [27] and is widely used as a tool for evaluating GPD. The originally reported Cronbach's alpha for internal consistency was 0.91 for the K10 [28] and 0.92 to 0.95 for the IES-R [24]. In this study, Cronbach's alphas of 0.91 for the IES-R and 0.89 for the K10 were obtained.

Dispositional empathy was evaluated using the IRI [19]. The IRI is a 28-item self-report measure answered on a 5-point Likert scale. It consists of four subscales (PT, FS, EC, and PD), and each subscale contains seven different items (score ranges from 0 to 28). A previous paper reported Cronbach's alphas of 0.65 for PT, 0.76 for FS, 0.77 for EC, and 0.76 for PD [29]. In this study we obtained Cronbach's alphas of 0.63 for PT, 0.62 for FS, 0.57 for EC, and 0.65 for PD.

In addition to these psychological measures, the following information was collected based on the previous report by Berger and colleagues [7]: age, sex, marital status, rank, unit (e.g., medical, airlift, others), previous disaster relief experience, exposure to human bodies during relief efforts, and previous psychiatric treatment history.

Statistical analyses

First, Pearson correlation analyses were performed to explore the correlation between dispositional empathy and PTSR or GPD. Second, analysis of variance was used for the univariate analyses of each personal attribute. Finally, hierarchical linear regression analyses were conducted to investigate factors related to PTSR and GPD. In Step 1, personal attributes including age, sex, marital status, previous deployment experience, psychiatric treatment history were entered as covariates. In Step 2, work-related factors such as rank, unit (e.g., medical or airlift), and exposure to bodies were added as covariates. In Step 3, dispositional empathy evaluated using the four subscales of the IRI (PT, FS, EC, and PD) that were entered as predictor variables.

We used a significance level of $p < .05$. IBM SPSS Statistics for Windows version 22 was used for the statistical tests [30].

Results

Personal attributes and the results of the univariate analyses

The average age of the participants was 35.59 ± 7.99 years (mean ± *SD*). As Table 1 demonstrates, those with no previous disaster relief experience scored significantly higher on both PTSR and GPD than those with previous disaster relief experience. In addition, women, officers, and individuals assigned to medical units showed significantly higher scores on GPD than did men, those who were Enlisted/Private, and individuals assigned to "others" units, respectively.

Psychological measures and correlation analyses

Table 2 presents the summary statistics for the psychological measures and the results of the Pearson correlation analyses between the measures. IES-R was significantly correlated with two IRI subscales: FS ($r = .28$, $p < .001$) and PD ($r = .25$, $p < .001$). K10 showed a significant correlation with three IRI subscales: PD ($r = .35$, $p < .001$), FS ($r = .23$, $p < .001$), and EC ($r = .18$, $p < .01$). There were significant correlations between the IRI subscales, except for PT and PD.

Table 1 Personal attributes and the results of the univariate analyses

			PTSR		GPD	
	N	%	Mean	*SD*	Mean	*SD*
Sex						
Male	214	94.3	4.6	6.7	12.7	3.6
Female	13	5.7	7.7	6.3	17.2***	8.0
Marital status						
Single	81	35.7	4.0	5.9	12.4	3.5
Married	146	64.3	5.2	7.1	13.2	4.4
Rank						
Enlisted/Private	143	63.0	4.3	5.8	12.3	3.1
Officer	84	37.0	5.6	7.9	13.9**	5.3
Unit						
Medical	53	23.3	5.9	7.1	14.1[a]	5.3
Airlift	97	42.7	4.8	7.5	13.0	3.8
Others	77	33.9	3.9	5.3	12.0	3.2
Disaster relief experience						
Yes	193	85.0	4.3	6.1	12.6	3.9
No	34	15.0	7.5*	8.9	14.9**	4.6
Exposure to bodies						
No	216	95.2	4.8	6.8	12.9	4.1
Yes	11	4.8	3.5	4.4	13.5	4.6
Psychiatric treatment history						
No	219	98.2	4.8	6.7	12.9	4.1
Yes	4	1.8	8.5	7.2	11.0	2.0

N = 227. *PTSR* Posttraumatic stress response evaluated by the Impact of Event Scale-Revised, *GPD* General psychological distress evaluated by the Kessler Psychological Distress Scale, *SD* standard deviation

[a]Individuals who were assigned to medical units showed significantly higher scores than others ($p < .05$, multiple comparisons with the Bonferroni correction)

*$p < .05$, ** $p < .01$, *** $p < .001$

Hierarchical linear regression analyses

The results of the hierarchical linear regression analyses for high PTSR and GPD are shown in Table 3. It is reported that any variance inflation factor (VIF) exceeds 10 and tolerance value lower than 0.10 indicates a potential problem of multicollinearity [31]. In this study, variance inflation factor (VIF) ranged from 1.007 to 1.621 and tolerance ranged from 0.617 to 0.993 throughout the hierarchical linear regression analyses, no multicollinearity was observed. Regarding the correlates of PTSR, significant associations were observed for two IRI subscales: FS ($\beta = 0.21$, SE = 0.11, $p < .01$) and PD ($\beta = 0.18$, SE = 0.13, $p < .05$). Having no experience of disaster relief was also significantly associated with high PTSR ($\beta = 0.15$, SE = 1.3, $p < .05$). For the correlates of high GPD status, significant relations were shown for PD ($\beta = 0.28$, SE = 0.07, $p < .001$), marital status (married, $\beta = 0.22$, SE = 0.61, $p < .01$), being female ($\beta = 0.18$, SE = 1.15, $p < .01$), medical unit ($\beta = 0.18$, SE = 0.68, $p < .05$), and no disaster relief experience ($\beta = 0.13$, SE = 0.73, $p < .05$). Therefore, the

Table 2 Results of the psychological measures and Pearson correlation analyses

	IES-R	K10	IRI_PT	IRI_FS	IRI_EC	IRI_PD	Mean	SD	Median	Range	Cronbach's alpha
IES-R	–	.59***	.07	.28***	.05	.25***	4.77	6.70	2	0–40	0.91
K10		–	.13	.23***	.18**	.35***	12.91	4.09	11	10–39	0.89
IRI_PT			–	.14*	.43***	.04	15.90	4.09	16	5–28	0.63
IRI_FS				–	.22**	.39***	9.67	4.28	9	0–22	0.62
IRI_EC					–	.28***	16.89	3.59	17	8–28	0.57
IRI_PD						–	10.31	3.88	10	2–22	0.65

Note. *N* = 227. *IES-R* Impact of Event Scale-Revised, *K10* Kessler Psychological Distress Scale, *IRI* Interpersonal Reactivity Index, *PT* Perspective Taking, *FS* Fantasy, *EC* Empathic Concern, *PD* Personal Distress, *SD* standard deviation
*$p < .05$, ** $p < .01$, *** $p < .001$

two IRI subscales, FS and PD, showed the largest standardized coefficient β in the multiple linear regression models for PTSR and GPD, respectively.

Discussion

We examined the associations between dispositional empathy and the mental health status (PTSR and GPD) of JGSDF personnel who were engaged in the international disaster relief activity after Typhoon Yolanda in 2013. High PTSR was significantly related to both high FS and PD. High GPD was significantly related to high PD. To our knowledge, this is the first paper to report a link between psychological distress or posttraumatic stress and dispositional empathy among disaster workers using quantitative empathy measures.

Table 3 Results of the hierarchical multiple linear regression analysis

	PTSR Hierarchial Models			GPD Hierarchial Models		
	Standardized Coefficient β			Standardized Coefficient β		
	Step 1	Step 2	Step 3	Step 1	Step 2	Step 3
Personal Attributes						
Age	0.02	0.02	0.02	−0.05	−0.05	− 0.04
Sex[a]	0.11	0.11	0.07	0.26***	0.23**	0.18**
Marital status[b]	0.11	0.12	0.13	0.19**	0.18*	0.22**
Disaster relief experience[c]	−0.18**	− 0.17*	−0.15*	− 0.19**	−0.17*	− 0.13*
Psychiatric treatment history[c]	0.09	0.09	0.1	−0.05	−0.05	− 0.06
Work-related factors						
Rank[d]		0.03	0.01		0.09	0.04
Medical unit[c]		0.09	0.1		0.18*	0.18*
Airlift unit[c]		0.10	0.06		0.16*	0.12
Exposure to bodies[c]		−0.06	−0.03		0.03	0.06
Dispositional Empathy						
IRI_PT			0.05			0.04
IRI_FS			0.21**			0.08
IRI_EC			−0.11			0.03
IRI_PD			0.18*			0.28***
Statistics						
R^2	0.057	0.071	0.164	0.13	0.166	0.271
ΔR^2		0.014	0.093		0.036	0.106
F	2.635*	1.815	3.150 ***	6.475***	4.696***	5.984***

N = 227. *PTSR* Posttraumatic stress response evaluated by the Impact of Events Scale-Revised, *GPD* General psychological distress evaluated by the Kessler Psychological Distress Scale, *IRI* Interpersonal Reactivity Index, *PT* Perspective Taking, *FS* Fantasy, *EC* Empathic Concern, *PD* Personal Distress
[a]Dummy variable was created (male = 0, female = 1). [b]Dummy variable was created (single = 0, married = 1). [c]Dummy variables were created (no = 0, yes = 1).
[d]Dummy variables were created (enlisted/private = 0, officer = 1)
*$p < .05$, ** $p < .01$, *** $p < .001$

PD reflects emotional dispositional empathy and represents "self-oriented" feelings of personal anxiety and unease in tense interpersonal settings. Previous research that targeted clinical physicians reported that PD was closely related to secondary traumatic stress [32]. Cognitive neuroscience studies have outlined control mechanisms that regulate whether someone's empathic reactions are self- or other-oriented, indicating the importance of being aware of the distinction between experiences of the self and others [33, 34]. Our study suggests that individuals with high PD—who have a poor ability to distinguish between self- and other-oriented empathic reactions—are prone to suffering from psychological distress when faced with persons experiencing adversity.

FS, which is the tendency to transpose oneself imaginatively into the feelings and actions of fictitious characters, was also extracted as a significant factor related to high PTSR in this study. Ursano and colleagues have shown the importance of "identification with disaster victims" as a mechanism through which relief workers experience secondary trauma [17]. Cetin and colleagues also reported results that support this finding [15] and warned against excessive identification with disaster victims. Considering the conceptual similarity between FS, which is a type of dispositional empathy, and "identification with disaster victims," our results also support these previous findings.

Previous disaster relief-related literature suggests the importance of maintaining professional distance and avoiding excessive empathy and identification with victims [8, 15, 17, 35]. A similar trend has been observed in the field of clinical medicine; "detached concern"—a purely cognitive understanding of patients' emotions, while establishing emotional distance to maintain objectivity and limit exposure to negative emotions—has been traditionally recommended for physicians [36]. Given that those with high FS or PD are prone to suffering from psychological distress when faced with distressed individuals, it is likely that maintaining professional or emotional distance, such as "detached concern," is especially helpful for such emergency relief workers in order to minimize their psychological distress. However, this does not necessarily suggest that a complete absence of empathy is appropriate. Empathy is multifaceted; "other-oriented" empathy provide individuals with a variety of positive effects such as compassion satisfaction [37] and positive clinical outcomes [38]. One study targeted at physicians reported that compassion satisfaction was strongly associated with EC and PT, while compassion fatigue was more closely related to PD [32]. Therefore, an educational intervention that could reinforce other-oriented empathic reactions while inhibiting self-oriented empathic reactions might be effective for mitigating the psychological distress of emergency relief workers. It will be crucial to examine the effectiveness of such educational interventions through in-depth follow-up studies. These programs may specifically target workers with high PD or FS in order to prevent their posttraumatic mental health difficulties.

In this study, those with no disaster relief experience were identified as being at risk for both high PTSR and GPD, and women, married individuals, and medical unit were identified as being at risk for high GPD. Previous studies that focused on body handlers also reported that women and inexperienced workers had higher levels of distress than men and experienced workers [39]. Our results are consistent with this previous report. As for marital status, the previous literature has reported that unmarried individuals are more prone to suffer from psychological distress than those who are married [40]. Although our study demonstrated the opposite result, we theorize that being married could be not only protective but also risk factor depending on the marital relationship or family situation. For example, for the married personnel who have not built a good marital relationship, the existence of spouse could work as a concern rather than a social support when they are suddenly assigned for disaster relief work. Such background might induce inconsistent outcomes. Since medical staff were more likely to suffer from direct or indirect traumatic stress in such a major disaster, it was reasonable that being a member of medical unit was identified as the risk factor for high GPD.

Limitations

Our findings should be interpreted within the context of some limitations. First, our study participants were limited to JGSDF personnel and they did not include other defense services; therefore, our results do not represent all JGSDF personnel engaged in disaster relief activities in the Philippines. Second, this study employed a registered (non-anonymous) questionnaire, which has been reported to cause participants to conceal their symptoms, as compared to an anonymous questionnaire [41]. Furthermore, the Japanese sociocultural background strongly stigmatizes the expression of emotional suffering [42]. Thus, there is a strong possibility that participants' psychological effects were underreported in this study. Third, our cross-sectional study design limits the causal association between the dependent and the independent variables. Finally, this study did not examine other factors that might confound our findings (e.g., pre-deployment mental health status, personal characteristics for coping with stress, previous traumatic experiences, numbers of years of disaster relief experience, compassion satisfaction, and major life event experience). Further studies that include such information are needed to more rigorously identify the psychological effects of these factors for disaster workers.

Conclusions

Despite some limitations, we demonstrated that PD and FS, which are subscales of the IRI, are related to psychological distress among disaster workers. Situations that increase the risk of secondary trauma are not limited to disaster relief activities but also include humanitarian aid, such as medical and welfare activities. More precise and better understanding of the relationship between dispositional empathy and psychological distress is needed to design better educational interventions to protect the mental health of people who engage in such activities.

Abbreviations

EC: Empathic Concern; FS: Fantasy; GPD: General psychological distress; IES-R: Impact of Events Scale-Revised; IRI: Interpersonal Reactivity Index; JGSDF: Japan Ground Self-Defense Force; K10: Kessler Psychological Distress Scale; PD: Personal Distress; PT: Perspective Taking; PTSR: Posttraumatic stress response

Acknowledgements

We wish to thank all the participants and medical staff of the JGSDF who supported our research. The authors would also like to thank Dr. Yumi Suzuki of the International College of Arts and Sciences, Fukuoka Women's University, Fukuoka, Japan, for use of the Japanese version of the IRI. The views expressed in this article are those of the authors and do not reflect the position or policy of the National Defense Medical College or the Japan Ministry of Defense.

Funding

This work was supported by the Japanese Society for the Promotion of Science KAKENHI Grant number 26461779.

Authors' contributions

MN conceived and designed the study, and developed it in discussion with JS, MT, TS, HT, AY, and KS. MN, TF, and FW were involved in the acquisition and analysis of the data, and all authors participated in the interpretation of the data. MN wrote the first draft of the article and all authors contributed to critically revising the paper. Finally, all authors read and approved the final manuscript.

Consent for publication

Not applicable.

Competing interests

The authors declare that they have no competing interests.

Author details

[1]Division of Behavioral Science, National Defense Medical College Research Institute, 3-2 Namiki, Tokorozawa, Saitama 359-8513, Japan. [2]Department of Psychiatry, School of Medicine, National Defense Medical College, 3-2 Namiki, Tokorozawa, Saitama, Japan. [3]Japan Ground Self-Defense Force Medical School, 1-2-24, Ikejiri, Setagaya-ku, Tokyo, Japan.

References

1. National Disaster Risk Reduction and Management Council. Final report re: effects of typhoon "Yolanda" (Haiyan). In: NDRRMC update; 2013. http://ndrrmc.gov.ph/attachments/article/1329/FINAL_REPORT_re_Effects_of_Typhoon_YOLANDA_(HAIYAN)_06-09NOV2013.pdf. Accessed 24 Apr 2018.
2. Cabinet Office of Japan. International contributions of Japan self-defense forces. In: We are Tomodachi; 2014. http://www.japan.go.jp/tomodachi/2014/spring-summer2014/international_contributions_of_apan.html. Accessed 24 Apr 2018.
3. Norris FH, Friedman MJ, Watson PJ, Byrne CM, Diaz E, Kaniasty K. 60,000 disaster victims speak: part I. an empirical review of the empirical literature, 1981–2001. Psychiatry. 2002;65:207–39.
4. Perrin MA, DiGrande L, Wheeler K, Thorpe L, Farfel M, Brackbill R. Differences in PTSD prevalence and associated risk factors among world trade center disaster rescue and recovery workers. Am J Psychiatry. 2007;164:1385–94.
5. Figley CR. Compassion fatigue as secondary traumatic stress disorder. In: Figley CR, editor. Compassion fatigue: coping with secondary traumatic stress disorder in those who treat the traumatized. New York: Routledge; 1995. p. 1–20.
6. Benedek DM, Fullerton C, Ursano RJ. First responders: mental health consequences of natural and human-made disasters for public health and public safety workers. Annu Rev Public Health. 2007;28:55–68.
7. Berger W, Coutinho ES, Figueira I, Marques-Portella C, Luz MP, Neylan TC, et al. Rescuers at risk: a systematic review and meta-regression analysis of the worldwide current prevalence and correlates of PTSD in rescue workers. Soc Psychiatry Psychiatr Epidemiol. 2012;47:1001–11. https://doi.org/10.1007/s00127-011-0408-2.
8. Fullerton CS, McCarroll JE, Ursano RJ, Wright KM. Psychological responses of rescue workers: fire fighters and trauma. Am J Orthop. 1992;62:371–8.
9. Guo YJ, Chen CH, Lu ML, Tan HK, Lee HW, Wang TN. Posttraumatic stress disorder among professional and non-professional rescuers involved in an earthquake in Taiwan. Psychiatry Res. 2004;127:35–41. https://doi.org/10.1016/j.psychres.2004.03.009.
10. Marmar CR, Weiss DS, Metzler TJ, Ronfeldt HM, Foreman C. Stress responses of emergency services personnel to the Loma Prieta earthquake interstate 880 freeway collapse and control traumatic incidents. J Trauma Stress. 1996;9:63–85.
11. Leffler CT, Dembert ML. Posttraumatic stress symptoms among U.S. navy divers recovering TWA flight 800. J Nerv Ment Dis. 1998;186:574–7.
12. Ursano RJ, McCarroll JE. Exposure to traumatic death: the nature of the stressor. In: Ursano RJ, McCaughey BG, Fullerton CS, editors. Individual and community responses to trauma and disaster: the structure of human chaos. Cambridge: Cambridge University Press; 1994. p. 46–71.
13. Alexander DA, Wells A. Reactions of police officers to body-handling after a major disaster. A before-and-after comparison. Br J Psychiatry. 1991;159:547–55.
14. Jones DR. Secondary disaster victims: the emotional effects of recovering and identifying human remains. Am J Psychiatry. 1985;142:303–7.
15. Cetin M, Kose S, Ebrinc S, Yigit S, Elhai JD, Basoglu C. Identification and posttraumatic stress disorder symptoms in rescue workers in the Marmara, Turkey, earthquake. J Trauma Stress. 2005;18:485–9. https://doi.org/10.1002/jts.20056.
16. Regehr C, Goldberg G, Hughes J. Exposure to human tragedy, empathy, and trauma in ambulance paramedics. Am J Orthop. 2002;72:505–13.
17. Ursano RJ, Fullerton CS, Vance K, Kao TC. Posttraumatic stress disorder and identification in disaster workers. Am J Psychiatry. 1999;156:353–9. https://doi.org/10.1176/ajp.156.3.353.
18. Decety J, Svetlova M. Putting together phylogenetic and ontogenetic perspectives on empathy. Dev Cogn Neurosci. 2012;2:1–24. https://doi.org/10.1016/j.dcn.2011.05.003.
19. Davis MH. Measuring individual differences in empathy: evidence for a multidimensional approach. J Pers Soc Psychol. 1983;44:113–26. https://doi.org/10.1037/0022-3514.44.1.113.
20. Batson CD, Fultz J, Schoenrade PA. Distress and empathy: two qualitatively distinct vicarious emotions with different motivational consequences. J Pers. 1987;55:19–39.
21. Stepien KA, Baernstein A. Educating for empathy. A review. J Gen Intern Med. 2006;21:524–30.
22. Figley CR. Compassion fatigue: Psychotherapists' chronic lack of self care. J Clin Psychol. 2002;58:1433–41. https://doi.org/10.1002/jclp.10090.
23. Klimecki O, Singer T. Empathic distress fatigue rather than compassion fatigue? Integrating findings from empathy research in psychology and social neuroscience. In: Oakley B, Knafo A, Madhavan G, Wilson D, editors. Pathological altruism. New York: Oxford University press; 2012. p. 368–83.
24. Asukai N, Kato H, Kawamura N, Kim Y, Yamamoto K, Kishimoto J, et al. Reliability and validity of the Japanese-language version of the impact of event scale-revised (IES-R-J): four studies of different traumatic events. J Nerv Ment Dis. 2002;190:175–82.
25. Furukawa TA, Kawakami N, Saitoh M, Ono Y, Nakane Y, Nakamura Y, et al. The performance of the Japanese version of the K6 and K10 in the world

mental health survey Japan. Int J Methods Psychiatr Res. 2008;17:152–8. https://doi.org/10.1002/mpr.257.
26. Weiss DS, Marmar CR. The impact of event scale-revised. In: Wilson JP, Keane TM, editors. Assessing psychological trauma and PTSD. New York: The Guilford Press; 1997. p. 339–411.
27. Kessler RC, Andrews G, Colpe LJ, Hiripi E, Mroczek DK, Normand SL, et al. Short screening scales to monitor population prevalences and trends in non-specific psychological distress. Psychol Med. 2002;32:959–76.
28. Sakurai K, Nishi A, Kondo K, Yanagida K, Kawakami N. Screening performance of K6/K10 and other screening instruments for mood and anxiety disorders in Japan. Psychiatry Clin Neurosci. 2011;65:434–41.
29. Himichi T, Osanai H, Goto T, Fujita H, Kawamura Y, Davis MH, et al. Development of a Japanese version of the interpersonal reactivity index. Shinrigaku Kenkyu. 2017;88:61–71.
30. Corp IBM. SPSS statistics for windows version 22.0.0. Armonk: IBM Corp; 2013.
31. Hair JF, Black WC, Babin BJ, Anderson RE. Multivariate data analysis. 7th ed. Upper Saddle River: Pearson Prentice Hall; 2010.
32. Gleichgerrcht E, Decety J. Empathy in clinical practice: how individual dispositions, gender, and experience moderate empathic concern, burnout, and emotional distress in physicians. PLoS One. 2013;8:e61526. https://doi.org/10.1371/journal.pone.0061526.
33. Decety J, Jackson PL. The functional architecture of human empathy. Behav Cogn Neurosci Rev. 2004;3:71–100. https://doi.org/10.1177/1534582304267187.
34. Decety J, Lamm C. Human empathy through the lens of social neuroscience. Sci World J. 2006;6:1146–63. https://doi.org/10.1100/tsw.2006.221.
35. Pross C. Burnout, vicarious traumatization and its prevention. Torture. 2006;16:1–9.
36. Fox R, Lief H. Training for "detached concern" in medical students. In: Lief HI, Lief VF, Lief NR, editors. The psychological basis of medical practice. New York: Harper & Row; 1963. p. 12–35.
37. Sodeke-Gregson EA, Holttum S, Billings J. Compassion satisfaction, burnout, and secondary traumatic stress in UK therapists who work with adult trauma clients. Eur J Psychotraumatol. 2013;4. https://doi.org/10.3402/ejpt.v4i0.21869.
38. Derksen F, Bensing J, Lagro-Janssen A. Effectiveness of empathy in general practice: a systematic review. Br J Gen Pract. 2013;63:e76–84.
39. McCarroll JE, Ursano RJ, Fullerton CS, Lundy A. Traumatic stress of a wartime mortuary: anticipation of exposure to mass death. J Nerv Ment Dis. 1993;181:545–51. https://doi.org/10.1097/00005053-199309000-00003.
40. Fullerton CS, Ursano RJ, Wang L. Acute stress disorder, posttraumatic stress disorder, and depression in disaster or rescue workers. Am J Psychiatry. 2004;161:1370–6.
41. McLay RN, Deal WE, Murphy JA, Center KB, Kolkow TT, Grieger TA. On-the-record screenings versus anonymous surveys in reporting PTSD. Am J Psychiatry. 2008;165:775–6. https://doi.org/10.1176/appi.ajp.2008.07121960.
42. Goto T, Wilson JP. A review of the history of traumatic stress studies in Japan: from traumatic neurosis to PTSD. Trauma Violence Abuse. 2003;4:195–209 doi: July 1, 2003. https://doi.org/10.1177/1524838003004003001.

Depression and glycaemic control among type 2 diabetes patients: a cross-sectional study in a tertiary healthcare facility in Ghana

Josephine Akpalu[1], Ernest Yorke[1], Joana Ainuson-Quampah[2], Williams Balogun[3] and Kwame Yeboah[4*]

Abstract

Background: Diabetes and depression are both chronic debilitating conditions, and their coexistence has been associated with adverse outcomes. In this study, we investigated the association between glycaemic control and depression in type 2 diabetes (T2DM) patients attending a tertiary healthcare facility in Ghana.

Methodology: In a cross-sectional study design, Patient Health Questionnare-9 (PHQ-9) was used to assess depression in 400 T2DM, aged 30–65 years. Anthropometric characteristics and blood pressure were measured. Venous blood was collected to measure the levels of glycated haemoglobin (HbA1c).

Results: The prevalence of depression was 31.3% among T2DM patients. Female gender, being unmarried, frequent intake of alcohol, previous smoking status and insulin use were associated with increased odds of depression, whereas being educated above basic school level was associated with a decreased odds of depression. In a multivariable logistic regression model, being unmarried and poor glycaemic control were associated with an increase in odds of depression after adjusting for age, gender, and social factors. The association between depression and glycaemic control was attenuated when clinical factors were introduced into the model.

Conclusion: In our study population, we found that depression is common among Ghanaians with T2DM, and not associated with poor glycaemic control in a fully multivariable-adjusted model.

Keywords: Depression, Type 2 diabetes mellitus, Glycaemic control, Ghana

Background

The prevalence of diabetes mellitus has reached epidemic levels globally resulting in enormous human, economic and social cost worldwide. Currently, 415 million people are living with diabetes, 75% of whom live in low and middle-income countries; this number has been projected to increase to 642 million by 2040 [1]. Depression is also a chronic disease that affects about 340 million people at any given time worldwide [2]. The temporal relationship between diabetes and depression has been found to be bi-directional; patients with depression have an increased risk of 1.6 fold of developing diabetes, whereas diabetes patients are twice as likely to be depressed, compared to non-diabetes individuals [3–5].

The presence of depressive symptoms may affect T2DM patient's adherence to diabetes self-care regimen, particularly diabetic medications, dietary modifications and exercise [6]. Compared to non-depressed T2DM patients, depressed T2DM patients have relatively higher glycated haemoglobin (HbA1c) and increased prevalence of microvascular and macrovascular complications [7–9]. Screening and treatment of depression in diabetes patients have been reported to favourably improve glycemic control, as well as prevent or delay diabetes-related complications [4]. However, the recognition and treatment of depression among patients with diabetes have been found to be less than optimum [10]. Moreover,

* Correspondence: kyeboah@ug.edu.gh; melvinky@gmail.com
[4]Department of Physiology, School of Biomedical and Allied Health Sciences, University of Ghana, Accra, Ghana
Full list of author information is available at the end of the article

in low and middle-income countries including Ghana, there is a dearth of data on the burden of depression among diabetes patients [11, 12].

In this study, we investigated the association between glycaemic control and depression among T2DM patients attending a tertiary care facility in Ghana. We hypothesized that compared to non-depressed diabetes patients, diabetes patients with depression will have poor glycaemic control.

Methodology

The study was a cross-sectional design, conducted at the National Diabetes Management and Research Centre, Korle Bu Teaching Hospital, Accra, Ghana. The minimum sample size was calculated based on the hypothetical prevalence rates of depression and glycaemic control to be 26% and 15% [13] respectively; 340 patients were required to achieve a power of 80% and α of 0.05. In all, 400 T2DM patients, aged between 30 and 65 years, were enrolled into the study by systematic random sampling of every fourth consenting patient visiting the clinic. Patients with type 1 diabetes, pregnant women and those aged less than 30 years at diagnosis or patients older than 65 years were excluded from the study. In addition, patients with other causes of depression such as loss of a close family member within past 4 months and medication/history of depression or manic/hypomanic episode were excluded from the study. The socio-demographic characteristics such as age, gender, education, employment, alcohol & smoking status, as well as clinical data like duration of diabetes, diabetes medication, hypertension and antihypertensive medication were collected using structured questionnaires.

Depression was screened using Patient Health Questionnaire-9 (PHQ-9). The PHQ-9 is an instrument that has been validated in sub-Saharan Africans [14, 15] and in diabetes patients [16] for the detection of general depressive symptoms. The PHQ-9 assesses how often the respondent has experienced specific symptoms over the past 2 weeks, assigning values of 0 to 3 points (0 - not at all, 1 - several days, 2 - more than half of the days, 3 - nearly every day) [17]. Major depressive disorder was defined as the presence of at least five symptoms, reported for more than half the days in the past 2 weeks, including depressed mood or anhedonia, as well as the thought of suicide or better dead [18].

Blood pressure was measured after 5 min rest using an automated digital blood pressure monitor (Omron 907XL pro, Healthcare, Inc., Vernon Hills, IL), with the patients seated comfortably with a back support and arm resting on a table. Body weight and height were measured with a Seca 740 scale and a stadiometer respectively, and the body mass index (BMI) computed using the formula: weight in kilogrammes divided by the height in metres squared.

Venous blood was drawn from each participant for the measurement of glycated haemoglobin (HbA1c) using the boronate affinity chromatography method on PDQ Plus HPLC autoanalyzer (Primus Diagnostics, Trinity Biotech, Ireland). Good glycaemic control was defined as HBA1c of less than 7% [19]. Ethical approval was sought and obtained from the Ethical and Protocol Review Committee of the College of Health Sciences, University of Ghana (Protocol ID MS-Et/M.6-P4.4/2012–13) and each patient provided written voluntary informed consent after the rationale and procedure of the study were thoroughly explained. Patients found to be depressed we referred to the Psychiatry department for further assessment and possible management.

Statistical analysis

Data was analysed using SPSS version 18. Data was presented as mean with standard deviation for continuous variables and as proportions for categorical variables. The study subjects were dichotomized based on the presence or absence of depression. Differences between the two groups with regards to their socio-demographic and clinical variables as well as HbA1c were assessed. The chi-squared (χ^2) test was used for the comparison of categorical variables and Students t-test for continuous measures. Logistic regression models were performed to determine the change in odds of depression and glycaemic control after adjusting for confounding variables. The level of significance was set at $p < 0.05$.

Results

In our study population with a high representation of females (male: female = 1:4), 125 (31.3%) of the participants were found to have depression. Age, duration of diabetes and BMI were comparable for T2DM patients with or without depression (T-test, p-values> 0.05). Female gender, marital status, educational level, alcohol intake and smoking status were associated with depression (χ^2, p-values< 0.05). T2DM patients with depression had higher systolic blood pressure and glycated haemoglobin level than T2DM patients without depression (T-test, $p < 0.05$; Table 1).

In unadjusted logistic regression models, being female (OR = 2.84), unmarried (OR = 1.63), regular alcohol consumer (OR = 5.47), former smoker (OR = 1.28), using insulin (OR = 1.3) and having poor glycaemic control (OR = 1.82) were associated with an increased odds of depression (Table 2). Multivariable logistic regression models were constructed to analyze the relationship between depression versus glycaemic control status and marital status, with sequential adjustments for social and clinical factors. Poor glycaemic control was associated with an increase in

Table 1 General characteristics of participants by depression status

	T2DM without depression	T2DM with depression	All Patients	Test statistic	*P*
N (%)	275 (68.7)	125 (31.3)	400		
Age	52.9 ± 8.5	52.2 ± 9	52.7 ± 8.7	t (0.79)	0.48
Duration of diabetes, yrs	9.1 ± 7.3	9.5 ± 6.3	9.2 ± 7	t (0.56)	0.57
Females, n (%)	208 (75.6)	106 (84.6)	314 (78.5)	X^2 (6.72)	0.01
Married n (%)	190 (69.1)	72 (57.6)	262 (65.5)	X^2 (5.02)	0.02
Employed n (%)	194 (70.5)	83 (66.4)	277 (69.2)	X^2 (0.69)	0.41
Education				X^2 (5.04)	0.02
Primary or less	68 (24.7)	41 (32.8)	109 (27.3)		
Junior grade	119 (43.3)	55 (44)	174 (43.5)		
High school	50 (18.2)	19 (15.2)	69 (17.3)		
Tertiary	38 (13.8)	10 (8)	48 (12)		
Alcohol consumption				X^2 (4.86)	0.035
Doesn't drink	212 (77.1)	92 (73.6)	304 (76)		
Occasional	61 (22.2)	21 (16.8)	90 (22.5)		
Always	2 (0.7)	3 (2.4)	5 (1.3)		
Smoking status				X^2 (5.48)	0.04
Never	260 (94.5)	116 (92.8)	376 (94)		
Previous	14 (5.1)	8 (6.4)	22 (5.5)		
Current	1 (0.4)	1 (0.8)	2 (0.5)		
BMI (mean ± SD)	30.2 ± 6.6	29.4 ± 5.6	29.9 ± 6.3	t (1.18)	0.24
Obesity classification				X^2 (3.99)	0.076
Normal	56 (20.4)	24 (19.2)	80 (20.1)		
Overweight	89 (32.4)	41 (32.8)	130 (32.7)		
Obese	128 (46.5)	60 (48)	188 (47.2)		
Waist circumferece	99.9 ± 13	99.2 ± 11.7	99.7 ± 12.6	t (0.54)	0.58
WHR	0.93 ± 0.11	0.94 ± 0.09	0.94 ± 0.1	t (0.96)	0.34
Hypertension n (%)	219 (79.6)	99 (79.2)	318 (79.5)		0.39
Systolic BP, mmHg	126 ± 26	133 ± 21	132 ± 23	t (2.16)	0.03
Diastolic BP, mmHg	81 ± 12	80 ± 12	81 ± 12	t (0.77)	0.44
Heart rate, bpm	80 ± 15	81 ± 12	80 ± 14	t (0.71)	0.48
FPG, mol/l	9.2 ± 5.5	9.9 ± 4.3	9.4 ± 5.1	t (1.38)	0.17
HbA1c, %	9.4 ± 2.8	10.2 ± 3	9.9 ± 2.9	t (2.52)	0.013

WHR waist-hip ratio, *BMI* body mass index, *BP* blood pressure, *FPG* fasting plasma glucose, *HbA1c* glycated haemoglobin, *t* T-test statistic, X^2 chi-square statistic

odds of depression, even after adjustment for age and gender (AOR = 1.4, $p = 0.037$), as well as social factors (AOR = 1.25, $p = 0.047$); the association was however not significant after the introduction of clinical factors into the model (AOR = 1.04, $p = 0.286$). Being unmarried was associated with increased odds of depression in the fully adjusted model (AOR = 1.47, $p = 0.046$; Table 3).

Discussion

Our study has shown that depression is present in about one-third of T2DM patients after screening, and depression was associated with poor glycaemic control. Patients with diabetes have twice the odds of developing depression compared with those without diabetes [4, 5]. Depression in T2DM patients has been studied extensively in populations from high-income countries, however, data from lower-income countries such as Ghana are sparse [11, 12].

The prevalence of depression among T2DM patients in our study was similar to that reported in other studies. In a meta-analysis of 42 studies involving over 21,000 adult patients, clinically significant depression was diagnosed in 31% of T2DM patients [5]. Comparable results have also been reported among adult patients with diabetes in Greece (33.4%) [20], rural Bangladesh

Table 2 Unadjusted logistic regression of depression with socio-demographic and clinical factors

	OR (95% CI)	Wald's	*p*
Female gender (Ref: Males)	2.84 (1.67–4.07)	4.59	< 0.001
Age (per 1 year change)	1.303 (0.84–1.68)	1.5	0.13
Duration of diabetes ≥10 years (Ref < 10 yrs)	1.05 (0.81–1.46)	0.32	0.76
Unmarried (Ref: Married)	1.63 (1.05–2.54)	2.17	0.003
Above basic school education (Ref: Basic school)	0.64 (0.4–0.93)	2.07	0.037
Alcohol status (Ref: Never)			
Occasional	1.1 (0.66–1.74)	0.39	0.711
Always	5.47 (1.56–13.03)	3.14	0.002
Former Smokers (Ref: Non-smokers)	1.28 (1.05–3.84)	0.75	0.041
BMI (ref: Nornal)			
Overweight	1.07 (0.55–2.1)	0.2	0.851
Obese	0.9 (0.47–1.76)	0.3	0.761
Hypertension (ref: Non-hypertensive)	1.13 (0.87–1.85)	0.63	0.536
Insulin use (Ref: Oral Hypoglycaemic drugs)	1.3 (1.18–1.62)	3.24	0.001
Poor glycaemic control (Ref: HbA1c < 7%)	1.82 (1.32–2.48)	3.72	< 0.001

(30%) [21] and in the UK (25%) [22]. In contrast to our findings, relatively lower prevalence of depression was found in studies from rural Pakistan (14.7%) [23] and Brazil (18.6%) [24], with a much lower rate in the United States (8.3%) [25]. On the other hand, using different depression assessment tools, higher rates of depression were reported in urban centers in Iran (71.8%) and Pakistan (43.5%) [11, 26]. The wide variation in depression across various studies may be attributed to the difference in the socio-cultural background of the participants. In screening for depression in the various these studies, different assessment tools with varying sensitivity and specificity to detect depression were used [16].

Very few studies in Africa have evaluated the occurrence of depression and its effects among patients with diabetes [12]. However available studies from Nigeria reported the prevalence of depression among T2DM patients within the range of 19.4% to 30%. [27–29]. Depression in the general population in Ghana was reported to be rare decades ago, [30] however, in recent years the prevalence has been shown to be comparable to that in western countries [30]. The WHO reported a population-based prevalence of mild depression to be 6.7% among Ghanaian adults > 50 years of age, far lower than the findings of the current study [31]. Indeed different studies have reported the prevalence of depression in different Ghanaian populations to be within the range of 3.8 to 9.9% [31–33], and whereas 24.5% of patients referred to a psychiatry clinic were diagnosed with depression [34].

In general, the co-existence of diabetes and depression worldwide has been shown to vary by type of diabetes and the socio-economic status of populations studied [35]. Depression and other psychological problems tend to be more common in developing countries compared

Table 3 Multivariable regression of depression with marital status, medication adherence and glycaemic control

	Unmarried	Wald's (p)	Poor glycaemic control	Wald's (p)
Model 1	1.63 (1.15–2.54)	2.42 (0.016)	1.82 (1.32–2.48)	3.72 (< 0.001)
Model 2	1.54 (1.1–2.41)	2.16 (0.031)	1.4 (1.27–2.39)	2.09 (0.037)
Model 3	1.48 (1.09–2.33)	2.02 (0.042)	1.25 (1.17–2.04)	1.98 (0.047)
Model 4	1.46 (1.12–2.31)	2.05 (0.04)	1.04 (0.85–2.29)	0.56 (0.286)
Model 5	1.47 (1.11–2.37)	1.99 (0.046)	–	

This Table represents multivariable logistic regression analyses with depression status as dependent variable, and either marital status, medication adherence or glycaemic control as an independent variable in separate models (Model 1). Further adjustments to the models were performed by introducing variables sequentially as indicated below:
Model 1: Unadjusted
Model 2: Model 1 + age & gender
Model 3: Model 2 + social factors (education, employment, alcohol & smoking status)
Model 4: Model 3 + clinical factors (duration of diabetes, diabetes medication & hypertension)
Model 5: Model 4 + Glycaemic control

with developed countries [36–38]. Possible explanations for this observation include higher level of gender inequalities, social insecurity, lower level of education, greater level of poverty and financial constraints among others [37, 38]. Female gender, unmarried status and a lower level of education, all of which have socio-economic implications, were associated with depression in this study. These results are supported by similar findings in both the general population [37, 38] as well as among people with diabetes [22, 39].

Contrary to various study reports, we did not find significant association between poor glycaemic control and depression. Some studies have reported that depressed T2DM patients have higher HbA1c levels compared with non-depressed individuals [25, 40, 41]. The coexistence of depression with diabetes has been reported to be significantly associated with poor glycaemic control [42]. However, this association has not been demonstrated in all studies [43]. In systematic reviews and meta-analysis, depression was found to be weakly correlated with glycaemic status [44]. In type 1 diabetes patients, the association between depression and glycaemic control exist in younger patients, and not in adult patients [45]. The findings of our study indicate that, clinical factors like diabetes duration, medication and hypertension status are important factors that link depression to glycaemic status. It must be noted also that predictors of depression in non-diabetes population in Ghana has not been well studied. However, it is worth noting that there is evidence that remission of depression can result in the improvement of glycaemic control [7]. In addition, depression is said to impair good self-care practices resulting in poor adherence to medication, as well as other diabetes management regimens [46]. Diabetes patients with comorbid depression have been found to have fewer days adherence to dietary, exercise and self-monitoring recommendations, with a 2.3 fold increased odds of missing medication doses compared with those without depression [47].

The findings of this study indicate that, compared to unmarried participants, currently married participants had lower risk prevalence of depression. Studies have shown marriage is strongly and positively associated with psychological well-being for men and women. On average, the currently married report higher levels of psychological well-being (measured by lower rates of depression, substance abuse, and alcoholism) than never-married, divorced, widowed, or separated individuals [48, 49]. Spousal support is among the important sources of psychological fortitude during chronic illness like diabetes, although there is a possibility of disruptions in the marital relationship during chronic illness [48]. The importance of marital support in diabetes management might stem from the other spouse helping the ailing spouse to adhere to diabetes medication and self-management practices. Even with married patients, Katz [50] reported that the self-management behavior of husbands with diabetes often deteriorates when conflict exists with their wives. In addition, the belief of a spouse in the importance of glycemic control predicts such control better than the patient's beliefs [49]. However, in this study, we did not investigate in the quality of intimacy in married participants, as well as the beliefs of the spouse on diabetes management practices.

Limitation of the study

The major limitation of our study is that the results may not reflect the true burden of depression in the general T2DM population since patients were selected from a specialized tertiary hospital in urban Ghana. Possible replication of this study in a primary health care setting in suburban or rural communities to confirm these findings will be vital. Our study did not include non-diabetes controls for comparison, limiting the interpretation of the possible role of diabetes in depression. Also, being a cross-sectional study by design, we cannot deduce the 'cause-effect' relationship between diabetes and depression from our findings; a longitudinal study design will be needed to investigate this relationship.

Conclusions

The findings of our study have shown that depression is quite common among Ghanaian patients with T2DM. Poor glycaemic control was not associated with depression among T2DM patients in our study. Marriage was found to be protective against depression. Future studies may investigate the role of quality of marital intimacy and spousal beliefs on depression.

Abbreviations

HbA1c: Glycated haemoglobin; MMAS: Morisky Medication Adherence Scale; PHQ-9: Patient Health Questionnaire-9; T2DM: Type 2 diabetes mellitus; WHO: World Health Organization

Acknowledgements

The authors wish to acknowledge Prof Albert G.B, Amoah, Prof Richard Adanu and Prof Olugbenga Ogedegbe and his team for their tremendous support before, during and after this project. We also wish to acknowledge the contributions of Margaret Reynolds and Naa in the acquisition of data.

Funding

No funding was available for the study.

Authors' contributions

JA was involved in the conception, design, acquisition of data, interpretation of data and initial drafting of the manuscript. EY participated in conception, design, acquisition of data and interpretation of data. KY was involved in the conception, design, analysis and interpretation of data. JAQ participated in the conception, design, acquisition of data and interpretation of data. WB participated in the conception, design and interpretation of data. All authors critically reviewed the manuscript for important intellectual content and agreed on the version to be published.

Consent for publication
Not applicable.

Competing interests
The authors declare that they have no competing interests.

Author details
[1]Department of Medicine & Therapeutics, School of Medicine & Dentistry, University of Ghana, Accra, Ghana. [2]Department of Dietetics, School of Biomedical and Allied Health Sciences, University of Ghana, Accra, Ghana. [3]College of Medicine, University of Ibadan, Ibadan, Nigeria. [4]Department of Physiology, School of Biomedical and Allied Health Sciences, University of Ghana, Accra, Ghana.

References
1. IDF Diabetes atlas: Seventh edition. www.diabetesatlas.org. Assessed 12 Aug 2016.
2. Greden JF. Physical symptoms of depression: unmet needs. J Clin Psychiatry. 2003;64(Suppl. 7):5–11.
3. Mezuk B, Eaton WW, Albrecht S, Golden SH. Depression and type 2 diabetes over the lifespan. Diabetes Care. 2008;31:2383–90.
4. Ali S, Stone MA, Peters JL, Davies MJ, Khunti K. The prevalence of co-morbid depression in adults with type 2 diabetes: a systematic review and meta-analysis. Diabet Med. 2006;23:1165–73.
5. Anderson RJ, Freedland KE, Clouse RE, Lustman PJ. The prevalence of comorbid depression in adults with diabetes: a meta-analysis. Diabetes Care. 2001;24:1069–78.
6. Gonzalez JS, Peyrot M, McCarl LA, Collins EM, et al. Depression and diabetes treatment nonadherence: a meta-analysis. Diabetes Care. 2008;31:2398–403.
7. Lustman PJ, Anderson RJ, Freedland KE, De Groot M. Depression and poor glycemic control: a meta-analytic review of the literature. Diabetes Care. 2000;23:934–42.
8. De Groot M, Anderson R, Freedland KE, Clouse RE, Lustman PJ. Association of depression and diabetes complications: a meta-analysis. Psychosom Med. 2001;63:619–30.
9. Roy T, Lloyd CE, Parvin M, Mohiuddin GB, Rahman M. Prevalence of co-morbid depression in out-patients with type 2 diabetes mellitus in Bangladesh. BMC Psychiatry. 2012;12:123.
10. Katon WJ, Simon G, Russo J, et al. Quality of depression care in a population-based sample of patients with diabetes and major depression. Med Care. 2004;42:1222–9.
11. Khuwaja AK, Lalani S, Dhanani R, Azam IS, et al. Anxiety and depression among outpatients with type 2 diabetes: a multi-Centre study of prevalence and associated factors. Diabetology Metab Syndr. 2010;2(72):1–7.
12. Patel V, Kim Y. Contribution of low- and middle-income countries to research published in leading general psychiatry journals, 2002-2004. Br J Psychiatry. 2007;190:77–8.
13. Heckbert SR, et al. Depression in relation to long-term control of glycemia, blood pressure, and lipids in patients with diabetes. J Gen Intern Med. 2010; 25:524–9.
14. Weobong B, Akpalu B, Doku V, Owusu-Agyei S, et al. The comparative validity of screening scales for postnatal common mental disorder in Kintampo, Ghana. J Affect Disord. 2009;113:109–17.
15. Adewuya AO, Ola BA, Afolabi OO. Validity of the patient health questionnaire (PHQ-9) as a screening tool for depression amongst Nigerian university students. J Affect Disord. 2006;96:89–93.
16. van Steenbergen-Weijenburg KM, de Vroege L, Ploeger RR, et al. Validation of the PHQ-9 as a screening instrument for depression in diabetes patients in specialized outpatient clinics. BMC Health Serv Res. 2010;10:235–41.
17. Kroenke K, Spitzer RL, Williams JB. The PHQ-9: validity of a brief depression severity measure. J Gen Intern Med. 2001;16:606–13.
18. Manea L, Gilbody S, McMillan D. Optimal cut-off score for diagnosing depression with the patient health questionnaire (PHQ-9): a meta-analysis. Can Med Assoc J. 2012;184:E191–6.
19. American Diabetes Association. Standards of Medical Care in Diabetes 2014: Position statement of the American Diabetes Association. Diabetes Care. 2014;37:S14–80.
20. Sotiropoulou A, Papazatiropoulou A, Apostolou O, Kokolaki A, Gikas A, Pappas S. Prevalence of depressive symptoms among non-insulin treated Greek type 2 diabetes subjects. BMC Res Notes. 2008;1:101.
21. Asghar S, Hussain A, Sm A, Khan AK, Magnusssson A. Prevalence of depression and diabetes: a population-based study from rural Bangladesh. Diab Med. 2008;24:124–7.
22. Collins MM, Corcorant P, Perry IJ. Anxiety and depression symptoms in patients with diabetes. Diabet Med. 2009;26:153–61.
23. Zahid N, Asghar S, Claussen B, Hussain A. Depression and diabetes in rural community in Pakistan. Diabetes Res Clin Pract. 2008;29:124–7.
24. Papelbaum M, Moreira RO, Coutinho W, Kupfer R, Zagury L, Freitas S, Appolinário JC. Depression, glycemic control and type 2 diabetes Marcelo. Diabetol Metab Syndr. 2011;3:26.
25. Li C, Ford ES, Strine TW, Mokdad AH. Prevalence of depression among US adults with diabetes: findings from 2006 behavioral risk factor surveillance system. Diabetes Care. 2008;31:105–7.
26. Khamseh ME, Baradaran HR, Rajabali H. Depression and diabetes in Iranian patients: a comparative study. Int J Psychiatry Med. 2007;37:81–6.
27. James BO, Morakinyo O, Eze GO, Lawani AO, Omoaregba JO. Depression and subjective quality of life among outpatients with diabetes mellitus at a teaching hospital in Nigeria. Ment Health Fam Med. 2010;7:179.
28. Akinlade K, Ohaeri J, Suberu M. The psychological condition of a cohort of Nigerian diabetic subjects. Afr J Med Med Sci. 1996;25:61.
29. Agbir T, Audu M, Adebowale T, Goar S. Depression among medical outpatients with diabetes: a cross-sectional study at Jos University teaching hospital, Jos, Nigeria. Ann Afr Med. 2010;9(1):5-10.
30. Read UM, Doku VCK. Mental Health Research in Ghana: a literature review. Ghana Med J. 2012;46(2 Suppl):29–38.
31. Thapa SB, Martinez P, Clausen T. Depression and its correlates in South Africa and Ghana among people aged 50 and above: findings from the WHO study on global ageing and adult health. J Psychiatry. 2014;17:1–6.
32. Weobong B, Asbbroek AHA, Soremekun S, Danso S, et al. Determination of postnatal depression in rural Ghana: finding from the DON population-based cohort study. Depress Anxiety. 2015;32:108–19.
33. Weobong B, Asbbroek AHA, Soremekun S, Kirkwood BR. Prevalence and determinants of antenatal depression among pregnant women in a predominantly rural population in Ghana: the Don population-based study. J Affect Disord. 2014;165:1–7.
34. Turkson SN. Psychiatric diagnosis among referred patients in Ghana. East Afr Med J. 1998;75(6):336–8.
35. Egede LE, Ellis C. Diabetes and depression: global perspectives. Diab Res Clin Pract. 2010;87:302–12.
36. Stein DJ, Gureje O. Depression and anxiety in the developing world: is it time to medicalize their suffering. Lancet. 2004;364:233–4.
37. Mirza I, Jenkins R. Risk factors, prevalence, and treatment of anxiety and depressive disorders in Pakistan: systemic review. BMJ. 2004;328:794.
38. Khuwaja AK, Kadir MM. Gender differences and clustering patterns of behavioral risk factors for chronic non-communicable diseases: community-based study from a developing country. Chronic Illn. 2010;6: 163–70.
39. Egede LE, Zheng D, Simpson K. Comorbid depression is associated with increased health care use and expenditures in individuals with diabetes. Diabetes Care. 2002;25:464–70.
40. Richardson LK, Egede LE, Mueller M, Echols CL, Gebregziabher M. Longitudinal effects of depression on glycemic control in veterans with type 2 diabetes. Gen Hosp Psychiatry. 2008;30:509–14.
41. Wagner JA, Abbot GL, Heapy A, Yong I. Depressive symptoms and diabetes control in African Americans. J Immigr Minor Health. 2009;11:66–70.
42. Lustman PJ, Clouse RE. Depression in diabetic patients: the relationship between mood and glycemic control. Journal of Diabetes and its Complications. 2005;19(2):113-22.
43. Kaulgud RS, NekarMS SKJ, Joshi RR, Vijayalakshmi PB. Study of depression in patients with diabetes compared to non-diabetics among elderly population and its association with blood sugar, HbA1c values. Int J Bio Res. 2013;04:55–61.
44. Ismail K, Winkley K, Rabe-Hesketh S. Systematic review and meta-analysis of randomised controlled trials of psychological interventions to improve glycaemic control in patients with type 2 diabetes. Lancet. 2004;363(9421): 1589–97.

45. Winkley K, Landau S, Eisler I, Ismail K. Psychological interventions to improve glycaemic control in patients with type 1 diabetes: systematic review and meta-analysis of randomised controlled trials. BMJ. 2006;333(7558):65.
46. Egede LE. Effects of depression on self-management behaviours and health outcomes in adults with type 2 diabetes. Curr Diabetes Rev. 2005;1:235–43.
47. Gonzalez S, Sa S, Cagliero E, Wexler DJ, et al. Depression, self-care and medication adherence in type 2 diabetes: relationships across the full range of symptoms severity. Diabetes Care. 2007;30:2222–7.
48. Frech A, Williams K. Depression and the psychological benefits of entering marriage. J Health Soc Behav. 2007;48(2):149–63.
49. Trief PM, Sandberg J, Greenberg RP, Graff K, Castronova N, Yoon M, Weinstock RS. Describing support: a qualitative study of couples living with diabetes. Fam Syst Health. 2003;21(1):57.
50. Trief PM, Ploutz-Snyder R, Britton KD, Weinstock RS. The relationship between marital quality and adherence to the diabetes care regimen. Ann Behav Med. 2004;27(3):148–54.

6

Prevalence of positive depression screen among post miscarriage women

Steve Kyende Mutiso*, Alfred Murage and Abraham Mwaniki Mukaindo

Abstract

Background: Miscarriages are a common pregnancy complication affecting about 10–15% of pregnancies. Miscarriages may be associated with a myriad of psychiatric morbidity at various timelines after the event. Depression has been shown to affect about 10–20% of all women following a miscarriage. However, no data exists in the local setting informing on the prevalence of post-miscarriage depression. We set out to determine the prevalence of positive depression screen among women who have experienced a miscarriage at the Aga Khan University hospital, Nairobi.

Methods: The study was cross-sectional in design. Patients who had a miscarriage were recruited at the post-miscarriage clinic review at the gynecology clinics at Aga Khan University Hospital, Nairobi. The Edinburgh postpartum depression scale was used to screen for depression in the patients. Prevalence was calculated from the percentage of patients achieving the cut -off score of 13 over the total number of patients.

Results: A total of 182 patients were recruited for the study. The prevalence of positive depression screen was 34.1% since 62 of the 182 patients had a positive depression screen. Moreover, of the patients who had a positive depression screen, 21(33.1%) had thoughts of self-harm.

Conclusion: A positive depression screen is present in 34.1% of women in our population two weeks after a miscarriage. Thoughts of self-harm are present in about a third of these women (33.1%) hence pointing out the importance of screening these women using the EPDS after a miscarriage.

Keywords: post-miscarriage, depression, prevalence

Background

A miscarriage is the premature loss of a fetus prior to viability. This may have different definitions depending on a regions' definition of the cusp of viability but the World Health Organization (WHO) defines it as the premature loss of a fetus up to 23 weeks of pregnancy and weighing up to 500 g [1]. Miscarriages are among the most common complication of pregnancy occurring in about 10–15% of pregnancies that are considered low-risk [2, 3]. Most of these miscarriages occur in the first trimester with a steady decline on the frequency of miscarriages up to about 20 weeks [4]. More so, more than 75% of miscarriages occur prior to 18 weeks [4]. A miscarriage can either be spontaneous or induced in etiology [5]. Spontaneous miscarriages have a myriad of causes including chromosomal abnormalities, uterine anomalies and environmental agents such as alcohol intake or cigarette smoking [6, 7].

Whether they are spontaneous or induced miscarriages have a significant implication in psychiatric morbidity of the involved women [8, 9]. However, induced miscarriages have been associated with higher rates of psychiatric complications compared to spontaneous ones [10]. Psychiatric illnesses have been shown to be a major complication of miscarriages with various psychiatric morbidities being linked to it including depression, anxiety and even post-traumatic stress disorders [9, 11, 12]. Furthermore, such psychiatric illnesses have been shown to have an implication in subsequent pregnancies with women who have had psychiatric morbidity being shown to be at higher risk of redeveloping

* Correspondence: steve_mutiso@yahoo.com
Department of Obstetrics and Gynaecology, Aga Khan University hospital, Nairobi, Kenya

the conditions in pregnancy and also other psychiatric conditions [12].

Depression in women who have had a miscarriage occurs at various timelines after the miscarriage episode [13]. Starting as early as within 10 days and being able to last a woman's lifetime, depressive illness seems to be of significant burden after a miscarriage [14]. Moreover, women experiencing a miscarriage have varied socio-cultural backgrounds as opposed to women going through a term pregnancy with a live outcome [15]. Furthermore, pregnant women in the region have also been shown to be of different socio-cultural backgrounds as compared to a Caucasian population [16]. Women in the region are married at an earlier age, with most living in the confines of an extended family and have wrong conceptions about the causation and implications of a miscarriage [4]. These varied factors argue out the importance of a regional study to look at the implications of miscarriages on depression. Various studies, conducted worldwide but none in Africa, have analyzed the prevalence of depression following a miscarriage with rates of 10–20% being described [14, 17]. Depression has also been shown to be significantly higher after a miscarriage compared to women who have not had a history of miscarriage [18, 19].

There is paucity of local literature with regards to incidence of depression after a miscarriage and the factors influencing its occurrence with no studies published with regards to its prevalence in the African population. Henceforth, we set out to determine the prevalence of depressive illness in patients after a miscarriage at a private tertiary teaching hospital in Kenya.

Methods

Objective

To determine the prevalence of positive depression screen for women who have experienced a miscarriage at the Aga Khan University Hospital Nairobi.

Study design

The study was a cross-sectional study where we examined both the exposure to a miscarriage to the outcome of depression at the same time.

Study setting and participants

The study was conducted at the Aga Khan University hospital Nairobi (AKUH, N). Participants were recruited from the Gynecology Clinics, which run daily, at the clinic review after a miscarriage. A miscarriage was defined as a pregnancy loss occurring at or before 23 weeks of a pregnancy or the miscarriage of a fetus of less than 500 g. Participants had some sort of treatment of the miscarriage including expectant, medical or surgical management. The clinic review was usually scheduled 2 weeks after the miscarriage but had a range of between one and 3 weeks. We further explore the choice of the study participants in the discussion.

Inclusion and exclusion criteria

We included women in the reproductive age group (15–49 years) who had experienced a miscarriage which were either spontaneous or induced. We excluded other forms of early pregnancy losses like women with a diagnosed ectopic pregnancy in order to eliminate it compounding the analysis of the impact of the mode of treatment on prevalence of depression. Women with previously diagnosed depression were also excluded.

Study procedures

Participants were required to sign consent to be included in the study after which two types of data were collected from the patient. A demographics tool and the Edinburgh Postnatal Depression scale (EPDS) [20] was administered to the patient. The data collection tools were administered by the principal investigator and a research assistant (a nurse in the gynecology clinic). Women were approached in the triage room after triage had been done. We approached a total of 202 women to get the sample size of 182 women – 20 women declined to be included.

Study tools

The study used two tools to collect information from the patients – a demographics tool and the EPDS.

The demographics tool was created for the study which collected the patients file number, age and other associated factors that may impact on the occurrence of post-miscarriage depression. These factors included the patient's age, educational background, gestation at miscarriage, marital status, planning of the pregnancy, social support, mode of treatment of the miscarriage, number of prior miscarriages, mode of conception and prior pregnancy outcome.

Depression symptoms were measured using the Edinburgh Postnatal Depression Scale (Additional file 1) [20]. This tool is a 10 item questionnaire that inquires on the presence of depressive symptoms in the period preceding the interview. Participant's responses regarding the frequency of symptoms are scored from 0 to 3. Total score may range from 0 to 30 [17]. A score of 13 and above was deemed screen-positive and indicative of a high likelihood of depression as used in prior studies [17]. The checklist and the demographics tool were administered by the principal investigator or a research assistant to patients coming for the post miscarriage clinic review at the Gynecology clinic.

Sample size and sampling method

There are no baseline prevalence studies from our population but from published literature from studies conducted worldwide but not in Africa [14] it is estimated that post miscarriage depression occurs in about 10–20% of women. More so, a study done in the AKUH, N using the EPDS for detection of postnatal depression in mothers revealed a prevalence rate of 13% [21]. This being the same setup we may assume the prevalence of post-miscarriage depression may likely be similar to the rate of postnatal depression and hence use it in the sample size calculation.

Sample size was calculated from a formula for estimating a population prevalence [22].

$$n = \frac{Z^2P(1\text{-}P)}{d^2}$$

Where: n = Required sample size. Z = Z statistic for a 95% confidence interval [1.96]. P = Expected prevalence of Post miscarriage depression at AKUH, N. d = Precision around expected prevalence ±0.05. Substituting for the equation:

$$n = \frac{1.96^2 \times 0.13(1\text{-}0.13)}{0.05^2}$$

$$n = 173.$$

The patients were selected by a consecutive sampling method.

Data management and analysis

The prevalence of positive depression screen for women who have experienced a miscarriage was determined as a percentage of patients who screened positive from the total participants. Descriptive statistics for continuous variables, such as age and gestation age at the miscarriage, were done to describe the baseline characteristics of women in the screen – positive and screen – negative groups. The statistical package for the social sciences (SPSS) version 22 was used for data analysis. Data were represented in tables and graphs.

Ethical considerations

Ethical approval was obtained from the Research and Ethics committee at the AKUH, N. Participants were recruited after obtaining written informed consent as per study protocol. Patients had the right to refuse or withdraw from the study at any point and this did not impact on the quality of care received subsequently. The study used alternative study numbers to maintain patient privacy and confidentiality. The data collection forms were safely kept in a locked cabinet to which only the primary investigator and the research assistant had access to. Patient who screened positive for post-miscarriage depression had an appointment booked for further evaluation and management by the psychiatrist, this however was at their own cost. Around 80% (50 of the 62) of women referred attended a psychiatrist follow up, the number included the women who had suicidal ideation and they were offered appropriate counselling and follow up.

Results

A total of 182 patients were recruited for the study. The patients were recruited from the outpatient gynecological clinics at the AKUH. No patients were excluded from this number since they all had their documentation in full.

Patient characteristics

The age of the patients recruited varied from as low as 17 years to the oldest being 45 years old. The mean age was 29.42 (SD = 5.6) years as shown in Table 1.Most of the patients had a university/college level of education

Table 1 Patient characteristics including age, gestational age at miscarriage, level of education, marital status, pregnancy planning, social support, others being aware of pregnancy, number of prior miscarriages, mode of conception and prior pregnancy outcome

Variable	Description	Value
Age	Mean (SD)	29.42 (±5.6) years
Gestational age at miscarriage in weeks	Mode (*n*)	8 weeks (41 women)
Level of education	Primary *n*(%)	4 (2.2%)
	Secondary *n*(%)	19 (10.4%)
	College/University *n*(%)	159 (87.4%)
Marital status	Single *n*(%)	34 (18.7%)
	Married *n*(%)	148 (81.3%)
Pregnancy planning	Planned *n*(%)	132 (72.5%)
	Unplanned *n*(%)	50 (27.5%)
Social Support	Lives alone *n*(%)	19 (10.4%)
	Lives with others *n*(%)	163 (89.6%)
Others aware of pregnancy	Yes *n*(%)	158 (86.8%)
	No *n*(%)	24 (13.2%)
Prior Miscarriage	None *n*(%)	124 (68.1%)
	1 *n*(%)	44 (24.2%)
	2 *n*(%)	6 (3.3%)
	3 *n*(%)	8 (4.4%)
Mode of Conception	Spontaneous *n*(%)	173 (95.0%)
	Assisted *n*(%)	9 (5.0%)
Prior Pregnancy Outcome	None *n*(%)	76 (41.8%)
	Miscarriage *n*(%)	38 (20.9%)
	Live Birth *n*(%)	68 (37.4%)

(87.4%; *n* = 159) with less having a primary level (2.2%; *n* = 4) or secondary level of education (10.4%; *n* = 19).

The gestational age at miscarriage varied from 3 weeks to the maximum of 23 weeks with the mode gestational age being 8 weeks(22.5%; *n* = 41). A large percentage (81.3%; *n* = 148) of the patients were married with also a high percentage of the pregnancies being planned (72.5%; *n* = 132). A high proportion of these women with miscarriages had social support with 89.6% (*n* = 163) living with other individuals and this corresponded to the high percentage of them having another individual aware of their pregnancy (86.8%; *n* = 158). This information is also displayed in Table 1. Furthermore, 68.1% (*n* = 124) of the women recruited had not experienced a previous miscarriage with about a quarter having experienced one prior miscarriage (24.2%; *n* = 44) and much less having had 2(3.3%; *n* = 6) or 3(4.4%; *n* = 8) prior miscarriages. Most women had conceived spontaneously (95%; *n* = 173) with 37.4% (*n* = 68) having had a live birth in their previous pregnancy (Table 1).

Almost half of the miscarriages seen were managed medically (47.3%; *n* = 86) with a small percentage (6%; *n* = 11) requiring a combination of more than one mode of *treatment* (Fig. 1).

Prevalence of positive depression screen

The prevalence for positive depression screen in post miscarriage patients from the present study is estimated at 34.1%. In the recruited patients, 62 of the 182 participants scored 13 or more in the EPDS and had a positive screen for post miscarriage depression (Fig. 2). Patients who had a positive depression screen were referred for psychiatric review at their convenience and cost. This study did not envisage further follow up of these participants.

Self-harm

The last question of the EPDS assesses thoughts of self-harm and because of it implication it's important to highlight the outcome result of this question. Out of the 62 participants who had a positive depression screen, 21(33.8%) had thoughts of self-harm which were distributed as shown in Fig. 3.

Discussion

Miscarriages are common especially in early pregnancy and with the growing concern about its mental health implications, it's an area of growing interest in obstetrics and gynaecology. The present study set out to determine the prevalence of positive depression screen among women who have had a miscarriage.

The present study recruited 182 women who had miscarriage and screened them after having had treatment for the miscarriage. The patients recruited had a mean age of 29.42 years with the youngest being 17 years and the oldest 45 years. More so, although it is known that miscarriages tend to increase with advancing age [23], most of our patients were mainly 26 to 31 year olds which represented 47.3% of all the patients. This can be attributed to the particular demographic the hospital serves which includes young working women and hence may not be a true representation of the occurrence of miscarriages with age.

The mode gestational age at miscarriage was 8 weeks. This is in keeping with previous studies in miscarriages as most are seen within the first trimester and tend to reduce with advancing age [24]. This pattern also been

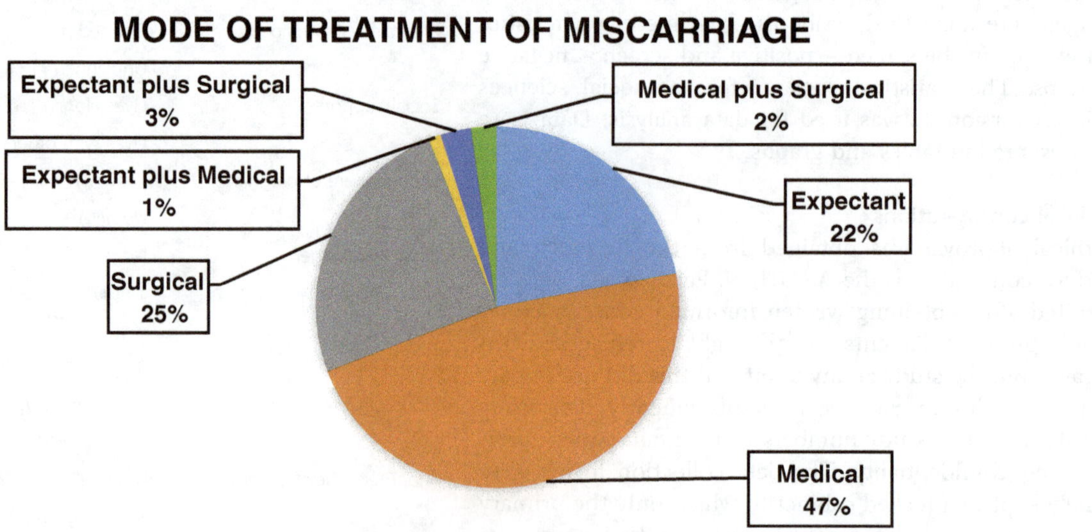

Fig. 1 Mode of treatment of miscarriages

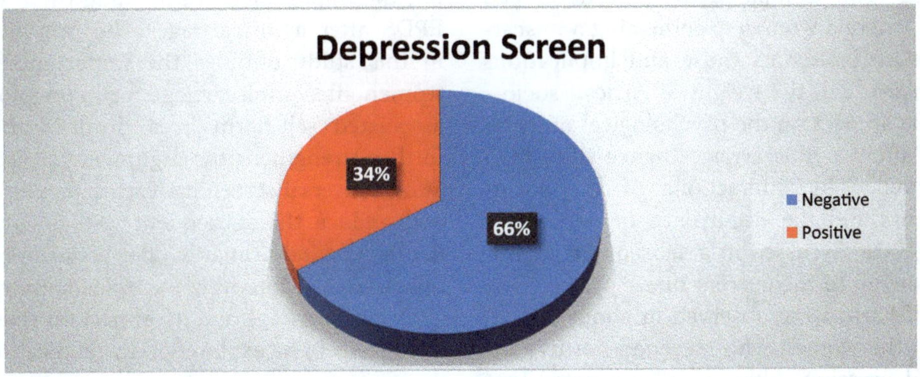

Fig. 2 Depression screen result

documented in a local study that documented miscarriages with advancing gestational age [4]. It was observed that their peak age of miscarriages was at 6 weeks with around 25% of the pregnancies observed resulting in miscarriage. The cause of the high incidence of miscarriage in early pregnancy has not well elucidated although there is increasing concern that it may be as a result of disorders in genetic makeup of the pregnancy and placentation with low levels of angiogenic markers also playing a key role [25].

Most of women recruited in this study had an advanced level of education with 87.4% having a college or university level education. This is in keeping with studies done in pregnant women from a similar population. Majority of the women recruited were married (81.3%) and more of their pregnancies were planned (72.5%). This again just points out to the social strata of most patients with a miscarriage in our setting [4]. In the present study, 89.6% of the women recruited had social support meaning they did not live alone and consequently, 86.8% reported that the pregnancy ending in miscarriage was known to another person. This again points out to the social setting of the women recruited with expectations that most of them would plan a pregnancy after marriage and hence wouldn't be living alone and probably a another person would know about their miscarriage. This in turn may impact on the occurrence of prevalence found in this population, we may postulate that this prevalence may be different in a population with a lesser proportion of social support.

The prevalence of positive depression screen in post miscarriage women in our study was 34.1%. Sixty two of the 182 women had an EPDS score of 13 or more. This is the highest prevalence of positive depression screen after a miscarriage reported in recent literature. Previous studies reported a prevalence ranging from as low as 10% to as high as 28.7% [14, 15]. The high prevalence in our study is a novel finding with regards to depression after a miscarriage. The occurrence of depression after a miscarriage has been strongly attributed to socio-cultural beliefs [26, 27]. More so, in the African context many myths exist in regards to the cause and future implications of miscarriage [16]. These myths do influence the ability of a woman to seek psychological help after a miscarriage and go through the proper grief process and subsequently explain the high prevalence of depression

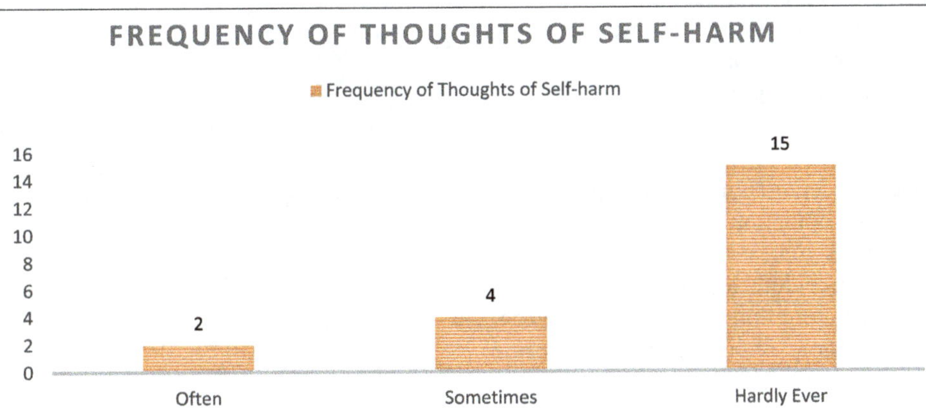

Fig. 3 Frequency of Thoughts of Self harm

after a miscarriage [26]. Compared to more developed western societies, where a woman experiencing a miscarriage may understand better its cause and implications to future pregnancies [23], the weight of African socio--cultural beliefs may impact on the psychological morbidity experienced after a miscarriage hence the high prevalence observed. The interactions of the socio-demographic factors and the occurrence of depression after a miscarriage are discussed in a subsequent manuscript that's a follow up to the current one.

Thoughts of self-harm were observed in about a third (33.8%; $n = 21$) of the women who screened positive for post miscarriage depression. Although it was noted that most of the women hardly ever had these thoughts, it is concerning that they are present in the setting of post miscarriage depression. No studies have been done in post miscarriage women assessing their thoughts of self-harm, however in postnatal women assessed with the EPDS the prevalence reported varies from around 4–20% [28, 29]. The occurrence of self-harm was further correlated to risk factors such as younger maternal age, being single, history of childhood abuse and associated symptoms of sleep disturbance and anxiety [28, 29]. Although the present study was not powered to investigate these factors, we can posit that the same factors may play a role in women with a positive depression screen after a miscarriage.

Limitations and future directions

The limitations of the study included not being able to confirm clinical depression using a psychiatric consult which was due to financial constraints due to a limited budget. But this may be a study to undertake now that we have shown that post miscarriage depression is an area of concern in the field of obstetrics and gynaecology. The other limitation was lack of further follow up of the women who had a positive depression screen to elucidate whether this number waned off with passing time. This would have aided in further understanding of the psychological evolution of the depressive episode. This was also due to the constraint of time the study was to be carried out in but we hope further studies can be done to elucidate this in our population.

Conclusion

In conclusion, a positive depression screen is present in 34.1% of women in our population 2 weeks after a miscarriage. More so, factors that seem to impact on the positive depression screen include a younger age, a lower education level, an older gestational age at miscarriage, being single, an assisted mode of conception and a prior miscarriage – these have been further explored in a subsequent manuscript. Thoughts of self-harm are present in about a third of these women (33.1%) hence pointing out the importance of screening these women using the EPDS after a miscarriage. The prevalence documented in this study outlines the importance of screening of women after a miscarriage for depression, more so, with associated self-harm in a third of these women this further strengthens the argument for universal screening. With universal screening, earlier pick up of these women may reduce the subsequent well documented effects of depression and primarily offer better universal care after a miscarriage. Moreover, the role of universal counselling after a miscarriage and its impact on reduction of depression needs to be explored in the clinical setting.

Acknowledgements
The management, staff, faculty members, and my colleagues for their invaluable input and for being a great source of support to me during this study.

Funding
This study was funded by a research grant offered for postgraduate trainees at the Aga Khan University Hospital. The funding had no role in the collection, analysis and interpretation od result findings.

Authors' contributions
MSK was involved in the development of the research question, collection of data, analysis of the data, drafting of the manuscript and final approval of the manuscript. MA was involved in the analysis of the data, drafting of the manuscript and final approval of the manuscript. MM was involved in the development of the research question, analysis of the data, drafting of the manuscript and final approval of the manuscript.

Consent for publication
No patients' individual data was used in the present study and hence no consent was needed for publication.

Competing interests
The authors have no competing interests to declare with regards to the present study.

References
1. World Health Organisation. WHO: recommended definitions, terminology and format for statistical tables related to the perinatal period and use of a new certificate for cause of perinatal deaths. Modifications recommended by FIGO as amended October 14, 1976. Acta Obstet Gynecol Scand. 1977; 56(3):247–53.
2. Tong S, Kaur A, Walker SP, Bryant V, Onwude JL, Permezel M. Miscarriage risk for asymptomatic women after a normal first-trimester prenatal visit. Obstet Gynecol. 2008;111(3):710–4.
3. Zinaman MJ, Clegg ED, Brown CC, O'Connor J, Selevan SG. Estimates of human fertility and pregnancy loss. Fertil Steril. 1996;65(3):503–9.
4. Dellicour S, Aol G, Ouma P, Yan N, Bigogo G, Hamel MJ, et al. Weekly miscarriage rates in a community-based prospective cohort study in rural western Kenya. BMJ Open. 2016;6(4):e011088.
5. Swanson KM. Predicting depressive symptoms after miscarriage: a path analysis based on the Lazarus paradigm. J Womens Health Gend Based Med. 2000;9(2):191–206.
6. Hemming K. Causation or association: running before we can walk? BJOG. 2014;121(11):1385.
7. Liu Y, Liu Y, Zhang S, Chen H, Liu M, Zhang J. Etiology of spontaneous abortion before and after the demonstration of embryonic cardiac activity in women with recurrent spontaneous abortion. Int J Gynaecol Obstet. 2015;129(2):128–32.

8. Klier CM, Geller PA, Neugebauer R. Minor depressive disorder in the context of miscarriage. J Affect Disord. 2000;59(1):13–21.
9. Coleman PK. Abortion and mental health: quantitative synthesis and analysis of research published 1995-2009. Br J Psychiatry. 2011;199(3):180–6.
10. Broen AN, Moum T, Bodtker AS, Ekeberg O. Psychological impact on women of miscarriage versus induced abortion: a 2-year follow-up study. Psychosom Med. 2004;66(2):265–71.
11. Bianchi-Demicheli F. Psychiatric and psychological consequences of abortion. Rev Medicale Suisse. 2007;3(98):401–2. 4, 6-7
12. McCarthy FP, Moss-Morris R, Khashan AS, North RA, Baker PN, Dekker G, et al. Previous pregnancy loss has an adverse impact on distress and behaviour in subsequent pregnancy. BJOG. 2015;122(13):1757–64.
13. Fergusson DM, Horwood LJ, Boden JM. Abortion and mental health disorders: evidence from a 30-year longitudinal study. Br J Psychiatry. 2008;193(6):444–51.
14. Sham A, Yiu M, Ho W. Psychiatric morbidity following miscarriage in Hong Kong. Gen Hosp Psychiatry. 2010;32(3):284–93.
15. Reardon DC, Cougle JR. Depression and unintended pregnancy in the National Longitudinal Survey of youth: a cohort study. BMJ. 2002;324(7330):151–2.
16. Abiola AO, Ajayi A, Umeh CS, Adegbesan-Omilabu MO, Olufunlayo TF, Akodu BA. Knowledge, prevalence and psychological effect of miscarriage among women of reproductive age group attending obstetrics and gynaecology clinics of Lagos University teaching hospital, Nigeria. Niger Postgrad Med J. 2013;20(4):319–24.
17. Neugebauer R. Depressive symptoms at two months after miscarriage: interpreting study findings from an epidemiological versus clinical perspective. Depress Anxiety. 2003;17(3):152–61.
18. Neugebauer R, Kline J, O'Connor P, Shrout P, Johnson J, Skodol A, et al. Determinants of depressive symptoms in the early weeks after miscarriage. Am J Public Health. 1992;82(10):1332–9.
19. Radloff LS. The CES-D scale: a self-report depression scale for research in the general population. Appl Psychol Meas. 1977;1(3):385–401.
20. Cox JL, Holden JM, Sagovsky R. Detection of postnatal depression. Development of the 10-item Edinburgh postnatal depression scale. Br J Psychiatry. 1987;150:782–6.
21. Khadija W. Prevalence of postpartum depression using the Edinburgh postpartum depression scale at the Aga khan university hospital, Nairobi Aga khan university hospital; 2011.
22. Pourhoseingholi MA, Vahedi M, Rahimzadeh M. Sample size calculation in medical studies. Gastroenterol Hepatol Bed Bench. 2013;6(1):14–7.
23. Gerdts C, Dobkin L, Foster DG, Schwarz EB. Side effects, physical health consequences, and mortality associated with abortion and birth after an unwanted pregnancy. Womens Health Issues. 2016;26(1):55–9.
24. Sapra KJ, Joseph KS, Galea S, Bates LM, Louis GM, Ananth CV. Signs and symptoms of early pregnancy loss: a systematic review. Reproductive sciences (thousand oaks, Calif). 2016.
25. Andersen LB, Dechend R, Karumanchi SA, Nielsen J, Joergensen JS, Jensen TK, et al. Early pregnancy angiogenic markers and spontaneous abortion: an Odense child cohort study. Am J Obstet Gynecol. 2016;215(5):594.e1–e11.
26. Obi SN, Onah HE, Okafor II. Depression among Nigerian women following pregnancy loss. Int J Gynaecol Obstet. 2009;105(1):60–2.
27. Kulathilaka S, Hanwella R, de Silva VA. Depressive disorder and grief following spontaneous abortion. BMC Psychiatry. 2016;16:100.
28. Kim JJ, La Porte LM, Saleh MP, Allweiss S, Adams MG, Zhou Y, et al. Suicide risk among perinatal women who report thoughts of self-harm on depression screens. Obstet Gynecol. 2015;125(4):885–93.
29. Sit D, Luther J, Buysse D, Dills JL, Eng H, Okun M, et al. Suicidal ideation in depressed postpartum women: associations with childhood trauma, sleep disturbance and anxiety. J Psychiatr Res. 2015;66-67:95–104.

Determinants of antenatal depression and postnatal depression in Australia

Felix Akpojene Ogbo[1,2*], John Eastwood[2,3,4,5,6], Alexandra Hendry[2,7], Bin Jalaludin[2,8], Kingsley E. Agho[1], Bryanne Barnett[9] and Andrew Page[1,2]

Abstract

Background: Depression is a leading source of morbidity and health loss in Australian women. This study investigates the determinants of antenatal depressive symptoms and postnatal depressive symptoms in an Australian population, including people from culturally and linguistically diverse (CALD) backgrounds.

Method: The study used a retrospective cohort of mothers of all live births in public health facilities in 2014 ($N = 17{,}564$) within South Western Sydney Local Health District and Sydney Local Health District in New South Wales, Australia. Prevalence of antenatal and postnatal depressive symptoms were estimated for the cohort. Multivariate logistic regression models were conducted to investigate the sociodemographic, psychological and health service determinants of antenatal and postnatal depressive symptoms, measured using the Edinburgh Postnatal Depression Scale (EPDS).

Results: The prevalence of antenatal and postnatal depressive symptoms was 6.2% and 3.3% of the cohort, respectively. Significant risk factors for maternal depressive symptoms during pregnancy were, a lack of partner support, history of intimate partner violence, being from the CALD population and low socioeconomic status. Self-reported antenatal depressive symptoms were strongly associated with postnatal depressive symptoms. Risk factors for postnatal depressive symptoms were similar to those for antenatal depressive symptoms, as well as assisted delivery.

Conclusion: Factors relating to demographic and psychosocial disadvantage were associated with subsequent antenatal and postnatal depressive symptoms in New South Wales, Australia. Our study suggests that screening for probable depression and timely referral for expert assessment of at-risk mothers may be an effective strategy to improve maternal mental health outcomes.

Keywords: determinants, antenatal, depression, perinatal, postnatal, Australia, pregnancy

Background

Depression is a major public health issue worldwide and was among the leading source of health loss in terms of disability-adjusted life years among Australian women of reproductive age in 2016 [1, 2]. Maternal depression during pregnancy (antenatal depression) and postnatal depression have both short- and long-term consequences for the mother, the child and family. For the infant, these may include low birth weight, psychological issues, increased risk of experiencing diarrhoea and suboptimal infant feeding patterns [3–6]. Lower rates of immunisation, and reduced growth and developmental trajectories have also been reported in infants whose mothers had perinatal depression [7]. In addition, stress, poor social interaction and lost productivity have been documented in pregnant women with depression [8, 9].

In Australia, recent studies have indicated that maternal depression during pregnancy is associated with adverse perinatal outcomes [10, 11]. Other Australian studies have reported higher prevalence for antenatal depression, from 6% [4, 10] to 17% [12] and postnatal depression, from 6% to 12% [4, 12, 13]. A study conducted among women living in a socioeconomically disadvantaged community in South Australia indicated that the incidence of antenatal

* Correspondence: f.ogbo@westernsyndey.edu.au
[1]Translational Health Research Institute, School of Medicine, Western Sydney University, Campbelltown Campus, Locked Bag 1797, Penrith, NSW 2571, Australia
[2]Ingham Institute for Applied Medical Research, University of New South Wales, 1 Campbell Street, Liverpool, NSW 2170, Australia
Full list of author information is available at the end of the article

depressive symptoms over a seven-month period was 30%, reflecting variation in the burden of perinatal depression in women across the socioeconomic scale [14].

Previous studies conducted in Australia have shown a range of factors associated with antenatal and postnatal depression. Risk factors for antenatal depression include low self-esteem, anxiety, low social support, negative cognitive style, major life events, low income and history of abuse [12, 14], domestic violence during pregnancy and having recently hit someone else in anger [14]. Risk factors for postnatal depression include antenatal depression and history of depression [12], poor health status of the mother, not breastfeeding, difficult financial situation and being born overseas [13]. Furthermore, analysis of data from the beyondblue National Depression Program in Australia found that antenatal depression, a prior history of depression and limited partner support were the strongest risk factors for postnatal depression [15].

The Edinburgh Postnatal Depression Scale (EPDS) is routinely used for pregnant women in many Australian primary health care settings to identify and refer for expert assessment and management, women who may be experiencing or are at risk of perinatal depression. The National Postnatal Depression Program recommends the EPDS as a screening device for perinatal depression, and advocates for ongoing research in perinatal depression to inform policy formulation, and targeted and evidence-based initiatives [4, 16]. Accordingly, the present study aimed to investigate socioeconomic, psychosocial and health service determinants of maternal depressive symptoms during pregnancy and postnatal depressive symptoms in Australia, including people from culturally and linguistically diverse (CALD) populations.

Methods

Data source

The study was based on a retrospective cohort of mothers of all live births ($N = 17{,}564$) in public health facilities within South Western Sydney Local Health District (SWSLHD) and the Sydney Local Health District (SLHD) in 2014, in the state of New South Wales (NSW), Australia. Antenatal data, routinely collected by qualified midwives, were linked to routinely collected postnatal data (by skilled community health nurses), using individual identifiers. These data were stored in the Information Management & Technology Division (IM&TD) database of the health districts. After ethics approvals were obtained, the data were cleaned and coded for analysis.

Study setting

SWSLHD and SLHD represent approximately 52 % of the Sydney metropolitan region, with a population of over 1,457,100 people. This region of Sydney has one of Australia's most culturally diverse populations [17, 18], with approximately 50 % of mothers born overseas, with mothers from Middle Eastern countries (10%), South East Asia (8%) and Southern Asia (8%) most commonly represented [19]. The health districts provide health services to a socioeconomically diverse population, with some geographic areas in South Western Sydney representing some of the most socioeconomically disadvantaged and advantaged areas in the Sydney metropolitan region [10].

Risk factors

Study variables included: maternal age (categorised as less than 20 years, 20–34 years or over 35 years); area-based socioeconomic status (SES, categorised as low, medium or high); partner support (categorised as Yes or No/unsure); culturally and linguistically diverse (CALD, categorised as Yes or No); history of physical intimate partner violence (IPV, categorised as Yes or No); fear of partner/ex-partner (categorised as Yes or No); history of pre-existing antenatal health problems (such as diabetes mellitus and hypertension, categorised as Yes or No); and type of delivery (categorised as normal vaginal, assisted vaginal or caesarean delivery). Sociodemographic, psychological and health service data were collected in the first prenatal clinic visit for the index pregnancy, and information on the type of delivery was collected soon after birth.

Area-based SES was measured using the Socio-Economic Index for Areas (SEIFA), based on the mother's address. SEIFA is a measurement indicator developed by the Australian Bureau of Statistics that ranks areas in Australia according to relative socio-economic advantage and disadvantage [20]. Deciles of SES were categorised into high (top 10% of the population), medium (middle 80% of the population) and low (bottom 10% of the population) groups, consistent with previous publications [10, 19]. CALD is a term used for communities with diverse language, ethnic background, nationality, dress, traditions, food, societal structures, art and religion characteristics [21]. IPV information was collected during antenatal period based on the NSW Routine Domestic Violence Screening policy, where mothers were asked: "Within the last 12 months, have you been hit, slapped or hurt in other ways by your partner or ex-partner (physical IPV)?" or "Are you frightened of your partner or ex-partner (psychological IPV)?"

Outcome variables

In the present study, maternal depressive symptoms during pregnancy and postnatal depressive symptoms were the main outcomes, measured using the EPDS, which has been validated in the antenatal and postnatal periods [22–24]. The EPDS has been recommended as a screening tool for perinatal depression among women in Australia [4]. Midwives collected information on sociodemographic and psychosocial characteristics, and maternal depressive symptoms during pregnancy at the first antenatal care visit. For non-English speaking mothers, the English version of the EPDS was administered through qualified interpreters, certified by the National Accreditation Authority for Translators and Interpreters in Australia. The overall number of antenatal depressive symptoms was calculated to achieve a total score (out of 30) and was then coded as a categorical variable (score < 13 or score ≥ 13), with a score of greater or equal to 13 suggestive of antenatal depressive symptoms [24].

Data on postnatal depressive symptoms were collected within the first six weeks of birth. The total number of postnatal depressive symptoms was also tallied to obtain a total score (out of 30) and was then coded as a categorical variable (score < 13 or score ≥ 13) to indicate scores suggestive of postnatal depressive symptoms [24]. In the present analysis, the EPDS cut-points used to indicate probable depression were selected based on previously published studies [10, 13, 25, 26] and the NSW government guidelines on improving mental health outcomes for parents and infants [27].

The EPDS is the most common and acceptable screening tool for identifying depressive symptoms in the perinatal period worldwide, with a reported sensitivity of 68–86% and specificity of 78–96% [23, 24]. In Australia, a study that used the EPDS among a sample of 4148 women, reported a sensitivity of 100% and specificity of 89% [28]. Studies have reported a positive predictive value (PPV) for clinical depression [23] and a PPV of approximately 70% with an EPDS score of > 12 [24, 28, 29].

Statistical analysis

Preliminary analyses involved a series of frequencies and cross-tabulations to estimate the prevalence of antenatal and postnatal depressive symptoms by study variables. This was followed by univariate logistic regression analysis to examine all potential risk factors associated with antenatal and postnatal depressive symptoms. Only those variables with *P*-value < 0.1 in univariate models were then entered into a multivariate model to estimate the factors associated with antenatal and postnatal depressive symptoms. Univariate and multivariate odds ratios (ORs) and their 95% confidence intervals were reported in the present study.

Missing data

The study investigated the potential effect of missing data on observed odds ratios in sensitivity analyses, which were conducted on an imputed data set based on the original cohort comprising complete outcome data (Figs. 1 and 2). Multivariate imputation by chained equation was used to impute missing information on study factors included in the analysis. This approach assumes that data were missing at random and that the characteristics of known participants can be used to calculate the characteristics of participants with missing data [30]. Sensitivity analyses were conducted using the *ice* command in Stata software (Stata Corp, V.15.0, College Station, TX, USA), based on 25 multiple imputations [31]. Revised odds ratios and corresponding confidence intervals were estimated from the imputed dataset, using the *mim* command.

Results

Antenatal depressive symptoms (EPDS ≥13)

The prevalence of mothers who reported depressive symptoms during pregnancy was 6.2% in the cohort and was higher among mothers who reported psychological IPV (28%) or physical IPV (32%) [Table 1]. The prevalence of ANC depressive symptoms was higher in people from the CALD background (8.0%) compared to those from the non-CALD group (4.0%). A lack of partner support (OR = 6.1, 95% CI: 4.6–7.9, $P < 0.001$) and being from the CALD group (OR = 2.0, 95% CI: 1.6–2.4, $P < 0.001$) were associated with antenatal depressive symptoms. Intimate partner violence was associated with depressive symptoms during pregnancy compared to mothers with no history of IPV (OR = 2.6, 95% CI: 1.6–4.2, P < 0.001 for physical IPV and OR = 4.8, 95% CI: 3.0–7.8, P < 0.001 for psychological IPV). Mothers from high SES group were significantly less likely to experience depressive symptoms during pregnancy compared to mothers from low SES group (OR = 0.5, 95% CI: 0.3–0.7, P < 0.001) [Table 1].

Postnatal depressive symptoms (EPDS ≥13)

The prevalence of postnatal depressive symptoms was 3.3%, and maternal depressive symptoms during pregnancy were strongly associated with postnatal depressive symptoms (OR = 6.7, 95%CI: 4.9–9.3, $P < 0.001$) [Table 2]. Compared to mothers from the low SES group, mothers from higher SES group were less likely to experience postnatal depressive symptoms (OR = 0.7, 95% CI: 0.5–0.9, $P = 0.010$ for middle SES group and OR = 0.5, 95% CI: 0.3–0.8, $P = 0.025$ for high SES group). The prevalence of postnatal depressive symptoms was higher in mothers from the CALD group (4.2%), and mothers who identified as being from the CALD group were also more likely to experience postnatal depressive symptoms compared to those, not from the CALD group (OR = 1.5, 95%CI 1.1–2.0, $P = 0.002$). Psychological IPV was strongly associated with postnatal depressive symptoms (OR = 5.3, 95% CI: 2.5–11.0, $P < 0.001$), and mothers who had a caesarean section were more likely to experience postnatal depressive symptoms compared to those

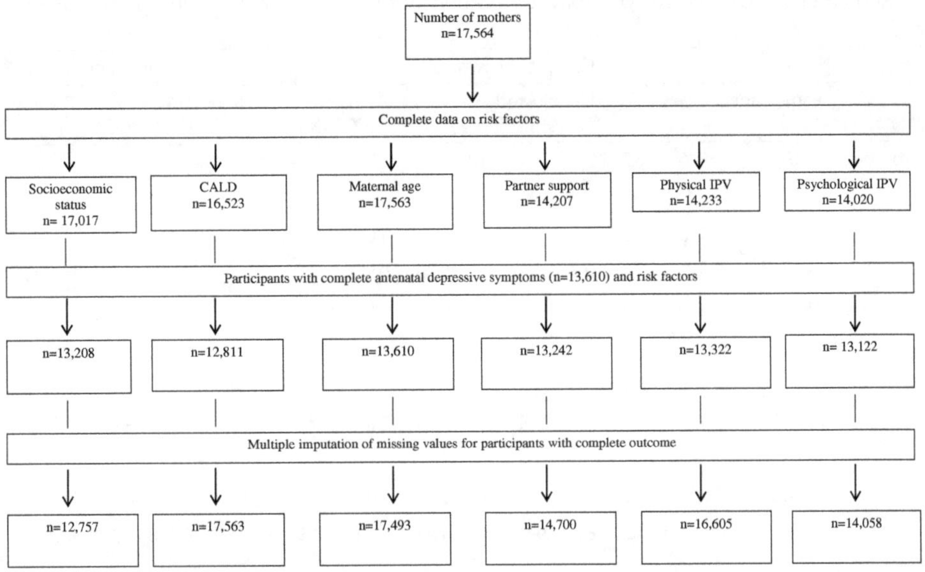

Fig. 1 Flow chart of available data on antenatal depressive symptoms and risk factors in South Western Sydney Local Health District and Sydney Local Health District in New South Wales, Australia (2014)

who had normal vaginal delivery (OR = 1.7, 95%CI: 1.3–2.3, P < 0.001).

Stratified analyses showed no substantial, significant differences between CALD and non-CALD groups. For example, mothers who experienced physical and psychological IPV were almost equally distributed in both groups (50% in both groups for physical IPV, and 49.0% and 51.0% among non-CALD and CALD population for psychosocial IPV, respectively). The revised odds ratios from sensitivity analyses were not markedly different from the complete case analysis (except for the association between younger maternal age and antenatal depressive symptoms), indicating that missing data did not substantially affect the observed findings.

Discussion

The prevalence of maternal depressive symptoms during pregnancy was 6.2%, with a higher prevalence observed in mothers with a history of IPV. The analysis showed that a lack of partner support, IPV, being from the

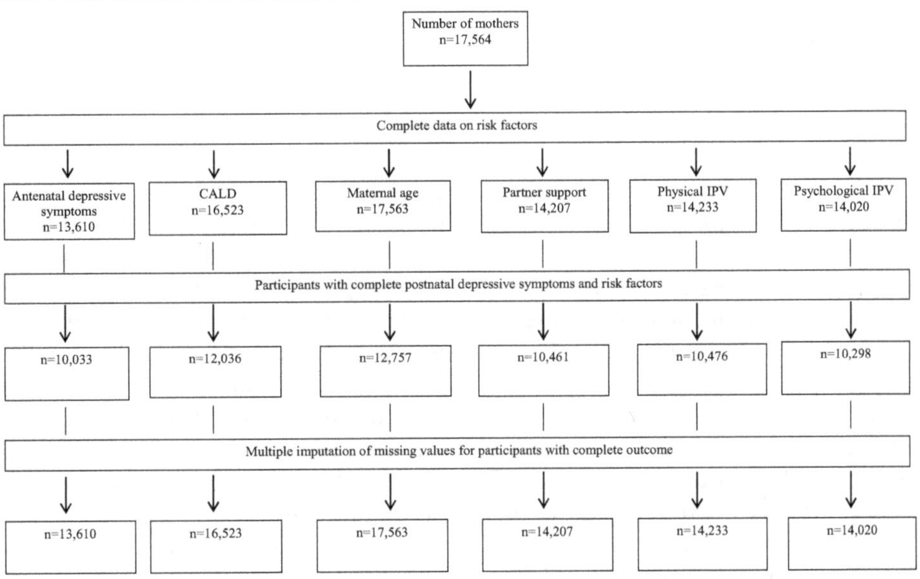

Fig. 2 Flow chart of available data on postnatal depressive symptoms and risk factors in South Western Sydney Local Health District and Sydney Local Health District in New South Wales, Australia (2014)

Table 1 Study factors and antenatal depressive symptoms of mothers from South Western Sydney and Sydney Local Health Districts in 2014 ($N = 17{,}564$)

Outcome	Participants	Cases	%	Complete cases				Multiple imputation [a]			
				Unadjusted OR (95%CI)	P value	Adjusted OR (95%CI)	P value	Unadjusted OR (95%CI)	P value	Adjusted OR (95%CI)	P value
Antenatal depressive symptoms	13,610	846	6.2								
Socio-economic status											
Low	5716	450	7.9	1.0		1.0		1.0		1.0	
Medium	5968	321	5.4	0.6 (0.5–0.7)	< 0.001	0.8 (0.7–1.0)	0.060	0.6 (0.5–0.7)	< 0.001	0.8 (0.7–0.9)	< 0.001
High	1524	43	2.8	0.3 (0.2–0.4)	< 0.001	0.5 (0.3–0.7)	0.001	0.3 (0.2–0.4)	< 0.001	0.5 (0.4–0.5)	< 0.001
CALD group											
No	6173	278	4.5	1.0		1.0		1.0		1.0	
Yes	6638	528	8.0	1.8 (1.5–2.1)	< 0.001	2.0 (1.6–2.4)	< 0.001	1.6 (1.6–1.7)	< 0.001	1.8 (1.7–1.9)	< 0.001
Supportive Partner											
Yes	12,805	666	5.2	1.0		1.0		1.0		1.00	
No/unsure	437	140	32.0	8.5 (6.9–10.6)	< 0.001	6.1 (4.6–7.9)	< 0.001	8.5 (8.2–8.9)	< 0.001	6.1 (5.9–6.4)	< 0.001
Antenatal health problems											
No	8573	465	5.4	1.0		1.0		1.0		1.0	
Yes	3774	273	7.2	1.3 (1.1–1.5)	< 0.001	1.2 (1.0–1.5)	0.003	1.3 (1.3–1.4)	< 0.001	1.2 (1.2–1.3)	< 0.001
Physical intimate partner violence											
No	13,140	182	5.9	1.0		1.0		1.0		1.0	
Yes	777	50	27.5	6.0 (4.3–8.4)	< 0.001	2.6 (1.6–4.2)	< 0.001	6.4 (6.1–6.8)	< 0.001	3.1 (2.9–3.4)	< 0.001
Psychological intimate partner violence											
No	12,989	768	5.9	1.0		1.0		1.0		1.0	
Yes	133	43	32.3	7.0 (5.2–11.0)	< 0.001	4.8 (3.0–7.8)	< 0.001	8.0 (7.6–8.5)	< 0.001	4.1 (3.8–4.4)	< 0.001
Maternal age group											
20–34 years	9382	571	6.1	1.0		1.0		1.0		1.0	
> 35 years	3206	207	6.5	1.0 (1.1–2.5)	0.452	1.0 (0.8–1.2)	0.624	1.0 (1.0–1.1)	< 0.001	1.1 (1.0–1.1)	< 0.001
< 20 years	243	24	9.9	1.7 (1.1–2.6)	0.017	1.4 (0.8–2.5)	0.178	1.5 (1.4–1.6)	< 0.001	1.3 (1.2–1.4)	< 0.001

Data on risk factors and antenatal depressive symptoms were collected at the first antenatal clinic visit. Multivariate model adjusted for variables with p-value < 0.1 in univariate analysis. The variables include maternal age, socioeconomic status, CALD group, supportive partner, history of physical intimate partner violence, antenatal health problems and history of fear of partner/ex-partner

CALD culturally and linguistically diverse

[a] Sensitivity analyses following multiple imputations for missing values

CALD population and low SES group were associated with maternal depressive symptoms during pregnancy. The prevalence of postnatal depression was 3.3%, and the risk factors for postnatal depressive symptoms were assisted delivery (caesarean section), low SES, psychological IPV, being from the CALD population and antenatal depressive symptoms.

The impact of antenatal depression on perinatal outcomes in the study participants has been documented [10] and was consistent with previous reports [5, 11]. Similarly, most of the previously established risk factors for antenatal depression in other contexts also played a role in predicting maternal depressive symptoms during pregnancy in the current study. A number of the identified risk factors are amenable to initiatives, suggesting that well-targeted interventions and policies may be helpful in reducing the burden of antenatal depression. For example, IPV and a lack of partner support were the strongest risk factors for antenatal depressive symptoms in the present study, consistent with evidence from previous reports [12, 32]. The Australian, State and Territory governments commitment to reducing perinatal depression, IPV and improve partner support are broader initiatives needed to improve the social-emotional and physical health of both mother and infant health [33–35].

In the state of NSW, there are facility- and community-based interventions that aim to identify vulnerable mothers with probable depressive episodes quickly, and referral for expert assessment and

Table 2 Study factors and postnatal depressive symptoms of mothers from South Western Sydney and Sydney Local Health Districts in 2014 (N = 17,564)

				Complete cases				Multiple imputation [a]			
Outcome	Participants	cases	%	Unadjusted OR (95%CI)	P value	Adjusted OR (95%CI)	P value	Unadjusted OR (95%CI)	P value	Adjusted OR (95%CI)	P value
Postnatal depressive symptoms	12,757	425	3.3								
Maternal age group											
20–34 years	8605	291	3.4	1.0		1.0		1.0		1.0	
> 35 years	3170	101	3.2	0.9 (0.7–1.1)	0.638	0.8 (0.6–1.2)	0.422	0.9 (0.9–1.0)	0.002	0.7 (0.8–0.9)	< 0.001
< 20 years	228	8	3.5	1.0 (0.5–2.1)	0.936	1.3 (0.5–3.)	0.525	1.1 (0.9–1.2)	0.094	0.9 (0.8–1.1)	0.862
Socio-economic status											
Low	4964	211	4.3	1.0		1.0		1.00		1.0	
Medium	5877	162	2.8	0.6 (0.5–0.7)	< 0.001	0.7 (0.5–0.9)	0.010	0.6 (0.6–0.7)	< 0.001	0.7 (0.7–0.8)	< 0.001
High	1559	36	2.3	0.5 (0.3–0.7)	0.001	0.5 (0.3–0.8)	0.025	0.5 (0.4–0.5)	< 0.001	0.5 (0.5–0.6)	< 0.001
Antenatal depressive symptoms											
EPDS < 13	9405	225	2.4	1.0		1.0		1.00		1.0	
EPDS ≥13	628	97	15.5	8.5 (6.5–11.0)	< 0.001	6.7 (4.9–9.3)	< 0.001	8.5 (8.2–8.8)	< 0.001	6.9 (6.6–7.2)	< 0.001
CALD group											
No	6031	162	2.7	1.0		1.0		1.0		1.0	
Yes	6005	252	4.2	1.6 (1.3–1.9)	< 0.001	1.5 (1.1–2.0)	0.002	1.4 (1.4–1.5)	< 0.001	1.3 (1.2–1.4)	< 0.001
Supportive Partner											
Yes	10,131	299	3.0	1.0		1.0		1.0		1.00	
No/unsure	103	36	10.9	1.0 (0.6–1.6)	0.973	3.1 (2.0–4.9)	< 0.001	3.8 (3.6–4.0)	< 0.001	2.9 (2.7–3.2)	< 0.001
Antenatal health problems											
No	8566	256	3.0	1.0		1.0		1.0		1.0	
Yes	3177	123	3.9	1.3 (1.0–1.6)	0.400	1.1 (0.8–1.4)	0.287	1.3 (1.2–1.3)	< 0.001	1.2 (1.2–1.3)	< 0.001
Physical intimate partner violence											
No	10,339	329	3.1	1.0		1.0		1.0		1.0	
Yes	137	11	8.0	2.8 (1.5–5.3)	0.001	0.9 (0.3–2.3)	0.864	3.2 (2.9–3.5)	< 0.001	1.5 (1.3–1.7)	< 0.001

Table 2 Study factors and postnatal depressive symptoms of mothers from South Western Sydney and Sydney Local Health Districts in 2014 (N = 17,564) *(Continued)*

				Complete cases				Multiple imputation [a]			
Outcome	Participants	cases	%	Unadjusted OR (95%CI)	P value	Adjusted OR (95%CI)	P value	Unadjusted OR (95%CI)	P value	Adjusted OR (95%CI)	P value
Psychological intimate partner violence											
No	10,196	317	3.1	1.0		1.0		1.0		1.0	
Yes	102	15	14.7	5.5 (3.1–9.6)	< 0.001	5.3 (2.5–11.0)	< 0.001	5.7 (5.3–6.2)	< 0.001	4.6 (4.1–5.1)	< 0.001
Type of delivery [b]											
Normal vaginal	7865	219	2.8	1.0		1.0		1.0		1.0	
Assisted vaginal	1408	55	3.9	1.4 (1.0–1.9)	0.014	1.3 (0.8–2.0)	0.166	1.2 (1.2–1.3)	< 0.001	1.3 (1.2–1.4)	< 0.001
Caesarean section	3448	151	4.4	1.6 (1.3–2.0)	< 0.001	1.7 (1.3–2.3)	< 0.001	1.4 (1.4–1.5)	< 0.001	1.4 (1.3–1.5)	< 0.001

Information on maternal age, supportive partner, physical and psychological intimate partner violence, socio-economic status, antenatal depressive symptoms, CALD and antenatal health problems were collected during the antenatal period

CALD culturally and linguistically diverse

[a] Sensitivity analyses following multiple imputations for missing values

[b] Information on the type of delivery was collected soon after birth; and data on postnatal depressive symptoms were collected within the first six weeks post-birth. Multivariate model adjusted for variables with p-value < 0.1 in univariate analysis. The variables include maternal age, antenatal depressive symptoms, socioeconomic status, CALD, supportive partner, history of physical intimate partner violence, antenatal health problems, history of fear of partner/ex-partner and type of delivery

subsequent management [34, 36–38]. While those initiatives are important and reportedly well-received, it is also worth noting that risk factors for antenatal depression are multi-faceted, and would require multidisciplinary and multi-agency intervention approaches that are targeted, collaborative and coordinated to improve health outcomes [39]. More recently, the NSW government has begun moving to a more patient-centred integrated health system, with connected service provision across different providers [40]. Aspects of the strategy have been shown to identify barriers to care and facilitate care for vulnerable families, including those with depressive symptoms [41, 42]. Scaling up such an approach for at-risk mothers will improve not only maternal and infant health, but also the family's social interaction and long-term productivity.

The study found that the prevalence of antenatal depressive symptoms was similar to a previous national report [4]. This finding underscores the utility of the EPDS, applied in the Australian primary health care setting, to promptly identify women with probable depression and referral for professional assessment. Our study indicated that the proportion of women who reported postnatal depressive symptoms was lower than the national prevalence (19%) [43] and prior studies from Australia (6.2–10.4%) [11, 13, 44]. However, a recent systemic review found that depression among Australian women ranged from 2.6% to 43.9%, highlighting the disparities in mental health burden across the lifespan [43, 45].

A plausible explanation for the low prevalence of postnatal depressive symptoms in our study may be due to the period in which the data were collected. The postnatal data were collected within the first six weeks' post-birth, while the national survey was based on the first year of the birth of the child. Additionally, the prevalence of postnatal depressive symptoms may have varied from previous studies because of the impact of the integrated perinatal care initiatives [36, 46] and other family-centred services in the region [47]. Formal evaluation of the perinatal care interventions is warranted to determine the extent to which the initiatives have been context-specific.

Mothers from low SES groups and being from the CALD group were at risk of experiencing pre- and/or post-pregnancy depressive symptoms, in line with previous studies [12, 14]. Plausible reasons for why being from the CALD group increases the risk of prenatal and/or postnatal depressive symptoms among mothers have been highlighted in Australia. These include socio-cultural barriers (e.g., cultural norms, language and traditional gender roles); structural barriers (e.g., a lack of knowledge of available services and issues with access); service-related barriers (e.g., culturally-inappropriate service models or a perception of such services); domestic violence problems [48], and alcohol and other drugs issues [49]. A number of those barriers may also apply to mothers from low SES groups, as well as issues of limited uptake of health messages associated with mothers from low-income households [50]. Although being from the CALD group is not modifiable or improvement in SES status can be a long-term project; targeted and culturally-appropriate initiatives that are specific to mothers in those populations will improve health outcomes. A report from Australia estimated that maternal perinatal depression cost the Australian economy 171 million dollars in 2012, and the majority of the burden was attributable to lost productivity in the workplace [35]. This report further highlights the fact that routine screening for perinatal depression and subsequent referral for further assessment of vulnerable women is essential to improving health and economic productivity.

The study has a number of policy and pragmatic implications for health professionals, health administrators, researchers and the public. Our study provides risk factors for antenatal and postnatal depressive symptoms in Australia, as well as among people from culturally diverse communities, using routinely collected and context-specific data. Evidence has shown that strong government support is critical to health interventions aimed at identifying and/or treating diseases in the early stages [4, 16]. The NSW government SAFE START policy framework is one of such support, aimed at providing planned, coordinated and complete psychosocial assessment, depression screening and follow-up care and support for mothers and babies during the perinatal period [36]. Although the SAFE START initiative is still active in NSW, in 2015, the Australian federal government stopped a funding agreement with the states and territories government for a National Perinatal Depression Initiative (NPDI) which provided new parents access to screening and counselling services since the year 2008 [51]. Studies that evaluate the impact of the NPDI and other sub-national policy responses and interventions to perinatal depression may be warranted in Australia to measure where improvements have been made, where opportunities are or where challenges occur. Further studies on the impact and possible referral pathways of moderate perinatal depression may also be needed.

Study limitations and strengths

The study has a number of limitations. First, the outcome of interest and some of the risk factors (e.g., IPV) were based on self-report, which is a possible source of recall or measurement bias that may have underestimated or overestimated the association between the risk factors and outcomes. Second, the study used routinely collected data for the analyses of risk factors for antenatal depressive symptoms, and the establishment of clear temporal relationships cannot be determined for such associations, where study factors data and antenatal depressive information were collected contemporaneously. Nonetheless, the study provides evidence on clear temporal relationships between the study factors and postnatal depressive symptoms. Third, unmeasured covariates such as the impact of social support and family structure may be a limitation of the study. Fourth, our study was unable to differentiate mothers with pre-existing clinical depression from those with first-ever perinatal depressive symptoms. A stratified analysis of pre-existing and first-ever perinatal depression would have provided additional information on the health status of mothers. Despite these limitations, we take advantage of the routine and consistently collected maternal and infant data in Sydney, Australia to provide context-specific evidence to inform policy decision-making and initiatives. Also, the observed odds ratios are unlikely to be affected by missing data as we considered the potential bias due to missing data in a sensitivity analysis that imputed missing information.

The EPDS is a screening tool, and may not identify all mothers with depressive episodes, as some mothers with high scores may not have clinical depression, while some mothers with low scores may underestimate, or not wish to report distress. The use of the EPDS as the measure for probable depression diagnosis may be less ideal as an assessment of depressive symptoms in the postnatal period may due to extra postpartum duties associated with the arrival of a newborn. Possible limitations of the EPDS tool and an alternative device were recently highlighted [52], similar to previously published shortcomings [53, 54] and alternatives to the EPDS [55, 56]. Nevertheless, it is important to note that even if a screening tool is error-free, its interpretation (i.e., the assignment of a positive or negative outcome) may still be incorrect [57].

Despite the limitations of the EPDS, it is an extremely valuable tool for researchers to evaluate the impact of preventive programs and for clinicians to promptly identify mothers who may be experiencing or are at risk for perinatal depression [4, 16]. Also, the EPDS is unique and designed for use in the perinatal period as it does not measure somatic symptoms associated with depression, as symptoms like weight change and sleep difficulties are associated with normal pregnancies.

Conclusion

The prevalence of antenatal depressive symptoms was higher in mothers with a history of IPV. A lack of partner support, IPV, being from the CALD population and low SES group were risk factors for antenatal and postnatal depressive symptoms. Antenatal depressive symptoms were strongly associated with postnatal depressive symptoms. The study suggests that screening for probable depression and referral for expert assessment may help to identify at-risk mothers of perinatal depression promptly, and may create pathways for improved maternal mental health care.

Abbreviations

CALD: Culturally and linguistically diverse; EPDS: Edinburgh postnatal depression scale; IPV: Intimate partner violence; NPDI: National perinatal depression initiative; NSW: New South Wales; SES: Socio-economic status; SLHD: Sydney Local Health District; SWSLHD: South Western Sydney Local Health District

Acknowledgements

The authors are grateful to all the health professionals in South Western Sydney and Sydney Local Health Districts who spent time entering the data, and also to personnel in the Information Management & Technology Division for the time spent on generating the data for this analysis.

Funding

This study received no specific grant from any funding agency in the public, commercial or not-for-profit sectors.

Authors' contributions

FAO contributed to the conceptualisation of the research idea, performed the analysis, interpreted results, drafted the original manuscript and critically revised the manuscript as submitted. JE conceptualised the study idea, obtained and prepared the data, interpreted results and critically revised the manuscript. AH obtained and prepared the data for analysis. BJ contributed to data preparation, results interpretation and critically revised the manuscript. AP, KA and BB provided guidance on the analysis, interpreted results and critically revised the manuscript. All authors read and approved the final manuscript as submitted.

Consent for publication

Not applicable

Competing interests

The authors declare that they have no competing interests.

Author details

[1]Translational Health Research Institute, School of Medicine, Western Sydney University, Campbelltown Campus, Locked Bag 1797, Penrith, NSW 2571, Australia. [2]Ingham Institute for Applied Medical Research, University of New South Wales, 1 Campbell Street, Liverpool, NSW 2170, Australia. [3]School of Women's and Children's Health, University of New South Wales, Kensington, Sydney, NSW 2052, Australia. [4]Menzies Centre for Health Policy, Charles Perkins Centre, School of Public Health, Sydney University, Sydney, NSW 2006, Australia. [5]School of Public Health, Griffith University, Gold Coast, QLD 4222, Australia. [6]Department of Community Paediatrics, Sydney Local Health District, Croydon Community Health Centre, 24 Liverpool Rd, Croydon, NSW 2132, Australia. [7]National Centre for Immunisation Research and Surveillance, The Children's Hospital at Westmead, Locked Bag 4001, Westmead, NSW

2145, Australia. [8]Healthy People and Places Unit, South Western Sydney Local Health District, Liverpool, NSW, Australia. [9]St John of God Health Care, Blacktown, NSW, Australia.

References

1. Institute for Health Metrics and Evaluation. GBD Compare Seattle, WA, USA: IHME, University of Washington; 2016 [November 22 2017]. Available from: http://vizhub.healthdata.org/gbd-compare.
2. Hay IS, Abajobir AA, Abate KH, Abbafati C, Abbas KM, Abd-Allah F, et al. Global, regional, and national disability-adjusted life-years (DALYs) for 333 diseases and injuries and healthy life expectancy (HALE) for 195 countries and territories, 1990–2016: a systematic analysis for the global burden of disease study 2016. Lancet. 2017;390(10100):1260–344.
3. Dias CC, Figueiredo B. Breastfeeding and Depression: a systematic review of the literature. J Affect Disord. 2015;171:142–54.
4. beyondblue National Postnatal Depression Program. The beyondblue National Postnatal Depression Program Prevention and Early Intervention 2001–2005. 2005.
5. Grigoriadis S, EH VP, Mamisashvili L, Tomlinson G, Dennis C-L, Koren G, et al. the impact of maternal depression during pregnancy on perinatal outcomes: a systematic review and meta-analysis. The Journal of clinical psychiatry. 2013;74(4):321–41.
6. Gentile S. Untreated depression during pregnancy: short-and long-term effects in offspring. A systematic review. Neuroscience. 2015
7. Rahman A, Iqbal Z, Bunn J, Lovel H, Harrington R. Impact of maternal depression on infant nutritional status and illness: a cohort study. Arch Gen Psychiatry. 2004;61(9):946–52.
8. Zuckerman B, Amaro H, Bauchner H, Cabral H. Depressive symptoms during pregnancy: relationship to poor health behaviors. Am J Obstet Gynecol. 1989;160(5):1107–11.
9. Gotlib IH, Hammen CL. Handbook of depression. New York, USA: Guilford Press; 2008.
10. Eastwood J, Ogbo FA, Hendry a, Noble J. page a, early years research group. The impact of antenatal depression on perinatal outcomes in Australian women. PLoS One. 2017;12(1):e0169907. https://doi.org/10.1371/journal.pone.0169907.
11. Navaratne P, Foo XY, Kumar S. Impact of a high Edinburgh postnatal depression scale score on obstetric and perinatal outcomes. Sci Rep. 2016;6
12. Leigh B, Milgrom J. Risk Factors for antenatal depression, postnatal depression and parenting stress. BMC psychiatry. 2008;8(1):1.
13. Eastwood JG, Phung H, Barnett B. Postnatal depression and socio-demographic risk: factors associated with Edinburgh depression scale scores in a metropolitan area of new South Wales, Australia. Australian & New Zealand Journal of Psychiatry. 2011;45(12):1040–6.
14. Edwards B, Galletly C, Semmler-Booth T, Dekker G. Antenatal psychosocial risk factors and depression among women living in socioeconomically disadvantaged suburbs in Adelaide, South Australia. Australian & New Zealand Journal of Psychiatry. 2008;42(1):45–50.
15. Milgrom J, Gemmill AW, Bilszta JL, Hayes B, Barnett B, Brooks J, et al. Antenatal risk factors for postnatal depression: a large prospective study. J Affect Disord. 2008;108(1):147–57.
16. beyondblue. Clinical practice guidelines for depression and related disorders—anxiety, bipolar disorder and puerperal psychosis—in the perinatal period. A guideline for primary care health professionals. Melbourne, Australia: beyondblue, 2011.
17. South Western Sydney Local Health District. Research Strategy for South Western Sydney Local Health District 2012–2021. Sydney, Australia: South Western Sydney Local Health District; 2012.
18. Sydney Local Health District. Planning online: Sydney local Health District; 2016 [22 June 2016]. Available from: https://www.slhd.nsw.gov.au/planning/profiles.html.
19. Ogbo FA, Eastwood J, Page A, Arora A, McKenzie A, Jalaludin B, et al. prevalence and determinants of cessation of exclusive breastfeeding in the early postnatal period in Sydney, Australia. Int Breastfeed J. 2017;12(1):16.
20. Australian Bureau of Statistics. Technical Paper: Socio-Economic Indexes for Areas (SEIFA) 2011, 2013. Commonwealth of Australia: Canberra.
21. Australian Bureau of Statistics. Culturally and linguistically diversity (CALD) characteristics 2016 [cited 2017 18 January]. Available from: http://www.abs.gov.au/ausstats/abs@.nsf/Lookup/by%20Subject/4529.0.00.003~2014~Main%20Features~Cultural%20and%20Linguistic%20Diversity%20(CALD)%20Characteristics~13.
22. Murray D, Cox JL. Screening for depression during pregnancy with the Edinburgh depression scale (EDDS). Journal of reproductive and infant psychology. 1990;8(2):99–107.
23. Murray L, Carothers AD. The validation of the Edinburgh post-natal depression scale on a community sample. Br J Psychiatry. 1990;157(2):288–90.
24. Cox JL, Holden JM, Sagovsky R. Detection of postnatal depression. Development of the 10-item Edinburgh postnatal depression scale. Br J Psychiatry. 1987;150(6):782–6.
25. Hannah P, Adams D, Lee A, Glover V, Sandler M. Links Between early post-partum mood and post-natal depression. Br J Psychiatry. 1992;160(6):777–80.
26. Kohlhoff J, Hickinbotham R, Knox C, Roach V, Barnett Am B. Antenatal psychosocial assessment and depression screening in a private hospital. Aust N Z J Obstet Gynaecol. 2016;56(2):173–8.
27. NSW Department of Health. NSW Health/Families NSW Supporting Families Early Package – SAFE START Guidelines: Improving Mental Health Outcomes for Parents & Infants. In: Health Mo, editor. Sydney NSW Health 2010. p. 9–10.
28. Boyce P, Stubbs J, Todd A. The Edinburgh postnatal depression scale: validation for an Australian sample. Aust N Z J Psychiatry. 1993;27(3):472–6.
29. Leverton T, Elliott S. Is the EPDS a magic wand?: 1. A comparison of the Edinburgh Postnatal Depression Scale and health visitor report as predictors of diagnosis on the Present State Examination. 2000.
30. Sterne JA, White IR, Carlin JB, Spratt M, Royston P, Kenward MG, et al. Multiple imputation for missing data in epidemiological and clinical research: potential and pitfalls. BMJ. 2009;338:b2393.
31. Spratt M, Carpenter J, Sterne JA, Carlin JB, Heron J, Henderson J, et al. Strategies for multiple imputation in longitudinal studies. Am J Epidemiol. 2010;172(4):478–87.
32. Biaggi A, Conroy S, Pawlby S, Pariante CM. Identifying the women at risk of antenatal anxiety and depression: a systematic review. J Affect Disord. 2016; 191:62–77.
33. Australian Government Department of Social Services. The National Plan to Reduce Violence against Women and their Children 2010–2022 (the National Plan). In: Department of Social Services, editor. Canberra 2011.
34. Australian Department of Human Services. Family and Domestic Violence Strategy 2016–2019. Can Underwrit. 2016;
35. Deloitte Access Economics. The cost of perinatal depression in Australia. Canberra, ACT: Deloitte, 2012.
36. New South Wales Ministry of Health. SAFE START Strategic Policy. In: Mental Health and Drug and Alcohol Office, editor. Sydney, Australia: NSW Health; 2010.
37. NSW Ministry of Health. Violence Prevention and Response Unit. Domestic Violence Routine Screening Program: Snapshot Report 9. 2012.
38. NSW Health. SAFE START guidelines: improving mental health outcomes for parents and infants. NSW Health: Sydney, Australia; 2010.
39. Katz I. Community interventions for vulnerable children and families: Participation and power. Communities, Children and Families Australia. 2007;3(1):19.
40. New South Wales Ministry of Health. NSW Integrated Care Online: NSW Health; 2017 [cited 2017 14 August]. Available from: http://www.health.nsw.gov.au/integratedcare/Pages/default.aspx.
41. Eastwood J, Miller E. Healthy homes and Neighbourhoods integrated care initiative 2016 [February 2017]. Available from: http://www.health.nsw.gov.au/wohp/Documents/mc7-miller-eastwood.pdf.
42. Northern NSW Local Health District. NNSW integrated care strategy – status report may 2016. New South Wales: Northern NSW Local Health District; 2016.
43. Australian Institute of Health and Welfare. Experience of perinatal depression: data from the 2010 Australian National Infant Feeding Survey. Canberra: AIHW, 2012 Contract No.: PHE 161.
44. Eastwood JG, Jalaludin BB, Kemp LA, Phung HN, Barnett BE. Relationship of postnatal depressive symptoms to infant temperament, maternal expectations, social support and other potential risk factors: findings from a large Australian cross-sectional study. BMC pregnancy and childbirth. 2012;12(1):148.
45. Rich JL, Byrne JM, Curryer C, Byles JE, Loxton D. Prevalence and correlates of depression among Australian women: a systematic literature review, January 1999-January 2010. BMC research notes. 2013;6(1):424.

46. South Western Sydney Local Health District. SWSLHD mental health service: a clinical stream of south western Sydney local Health District. Sydney: SWSLHD; 2013.
47. Karitane. Mental Health Services: Karitane; 2017 [cited 2017 14 August]. Available from: https://karitane.com.au/page/our-services/mental-health-services.
48. Sawrikar P, Katz I. Enhancing family and relationship service accessibility and delivery to culturally and linguistically diverse families in Australia (Vol. 3/ 2008). Australian Institute of Family Studies, AFRC Issues, Australian Family Relationships Clearinghouse: Melbourne; 2008.
49. Browne J, Renzaho A. Prevention Of alcohol and other drug problems in culturally and linguistically diverse communities. Prevention. research quarterly. 2010;13:1–24.
50. Bowes J, Grace R. Review of early childhood parenting, education and health intervention programs for indigenous children and families in Australia. Canberra: Australian Institute of Health and Welfare & Melbourne: Australian Institute of Family Studies. 2014;
51. David Lewis. National Perinatal Depression Initiative loses federal funding; states, territories 'hard-pressed' to cover cuts Online: ABC; 2015 [cited 2017 31 July]. Available from: http://www.abc.net.au/news/2015-06-19/ government-pulls-funding-from-perinatal-depression-program/6560266.
52. Matthey S, Agostini F. Using the Edinburgh postnatal depression scale for women and men—some cautionary thoughts. Archives of women's mental health. 2017;20(2):345–54.
53. Cox J, Holden J. Perinatal mental health: a guide to the Edinburgh postnatal depression scale (EPDS): Royal College of psychiatrists; 2003.
54. Allison KC, Wenzel A, Kleiman K, Sarwer DB. Development of a brief measure of postpartum distress. J Women's Health. 2011;20(4):617–23.
55. Somerville S, Byrne SL, Dedman K, Hagan R, coo S, Oxnam E, et al. detecting the severity of perinatal anxiety with the perinatal anxiety screening scale (PASS). J Affect Disord. 2015;186:18–25.
56. Brodey BB, Goodman SH, Baldasaro RE, Brooks-DeWeese A, Wilson ME, Brodey IS, et al. Development of the perinatal depression inventory (PDI)-14 using item response theory: a comparison of the BDI-II, EPDS, PDI, and PHQ-9. Archives of women's mental health. 2016;19(2):307–16.
57. Rothman KJ, Greenland S, Lash TL. Modern epidemiology. Philadelphia, USA: Lippincott Williams & Wilkins; 2008.

8

Cross-sectional relationship of perceived familial protective factors with depressive symptoms in vulnerable youth

Hanna E. Schwendemann[1*], Heidi Kuttler[2], Thomas Mößle[3] and Eva Maria Bitzer[1]

Abstract

Background: There are multiple negative consequences associated with heavy episodic drinking and close associations between substance abuse and depression, alcohol-intoxicated adolescents (AIA) represent a vulnerable group. We aim to add to the current literature by investigating the cross-sectional relationship of perceived familial protective factors with depressive symptoms in AIA in hospitals, with respect to sex. Depression is among the 10 leading causes of disabilities during childhood and adolescence, with girls being more vulnerable than boys. Considerable evidence reveals a strong association between depression and alcohol abuse. The family provides the possibility to positively influence depressive symptoms.

Methods: We present cross-sectional data of a German multisite, epidemiological cohort study on AIA. By using youth's self-reports, we assessed sociodemographic data, as well as data on perceived familial protective factors and depressive symptoms using items of the Communities that Care Youth Survey instrument. We performed descriptive and multigroup analyses to evaluate the measurement invariance of the used instruments. Moreover, to investigate the relationships between the constructs, we used structural equation modelling.

Results: The study sample comprised 342 AIA, with a mean age of 15.5 years (SD = 1.2; 48.1% girls). The final structural equation model achieved an acceptable model fit of χ^2 (69, 342) = 110.056; $p = .001$; TLI = 0.97; CFI = 0.98; RMSEA = 0.046; SRMR = 0.042, and the rewards for prosocial involvement in the family context correlated significantly negatively with present depressive symptoms, (ß = – 0.540, $p <$ 0.001). The effects were stronger in boys (ß = – 0.576, $p <$ 0.001) than in girls (ß = – 0.519, $p <$ 0.001).

Conclusion: In vulnerable youth in Germany, depressive symptoms are correlated to good experiences within the family. Future research should assess whether interventions that enhance parental support reduce the risk of depressive symptoms in AIA. Our findings highlight the need for family-based prevention programmes, particularly for AIA with an increased risk of depression.

Keywords: depressive symptoms, adolescents, familial protective factors, resilience, family structure

Background

Approximately 15–20% of all children and adolescents experience depressive symptoms during childhood and adolescence, and depression is among the 10 leading causes of disability in this age group [1–4]. In Germany, almost 18% of children and adolescents experience such symptoms at least once in their lifetime, and in 4% of German adolescents, depression persists for a minimum of 2 years [2, 5]. Depressive symptoms in youth are a predictor of depression in adulthood [3, 5]. The female sex is an established factor for depression, with the risk in puberty for girls being twice as high as that for boys [6, 7].

Alcohol is one of the most significant risk factors for morbidity and mortality in young people worldwide, and alcohol misuse and episodic heavy drinking is a significant public health concern [8, 9]. More than one-third of 15–16-year olds in Europe have reported excessive alcohol consumption in the last 30 days, and 13% have

* Correspondence: hanna.schwendemann@ph-freiburg.de
[1]Pädagogische Hochschule Freiburg/University of Education, Kunzenweg 21, 79117 Freiburg, Germany
Full list of author information is available at the end of the article

been intoxicated in the last 30 days [10]. Regular, augmented, or excessive alcohol consumption is often associated with alcohol abuse in later life, as well as with depression during adolescence. Both frequency and extent of alcohol consumption have emerged as significant predictors of higher levels of depression [11–17], and heavy episodic drinking in adolescence can furthermore be an indicator of already existing disorders. Hospitalised intoxicated adolescents are a vulnerable group whose healthy development is endangered. At the same time, the hospitalization of adolescents because of excessive alcohol consumption presents an opportunity to initiate preventive efforts [18].

Models of risk and protective factors have predicted the onset and progression of disorders [19–22]. The Social Development Model (SDM) provides a framework for explaining healthy or problematic development, in which family environment and social interactions emerge as relevant factors influencing youth's development [19, 23, 24]. It is evident that (1) opportunities for prosocial involvement and interaction with others, (2) the degree of involvement and interaction, (3) the skills to participate, and (4) receiving rewards for prosocial involvement lead to bonding processes within the social environment and act as protective factors [23, 25–27]. Less attachment to parents as well as family conflicts are risk factors for depression [6]. Currently, few studies have investigated the relationship between resilience, protective factors, and problem behaviour or mental disorders in young people [5, 28].

The family, as an instant, lasting, and influential environment for children and youth, protects against the development of psychopathology and provides opportunities for preventive interactions [29–31]. Parents are the central caretakers of children and youth, may influence their attitudes and behaviours, and contribute to their socialisation [32, 33]. Adolescents' family relationship, family climate, and cohesion can be a risk or a protective factor against depression [5, 34, 35]. Better parent–adolescent communication, parental connectedness, shared activities, and warmth are associated with fewer mental disorders and are strongly protect against depressive symptoms [7, 36].

In this study, we present cross-sectional results of a German multisite, epidemiological cohort study on adolescents hospitalised due to alcohol intoxication (International Classification of Diseases, Tenth Revision (ICD 10) F10.0). Because of the multiple negative consequences associated with heavy episodic drinking and close associations between substance abuse and depression, alcohol-intoxicated adolescents (AIA) represent a vulnerable group. The influence of protective factors in the context of depressive symptoms in AIA has not been well studied. We aim to add to the current literature by investigating the cross-sectional relationship of family protective factors with depressive symptoms in AIA, using the SDM.

In the current study, we examined whether according to the SDM, opportunities for prosocial involvement in the family context lead to rewards for prosocial involvement and cause a good attachment to the mother and father. Furthermore, we investigated whether in compliance with the SDM, good bonding to one's parents reduces depressive symptoms in AIA. Because depressive symptoms vary with sex, we analysed whether group differences existed in AIA.

Methods

Study design

We collected cross-sectional data in a German multisite, epidemiological cohort study, conducted between June 2012 and October 2013. The survey was conducted in co-operation with 10 prevention centres throughout Germany applying the national prevention programme HaLT/"Close to the limit" [9]. This programme targets youth aged 11–17 years hospitalised with acute alcohol intoxication (ICD-10 F10.0) diagnosed by the referring physician in the emergency room. It aims to prevent the stabilisation of heavy alcohol consumption among children and adolescents [9]. HaLT involves two components: a proactive strategy/structural prevention component in the community setting and a reactive strategy, where social workers execute a brief intervention. This intervention is based on motivational interviewing, at patients' bedside, typically the day after the intoxication incident [9, 37, 38]. To conduct the current survey, the trained social workers recruited the survey participants before the brief intervention and interviewed AIA aged 13–18 years, during their hospital stay.

We defined inclusion criteria (participants should be aged 13–18 years and hospitalised due to alcohol intoxication) and exclusion criteria (not in the desired age group and another reason for hospitalisation). Informed consent of both parents and adolescents was collected by the social workers, who subsequently handed over a written questionnaire to the adolescents. Prevention centres documented all cases of acute alcohol intoxication during the study period and number of study participants. The study participation was 69%. Non-participation was based on either refusal to participate in the survey (15.5%), acute need of support (10.9%), or low literacy (4.6%) [39]. The participating adolescents received a USB flash drive and a 10-Euro voucher as an incentive.

Measures

Perceived familial protective factors and depressive symptoms were assessed based on self-reports of the youth as well as sociodemographic data (sex, age, and family structure).

Familial protective factors

Perceived familial protective factors were recorded using the German version [40] of the Communities That Care (CTC) Youth Survey instrument [19]. The CTC instrument is designed to assess a broad set of risk and protective factors across different domains: community, school, family, peers, and individuals, as well as health and behavioural outcomes [19].

The CTC instrument evolved from the SDM and has been used in the USA and other countries. In Germany, there is an adapted German version of the CTC instrument, which we used in our study [41, 42]. For our analysis, four scales of the CTC-protective family domain with 11 items are included. This selection is based on our previous study on the psychometric properties of the CTC instrument [18]. The attachment of adolescents to their mother and father is measured by three items each. For example, "Do you feel close to your mother?" and "Do you feel close to your father?" Opportunities for prosocial involvement in the family context are measured by three items (e.g., "My parents notice when I am doing a good job and let me know about it") and rewards for prosocial involvement by two items (e.g., "My parents ask me what I think before most family decisions affecting me are made"). The response categories for the attachment to the mother and father are measured using the following scores: 1 = 'no', 2 = 'rather no', 3 = 'rather yes', and 4 = 'yes'. Response categories for opportunities and rewards for prosocial involvement ranged from 1 = 'very wrong' to 4 = 'very right'. When summing each scale, high scores represent high familial protection. The Cronbach's α of the scales are sufficient, attachment to mother: α = 0.80, attachment to father: α = 0.88, opportunities for prosocial involvement: α = 0.74, and rewards for prosocial involvement: α = 0.87 [18].

We followed the recommendation of Arthur et al. (2007) to calculate cut-off values for the scales (whether protective factor is present) [43]. This implies three steps: 1) identifying the scale mean, 2) calculating the mean absolute deviation (MAD) according to Leys (2013) [44], 3) deducting the scale mean with 15*MAD (cut-off points: attachment to mother = 2.85, attachment to father = 2.85, opportunities for prosocial involvement = 3.26, and rewards for prosocial involvement = 3.39) [45].

Depressive symptoms

We assessed depressive symptoms with the following items of the CTC instrument [19]: "Sometimes I think life is not worth it," "All in all, I am inclined to think I am a failure," and "In the past year, have you felt depressed or sad MOST days, even if you felt okay sometimes?" The response options ranged as follows: 1 = 'no', 2 = 'rather no', 3 = 'rather yes', and 4 = 'yes'. Cronbach's α in our AIA sample was 0.80.

To analyse present depressive symptoms, we summed the answers of all three items of the scale. We assumed depressive symptoms, if at least one answer to one of the three items was 'yes' or 'rather yes', and the sum of the added values has more than 6 points. A recent study on American students (age M = 19.2, SD = 0.44 years) showed a high accuracy of the four-item depression scale of the CTC instrument compared with the Patient Health Questionnaire with 9 items (PHQ-9). The four items reflect the Diagnostic and Statistical Manual of Mental Disorders-5 criteria very well, and three of the four items measure cognitive symptoms, which are strongly discriminant of other depressive symptoms [46].

Statistical analysis

We calculated frequencies and tested patterns of the missing values. The overall frequency of missing values was low (77.8% of respondents with less than 5% missing data). The missing values were either completely missing at random or missing at random.

Descriptive statistics (mean and proportions) were calculated, and the data were checked for normality. We analysed the construct validity of the familial protective scales and depressive symptoms through confirmatory factor analysis (CFA). As advised by Cole (2007), we allowed correlations between residual terms of the attachment to the mother and father scales, that are implied by the measurement strategy, which are the equally expressed items of the mother and father [47].

We performed structural equation modelling (SEM) to investigate the relationship between the family protective factors and depressive symptoms in AIA using the SDM.

First, we tested the measurement invariance of the SEM multigroup modelling with respect to sex. Configural invariance is present if the factor structure, loading pattern, and intercepts are similar in both groups [48]. For testing weak invariance, the factor loadings are set equal across groups. If this models proves the stage, structural relationship between groups, such as factor correlations, can be examined and compared across groups [49]. Strong invariance is tested by additionally constraining the intercepts to be equal across groups. Confirmation allows a comparison of latent means and regression parameters between groups [50–52]. The nested model is compared with the previous less restricted model by a χ^2 difference test. As noted by Chen (2007), χ^2 differences have the same problem as absolute χ^2 tests by being highly sensitive to the sample size and violations of the normality assumption. Therefore, goodness-of-fit statistics are recommended. When the sample size is adequate ($n > 300$), a change of the Δ comparative fit index (CFI) ≤ − 0.010 supplemented by a change in the Δ root mean square error of approximation (RMSEA) ≤ 0.015 indicates invariance [53]. An analysis of partial measurement invariance is possible, if the nested model is worse than the previous model. Partial invariance is present if at any of the restrictions of the aforementioned stages are freed for some indicators to improve the model fit [48]. If at one stage, partial invariance is present, then this partial model is the basis for the next step of assessing measurement invariance [48].

To analyse the differences in path coefficients with respect to sex, we performed model comparisons by using the χ^2 differences of the restricted model (equal constraint regressions) and the model without the restriction. For model comparisons, we used the Satorra–Bentler-scaled χ^2 difference test using difference test scaling correction and the differences in the degree of freedom [54].

We applied the maximum likelihood estimator with robust standard errors (MLR) to obtain appropriate fit indices [55]. We used the CFI, Tucker–Lewis Index (TLI), and RMSEA to evaluate the model fit. Furthermore, we checked the standardised root mean square residual (SRMR < 0.1). The following parameter estimates and goodness-of-fit statistics describe an acceptable model fit; CFI and TLI ≥ 0.90, RMSEA ≤0.08. Moreover, a good model fit is represented by the following estimates; CFI and TLI ≥ 0.97 and RMSEA ≤0.05, which were used to evaluate the model data [56].

For the descriptive and multivariate analyses, we used SPSS Version 22 (IBM Corp. Released 2013. IBM SPSS Statistics for Windows, Version 22.0. Armonk, NY: IBM Corp). For the CFA, SEM, and measurement invariance tests, we used R (Version 3.2.4) with the missForest, semTools and lavaan packages (0.5–20) [55, 57, 58].

Results

Subject characteristics

The study cohort consisted of 342 AIA in hospital, with a mean age of 15.5 years (SD = 1.2, 48.1% girls). Among all adolescents, 46.8% lived in a traditional family. Among the remaining 53.2% of adolescents, most lived with a single mother (Table 1).

Confirmatory factor analysis

First, we investigated the latent structure of the perceived familial protective factors and depressive symptoms. The four familial protective scales (χ^2 (35; 342) = 56.380, $p = 0.012$; TLI = 0.979; CFI = 0.985; RMSEA = 0.047, SRMR = 0.029) and depressive symptoms represented independent factors. All estimated measurement loadings were significant, and the goodness-of-fit statistics was acceptable (Figs. 1 and 2).

Table 1 Sociodemographic variables of the study population ($n = 342$)

	N valid	*n* (%)
Female sex	337	162 (48.1)
Traditional family[a]	340	159 (46.8)
Familial protective factors		
Attachment to mother (good)	321	198 (61.7)
Attachment to father (good)	316	159 (50.3)
Opportunities for prosocial involvement (good)	324	173 (53.4)
Rewards for prosocial involvement (good)	323	166 (51.4)
Depressive Symptoms	337	104 (30.9)
Sometimes I think life is not worth it	332	97 (29.2)
All in all, I am inclined to think I am a failure	331	72 (21.2)
In the past year have you felt depressed or sad MOST days, even if you felt okay sometimes?	331	88 (26.6)
Age	310	M = 15.5 (SD = 1.2)
≤ 13		18 (5.8)
14–15		120 (35.1)
16–17		169 (49.4)
≥ 18		3 (0.9)

M mean, *SD* standard deviation
[a]traditional family – living with both parents

Relationship between perceived familial protective factors and depressive symptoms

We analysed the relationship of perceived familial protective factors with depressive symptoms using the SDM (χ^2 (69, 342) = 162.847; $p < 0.001$; TLI = 0.94; CFI = 0.95; RMSEA = 0.070; SRMR = 0.065). In the SDM, opportunities for prosocial involvement in the family led to rewards for this involvement. Positive engagement in the family context resulted in a good attachment to the mother and father. We assume, that there is a possibility that the SDM is conceivable in either direction; Therefore, we analysed the SEM vice versa. This led to the model that fitted best to the data. The SDM-reverse model achieved a better model fit of χ^2 (69, 342) = 110.056; $p = 0.001$; TLI = 0.97; CFI = 0.98; RMSEA = 0.046; SRMR = 0.042; Fig. 3).

Because of the cross-sectional data, we analysed the influence of depressive symptoms on perceived rewards for prosocial involvement as well, which resulted in a comparable model adjustment (χ^2 (67, 342) = 107.947; $p = 0.001$; TLI = 0.97; CFI = 0.98; RMSEA = 0.047; SRMR = 0.038).

Our cross-sectional analysis revealed that a good attachment to the mother (ß = 0.815, $p < 0.001$) and father (ß = 0.447, $p < 0.001$) led to opportunities for prosocial involvement in the family context. Opportunities for prosocial involvement were significantly positively associated with rewards for prosocial involvement in the family context (ß = 0.844, $p < 0.001$). The SEM showed that rewards

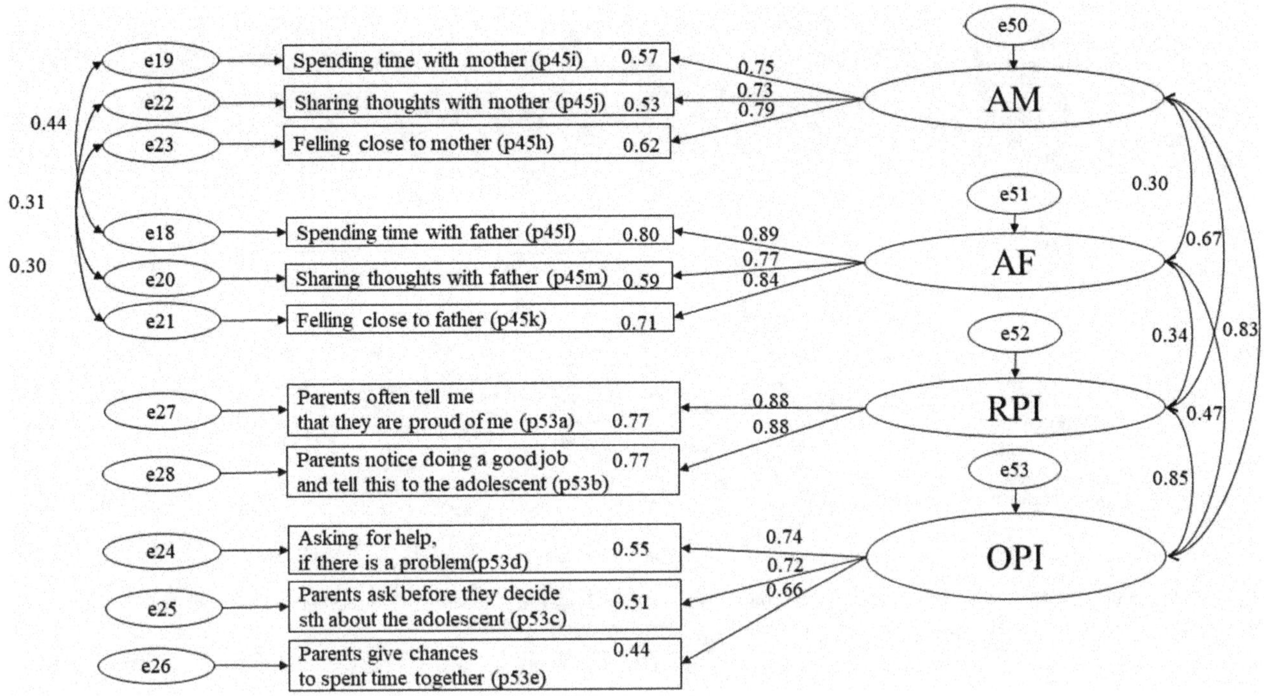

Fig. 1 CFA of familial protective factors, AM – attachment to mother / AF – attachment to father/ OPI – opportunities for prosocial involvement / RPI – rewards for prosocial involvement

for prosocial involvement were significantly negatively related to depressive symptoms. The higher the perceived familial rewards for prosocial involvement were pronounced, the lower was the symptom appearance of depression (ß = – 0.540; $p <$ 0.001). Vice versa, we observed that adolescents with higher levels of depressive symptoms perceived lower rewards for prosocial involvement in the family context (ß = – 0.538, $p < 0.001$).

Measurement invariance

Table 2 shows the results of the hierarchical measurement invariance with respect to sex. The fit statistics of the analysis showed that configural and weak invariance can be assumed. With respect to strong invariance, the changes in the CFI and RMSEA compared with the weak model were larger than – 0.010 and 0.015, respectively. In order to test partial weak invariance, the modification indices for individual parameters were examined. By freeing the loadings of the items p45h ("Feeling close to mother") and r28a ("Sometimes I think life is not worth it"), the ΔCFI and ΔRMSEA were below their cut-off points, indicating a partial strong invariance.

Familial protective factors and depressive symptoms with respect to sex

We analysed the final SEM model for differences between boys and girls, using multigroup analysis. We tested the nested model, where we constrained the path

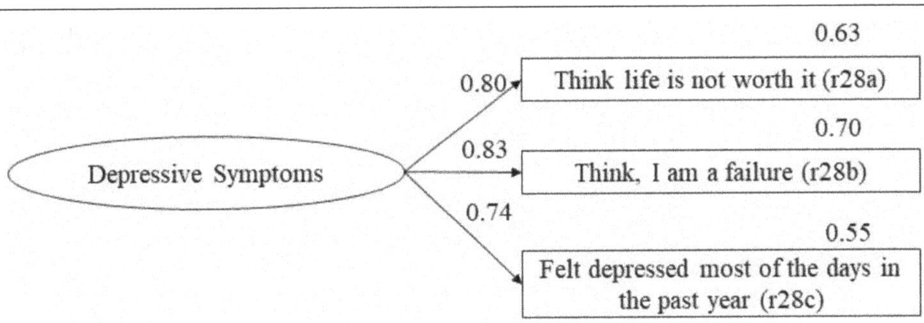

Fig. 2 CFA of depressive symptoms

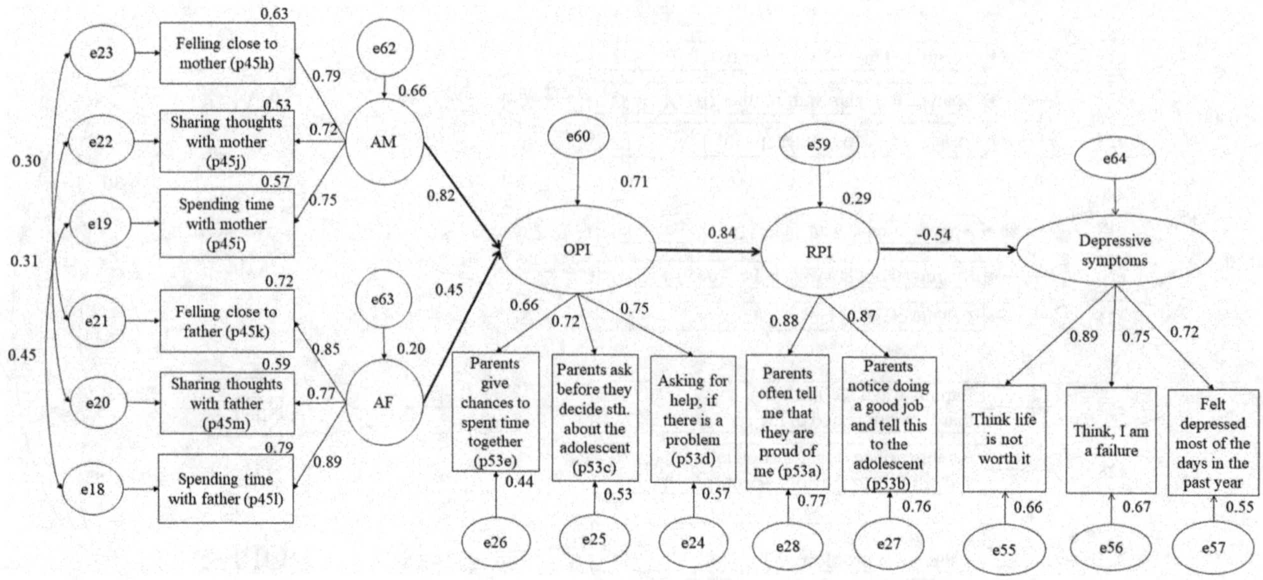

Fig. 3 SEM of familial protective factors and depressive symptoms in AIA (n = 342),: AM – attachment to mother / AF – attachment to father / OPI – opportunities for prosocial involvement / RPI – rewards for prosocial involvement

coefficients of the SEM against the unconstrained model. Sex showed a moderating effect on the SEM $\Delta\ \chi^2 =$ 11.335 (Δ df = 4, $p = 0.023$). Compared with girls, boys perceive their mothers and fathers to provide less opportunities for prosocial family involvement (mothers: boys, ß = 0.727, $p < 0.001$ and girls, ß = 0.857, $p < 0.001$; fathers: boys, ß = 0.399, $p < 0.001$ and girls: ß = 0.462, $p < 0.001$). For engagement in the family, boys perceive more rewards (ß = 0.867, $p < 0.001$) than do girls (ß = 0.843, $p <$ 0.001). These rewards significantly reduce depressive symptoms in both boys (ß = – 0.576, $p < 0.001$) and girls (ß = – 0.519, $p < 0.001$). A comparison of the latent means between girls and boys in the multigroup analysis revealed that boys were less affected by depressive symptoms (ΔM = – 0.438; Wald-z = – 4.588; $p < 0.001$) and less attached to their mothers (ΔM = – 0.276; Wald-z = – 3.621; $p < 0.001$) than were girls (Fig. 4).

Discussion

In this study, we analysed cross-sectional data of the vulnerable target population of AIA with respect to perceived familial protective factors and their relationship to depressive symptoms during hospital stay.

One-third of AIA experience depressive symptoms. The prevalence of depressive symptoms in AIA is comparable with that in representative samples [39]. Furthermore, more than 50% of AIA grow in non-traditional families, which accounts for an important risk factor for mental disorders, such as depression [5, 34]. A comparison of perceived familial resources of AIA with those of a representative sample of adolescents clearly showed that AIA have fewer opportunities and rewards for prosocial involvement, but the attachment to parents was almost the same in AIA and representative samples [59, 60].

We proved that the CTC scales used to measure perceived familial protective factors and depressive symptoms represent independent latent factors using CFA. The SEM was partial strong invariant in boys and girls, which is an important prerequisite for meaningful group comparisons.

Our data fit best to a SEM resembling a sort of 'reversed SDM'. According to the SDM, opportunities

Table 2 Results of the measurement invariance analysis of the SEM comparing boys and girls (MLR estimator)

Model	χ^2	*df*	$\Delta\ \chi^2$	*p*	CFI	ΔCFI	RMSEA	ΔRMSEA
Thresholds						≤ – 0.010		≤ 0.015
Configural invariance	245.462	134		< 0.001	0.950		0.074	
Weak invariance	254.394	143	8.932	< 0.001	0.950	−0.000	0.072	0.002
Strong invariance	284.859	152	30.465	< 0.001	0.941	−0.009	0.076	−0.002
Partial strong invariance[a]	266.094	151	11.700	< 0.001	0.949	−0.001	0.071	0.001

[a]Freeing of the intercepts of the items p45h and r28a

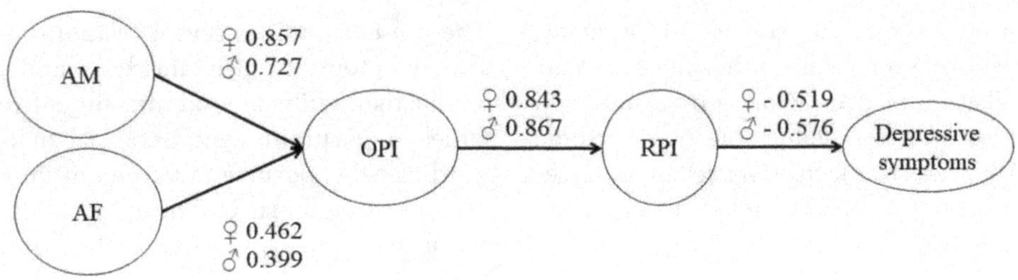

Fig. 4 SEM of familial protective factors and depressive symptoms in AIA – differences across sex (n = 342): AM – attachment to mother /AF – attachment to father / OPI – opportunities for prosocial involvement / RPI – rewards for prosocial involvement

and rewards for prosocial engagement are important for fostering familial prosocial socialisation that results in attachment to both parents [26, 61]. Our final model indicates that a good attachment to the mother and father offers opportunities for prosocial involvement in the family context, which results in rewards for prosocial involvement and reduces depressive symptoms. In adolescence, a good relationship to both parents is central for gaining autonomy. Parents with a secure attachment are more responsive and more supportive toward their children to gain autonomy and enable decision-making in adolescents. The search for physical closeness in childhood is replaced with communication about thoughts and feelings of the adolescents [62–64]. The phenomenon of a reverse-SDM path in vulnerable youth should be investigated in a representative sample of adolescents.

As indicated in the literature, adolescents' family relationship, family climate, and cohesion protect against depression [5, 34, 35]. We showed that in AIA, perceived parental rewards for prosocial involvement as developmental resources are negatively correlated with depressive symptoms. This result helps social workers to support AIA and their family in the situation of hospitalisation as an important starting point for addressing preventive interventions.

Multigroup analysis revealed that these results are valid for both boys and girls. However, significant differences existed between boys and girls. Girls perceive having more opportunities to engage in the family context obtained from their mothers, but boys perceive getting more rewards for prosocial involvement. These rewards result in a significantly stronger reduction of depressive symptoms in boys. With respect to mean differences in depressive symptoms in AIA, we observed that girls had more depressive symptoms than did boys. Studies have reported considerable sex differences not only in the number of depressive symptoms but also in the structure of protective factors. For instance, spending time with the family is particularly protective for boys buffering depressive symptoms [65, 66].

The fact that 53.2% of AIA live with only one parent as well as the negative influence of familial protective factors on depressive symptoms highlights the importance of integrating mothers and fathers within the context of AIA. Furthermore, when working with AIA having depressive symptoms, focus should be placed on familial protective factors. Parental support and emotional warmth confer protective against depressive symptoms [35, 67]. Increasing familial protective factors predicts a decrease in depressive disorders [5]. The incidence rate of depression is considerably higher in adolescents with low parental support than in their high parental support counterparts [1]. AIA have less familial protective factors than representative samples, are more likely to live with a single parent, and have a higher risk of depressive symptoms. Therefore, in AIA, it is necessary to thoroughly evaluate depressive symptoms, family structure, familial protective factors, and sex to prevent a problematic development. One possibility for developing familial protective resources is the 'Strengthening Families Programme', which addresses parents and their vulnerable youth to improve familial communication and interaction, clarifying rules and emphasising caring and warm relationship [68, 69].

The protective function of family factors is particularly important for single parents because the risk factors for mental disorders and substance abuse in adolescence accumulate when there are, for example, family conflicts, financial problems, and lack of joint activities [70]. This risk is especially present in boys [71]. Addressing family protective factors and integrating the second parent, which is the father in most cases, can be an important resource in the family environment of adolescents. Familial protective factors are correlated with depressive symptoms in AIA; therefore, the opportunity to address these factors in the context of hospitalisation should be used.

Strengths and limitations

One of the strengths of this study is the multicentre design integrating vulnerable youth during their hospital stay. It is difficult to reach AIA in routine care, but our study consulted in collaboration with social workers examined more than 300 AIA at 10 hospitals in Germany. We assessed depressive symptoms in hospitalised AIA and perceived familial protective factors; our results add to the scarce literature on this vulnerable target group. We assessed familial protective factors via self-reports because of the survey setting; the feasibility of this empirical inquiry has been indicated in the literature [5, 34, 36, 72]. To confirm the assessment of depression, we cross-checked AIA self-reported depression with the estimated need to initiate social support (i.e., contacting the youth welfare office, drug and family counselling) collected from trained social workers. AIA reporting depressive symptoms received more offers of social support than did the youth not reporting depressive symptoms [39, 45].

Our results are limited by the fact that we only assessed depressive symptoms with three items of the CTC instrument and not via a standardised instrument, such as the PHQ-9, the Beck Depression Inventory, or a diagnostic interview [46]. In this study, we used the CTC instrument to obtain an impression of depressive symptoms in AIA. Briefly, we did not want to diagnose depression, but rather to identify the need for action in adolescents and provide this information to health care professionals outside the hospital setting. It must be considered that we asked the youth for depressive symptoms in the year before hospitalisation. In our analyses, we could only evaluate the relationship of perceived familial protective factors with reported depressive symptoms at the hospital because of the cross-sectional nature of the data. Data on the mid-term development (a 6-month follow-up) of depressive symptoms are available, but were not included in the present study because its small sample size did not allow for a valid analysis. Furthermore, this decision was taken due to differing time spans in the assessment of depressive symptoms. At the hospital, items were used with the original wording, and at T1, the time span was changed for the 6 months since hospitalisation [39].

In addition to familial influences on depressive symptoms, peers play an important role in the lives of adolescents. Their influence can limit the influence of parents [7, 73]. This idea may be integrated in further research on factors protecting against depressive symptoms in AIA, but was not included in the present analysis.

Future research should evaluate the medium-term effects of protective factors on the development of depressive symptoms in AIA. The emergency setting could be used for assessing the risk profiles of AIA that focus on developmental hazards, as well as individual and familial protective factors to identify at-risk groups and offer opportunities for interventions. An intervention study would provide a good opportunity to investigate the medium-term effects of interventions in enhancing familial protective factors in AIA.

Conclusion

The present findings reveal relationships among depressive symptoms in girls and boys and good experiences within the family, a good attachment to the mother and father, opportunities for prosocial involvement, and rewards for this positive involvement in the family context. The cross-sectional buffering effect of rewards for prosocial involvement is particularly strong in boys. Identifying depressive symptoms in hospitals can be an important starting point for preventive programmes and early interventions to reduce the existing symptoms by reinforcing familial resources; additionally, familial protective factors are helpful for addressing the needs of adolescents at a risk of major depression.

Future research should investigate whether interventions that enhance parental support reduce the risk of depressive symptoms in adolescents after alcohol intoxication. Strengthening familial protective factors may influence the onset of symptoms, and existing symptoms may also be affected by familial resources, such as family climate and social support [5]. Our findings highlight the need for family-based prevention programmes, particularly for AIA having an increased risk of depression.

Abbreviations

AIA: Alcohol intoxicated adolescents; CFA: Confirmatory factor analysis; CFI: Comparative fit index; CTC: Communities that care youth survey instrument; MAD: Mean absolute deviation; MLR: Maximum likelihood estimator with robust standard errors; PHQ-9: Patient health questionnaire with 9 items; RMSEA: Root mean square error of approximation; SDM: Social development model; SEM: Structural equation model; SRMR: Standardised root mean square residual; TLI: Tucker–Lewis Index

Acknowledgements

The authors thank all adolescents and parents for their participation, as well as the hospital staff for their vast support. Thanks to all the social workers in the HaLT-prevention-centres in Bad Homburg, Berlin, Bielefeld, Kassel, Leipzig, Lörrach, Rastatt/Baden-Baden, Schweinfurt, Wiesbaden, and Worms. The authors thank Mr. F. Groeger-Roth from the Federal Prevention Council of Lower Saxony (Landespräventionsrat Niedersachsen) and Prof. Dr. R. Soellner, Universität Hildesheim. We also thank the RiScA-Group (Risk and Protective Factors in the Context of Acute Alcohol Intoxication in Childhood and Adolescence group), which includes (in addition to the authors Hanna Schwendemann, Heidi Kuttler and Eva Maria Bitzer) Stefanie Bumke, Cornelius Groß, Ludwig Kraus, Daniela Pionthek, Olaf Reis, and Ullrich Zimmermann.

Authors' contribution

HS planned and performed the data analysis and drafted the manuscript. HK conceived the study and participated in its design, coordination, and data acquisition. TM played an advisory role in performing the data analysis and interpreting its results. EMB provided substantial input to the study design, statistical analysis, and data interpretation. HK, TM, and EMB revised the manuscript critically for important intellectual content.

Funding

The study was funded by the German Ministry of Health (grant ID: IIA5 – 2511DSM220), which played no role in the study design, data collection, analysis, and interpretation or manuscript drafting.

Consent for publication
Not applicable

Competing interests
On behalf of all authors, the corresponding author declares having no competing interests.

Author details
[1]Pädagogische Hochschule Freiburg/University of Education, Kunzenweg 21, 79117 Freiburg, Germany. [2]Cooptima, Talweg 44, 79540 Lörrach, Germany. [3]State Police College Baden-Württemberg, Sturmbühlstraße 250, 78054 Villingen-Schwenningen, Germany.

References
1. Seeley J, Stice E, Rohde P. Screening for depression prevention: identifying adolescent girls at high risk for future depression. J Abnorm Psychol. 2009; 118:161–70. https://doi.org/10.1037/a0014741.
2. Barkmann C, Schulte-Markwort M. Prevalence of emotional and behavioural disorders in German children and adolescents: a meta-analysis. J Epidemiol Community Health. 2012;66:194–203. https://doi.org/10.1136/jech.2009.102467.
3. Costello EJ, Foley Debra L, Angold A. 10-year research update review: the epidemiology of child and adolescents psychiatric disordern: II. Developmental epidemiology. J AM ACAD Child Adolesc Psychiat. 2006;45: 8–24. https://doi.org/10.1097/01.chi.0000184929.41423.c0.
4. Mokdad AH, Forouzanfar MH, Daoud F, Mokdad AA, El Bcheraoui C, Moradi-Lakeh M, et al. Global burden of diseases, injuries, and risk factors for young people's health during 1990–2013: a systematic analysis for the global burden of disease study 2013. Lancet. 2016;387:2383–401. https://doi.org/10.1016/S0140-6736(16)00648-6.
5. Klasen F, Otto C, Kriston L, Patalay P, Schlack R, Ravens-Sieberer U. Risk and protective factors for the development of depressive symptoms in children and adolescents: results of the longitudinal BELLA study. Eur Child Adolesc Psychiat. 2014; https://doi.org/10.1007/s00787-014-0637-5.
6. Belhadj Kouider E, Petermann F. Common risk factors of depressive and anxiety Symptomatics in childhood and adolescence: a systematic review from Transdiagnostic perspectives. Fortschr Neurol Psychiatr. 2015;83:321–33. https://doi.org/10.1055/s-0035-1553089.
7. Patton GC, Sawyer SM, Santelli JS, Ross DA, Afifi R, Allen NB, et al. Our future: a lancet commission on adolescent health and wellbeing. Lancet. 2016;387:2423–78. https://doi.org/10.1016/S0140-6736(16)00579-1.
8. Catalano RF, Fagan AA, Gavin LE, Greenberg MT, Irwin CE, Ross DA, Shek DTL. Worldwide application of prevention science in adolescent health. Lancet. 2012;379:1653–64.
9. Diestelkamp S, Arnaud N, Sack P-M, Wartberg L, Daubmann A, Thomasius R. Brief motivational intervention for adolescents treated in emergency departments for acute alcohol intoxication - a randomized-controlled trial. BMC Emerg Med. 2014;14:13. https://doi.org/10.1186/1471-227X-14-13.
10. ESPAD Group. ESPAD report 2015: results from the European school survey project on alcohol and other drugs. Luxembourg; 2016.
11. Cairns KE, Yap, Hui MB, Pilkington PD, Jorm AF. Risk and protective factors for depression that adolescents can modify: a systematic review and meta-analysis of longitudinal studies. J Affect Dis. 2014;169:61–75. https://doi.org/10.1016/j.jad.2014.08.006.
12. Bitzer EM, Grobe TG, Schilling E, Dörning H, Schwartz F. Schwerpunktthema: Alkoholmissbrauch bei Jugendlichen. Focus topic: Alcohol abuse in adolescents. Asgard-Verl: St. Augustin; 2009.
13. Behrendt S. Buchbesprechungen. Book reviews. Sucht. 2008;54:354–61.
14. Buchmann AF, Schmid B, Blomeyer D, Zimmermann US, Jennen-Steinmetz C, Schmidt MH, et al. Drinking against unpleasant emotions: possible outcome of early onset of alcohol use? Alcohol Clin Exp Res. 2010;34:1052–7. https://doi.org/10.1111/j.1530-0277.2010.01180.x.
15. Buchmann AF, Schmid B, Blomeyer D, Becker K, Treutlein J, Zimmermann US, et al. Impact of age at first drink on vulnerability to alcohol-related problems: testing the marker hypothesis in a prospective study of young adults. J Psychiat Res. 2009;43:1205–12. https://doi.org/10.1016/j.jpsychires.2009.02.006.
16. Skogen JC, Sivertsen B, Lundervold AJ, Stormark KM, Jakobsen R, Hysing M. Alcohol and drug use among adolescents: and the co-occurrence of mental health problems. Ung@hordaland, a population-based study. BMJ Open. 2014;4:e005357. https://doi.org/10.1136/bmjopen-2014-005357.
17. Edwards AC, Heron J, Dick DM, Hickman M, Lewis G, Macleod J, Kendler KS. Adolescent alcohol us is positively associated with later depression in a population-based U.K. cohort. J Stud Alcohol Drugs. 2014;75:758–65.
18. Kuttler H, Schwendemann H, Bitzer EM. Familial risk and protective factors in alcohol intoxicated adolescents: psychometric evaluation of the family domain of the communities that care youth survey (CTC) and a new short version of the childhood trauma questionnaire (CTQ). BMC Pediatr. 2015;15: 1–14. https://doi.org/10.1186/s12887-015-0471-z.
19. Arthur MW, Hawkins JD, Pollard JA, Catalano RF, Baglioni AJ Jr. Measuring risk and protective factors for substance use, delinquency, and other adolescent problem behaviors: the communities that care youth survey. Eval Rev. 2002;26:575–601. https://doi.org/10.1177/0193841022237850.
20. Bond L, Lyndal T, Tombourou JW, Patton GC, Catalano RF. Improving the lives of young victorians in our community: a survey or risk and protective factors. Centre for Adolescent Health: Melbourne; 2000.
21. Sawyer SM, Afifi RA, Bearinger LH, Blakemore S-J, Dick B, Ezeh AC, Patton GC. Adolescence: a foundation for future health. Lancet. 2012;379:1630–40. https://doi.org/10.1016/S0140-6736(12)60072-5.
22. Viner RM, Ozer EM, Denny S, Marmot M, Resnick M, Fatusi A, Currie C. Adolescence and the social determinants of health. Lancet. 2012;379:1641–52.
23. Catalano RF, Hawkins JD. The social development model. In: Hawkins JD, editor. A theory of antisocial behavior: Deliquency and crime therories; 1996. p. 149–97.
24. Masten AS. Global perspectives on resilience in children and youth. Child Dev. 2014;85:6–20. https://doi.org/10.1111/cdev.12205.
25. Cohen AL. The social development model. EBSCO Research Starters; 2008. p. 1–7.
26. Hawkins JD, Weis JG. The social development model: an integrated approach to delinquency prevention. J Prim Prev. 1985;6:73–97. https://doi.org/10.1007/BF01325432.
27. Schubert H. Evaluation des Modellproprogramms "communities that care" in Niedersachsen: Theoretische Grundlagen und empirische Befunde zur sozialräumlichen Prävention in Netzwerken. Evaluation of the model program "communities that care" in lower Saxony: theoretical basics and empirical findings on sociospatial prevention in networks. Köln: Verl. Sozial, Raum, Management; 2013.
28. Lyssenko L, Rottmann N, Bengel J. Research on psychological resilience. Relevance for prevention and health promotion. Bundesgesundheitsblatt Gesundheitsforschung Gesundheitsschutz. 2010;53:1067–72. https://doi.org/10.1007/s00103-010-1127-7.
29. Bengel J, Meinders-Lücking F, Rottmann N. Schutzfaktoren bei Kindern und Jugendlichen: stand der Forschung zu psychosozialen Schutzfaktoren für Gesundheit. Protective factors in children and adolescents: state of research on psychosocial protection factors for health. Köln: Bundeszentrale für Gesundheitliche Aufklärung; 2009.
30. Werner EE. The children of Kauai: resiliency and recovery in adolescence and adulthood. J Adolesc Health. 1992;13:262–8.
31. Masten AS. Regulatory processes, risk, and resilience in adolescent development. Ann New York Acad Sci. 2004;1021:310–9. https://doi.org/10.1196/annals.1308.036.
32. Tapia JA, Rueda C, Fuentes CA. Development and validation of the family motivational Questionnaiere (FMC-Q). Psicothema. 2013;25:266–74. https://doi.org/10.7334/psicothema2012.218.
33. Véronneau M-H, Dishion TJ. Predicting change in early adolescent problem behavior in the middle school years: a Mesosystemic perspective on parenting and peer experiences. J Abnorm Child Psychol. 2010;38:1125–37. https://doi.org/10.1007/s10802-010-9431-0.
34. Piko BF, Luszczynska A, Fitzpatrick KM. Social inequalities in adolescent depression: the role of parental social support and optimism. Int J Soc Psychiat. 2013;59:474–81. https://doi.org/10.1177/0020764012440788.
35. Costello D, Swendsen J, Rose J, Dierker L. Risk and protective factors associated with trajectories of depressed mood from adolescence to early adulthood. J Consult Clin Psychol. 2008;76:173–83. https://doi.org/10.1037/0022-006X.76.2.173.
36. van Voorhees B, Paunesku D, Kuwabara S, Basu A, Gollan J, Hankin B, et al. Protective and vulnerability factors predicting new-onset depressive episode in a representative of U.S. adolescents. J Adolesc Health. 2008;42:605–16. https://doi.org/10.1016/j.jadohealth.2007.11.135.

37. Wolstein J, Wurdak M, Stürmer M. Evaluation des Alkoholpräventionsprojektes HaLT - Hart am Limit in Bayern. München: Evaluation of the alcohol prevention project HaLT - Hart am Limit in Bavaria; 2011.
38. Steiner M., Knittel T. The national pilot project HaLT – scientific monitoring. 2007. http://www.prognos.com/fileadmin/pdf/publikationsdatenbank/HaLT%20Short%20Report.pdf. Accessed 6 Jul 2016.
39. Kuttler H, Schwendemann H, Reis O, Bitzer EM. Developmental hazards among young alcohol intoxicated patients. J Adolesc Health. 2016;59:87–95. https://doi.org/10.1016/j.jadohealth.2016.03.022.
40. Groeger-Roth F, Frisch JU, Benit N, Soellner R. Risikofaktoren für problematischen Substanzkonsum von Jugendlichen – Zur Anwendbarkeit des communities that care Schülersurveys auf kommunaler Ebene. Risk factors for problematic substance use – is the communities that care youth survey applicable in german communities? Sucht. 2015;61:237–49. https://doi.org/10.1024/0939-5911.a000379.
41. Groeger-Roth F. Lokale Risiko- und Schutzfaktoren für Jugendkriminalität. Die Rolle von sozialräumlichen Unterschieden für die kommunale Prävention. Local risk and protection factors for juvenile crime. The role of socio-spatial differences for community prevention. Social spatial work in the offenders assistance. Sozialräumliches Arbeiten in der Straffälligenhilfe. 2012:73–89.
42. Groeger-Roth F. dt. Version des CTC - Itemkennwerte 11/2013. Frankfurt.
43. Arthur MW, Briney JS, Hawkins JD, Abbott RD, Brooke-Weiss BL, Catalano RF. Measuring risk and protection in communities using the communities that care youth survey. Eval Program Plann. 2007;30:197–211. https://doi.org/10.1016/j.evalprogplan.2007.01.009.
44. Leys C, Ley C, Klein O, Bernard P, Licata L. Detecting outliers: do not use standard deviation around the mean, use absolute deviation around the median. J Exp Soc Psychol. 2013;49:764–6. https://doi.org/10.1016/j.jesp.2013.03.013.
45. Schwendemann H, Kuttler H, Bitzer EM. Entwicklungsgefährdung bei Jugendlichen mit Alkoholintoxikation prognostizieren. Predict developmental risk in adolescents with alcohol intoxication. Sucht. 2015;61:223–36. https://doi.org/10.1024/0939-5911.a000378.
46. Rhew IC, Monahan KC, Oesterle S, Hawkins JD. The communities that care brief depression scale: psychometric properties and criterion validity. J Community Psychol. 2016;44:391–8. https://doi.org/10.1002/jcop.21766.
47. Cole DA, Ciesla JA, Steiger JH. The insidious effects of failing to include design-driven correlated residuals in latent-variable covariance structure analysis. Psychol Methods. 2007;12:381–98. https://doi.org/10.1037/1082-989X.12.4.381.
48. Vandenberg RJ, Lance CE. A review and synthesis of the measurement invariance literature: suggestions, practices, and recommendations for oragnisational research. Organ Res Methods. 2000;3:4–70. https://doi.org/10.1177/109442810031002.
49. van de Schoot R, Schmidt P, DeBeuckelaer A. Measurement invariance. Lausanne: Frontiers Media SA; 2015.
50. Weiber R, Mühlhaus D. Strukturgleichungsmodellierung: Eine anwendungsorientierte Einführung in die Kausalanalyse mit Hilfe von AMOS, SmartPLS und SPSS. Structural equation modeling: an application-oriented introduction to causal analysis using AMOS, SmartPLS and SPSS. 2nd ed. Berlin: Springer Gabler; 2014.
51. Little TD. Longitudinal structural equation modeling. Guildford: New York [u. a.]; 2013.
52. Meredith W, Teresi JA. An essay on measurement and factorial invariance. Med Care. 2006;44:S69–77. https://doi.org/10.1097/01.mlr.0000245438.73837.89.
53. Chen FF. Sensitivity of goodness of fit indexes to lack of measurement invariance. Struct Equation Model Multidisciplinary J. 2007;14:464–504. https://doi.org/10.1080/10705510701301834.
54. Satorra A, Bentler PM. A scaled difference Chi-Square test statistic for moment structure analysis. Psychometrica. 2001;66:507–14. https://doi.org/10.1007/BF02296192.
55. Rosseel Y. Lavaan: an R package for structural equation modeling. J Stat Softw. 2012;48:1–36. https://doi.org/10.18637/jss.v048.i02.
56. Byrne BM. Structural equation modeling with AMOS: basic concepts, applications, and programming. 2nd ed. New York: Routledge; 2010.
57. Oberski D. Lavaan.Survey: an R package for complex survey analysis of structural equation modeling. J Stat Softw. 2014;57:1–27. https://doi.org/10.18637/jss.v057.i01.
58. Stekhoven DJ. Using the missForest package. 2011. http://stat.ethz.ch/education/semesters/ss2012/ams/paper/missForest_1.2.pdf. Accessed 6 Jul 2016.
59. Frisch JU, Soellner R, Groeger-Roth F. Community based prevention: does communities that care (CTC) methodology apply to Germany? San Fransico; 2.6.2016.
60. Soellner R, Frisch JU, Reder M. Communities That Care: Schülerbefragung in Niedersachsen. Hildesheim: Universitätsverlag Hildesheim; 2016.
61. Huang B, Kosterman R, Catalano RF, Hawkins JD, Abbott RD. Modeling mediation in the etiology of violent behavior in adolescence: a test of the social development model. Criminology. 2001;39:75–108. https://doi.org/10.1111/j.1745-9125.2001.tb00917.x.
62. Zimmermann P, Iwanski A. Bindung und Automnomie im Jugendalter. In: Neider A, Bleckmann P, Brisch KH, editors. Krisenbewältigung, Widerstandskräfte, Soziale Bindungen im Kindes- und Jugendalter // Bindung und Jugend: Individualität, Gruppen und Autonomie. 1st ed. Stuttgart: Verl. Freies Geistesleben; Klett-Cotta; 2014. p. 12–35.
63. Koehn AJ, Kerns KA. Parent-child attachment: meta-analysis of associations with parenting behaviors in middle childhood and adolescence. Attach Hum Dev. 2017:1–28. https://doi.org/10.1080/14616734.2017.1408131.
64. Amann U. Substanzmissbrauch im Jugendalter und Bindungserfahrungen: wissenschaftliche Ergebnisse und Erfahrungen aus der Praxis der Jugend-Suchtstation clean.kick und clean.kids. In: Neider A, Bleckmann P, Brisch KH, editors. Krisenbewältigung, Widerstandskräfte, Soziale Bindungen im Kindes- und Jugendalter // Bindung und Jugend: Individualität, Gruppen und Autonomie. 1st ed. Stuttgart: Verl. Freies Geistesleben; Klett-Cotta; 2014. p. 112–38.
65. Piko BF, Kovacs E, Fitzpatrick KM. What makes a difference? Understanding the role of protective factors in Hungarian adolescents' depressive symptomatology. Eur Child Adolesc Psychiat. 2009;18:617–24. https://doi.org/10.1007/s00787-009-0022-y.
66. Formoso D, Gonzales NA, Aiken LS. Family conflict and children's internalizing and externalizing behavior: protective factors. Am J Community Psychol. 2000;28:175–99. https://doi.org/10.1023/A:1005135217449.
67. Connor J, Rueter M. Parent-child relationships as systems of support or risk for adolescent suicidality. J Fam Psychol. 2006;20:143–55. https://doi.org/10.1037/0893-3200.20.1.143.
68. Stappenbeck J, Wendell A, Thomasius R. Evaluation des familienbasierten Programms Familien stärken zur Prävention von Sucht- und Verhaltensproblemen bei Jugendlichen. Evaluation of the family based program "strengthening families" to prevent addictive and behavior problems in adolescents. Gesundheitswesen. 2015;77:S74–5. https://doi.org/10.1055/s-0032-1333246.
69. Stolle M, Sack P-M, Stappenbeck J, Thomasius R. Familienbasierte Prävention bei Kindern und Jugendlichen. Family-based prevention in children and adolescents. SUCHT - Zeitschrift für Wissenschaft und Praxis / J Addict Res Pract. 2010;56:51–60. https://doi.org/10.1024/0939-5911/a000010.
70. Klocke A. Gesundheit der Kinder in Einelternfamilien. Childrens health in one-parent families. Gesundheitswesen. 2012;74:70–5. https://doi.org/10.1055/s-0032-1312634.
71. Tomcikova Z, Veselska ZD, Geckova AM, Van Dijk JP, Reijneveld SA. Adolescents' drinking and drunkenness more likely in one-parent families and due to poor communication with mother. Cent Eur J Public Health. 2015;23:54–8. https://doi.org/10.21101/cejph.a3951.
72. Fergusson DM, Beautrais AL, Horwood LJ. Vulnerability and resiliency to suicidal behaviours in young people. Psychol Med. 2003;33:61–73.
73. Lohaus A, Vierhaus M. Entwicklungspsychologie des Kindes- und Jugendalters für bachelor. Developmental Psychology of childhood and adolescence for bachelor. 3rd ed. Berlin: Springer; 2015.

Factors associated with persistent posttraumatic stress disorder among U.S. military service members and veterans

Richard F. Armenta[1,2*], Toni Rush[3], Cynthia A. LeardMann[1,2], Jeffrey Millegan[4], Adam Cooper[1], Charles W. Hoge[5] and for the Millennium Cohort Study team

Abstract

Background: Posttraumatic stress disorder (PTSD) can have long-term and far-reaching impacts on health and social and occupational functioning. This study examined factors associated with persistent PTSD among U.S. service members and veterans.

Methods: Using baseline and follow-up (2001–2013) questionnaire data collected approximately every 3 years from the Millennium Cohort Study, multivariable logistic regression was conducted to determine factors associated with persistent PTSD. Participants included those who screened positive for PTSD using the PTSD Checklist–Civilian Version at baseline ($N = 2409$). Participants were classified as having remitted or persistent PTSD based on screening negative or positive, respectively, at follow-up.

Results: Almost half of participants ($N = 1132$; 47%) met criteria for persistent PTSD at the first follow-up; of those, 804 (71%) also screened positive for PTSD at the second follow-up. Multiple factors were independently associated with persistent PTSD in an adjusted model at the first follow-up, including older age, deployment with high combat exposure, enlisted rank, initial PTSD severity, depression, history of physical assault, disabling injury/illness, and somatic symptoms. Among those with persistent PTSD at the first follow-up, additional factors of less sleep, separation from the military, and lack of social support were associated with persistent PTSD at the second follow-up.

Conclusions: Combat experiences and PTSD severity were the most salient risk factors for persistent PTSD. Comorbid conditions, including injury/illness, somatic symptoms, and sleep problems, also played a significant role and should be addressed during treatment. The high percentage of participants with persistent PTSD supports the need for more comprehensive and accessible treatment, especially after separation from the military.

Keywords: Post-traumatic stress disorder, PTSD, Military, Combat, Veterans

Background

Posttraumatic stress disorder (PTSD) is one of the most common health conditions among U.S. service members, with an estimated prevalence between 5% and 20% among the 2.7 million who have deployed to Iraq and Afghanistan since 2001, depending primarily on level of combat exposure [1, 2]. PTSD has been associated with a nearly 200% increase in hospitalizations among active duty service members between 2006 and 2012, and is a leading diagnosis in Department of Veterans Affairs medical settings [3]. However, these statistics underestimate the impact of PTSD since many service members in need of treatment do not seek care [1].

The course of PTSD varies, but symptoms can become persistent and last years or even a lifetime [4–7]. Persistent PTSD has been associated with long-term neurobiological changes and comorbidities that can have profound effects on physical and mental health functioning [8–11]. These changes may affect the person's psychological, behavioral, and physical health [12–14], decreasing one's quality of life and manifesting in the form of increased rates of

* Correspondence: richard.f.armenta.ctr@mail.mil
[1]Deployment Health Research Department, Naval Health Research Center, 140 Sylvester Road, San Diego, CA 92106-3521, USA
[2]The Henry M. Jackson Foundation for the Advancement of Military Medicine, Inc, Bethesda, MD, USA
Full list of author information is available at the end of the article

cardiovascular disease [12, 15], hypertension, obesity [12, 16], immune-mediated disorders [17], and mortality. In addition, PTSD often co-occurs with depression, anxiety, and substance abuse [1, 18], all of which have been linked to suicidal behaviors [19]. As a direct effect of PTSD or an indirect result of comorbid health effects, important social interactions involving intimate relationships, such as marriage, are also often negatively affected, leading to decreased support and further worsening of symptoms [20]. Ongoing PTSD has been associated with increased disability, decreased productivity, and decreased fitness, thereby limiting one's ability to continue to serve in the military or function in other occupational settings [21]. The longer PTSD remains untreated, the greater the probability that this stress-related disorder will lead to a health complication [22]. Therefore, understanding the mechanisms related to the persistence of PTSD symptoms is critical to the life and well-being of service members, veterans, and their families.

Limited research has examined factors associated with persistent PTSD among U.S. veterans of the Vietnam conflict [23–25] and World War II [26], as well as British veterans of the recent Iraq conflict [27]. In these studies, combat severity was associated with higher occurrence of PTSD and persistence of symptoms [23–26]. Other notable factors associated with persistent PTSD included lack of social support [23, 26, 27], preexisting depression [24], and reporting of multiple physical symptoms [13, 27]. Other studies have found that PTSD symptoms may continue to increase over time [4]. Studies that are more comprehensive involving U.S. cohorts and a more comprehensive range of potential risk and protective factors are lacking. Understanding the broad interactions of various risk factors in the development of persistent PTSD among U.S. military personnel is essential to providing specialized multidisciplinary treatment for service members and veterans.

This study is the first, to our knowledge, to prospectively assess persistent PTSD symptoms among U.S. military personnel serving since the start of operations in Iraq and Afghanistan. The primary objective of this study was to estimate rates of persistent PTSD and identify factors associated with persistent symptoms among participants in the Millennium Cohort Study, a large cohort study of service members and veterans from all service branches and components [28, 29].

Method

Launched in 2001, the Millennium Cohort Study was designed to examine the impact and long-term health effects associated with military service. Between 2001 and 2013, four separate groups of service members, referred to as panels, were enrolled. Participants were randomly selected from U.S. military personnel and asked to complete a comprehensive web-based or paper survey approximately every 3 years. A detailed description of the Millennium Cohort Study methodology has been published elsewhere [28, 29].

The present study included Millennium Cohort participants who enrolled in the first or second panel. Participants must have completed at least two questionnaires, the 2004–2006 and 2007–2008 surveys, approximately 3 years apart ($N = 63{,}589$). Data from the 2004–2006 survey cycle and 2007–2008 survey cycle are referred to as "baseline" and "first follow-up," respectively, for the purposes of this paper. To be eligible for this analysis, participants must have screened positive for PTSD at baseline ($N = 2992$). After excluding those with missing data for the key outcome or predictor variables, the study population between baseline and the first follow-up included 2409 individuals (80.5% of the eligible sample). In addition, participants who screened positive for PTSD at first follow-up had complete data for the covariates of interest, and those who had follow-up data at the subsequent 2011–2013 survey cycle ($N = 822$) were assessed for persistent PTSD at the "second follow-up."

Outcome

PTSD was assessed using the PTSD Checklist–Civilian Version (PCL-C), a 17-item measure that asks participants to self-report the severity of each item in the past month. PCL-C responses are scored with a 5-point Likert scale ranging from 1 ("not at all") to 5 ("extremely"), with a possible total score of 17 to 85. Based on the DSM-IV-TR, participants screened positive for PTSD if they reported a moderate or higher level (scoring ≥3) for at least one intrusion, at least three avoidance, and at least two hyperarousal symptoms [30]. This DSM-IV-TR criterion for scoring the PCL-C has been shown to correspond to a total cutoff of 44 in military personnel, a sufficiently high threshold for estimating prevalence in a population study [31, 32]. Participants who met these criteria at follow-up were defined as having persistent PTSD, and those who no longer screened positive were defined as having remitted. A continuous PTSD severity score at baseline was also included in analyses to determine whether those with higher initial PTSD scores were more likely to have persistent PTSD. PTSD severity scores were modeled as a 10 point change based on the standard deviation and what might be considered a clinically relevant change in scores.

Covariates

Demographic and military characteristics were obtained at baseline from personnel files from the Defense Manpower Data Center and included sex, birth cohort, race/ethnicity, marital status, educational level, service branch, military component, pay grade, military separation, and military occupation. All other covariates, with the exception of deployment, were measured at baseline for the first analysis (i.e., persistent PTSD assessed at the first follow-up) and at the first follow-up for the second analysis (i.e., persistent PTSD assessed at the second follow-up).

Deployment experience in support of the operations in Iraq and Afghanistan prior to the first follow-up was determined using Department of Defense electronic military records. Combat experiences were assessed at the first follow-up using a 12-item modified version of the Walter Reed Combat Experiences Scale (e.g., being attacked or ambushed, seeing dead bodies, knowing someone seriously injured or killed), with an aggregate score of 1–12 representing more variation in type of combat experiences. Deployment and combat experience/severity were combined into one variable with five categories reflecting no deployment, deployment without combat, and deployment with low combat (score, 1–3), medium combat (score, 4–10), and high combat (score, > 10), using methods similar to prior studies [1].

Depression was assessed by self-reporting "ever" being diagnosed with depression by a medical professional or screening positive on the 8-item Primary Care Evaluation of Mental Disorders Patient Health Questionnaire depression scale (PHQ-8) [33]. Based on DSM-IV-TR criteria, participants screened positive for depression if they met the following criteria: responded "more than half the days" or "nearly every day" to at least 5 of the 8 items, in which one of the endorsed items was a depressed mood or anhedonia. Participants were also asked if they had ever been diagnosed with manic disorder or schizophrenia, or had been prescribed a medication to treat anxiety, panic, or depression.

Functional physical health was assessed using the physical component summary score derived from the Medical Outcomes Study Short Form 36-Item Health Survey for Veterans [34]. Continuous scores, in which higher scores represent better health, were collapsed into three categories; consistent with previous methodology, "low" and "high" represented scores below the 15th percentile and above the 85th percentile, respectively [35]. Multiple physical symptoms were assessed using the 15-items from the Patient Health Questionnaire (PHQ-15) [36]. The first 13 items are rated on a 0 ("not bothered at all") to 2 ("bothered a lot") scale for the past month; the remaining two items, sleeping trouble and fatigue, are rated on a 0 to 3 scale for the past 2 weeks and were adapted to the 0 to 2 response scale using the validated approach of Kroenke et al. [36]. Scores were summed, and a cutoff score of 15 was used to indicate impairment. A score of ≥15 has been shown to be significantly associated with increased impairment and higher utilization of health care services, and has been used in other military studies [13].

Behavioral characteristics (e.g., body mass index [BMI], sleep, tobacco use, alcohol use) were based on self-reported data assessed at baseline. BMI was categorized as underweight (< 18.5 kg/m^2), normal weight (18.5–24.9 kg/m^2), overweight (25.0–29.9 kg/m^2), and obese (≥ 30 kg/m^2); underweight and normal weight were combined due to low numbers of underweight individuals. Sleep duration was categorized into three groups: < 4 h, 4–6 h, and > 6 h. Tobacco use was categorized as current smoker, past smoker, and nonsmoker, and based on questions about ever smoking 100 cigarettes, current smoking, and successfully quitting smoking. Alcohol-related problems were assessed using the five PHQ items and based on one or more affirmative responses [37]. Social support was measured by how much participants reported being bothered by "having no one to turn to when they have a problem" in the last 4 weeks, and dichotomized to "not bothered at all/bothered a little" and "bothered a lot." Each stressful life experience was assessed as a binary variable based on endorsement of divorce, financial problems, physical assault, sexual assault, illness or death of a loved one, and personal disabling illness or injury. This study was approved by the Institutional Review Board at the Naval Health Research Center and all participants provided voluntary written informed consent.

Statistical analysis

Descriptive analyses and chi-square tests were used to compare demographic, behavioral, and military characteristics by PTSD persistence. Bivariate logistic regression was conducted to determine factors associated with persistent PTSD. Multivariable logistic regression models, for both the first and second follow-ups, were derived using a backwards elimination process that initially included all variables associated with PTSD in the unadjusted models ($p < 0.20$) [38, 39]. Factors were manually removed sequentially until the final model included only those that were significantly associated with PTSD ($p < 0.05$) or confounded the relationship between any covariate and PTSD by >10% [40]. Collinearity was assessed using variance inflation factors and condition indices. All analyses were conducted using SAS software, version 9.3 (SAS Institute Inc., Cary, N.C.).

Results

Of the 2409 service member participants who met criteria for PTSD at baseline, the mean age was 32.2 years (SD = 10.2), 65% were male, and 71% were non-Hispanic white. 49% of the sample deployed between 2001 and the first follow-up visit; of those, 90% reported experiencing combat.

Overall, 1123 (47%) service members had persistent PTSD at the first follow-up (2007–2008). In bivariate analyses (Table 1), numerous characteristics were significantly associated (all $p < 0.05$) with persistent PTSD, including birth year prior to 1960 (vs. 1980 or later), lower educational level, being married, being in the Army or Marine Corps, having an enlisted pay grade, having a history of deployment with moderate to severe combat, reporting greater PTSD severity at baseline, presence of another mental health condition (i.e., depression, manic disorder, schizophrenia), use of psychotropic medication, higher BMI (i.e., obese), lower physical functioning, screening positive for multiple physical symptoms, short sleep duration (≤ 4 h), being a current smoker, and history of stressful experiences (e.g., sexual assault, divorce, physical assault, disabling illness or injury).

In the final multivariable model (Table 2), factors that remained significantly associated with persistent PTSD at the first follow-up period (2007–2008) included older age, enlisted pay grade (with junior enlisted pay grade having highest odds), deployment with moderate or higher combat experiences, higher baseline PCL-C score, multiple physical symptoms (PHQ-15 score ≥ 15), depression, prior experience of physical assault, or disabling injury/illness. High combat exposure (OR = 3.91) and severity of PTSD symptoms at baseline (OR = 1.59 for each 10-point increment on the PCL) were the strongest risk factors for persistent PTSD.

Of the 1792 participants who screened positive for PTSD at baseline and had available data from the three survey cycles, 592 (33.0%) screened positive for PTSD on both follow-up questionnaires. Among those who screened positive for PTSD at the first follow-up and had available data at the second follow-up ($N = 822$), 585 (71.2%) continued to screen positive at the second follow-up visit. In addition to many of the aforementioned factors associated with persistent PTSD, separation from the military, sleeping less than 4 h per night, and lack of social support were associated with persistence of PTSD at the second follow-up (Table 2).

Discussion

PTSD is one of the most common disabling disorders among U.S. service members and veterans, and it often becomes a chronic condition. In this study, we found that 47% of those who screened positive for PTSD at baseline were still positive for PTSD at follow-up approximately 3 years later; of those, over 70% remained positive for PTSD at the second follow-up approximately 6 years later.

Results from this study indicate that the intensity of combat exposure during the recent operations in Iraq and Afghanistan is a strong risk factors for persistent PTSD. This finding is consistent with other research that suggests combat exposure, compared with other types of trauma, confers a uniquely high risk of persistent PTSD, with strong linear associations related to combat intensity [2, 27, 41, 42]. Conversely, individuals who deployed without experiencing combat were more likely to screen negative for PTSD at follow-up compared with those who did not deploy. This protective association among non-combat deployers is likely due to the well-known healthy warrior effect, in which healthier service members are more likely to deploy than service members experiencing medical problems [43].

In addition to combat intensity, a number of other important risk factors for PTSD chronicity were identified, in particular indicators of psychological or physical health comorbidities. Not surprisingly, PTSD severity at baseline was strongly associated with persistence of symptoms. However, even after adjusting for PTSD severity and other variables, comorbid health conditions, which are common among those with PTSD, still emerged as important and independent risk factors of persistent PTSD. These findings indicate that those with comorbid conditions, such as depression or multiple physical symptoms, may be different in some ways than those with the single condition of PTSD. These comorbid conditions a may lead to increased dysregulation of neuroendocrine and autonomic nervous system or interoceptive functions. These comorbid conditions could also be linked to pain perception changes or physical symptoms acting as reminders of the traumatic event, either directly from injury that occurred as part of the trauma or indirectly through physiological mechanisms associated with bodily sensations [44]. For these and other reasons, it may be more difficult to effectively treat and care for individuals with PTSD who have other additional conditions.

One notable finding was that participants who reported sleeping less than 4 h per night at the first follow-up survey were more likely to screen positive for PTSD at the second follow-up, suggesting that sleep is an important predictor of long-term persistent PTSD. Sleep problems are common among service members who have deployed, independent of PTSD, and research has shown that those who develop disruptions in normal sleep patterns after a traumatic event are more likely to develop PTSD [45]. Additionally, sleep problems may result from the PTSD symptoms themselves, such as hypervigilance and recurrent nightmares. Sleep problems are also associated with comorbid conditions. Given these multiple interrelated health associations, treatment of persistent PTSD symptoms may include comprehensive approaches that address comorbid physical health problems, chronic pain, and sleep problems [44, 46].

Table 1 Frequencies and Unadjusted Odds Ratios of Characteristics Measured in 2004–2006 by Persistent PTSD at the First Follow-Up for Millennium Cohort Participants ($N = 2409$)

Variables	Persistent PTSD					
	No ($N = 1286$)		Yes ($N = 1123$)		OR	95% CI
Demographics	Number	Percent	Number	Percent		
Sex						
Male	823	64.0	742	66.1	1.0	
Female	463	36.2	381	33.9	0.91	0.77–1.08
Birth year*						
Prior to 1960	145	11.3	172	15.3	1.60	1.23–2.10
1960–1969	326	25.4	286	25.5	1.19	0.95–1.48
1970–1979	419	32.6	372	33.1	1.20	0.98–1.47
1980 or later	396	30.8	293	26.1	1.0	
Education*						
Some college or less	1019	79.2	936	83.3	1.0	
Bachelor's degree or higher	267	20.8	187	16.7	0.76	0.62–0.94
Race/ethnicity						
Non-Hispanic White	928	72.2	781	69.5	1.0	
Non-Hispanic Black	132	10.3	146	13.0	1.31	1.02–1.69
Other	226	17.6	196	17.5	1.03	0.83–1.28
Marital status*						
Never married	532	41.4	403	35.9	1.0	
Married	615	47.8	587	52.3	1.26	1.06–1.50
Other	139	10.8	133	11.8	1.26	0.96–1.66
Military Characteristics						
Service branch*						
Army	753	58.6	722	64.3	1.44	1.14–1.81
Navy/Coast Guard	216	16.9	162	14.4	1.12	0.84–1.51
Marine Corps	95	7.4	91	8.1	1.44	1.01–2.05
Air Force	222	17.3	148	13.2	1.0	
Service component						
Active duty	656	51.0	6594	52.9	1.08	0.92–1.27
Reserve/National Guard	630	49.0	529	47.1	1.0	
Pay grade*						
E1–E4	607	46.2	556	49.5	1.66	1.27–2.17
E5–E9	496	38.6	466	41.5	1.70	1.29–2.24
Officer	183	14.2	101	9.0	1.0	
Military separation						
No	1038	80.7	877	78.1	1.0	
Yes	248	19.3	246	21.9	1.17	0.96–1.43
Military occupation						
Combat	231	18.0	217	19.3	0.96	0.73–1.35
Health care	133	10.3	126	11.2	1.0	
Other	922	71.7	780	69.5	0.89	0.69–1.16
Deployment experience[a,]*						
Nondeployed	675	52.5	555	61.4	1.0	

Table 1 Frequencies and Unadjusted Odds Ratios of Characteristics Measured in 2004–2006 by Persistent PTSD at the First Follow-Up for Millennium Cohort Participants ($N = 2409$) *(Continued)*

Variables	Persistent PTSD					
	No ($N = 1286$)		Yes ($N = 1123$)		OR	95% CI
Demographics	Number	Percent	Number	Percent		
Deployed without combat	91	7.1	28	5.2	0.34	0.22–0.54
Deployed, low combat	162	12.6	73	6.5	0.55	0.41–0.74
Deployed, moderate combat	320	24.9	369	32.9	1.41	1.17–1.70
Deployed, high combat	38	2.9	98	8.7	3.13	2.12–4.63
Medical Characteristics						
PTSD severity at baseline (mean, SD per 10-point change in score)[b,*]	50.8	9.7	57.6	11.3	1.84	1.70–2.01
Depression[c,*]						
No	538	41.8	277	24.7	1.0	
Yes	748	58.2	846	75.3	2.20	1.84–2.62
Manic*						
No	1238	96.3	1025	91.3	1.0	
Yes	48	3.7	98	8.7	2.47	1.73–3.52
Schizophrenia*						
No	1271	98.8	1090	97.1	1.0	
Yes	15	1.2	33	2.9	2.56	1.39–4.75
Psychotropic medication[d,*]						
No	1024	79.6	767	68.3	1.0	
Yes	262	20.4	356	31.7	1.81	1.51–2.18
BMI categories[e,*]						
Under/normal weight	457	35.5	365	32.5	1.0	
Overweight	582	45.3	486	43.3	1.04	0.87–1.26
Obese	247	19.2	272	24.2	1.38	1.11–1.72
Physical component score*						
Low	148	11.5	229	20.4	1.0	
Mid	907	70.5	760	67.7	0.54	0.43–0.68
High	231	18.0	134	11.9	0.37	0.28–0.50
Multiple somatic symptoms score*						
< 15	1079	83.9	778	69.3	1.0	
≥ 15	207	16.1	345	30.7	2.31	1.90–2.81
Behavioral Characteristics						
Sleep duration*						
< 4 h/day	230	17.9	310	27.6	1.41	1.11–1.78
4–6 h/day	358	27.8	368	23.9	1.15	0.82–1.61
> 6 h/day	698	54.3	545	48.5	1.0	
Smoking*						
Past smoker/nonsmoker	934	72.6	778	69.2	1.0	
Current smoker	352	27.4	3345	30.7	1.17	0.98–1.40
Alcohol-related problems						
No	960	74.6	826	73.5	1.0	
Yes	326	25.4	297	26.5	1.06	0.88–1.27
Stressful Experiences						

Table 1 Frequencies and Unadjusted Odds Ratios of Characteristics Measured in 2004–2006 by Persistent PTSD at the First Follow-Up for Millennium Cohort Participants ($N = 2409$) *(Continued)*

Variables	Persistent PTSD					
	No ($N = 1286$)		Yes ($N = 1123$)		OR	95% CI
Demographics	Number	Percent	Number	Percent		
Divorced*						
No	778	60.5	600	53.4	1.0	
Yes	508	39.5	523	46.6	1.33	1.14–1.57
Financial problems*						
No	923	71.8	765	68.1	1.0	
Yes	363	28.2	358	31.9	1.19	1.00–1.42
Sexual assault*						
None	893	69.4	722	64.3	1.0	
Harassment	158	12.3	149	13.3	1.17	0.91–1.49
Assault	235	18.3	252	22.4	1.33	1.08–1.62
Physical assault*						
No	1032	80.3	791	70.4	1.0	
Yes	254	19.7	332	29.6	1.70	1.41–2.06
Ill/Death of a loved one*						
No	326	25.3	229	20.4	1.0	
Yes	960	74.7	894	79.6	1.33	1.09–1.61
Disabling illness/injury*						
No	989	76.9	725	64.6	1.0	
Yes	297	23.1	398	35.4	1.82	1.53–2.19

BMI =body mass index, *CI* =confidence interval, *OR* =odds ratio, *PHQ* =Patient Health Questionnaire, *PTSD* =posttraumatic stress disorder
[a]Deployments include those which occurred prior to the 2007 survey date and were in support of operations in Iraq and Afghanistan
[b]PTSD severity at baseline was included as a continuous variable to adjust for varying PTSD scores. Results were modeled using a 10 point change in the severity score based on the standard deviation and what would be considered a clinically relevant change the PTSD score
[c]Depression includes diagnosis by a medical professional or screening positive on the PHQ-9
[d]Endorsed "yes" to survey question, "Are you currently taking any medicine for anxiety, depression, or stress?"
[e]BMI categories: under/normal weight (≤24.9 kg/m2), overweight (25.0–29.9 kg/m2), and obese (≥30 kg/m2)
*Variable significant at $p < 0.20$ using chi-square testing

An important aspect of PTSD treatment is having adequate social support. We found that being bothered a lot by not having someone to turn to was associated with persistent PTSD at the second follow-up. Research shows that social relationships can help with treatment compliance, coping with intrusive symptoms, and sharing feelings and thoughts that are experienced with PTSD. Social support both during and following deployment has been shown to be associated with lower PTSD severity [47]. Additionally, separation or retiring from the military was associated with persistent PTSD between the first and second follow-up visits, which may also relate in part to changes in social relationships after transitioning from the military. It is also likely that persistent PTSD itself led to medical discharge from the military for some study participants [48].

Participants born before 1980 were more likely to have persistent PTSD. Military studies have generally observed that the risk of PTSD is highest in younger age groups; however, when examining persistence or chronicity, studies have more often shown an association with older age [27, 49]. Studies among aging war veterans and Holocaust survivors have reported that PTSD severity increases in older trauma survivors [49].

We did not find an association between reported history of sexual trauma and persistent PTSD in adjusted models, though there was an association in unadjusted models. Sexual assault has been shown to be one of the most significant types of traumatic events in predicting PTSD and other mental health outcomes [50, 51]. In our analysis, the null association with sexual assault may be attributable to the small number of sexual assault cases or high correlation with other statistically significant variables such as physical assault. It is also possible that the measure of sexual assault was less than optimal and thus could have missed some cases of sexual assault or lead to misclassification. Further research to examine the role of sexual trauma in PTSD persistence is needed.

Table 2 Multivariable Regression Analysis of Predictors of Persistent PTSD at the First (2007–2008) and Second Follow-Ups (2011–2013)

	First Follow-Up (*N* = 2409) (47% With Persistent PTSD)		Second Follow-Up (*N* = 822) (71.2% With Persistent PTSD)	
Characteristic*	OR	95% CI	OR	95% CI
Birth year				
Prior to 1960	2.34	1.68–3.54	2.68	1.53–4.68
1960–1969	1.71	1.25–2.36	2.11	1.32–3.36
1970–1979	1.42	1.11–1.83	1.40	0.91–2.14
1980 or later	1.00		1.00	
Pay grade				
Junior enlisted (E1–E4)	2.10	1.50–2.93		
Senior enlisted (E5–E9)	1.68	1.25–2.27		
Officer	1.00			
Deployment experience[a]				
Nondeployed	1.00		1.00	
Deployed without combat	0.56	0.36–0.90	0.91	0.33–2.51
Deployed, low combat	0.73	0.53–1.00	1.77	0.90–3.50
Deployed, moderate combat	1.72	1.39–2.12	1.44	0.98–2.12
Deployed, high combat	3.91	2.56–5.96	2.63	1.27–5.42
PTSD severity at baseline[b]				
Per 10 point change in score	1.59	1.45–1.74	1.23	1.06–1.43
Multiple somatic symptoms score				
< 15	1.00			
≥ 15	1.47	1.18–1.83		
Depression[c]				
No	1.00		1.00	
Yes	1.50	1.23–1.83	2.33	1.63–3.33
Physical assault				
No	1.00			
Yes	1.25	1.01–1.54		
Sleep duration				
< 4 h per day			1.75	1.15–2.69
4–6 h per day			1.08	0.74–1.58
> 6 h per day			1.00	
Separation from military				
No			1.00	
Yes			1.57	1.12–2.21
Social support				
Not bothered/bothered a little			1.00	
Bothered a lot			1.51	1.09–2.10
Disabling injury/illness				
No	1.00			
Yes	1.35	1.11–1.66		

CI =confidence interval, *OR* =odds ratio, *PHQ* =Patient Health Questionnaire, *PTSD* =posttraumatic stress disorder
[a]Deployments include those which occurred any time prior to the 2007 survey date and were in support of operations in Iraq and Afghanistan
[b]PTSD severity at baseline was included as a continuous variable to adjust for varying PTSD scores. Results were modeled using a 10 point change in the severity score based on the standard deviation and what would be considered a clinically relevant change the PTSD score
[c]Depression includes diagnosis by a medical professional or screening positive on the PHQ-9
*All variables with OR and 95% CI are significant at the alpha < 0.05 level

Study limitations and strengths

The results of our study must be interpreted with some limitations in mind. The study population consisted of a sample of responders to the Millennium Cohort questionnaire and may not be representative of the overall military population. However, investigations of potential biases have found the cohort to be highly representative, without evidence that participation is influenced by poor health or other key factors that would relate to health outcomes analyses [52, 53]. Self-reported survey data may be subject to recall and reporting biases; however, there was high consistency in associations between time periods. It is still possible that participants could inaccurately recall information across time periods. While the PCL-C is a screening tool for and not diagnostic of PTSD, it has strong demonstrated validity, and the associations with PCL severity found in this study were consistent with other research [31]. The follow-up period (3 years between surveys) was relatively long, and we were not able to study PTSD treatment received in military, veteran, or civilian settings by cohort participants. Thus, it was not possible to look at the trajectory of fluctuations in symptomatology over shorter periods of time, the effectiveness of treatment that may have been received, or other factors related to service utilization, such as receiving medical disability for PTSD or related health conditions. We did not assess lifetime or childhood trauma history, which may increase the risk of persistent PTSD; this should be included in future studies. Our assessment of social support was limited to one item, thus further studies should include a more comprehensive measure of social support to better understand how it is associated with persistent PTSD. Finally, 19.5% of participants were excluded due to missing data. In examining those with missing data compared to those with no missing data for all covariates we found that only three (sex, birth cohort, and race/ethnicity) were statistically different, albeit the differences were less than 5%. Further, In a bivariate sensitivity analysis using all data available for race, sex, and birth cohort there were no significant differences in associations with persistent PTSD when compared with bivariate analysis using only observations with complete data (data not shown). These additional analyses indicated that the missingness likely did not impact the results.

Despite these limitations, this study has many notable strengths. To our knowledge, this is the first study to longitudinally examine persistent PTSD among a large cohort of U.S. service members and veterans. The sampling method was population based and represents all service branches. The study methodology using the PCL-C allowed for the detection of individuals suffering from PTSD who may not seek care [1]. Finally, due to the prospective and comprehensive nature of the survey, we were able to examine multiple risk factors.

Conclusions

Understanding correlates of PTSD chronicity is critical to the long-term health and well-being of service members and veterans. Almost half of participants who screened positive for PTSD at baseline had persistent PTSD at the first-follow-up; among those, over two thirds had persistent PTSD at the second follow-up. Given the large number of factors associated with PTSD persistence, our study highlights the importance of holistic collaborative care models that address complex interrelated comorbid health conditions, including depression, generalized physical symptoms, and sleep problems [32].

Acknowledgements

In addition to the authors, Millennium Cohort Study team includes Valerie Stander, PhD; Gia Gumbs, MPH; Steven Speigle; Cynthia LeardMann, MPH; Gordon Lynch; Beverly Sheppard; Lauren Bauer, MPH; Chris Phillips, MD, MPH; William Lee; Jennifer Walstrom; Daniel Trone, PhD; Anna Rivera, MPH; Denise Lovec-Jenkins; Ben Porter, PhD; Anet Petrosyan; Rudolph Rull, PhD; Anna Bukowinski, MPH; Teresa Powell, MS; Danielle Mitchell, MPH; Evelyn Sun, MPH; Jacqueline Pflieger, PhD; Deborah Bookwalter, ScD; Richard Armenta, PhD; Toni Geronimo, MPH; Claire Kolaja, MPH; Kyna Long, MS; Isabel Jacobson, MPH; Alejandro Esquivel; Rayna Matsuno, PhD; Dennis Faix, MD, MPH; Carlos Carballo, MA; Satbir Boparai, MBA; Kelly Woodall, MPH; Chiping Nieh, PhD. The authors also thank the professionals from the US Army Medical Research and Materiel Command, especially those from the Military Operational Medicine Research Program, Fort Detrick, Maryland, Scott L. Seggerman from the Management Information Division, Defense Manpower Data Center, and the Millennium Cohort Study participants.

Funding

The Millennium Cohort Study is funded through the Military Operational Medicine Research Program, United States Army Medical Research and Materiel Command (Fort Detrick, Maryland).

Disclaimer

Report No. 17–39 was supported by the Military Operational Medicine Research Program under work unit no. 60002. The views expressed in this article are those of the authors and do not necessarily reflect the official policy or position of the Department of the Navy, Department of the Army, Department of the Air Force, Department of Veterans Affairs, Department of Defense, or the U.S. Government. Approved for public release; distribution unlimited. Human subjects participated in this study after giving their free and informed consent. This research has been conducted in compliance with all applicable federal regulations governing the protection of human subjects in research (NHRC.2000.0007).

Authors' contributions

RFA helped conceptualize the manuscript, conducted the statistical analysis, drafted the manuscript, and completed final edits of the manuscript. TR helped conceptualize the manuscript, assisted with data analysis, and provided critical review of the manuscript. CAL, JM, and CWH provided subject matter expertise, and critically revised the manuscript. AC helped draft the manuscript and provided critical review of the manuscript. All authors read and approved the final manuscript.

Consent for publication
Not applicable

Competing interests
The authors declare that they have no competing interests.

Author details
[1]Deployment Health Research Department, Naval Health Research Center, 140 Sylvester Road, San Diego, CA 92106-3521, USA. [2]The Henry M. Jackson Foundation for the Advancement of Military Medicine, Inc, Bethesda, MD, USA. [3]Department of Family Medicine and Public Health, La Jolla, University of California, San Diego, School of Medicine, San Diego, CA, USA. [4]Directorate of Mental Health, Naval Medical Center San Diego, San Diego, CA, USA. [5]Walter Reed Army Institute of Research, Silver Spring, MD, USA.

References

1. Hoge CW, Castro CA, Messer SC, McGurk D, Cotting DI, Koffman RL. Combat duty in Iraq and Afghanistan, mental health problems, and barriers to care. N Engl J Med. 2004;351(1):13–22.
2. Kok BC, Herrell RK, Thomas JL, Hoge CW. Posttraumatic stress disorder associated with combat service in Iraq or Afghanistan: reconciling prevalence differences between studies. J Nerv Ment Dis. 2012;200(5):444–50.
3. Armed Forces Health Surveillance Center (AFHSC). Summary of mental disorder hospitalizations, active and reserve components, U.S. armed forces, 2000–2012. *MSMR*. 2013;20(7):4–11. discussion 10-11
4. Vasterling JJ, Aslan M, Proctor SP, Ko J, Marx BP, Jakupcak M, Schnurr PP, Gleason T, Huang GD, Concato J. Longitudinal examination of posttraumatic stress disorder as a long-term outcome of Iraq war deployment. Am J Epidemiol. 2016;184:796–805.
5. Doron-LaMarca S, Niles BL, King DW, King LA, Pless Kaiser A, Lyons MJ. Temporal associations among chronic PTSD symptoms in US combat veterans. J Trauma Stress. 2015;28(5):410–7.
6. Marmar CR, Schlenger W, Henn-Haase C, Qian M, Purchia E, Li M, Corry N, Williams CS, Ho C-L, Horesh D. Course of posttraumatic stress disorder 40 years after the Vietnam war: findings from the National Vietnam Veterans Longitudinal Study. JAMA Psychiatry. 2015;72(9):875–81.
7. O'Toole BI, Catts SV, Outram S, Pierse KR, Cockburn J. The physical and mental health of Australian Vietnam veterans 3 decades after the war and its relation to military service, combat, and post-traumatic stress disorder. Am J Epidemiol. 2009;170(3):318–30.
8. Heim C, Nemeroff CB. Neurobiology of posttraumatic stress disorder. CNS Spectr. 2009;14(1):13–24.
9. Asnaani A, Reddy MK, Shea MT. The impact of PTSD symptoms on physical and mental health functioning in returning veterans. J Anxiety Disord. 2014; 28(3):310–7.
10. Goldberg J, Magruder KM, Forsberg CW, Kazis LE, Üstün TB, Friedman MJ, Litz BT, Vaccarino V, Heagerty PJ, Gleason TC. The association of PTSD with physical and mental health functioning and disability (VA cooperative study# 569: the course and consequences of posttraumatic stress disorder in Vietnam-era veteran twins). Qual Life Res. 2014;23(5):1579–91.
11. Sherin JE, Nemeroff CB. Post-traumatic stress disorder: the neurobiological impact of psychological trauma. Dialogues Clin Neurosci. 2011;13(3):263–78.
12. McFarlane AC. The long-term costs of traumatic stress: intertwined physical and psychological consequences. World Psychiatry. 2010;9(1):3–10.
13. Hoge CW, Terhakopian A, Castro CA, Messer SC, Engel CC. Association of posttraumatic stress disorder with somatic symptoms, health care visits, and absenteeism among Iraq war veterans. Am J Psychiatry. 2007;164(1):150–3.
14. Pacella ML, Hruska B, Delahanty DL. The physical health consequences of PTSD and PTSD symptoms: a meta-analytic review. J Anxiety Disord. 2013; 27(1):33–46.
15. Beristianos MH, Yaffe K, Cohen B, Byers AL. PTSD and risk of incident cardiovascular disease in aging veterans. Am J Geriatr Psychiatry. 2016;24(3):192–200.
16. LeardMann CA, Woodall KA, Littman AJ, Jacobson IG, Boyko EJ, Smith B, Wells TS, Crum-Cianflone NF. Post-traumatic stress disorder predicts future weight change in the millennium cohort study. Obesity. 2015;23(4):886–92.
17. Gupta MA. Review of somatic symptoms in post-traumatic stress disorder. Int Rev Psychiatry. 2013;25(1):86–99.
18. Santiago PN, Wilk JE, Milliken CS, Castro CA, Engel CC, Hoge CW. Screening for alcohol misuse and alcohol-related behaviors among combat veterans. Psychiatr Serv. 2010;61(6):575–81.
19. Oquendo MA, Friend JM, Halberstam B, Brodsky BS, Burke AK, Grunebaum MF, Malone KM, Mann JJ. Association of comorbid posttraumatic stress disorder and major depression with greater risk for suicidal behavior. Am J Psychiat. 2003;160(3):580–2.
20. Allen ES, Rhoades GK, Stanley SM, Markman HJ. Hitting home: relationships between recent deployment, posttraumatic stress symptoms, and marital functioning for Army couples. J Fam Psychol. 2010;24(3):280–8.
21. Lim D, Sanderson K, Andrews G. Lost productivity among full-time workers with mental disorders. J Ment Health Policy Econ. 2000;3(3):139–46.
22. McEwen BS. Central effects of stress hormones in health and disease: understanding the protective and damaging effects of stress and stress mediators. Eur J Pharmacol. 2008;583(2–3):174–85.
23. Green BL, Grace MC, Lindy JD, Gleser GC, Leonard A. Risk factors for PTSD and other diagnoses in a general sample of Vietnam veterans. Am J Psychiatry. 1990;147(6):729–33.
24. Koenen KC, Stellman JM, Stellman SD, Sommer JF Jr. Risk factors for course of posttraumatic stress disorder among Vietnam veterans: a 14-year follow-up of American legionnaires. J Consult Clin Psychol. 2003;71(6):980–6.
25. Roy-Byrne P, Arguelles L, Vitek ME, Goldberg J, Keane TM, True WR, Pitman RK. Persistence and change of PTSD symptomatology–a longitudinal co-twin control analysis of the Vietnam era twin registry. Soc Psychiatry Psychiatr Epidemiol. 2004;39(9):681–5.
26. Jankowski MK, Schnurr PP, Adams GA, Green BL, Ford JD, Friedman MJ. A mediational model of PTSD in world war II veterans exposed to mustard gas. J Trauma Stress. 2004;17(4):303–10.
27. Rona RJ, Jones M, Sundin J, Goodwin L, Hull L, Wessely S, Fear NT. Predicting persistent posttraumatic stress disorder (PTSD) in UK military personnel who served in Iraq: a longitudinal study. J Psychiatr Res. 2012; 46(9):1191–8.
28. Ryan MA, Smith TC, Smith B, Amoroso P, Boyko EJ, Gray GC, Gackstetter GD, Riddle JR, Wells TS, Gumbs G, et al. Millennium cohort: enrollment begins a 21-year contribution to understanding the impact of military service. J Clin Epidemiol. 2007;60(2):181–91.
29. Gray GC, Chesbrough KB, Ryan MA, Amoroso P, Boyko EJ, Gackstetter GD, Hooper TI, Riddle JR. The millennium cohort study: a 21-year prospective cohort study of 140,000 military personnel. Mil Med. 2002;167(6):483–8.
30. Weathers F, Litz B, Herman D, Huska JA, Keane T. The PTSD checklist (PCL): reliability, validity, and diagnostic utility. San Antonio: Paper presented at: Annual Meeting of International Society for Traumatic Stress Studies; 1993.
31. Terhakopian A, Sinaii N, Engel CC, Schnurr PP, Hoge CW. Estimating population prevalence of posttraumatic stress disorder: an example using the PTSD checklist. J Trauma Stress. 2008;21(3):290–300.
32. Hoge CW. Neuropsychiatric illnesses in war veterans. In: FA KDL, Hauser SL, Longo DL, Jameson JL, Loscaizo J, editors. Harrisons textbook of medicine. 19th ed. New York: McGraw Hill; 2015.
33. Kroenke K, Strine TW, Spitzer RL, Williams JB, Berry JT, Mokdad AH. The PHQ-8 as a measure of current depression in the general population. J Affect Disord. 2009;114(1–3):163–73.
34. Kazis LE, Lee A, Spiro Iii A, Rogers W. Measurement comparisons of the medical outcomes study and veterans SF-36® health survey. Health Care Financ Rev. 2004;25(4):43.
35. LeardMann CA, Smith TC, Smith B, Wells TS, Ryan MA. Baseline self reported functional health and vulnerability to post-traumatic stress disorder after combat deployment: prospective US military cohort study. BMJ. 2009;338: b1273.
36. Kroenke K, Spitzer RL, Williams JB. The PHQ-15: validity of a new measure for evaluating the severity of somatic symptoms. Psychosom Med. 2002; 64(2):258–66.
37. Jacobson IG, Ryan MA, Hooper TI, Smith TC, Amoroso PJ, Boyko EJ, Gackstetter GD, Wells TS, Bell NS. Alcohol use and alcohol-related problems before and after military combat deployment. JAMA. 2008;300(6):663–75.
38. Maldonado G, Greenland S. Simulation study of confounder-selection strategies. Am J Epidemiol. 1993;138(11):923–36.
39. Mickey RM, Greenland S. The impact of confounder selection criteria on effect estimation. Am J Epidemiol. 1989;129(1):125–37.
40. Skelly AC, Dettori JR, Brodt ED. Assessing bias: the importance of considering confounding. Evid Based Spine Care J. 2012;3(01):9–12.

41. Xue C, Ge Y, Tang B, Liu Y, Kang P, Wang M, Zhang L. A meta-analysis of risk factors for combat-related PTSD among military personnel and veterans. PLoS One. 2015;10(3):e0120270.
42. Prigerson HG, Maciejewski PK, Rosenheck RA. Combat trauma: trauma with highest risk of delayed onset and unresolved posttraumatic stress disorder symptoms, unemployment, and abuse among men. J Nerv Ment Dis. 2001; 189(2):99–108.
43. Larson GE, Highfill-McRoy RM, Booth-Kewley S. Psychiatric diagnoses in historic and contemporary military cohorts: combat deployment and the healthy warrior effect. Am J Epidemiol. 2008;167(11):1269–76.
44. Yehuda R, Hoge CW, McFarlane AC, Vermetten E, Lanius RA, Nievergelt CM, Hobfoll SE, Koenen KC, Neylan TC, Hyman SE. Post-traumatic stress disorder. Nat Rev Dis Primers. 2015;1:15057.
45. Gehrman P, Seelig AD, Jacobson IG, Boyko EJ, Hooper TI, Gackstetter GD, Ulmer CS, Smith TC. Predeployment sleep duration and insomnia symptoms as risk factors for new-onset mental health disorders following military deployment. In: DTIC Document; 2013.
46. Krystal JH, Pietrzak RH, Rosenheck RA, Cramer JA, Vessicchio J, Jones KM, Huang GD, Vertrees JE, Collins J, Krystal AD. Sleep disturbance in chronic military-related PTSD: clinical impact and response to adjunctive Risperidone in the veterans affairs cooperative study# 504. J Clin Psychiatry. 2016;77(4):483–91.
47. Han SC, Castro F, Lee LO, Charney ME, Marx BP, Brailey K, Proctor SP, Vasterling JJ. Military unit support, postdeployment social support, and PTSD symptoms among active duty and National Guard soldiers deployed to Iraq. J Anxiety Disord. 2014;28(5):446–53.
48. Creamer M, Carboon I, Forbes AB, McKenzie DP, McFarlane AC, Kelsall HL, Sim MR. Psychiatric disorder and separation from military service: a 10-year retrospective study. Am J Psychiat. 2006;163:733–4.
49. Schnurr PP, Lunney CA, Sengupta A, Waelde LC. A descriptive analysis of PTSD chronicity in Vietnam veterans. J Trauma Stress. 2003;16(6):545–53.
50. Millegan J, Milburn EK, LeardMann CA, Street AE, Williams D, Trone DW, Crum-Cianflone NF. Recent sexual trauma and adverse health and occupational outcomes among US Service women. J Trauma Stress. 2015; 28(4):298–306.
51. Millegan J, Wang L, LeardMann CA, Miletich D, Street AE. Sexual trauma and adverse health and occupational outcomes among men serving in the US military. J Trauma Stress. 2016;29:132–40.
52. Smith B, Wingard DL, Ryan MA, Macera CA, Patterson TL, Slymen DJ. U.S. military deployment during 2001-2006: comparison of subjective and objective data sources in a large prospective health study. Ann Epidemiol. 2007;17(12):976–82.
53. Wells TS, Jacobson IG, Smith TC, Spooner CN, Smith B, Reed RJ, Amoroso PJ, Ryan MA. Prior health care utilization as a potential determinant of enrollment in a 21-year prospective study, the millennium cohort study. Eur J Epidemiol. 2008;23(2):79–87.

Work-related adverse events leaving their mark: a cross-sectional study among Dutch gynecologists

Melanie A. M. Baas[1†], Karel W. F. Scheepstra[1,2†], Claire A. I. Stramrood[3], Ruth Evers[4], Lea M. Dijksman[5,6] and Maria G. van Pampus[1*]

Abstract

Background: Health care professionals who are frequently coping with traumatic events have an increased risk of developing a posttraumatic stress disorder. Research among physicians is scarce, and obstetrician-gynecologists may have a higher risk. Work-related traumatic events and posttraumatic stress disorder among obstetricians-gynecologists and the (desired) type of support were studied.

Methods: A questionnaire was emailed to all members of the Dutch Society of Obstetrics and Gynaecology, which included residents, attending, retired and non-practicing obstetricians-gynecologists. The questionnaire included questions about personal experiences and opinions concerning support after work-related events, and a validated questionnaire for posttraumatic stress disorder.

Results: The response rate was 42.8% with 683 questionnaires eligible for analysis. 12.6% of the respondents have experienced a work-related traumatic event, of which 11.8% met the criteria for current posttraumatic stress disorder. This revealed an estimated prevalence of 1.5% obstetricians-gynecologists with current posttraumatic stress disorder. 12% reported to have a support protocol or strategy in their hospital after adverse events. The most common strategies to cope with emotional events were: to seek support from colleagues, to seek support from family or friends, to discuss the case in a complication meeting or audit and to find distraction. 82% would prefer peer-support with direct colleagues after an adverse event.

Conclusions: This survey implies that work-related events can be traumatic and subsequently can lead to posttraumatic stress disorder. There is a high prevalence rate of current posttraumatic stress disorder among obstetricians-gynecologists. Often there is no standardized support after adverse events. Most obstetrician-gynecologists prefer peer-support with direct colleagues after an adverse event. More awareness must be created during medical training and organized support must be implemented.

Keywords: Adverse events, Second victim, Obstetrician-gynecologist, Psychotrauma, Posttraumatic stress disorder, PTSD

Background

Professionals frequently coping with traumatic events have an increased risk of developing a posttraumatic stress disorder (PTSD). Groups at risk include military personnel, rescue workers, police, firefighters, and ambulance personnel. Similarly, hospital physicians cope with events such as severe illness, life-threatening situations and death frequently [1, 2]. However, research about traumatic events and PTSD among hospital physicians is scarce, and as a result the effects of work-related traumatic events may be underestimated. Overall, mental health problems in health care professionals may jeopardize the safety and quality of health care provided, with decreased productivity [3], high collateral costs [4], and medical errors [5–7]. Fortunately, the importance of physicians own mental health to foster optimal patient care is emphasized as a new competency in the

* Correspondence: m.g.vanpampus@olvg.nl
†Equal contributors
1Department of Obstetrics and Gynecology, OLVG, PO box 95500, 1090 HM Amsterdam, The Netherlands
Full list of author information is available at the end of the article

CanMEDS framework [8]. The widely used CanMEDS framework was developed to define the necessary competencies for physicians. It provides a comprehensive foundation for medical education and practice for many (future) physicians in a dozen countries.. Obstetrician-Gynecologists (ObGyns) may be at increased risk of experiencing traumatic events since pregnancy and childbirth are expected to be joyful times, but can include severe complications, including stillbirth or maternal death with high emotional impact on the physician, midwife or nurse [9–13].

Posttraumatic stress disorder

Whereas many types of work-related events can be marked as adverse, not all adverse events are traumatic. A traumatic event according to DSM-IV (Diagnostic and Statistical Manual of Mental Disorders) [14] is to experience or directly witness actual or threatened death, serious injury or a threat to the physical integrity of themselves or others. Furthermore, it was obligatory that the response involved intense fear, helplessness or horror. In the recently published fifth version of the DSM [15] this last criterion is removed, since it proved to have no utility in predicting the onset of PTSD. In particular, professionals did not always have these emotions at time of the event, while they did develop PTSD symptoms [16]. Furthermore, in the DSM-5, criterion A4 is added, specifically concerning professionals who have never been in direct danger, but can learn about consequences of traumatic events as part of their job [16].

Not all who experience a traumatic event develop PTSD: 80% of the general Dutch population will experience at least one traumatic event during their life, with a lifetime prevalence rate of PTSD being 7.4% [17]. A traumatic event can lead to a period of posttraumatic stress symptoms with intrusions, avoidance, negative cognitions and mood, and hyperarousal, but often these symptoms decline. When these symptoms last for at least one month, and lead to significant impairment in social, occupational or other important areas of functioning, PTSD can be diagnosed [15]. Risk factors for developing PTSD after experiencing a traumatic event include female gender, poor social support, prior trauma exposure, prior mental disorder and continuing stressors [18].

Second victims

In 2000, the term second victim was introduced to address the impact of work-related adverse events on health care professionals [19]. Second victims can be defined as *"healthcare providers who are involved in an unanticipated adverse patient event, in a medical error and/or a patient related injury and become victimized in the sense that the provider is traumatized by the event"* [20]. The reported prevalence of second victims among health care providers varies from 10.4 to 46% [21–24]. The second victim can have continued emotional distress, leading to a posttraumatic stress disorder.

Studies about traumatic events and PTSD among health care professionals in general have low response rates and show a widely varying prevalence of PTSD or PTS-symptoms [1]. Studies among midwives, labor ward nurses and obstetricians reported a prevalence of moderate to severe work-related PTS-symptoms of 26–36%, with the most frequently reported traumatic events being fetal demise/neonatal death, shoulder dystocia (obstetric emergency during vaginal delivery that requires additional obstetric manoeuvres to deliver the fetus after the head has been born. It is associated with perinatal morbidity and mortality), and infant rescusitation [25–27].

Support and coping after adverse events

It is unknown how many Dutch hospitals have implemented support strategies for health care professionals, but the absence of these strategies in many high risk specialties, such as anesthesiology is experienced as a common problem [28]. In addition, there is a low likelihood of a physician asking for help, due to perceived barriers (doubts about confidentiality, fear of negative impact on career, stigma [29], a low awareness of support options and time constraints [30].

More is known about the coping strategies of health care professionals after adverse events. The five most common coping mechanisms among American obstetricians are: asking support from a colleague, asking support from family or friends, exercising or performing hobbies, writing a formal case report or undertaking religious activities [10]. Other research supports this finding that physicians mainly wish for peer-support from colleagues after adverse events [30].

Aim of the study

The aim of this study was to study the prevalence of work-related traumatic events (according to the DSM-IV A-criterion for posttraumatic stress disorder) among ObGyns, and to describe the prevalence of PTSD among ObGyns. Furthermore, we explored the current coping and professional support after work-related adverse events and the desired type of support. It was hypothesized that work-related events could be traumatic and lead to PTSD among ObGyns and current coping and support would be considered insufficient.

Methods

Population and procedure

The current study used the membership database of the Dutch Society of Obstetrics & Gynecology (NVOG). Permission to access and use this non-public database was granted by the NVOG. This database includes all resident and attending ObGyns in the Netherlands, as well as retired and non-practicing ObGyns. Of the 1596 members, 1578 members with a registered email address were included, which equals 98.9% of the NVOG population. Since the database did not differentiate between retired and non-practicing ObGyns, we considered all non-working ObGyns younger than 60 years into ObGyns with other jobs, and non-working ObGyns older than 60 years as retired. The link to the questionnaire was sent by email using an anonymous (non-traceable) link. All physicians received an invitation to participate in March 2014 by email, and two reminders during a 7.5 week period. The survey was piloted among a small group of resident and attending ObGyns for face validity, after which no substantial changes were made.

Measurements

The survey consisted of 32 questions, starting with demographics (5 questions), personal experiences about work-related adverse events, coping and support provided (12 questions), desired support (2 questions) and one statement question. Lastly, when a work-related traumatic event was experienced during their career (PTSD-criterion A according to DSM-IV, 2 questions), at least once and more than four weeks ago, they also completed the Trauma Screening Questionnaire (TSQ) [31]. The TSQ is a validated 10-item screening instrument corresponding to a provisional diagnosis of PTSD according to the DSM-IV [14]. The Dutch psychometric properties are validated with Cronbach's alphas from 0.71 to 0.91. A cut-off value of 6 or higher was used [32]. The original Dutch questionnaire and the English translation are included as Additional files 1 and 2 to this manuscript. The survey was part of a larger questionnaire among ObGyns about mental health after work-related adverse events.

Statistical analysis

Descriptive and statistical analyses were performed with SPSS 18.0 for Windows. For the 4-point Likert scale questions, median scores for central tendency, interquartile range (IQR, 25–75%) and frequencies for distribution were calculated. Independents t-tests (for continuous variables) or Fisher's exact tests (for categorical variables) were used to compare subgroups. All variables are reported with numbers (%) or mean ± standard deviation. A p-value of less than .05 was considered statistically significant. Open answers were independently categorized by two authors (KS and MB), and subsequently analyzed by two independent assessors(KS, MS). Any disagreement was discussed until consensus was achieved. The overall interrater reliability was moderate, with Cohen's kappa's of 0.44 or higher [33].

Results

Respondent and population characteristics

Table 1 shows the characteristics of the respondents ($n = 683$) and reference population. The sample was found to be a good representation of the NVOG members, as the response rates in the subgroups (age, gender, level of training) corresponded to the overall NVOG population. Of all the residents ($n = 394$), 184 (47.8%) responded, so the highest response rate was among residents, followed by attending ObGyns (45.7%). Retired and non-practicing ObGyns had a response rate of 25.3%. The majority of the respondents were female (65.3%), with a varying distribution among the subgroups. The percentages varied from 85% female residents to 14% female among retired ObGyns. This distribution corresponded to the tendency of having an increasing amount of young female medical doctors in the Netherlands. Work experience in obstetrics and gynecology ranged from 0.5 to 46.0 years. The respondent demographics are shown in Table 2.

Posttraumatic stress disorder

The outcomes of the TSQ are shown in Table 3. 86 (12.6%) of the respondents reported having experienced at least one traumatic event during their work as an ObGyn and thereby met DSM-IV criterion A. One of them did not continue answering the TSQ, leading to 85 respondents completing the TSQ. 10 (11.8%) subjects screened positive for a current PTSD diagnosis. This equaled a prevalence of 1.5% among all ObGyns, and 1.4% among the ObGyns that are currently practicing (residents and attending). Among the remaining 75 ObGyns without current PTSD who did experience a traumatic event, 60.0% reported having experienced multiple work related PTS-symptoms earlier in their career. The sample size was not large enough to perform subgroup analysis on PTSD or PTS-symptoms earlier in life. The most commonly reported adverse events were neonatal death, maternal death, severe neonatal and maternal complications, patient aggression or violence towards healthcare professionals, medical errors and interpersonal conflicts with colleagues. Twenty-one respondents mentioned they did not wish to describe the traumatic event because of fear of loss of anonymity, three were not applicable (did not describe an event).

Work-related emotional stressors

Of all ObGyns, 230 (33.7%) have at some point considered leaving their medical profession. The most common reasons were a high workload, varying shifts, high responsibility, work/life imbalance, conflicts with colleagues, new interests and work culture related problems. 21.1% reported having faced a complaint at the disciplinary board, and this percentage increased with

Table 1 Demographic characteristics of respondents and NVOG population

Variable	Respondents $N = 683$	NVOG population $N = 1596$
ObGyn		
Resident	184 (26.9)	394 (24.7)
Attending	442 (64.7)	975 (61.1)
Non-practicing	21 (3.1)	18 (1.1)[a]
Retired	36 (5.3)	209 (13.1)[a]
Gender		
Male	237 (34.7)	663 (41.5)
Female	446 (65.3)	933 (58.5)
Age		
25–34	155 (22.7)	329 (21.2)
35–44	211 (30.9)	433 (27.9)
45–54	152 (22.3)	339 (21.8)
55–64	115 (16.8)	258 (16.6)
65 and older	50 (7.3)	194 (12.5)
Years in practice		
Mean ± SD	17.4 ± 10.7	Unknown
Range	0.5–46	Unknown
Complaints at disciplinary board	144 (21.1)	Unknown

All variables are in number (%), or mean ± standard deviation
NVOG Dutch Society of Obstetrics & Gynecology, *ObGyns* Obstetrician-gynecologists
[a]Calculated numbers. The NVOG did not differentiate between retired and not-practicing ObGyns. We counted ObGyns younger than 60 years as non-practicing, older than 60 years as retired

years in practice: 1.6% of the residents, 26.7% of the attending, 38.1% of the non-practicing and 41.7% of the retired ObGyns (Table 2). The group that had considered leaving the profession had a significantly higher PTSD prevalence rate (0.7% vs 3.0%, $p = 0.01$).

Respondents experienced the following events as high emotional impact stressors: missing a diagnosis (64.3%), doubting a medical decision (44.5%), life-threatening moments (43.2%), death of a patient (37.6%), feeling they could not help the patient (24.3%), bad news conversations (16.1%) (Fig. 1). Other stressors reported (23.1%) included severe complications, conflicts with colleague, patient and disciplinary board complaints, discontented patients and patient aggression or violence.

Table 2 Demographic variables per subgroup

	Total ($n = 683$)	Resident ($n = 184$)	Attending ($n = 442$)	Non-practicing ($n = 21$)	Retired ($n = 36$)
Gender					
Male	237 (34.7)	27 (14.7)	165 (37.3)	14 (66.7)	31 (86.1)
Female	446 (65.3)	157 (85.3)	277 (62.7)	7 (33.3)	5 (13.9)
Age					
25–34	155 (22.7)	146 (79.3)	9 (2.0)	0	0
35–44	211 (30.9)	38 (20.7)	169 (38.2)	1 (4.8)	3 (8.3)
45–54	152 (22.3)	0	149 (33.7)	3 (14.3)	0
55–64	115 (16.8)	0	107 (24.2)	6 (28.6)	2 (5.6)
65 and older	50 (7.3)	0	8 (1.8)	11 (52.4)	31 (86.1)
Years in practice					
Mean ± SD	17.4 ± 10.7	5.3 ± 2.4	20.6 ± 8.3	29.5 ± 9.3	32.4 ± 7.9
Complaints at the disciplinary board	144 (21.1)	3 (1.6)	118 (26.7)	8 (38.1)	15 (41.7)

All variables are in number (%), or mean ± standard deviation

Table 3 Posttraumatic stress disorder measurements

	Total (*n* = 683)	Practicing (*n* = 626)		Not practicing (*n* = 57)	
		Resident (*n* = 184)	Attending (*n* = 442)	Other job (*n* = 21)	Retired (*n* = 36)
PTSD					
DSM-IV criterion A (%)	86 (12.6)	14 (7.6)	67 (15.2)	3 (14.3)	3 (8.3)
Above cut-off[a] (%)	10 (1.5)	1 (7.1)	8 (12.1)	0 (0.0)	1 (33.3)

All variables are in number (%) of mean ± standard deviation
DSM-IV Diagnostic and Statistical Manual of Mental Disorders, *PTSD* Posttraumatic Stress Disorder, *TSQ* Trauma Screening Questionnaire
[a]Measured with a a TSQ cut-off value of 6 or higher. TSQ was completed by *n* = 85

Coping

The most commonly used coping strategies after emotional events (Fig. 2) were gaining support from colleagues (87.4%), gaining support from family or friends (72.2%), discussing the case in a complication meeting or audit (42.6%), finding distraction (33.8%) and practicing sports or other hobbies (26.4%). Among the respondents, 5.1% increased their use of alcohol, drugs and/or nicotine and 1.5% used medication they normally would not use. Furthermore, 0.6% gave up practicing as an ObGyn as a result of emotional stressors. When asked where they learned their coping strategies, 53% reported never having formally learned, 22.5% during a peer support group, 10.5% during specialist training, 4.8% during medical school, 4.8% during additional specialist courses and 33.8% learned through other ways. With the statement that there is room to express emotions on the ward or within their department after experiencing an emotional event, 80.8% agreed. Not many ObGyns (4.8%) agreed with the statement that having sleepless nights due to an adverse event means that you are not made to be an ObGyn. One in two ObGyns (55.2%) of the respondents have become more defensive in their decision making and 24.4% changed their work habits as a result of adverse events (e.g. no longer doing nightshifts, not performing surgery alone or no longer performing vaginal breech deliveries).

Current and desired support

Of all ObGyns, 410 (60.0%) thought the current support services after adverse events are insufficient. Of these 410 respondents, 255 (62.3%) reported that their department or hospital has no support protocol or strategy, 105 (25.7%) were not aware whether there is a protocol and 49 (12.0%) do have a protocol. When asked about preferences for support after an adverse event, most ObGyns (82.0%) would prefer peer support from direct colleagues. 29.9% would like support from a professional (psychologist or counsellor), 22.3% would prefer peer support from indirect colleagues (non-ObGyn physicians) and 10% would like to have a buddy appointed. 86.1% stated that the culture concerning the support after adverse events should change.

Discussion

In this large-scale study with a good response rate, our work-related PTSD prevalence among ObGyns (1.5%) is comparable to the general prevalence rate of current PTSD in the Netherlands (1.3%) [17]. However, this common prevalence is mostly not work-related, and with this in mind we conclude the work-related prevalence of PTSD among ObGyns is high compared to the general Dutch population. On the other hand, our estimated prevalence rate is low compared to other studies on prevalence rates of posttraumatic stress among health care professional in general (10.4–43.3%) [7, 21–24] and

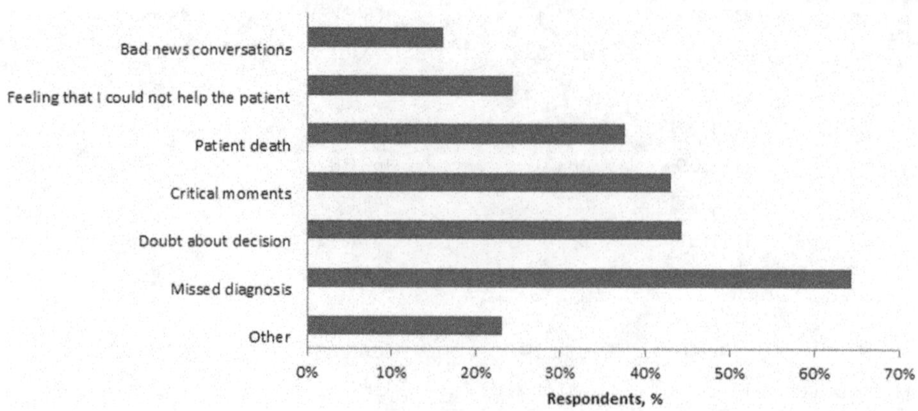

Fig. 1 Events with high emotional impact

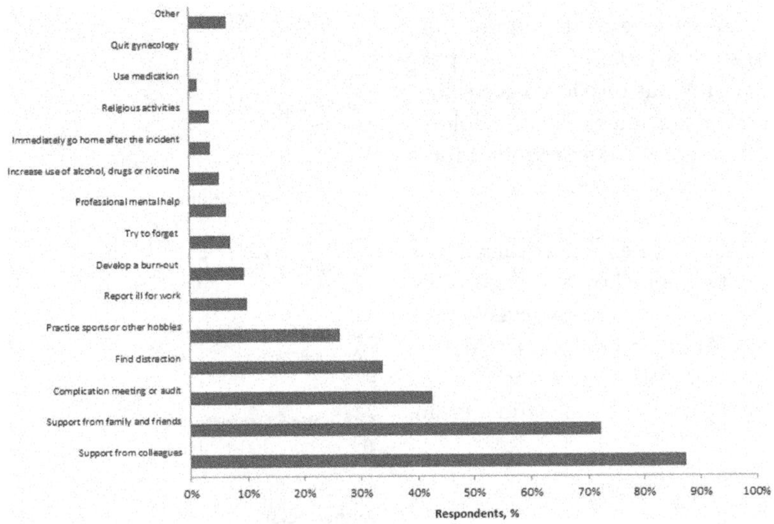

Fig. 2 Coping strategies

labor and delivery ward personnel (32–36%) [25–27]. However, a variety in definitions, questionnaires, stressor criterions, countries and professions is making comparison of results difficult. For instance, only one research group tried to determine a presumptive diagnosis of PTSD instead of posttraumatic stress in general, by applying the DSM-IV symptomcluster criteria to the Secondary Traumatic Stress Scale [25, 27]. It is needless to say that ObGyns who did not meet full criteria for PTSD may still have significant impairment, and it is important to look beyond a DSM-diagnosis.

Among the ObGyns without current PTSD who did experience a traumatic event, 59.2% report having experienced multiple work-related PTS-symptoms earlier in their career. Unfortunately, due to the retrospective aspect of this study, we cannot differentiate between physiological adaption, an Acute Stress Disorder or previous PTSD. Nonetheless, we conclude that psychological distress after a work-related adverse event is common.

While the CanMEDS framework is used during medical training in the Netherlands, the current study implies that coping and support are not learned during specialist training. Of the Dutch ObGyns, 60% think that the current support strategies are insufficient and only 12% reports that support services are available in their hospital/department. This corresponds to recent studies in which the institutional support for hospital-based physicians or nurses is considered low, and most support was to be expected from colleagues, family and friends [34–37]. With strong social support being an important protective factor for PTSD and gathering social support being a common coping mechanism in our sample, the role of educating health care professionals to support their colleagues after adverse events is crucial.

As a consequence of adverse events, ObGyns may become more defensive, adjust their work conditions and consider quitting their profession. One third of all Dutch ObGyns considered giving up gynecological practice, which is higher than findings from prior research (1 in 10) [10]. However, in the present study the questions about considering giving up practicing did not differentiate between this being due to experiencing adverse events or because of other reasons. The results of this current study confirmed self-medication with (increased use of) drugs, nicotine and/or medication after experiencing an adverse event [23, 38] as a coping style used by some physicians after experiencing an adverse work-related event.

In accordance with prior research,[30] situations described as high emotional impact are not necessarily the most extreme cases. Some physicians experience (multiple) minor complications as traumatic, whereas others experience disciplinary complaints or conflicts with colleagues as more stressful. We consider work conflicts and patient aggression or violence as work-related adverse events as well. These may concern all health care professionals and we therefore emphasize some form of support or guidance after such events as well.

Strengths and limitations

One of the strengths of this study includes the large sample size ($n = 683$), as well as a high response rate of 42.8%. Although a recent study among Danish obstetricians and midwives about feelings and concerns after traumatic childbirth reached an even high response rate (59%) [39], our response rate is considerably higher than some previous studies (5–16%) [25–27]. There are also several limitations to this study. Since avoidance is inherent to PTSD and may lead to non-response, the PTSD-prevalence of 1.5% may be an underestimation. Due to the anonymous design of the study, a non-responder analysis was not possible. Secondly, PTSD criterion A was measured according to DSM-IV, in which experiencing intense fear, helplessness or horror right after the event was still required for a PTSD-diagnosis. In the DSM-5 this criterion has been removed, which is of particular interest since during work-related traumatic events there is often 'the professional kicking in,' and emotions are postponed or neglected. This could have led to underdiagnosing traumatic events and thereby work-related PTSD. Another limitation is that a clinical interview is necessary for diagnosing PTSD, and therefore the prevalence rate in our study is an estimated prevalence.

Implications and recommendations

For future research, we would advise to include questions about the time that has passed since the traumatic event, and to include possible confounders for developing PTSD after experiencing a traumatic event [40], which could help identifying and supporting high-risk individuals. If possible, a longitudinal design would be of great interest.

We suggest that all hospitals increase awareness among residents and attending physicians, and standardized support after adverse events should be implemented. Also, education on coping strategies should be expanded in medical training, to optimize peer support by colleagues.

Lastly, we suggest further evaluation of the most effective support methods and the effect on quality and safety of health care. We stimulate exploration of this topic among other medical specialties as well, since adverse events concern most health care professionals.

Conclusion

This is the first large-scale study about work-related adverse events, coping, support and PTSD among Dutch ObGyns. Findings imply that there is a substantial group of ObGyns who experienced at least one work-related traumatic event (according to the DSM-IV criteria for PTSD), and that this can lead to work-related PTSD. As hypothesized, it was found that respondents consider the support after adverse events to be insufficient, and coping is not learned during medical and specialist training. There is potential for a change of culture, and creating a professional peer support system.

Abbreviations

DSM: Diagnostic and Statistical Manual of Mental Disorders; NVOG: Dutch Society of Obstetrics & Gynecology; ObGyns: Obstetrician-gynecologists; PTS: Post-Traumatic stress; PTSD: Post-Traumatic stress disorder; TSQ: Trauma screening questionnaire

Acknowledgements

We would like to thank the Dutch Association of Obstetrics and Gynecology (NVOG) and its members for their cooperation.

Funding

Not applicable.

Authors' contributions

MB, MvP, RE and CS designed the study. KS and MB collected and analyzed the data with support of LD. MB and KS drafted the manuscript and have contributed equally. All authors contributed to and approved the final manuscript.

Consent for publication

Not applicable.

Competing interests

The authors declare that they have no competing interests.

Author details

[1]Department of Obstetrics and Gynecology, OLVG, PO box 95500, 1090 HM Amsterdam, The Netherlands. [2]Department of Psychiatry, Academic Medical Center, PO Box 22660, 1100 DD Amsterdam, The Netherlands. [3]Department of Obstetrics and Gynecology, University Medical Center Utrecht, PO Box 85500, 3508GA Utrecht, The Netherlands. [4]Talmor, Andreas Bonnstraat 20hs, 1091AZ Amsterdam, The Netherlands. [5]Department of Research and Epidemiology, OLVG, PO box 95500, 1090 HM Amsterdam, The Netherlands. [6]Department of Research and Epidemiology, St. Antoniusziekenhuis, PO Box 2500, 3430EM Nieuwegein, The Netherlands.

References

1. Robertson N, Perry A. Institutionally based health care workers ' exposure to Traumatogenic events : systematic review of PTSD presentation. J Trauma Stress. 2010;23(3):417–20.
2. Coby J, Boer D, Lok A, Van E, Duivenvoorden HJ, Bakker AB, et al. Social science & medicine work-related critical incidents in hospital-based health care providers and the risk of post-traumatic stress symptoms, anxiety, and depression : a meta-analysis. Soc Sci Med. 2011;73(2):316–26. https://doi.org/10.1016/j.socscimed.2011.05.009.
3. Dewa CS, Loong D, Bonato S, Thanh NXJP. How does burnout affect physician productivity? A systematic literature review. BMC Health Serv Res. 2014;14:325.
4. Dewa CS, Jacobs P, Thanh NXLD. An estimate of the cost of burnout on early retirement and reduction in clinical hours of practicing physicians in Canada. BMC Health Serv Res. 2014;14:254.
5. Shanafelt TD, Bradley KA, Wipf JE, Back AL. Burnout and self-reported patient care in an internal medicine residency program. Ann Intern Med. 2002;136(5):358–67.
6. Wagner C, Zegers M, de Bruijne M. Onbedoelde en potentieel vermijdbare schade bij snijdende specialismen. [Unintended and potential preventable damage in surgical specialties]. Ned Tijdschr Geneeskd. 2009;153:B62.
7. Ruitenburg MM, Frings-dresen MHW, Sluiter JK. The prevalence of common mental disorders among hospital physicians and their association with self-reported work ability : a cross-sectional study. BMC Health Serv Res. 2012; 12(1):1. Available from: BMC Health Services Research
8. Frank J. The CanMEDS 2005 physician competency framework. Better standards Better physicians Better care 2005;
9. Rice H, Warland J. Bearing witness: midwives experiences of witnessing traumatic birth. Midwifery. 2013;29(9):1056–63.
10. Gold KJ, Kuznia AL, Hayward RA. How physicians cope with stillbirth or neonatal death: a national survey of obstetricians. Obstet Gynecol. 2008; 112(1):29–34.
11. Nuzum D, Meaney S. The impact of stillbirth on consultant obstetrician gynaecologists: a qualitative study. BJOG. 2014;121:1020–8.
12. Cauldwell M, Chappel L, Murtagh G, Bewley S. Learning about maternal death and grief in the profession: a pilot qualitative study. Acta Obstet Gynecol Scand. 2015;94:1346–53.

13. Leinweber J, Mph Å, Rowe HJ. The costs of " being with the woman ": secondary traumatic stress in midwifery. Midwifery [Internet]. 2010;26(1):76–87. https://doi.org/10.1016/j.midw.2008.04.003.
14. American Psychiatric Association. Diagnostic and statistical manual of mental disorders (fourth edition). Washington, DC: American Psychiatric Association; 1994.
15. American Psychiatric Association. Diagnostic and statistical manual of mental disorders (fifth edition). Washington, DC: American Psychiatric Association; 2013.
16. Friedman MJ, Resick PA, Bryant RA, Brewin C. Considering PTSD for DSM-5. Depress Anxiety. 2011;28:750–69.
17. de Vries GJ, Olff M. The lifetime prevalence of traumatic events and posttraumatic stress disorder in the Netherlands. J Trauma Stress. 2009; 22:259–67.
18. Olff M. De posttraumatische stressstoornis. Ned Tijdschr Geneeskd. 2013; 157(26):A5818.
19. Wu A. Medical Error: the second victim. BMJ. 2000;320:726–7.
20. Scott SD, Hirschinger LE, Cox KR, Mccoig M, Brandt J, Hall LW. The natural history of recovery for the healthcare provider "second victim" after adverse patient events. Qual Saf Heal Care. 2009;18(5):326
21. Scott SD, Hirschinger LE, Cox KR, McCoig M, Hahn-Cover K, Epperly KM, Philips ECHL. Caring for our own: deploying a systemwide second victim rapid response team. Jt Comm J Qual Patient Saf. 2010;36(5):233–40.
22. Lander LI, Connor JA, Shah RK, Kentala E, Healy GBRD. Otolaryngologists' responses to errors and adverse events. Laryngoscope. 2006;116(7):1114–20.
23. Seys D, Wu AW, Gerven E Van, Vleugels A, Panella M, Scott SD, et al. Evaluation & the Health Professions after Adverse Events: A Systematic Review. Eval Heal Prof. 2013:36(2):135–62.
24. Wolf ZR, Serembus JF, Smetzer J, Cohen HCM. Responses and concerns of healthcare providers to medication errors. Clin Nurse Spec. 2000;14(6):278–87.
25. Beck CT, Logiudice J, Gable RK. A Mixed-Methods Study Of Secondary Traumatic Stress In Certified Nurse-Midwives : Shaken Belief In The Birth Process. 2015.
26. Sheen K, Spiby H, Slade P. International journal of nursing studies exposure to traumatic perinatal experiences and posttraumatic stress symptoms in midwives: prevalence and association with burnout. Int J Nurs Stud. 2015; 52(2):578–87. https://doi.org/10.1016/j.ijnurstu.2014.11.006.
27. Beck CT, Gable RK. A mixed methods study of secondary traumatic stress in labor and delivery nurses. JOGNN. 2012;747–60.
28. Boyle D, O'Connell D, Platt FWAR. Disclosing errors and adverse events in the intensive care unit. Crit Care Med. 34(5):1532–7.
29. Van Gerven E, Van der Elst T, Vandenbroeck S, Dierickx S, Euwema M, Sermeus W, et al. Increased risk of burnout for physicians and nurses involved in a patient safety incident. Med Care. 2016;54(10):937–43.
30. Hu Y, Fix M, Hevelone N, Lipsitz S, Greenberg C, Weissman J, et al. Physicians' needs in coping with emotional stressors: the case for peer support. Arch Surg. 2012;147(3):212–7.
31. Brewin C, Rose S, Andrews B, Green J, PT P, McEvedy C, et al. Brief screening instrument for post-traumatic stress disorder. Br J Psychiatry. 2002;181:158–62.
32. Dekkers A, Olff M, Naring G. Identifying persons at risk for PTSD after trauma with TSQ in the Netherlands. Communit Ment Heal J. 2010;46(1):20–5.
33. Landis J, Koch G. Measurement of observer agreement for categorical data. Biometrics. 1977;33:159–74.
34. Joesten L, Cipparrone N, Okuno-Jones S, Dubose ER. Assessing the perceived Level of Institutional Support for the Second Victim after a PAtient Safety EVent. J Patient Saf. 2015;11(2):73–8.
35. Mira JJ, Lorenzo S, Carrillo I, Ferrús L, Pérez-Pérez P, Iglesias F, et al. Interventions in health organisations to reduce the impact of adverse events in second and third victims. BMC Health Serv Res. 2015;15(1):341.
36. Ullström S, Andreen Sachs M, Hansson J, Ovretveit J, Brommels M. Suffering in silence: a qualitative study of second victims of adverse events. BMJ Qual Saf. 2014;23(4):325–31.
37. Waterman A, Garbutt J, Hazel E, Dunagan W, Levinson W, Fraser V, et al. The emotional impact of medical errors on practicing physicians in the United States and Canada. Jt Comm J Qual Patient Saf. 2007;33(8):467–76.
38. van Gerven E, Deweer D, Scott S, Panella M, Euwema M, Sermeus W, et al. Personal, situational and organizational aspects that influence the impact of patient safety incidents: a qualitative study. Rev Calid Asist. 2016;31:34-46.
39. Schrøder K, Jørgensen JANS, Lamont RF, Hvidt NC. Blame and guilt – a mixed methods study of obstetricians ' and midwives ' experiences and existential considerations after involvement in traumatic childbirth. Acta Obstet Gynecol Scand. 2016;95(7):735–45.
40. Skogstad M, Skorstad M, Lie A, Conradi HS, Heir T, Weisæth L. Work-related post-traumatic stress disorder. Occup Med. 2013;63(3):175–82.

Trauma exposure and the mediating role of posttraumatic stress on somatic symptoms in civilian war victims

Naser Morina[1*], Ulrich Schnyder[1], Richard Klaghofer[1], Julia Müller[2,3] and Chantal Martin-Soelch[4]

Abstract

Background: It has been well documented that the exposure to war has a negative effect on the psychological health of civilian. However, little is known on the impact of war exposure on the physical health of the civilian population. In addition, the link between trauma exposure and somatic symptoms remain poorly understood. This cross-sectional study examined levels of somatic symptoms in the aftermath of war, and the mediating role of posttraumatic stress symptoms in the relationship between trauma exposure and somatic symptoms.

Methods: Civilian war survivors ($N = 142$) from Kosovo were assessed for potentially traumatic events, posttraumatic stress symptoms, and somatic symptoms. Data were analyzed using mediation analyses. Posttraumatic stress disorder (PTSD) symptoms were categorized based on King's four factor model (Psychol Assessment. 10: 90-96, 1998).

Results: Participants reported on average more than 5 types of traumatic exposure. The cut-off indicative for PTSD was exceeded by 26.1% of participants. Symptom levels of PTSD were associated with somatic symptoms. The relationship between trauma exposure and somatic symptoms was partly mediated by the active avoidance and hyperarousal symptom clusters of PTSD.

Conclusion: Active avoidance and hyperarousal symptoms seem to play a key role in traumatized people suffering from somatic symptoms.

Keywords: Trauma, PTSD symptom cluster, Active avoidance, Numbing, Hyperarousal, Somatic symptoms, Civilian, War, Victims

Background

Civilian populations exposed to trauma, such as military persecution and war, often suffer from a variety of psychological complaints including anxiety, depression, and posttraumatic stress symptoms. For instance, prevalence rates of 48% and 42% for mood and anxiety disorders, respectively, were found in Kosovar civilian adults having survived the war [1].

Somatization symptoms, i.e., somatic symptoms for which no or no sufficient organic causes are found, are frequently found to be related with posttraumatic stress disorder (PTSD), regardless of the traumatic event [2]. For example, in war veterans, combat stress reactions and PTSD were related to somatization symptoms, i.e. pain [3, 4]. Similar findings were found among a sample of factory accident survivors, where PTSD severity was positively correlated with somatization [5]. Disaster survivors suffering from PTSD reported more physical symptoms than those without PTSD [6], a finding that was also found 14 years after the genocide in Ruanda [7]. Another study found in a refugee population an association of somatization with PTSD severity [8]. Andreski et al. [9] found in their prospective study of PTSD and somatization, that PTSD increased the risk of developing somatization symptoms but that new PTSD cases were not elevated in people with a somatization disorder. Taken together, it seems that somehow PTSD may mediate the development of somatization following a traumatic event [10–12].

* Correspondence: naser.morina@usz.ch
[1]Department of Consultation-Liaison-Psychiatry and Psychosomatic Medicine, University Hospital, University of Zurich, Culmannstrasse 8, 8091 Zurich, Switzerland
Full list of author information is available at the end of the article

Various studies have examined the role of the different PTSD clusters on somatic symptoms. As such, studies have found that specific PTSD symptoms, e.g., hyperarousal may cause repeated muscle tension that could result in somatization complaints [13]. In other studies intrusive re-experiencing symptoms [6] and numbing [14] also predicted somatic symptoms in PTSD patients. There are various theoretical models to explain the association between posttraumatic stress and somatization health symptoms. For example, the shared vulnerability [15, 16] and mutual maintenance model [17], and a recent extension, the perpetual avoidance model [18], propose that individuals with PTSD and somatization symptoms have shared vulnerability to both conditions, or alternatively, that pain symptoms and posttraumatic stress symptoms interact with each other.

While there is a considerable amount of literature addressing survivors of combat, motor vehicle accidents and interpersonal trauma, war and postwar civilian populations have been less studied to date [19, 20]. To the best of our knowledge, no studies have examined war-traumatized civilians in terms of the differential relationship of each posttraumatic stress symptom cluster and somatic problems. This cross-sectional study aimed at investigating the relationship between trauma, posttraumatic stress symptoms and somatization symptoms in postwar civilians, i.e., Kosovar civilians more than a decade after the war. We hypothesized that despite the relatively long time lapse since the end of war, participants would suffer from clinically relevant symptoms of posttraumatic stress and somatization symptoms, and that specific PTSD symptom clusters would be associated with somatization symptoms.

Methods

Participants and procedure

The study was approved by the ethics committee of the Canton Zurich, Switzerland. Because no ethics committee was available in Kosovo, the study was approved by the Ministry of Education of Kosovo. A random sample of adult civilians from the general population of three different regions of Kosovo who had been exposed to potentially traumatic events (PTE) during the war in 1998/1999 was surveyed 10 years afterwards. Participants were included if they had been born within the territory of Kosovo; were adults, e.g. above 18 years old; had experienced at least one war-related PTE. People were excluded if they had not been residing permanently in Kosovo during the war or if they had executed higher military functions during the war. Interviews were conducted on a one-to-one verbal administration, in which the instructions and questions were read out to the participants in their native language by master-level students of clinical psychology. The details of sampling techniques and characteristics of the sample have been described in a previous publication [21].

Measures

To pursue semantic equivalence to the original measures, the Albanian translations were conducted in accordance with the standardized translation and back-translation procedure [22]. Natively Albanian-speaking health professionals conducted the translation. The measures were tested in a pilot phase, for which 5 participants were randomly selected and then the first author, whose native language is Albanian and a native Albanian-speaking psychiatrist compared source and back-translation and adapted the translations where necessary.

Traumatic events and PTSD symptoms

Exposure to various types of potentially traumatic events was assessed using a measure derived from combining the trauma event list of the Harvard Trauma Questionnaire [23], and the first part of the Posttraumatic Diagnostic Scale (PDS; [26]), resulting in a total of 23 items. Participants indicate if a given potentially traumatic event was experienced and/or witnessed. Subsequently, participants' overall trauma exposure is established by summing up the number of types of trauma they had been exposed to. The severity of 17 PTSD symptoms according to the Diagnostic and Statistical Manual of Mental Disorders 4th edition (DSM-IV; [24]) criteria was assessed using the PDS [25, 26]. The frequency of each symptom in the last month was rated on a 4-point scale ranging from 0 = "*never*" up to 3 = "*5 times per week or more/nearly always*"), yielding a total severity score ranging from 0 to 51. Besides the assessment of symptom levels, the PDS allows making a categorical probable diagnosis of PTSD according to DSM-IV criteria, which requires at least one symptom of re-experiencing, three of avoidance, and two of hyperarousal. The PDS has demonstrated good psychometric properties [26]. The internal consistency in the current sample was $\alpha = .96$.

To take into account the changes of PTSD in the DSM 5 the symptoms of PTSD in this sample were subdivided into four factors according to King and colleagues emotional numbing model of PTSD [27]. The model was first tested in treatment-seeking male veterans resulting in four correlated factors of Re-experiencing, Avoidance, Numbing, and Hyperarousal and was confirmed in other trauma-related populations, such as refugees [28].

Somatization symptoms

Somatic symptoms were assessed using the 12-item somatization subscale of the Symptom Checklist-90-revised (SCL-90-R; [29]). The SCL-90-R has been translated in many languages and used in different cultural contexts [30, 31]. Each of the 12 symptoms was assessed for the last week on a 5-point Likert scale ranging from 0=*"not at all"* to 4 = *"extremely"* (range: 0–48). Items scored as 2 = *"moderately"* or above are considered as positive responses, yielding a total count of somatization symptoms. The somatization subscale in our study demonstrated good internal consistency (Cronbach's alpha = .90).

Statistical analysis

All analyses were conducted using SPSS 23 (SPSS inc., Chicago, IL, USA). There were less than 5% missing data on any of the variables included in the analyses. Descriptive characteristics were calculated for all outcome variables and are given in terms of means (M) and standard deviations (SD) in continuous variables, and counts and percentages in categorical variables. The mediating role of posttraumatic stress in the relationship between trauma and somatization symptoms was investigated by a statistical mediation analysis approach developed by Preacher and Hayes [32, 33]. The indirect method of this approach uses bootstrapping, which includes random resampling from the original data, with 5'000 pseudo bootstrap samples being generated. Following this, point estimates for specific and total indirect effects for each sample are provided, which then can be used to calculate indirect effects and their confidence intervals (95% CIs). The CIs are then used to define if the effects are statistically significant at $p < .05$. The use of bootstrap models is especially suggested for small sample sizes [34]. We performed a model for somatization symptoms as outcome variable, where trauma exposure was an independent variable, and the mediator variables were the four sub clusters of posttraumatic stress symptoms (re-experiencing, active avoidance, numbing and hyperarousal). All analyses were controlled for gender, age, education and employment status.

Results

Sample characteristics

Approximately half of the 142 assessed participants were female ($n = 80$, 56.4%). Mean age of the participants was 43.8 years (SD = 6.12), education was 10.4 years of education (SD = 3.6), and 35% were working at least part time or undergoing vocational training, whereas the remaining 65% were not employed.

Trauma exposure and symptom severity

Participants had experienced or witnessed a mean of 5.3 (SD = 4.2) types of potentially traumatic events (see Table 1). The most frequently reported PTE's were: *"lack of shelter" (51.4%), "lack of food or water"* (44.4%), *"being close to death"* (39.9%) and *"combat situation"* (35.9%). The least frequently reported lifetime traumatic events included sexual violence (between 1.4% and 2.1%).

The PDS cut-off score for probable PTSD was exceeded by 26.1% of participants. Participants with probable PTSD and no PTSD did not differ on sociodemographic variables (age: $p = .195$; gender: $p = .406$).

The severity score for somatization symptoms on the SCL-90-R was 10.3 (SD = 8.5) Participants reported on average 3.3 (SD = 3.3) different somatization symptoms with a range of 0 to 12.

Women had higher levels of somatization symptoms ($p = .004$) than men, whereas levels of PTSD symptoms were similar between men and women ($p = .290$). Participants with a probable diagnosis of PTSD showed higher scores on somatization symptoms (see Table 2).

Relationship between PTSD and somatization symptoms

The results from the mediation analysis are presented in Table 3 (see Fig. 1 for diagrammatic representation of the tested model). According to the mediation analyses, trauma exposure was significantly associated with somatization symptoms. Trauma exposure was significantly associated with posttraumatic re-experiencing, active avoidance, numbing and hyperarousal. With respect to the effect of posttraumatic stress symptoms (mediator) on somatization symptoms (outcome), only active avoidance and hyper-arousal were significantly associated with somatization symptoms. Posttraumatic stress thus partly mediated the relationship between trauma exposure and somatization symptoms, accounting for 37% of the variance in somatization symptoms. There was a significant indirect negative effect of posttraumatic stress symptoms on somatization symptoms via active avoidance and a significant indirect positive effect of posttraumatic stress symptoms via hyperarousal.

Discussion

In this cross-sectional study, we examined the relationship between trauma exposure, posttraumatic stress symptoms and the level of somatization symptoms in a randomly selected sample of Kosovar civilian war survivors ($N = 142$). Substantial trauma exposure and high levels of clinically relevant symptoms of PTSD and somatization symptoms were found. Somatization symptoms correlated significantly with PTSD symptoms. In mediation analyses, the relationship between traumatic exposure and somatization symptoms was partly mediated by active avoidance and by posttraumatic hyperarousal, accounting for 37% of the variance in somatization symptoms.

As expected, compared to non-conflict countries, lifetime trauma exposure was substantial in the civilian population in Kosovo [35–37]. This is unsurprising since the cohort was sampled from a war-affected region.

Table 1 Trauma exposure reported by $N = 142$ civilian war survivors in post-war Kosovo region

Trauma type	*n*	%
Lack of shelter	73	51.4%
Lack of food or water	63	44.4%
Being close to death	56	39.4%
Combat situation	51	35.9%
Ill health without access to medical care	51	35.9%
Natural disaster	46	32.4%
Serious accident, fire or explosion	45	31.7%
Life-threatening illness	45	31.7%
Serious physical injury	41	28.9%
Forced separation from family member	40	28.2%
Murder of one or more strangers	36	25.4%
Unnatural death of a family member or friend	35	24.6%
Murder of a family member or friend	34	23.9%
Enforced isolation from others	23	16.2%
Torture	21	14.8%
Non-sexual assault by a stranger	21	14.8%
Imprisonment	19	13.4%
Disappearance or kidnapping	14	9.9%
Non-sexual assault by a family member or someone you know	11	7.7%
Brainwashing	6	4.2%
Sexual assault by a family member or someone you know	3	2.1%
Sexual assault by a stranger	2	1.4%
Sexual contact when you were younger than 18 with someone who was 5 or more years older than you	2	1.4%

Notes: Potentially traumatic events

Further, the high rates of probable PTSD (26%) and the high levels of somatization symptoms in the present sample are in line with earlier studies conducted in the post-war Balkans [1, 38, 39].

In addition, consistent with findings in the previous literature, female gender was associated with higher scores on somatization symptoms [40–42]. However, PTSD in the present study was equally found in women and men, which is in contrast to the epidemiological literature, but has been shown in samples of military personnel [43]. There is evidence, though, that gender may play a mediating role in the relationship of trauma and somatization symptoms, with females developing more somatization complaints as compared to men [9, 40]. This pattern overlaps with the robust finding of more females developing PTSD than males [44].

One of the interesting findings in this study was the differential role of PTSD symptom clusters on somatization symptoms. Specifically, we found that arousal mediated the association between trauma exposure and somatization symptoms using the PTSD cluster's classification by King and colleagues [27]. A comparable result was found by McFarlane et al. [6] in a sample of fire-fighters. The present study adds to the previous literature, however, by subdividing the avoidance cluster into active avoidance and numbing to the model. It is also conceivable that the numbing symptoms overlap with alexithymia and depressive symptoms, which have been shown to mediate the association of trauma exposure on somatization in major depression [45]. In addition, it is possible that passive avoidance may contribute to somatization presentations, as shown in the Escalona and Colleagues study [14], because these responses can include social and emotional withdrawal, which in turn might increase awareness of and focus on internal sensory perception. Avoidance behaviors in people suffering from pain can be attributed, in part, to catastrophizing about the severity of the pain as a predominant somatic symptom and the patient's inability to function, which may contribute to fear of pain and lead to avoidance of activities [46].

Active avoidance is a mediator of the relationship between trauma and somatic symptoms in a negative direction. This means the more one avoids situations and thoughts that remind him of the trauma, the less somatization symptoms one has. Further, this could mean, if someone is avoidant of thoughts and feelings, he is not very good at recognizing how he feels and so reports lower levels of subjective somatic symptoms. There has also been considerable attention given to the bidirectional relationship between PTSD and posttraumatic somatization symptoms such as pain. As Sharp and Harvey (Sharp & Harvey, 2001) have argued, PTSD patients can have their trauma memories triggered by episodes of pain because their pain is associated with the experience of the traumatic event. Conversely, posttraumatic stress can exacerbate pain by (a) increasing

Table 2 Somatization severity and symptom count by PTSD diagnosis ($N = 142$)

	PTSD ($n = 37$)		No PTSD ($n = 105$)		t-test
	M	SD	M	SD	
Somatization Severity	15.9	8.8	8.3	7.5	5.104***
Somatization Symptom Count	5.65	3.38	2.57	2.29	−4.130***

Notes: Somatization: subscale Somatization SCL-90-R, PTSD PTSD in posttraumatic diagnostic scale
***$p < .001$

Table 3 Results of analyses examining the mediating role of PTSD symptoms on the relationship between trauma exposure and somatization symptoms

		DV - Somatization Symptoms				
Independent variable (*IV*)	Mediating variable (*MV*)	Direct effects (c')	Total effects (c)			
Trauma		**.45****	**.62*****	Adj. $R^2 = .37$, $F(9,132) = 10.36$, $p < .001$		
		Effect of *IV* on *MV* (*a*)	Effect of *MV* on *DV* (*b*)	Indirect effects (*a x b*)	95% CI Low	95% CI High
Trauma	Re-experiencing	**.28****	.40	.115	−.044	.367
Trauma	Active Avoidance	**.16*****	**−.91***	**−.150***	−.360	−.036
Trauma	Numbing	**.18****	.19	.035	−.097	.284
Trauma	Hyperarousal	**.24*****	**.68****	**.166***	.011	.358

Notes: * $p < 0.05$; ** $p < 0.01$; *** $p < 0.001$. Re-experiencing = Re-experiencing subscale of PTSD in PDS; Active Avoidance = Avoidance subscale of PTSD in PDS; Numbing = Numbing subscale of PTSD in PDS; Hyperarousal = Hyperarousal subscale of PTSD in PDS; Somatization: Subscale Somatization SCL-90-R

arousal, (b) elevating muscle tension, (c) promoting vigilance to pain sensations, and (d) exaggerating negative appraisals about the severity of the pain experience.

Additional war-related consequences, such as social problems, may complicate the understanding of etiology, assessment, and course of treatment. In a low-income country such as Kosovo, socio-economic hardship and health problems might additionally be associated. Beyond this, it has been suggested that among some non-western, collectivistic cultures, somatization symptoms are among the most frequent presentations of trauma survivors [47, 48]. In Kosovo, it is conceivable that being psychologically ill might be socially unacceptable, whereas presenting somatization symptoms is more acceptable in Kosovarian people.

This study has several limitations. First, our results are based on self-reports assessed by questionnaires which usually have lower reliability than structured clinical interviews. However, because questionnaires were administered within a personal interview conducted by trained clinical psychology master students, we expect sufficient reliability. Another limitation is the use of instruments that have not yet been validated in Albanian. However, translations and back-translations were thoroughly performed by experienced and natively speaking interpreters in mental health and after consensus discussions adapted by mental health care providers, if necessary, in order to achieve maximum quality. The long period between the war and our assessment might have induced inaccurate recall; moreover, it is not clear whether the problems reported by participants were a consequence of the war, the current social situation and living conditions, or other adversities participants had been exposed to during the course of their lifetime. Finally, the cross-sectional approach of the present study does not allow to draw any conclusions regarding causal relationships between trauma exposure and the presence of somatization symptoms. However, our findings allow us to generate specific hypotheses regarding possible mechanisms and causal factors contributing to the prominent somatization symptoms in traumatized civilian war survivors. These precise assumptions about etiological mechanisms linking trauma exposure to somatization symptoms must be investigated in further research with longitudinal designs.

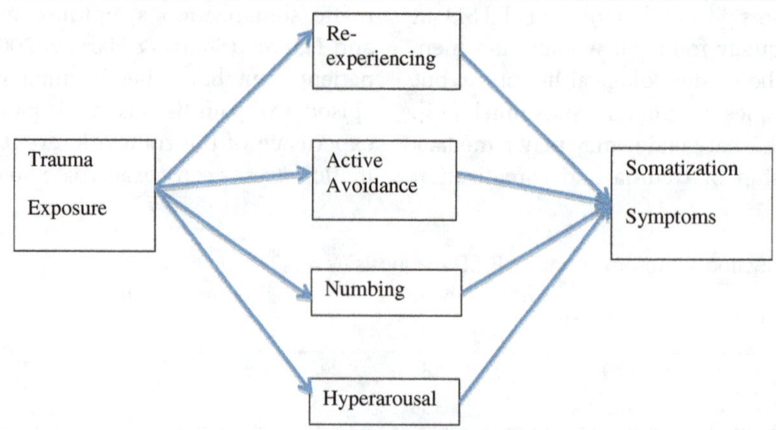

Fig. 1 Model of mediation analyses investigating the relationship between trauma, posttraumatic stress symptoms and somatization outcomes

Conclusions

More than a decade after the end of the Kosovo war, the presence of posttraumatic stress and somatic symptoms in the civilian population exposed to war is still substantial. Symptoms of posttraumatic mental health and somatic symptoms are highly associated, indicating a complex underlying mechanism. This study suggests that specific symptoms of PTSD, namely active avoidance and hyperarousal patterns, partially mediate this association. Active avoidance was associated with less somatic symptoms, whereas hyperaraousal was relate do more somatic symptoms. Therefore, when civilian survivors of war present with somatic complaints in primary care, mental health problems should always be taken into account as a differential diagnosis. The main approach should be the development of combined or stepped care treatments in terms of a bio-psycho-social model [49]. Finally, in the future, longitudinal studies with larger sample sizes allowing for multivariate analyses should be conducted in order to investigate underlying mechanisms, predictors, and causal factors.

Abbreviations

CI: Confidence interval; DSM-IV: Diagnostic and statistical manual of mental disorders 4th edition; M: Means; PDS: Posttraumatic diagnostic scale; PTE: potentially traumatic events; PTSD: Posttraumatic stress disorder; SCL-90-R: Symptom Checklist-90-revised; SD: Standard deviations

Acknowledgments

We would like to thank all participants, the interviewers, and the Swiss Parrotia Foundation for their trust and support.

Funding

The study was partially funded by the Parrotia Foundation, Switzerland. The funder played no role in the design and conduct (i.e. data collection, analysis, interpretation) of this study.

Authors' contributions

NM was involved in the conception and design of the study, the acquisition, analysis and interpretation of the data, and the drafting of the manuscript. He is accountable for all aspects of the work. US was involved in the conception of the study, in the analysis and interpretation of the data and the drafting of the manuscript. RK was involved in the analysis and interpretation of the data and the drafting of the manuscript. JM was involved in the conception and design of the study, interpretation of the data, and the drafting of the manuscript. CMS was involved in the analysis and interpretation of the data and the drafting of the manuscript. All authors read and approved the final manuscript.

Consent for publication

Not applicable.

Competing interests

The authors declare that they have no competing interests.

Author details

[1]Department of Consultation-Liaison-Psychiatry and Psychosomatic Medicine, University Hospital, University of Zurich, Culmannstrasse 8, 8091 Zurich, Switzerland. [2]Psychiatric Services Thurgau, 8596 Münsterlingen, Switzerland. [3]Paracelsus Medical University, Salzburg, Austria. [4]Division of Clinical and Health Psychology, Department of Psychology, University of Fribourg, 1700 Fribourg, Switzerland.

References

1. Priebe S, et al. Mental disorders following war in the Balkans: a study in 5 countries. Arch Gen Psychiatry. 2010;67(5):518.
2. Sack M, et al. Trauma prevalence and somatoform symptoms: are there specific somatoform symptoms related to traumatic experiences? J Nerv Ment Dis. 2007;195(11):928–33.
3. Shalev A, Bleich A, Ursano RJ. Posttraumatic stress disorder: somatic comorbidity and effort tolerance. Psychosomatics. 1990;31(2):197–203.
4. Solomon Z, Mikulincer M. Combat stress reactions, post traumatic stress disorder and somatic complaints among Israeli soldiers. J Psychosom Res. 1987;31(1):131–7.
5. Elklit A, Christiansen DM. Predictive factors for somatization in a trauma sample. Clin Pract Epidemiol Ment Health. 2009;5:1.
6. McFarlane AC, et al. Physical symptoms in post-traumatic stress disorder. J Psychosom Res. 1994;38(7):715–26.
7. Rieder H, Elbert T. The relationship between organized violence, family violence and mental health: findings from a community-based survey in Muhanga, southern Rwanda. Eur J Psychotraumatol. 2013;4. https://doi.org/10.3402/ejpt.v4i0.21329.
8. Spiller TR, et al. Somatisation and anger are associated with symptom severity of posttraumatic stress disorder in severely traumatised refugees and asylum seekers. Swiss Med Wkly. 2016;146:w14311.
9. Andreski P, Chilcoat H, Breslau N. Post-traumatic stress disorder and somatization symptoms: a prospective study. Psychiatry Res. 1998;79(2):131–8.
10. Gupta MA. Review of somatic symptoms in post-traumatic stress disorder. Int Rev Psychiatry. 2013;25(1):86–99.
11. Pacella ML, Hruska B, Delahanty DL. The physical health consequences of PTSD and PTSD symptoms: a meta-analytic review. J Anxiety Disord. 2013; 27(1):33–46.
12. Afari N, et al. Psychological trauma and functional somatic syndromes: a systematic review and meta-analysis. Psychosom Med. 2014;76(1):2–11.
13. Liedl A, et al. Support for the mutual maintenance of pain and post-traumatic stress disorder symptoms. Psychol Med. 2010;40(7):1215–23.
14. Escalona R, et al. PTSD and somatization in women treated at a VA primary care clinic. Psychosomatics. 2004;45(4):291–6.
15. Asmundson GJG, Katz J. Understanding the co-occurrence of anxiety disorders and chronic pain: state-of-the-art. Depress Anxiety. 2009;26(10):888–901.
16. Asmundson GJG, et al. PTSD and the experience of pain: research and clinical implications of shared vulnerability and mutual maintenance models. Can J Psychiatr. 2002;47(10):930–7.
17. Sharp TJ, Harvey AG. Chronic pain and posttraumatic stress disorder: mutual maintenance? Clin Psychol Rev. 2001;21(6):857–77.
18. Liedl A, Knaevelsrud C. Chronic pain and PTSD: the perpetual avoidance model and its treatment implications. Torture. 2008;18(2):69–76.
19. Teodorescu DS, et al. Chronic pain in multi-traumatized outpatients with a refugee background resettled in Norway: a cross-sectional study. BMC Psychol. 2015;3(1):7.
20. Carlsson JM, et al. Mental health and health-related quality of life: a 10-year follow-up of tortured refugees. J Nerv Ment Dis. 2006;194(10):725–31.
21. Schick M, et al. Trauma, mental health and intergenerational associations in Kosovar families 11 years after the war. Eur J Psychotraumatol. 2013;4. https://doi.org/10.3402/ejpt.v4i0.21060.
22. Bontempo R. Translation fidelity of psychological scales: an item response theory analysis of an individualism-collectivism scale. J Cross-Cult Psychol. 1993;24:149–66.
23. Mollica RF, et al. The Harvard trauma questionnaire. Validating a cross-cultural instrument for measuring torture, trauma, and posttraumatic stress disorder in Indochinese refugees. J Nerv Ment Dis. 1992;180(2):111–6.
24. APA. Diagnostic and statistical manual of mental disorders: *DSM-IV*. 4th ed. Washington: APA; 1994.
25. Foa EB. PDS (posttraumatic stress diagnostic scale) manual. Minneapolis: National Computer Systems; 1995.
26. Foa EB, et al. The validation of a self-report measure of posttraumatic stress disorder: the posttraumatic diagnostic scale. Psychol Assess. 1997;9(4):445–51.
27. King DW, et al. Confirmatory factor analysis of the clinician-administered PTSD scale: evidence for the dimensionality of posttraumatic stress disorder. Psychol Assessment. 1998;10(2):90–6.
28. Palmieri PA, Marshall GN, Schell TL. Confirmatory factor analysis of posttraumatic stress symptoms in Cambodian refugees. J Trauma Stress. 2007;20(2):207–16.
29. Derogatis LR. SCL-90-R: administration, scoring and procedure manual - I. Baltimore: John Hopkins; 1977.

30. Ventevogel P, et al. Properties of the Hopkins symptom Checklist-25 (HSCL-25) and the self-reporting questionnaire (SRQ-20) as screening instruments used in primary care in Afghanistan. Soc Psychiatry Psychiatr Epidemiol. 2007;42(4):328–35.
31. Mollica RF, et al. Indochinese versions of the Hopkins symptom Checklist-25: a screening instrument for the psychiatric care of refugees. Am J Psychiatry. 1987;144(4):497–500.
32. Preacher KJ, Hayes AF. Asymptotic and resampling strategies for assessing and comparing indirect effects in multiple mediator models. Behav Res Methods. 2008;40(3):879–91.
33. Hayes AF. Beyond baron and Kenny: statistical mediation analysis in the new millenium. Comm Mon. 2009;76:408–20.
34. Shrout PE, Bolger N. Mediation in experimental and nonexperimental studies: new procedures and recommendations. Psychol Methods. 2002;7(4):422–45.
35. Perkonigg A, et al. Traumatic events and post-traumatic stress disorder in the community: prevalence, risk factors and comorbidity. Acta Psychiatr Scand. 2000;101(1):46–59.
36. National Institute of Mental Health. Statistics. 2012. Retrieved June 16, 2012 from: http://www.nimh.nih.gov/statistics .
37. Kessler RC, et al. Posttraumatic stress disorder in the National Comorbidity Survey. Arch Gen Psychiatry. 1995;52(12):1048–60.
38. Kashdan TB, Morina N, Priebe S. Post-traumatic stress disorder, social anxiety disorder, and depression in survivors of the Kosovo war: experiential avoidance as a contributor to distress and quality of life. J Anxiety Disord. 2009;23(2):185–96.
39. Morina N, Ford JD. Complex sequelae of psychological trauma among Kosovar civilian war victims. Int J Soc Psychiatry. 2008;54(5):425–36.
40. McCall-Hosenfeld JS, et al. The association of interpersonal trauma with somatic symptom severity in a primary care population with chronic pain: exploring the role of gender and the mental health sequelae of trauma. J Psychosom Res. 2014;77(3):196–204.
41. Haug TT, Mykletun A, Dahl AA. The association between anxiety, depression, and somatic symptoms in a large population: the HUNT-II study. Psychosom Med. 2004;66(6):845–51.
42. Morina N, et al. Somatic distress among Kosovar civilian war survivors: relationship to trauma exposure and the mediating role of experiential avoidance. Soc Psychiatry Psychiatr Epidemiol. 2010;45(12):1167–77.
43. Norris FH, Slone LB. The epidemiology of trauma and PTSD. In: Friedman MJ, Keane TM, Resick PA, editors. in Handbook of PTSD: science and practice. New York: Guilford Press; 2007. p. 78–98.
44. Olff M, et al. Gender differences in posttraumatic stress disorder. Psychol Bull. 2007;133(2):183–204.
45. Gulec MY, et al. Effects of childhood trauma on somatization in major depressive disorder: the role of alexithymia. J Affect Disord. 2013;146(1):137–41.
46. Vlaeyen JW, Linton SJ. Fear-avoidance and its consequences in chronic musculoskeletal pain: a state of the art. Pain. 2000;85(3):317–32.
47. Kirmayer LJ, Young A. Culture and somatization: clinical, epidemiological, and ethnographic perspectives. Psychosom Med. 1998;60(4):420–30.
48. Ford CV. Somatic symptoms, somatization, and traumatic stress: an overview. Nordic Journal of Psychiatry. 1997;51(1):5–13.
49. Otis JD, et al. The development of an integrated treatment for veterans with comorbid chronic pain and posttraumatic stress disorder. Pain Med. 2009;10(7):1300–11.

12

Compromised dynamic cerebral autoregulation in patients with generalized anxiety disorder: a study using transfer function analysis

Zhen-Ni Guo[1,2†], Shan Lv[1†], Jia Liu[3], Zan Wang[1], Hang Jin[1], Quanli Qiu[3], Xin Sun[2*] and Yi Yang[1,2*]

Abstract

Background: Patients with generalized anxiety disorder (GAD) usually present with various neurological symptoms, but the mechanisms remain unclear. We aimed to analyze the characteristics of dynamic cerebral autoregulation (dCA) in patients with GAD.

Methods: Patients (aged ≥18 years) who were diagnosed with GAD were enrolled in this study. Medically and psychiatrically healthy volunteers were recruited as controls. Subjects received the Hamilton Rating Scale for Anxiety (HAMA) and 17-item Hamilton Depression Rating Scale (HAMD) evaluation. Noninvasive continuous arterial blood pressure and bilateral middle cerebral artery blood flow velocity were recorded simultaneously from each subject. Transfer function analysis was used to derive the autoregulatory parameters, including phase difference, gain, and coherence function.

Results: A total of 57 patients with GAD and 40 healthy volunteers were enrolled. We found that the phase difference values were significantly compromised in patients with GAD. In the Spearman correlation analysis, the phase difference values were negatively correlated with the HAMA scores and the HAMD scores. In the multiple linear regression analysis, GAD is negatively correlated with the phase difference values, whereas age is positively correlated with the phase difference values.

Conclusions: Our results suggested that the dCA was compromised in patients with GAD and negatively correlated with the score of anxiety. Improving the dCA may be a potential therapeutic method for treating the neurological symptoms of GAD patients.

Keywords: Generalized anxiety disorder, Dynamic cerebral autoregulation, Transcranial Doppler

Background

Generalized anxiety disorder (GAD) is one of the most common mental disorders in the world [1, 2] and can negatively affect the life quality of patients and disrupt important activities of daily living [1]. Patients with GAD usually present with various neurological symptoms, such as dizziness, headache, and sleep disorders; the mechanisms of these symptoms, however, remain unclear. It has been reported that in patients with GAD, the cerebral hemodynamics show abnormal manifestations [3, 4], which may be a reason for the neurological symptoms of GAD.

Cerebral autoregulation, which protects the brain tissue from hyperperfusion or hypoperfusion, is critical in regulating cerebral hemodynamics and has been found to play an important role in many neurological diseases [5–7]. Previous studies found that the factors involved in cerebral autoregulation regulation, such as neuroregulation, myogenic response, and endothelial regulation, etc., are dysfunctional in patients with GAD

* Correspondence: sjnksunxin@163.com; doctoryangyi@163.com
†Zhen-Ni Guo and Shan Lv contributed equally to this work.
[2]Clinical Trail and Research Center for Stroke, Department of Neurology, The First Hospital of Jilin University, Chang Chun, China
[1]Department of Neurology, The First Hospital of Jilin University, Xinmin Street 71#, Chang Chun 130021, China
Full list of author information is available at the end of the article

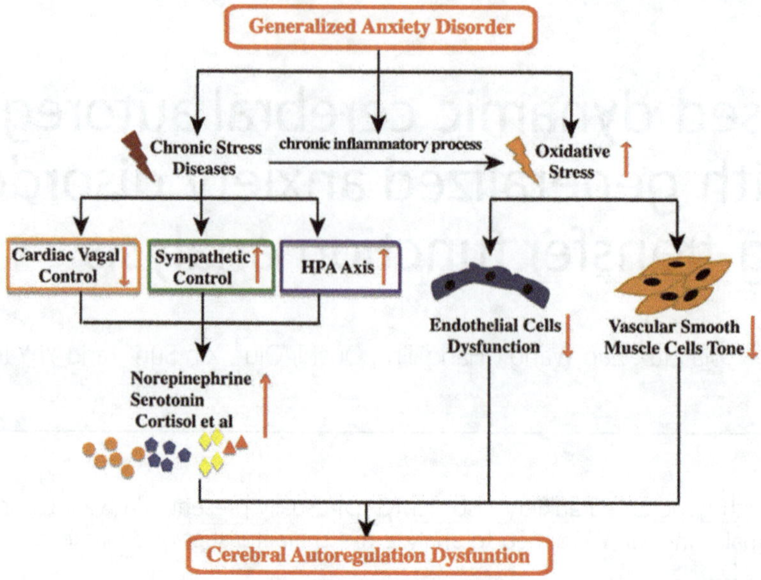

Fig. 1 Hypothesis between generalized anxiety disorder (GAD) and cerebral autoregulation impairment. In patients with GAD, neuroregulation, myogenic response, and endothelial regulation may be dysfunctional, which could damage cerebral autoregulation

(Fig. 1) [8–12]. Our previous study also showed that patients with GAD cannot maintain normal cerebral blood flow velocity from supine to standing [13]. These data imply that cerebral autoregulation may be impaired in GAD patients.

Cerebral autoregulation is divided into static cerebral autoregulation and dynamic cerebral autoregulation (dCA), and the dCA is more sensitive to pathological situations [14, 15]. When dCA is measured, continuous cerebral blood flow velocities (assessed using transcranial Doppler) and continuous finger blood pressure (assessed using a servo-controlled plethysmograph) were recorded simultaneously. These data were then analyzed using transfer function analysis, an approach used to analyze dCA based on spontaneous fluctuations of blood pressure and cerebral blood flow velocities at rest [16, 17]. In previous studies, dCA calculated by transfer function analysis has been applied in healthy subjects [18], cerebrovascular disease [5, 19], cognitive impairment [6], etc. However, dCA has not been studied in patients with GAD.

In this study, we hypothesize that dCA is compromised in patients with GAD. If our hypothesis is valid, dCA may serve as a potential therapeutic target to improve the neurological symptoms in patients with GAD.

Methods

Participants

The prospective study design was approved by the ethics committee of the First Hospital of Jilin University under the guidelines of the Helsinki Declaration of 1975/1983. Written informed consent was obtained from all subjects. Patients whose chief complaint was poor sleep were selected for screening. Patients (aged ≥18 years) who met the *Diagnostic and Statistical Manual of Mental Disorders, Fourth Edition, Text Revision* criteria for GAD [20] were recruited from May 2016 to November 2016 in the outpatient unit of the Neurological Department. Patients who met Diagnostic and Statistical Manual of Mental Disorders criteria for Major Depressive Disorder were excluded. Patients were otherwise healthy, with no ascertained disorders in the nervous, cardiovascular, or respiratory systems and without hypertension, diabetes, or hyperlipidemia. The clinical workup consisted of laboratory tests (liver and kidney function tests, hematology profile, blood glucose tests, and blood lipid tests), blood pressure, electrocardiography, transcranial Doppler (EMS-9 PB, Delica, China), carotid ultrasound (IU22, Phillips, Andover, MA, USA), cranial computed tomography/magnetic resonance imaging, and physical examination. Patients were evaluated with the Hamilton Rating Scale for Anxiety (HAMA) [21] and the 17-item Hamilton Depression Rating Scale (HAMD) [22]. Medically and psychiatrically healthy volunteers were recruited as controls. Two blinded clinical psychiatrists evaluated the patients' mental health status.

Dynamic cerebral autoregulation (dCA) protocol

The examination of dCA was performed as reported in previous research [5, 7, 23]. Subjects were asked to avoid nicotine, caffeine, alcohol, and all kinds of sleep medicines for at least 24 h before the dCA examination. The examination was performed in a quiet, dedicated research room with minimal surrounding stimuli. First, the baseline arterial blood pressure was measured at the brachial artery using an automatic blood pressure monitor (Omron 711). Second, we simultaneously recorded continuous spontaneous arterial blood pressure on the middle finger using a servo-controlled plethysmograph (Finometer Pro, Netherlands) and continuous bilateral middle cerebral artery blood flow velocity at a depth of 45 mm to 60 mm with 2 MHz probes attached to a customized head frame (MultiDop X2, DWL, Sipplingen, Germany). End-tidal carbon dioxide was recorded using a capnograph with a facemask attached to the nasal cannula. Data were recorded for 10 min for further dCA examination analysis.

Data analysis

The dCA analysis was performed as previously reported [5, 7] and was analyzed blindly for each subject. Briefly, dCA data were analyzed using MATLAB (MathWorks, Natick, MA, USA). Beat-to-beat alignment of the data was achieved with a cross-correlation function to eliminate possible time lags. The relationship between dynamic changes in spontaneous arterial blood pressure and bilateral middle cerebral artery blood flow velocity was assessed with a transfer function analysis. For each recording, arterial blood pressure and bilateral cerebral artery blood flow velocity were divided into a number of data segments by a 60-s window with a 30-s overlap. For one segment of arterial blood pressure and bilateral cerebral artery blood flow velocity, the transfer function analysis was implemented as,

$$H(f) = \frac{S_{pv}(f)}{S_{pp}(f)}, \tag{1}$$

where $H(f)$ denotes the frequency response. $S_{pp}(f)$ is the auto-spectrum of arterial blood pressure, and $S_{pv}(f)$ is the cross-spectrum between arterial blood pressure and cerebral artery blood flow velocity. For each subject, $S_{pp}(f)$ and $S_{pv}(f)$ were averaged over the segments to improve statistical reliability. The gain $|H(f)|$ and phase difference $\phi(f)$ can then be computed as,

$$|H(f)| = \sqrt{\{|H_R(f)|^2 + |H_I(f)|^2\}}, \tag{2}$$

$$\varnothing(f) = \tan^{-1}\left[\frac{H_I(f)}{H_R(f)}\right], \tag{3}$$

where $H_R(f)$ and $H_I(f)$ are the real and imaginary parts of $H(f)$, respectively. Low phase difference and high gain values at a low frequency band (0.06-0.12 Hz) indicate that cerebral artery blood flow velocity follows changes of arterial blood pressure passively, thus suggesting impairment of autoregulation [16, 17]. We also calculated coherence function to quantify the linearity in the frequency domain using a routine provided by Signal Processing Toolbox in MATLAB with the Welch method for the estimation of power spectral density and hamming window for the reduction of spectral leakage. The recordings with averaged coherence < 0.4 at the low frequency band were considered with insufficient linearity and therefore excluded from the transfer function analysis.

Statistical analysis

The Statistical Package for the Social Sciences Version 17.0 (SPSS, IBM, West Grove, PA, USA) was used to analyze the data. Continuous data are expressed as mean and standard deviation. Comparison between two groups were analyzed using Student's t-tests. The discrete variables are expressed as the rate (percentage) and were analyzed using chi-squared and Fisher's exact tests. The Spearman correlation analysis was used to analyze the relationship between phase difference values and HAMA scores and the relationship between phase difference values and HAMD scores. Multiple linear regression analysis was used to explore the effects of covariates on phase or gain. Calculated two-tailed P values < 0.05 were considered statistically significant.

Results

Demographic information

In total, 57 patients with GAD (45.05 ± 14.83; 18 males) and 40 healthy volunteers were enrolled in the study. The baseline characteristics are presented in Table 1.

Table 1 Baseline characteristics, phase difference, and gain in the patients and controls

	GAD (n = 57)	Control (n = 40)	t /χ^2	p
Male, n (%)	18 (31.58%)	24 (60.00%)	6.773	0.009
Age (years)	45.05 ± 14.83	43.10 ± 11.51	0.698	0.487
HAMA	19.79 ± 5.93	3.60 ± 1.71	19.501	< 0.001
HAMD	13.96 ± 4.08	4.37 ± 1.33	16.534	< 0.001
Mean ABP, mmHg	89.12 ± 7.48	86.60 ± 9.73	1.443	0.152
Heart rate	76.07 ± 8.99	74.10 ± 8.20	1.101	0.274
End-title CO_2, mmHg	35.23 ± 3.12	35.16 ± 2.56	0.613	0.542
Phase difference, degree				
Left hemisphere	43.43 ± 14.39	55.00 ± 8.86	−4.891	< 0.001
Right hemisphere	43.30 ± 15.40	54.07 ± 9.36	− 4.273	< 0.001
Gain, %/%				
Left hemisphere	0.89 ± 0.31	0.85 ± 0.24	0.820	0.414
Right hemisphere	0.86 ± 0.29	0.86 ± 0.22	−0.064	0.949
Smoking, n (%)	12 (21.1)	7 (17.5)	0.188	0.664
Drinking, n (%)	4 (7.0)	1 (2.5)	0.646	0.310

GAD generalized anxiety disorder, *ABP* arterial blood pressure, *HAMA* Hamilton Rating Scale for Anxiety, *HAMD* Hamilton Depression Rating Scale

Dynamic cerebral autoregulation

GAD patients

The patients with GAD showed no difference in phase difference values between the left and right hemispheres. However, when compared with the healthy controls, the phase difference values of both hemispheres of GAD patients were significantly lower than the corresponding hemisphere of the healthy controls. In addition, there was no significant difference in the gain values between GAD patients and healthy controls in both the left and right hemispheres (Fig. 2, and Table 1).

Correlation analysis

In the Spearman correlation analysis, both the left and right phase difference values were negatively correlated to HAMA scores (left: $r = -0.365$, $p < 0.001$; right: $r = -0.348$, $p < 0.001$). Similarly, both the left and right phase difference values were negatively correlated to HAMD scores (left: $r = -0.350$, $p < 0.001$; right: $r = -0.363$, $p < 0.001$).

Multiple linear regression analysis

The associations between clinical factors and phase difference are shown in Table 2. GAD and age are found to be correlated with phase difference values. GAD is negatively correlated to phase difference, whereas age is positively correlated to phase difference after adjusting for covariates (Table 2). No factors were detected associated with gain.

Discussion

In the present study, we found that the dCA of both hemispheres in patients with GAD was significantly lower as compared with the healthy controls. In addition, the dCA function is negatively correlated with the anxiety score. Impaired dCA may be a mechanism underlying the neurological symptoms of GAD and thus may serve as a potential therapeutic target to alleviate the neurological symptoms in patients with GAD.

Generally, phase difference between arterial blood pressure and cerebral artery blood flow velocity at a certain frequency can be considered as time delay between these recordings. Therefore, lower phase difference (shorter time delay) indicates that blood flow changes in pace (passively) with fluctuations of blood pressure, suggesting that the distal arterioles and capillary do not respond to the changes of blood pressure. In contrast, notable phase difference (larger time delay) suggests that the phase of arterial blood

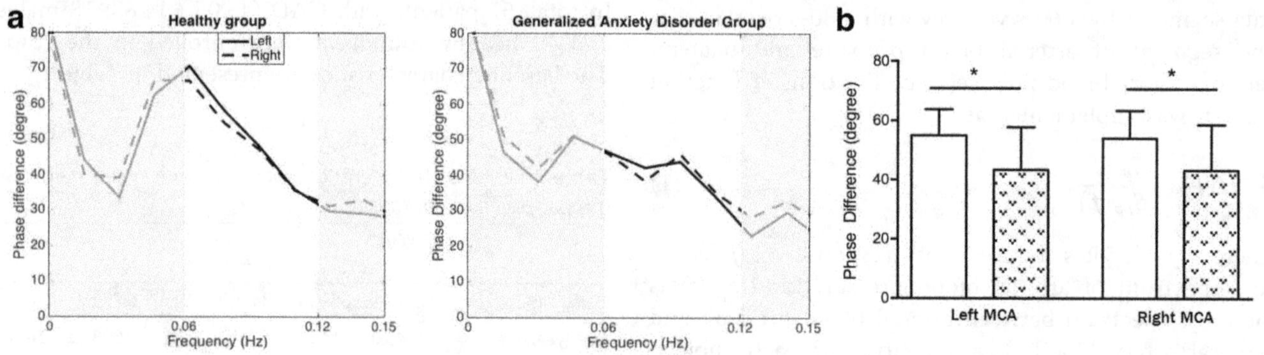

Fig. 2 a The phase difference and gain derived from the transfer function within significant interval 0.06-0.12 Hz are plotted. (–: left middle cerebral artery [MCA] and —: right MCA). Phase difference values (parameter of dynamic cerebral autoregulation) were significant compromised in patients with generalized anxiety disorder (GAD) compared with the healthy group, indicating an impairment of dynamic cerebral autoregulation in patients with GAD. There was no difference of the gain values between GAD group and healthy group. **b** Statistical analysis of phase differences and gains are shown. Phase difference values in the GAD group were significantly lower than the corresponding MCA of the healthy group. There was no difference in gain values in the two groups

Table 2 Multiple regression Coefficients for mean phase difference values of left and right hemisphere

Covariates	Unstandardized coefficients		Standardized coefficients	95% CI for β		*P*
	β	Std. Error		Lower Bound	Upper Bound	
Constant	63.819	21.494		21.105	106.534	0.004
Age (years)	0.240	0.092	0.248	0.057	0.422	0.011
Mean ABP, mmHg	−0.063	0.150	−0.041	−0.362	0.236	0.676
Heart rate	−0.075	0.143	−0.050	−0.360	0.210	0.604
End-title CO_2, mmHg	−0.229	0.389	−0.057	−1.003	0.544	0.557
Groups of mental disorder						
Control	Reference					
Generalized anxiety disorder	−11.052	2.629	−0.418	− 16.277	− 5.840	< 0.001
Gender						
Female	Reference					
Male	−0.143	3.024	0.005	−6.154	5.828	0.962
Smoking						
No	Reference					
Yes	−2.561	3.672	−0.078	−9.858	4.737	0.487
Drinking						
No	Reference					
Yes	−2.943	5.854	−0.050	−14.576	8.690	0.616

pressure is outpaced by the phase of cerebral artery blood flow velocity, implying that the distal arterioles and capillary do not comply with the changes in blood pressure. The reason why patients with GAD present with impaired dCA remains unclear and needs further investigation. As a chronic stress disease, lower cardiac vagal control and hyperactivity of the sympathetic and hypothalamic-pituitary-adrenal axis were reported in patients with GAD [24–29], leading to disorganized secretion of norepinephrine, serotonin, cortisol, etc. Some of these neuroendocrine substances are vasoactive substances that regulate cerebral autoregulation (Fig. 1).

The integrity of structure and function of the endothelium is essential to maintain a functional cerebral autoregulation [30–33]. However, in patients with GAD, both the structure and function of the endothelium may be damaged due to oxidative stress, which is another characteristic of GAD [34–36]. In addition, CRP [37], TNF-α, and IL-17 [38, 39] are increased in patients with GAD, indicating that the inflammatory process is activated and can induce endothelial cell dysfunction. Furthermore, oxidative stress can alter the vascular smooth muscle tone, another indispensable mechanism in regulating cerebral autoregulation, by changing reactive oxide species concentration (Fig. 1) [40].

As described above, the changes in neuroregulation, endothelial regulation, and myogenic response may collectively result in the impairment of dCA, leading to unstable cerebral blood flow in patients with GAD. A previous study by Kalk, et al. supports our findings [3]. They found that patients with untreated GAD showed increased perfusion in the left Broca's area and left occipitotemporal region, and venlafaxine-treated GAD patients showed increased cerebellar perfusion bilaterally [3]. In the present study, the impairment of dCA can result in abnormal cerebral perfusion. Our previous study also yielded some meaningful results: we found that patients with anxiety showed more pronounced decreases in cerebral blood flow velocity with abrupt standing, which indicates impaired dCA [4].

It is worth mentioning that phase difference values were negatively correlated with the HAMA scores, which suggests that as the HAMA scores increase, the phase difference values, i.e., dCA, tend to decrease. In addition, the negative correlation between phase difference values and HAMD scale suggests a potential impact of depressive symptoms on phase difference values. This phenomenon deserves further study in patients with major depressive disorder. The impairment of dCA in patients with GAD indicates that cerebral vascular function is a therapeutic target of GAD. Thus, methods to improve dCA may potentially relieve the neurological symptoms in patients with GAD.

Both the studies from Ortega-Gutierrez and Yams suggested that dCA remains intact in the elderly, though their intracranial arteries may be affected by atherosclerosis [41, 42]. In our study, we found age is a weak positive correlation to phase difference; the causes are not clear. One possible reason is that the patients we included were relatively young, and the age span is relatively small. However, this explanation is inadequate.

This study has some limitations. The first is the gender mismatch of the GAD group and controls. Because gender affect cerebral blood flow via complex mechanisms [43], we could not rule out the possible influence of sex on dCA. However, it is worth mentioning that the regression analyses suggest no effect of gender in our study. Second, we do not have the neuroendocrine results of our patients' blood to further support our results. Third, this is an observational study without in-depth mechanism research. Furthermore, large sample sizes and animal studies are needed. In addition, medication condition was not included in this article, which could potentially influence the results.

Conclusions

Our results suggested that the dCA was compromised in patients with GAD and negatively correlated with the score of anxiety. Improving the dCA may be a potential therapeutic method for treating the neurological symptoms of GAD patients.

Abbreviations

DCA: Dynamic cerebral autoregulation; GAD: Generalized anxiety disorder; HAMA: Hamilton rating scale for anxiety; HAMD: Hamilton Depression Rating Scale

Acknowledgments

This study was supported by Jie Zhang and Yang-Yang Zhou from the Center for Neurovascular Ultrasound, the First Hospital of Jilin University.

Funding

This project was supported by the National Natural Science Foundation of China to Zhen-Ni Guo (Grant No. 81501166), and the Young Elite Scientists Sponsorship Program by CAST to Zhen-Ni Guo. The founders were not involved in the design of the study, the data collection, the analysis or interpretation of data, or the writing of the manuscript.

Authors' contributions

Drafted the manuscript: YY, ZNG, SL. Revised the manuscript: XS, ZNG, SL. Drew the figures: ZNG, SL, XS, HJ. Acquisition of data: ZW, SL, HJ. Data analysis: JL, QLQ. Statistical analysis: ZNG, SL. Conceived and designed the manuscript: XS, YY. All authors read and approved the final manuscript.

Competing interests

The authors declare that they have no competing interests.

Author details

[1]Department of Neurology, The First Hospital of Jilin University, Xinmin Street 71#, Chang Chun 130021, China. [2]Clinical Trail and Research Center for Stroke, Department of Neurology, The First Hospital of Jilin University, Chang Chun, China. [3]Shenzhen Institutes of Advanced Technology, Chinese Academy of Sciences, Xueyuan Avenue, Shenzhen University Town, Shenzhen, China.

References

1. Locke AB, Kirst N, Shultz CG. Diagnosis and management of generalized anxiety disorder and panic disorder in adults. Am Fam Physician. 2015;91:617–24.
2. Phillips MR, Zhang J, Shi Q, Song Z, Ding Z, Pang S, Li X, Zhang Y, Wang Z. Prevalence, treatment, and associated disability of mental disorders in four provinces in China during 2001-05: an epidemiological survey. Lancet. 2009;373:2041–53.
3. Kalk NJ, Melichar J, Holmes RB, Taylor LG, Daglish MR, Hood S, Edwards T, Lennox-Smith A, Lingford-Hughes AR, Nutt DJ. Central noradrenergic responsiveness to a clonidine challenge in generalized anxiety disorder: a single photon emission computed tomography study. J Psychopharmacol. 2012;26:452–60.
4. Zhang HL, Guo ZN, Yang G, Yang L, Han K, Wu J, Xing Y, Yang Y. Compromised cerebrovascular modulation in chronic anxiety: evidence from cerebral blood flow velocity measured by transcranial Doppler sonography. Neurosci Bull. 2012;28:723–8.
5. Ma H, Guo ZN, Liu J, Xing Y, Zhao R, Yang Y. Temporal course of dynamic cerebral autoregulation in patients with intracerebral hemorrhage. Stroke. 2016;47:674–81.
6. Tarumi T, Dunsky DI, Khan MA, Liu J, Hill C, Armstrong K, Martin-Cook K, Cullum CM, Zhang R. Dynamic cerebral autoregulation and tissue oxygenation in amnestic mild cognitive impairment. J Alzheimer's Dis : JAD. 2014;41:765–78.
7. Guo ZN, Xing Y, Wang S, Ma H, Liu J, Yang Y. Characteristics of dynamic cerebral autoregulation in cerebral small vessel disease: diffuse and sustained. Sci Rep. 2015;5:15269.
8. Paulson OB, Strandgaard S, Edvinsson L. Cerebral autoregulation. Cerebrovasc Brain Metab Rev. 1990;2:161–92.
9. Makovac E, Meeten F, Watson DR, Herman A, Garfinkel SN, Critchley HD, Ottaviani C. Alterations in amygdala-prefrontal functional connectivity account for excessive worry and autonomic dysregulation in generalized anxiety disorder. Biol Psychiatry. 2016;80:786–95.
10. Fisher AJ, Newman MG. Heart rate and autonomic response to stress after experimental induction of worry versus relaxation in healthy, high-worry, and generalized anxiety disorder individuals. Biol Psychol. 2013;93:65–74.
11. Osika W, Montgomery SM, Dangardt F, Wahrborg P, Gan LM, Tideman E, Friberg P. Anger, depression and anxiety associated with endothelial function in childhood and adolescence. Arch Dis Child. 2011;96:38–43.
12. Munk PS, Isaksen K, Bronnick K, Kurz MW, Butt N, Larsen AI. Symptoms of anxiety and depression after percutaneous coronary intervention are associated with decreased heart rate variability, impaired endothelial function and increased inflammation. Int J Cardiol. 2012;158:173–6.
13. Guo ZN, Feng L, Yan X, Yang L, Huang S, Xing Y, Yang Y. Characteristics of cardio-cerebrovascular modulation in patients with generalized anxiety disorder: an observational study. BMC Psychiatry. 2017;17:259.
14. Dawson SL, Blake MJ, Panerai RB, Potter JF. Dynamic but not static cerebral autoregulation is impaired in acute ischaemic stroke. Cerebrovasc Dis. 2000;10:126–32.
15. Dawson SL, Panerai RB, Potter JF. Serial changes in static and dynamic cerebral autoregulation after acute ischaemic stroke. Cerebrovasc Dis. 2003;16:69–75.
16. Zhang R, Zuckerman JH, Giller CA, Levine BD. Transfer function analysis of dynamic cerebral autoregulation in humans. Am J Phys. 1998;274:H233–41.
17. Reinhard M, Roth M, Muller T, Czosnyka M, Timmer J, Hetzel A. Cerebral autoregulation in carotid artery occlusive disease assessed from spontaneous blood pressure fluctuations by the correlation coefficient index. Stroke. 2003;34:2138–44.
18. Barnes SC, Ball N, Haunton VJ, Robinson TG, Panerai RB. The cerebrocardiovascular response to periodic squat-stand maneuvers in healthy subjects: a time-domain analysis. Am J Physiol Heart Circ Physiol. 2017;313:H1240–8.
19. Chi NF, Ku HL, Wang CY, Liu Y, Chan L, Lin YC, Peng CK, Novak V, Hu HH, Hu CJ. Dynamic cerebral autoregulation assessment using extracranial internal carotid artery Doppler ultrasonography. Ultrasound Med Biol. 2017;43:1307–13.
20. American psychiatric association. Diagnostic and statistical manual of mental disorders, 4th., text revision. Washington, DC: American Psychiatric Association. 2000.

21. Hamilton M. The assessment of anxiety states by rating. Br J Med Psychol. 1959;32:50–5.
22. Hamilton M. A rating scale for depression. J Neurol Neurosurg Psychiatry. 1960;23:56–62.
23. Guo ZN, Xing Y, Liu J, Wang S, Yan S, Jin H, Yang Y. Compromised dynamic cerebral autoregulation in patients with a right-to-left shunt: a potential mechanism of migraine and cryptogenic stroke. PLoS One. 2014;9:e104849.
24. Thayer JF, Friedman BH, Borkovec TD. Autonomic characteristics of generalized anxiety disorder and worry. Biol Psychiatry. 1996;39:255–66.
25. Cameron OG, Smith CB, Lee MA, Hollingsworth PJ, Hill EM, Curtis GC. Adrenergic status in anxiety disorders: platelet alpha 2-adrenergic receptor binding, blood pressure, pulse, and plasma catecholamines in panic and generalized anxiety disorder patients and in normal subjects. Biol Psychiatry. 1990;28:3–20.
26. Reeves JW, Fisher AJ, Newman MG, Granger DA. Sympathetic and hypothalamic-pituitary-adrenal asymmetry in generalized anxiety disorder. Psychophysiology. 2016;53:951–7.
27. Dieleman GC, Huizink AC, Tulen JH, Utens EM, Creemers HE, van der Ende J, Verhulst FC. Alterations in HPA-axis and autonomic nervous system functioning in childhood anxiety disorders point to a chronic stress hypothesis. Psychoneuroendocrinology. 2015;51:135–50.
28. Lenze EJ, Mantella RC, Shi P, Goate AM, Nowotny P, Butters MA, Andreescu C, Thompson PA, Rollman BL. Elevated cortisol in older adults with generalized anxiety disorder is reduced by treatment: a placebo-controlled evaluation of escitalopram. Am J Geriatr Psychiatry. 2011;19:482–90.
29. Mantella RC, Butters MA, Amico JA, Mazumdar S, Rollman BL, Begley AE, Reynolds CF, Lenze EJ. Salivary cortisol is associated with diagnosis and severity of late-life generalized anxiety disorder. Psychoneuroendocrinology. 2008;33:773–81.
30. Ainslie PN, Murrell C, Peebles K, Swart M, Skinner MA, Williams MJ, Taylor RD. Early morning impairment in cerebral autoregulation and cerebrovascular CO2 reactivity in healthy humans: relation to endothelial function. Exp Physiol. 2007;92:769–77.
31. Guo ZN, Shao A, Tong LS, Sun W, Liu J, Yang Y. The role of nitric oxide and sympathetic control in cerebral autoregulation in the setting of subarachnoid hemorrhage and traumatic brain injury. Mol Neurobiol. 2016;53:3606–15.
32. White RP, Vallance P, Markus HS. Effect of inhibition of nitric oxide synthase on dynamic cerebral autoregulation in humans. Clin Sci. 2000;99:555–60.
33. Preckel MP, Leftheriotis G, Ferber C, Degoute CS, Banssillon V, Saumet JL. Effect of nitric oxide blockade on the lower limit of the cortical cerebral autoregulation in pentobarbital-anaesthetized rats. Int J Microcirc Clin Exp. 1996;16:277–83.
34. Emhan A, Selek S, Bayazit H, Fatih Karababa I, Kati M, Aksoy N. Evaluation of oxidative and antioxidative parameters in generalized anxiety disorder. Psychiatry Res. 2015;230:806–10.
35. Kaya MC, Bez Y, Karababa IF, Emhan A, Aksoy N, Bulut M, Gunes M, Atli A, Selek S. Decreased serum sulphydryl levels as a sign of increased oxidative stress in generalized anxiety disorder. Psychiatry Investig. 2013;10:281–5.
36. Bulut M, Selek S, Bez Y, Karababa IF, Kaya MC, Gunes M, Emhan A, Aksoy N, Sir A. Reduced PON1 enzymatic activity and increased lipid hydroperoxide levels that point out oxidative stress in generalized anxiety disorder. J Affect Disord. 2013;150:829–33.
37. Copeland WE, Shanahan L, Worthman C, Angold A, Costello EJ. Generalized anxiety and C-reactive protein levels: a prospective, longitudinal analysis. Psychol Med. 2012;42:2641–50.
38. Vieira MM, Ferreira TB, Pacheco PA, Barros PO, Almeida CR, Araujo-Lima CF, Silva-Filho RG, Hygino J, Andrade RM, Linhares UC, et al. Enhanced Th17 phenotype in individuals with generalized anxiety disorder. J Neuroimmunol. 2010;229:212–8.
39. Michopoulos V, Powers A, Gillespie CF, Ressler KJ, Jovanovic T. Inflammation in fear- and anxiety-based disorders: PTSD, GAD, and beyond. Neuropsychopharmacology. 2017;42:254–70.
40. Faraci FM. Reactive oxygen species: influence on cerebral vascular tone. J Appl Physiol. 2006;100:739–43.
41. Yam AT, Lang EW, Lagopoulos J, Yip K, Griffith J, Mudaliar Y, Dorsch NW. Cerebral autoregulation and ageing. J Clin Neurosci. 2005;12(6):643–6.
42. Ortega-Gutierrez S, Petersen N, Masurkar A, Reccius A, Huang A, Li M, Choi JH, Marshall RS. Reliability, asymmetry, and age influence on dynamic cerebral autoregulation measured by spontaneous fluctuations of blood pressure and cerebral blood flow velocities in healthy individuals. J Neuroimaging. 2014;24(4):379–86.
43. Liu W, Lou X, Ma L. Use of 3D pseudo-continuous arterial spin labeling to characterize sex and age differences in cerebral blood flow. Neuroradiology. 2016;58:943–8.

13

Functional connectivity of hippocampal subregions in PTSD: relations with symptoms

Bailee L. Malivoire[1], Todd A. Girard[1*], Ronak Patel[2] and Candice M. Monson[1]

Abstract

Background: Posttraumatic stress disorder (PTSD) is associated with abnormal hippocampal activity; however, the functional connectivity (FC) of the hippocampus with other brain regions in PTSD and its relations with symptoms warrants further attention. We investigated subregional hippocampal FC in PTSD during a resting state compared with a trauma-exposed control (TEC) group. Based on extant research, we targeted the FCs of the anterior and posterior hippocampal subregions with the amygdala, medial prefrontal cortex (mPFC), and the posterior cingulate (PCC).

Methods: Resting-state functional magnetic resonance images were acquired from 11 individuals with PTSD and 13 trauma-exposed controls. Anterior and posterior hippocampal FC was compared between groups. Within the PTSD and TEC groups, subregional hippocampal FC was correlated with scores on the Clinician-Administered PTSD Scale (CAPS) at time of scan and 4 months post-scan.

Results: Those with PTSD had significantly greater FC compared with the TEC group between the left posterior hippocampus and the bilateral PCC (g's > .96). Direct contrasts of the Fisher z-transformed coefficients indicated that the correlations between CAPS scores 4 months post scan and the FC between the left hippocampal head and the right PCC ($z = -2.07$, $p = .039$) as well as the FC between the right hippocampal tail and the right mPFC ($z = -2.19$, $p = .029$) were significantly greater in the PTSD group compared to the TEC group.

Conclusions: These results support between-group differences in posterior hippocampal FC and different relations with PTSD future symptoms, underscoring associations with the anterior and posterior hippocampus. These findings enrich our understanding of PTSD pathophysiology and provide support for future investigations of imaging biomarkers predictive of disease progression.

Keywords: Posttraumatic stress disorder, Functional magnetic resonance imaging, Hippocampus, Trauma symptoms, Resting state connectivity

Background

Approximately 10% of individuals exposed to a traumatic event go on to be diagnosed with posttraumatic stress disorder (PTSD), a debilitating psychiatric condition [1]. Neural differences have been noted among those with PTSD compared with those exposed to trauma but not diagnosed with the disorder [2, 3]. According to the widely-adopted neurocircuitry model, PTSD is primarily associated with structural and functional changes in the amygdala, medial prefrontal cortex (mPFC), and hippocampus [4, 5]. Investigation of neural correlates that are associated with greater likelihood of developing PTSD following trauma exposure enriches our understanding of disorder biomarkers and could guide therapeutic targets [6, 7]. The primary objective of the present study was to investigate subregional hippocampal neural correlates of current and future symptoms in PTSD.

Current theories of PTSD identify hippocampal dysfunction as a key contributor to hallmark symptoms of PTSD including trauma-related intrusions, difficulty voluntarily

* Correspondence: tgirard@psych.ryerson.ca
[1]Department of Psychology, Ryerson University, 350 Victoria St, Toronto, ON M5B 2K3, Canada
Full list of author information is available at the end of the article

recollecting trauma details, and overgeneralization of fear [1, 8, 9]. Moreover, individuals with PTSD demonstrate difficulties with everyday memory [10], working memory [11], and episodic memory [12, 13]. Given the integral role of the hippocampus in PTSD symptoms, memory, and related processes, it is of interest to understand how the role of the hippocampus in the neurocircuitry model differs between individuals with PTSD and a trauma-exposed control (TEC) group, and the functional connectivity within this system to PTSD symptoms.

Resting-state functional connectivity (rsFC) is commonly used to explore patterns of brain system activity in psychiatric conditions, such as PTSD [7, 14]. rsFC is a powerful tool that assesses correlated activity across brain regions over time during rest, permitting investigation of functional networks independent of a task to characterize abnormal intrinsic brain activity [7]. Thus, rsFC is a sensitive imaging technique that offers potential to identify imaging biomarkers of PTSD. rsFC studies in PTSD have found group differences in FC using whole-brain analyses [15], as well as using seed region-of-interest (ROI) analyses [16–18]. For instance, rsFC differences in hippocampal FC between PTSD and controls have been observed based on analyses using the amygdala [17, 18], the PCC [16], and the mPFC [19] as seed regions. However, functional magnetic resonance imaging (fMRI) research has largely focused on the hippocampus as a unitary structure. Given the different structural and functional connectivities of hippocampal subregions [20–22], investigating hippocampal rsFC at a subregional level may further elucidate the functional neurobiology of PTSD.

Anterior and posterior hippocampal subregions have distinct structural and functional connections and contribute to different emotional and cognitive processes (see [23] for a review). For example, the posterior hippocampus has connections with the pregenual ACC, the PCC, and the precuneus [21], and makes a greater contribution to the default mode network compared with the anterior hippocampus [20]. The posterior hippocampus specifically plays an important role in memory retrieval and spatial cognition [24]. In contrast, the anterior hippocampus is preferentially associated with the amygdala [22], the hypothalamic-pituitary-adrenal (HPA) axis, and the limbic prefrontal circuitry compared with the posterior hippocampus [20, 25]. Neuroimaging studies have linked anterior hippocampal activation with emotional memory [26] and reward-directed behaviour [27]. Anterior hippocampal-amygdala connections are thought to underlie atypical memory processes in PTSD, including flashbacks, intrusive thoughts, and nightmares [9], as well as overgeneralization of fear [28]. In sum, there is evidence to support differential roles of the anterior and posterior hippocampal subregions in memory processes, and PTSD symptoms and associated processes. Thus, here we investigated differential FC with these subregions to provide added insight into hippocampal FC in PTSD compared with TEC.

Limited prior research has investigated subregional hippocampal rsFC in PTSD. Chen and Etkin [20] compared anterior and posterior hippocampal rsFC between patients with Generalized Anxiety Disorder, PTSD, and non-traumatized controls. Compared with both the anxiety and control groups, connectivity to the PTSD group was diminished between the posterior hippocampus and brain regions part of the default mode network (associated with self-related cognitive processes) [29, 30], including the PCC and pregenual ACC. The PTSD and GAD groups differed from controls in their anterior hippocampal connectivity to the dorsal ACC/pre-supplementary motor area. Chen and Etkin [20] acknowledged the lack of a TEC group as a limitation: a TEC group is important to elucidating abnormal connectivity differences among individuals exposed to trauma who develop PTSD compared with those who do not. A recent study by Lazarov, Zhu, Suarez-Jimenez, Rutherford, and Neria [31] compared rsFC of the anterior and posterior hippocampus with brain regions within the salience and default-mode networks in PTSD patients and TECs. No between-group differences were evident when the hippocampus was treated as a homogenous structure. However, when investigating the anterior and posterior subregions separately, decreased rsFC was observed between the anterior hippocampus and the precuneus within the PTSD group compared with TEC. These recent studies [20, 31] highlight the importance of investigating subregional hippocampal rsFC.

rsFC can be used to predict PTSD symptoms measured by the Clinician Administered PTSD Scale (CAPS), a well--validated measure of PTSD symptom severity [32]. For instance, PCC/precuneus connectivity with the amygdala in PTSD patients is positively associated with CAPS scores and predictive of future symptoms 6 weeks later [33]. PCC connectivity with the right hippocampus, right amygdala, left mPFC, and left superior temporal gyrus are negatively correlated with CAPS scores [19, 34]. Moreover, the strength of the connectivity between the PCC and amygdala predicted PTSD symptom severity 1 to 6 months following the traumatic event [19]. Investigating relationships between FC and PTSD symptom severity can help identify possible biomarkers of PTSD or identify individuals with a greater predisposition for the disorder [19]. The hippocampus is a central structure in the neurocircuitry model of PTSD [4] and abnormal hippocampal connectivity is proposed to underlie key symptoms in PTSD [9]. Thus, subregional hippocampal rsFC may be predictive of PTSD symptom severity and could be a biomarker of the disorder; however this has not previously been investigated directly.

In sum, current theories of PTSD identify hippocampal dysfunction as a key contributor to hallmark symptoms of PTSD [1, 8, 9]. To our knowledge, only one study [31] has used subregional hippocampal seed regions to compare rsFC between PTSD and TEC groups. This level of analysis provides a more nuanced understanding of hippocampal connectivity. Moreover, given the integral role of the hippocampus in PTSD symptoms, subregional hippocampal rsFC is a likely predictor of PTSD symptom severity; however, no studies to date have investigated this association. The present study first compared subregional hippocampal rsFC with brain regions part of the neurocircuitry model between PTSD and TEC groups. A priori hypotheses were made based on previous rsFC research in PTSD and neuroanatomical connectivity. It was hypothesized that the PTSD and TEC groups would differ in rsFC between the anterior hippocampus and the amygdala and mPFC and between the posterior hippocampus and PCC. Secondly, the present study builds on existing literature by investigating the associations between subregional hippocampal rsFC and current PTSD symptoms, as well as the ability of subregional hippocampal rsFC to predict future symptoms. Given that the anterior and posterior hippocampal subregions contribute to different emotional and cognitive processes it was expected that these regions would differentially predict PTSD symptoms. Based on the literature reviewed above, we predicted that greater functional connectivity of the anterior hippocampus and lower connectivity of the posterior hippocampus would predict greater symptom severity.

Method

Participants

The current rsFC study sample ($N = 24$) comprised participants participating in larger studies of recently traumatized individuals; task-related fMRI data are reported by Patel, Girard, Pukay-Martin, and Monson [35]. Participant demographics and clinical characteristics are summarized in Table 1. At the time of scan, 11 participants met criteria for PTSD and the remaining 13 for the TEC group as determined by both CAPS and a psychodiagnostic assessment. CAPS has been demonstrated to have excellent reliability and validity for assessment of PTSD symptoms [32]. A CAPS score greater than 45 was required for a diagnosis of PTSD. In addition, consistent with Diagnostic and Statistical Manual of Mental Disorders, 4th Edition, (DSM-IV) criteria, the participants needed to endorse the presence of at least one re-experiencing symptom, three numbing or avoidance symptoms, and two hyperarousal symptoms. Diagnostic thresholds for these items were scores of at least one on frequency and two on intensity within the past month. CAPS was administered at the time of scan and 4 months post scan. The PTSD group was exposed to a variety of traumatic events including sexual assault ($n = 5$), physical assault and/or death threats ($n = 4$), witnessing a violent physical assault or death ($n = 1$), and combat exposure ($n = 1$).

Table 1 Participant demographics and clinical characteristics

Group	TEC ($n = 13$)	PTSD ($n = 11$)	p	d
Sex (male:female)	4:9	5:6	.459	0.31
Age	32 (10.4)	34 (13.6)	.623	0.17
Education	14.5 (2.1)	14.0 (2.5)	.560	−0.22
CAPS at scan	12.5 (10.0)	70.0 (14.2)	< .001	4.68
CAPS 4-mo post-scan	8.9 (16.5)	48.3 (26.2)	.002	1.80
BDI-II	6.0 (8.3)	18.9 (12.5)	.010	1.22
Time since trauma (mo)	10.0 (4–24)	12.0 (3–372)	.296	0.44

Sex differences are reported as frequency (n) and were evaluated with a Chi-square contingency test, Time since trauma is reported as medians (range) and compared with a Mann-Whitney U test (due to non-normality), and the remaining demographics are reported as Means (SD) using independent t tests. All contrasts were converted to Cohen's d to assess effect size
Abbreviations: *BDI* Beck Depression Inventory, *CAPS* Clinician Administered PTSD Scale, *mo* months, *PTSD* posttraumatic stress disorder, *TEC* trauma-exposed controls

The requirements for the TEC group were exposure to a traumatic event in accordance with criterion A of the CAPS and that they had a total CAPS score of less than 30 at time of scan. A cut-off score of 30 was selected to ensure the TEC group was diagnostically distinct from the PTSD group. The types of trauma exposure varied within the TEC group and included motor vehicle or biking accident ($n = 5$), witnessing a violent assault and/or death threats ($n = 4$), and direct exposure to physical assault or death ($n = 4$). As expected, the PTSD group had significantly higher CAPS scores at the time of scan and 4 months post-scan compared with the TEC group. The groups did not differ significantly in sex, age, education, or time since trauma (see Table 1).

Psychological comorbidities were assessed using either the Mini International Neuropsychiatric Interview ($n = 18$) [36] or the Structured Clinical Interview for DSM-IV ($n = 6$) [37] depending on study recruitment. Comorbid diagnoses within the PTSD group included anxiety ($n = 6$), major depressive ($n = 4$), and substance use ($n = 2$) disorders. Five PTSD participants were taking antidepressant medications at the time of assessment. With regard to the TEC group, only two participants were diagnosed with an anxiety disorder, and one had both alcohol abuse and substance dependence diagnoses; two participants were taking antidepressant medication. The Beck Depression Inventory-II (BDI-II) [38] was also used to assess depressive symptoms. As anticipated, compared with the TEC group, the PTSD group had significantly higher depression scores (see Table 1).

Brain image acquisition and preprocessing

Anatomical and resting-state fMRI images were acquired in an axial orientation using a 3-T Sigma MR System (GE Medical Systems, Milwaukee) located at Toronto Western Hospital. T_1-weighted anatomical scans were acquired using a fast spoiled gradient echo (FSPGR) sequence at a resolution of isotropic 1-mm^3 voxels (176 slices, 256-mm FOV, 256 × 256 matrix). As outlined below, these T_1 scans were used to co-register the resting-state functional scans, derive tissue-segmented maps, and determine normalization parameters. Resting-state data were collected for 308 s (TR = 2000 ms, TE = 30 ms, flip angle = 85°, 40 slices) at a spatial resolution of 3.125 × 3.125 × 4.0 mm^3 voxels (FOV = 200 mm). During the resting-state scan, participants laid face upward with their eyes open while viewing a black fixation cross on a white screen for 5 min. The resting state scans were preprocessed using the Data Processing & Analysis of Brain Imaging (DPABI) toolbox [39], which includes Data Processing Assistant for Resting-State fMRI Advanced (DPARSFAv3.2) and was run on MATLAB version 7.10.0 (The MathWorks, Natick, MA). Each participant's resting state scan consisted of 154 time points. The first 10 time points were removed for each participant for signal equilibrium and the remaining 144 images were preprocessed. The images were corrected for slice timing and a Friston 24-parameter head motion correction was applied, which regresses out head motion effects from the realigned images [40]. In addition, nuisance covariates including white matter and cerebrospinal fluid were regressed. White matter and cerebrospinal fluid masks were generated from each participant's segmentation map using a probability threshold of 0.99. The nuisance covariates were regressed from the time series using the CompCor method [41], which creates a combined white matter/cerebrospinal fluid mask and extracts the first five principal components to reduce noise related to respiratory and cardiac effects. Time points with too much motion were defined as volumes with FD (Jenkinson) > 0.2 mm and volumes two forward one back from these volumes [42], which is consistent with recommended DPABI methods [39]. Times points with motion above this threshold were regressed out.

The DARTEL tool [43] was used to normalize the functional images into a standard stereotaxic anatomical Montreal Neurological Institute (MNI) space. The normalized volumes were resampled to a voxel size of 3 mm^3. This process involved three steps including coregistration, segmentation, and writing normalization parameters. The images were smoothed with a 4-mm full-width, half-maximum isotropic Gaussian kernel, as in similar reports in the PTSD rsFC literature (e.g., [19]). Temporal filtering (0.01–0.1 Hz) was applied following smoothing to the time series of each voxel to reduce the effect of low and high frequency noise. Using the quality control feature of DPABI the accuracy of the coregistration, segmentation, and normalization of the images were checked. The head motion metrics were also reviewed for each participant. Lastly, a mean regression and standard deviation division standardization module was applied, in accord with recommendations to reduce the impact of nuisance variation on resting state fMRI measures [39].

Hypothesis-driven ROI-based analyses were used to directly target the study aims. This approach also mitigates the severity of correction for multiple tests. Based on a priori hypotheses, left and right ROIs for the hippocampus, mPFC, PCC, and amygdala were constructed using Mask for Region of Interest Analysis (MARINA) software [44]. The mPFC ROI was chosen to be comprehensive and included several regions shown to be implicated in PTSD pathophysiology, including the medial frontal gyrus and anterior cingulate [45], and to protect against Type 1 error involved in multiple ROI comparisons. As shown in Fig. 1, the hippocampal masks were manually sectioned into anterior and posterior ROIs using MRIcron [46], based on guidelines for anatomical segmentation of the hippocampal head and tail, respectively [47].

Data analysis

Spatially averaged time series from each ROI were extracted for each participant and used to generate FC maps using a voxel-wise method. The correlation coefficient map was converted into a Fisher's z map using the Fisher's z transformation to improve normality for

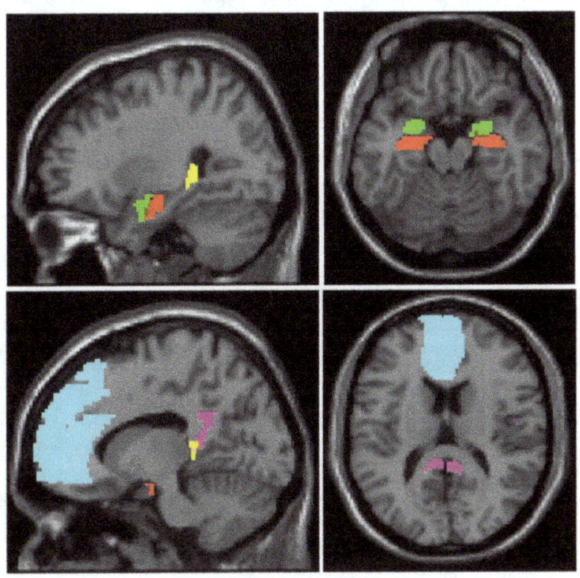

Fig. 1 The ROIs used in the present study displayed on a template brain. Red = anterior hippocampus; yellow = posterior hippocampus; green = amygdala; cyan = mPFC; magenta = PCC

analyses. The mean z values representing FC between each pair of ROIs were extracted for analysis. These FC coefficients were correlated with CAPS scores at the time of scan and for a subset for whom symptom data were available 4 months post-scan (TEC, $n = 10$; PTSD, $n = 6$;). Consistent with similar studies (e.g., [17]), we first conducted one-sample t-tests to examine between which regions correlated activity (FC coefficients) differed significantly from zero within the PTSD and TEC groups ($\alpha = .05$). However, to minimize Type 1 error and limit analyses to only meaningful FC relations, we only examined between-group differences when there were significant FC within at least one group.

Results

Within-group FCs

As shown in Table 2, many of the hippocampal FCs were significant within groups. More specifically, within the TEC group, the FCs between the left hippocampal head and the bilateral amygdala, bilateral mPFC, and left PCC were significant, as well as the FCs between the right hippocampal head and the amygdala ROIs bilaterally, and between the right hippocampal tail and the right amygdala. However, the left hippocampal tail failed to reveal any significant FCs with the other ROIs. In the PTSD group, FC values were significant between the bilateral hippocampal head and the bilateral amygdala, and between the left hippocampal tail and the bilateral PCC. FC did not differ significantly from zero between the right hippocampal tail and any of the ROIs. Five of the above FCs survived a Bonferroni correction ($p < .001$), with the most robust FCs between the hippocampal head and amygdala ROIs for both groups with medium-large effect sizes (see Table 2).

Between-group contrasts

As shown in Table 2, the mean FC values were higher in magnitude in the PTSD group than TEC across all hippocampal-ROI pairs, but they were also more variable. Among the FCs that were significant within groups, the correlated activation between the left hippocampal tail and the left PCC, $t(22) = 2.166$, $p = .041$, $g = .96$, and right PCC, $t(22) = 2.129$, $p = .045$, $g = .97$, was also significantly greater for the PTSD group compared to the TEC group and revealed comparably large effect sizes (Fig. 2).

Correlations with PTSD symptoms

Correlation analyses following up the two significant between-group FCs of the left hippocampal tail with bilateral PCC revealed that symptom severity 4 months post-scan was significantly predicted by the FC between the hippocampal tail and PCC in the left hemisphere, $r = -.87$, $p = .026$.

Further exploratory analyses between FCs and symptoms revealed that CAPS scores at the time of the scan were negatively associated with the FC between the right hippocampal head and the left ($r = -.64$, $p = .018$) and right mPFC ($r = -.76$, $p = .003$) for the TEC group. CAPS scores at the time of the scan were also negatively associated with the FC between the left hippocampal head and the left ($r = -.57$, $p = .042$; Fig. 3a) and right PCC ($r = -.64$, $p = .019$) for the TEC group. In the PTSD group, the above associations were of medium magnitude but failed to reach significance, $rs > -.44$, $ps > .181$.

CAPS scores 4 months post scan were negatively associated with FCs between the right hippocampal head and the right amygdala ($r = -.69$, $p = .029$) for the TEC group. This association was positive, but not significant within the PTSD group, $r = .27$, $p = .540$. Rather, within the PTSD group, CAPS scores 4 months post scan were negatively associated with FCs between the left hippocampal head and the left ($r = -.90$, $p = .014$; Fig. 3b) and right PCC, $r = -.87$, $p = .016$. Symptom severity 4 months post-scan was also significantly associated with FC between the right hippocampal tail and the right mPFC

Table 2 Means and standard deviations for the FC coefficients between the hippocampal head and tail with the amygdala, mPFC, and PCC regions

Group	Hippocampus		Amygdala		mPFC		PCC	
			Left	Right	Left	Right	Left	Right
PTSD	Head	Left	.64(.24)***	.57(.25)**	.31(.37)	.24(.41)	.24(.40)	.20(.44)
		Right	.45(.27)**	.58(.22)***	.31(.35)	.28(.37)	.22(.39)	.23(.40)
	Tail	Left	.27(.34)	.24(.37)	.33(.37)	.29(.39)	.33(.35)*	.35(.35)*
		Right	.22(.38)	.19(.39)	.18(.45)	.21(.42)	.21(.39)	.27(.38)
TEC	Head	Left	.64(.14)***	.43(.19)***	.23(.28)*	.18(.27)*	.16(.20)*	.12(.24)
		Right	.39(.22)***	.54(.16)***	.06(.19)	.04(.18)	−.04(.19)	−.01(.25)
	Tail	Left	.05(.23)	.07(.22)	.06(.15)	−.01(.17)	.08(.15)	.08(.20)
		Right	.08(.23)	.15(.23)*	.06(.19)	.04(.19)	.07(.21)	.09(.19)

*$p < .05$, **$p < .01$, ***$p < .001$ for the one-sample t-tests, rsFC > 0

FC values reported in the table are r coefficients to aid interpretation; analyses were conducted on the Fisher z-transformed coefficients to meet distribution assumptions

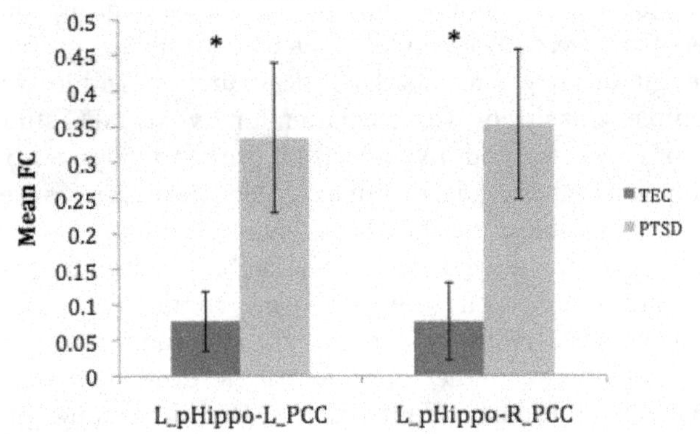

Fig. 2 The mean FC *r* values for the PTSD and TEC groups between the left hippocampal tail and the bilateral PCC. Error bars represent standard error

($r = -.85$, $p = .031$) within the PTSD group. The aforementioned associations were not significant within the TEC group, *rs* ranged from −.40 to .24, *ps* > .255. Direct contrasts of the Fisher z-transformed coefficients further indicated that the correlations between CAPS scores 4 months post scan and the FC between the left

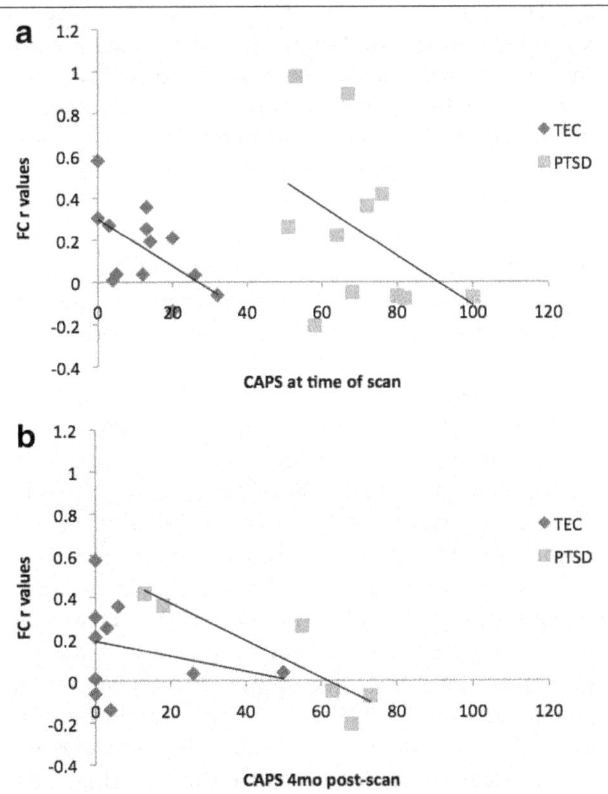

Fig. 3 Associations between PTSD symptoms (CAPS) and the FC between the left hippocampal head and the left PCC for the TEC and PTSD groups. There was a significant, negative correlation between (**a**) FC and symptoms for the TEC group at the time of scan ($R^2 = .33$) and (**b**) for the PTSD group for symptoms 4-months post-scan ($R^2 = .80$)

hippocampal head and the right PCC ($z = -2.07$, $p = .039$), as well as the FC between the right hippocampal tail and the right mPFC ($z = -2.19$, $p = .029$), were significantly greater in the PTSD than TEC group. The other tests of the correlations by group failed to reach significance.

Discussion

The present study provides empirical support for distinct rsFC among hippocampal subregions when investigating PTSD pathophysiology and its relation with PTSD symptoms. Comparing rsFC between groups we found greater rsFC between the posterior hippocampus and bilateral PCC in the PTSD group compared to the TEC group, which may reflect a biomarker of PTSD pathophysiology or of resilience in the TEC group. This relation on the left was also predictive of symptom severity 4 months post-scan.

Further analyses revealed lower FC between the anterior hippocampus and the bilateral PCC and FC between the posterior hippocampus and the left PCC and right mPFC in the PTSD sample that was associated with greater symptoms 4 months following the resting-state scan. In the TEC group, lower FC between the anterior hippocampus and the bilateral mPFC and PCC were associated with greater current PTSD symptom severity and lower FC between the anterior hippocampus and the right amygdala was associated with higher symptoms 4 months later. Notably, the left-head – right PCC and right-tail – right-mFPC predictors of CAPS scores 4 months post scan were also significantly greater in the PTSD than TEC group. These findings may reflect meaningful differential relations to symptoms reflective of pathophysiology. However, caution is warranted given their exploratory nature and the observation of greater variability and mean FCs in the PTSD group that may reflect psychometric sensitivity. Regardless, these relations warrant further investigation.

The correlation analyses extend previous research by demonstrating that PTSD symptoms were preferentially associated with anterior hippocampal rsFC. This finding is consistent with research that suggests the anterior hippocampus plays a greater role in PTSD symptoms and associated processes compared to the posterior hippocampus. Specifically, anterior hippocampal-amygdala FC is hypothesized to underlie the hallmark intrusion symptoms in PTSD, including intrusive thoughts, flashbacks, and nightmares [9], as well as overgeneralization of fear [28]. Moreover, anterior hippocampal FC is preferentially involved in emotional memory [26] and reward-directed behaviour [27], which may contribute to avoidance, a maladaptive behaviour that maintains PTSD symptoms. Specifically, it is proposed that following trauma exposure individuals with PTSD overconsolidate the traumatic memory, which is easily reactivated by trauma reminders and accompanied by conditioned emotional arousal. This leads to hypervigilance towards trauma-related cues and subsequent avoidance of trauma-related memories and reminders to minimize associated distress [48]. The avoidance could be conceptualized as a form of negative reinforcement that is rewarding for individuals with PTSD. Future research is warranted to investigate anterior hippocampal FC as a predictor of PTSD symptoms and its relationship with avoidance.

With respect to the group contrasts, the PTSD group revealed greater FC between the posterior hippocampus and PCC compared to TEC participants. Posterior hippocampal FC with the cingulate, precuneus, and visual cortices has been linked to spatial processing, including spatial memory and navigation [22]. There is preliminary support for greater impairment in PTSD compared to TEC samples on visuospatial copying tasks [49] and in constructing a cognitive map of a virtual environment [50]. The abnormal FC between the posterior hippocampus and PCC in PTSD compared to the TEC group may reflect differences in these processes and is a future direction for task-based imaging research. Moreover, the PCC and hippocampus are part of the default mode network, which is associated with self-referential thought processes and autobiographical memory [29]. Lower FC within the default mode network is more frequently observed across psychiatric and neurological conditions, with some variation across its subnetworks [30]. Hippocampal-PCC connectivity is associated with memory functions and the current enhanced FC may reflect a unique role of this subnetwork in PTSD. Previous research that has investigated differences in the default mode network between PTSD and TEC samples also support group differences in this network [16, 17]. Group rsFC differences between the hippocampus and PCC may reflect group differences in integration and contextualization of memories, which may contribute to threat hypersensitivity evident in PTSD [16]. Previous research comparing rsFC between individuals with PTSD and trauma-naïve controls has found there to be less hippocampal-PCC rsFC in the PTSD group compared to controls [16, 20]. This discrepancy from the greater FC observed here may be attributable to differences in data preprocessing, sample characteristics and a trauma-exposed versus trauma-naïve control group. These distinctions highlight the need for more consistent methodology across imaging studies and further assessment of moderating factors in PTSD research. Moreover, research is warranted comparing FC between individuals with PTSD, trauma-naïve controls, and TEC samples to characterize normal trauma-related changes in FC and FC specific to PTSD [3].

Two of the hypothesized group differences in rsFC, those between the anterior hippocampus and the amygdala and the posterior hippocampus and the mPFC, were unsupported in the present study. One possibility is that the subregional hippocampal-amygdala rsFC group differences were too subtle to detect with the current design or they may not have been present within this sample. Consistent with the latter, a previous rsFC study also failed to find hypothesized group differences in hippocampal-amygdala activity [51]. Moreover, as reported in Table 2, the FCs between anterior hippocampal ROIs with the amygdalae had the highest mean FC coefficients within each group and were comparable across groups. This finding may reflect that the functional connectivity between the hippocampal head and amygdala may remain robust and intact in PTSD under resting conditions or that this FC is similarly high in both trauma-exposed samples (PTSD and TEC); future comparison to a non-traumatized group will be valuable to assess these possibilities. Of note, a recent meta-analysis of task-based brain activation, revealed hippocampal and amygdala hyperactivity in PTSD in comparison to trauma-naïve samples but not TEC samples [2]. Interestingly, decreased connectivity between these regions was strongly associated with PTSD symptoms in the current TEC sample.

In contrast to the lack of group differences in hippocampal-mPFC rsFC in the present sample, Jin et al. [15] found weaker connectivity between the mPFC and the hippocampus in their PTSD group compared to trauma-naïve controls. Group FC differences are suggested to be a function of the type of comparison group (i.e., trauma-naïve controls versus TEC) [3]. It is possible that changes in hippocampal-mPFC FC are normal following exposure to trauma-related stress and do not differentiate individuals with PTSD from those exposed to trauma who did not develop PTSD. It is also possible that the mPFC ROI we used was too liberal to detect group differences or that group differences were not present in this sample. These are notable negative findings that require further investigation and replication.

Interpretations of the present study findings should be considered in light of the study's limitations. Firstly, although the ROIs were selected based on a priori hypotheses and the PTSD imaging literature, the small sample size constrains the positive predictive value of the findings. To address reproducibility concerns, we propose future pre-registration of larger-scale, collaborative replications [52, 53]. In addition, the sample was heterogeneous in the types of trauma exposure and time since trauma. In light of evidence that longer resting-state imaging time frames of 9–13 min may improve the test-retest reliability of the scans and FC estimates [54], future replication studies should consider using longer resting-state durations. Of note, post-hoc assessment of the potential relationship between time since trauma and CAPS scores failed to reveal any relations (data not shown). Future research with larger samples should investigate whether the associations found in this study are potentially moderated by type of trauma, time since trauma, and cumulative trauma load. Nonetheless, the current findings are valuable in demonstrating that there are common FC differences that distinguish PTSD and TEC samples. Consistent with previous studies investigating rsFC in PTSD (e.g., [16, 20]), participants had psychological comorbidities and were using antidepressant medication. It is unclear how medication use and psychological comorbidities affect rsFC. However, it is unlikely that the FC differences observed in the present study were solely attributable to medication use and psychological comorbidities given these confounds were present in both the PTSD and TEC groups. Depression scores significantly differed between groups and thus depression symptoms could be influencing the group differences found in the study; however, recruiting individuals with no depression affects generalizability and statistically covarying for depression can inappropriately remove true-score variance shared with diagnostic status [55]. Nonetheless, future neuroimaging research in PTSD is required to investigate the effects of medication use and comorbid symptoms on rsFC. Given heterogeneity of the mPFC and amygdala, another future direction could be to assess the potential of more nuanced rsFC between subregional hippocampal, amygdalar, and functionally distinct mPFC subregions, and their relations with PTSD symptoms. This work may also yield further insight into different symptom profiles. For instance, Nicholson et al. [56] observed differential rsFC between amygdala subregions among those with and without the dissociative subtype of PTSD.

Conclusions

This study is the first to investigate associations between anterior and posterior hippocampal rsFC and current and future PTSD symptoms and alludes to the anterior hippocampus as a potentially superior biomarker compared to the posterior hippocampus. The group differences in rsFC between the posterior hippocampus and the PCC may reflect a marker of resilience in individuals exposed to trauma who did not go onto develop the disorder. These findings underscore the importance of considering hippocampal subregions independently when investigating FC. This subregional approach extends our understanding of PTSD pathophysiology and provides support for future investigations of subregional hippocampal FC in PTSD and its use as a prognostic aid.

Abbreviations

ACC: Anterior cingulate cortex; BDI-II: Beck Depression Inventory-II; CAPS: Clinician-Administered PTSD Scale; DPABI: Data Processing & Analysis of Brain Imaging toolbox; DPARSFA: Data Processing Assistant for Resting-State fMRI Advanced; DSM-IV: Diagnostic and Statistical Manual of Mental Disorders, 4th Edition; FC: Functional connectivity; fMRI: Functional magnetic resonance imaging; FSPGR: Fast spoiled gradient echo; HPA: Hypothalamic-pituitary-adrenal; MARINA: Mask for Region of Interest Analysis; MNI: Montreal Neurological Institute; mPFC: Medial prefrontal cortex; PCC: Posterior cingulate cortex; PTSD: Posttraumatic stress disorder; ROI: Region-of-interest; rsFC: Resting-state functional connectivity; TEC: Trauma-exposed control

Acknowledgements

The researchers would like to thank the members of Dr. Candice Monson's IMPACT lab for their assistance in participant recruitment, screening, and assessment.

Funding

This research was funded by grants from New Initiatives Grant from the Faculty of Arts at Ryerson University, the Canadian Institutes of Health Research and National Institute of Mental Health. These funding bodies had no direct involvement in the design of the study and collection, analysis, or interpretation of data, or in writing the manuscript.

Authors' contributions

RP collected the resting-state scans as part of a separate investigation. BM and TG preprocessed and analyzed the resting-state fMRI data and wrote the manuscript. CM assisted in participant recruitment and contributed conceptual feedback to the manuscript. All authors read and approved the manuscript.

Competing interests

The authors declare that they have no competing interests.

Author details

[1]Department of Psychology, Ryerson University, 350 Victoria St, Toronto, ON M5B 2K3, Canada. [2]Department of Clinical Health Psychology, University of Manitoba, Winnipeg, MB, Canada.

References

1. American Psychiatric Association. Diagnostic and statistical manual of mental disorders. 5th ed. Arlington: American Psychiatric Publishing; 2013.
2. Patel R, Spreng RN, Shin LM, Girard TA. Neurocircuitry models of posttraumatic stress disorder and beyond: a meta-analysis of functional neuroimaging studies. Neurosci Biobehav Rev. 2012;36:2130–42.
3. Stark EA, Parsons CE, Van Hartevelt TJ, Charquero-Ballester M, McManners H, Ehlers A, et al. Post-traumatic stress influences the brain even in the absence of symptoms: a systematic, quantitative meta-analysis of neuroimaging studies. Neurosci Biobehav Rev. 2015;56:207–21.
4. Rauch SL, Shin LM, Phelps EA. Neurocircuitry models of posttraumatic stress disorder and extinction: human neuroimaging research—past, present, and future. Biol Psychiatry. 2006;60:376–82.
5. Rauch SL, Shin LM, Whalen PJ, Pitman RK. Neuroimaging and the neuroanatomy of PTSD. CNS Spectr. 1998;3:30–41.
6. Fornito A, Bullmore ET. What can spontaneous fluctuations of the blood oxygenation-level-dependent signal tell us about psychiatric disorders? Curr Opin Psychiatry. 2010;23:239–49.
7. Fox MD, Greicius M. Clinical applications of resting state functional connectivity. Front Syst Neurosci. 2010;4:1–13.
8. Brewin CR, Gregory JD, Lipton M, Burgess N. Intrusive images in psychological disorders: characteristics, neural mechanisms, and treatment implications. Psychol Rev. 2010;117:210–32.
9. Carrion VG, Wong SS. Can traumatic stress alter the brain? Understanding the implications of early trauma on brain development and learning. J Adolesc Health. 2012;51:23–8.
10. Bremner JD, Vermetten E, Afzal N, Vythilingam M. Deficits in verbal declarative memory function in women with childhood sexual abuse-related posttraumatic stress disorder. J Nerv Ment Dis. 2004;192:643–9.
11. Vasterling JJ, Duke LM, Brailey K, Constans JI, Allain AN, Sutker PB. Attention, learning, and memory performances and intellectual resources in Vietnam veterans: PTSD and no disorder comparisons. Neuropsychology. 2002;16:5–14.
12. Bremner JD, Scott TM, Delaney RC, Southwick SM, Mason JW, Johnson DR, et al. Deficits in short-term memory in posttraumatic stress disorder. Am J Psychiatr. 1993;150:1015–9.

13. Yehuda R, Keefe RS, Harvey PD, Levengood RA. Learning and memory in combat veterans with posttraumatic stress disorder. Am J Psychiatry. 1995; 152:137–9.
14. Greicius M. Resting-state functional connectivity in neuropsychiatric disorders. Curr Opin Neurol. 2008;21:424–30.
15. Jin C, Qi R, Yin Y, Hu X, Duan L, Xu Q, et al. Abnormalities in whole-brain functional connectivity observed in treatment-naive post-traumatic stress disorder patients following an earthquake. Psychol Med. 2014;44:1927–36.
16. Bluhm RL, Williamson PC, Osuch EA, Frewen PA, Stevens TK, Boksman K, Lanius RA. Alterations in default network connectivity in posttraumatic stress disorder related to early-life trauma. J Psychiatry Neurosci. 2009;34:187–94.
17. Sripada RK, King AP, Garfinkel SN, Wang X, Sripada CS, Welsh RC, Liberzon I. Altered resting-state amygdala functional connectivity in men with posttraumatic stress disorder. J Psychiatry Neurosci. 2012;37:241–9.
18. Zhang X, Zhang J, Wang L, Li R, Zhang W. Altered resting-state functional connectivity of the amygdala in Chinese earthquake survivors. Prog Neuro-Psychopharmacol Biol Psychiatry. 2016;65:208–14.
19. Zhou Y, Wang Z, Qin L, Wan J, Sun Y, Su S, et al. Early altered resting-state functional connectivity predicts the severity of post-traumatic stress disorder symptoms in acutely traumatized subjects. PLoS One. 2012;7:1–6.
20. Chen AC, Etkin A. Hippocampal network connectivity and activation differentiates post-traumatic stress disorder from generalized anxiety disorder. Neuropsychopharmacology. 2013;38:1889–98.
21. Poppenk J, Moscovitch M. A hippocampal marker of recollection memory ability among healthy young adults: contributions of posterior and anterior segments. Neuron. 2011;72:931–7.
22. Poppenk J, Evensmoen HR, Moscovitch M, Nadel L. Long-axis specialization of the human hippocampus. Trends Cogn Sci. 2013;17:230–40.
23. Chase HW, Clos M, Dibble S, Fox P, Grace AA, Phillips ML, Eickhoff SB. Evidence for an anterior–posterior differentiation in the human hippocampal formation revealed by meta-analytic parcellation of fMRI coordinate maps: focus on the subiculum. NeuroImage. 2015;113:44–60.
24. Nadel L, Hoscheidt S, Ryan LR. Spatial cognition and the hippocampus: the anterior–posterior axis. J Cogn Neurosci. 2013;25:22–8.
25. Fanselow MS, Dong HW. Are the dorsal and ventral hippocampus functionally distinct structures? Neuron. 2010;65:7–19.
26. Murty VP, Ritchey M, Adcock RA, LaBar KS. fMRI studies of successful emotional memory encoding: a quantitative meta-analysis. Neuropsychologia. 2010;48:3459–69.
27. Viard A, Doeller CF, Hartley T, Bird CM, Burgess N. Anterior hippocampus and goal-directed spatial decision making. J Neurosci. 2011;31:4613–21.
28. Admon R, Milad MR, Hendler T. A causal model of post-traumatic stress disorder: disentangling predisposed from acquired neural abnormalities. Trends Cogn Sci. 2013;17:337–47.
29. Andrews-Hanna JR, Smallwood J, Spreng RN. The default network and self-generated thought: component processes, dynamic control, and clinical relevance. Ann N Y Acad Sci. 2014;1316:29–52.
30. Menon V. Large-scale brain networks and psychopathology: a unifying triple network model. Trends Cogn Sci. 2011;15:483–506.
31. Lazarov A, Xi Z, Suarez-Jimenez B, Rutherford BR, Neria Y. Resting-state functional connectivity of anterior and posterior hippocampus in posttraumatic stress disorder. J Psychiatr Res. 2017;94:15–22.
32. Blake DD, Weathers FW, Nagy LM, Kaloupek DG, Gusman FD, Charney DS, Keane TM. The development of a clinician-administered PTSD scale. J Trauma Stress. 1995;8:75–90.
33. Lanius RA, Bluhm RL, Coupland NJ, Hegadoren KM, Rowe B, Theberge J, et al. Default mode network connectivity as a predictor of post-traumatic stress disorder symptom severity in acutely traumatized subjects. Acta Psychiatr Scand. 2010;121:33–40.
34. Qin L, Wang Z, Sun Y, Wan J, Su S, Zhou Y, Xu J. A preliminary study of alterations in default network connectivity in post-traumatic stress disorder patients following recent trauma. Brain Res. 2012;1484:50–6.
35. Patel R, Girard TA, Pukay-Martin N, Monson C. Preferential recruitment of the basolateral amygdala during memory encoding of negative scenes in posttraumatic stress disorder. Neurobiol Learn Mem. 2016;130:170–6.
36. Sheehan DV, Lecrubier Y, Sheehan KH, Janavs J, Weiller E, Keskiner A, et al. The validity of the MINI international neuropsychiatric interview (MINI) according to the SCID-P and its reliability. Eur Psychiatry. 1997;12:232–41.
37. First MB, Spitzer RL, Gibbon M, Williams JBW. Structured clinical interview for DSM-IV-TR axis I disorders, research version, patient edition with psychotic screen. Biometrics Research: New York; 2002.
38. Beck AT, Steer RA, Brown GK. Beck depression inventory-II. San Antonio. 1996;78:490–8.
39. Yan CG, Wang XD, Zuo XN, Zang YF. DPABI: data processing & analysis for (resting-state) brain imaging. Neuroinformatics. 2016;14:339–51.
40. Friston KJ, Williams S, Howard R, Frackowiak RS, Turner R. Movement-related effects in fMRI time-series. Magn Reson Med. 1996;35:346–55.
41. Behzadi Y, Restom K, Liau J, Liu TT. A component based noise correction method (CompCor) for BOLD and perfusion based fMRI. NeuroImage. 2007;37:90–101.
42. Jenkinson M, Bannister P, Brady M, Smith S. Improved optimization for the robust and accurate linear registration and motion correction of brain images. NeuroImage. 2002;17:825–41.
43. Ashburner J. A fast diffeomorphic image registration algorithm. NeuroImage. 2007;38:95–113.
44. Walter B, Blecker C, Kirsch P, Sammer, G, Schienle A, Stark R, Vaitl D. MARINA: an easy to use tool for the creation of MAsks for region of INterest analyses. Vol. 19. In 9th international conference on functional mapping of the human brain; 2003.
45. Shin LM, Rauch SL, Pitman RK. Amygdala, medial prefrontal cortex, and hippocampal function in PTSD. Ann N Y Acad Sci. 2006;1071:67–79.
46. Rorden C, Karnath HO, Bonilha L. Improving lesion-symptom mapping. J Cogn Neurosci. 2007;19:1081–8.
47. Boccardi M, Bocchetta M, Apostolova LG, Barnes J, Bartzokis G, Corbetta G, et al. Delphi definition of the EADC-ADNI harmonized protocol for hippocampal segmentation on magnetic resonance. Alzheimers Dement. 2015;11:126–38.
48. Yehuda R. Status of glucocorticoid alterations in post-traumatic stress disorder. Ann N Y Acad Sci. 2009;1179:56–69.
49. Gurvits TV, Lasko NB, Repak AL, Metzger LJ, Orr SP, Pitman RK. Performance on visuospatial copying tasks in individuals with chronic posttraumatic stress disorder. Psychiatry Res. 2002;112:263–8.
50. Tempesta D, Mazza M, Iaria G, De Gennaro L, Ferrara M. A specific deficit in spatial memory acquisition in post-traumatic stress disorder and the role of sleep in its consolidation. Hippocampus. 2012;22:1154–63.
51. Rabinak CA, Angstadt M, Welsh RC, Kenndy AE, Lyubkin M, Martis B, Phan KL. Altered amygdala resting-state functional connectivity in post-traumatic stress disorder. Front Psychiatry. 2011;2:1–8.
52. Button KS, Ioannidis JP, Mokrysz C, Nosek BA, Flint J, Robinson ES, et al. Power failure: why small sample size undermines the reliability of neuroscience. Nat Rev Neurosci. 2013;14:365–76.
53. Munafò MR, Nosek BA, Bishop DV, Button KS, Chambers CD, du Sert NP, et al. A manifesto for reproducible science. Nat Hum Behav. 2017;1:21.
54. Birn RM, Molloy EK, Patriat R, Parker T, Meier TB, Kirk GR, et al. The effect of scan length on the reliability of resting-state fMRI connectivity estimates. NeuroImage. 2013;83:550–8.
55. Miller GA, Chapman JP. Misunderstanding analysis of covariance. J Abnorm Psychol. 2001;110:40–8.
56. Nicholson AA, Densmore M, Frewen PA, Theberge J, Neufeld RWJ, McKinnon MC, Lanius RA. The dissociative subtype of posttramatic stress disorder: unique resting-state functional connectivity of basolateral and centromedial amygdala complexes. Neuropsychopharmacology. 2015;40:2317–26.

14

The relationship between addiction to smartphone usage and depression among adults

Aljohara A. Alhassan[1], Ethar M. Alqadhib[1], Nada W. Taha[1], Raneem A. Alahmari[2], Mahmoud Salam[3*] and Adel F. Almutairi[3]

Abstract

Background: Addiction to smartphone usage is a common worldwide problem among adults, which might negatively affect their wellbeing. This study investigated the prevalence and factors associated with smartphone addiction and depression among a Middle Eastern population.

Methods: This cross-sectional study was conducted in 2017 using a web-based questionnaire distributed via social media. Responses to the Smartphone Addiction Scale - Short version (10-items) were rated on a 6-point Likert scale, and their percentage mean score (PMS) was commuted. Responses to Beck's Depression Inventory (20-items) were summated (range 0–60); their mean score (MS) was commuted and categorized. Higher scores indicated higher levels of addiction and depression. Factors associated with these outcomes were identified using descriptive and regression analyses. Statistical significance was set at $P < 0.05$.

Results: Complete questionnaires were 935/1120 (83.5%), of which 619 (66.2%) were females and 316 (33.8%) were males. The mean ± standard deviation of their age was 31.7 ± 11 years. Majority of participants obtained university education 766 (81.9%), while 169 (18.1%) had school education. The PMS of addiction was 50.2 ± 20.3, and MS of depression was 13.6 ± 10.0. A significant positive linear relationship was present between smart phone addiction and depression ($y = 39.2 + 0.8x$; $P < 0.001$). Significantly higher smartphone addiction scores were associated with younger age users, ($\beta = -0.203$, adj. $P = 0.004$). Factors associated with higher depression scores were school educated users ($\beta = -2.03$, adj. $P = 0.01$) compared to the university educated group and users with higher smart phone addiction scores ($\beta = 0.194$, adj. $P < 0.001$).

Conclusions: The positive correlation between smartphone addiction and depression is alarming. Reasonable usage of smart phones is advised, especially among younger adults and less educated users who could be at higher risk of depression.

Keywords: Smartphone addiction, Depression, Age, Education, Middle East

Background

Addiction to smartphone usage is a common problem among adults worldwide. It manifests itself in the excessive usage of their phones, while engaged in other activities such as studying, driving, social gatherings and even sleeping [1]. However, many people fail to realize that addiction to smartphone usage is a serious issue that can have a negative effect on the person's thoughts, behavior, tendencies, feelings, and sense of well-being [2]. In particular, it can be a risk factor for depression, loneliness, anxiety and sleep disturbances [3]. As per the Mental Health Foundation in the United Kingdom, people with depression experience an unhappy mood, loss of interest or pleasure, feelings of guilt or low self-worth, disturbed sleep or appetite, low energy, and poor concentration. Depressive and anxiety disorders are two main common disorders that are highly prevalent globally, as over 300

* Correspondence: salamma@ngha.med.sa
[3]King Abdullah International Medical Research Center, King Saud bin Abdulaziz University for Health Sciences, Science and Technology Unit, Ministry of National Guard - Health Affairs, Riyadh 11426, Saudi Arabia
Full list of author information is available at the end of the article

million people are estimated to suffer from depression, which is equivalent to 4.4% of the world's population [4]. It is speculated that not only addiction to smartphone usage can affect one's mental and behavioral status, but also that those with mood disorders are more likely to become addicted to using their smartphones [5].

Numerous tools have been utilized in literature to assess the same phenomenon, but with different terms such as excessive smart phone usage, smartphone addiction, dependency on smart phones, internet addiction, problematic mobile phone usage, and so on. Remarkably, there was a tendency to use a non-pathological terminology, such as "Problematic Smartphone Use," rather than the term smartphone addiction [6]. Addiction manifests itself in various forms such as preoccupation, tolerance, lack of control, withdrawal, mood modification, conflict, lies, excessive use and loss of interest [7]. Several studies have found that women are more likely to develop an addiction to smartphone usage than men [8]. This was viewed as a positive way for people to stay connected in social relationships. One study clarified that women like to show affection to their families using their smartphones while men use phones for efficiency and practicality [3, 8]. Though there are several studies on this topic, no study has proven this connection so far. Smartphone addiction has been found to be correlated with various physical and psychological issues, as indicated in a number of studies that tested this relationship among various age groups. For example, one study found that people with depression, social anxiety and loneliness had different uses for their smartphones compared to others [9]. People with social anxiety made fewer outgoing calls, as well as, fewer text messages than those without social anxiety [9]. It was reported that high levels of smartphone addiction were correlated with low self-esteem, loneliness, depression and shyness [10].

Depression is a general reflection of the psychological wellbeing that is thought to be highly correlated with addiction to smartphone usage. The majority of studies on this issue revealed that there is a relationship between these two variables; however, all these studies were conducted in specific populations. In Turkey, females were more likely to develop an addiction to smartphone usage compared to males [11], while in Austria chronic stress, low emotional stability, female gender, young age and depression were associated with problematic mobile usage [12]. In Taiwan, adolescents with significant depression were more likely to have four or more symptoms of problematic cell phone usage [13]. Depression and anxiety disorders were reported around 18% among adults in Saudi Arabia [14]. Each community is unique in terms of its norms, practices, behaviors and traditions. Even within a single Middle Eastern setting, ethno-national affiliations may influence how people associate between insights and self-stigma [15]. Those residing in the Middle Eastern region consist of heterogeneous systems of social differentiation based on ethnic, linguistic, sectarian, familial, tribal, regional, socioeconomic, and national identities. Ethnic Arab people likewise follow more than one faith tradition. It is worth mentioning that Western cultural norms have been disseminated into the Arab world, but this effect has been experienced differently in communities and across societies [16]. The aim of this study was to investigate the relationship between addiction to smartphone usage and self-reported depression among a Middle Eastern population to better understand this relationship in such a region. This was fulfilled by presenting the prevalence of smart phone addiction and depression, describing the sample characteristics and identifying factors associated with both smartphone addiction and depression.

Methods

A cross-sectional study was conducted in 2017 by distributing a pre-validated web-based questionnaire through common social media networks, among the Saudi Arabian population. The usage of social networking channels guaranteed maximum distribution throughout various geographical regions and boosted the representativeness of the sample. A brief description of the study objectives was presented, and by convenience, those who agreed to respond to the questionnaire confirmed their agreement electronically. Incomplete questionnaires were dropped out. Participants were requested to report their nationality, age and region upon submission. Participants below 18 years of age were excluded. The data retrieved were stored in a private institutional server. This study was approved by the Institutional Review Board of the Saudi Ministry of National Guard Health Affairs (MNG-HA), Riyadh, Saudi Arabia (Rss 17/003). Participation was voluntary with assurance about the confidentiality of their information, as no identifiers or personal information were collected.

The data collection tool comprised of three sections, namely the participants' characteristics, the smart phone addiction assessment tool and the self-reported depression scale. These tools have been widely used in literature [11, 17]. Participants' characteristics were nationality, sex, age (years), level of education (school vs. university level), place of residence (region) and financial income level (<\$1500 vs. ≥\$1500). Participants with school educational level were those who stopped their education prior enrollment in university, while those with university educational levels were those either currently enrolled or have graduated from university. The level of smartphone addiction was assessed using the Smartphone Addiction Scale-Short Version (SAS-SV), which is a validated scale developed from the original Smartphone Addiction Scale (SAS) by Kwon 2013. It is a self-reported scale containing 10-items, each rated on a 6- point Likert scale from one "strongly disagree" to six "strongly agree". The total scores were summated, then converted to percentage mean scores (PMS), where higher scores indicated higher levels of smartphone addiction. In the original scale of SAS, the cut-off point was not reported [18]. A cutoff point at of 31/60 in males and 33/60 in females was utilized in the short version SAS by one Spanish-Belgium study [19]. Since no gender differences were reported between these cut off points [19], a cut-off point of score 32/60 or PMS = 53.3% was accounted in this study with subjects having PMS > 53% classified as excessive users or probably addicts. The concurrent validity and internal consistency were obtained for SAS-SV (Cronbach's alpha: 0.91) [18].

The Beck's Depression Inventory (BDI II) second edition is a tool used to assess the severity of depressive symptoms and to objectively quantify depression signs, but it's not a diagnostic tool. The BDI II consists of 20 items rated on a 4-point scale. The total score ranges from 0 to 60, as higher scores indicated higher levels of depression. Participants with scores 0–9 were classified as "having ups and downs but considered normal", 10–15 classified as "having mild mood disturbance", 16–19 classified as "borderline clinical depression", 20–29 classified as "having moderate depression", 30–39 classified with "severe depression" and ≥ 40 as having "extreme depression". This tool showed a Cronbach's alpha reliability coefficient of 0.89 [20]. The Arabic version that was used in this study was previously translated by another researcher with a coefficients alpha of 0.82 [21].

Data were analyzed using SPSS; IBM (version 24). Descriptive statistics including mean, standard deviation, frequency and percentages were used to present the participants' demographics and outcomes. The smart phone addiction and self-reported depression scores were analyzed as continuous variables and categorized qualitatively. Independent student t- test and one way ANOVA were used for bivariate analysis. Pearson's correlation was used to determine the nature and significance of relationship between the two outcome measures. Factors significantly associated with smart phone addiction and depression were presented after controlling for any possible confounder using two linear regression models.

Results

Sample characteristics

Response rate was 935/1120 (83.5%). The younger age group (18–35 years) were 609 (65.1%), followed by middle age group (36–54 years) 303 (32.4%) and older age group (≥55 years) 23 (2.5%), with a mean of age ± standard deviation 31.7 ± 11 years. Catchment areas varied between all regions of the Kingdom, with highest response in Central region 668 (71.5%) and least in Northern region 5(0.6%). Females comprised 619 (66.2%) and males 16 (33.8%) of the sample. The income of 418 (44.7%) was <$1300, while 517 (55.3%) was ≥$1300. Majority of sample 766 (81.9%) were university educated, while 169 (18.1%) were school educated, Table 1.

Smartphone addiction and Beck depression

The overall percentage mean score (PMS) of Smartphone Addiction scale (SAS-SV) was 50.2 ± 20.25, while the mean score of Beck depression scale was 13.6 ± 10.0. The responses to Beck Depression Scale and Smartphone Addiction Scale individual statments are enlisted in suppliment Additional file 1: Tables S1 and Additional file 2: Tables S2 respectively. Almost 19% can considered as non-addicted to smartphone usage (PMS = 0–30), 64% can considered as slightly addicted to smartphone usage (PMS = 31–70) and 17% as probably addicted to its usage (PMS = 71–100). In regards of depression, those classified as ups/downs to be normal were 39% (score 0–9), mild mood disturbance 25% (score 10–15), borderline clinical depression 12% (score 16–19), moderate depression 15% (score20–29), severe depression 7% (score 30–39) and extreme depression 1% (score ≥ 40). Qualitative characteristics of SAS-SV and Beck depression are illustrated in Figs. 1 and 2. A significant

Table 1 Description of sample characteristics

	N = 935 (100%)
Age (years)	
Young (18–35)	609 (65.1)
Middle (36–54)	303 (32.4)
Old (≥55)	23 (2.5)
x ± SD	31.7 ± 10.98
Gender	
Male	316 (33.8)
Female	619 (66.2)
Income	
Less than $1300	418 (44.7)
Between $1300 & $3700	316 (33.8)
More than $3700	201 (21.5)
Educational level	
School	169 (18.1)
University	766 (81.9)
Regional distribution	
North	5 (0.6)
South	47 (5.0)
Eastern	74 (7.9)
Western	121 (12.9)
Central	668 (71.5)
Others	20 (2.1)

Abbreviations: *x* mean, *SD* standard deviation

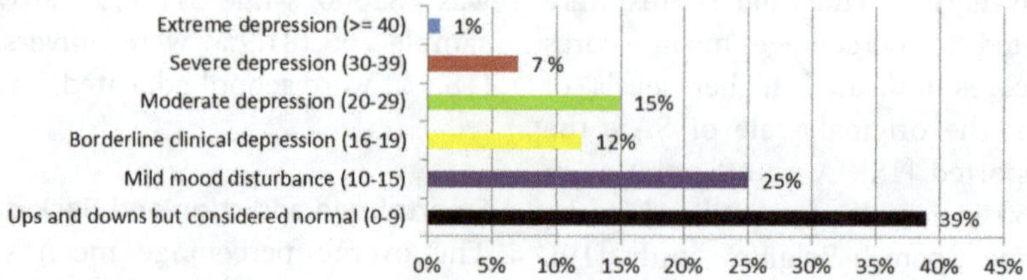

Fig. 1 Various levels of depression

positive relation was observed between addiction and depression scores y = 39.2 ± 0.81×, $P < 0.001$, Fig. 3.

Initial bivariate analysis showed that the younger age group (PMS = 51.3 ± 20.5) had significantly the highest addiction scores compared to the older age group, $P = 0.014$. Smartphone users with school education (PMS = 15.7 ± 11.3), those with income <$1300 (PMS = 14.6 ± 10.2) and younger age group (PMS = 14.2 ± 10.2) were significantly more depressed than their counter groups ($P = 0.003$, $P = 0.015$ and $P = 0.006$ respectively), Table 2.

Two linear regression models were constructed and revealed that the factors that were significantly associated with higher smartphone addiction scores were: a) younger age (β = – 0.203, adj. $P = 0.004$) compared to older age smartphone users. Significant factors associated with higher depression scores were: a) School educated users (β = – 2.034, adj. $P = 0.010$) compared to university educated users; b) Users with higher smartphone addiction scores (β = 0.194, adj. $P < 0.001$) compared to users with less addiction scores, Table 3.

Discussion

The association between smartphone addiction and depression has been discussed in previous studies, but which preceded the other remains debatable. In this study, there was a strong positive relationship between smartphone addiction and depression. A systematic review of 23 peer reviewed papers reported that depression was consistently related to problematic smartphone usage [22]. Depression in Lebanese and Austrian university students was also significantly associated with smartphone addiction [12, 23] or problematic mobile phone usage [13] respectively. In fact, one of the predisposing factors of smart phone addiction is increased stress levels followed by a decrease in self-control, which eventually leads to the over usage of smartphones [24]. It is worth mentioning, that no relationship between smartphone ownership and symptoms of depression were reported by one study, which entails that addiction is related to self-control rather than the possession of the phone itself [25]. However, a negative association between smartphone addiction and depression was reported by another study [26]. Furthermore, another study stated that familial social support was a significant predictor of smartphone addiction, as this addiction increased as individuals' familial support decreased [27]. There is no doubt that social relationships have been severely affected with the introduction of various social networks, and this phenomenon is commonly reported by the older generation who lived in the era before the introduction of smart phone technology. Unfortunately, there are gaps in literature on the probable association between smartphone addiction and social support [27]. Over usage of smartphones causes problems with attention and focusing, as these people are more likely to show more functional impairments that interfere with school, work and family life [28]. Young adults with personality type A who experience high stress level may lack positive stress coping mechanisms which makes them highly susceptible to smartphone addiction [8].

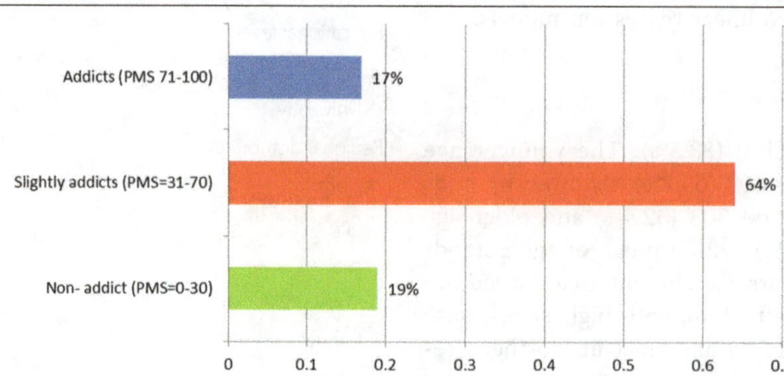

Fig. 2 Various levels of smart phone addiction

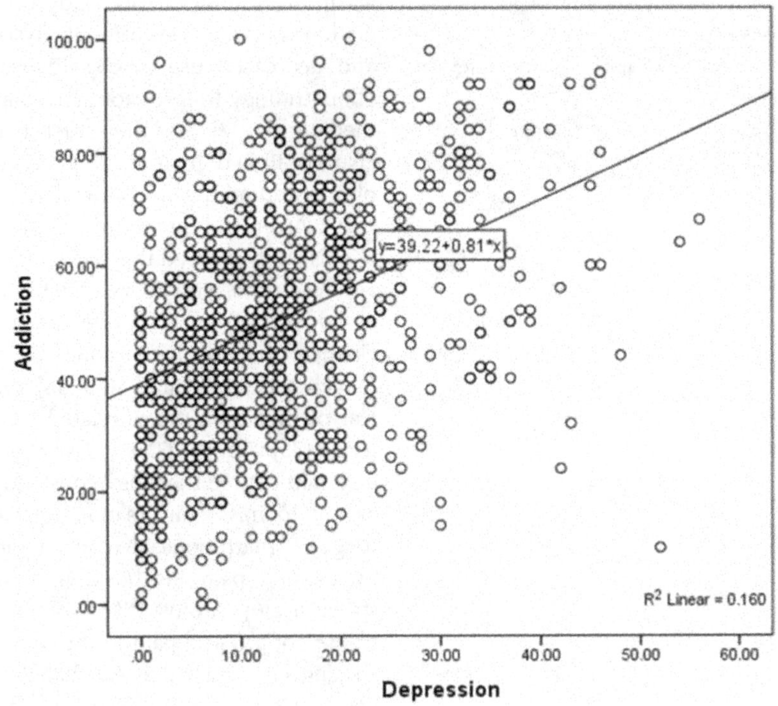

Fig. 3 Relationship between smart phone addiction and depression scores

Table 2 Scores of smart phone addiction and beck depression scales across sample characteristics

	Smart phone addiction (0–100) %mean score ± SD 50.2 ± 20.25	Beck depression (1–60) Mean score ± SD 13.6 ± 10.0
Gender		
Male	50.9 ± 22.2	13.3 ± 10.5
Female	49.9 ± 19.2	13.8 ± 9.8
	$t = 0.672$, $P = 0.502$	$t = -0.806$, $P = 0.420$
Age		
Young (18–35)	51.3 ± 20.5	14.2 ± 10.2
Middle (36–54)	48.9 ± 19.6	12.9 ± 9.5
Old (≥55)	40.2 ± 18.6	8.4 ± 8.96
	F = 4.301, df = 2, $P = 0.014$*	F = 5.167, df = 2, $P = 0.006$*
Educational level		
School	51.4 ± 20.9	15.7 ± 11.3
University	49.9 ± 20.1	13.2 ± 9.6
	$t = 0.724$, $P = 0.395$	$t = 8.786$, $P = 0.003$*
Income		
Less than $1300	50.2 ± 20.6	14.6 ± 10.2
Between $1300 & $3700	50.96 ± 19.8	13.4 ± 9.9
More than $3700	49.1 ± 20.3	12.1 ± 9.5
	F = 0.522, df = 2, $P = 0.594$	F = 4.221, df = 2, $P = 0.015$*

t = Student's t-test; F = one-way ANOVA
Abbreviations: *ANOVA* analysis of variance, *SD* standard deviation, *df* degree of freedom
P-value = statistically significant at < 0.05, % = percentage

Table 3 Significant factors associated with higher smart phone addiction and depression scores

Variables	Smart phone addiction β (t) Adj *P*-value	Beck depression β (t) Adj *P*-value
Gender		
Female[a]	0.675 (0.461)	−0.355(−0.536)
Male[b]	*Adj P* = 0.645	*Adj P* = 0.592
Age	−0.203 (−2.892)	−0.050(−1.582)
(Years)	*Adj P* = 0.004*	*Adj P* = 0.114
Educational level		
School[a]	−1.878 (− 1.077)	− 2.034(− 2.579)
University[b]	*Adj P* = 0.282	*Adj P* = 0.010*
Income		
< $1300[a]	2.285 (1.398)	−0.781(−1.058)
≥ $1300[b]	*Adj P* = 0.162	*Adj P* = 0.291
Smart Phone Addiction		0.194 (13.119)
(%mean score)	–	*Adj P* < 0.001*
Constant	56.729 (22.33)	7.703 (5.414)
	Adj P < 0.001*	*Adj P* < 0.001*

t = Student's t-test; [a]: reference group, [b]: compared group
Abbreviations: *β* coefficient of determination, *Adj* adjusted
*Statistically significant at $P < 0.05$

Observing the relationship between depression and smart phone addiction from an opposite perspective is also valid. Smartphone addiction can be a predisposing factor to depression, either indirectly or through a mediating effect. An association between smart phone addiction and altered lifestyle habits was found, with higher tendency among smart phone addicts to skip meals, to eat unhealthy diets, to gain weight, and to experience sleep disorders compared to less addicted smartphone users. These can be accounted as predisposing factors to depression [29]. Late night smartphone users indeed reported feeling tired (35.9%) and complained of less sleep quality (35.8%) [8]. This was confirmed by one Saudi study stating that higher problematic mobile usage scores were correlated with various unhealthy sleep hygiene, physical inactivity, dietary style and others [30]. One study reported that people with lower levels of self-perceived emotional or health conditions were more likely to exhibit an over usage of smartphones [31]. This indicates that these people are stuck in a vicious cycle. They are stressed from a certain emotional or health deficit, and then try to compensate or overcome this stress with on over usage of smart phones without realizing that this addiction itself leaves a negative impact on their social, emotional and physical wellbeing. On the other hand, an experimental study tried to determine the impact of not using a smart phone for 2 days. An alarming finding in this study was suggestive of an association between emotional dysregulation (suppression and decreased use of cognitive appraisal) and the psychopathology (depression, stress and anxiety) from social media loss [32]. Another study had claimed that neuroticism is linked in a chain-mediating effect with smartphone addiction and depression, all important variables that worsen the quality of life [33].

This study showed that the level of smart phone addiction was moderate, with 31.3% of subjects who can be accounted as addicts to smart phone usage. A meta-analysis paper claimed that the prevalence of smart phone addiction ranged between 39 and 40% [34]. One study proved that the fear of missing out was related to problematic smartphone usage [35]. Almost 60.9% of subjects in this study agreed to a certain degree that they constantly check their phones so as not to miss conversations between other people. Over usage of smartphones can actually impair the hand function by causing pain in the thumb and lowering the pinch strength [36]. Almost 33.8% of subjects in this study complained of physical pain in the wrist, back or neck. All these striking conclusions reveal that there is a clear association between smartphone usage addictions and various degrees of physical problems [37].

Younger individuals were more likely to be addicted than older individuals. A study from Turkey found that younger age groups had higher levels of smartphone overuse [12]. Generally, adolescents have a higher risk of smartphone addiction compared to adults, as they are more susceptible to accept new technologies than older generation groups [18]. Gender differences were not observed in this study, whether in relation to addiction or depression which was comparable to some studies in literature [19]. It was reported that males tend to use the internet mainly for online gaming, while females tend to use the internet for sending messages, chatting and blogging [26, 38]. Adults with higher educational level were less likely to have symptoms of depression, which was similar to results of a study conducted in 10 European countries [39]. A significant relationship between income and depression was noted as the people with lower income were more depressed. This was similar to findings of a Canadian study that found depression was less prevalent in those with a high income than those with a low income [23]. Younger adults seem to be more depressed than the older adults. This was consistent with findings in previous studies which can be attributed to the fact that younger adults are more susceptible to stressors such as social conflicts, marital relationships, raising children and others [40, 41].

Limitations

Few limitations have been observed in this study, mainly due to the retrospective nature of the study design and the method of data collection. Recall bias is expected to be minimal as smartphone usage is experienced on daily bases and participants won't have any difficulty recalling its influence on their various life aspects. Web-based surveys are usually linked to incentives, which make them prone to frauds. In this study, participation was both anonymous and free. The variable of marital status contracted errors during the extraction of data, and therefore was dropped out. There might be an association between marital status and the outcomes measured which could be investigated in future studies. Participation was not restricted to Saudi citizens and the job market in Saudi Arabia accommodates expatriate workers from all over the world, so the data collected is not only representative of the country itself. Generalizing the findings might not be self-limited to Saudi Arabia, as smart phone addiction is invading populations all over the world. Environmental and social characteristic of Saudi Arabia might be considered unique compared to other countries, but no studies have investigated the association between smart phone addiction and setting characteristics. The SAS-SV self-reported surveys grants researchers a reliable and valid assessment tool to identify addiction, yet a more accurate diagnosis is confirmed by a face to face assessment conducted by a clinical or behavioral expert. Depression is a sensitive outcome that cannot be linked exclusively to smartphone addiction; therefore the term "association" was used as a more conservative description of this relationship.

Conclusions

The positive correlation between smartphone addiction and depression is alarming. Reasonable usage of smart phones is advised, especially among younger adults and less educated users who could be at higher risk of depression. The relationship between depression and smartphone addiction is an escalating global concern that necessitates future studies to investigate further on this aspect.

Key points

- Depression is a mood disorder that is thought to be highly correlated with addiction to smart phone usage.
- An alarming positive correlation between addiction to smart phone usage and depression was found.
- Reasonable usage of smart phones is advised, especially among younger adults and less educated users who could be at higher risk of depression.

Abbreviations

BDI II: Beck's depression inventory; MNG-HA: Ministry of National Guard Health Affairs; MS: Mean score; PMS: Percentage mean score;
SAS: Smartphone Addiction Scale; SAS-SV: Smartphone addiction scale-short version; WHO: World Health Organization

Acknowledgements

This study was approved and monitored by King Abdullah International Medical Research Center, King Saud bin Abdulaziz University for Health Sciences, Riyadh, Saudi Arabia. The authors would like to thank the Research Office and the Institutional Review Board for their tremendous support.

Authors' contributions

All authors conceptualized and designed the study. AFM supervised the conduct of the study and data collection. AAA, EMA, NWT and RAA undertook the recruitment of subjects and managed the data. AFM and MS were accounted for the quality control. MS provided statistical advice on study design, data analysis and responded to reviewers' comments. All authors drafted the manuscript, and contributed substantially to its revision as submitted and agree to be accountable for all aspects of the work. All authors read and approved the final manuscript.

Competing interests

The authors declare that they have no competing interests.

Author details

[1]College of Rehabilitation and Health Sciences, Princess Noura Bint Abdulrahman University, Riyadh, Saudi Arabia. [2]King Abdullah International Medical Research Center, King Saud bin Abdulaziz University for Health Sciences, College of Applied Medical Sciences, Echography Cardiovascular Technology, Ministry of National Guard - Health Affairs, Riyadh, Saudi Arabia. [3]King Abdullah International Medical Research Center, King Saud bin Abdulaziz University for Health Sciences, Science and Technology Unit, Ministry of National Guard - Health Affairs, Riyadh 11426, Saudi Arabia.

References

1. Harwood J, Dooley J, Scott A, Joiner R. Constantly connected – the effects of smart-devices on mental health. Comput Hum Behav. 2014;34:267–72.
2. Edition F. Diagnostic and statistical manual of mental disorders. Arlington: American Psychiatric Publishing; 2013.
3. Gao Y, Li A, Zhu T, Liu X, Liu X. How smartphone usage correlates with social anxiety and loneliness. Peerj. 2016;4:e2197.
4. World Health Organization. Depression and other common mental disorders: global health estimates.
5. Zhang KZ, Chen C, Lee MK. Understanding the Role of Motives in smartphone Addiction. InPACIS. 2014. p. 131.
6. Bae SM. Smartphone addiction of adolescents, not a smart choice. J Korean Med Sci. 2017;32(10):1563–4.
7. Lee H, Kim JW, Choi TY. Risk factors for smartphone addiction in Korean adolescents: smartphone use patterns. J Korean Med Sci. 2017;32(10):1674–9.
8. Park N, Lee H. Nature of youth smartphone addiction in Korea: diverse dimensions of smartphone use and individual traits. J Commun Res. 2014; 51(1):100–32.
9. Wei R, Lo VH. Staying connected while on the move: cell phone use and social connectedness. New Media Soc. 2006;8(1):53–72.
10. Bian M, Leung L. Linking loneliness, shyness, smartphone addiction symptoms, and patterns of smartphone use to social capital. Soc Sci Comput Rev. 2015;33(1):61–79.
11. Demirci K, Akgönül M, Akpinar A. Relationship of smartphone use severity with sleep quality, depression, and anxiety in university students. J Behav Addict. 2015;4(2):85–92.
12. Augner C, Hacker G. Associations between problematic mobile phone use and psychological parameters in young adults. Int J Public Health. 2011; 57(2):437–41.
13. Yen C, Tang T, Yen J, Lin H, Huang C, Liu S, et al. Symptoms of problematic cellular phone use, functional impairment and its association with depression among adolescents in southern Taiwan. J Adolesc. 2009;32(4):863–73.
14. Al-Khathami AD, Ogbeide DO. Prevalence of mental illness among Saudi adult primary-care patients in Central Saudi Arabia. Saudi Med J. 2002;23(6):721–4.
15. Zisman-Ilani Y, Hasson-Ohayon I, Levy-Frank I, Tuval-Mashiach R, Roe D. Self-stigma, insight, and family burden among Israeli mothers of people with

serious mental illness: ethno-national considerations. Transcult Psychiatry. 2017;54(3):423–41.
16. Al-Krenawi A, Graham JR. Culturally sensitive social work practice with Arab clients in mental health settings. Health Soc Work. 2000;25(1):9–22.
17. Güzeller C, Coşguner T. Development of a problematic mobile phone use scale for Turkish adolescents. Cyberpsychol Behav Soc Netw. 2012;15(4):205–11.
18. Kwon M, Kim DJ, Cho H, Yang S. The smartphone addiction scale: development and validation of a short version for adolescents. PLoS One. 2013;8(12):e83558.
19. Lopez-Fernandez O. Short version of the smartphone addiction scale adapted to Spanish and French: towards a cross-cultural research in problematic mobile phone use. Addict Behav. 2017;64:275–80.
20. Lee E, Lee S, Hwang S, Hong S, Kim J. Reliability and validity of the Beck depression inventory-II among Korean adolescents. Psychiatry Investig. 2017;14(1):30.
21. Alansari BM. Internal consistency of an Arabic adaptation of the Beck depression inventory-II with college students in eighteen Arab countries. Soc Behav Personal Int J. 2006;34(4):425–30.
22. Elhai JD, Dvorak RD, Levine JC, Hall BJ. Problematic smartphone use: a conceptual overview and systematic review of relations with anxiety and depression psychopathology. J Affect Disord. 2017;207:251–9.
23. Matar Boumosleh J, Jaalouk D. Depression, anxiety, and smartphone addiction in university students- a cross sectional study. PLoS One. 2017; 12(8):e0182239.
24. Cho HY, Kim DJ, Park JW. Stress and adult smartphone addiction: Mediation by self-control, neuroticism, and extraversion. Stress and Health. 2017;33(5): 624–30.
25. Lemola S, Perkinson-Gloor N, Brand S, Dewald-Kaufmann J, Grob A. Adolescents' electronic media use at night, sleep disturbance, and depressive symptoms in the smartphone age. J Youth Adolesc. 2014;44(2):405–18.
26. Choi S, Kim D, Choi J, Ahn H, Choi E, Song W, et al. Comparison of risk and protective factors associated with smartphone addiction and internet addiction. J Behav Addict. 2015;4(4):308–14.
27. Aker S, Sahin MK, Sezgin S, Oguz G. Psychosocial factors affecting smartphone addiction in university students. J Addict Nurs. 2017;28(4):215–9.
28. Collier R. Mental health in the smartphone era. CMAJ. 2016;188(16):1141–2.
29. Kim Y, Lee N, Lim Y. Gender differences in the association of smartphone addiction with food group consumption among Korean adolescents. Public Health. 2017;145:132–5.
30. Alosaimi FD, Alyahya H, Alshahwan H, Al Mahyijari N, Shaik SA. Smartphone addiction among university students in Riyadh, Saudi Arabia. Saudi Med J. 2016;37(6):675.
31. Kim HJ, Min JY, Kim HJ, Min KB. Association between psychological and self-assessed health status and smartphone overuse among Korean college students. J Ment Health. 2017:1–6.
32. Elhai JD, Hall BJ, Erwin MC. Emotion regulation's relationships with depression, anxiety and stress due to imagined smartphone and social media loss. Psychiatry Res. 2018;261:28–34.
33. Gao T, Xiang YT, Zhang H, Zhang Z, Mei S. Neuroticism and quality of life: multiple mediating effects of smartphone addiction and depression. Psychiatry Res. 2017;258:457–61.
34. Davey S, Davey A. Assessment of smartphone addiction in Indian adolescents: a mixed method study by systematic-review and meta-analysis approach. Int J Prev Med. 2014;5(12):1500.
35. Liu Q, Zhou Z, Yang X, Kong F, Niu G, Fan C. Mobile phone addiction and sleep quality among Chinese adolescents: a moderated mediation model. Comput Hum Behav. 2017;72:108–14.
36. İNal EE, ÇetİntÜrk A, Akgönül M, Savaş S. Effects of smartphone overuse on hand function, pinch strength, and the median nerve. Muscle Nerve. 2015; 52(2):183–8.
37. AlAbdulwahab SS, Kachanathu SJ, AlMotairi MS. Smartphone use addiction can cause neck disability. Musculoskeletal Care. 2017;15(1):10–2.
38. Heo J, Oh J, Subramanian S, Kim Y, Kawachi I. Addictive internet use among Korean adolescents: a National Survey. PLoS One. 2014;9(2):e87819.
39. Ladin K. Risk of late-life depression across 10 European Union countries: deconstructing the education effect. J Aging Health. 2008;20(6):653–70.
40. Streiner D, Cairney J, Veldhuizen S. The epidemiology of psychological problems in the elderly. Can J Psychiatry. 2006;51(3):185–91.
41. Wade TJ, Cairney J. The effect of Sociodemographics, social stressors, health status and psychosocial resources on the age depression relationship. Can J Public Health Canadienne De Sante Publique. 2000;91(4):307–12.

15

Are changes in body-mass-index associated with changes in depressive symptoms? Findings of a population-based longitudinal study among older Germans

André Hajek* and Hans-Helmut König

Abstract

Background: The longitudinal relationship between BMI and depressive symptoms is not well understood. Therefore, we aimed at investigating the long-term association between body-mass-index (BMI) and depressive symptoms among older Germans.

Methods: Data were derived from a population-based longitudinal study of adults aged 40 and above in Germany (German Ageing Survey, DEAS). Four waves (2002–2014) were used. Depressive symptoms was assessed by the Center for Epidemiologic Studies Depression Scale (CES-D). Linear, quadratic and cubic terms were included for self-reported BMI. Fixed effects regressions were used to estimate the predictors of depressive symptoms.

Results: FE regressions showed a curvilinear effect of BMI on depressive symptoms in the total sample and in women, but not men, with significant gender differences. In sum, the greater the extreme of BMI (either higher or lower), the greater the risk for depressive symptoms in the total sample and in women.

Conclusion: Our findings indicate that the effect of BMI on depressive symptoms is by no means simple. The current study highlight the importance of comprehensive treatment of depression, which include management of (extreme) weight to manage depressive symptoms.

Keywords: Depressive symptoms, BMI, CES-D, Curvilinear effect, Longitudinal study

Background

It is expected that the number of individuals with excess weight increases markedly in the next decades as the mean age is expected to increase and the mean body weight gradually rises with age [1]. While there is large evidence that an increased body-mass-index (BMI) is associated with numerous adverse health-related *physical outcomes* such as a decreased physical function [2, 3], cardiovascular diseases, osteoarthritis, or cancer [4, 5], little is known about the consequences of weight changes on *psychological outcomes* such as depressive symptoms.

Cross-sectionally, the association between BMI and depressive symptoms has widely been studied, with mixed evidence. While some studies found a negative association between excess weight and depressive symptoms in older adults [6, 7], others found no association [8], whereas others found a positive association [9]. Equivocal results might be mainly explained by differences in statistical methods, culture and attitudes towards excess weight. The mixed evidence might also be explained by the curvilinearity in the relationship between BMI and depressive symptoms.

However, as already argued by Roberts and colleagues [10], longitudinal studies are needed to get insights into the causal relationship between BMI and depressive symptoms. By using longitudinal data, intraindividual changes can be investigated. Moreover, the problem of omitted variable bias can be solved [11]. Thus far, only a few longitudinal studies exist examining the effect of BMI on depressive symptoms among older adults [12–15],

* Correspondence: a.hajek@uke.de
Department of Health Economics and Health Services Research, Hamburg Center for Health Economics, University Medical Center Hamburg-Eppendorf, Hamburg, Germany

mainly indicating that excess weight increased the risk of subsequent depressive symptoms.

In addition, the *longitudinal relationship* between BMI and these outcome variables is not well understood. For example, do we become more depressed as we lose or increase weight? Or are changes in depressive symptoms not associated with weight changes? Or are changes in weight related to changes in depressive symptoms in a curvilinear pattern, with individuals becoming underweight and overweight scoring worse? Based on previous studies showing that underweight as well as overweight are associated with increased depressive symptoms [16, 17], we hypothesize that the greater the change to the extreme of BMI, the greater the risk of an increase in depressive symptoms. More specifically, factors associated with obesity such as poor body image, maladaptive eating behaviors or avoidance of physical activity might explain the relationship between obesity and depressive symptoms [18]. The relation between low weight and depressive symptoms might be explained by lifestyle factors (e.g., alcohol consumption) and chronic illnesses [19]. In addition, biological factors such as high density lipoprotein (HDL) cholesterol might play a role in this relationship [19].

Furthermore, we hypothesize that the relationship between changes in BMI and changes in depressive symptoms is stronger in women [20–22] than in men since extreme BMI values might carry greater stigma in women [23].

Consequently, we aimed at investigating the longitudinal relationship between intraindividual changes in BMI and intraindividual changes in depressive symptoms by using a large population-based longitudinal study of adults aged 40 and over (2002–2011) in Germany. Fixed effects regressions were used (with linear [BMI], quadratic [BMI*BMI] and cubic terms [BMI*BMI*BMI] for BMI) to examine whether changes in BMI are associated with changes in depressive symptoms, adjusting for several covariates. Furthermore, by using FE regressions, time-constant factors (both, unobserved and observed) were taken into consideration.

Methods

Sample

Currently, the German Ageing Survey (DEAS) has completed five survey waves, beginning in 1996. It is a nationally representative sample of the population aged 40 and over living in private households. The sample for the current study was drawn by a national probability sampling stratified by age, sex, and place of residence. Participants were interviewed by trained staff using a standardized questionnaire.

As depressive symptoms were quantified from the second wave onwards, we used data from wave 2 (2002) to wave 5 (2014). In the second wave 5194 subjects were interviewed, whereas 8200 subjects were interviewed in the third wave (2008). 4855 individuals were included in the fourth wave (2011), and 10,325 individuals participated in the fifth wave. The large discrepancies between the sample sizes by survey year can be explained by the introduction of new samples. For example, 6205 subjects were interviewed for the first time in the third wave and 1995 subjects have been interviewed in former waves (994 in the first wave and 1001 in the second wave). In the fourth wave, only panel-willing participants (individual willing to participate in a future wave) of the previous waves (wave 1: 1040; wave 2: 957; wave 3: 2858) have been re-questioned. Thus, the fourth wave is a pure panel survey. While 6002 individuals were interviewed for the first time in the fifth wave, 4323 individuals have been interviewed in former waves (888 in the first wave, 866 in the second wave and 2569 in the third wave). The baseline samples provide information to describe and investigate the current situation and social changes over time. In 1996, individuals of the birth cohorts 1911–1956 were used (2002: 1917–1962; 2008: 1923–1968; 2014: 1929–1974). A very recent study by Klaus et al. [24] displayed the sample design of the German Ageing Survey in detail. Moreover, detailed figures were given for the DEAS baseline samples 1996, 2002, 2008 and 2014 and the longitudinal samples 2002, 2008, 2011 and 2014.

Data were gathered from the German population living in private households aged 40 and over in 1996, whereas from 2002 even non-German nationals were included (random sampling of non-Germans nationals in the birth cohorts 1917–1962). The main reasons for a lack of follow-up data were refused further participation and health reasons. More details with regard to the sample composition and the sampling frame were provided elsewhere [25]. Prior to the interview, written informed consent was given. Individuals received a small incentive for participation (1996, 2002: telephone card; 2008: stamp album; 2011: €10) to increase response rate [26]. This was also done to increase response rate in groups, which are often underrepresented in surveys (e.g., low educated individuals or singles) [27].

Dependent variable

Depressive symptoms were assessed by means of the short version [28] of the Center for Epidemiologic Studies Depression Scale (CES-D, 15 items) [29], a well-validated scale with good psychometric properties [30]. The scale is the sum of all 15 items, ranging from 0 to 45 (high values indicate more depressive symptoms).

Independent variables

Our main variable of interest, BMI (linear, quadratic and cubic terms) was computed as self-reported weight in kilograms divided by height in square meters (kg/m^2). Quadratic and cubic terms were used to explore the possible nonlinear relationship between BMI and depressive symptoms over time. Furthermore, control variables were integrated in the main model: age, marital status (Ref.: married, living together with spouse; married, living separated from spouse; divorced; widowed; never married), (log) monthly household net income in Euro, employment status (Ref.: working; retired; other: not employed), and comorbidity (number of illnesses, e. g. osteoporosis or cancer). Moreover, the validated Rosenberg scale [31], consisting of ten items (from 1 = "strongly agree" to 4 = "strongly disagree"), was used to assess self-esteem. It was included as a potential confounder in our main regression model because it might affect the outcome variable. An index score was developed by averaging the items (higher values indicate higher level of self-esteem). Cronbach's alpha was .84. In addition, the number of important people in regular contact (0–9) was included.

Additionally, the time-invariant variable education was reported to describe the sample. It was measured by using the International Standard Classification of Education (ISCED-97) [32], with low (0–2), medium (3–4) and high education (5–6). We performed robustness checks by running regression models (sensitivity analysis) where we additionally controlled for functional health because it might affect the outcome variable. This was measured by the subscale "physical functioning" of the 36-Item Short Form Health Survey (SF-36) [33]. The individuals rated impairments in ten activities of daily living (e.g., bathing or lifting) on a three-point scale [34]. The items were transformed into a single scale (from 0 = worst score to 100 = best score). In addition, further analysis was conducted with BMI categories using the WHO thresholds: underweight ($BMI < 18.5\ kg/m^2$), normal weight ($18.5\ kg/m^2 \leq BMI < 25\ kg/m^2$), overweight ($25\ kg/m^2 \leq BMI < 30\ kg/m^2$), and obesity ($BMI \geq 30\ kg/m^2$). While the WHO thresholds additionally differentiate between obese grade I ($30\ kg/m^2 \leq BMI < 35\ kg/m^2$), obese grade II ($35\ kg/m^2 \leq BMI < 40\ kg/m^2$), and obese grade III ($BMI \geq 40\ kg/m^2$), it is worth stressing that these additional classifications were not used for reasons of simplicity.

Moreover, additional regression models were computed as follows: Depressive symptoms were replaced by log depressive symptoms to account for the skewness (linear FE regressions). In addition, depressive symptoms were considered as count data. Thus, FE Poisson regressions and FE negative binomial regressions were computed.

Furthermore, depressive symptoms were replaced by depression (CES-D ≥ 18 [30]). Consequently, conditional FE logistic regressions were used.

Moreover, self-esteem was excluded from our main regression model in further sensitivity analysis. In addition, very extreme BMI values were excluded from FE regression analysis in another sensitivity analysis.

Statistical analysis

First, descriptive characteristics and pattern of change for individuals included in linear FE regressions were reported. Second, pairwise correlations were reported to yield insights into the relation between BMI and depressive symptoms. Third, longitudinal regression analysis (linear FE regressions) was performed.

One of the main advantages of longitudinal data is that time-constant unobserved factors can be taken into account. This is crucial because these time-constant unobserved factors such as genetic disposition, or pessimism are often systematically correlated with the predictors [11]. If this correlation is present, not only pooled ordinary least squares (OLS) estimates but also random effects (RE) strategies are inconsistent [35]. Contrarily, fixed effects (FE) regressions provide consistent estimates (under the assumption of strict exogeneity) even if time-constant unobserved factors are correlated with the predictors [35]. Actually, some recent studies [36–38] have shown that FE regressions are the method of choice with depressive symptoms as outcome variable. The strict exogeneity assumptions means that FE estimates are biased under endogeneity. Endogeneity in turn can have different sources: (1) unobserved time-varying confounders, (2) reverse causality, simultaneity (Y also influences X), (3) measurement errors and (4) endogenous selection bias. Please see Brüderl and Ludwig for further details [39].

One of the main goals was to provide consistent estimate under rather weak assumptions [39]. Consequently, FE regressions were used. Sargan-Hansen tests supported this choice. A Sargan-Hansen test is a Hausman test with robust standard errors. The intuition of this test is that FE estimates are consistent. If the estimates of the RE regressions do not differ systematically, then RE regressions can be used (because they are more efficient since they use within- and between-information). The Sargan-Hansen test statistic was 214.1, $p < .0001$ (main model, total sample), suggesting that there were systematic differences between the coefficients observed using the FE and the RE regressions. In addition, the strengths and limitations of the FE model are discussed by Brüderl and Ludwig [39].

FE regressions solely use intraindividual changes (changes within individuals over time). Hence, the FE-estimator is also called 'Within-estimator'. Thus, the association between intraindividual changes in BMI and intraindividual changes in depressive symptoms was examined. However, for linguistic reasons, seemingly causal terminology was used in the current study, though this should be interpreted with great caution [39–41]. Please see the strengths and limitations section for further details. Further technical details are described elsewhere [35, 42, 43].

According to Cameron and Trivedi [35], it was tested whether the depressive symptoms variable has enough within variation ('xttab' and 'xttrans' in Stata) to obtain precise estimates. For example, in each wave only about 26% of the individuals with no depressive symptoms (= 0) in the data had no depressive symptoms in the next year. The remaining 74% became 1 or more. Thus, there is enough within-variation over time.

It is worth noting that individuals where BMI does not change did not contribute to the FE-estimator (no control group). However, as stated by Brüderl and Ludwig [39], by including age in our FE regression model (a so-called two-way FE regression model), the control group information is used for estimating the age effects. Thus, a general recommendation is to include age or period effects in FE regression analysis [39].

Results

Sample characteristics and pattern of change

Because we were interested in changes within individuals over time, only individuals were included in the FE estimates if they had changes in the outcome variable between the second and the fifth wave. Descriptive statistics for individuals included in FE regressions (total sample) are shown in Table 1. Data of 12,793 individuals were used. Besides, it is worth stating that the Stata command for FE regressions include individuals with one observation in computing the number of observations because these individuals deliver information about the between R^2, the overall R^2, the variance components, the constant, as well as the correlation between individual effects constant over time and the independent variables. However, it is also worth emphasizing that this does not affect the beta-coefficients and the standard errors. Thus, it is worth stressing that individuals with only one observation did not contribute to the beta-coefficients and the standard errors of the FE regression analysis. Please see for further details [44]. We used the 'xtreg' command with the 'fe' option for computing linear FE regressions.

Concerning the time-constant variables, which were not included in FE regressions as predictors, the majority was male (51.2%) and had a medium educational level (52.9%). The mean age was 63.5 years (±11.4 years, 40–95 years). Most of the individuals were married, living together with spouse (71.6%) and retired (53.2%). The mean number of important people in regular contact was 4.9 (±2.7), the mean self-esteem score was 3.4 (±0.4), the mean number of chronic diseases was 2.5 (±1.9), the mean BMI was 26.7 (±4.4, 15.2–69.1; men: 27.1 ± 4.0, 15.2–69.1; women: 26.3 ± 4.8, 15.2–68.8) and the mean depressive symptoms score was 6.7 (±6.1; skewness: 1.7).

The mean level of changes from wave 2 to wave 5 in BMI and depressive symptoms were positive in depressive symptoms (indicating more depressive symptoms over time) and BMI, i.e. overall mean level of change in depressive symptoms was 0.08 (±6.04) and overall mean level of change in BMI was 0.45 (±3.72).

Correlations

We computed cross-sectional Pearson correlations (Table 2) in order to gain some insight into the relationships between the variables.

Depressive symptoms were significantly associated with marital status ($r = .13$, $p < .001$), employment status (retired: $r = .03$, $p < .01$; other: .06, p < .001), the number of important people in regular contact ($r = -.08$, $p < .001$),

Table 1 Sample Characteristics for individuals included in fixed effects regressions (2002–2014, pooled)

Male: N (%)	10,142 (51.2)
Education: Low education (ISCED-97: 0–2): N (%)	1305 (9.4)
Education: Medium education (ISCED-97: 3–4): N (%)	7320 (52.9)
Education: High education (ISCED-97: 5–6): N (%)	5219 (37.7)
Age: Mean (SD), Range	63.5 (11.4), 40–95
Married, living together with spouse: N (%)	14,187 (71.6)
Employment status: Working: N (%)	7077 (35.7)
Employment status: Retired: N (%)	10,543 (53.2)
Employment status: Other: N (%)	2206 (11.1)
Number of important people in regular contact: Mean (SD), Range	4.9 (2.7), 0–9
Self-esteem (Rosenberg scale)	3.4 (0.4), 1.2–4
Number of chronic diseases: Mean (SD), Range	2.5 (1.9), 0–11
BMI: Mean (SD), Range	26.7 (4.4), 15.2–69.1
Depressive symptoms (CES-D): Mean (SD), Range	6.7 (6.1), 0–45
Observations	19,826
Number of individuals	12,793

Table 2 Pairwise cross-sectional correlations (with Bonferroni correction for multiple comparisons; 2002–2014, pooled)

	Depressive symptoms (CES-D)	Age	Marital status (Ref.: married, living together with spouse)	Employment status: retired (Ref.: Working)	Employment status: other	Number of important people in regular contact	Self-esteem (Rosenberg scale)	Number of chronic diseases	BMI
Depressive symptoms (CES-D)	1								
Age	0.0145	1							
Marital status (Ref.: married, living together with spouse)	0.128***	0.0683***	1						
Employment status: retired (Ref.: Working)	0.0276**	0.772***	0.0442***	1					
Employment status: other	0.0602***	−0.155***	0.00624	−0.377***	1				
Number of important people in regular contact	− 0.0739***	− 0.107***	− 0.114***	− 0.0784***	− 0.0163	1			
Self-esteem (Rosenberg scale)	−0.395***	−0.0343***	− 0.0699***	−0.0390***	− 0.0640***	0.0555***	1		
Number of chronic diseases	0.280***	0.365***	0.0607***	0.306***	−0.0401***	−0.0140	− 0.236***	1	
BMI	0.0438***	0.0412***	−0.0214+	0.0591***	0.00881	−0.0141	−0.0442***	0.185***	1
Observations	19,826								

*** $p < 0.001$, ** $p < 0.01$, * $p < 0.05$, + $p < 0.10$ (listwise deletion was used)

self-esteem ($r = -.40$, $p < .001$), the number of chronic diseases ($r = .28$, $p < .001$) and BMI ($r = .04$, $p < .001$), whereas depressive symptoms were not significantly associated with age.

Regression analysis

In Table 3, we used three model specifications for the total sample (columns 1–3), for men (columns 4–6) and for women (columns 7–9). In the first model specification, we included only the linear BMI term (besides potential confounders; column 1, 4 and 7). In the second model specification, we additionally used a quadratic term for BMI (column 2, 5 and 8). In the third model specification, a cubic term for BMI was included (column 3, 6 and 9). FE regressions revealed that the effect of BMI on depressive symptoms is curvilinear in the total sample and in women, but not men. To ease the interpretation, our (sex-specific) analysis is illustrated using "marginsplot" in Stata (Figs. 1 and 2). According to Fig. 1, there seems to be a curvilinear effect in women, i.e. the curve illustrates a steep decline in the outcome measure and reaches a plateau (normal weight and overweight). After that (excess weight), depressive symptoms increases. In contrast to that, there seems to be an almost linear relationship between depressive symptoms and BMI in men. More specifically, the greater the BMI, the lower depressive symptoms. There was a significant interaction between BMI with gender (linear: $p < .05$; quadratic: $p < .05$; cubic: $p < .05$).

In addition, depressive symptoms significantly increased with decreasing self-esteem and increasing comorbidity in the total sample and in both sexes, whereas depressive symptoms were not significantly associated with marital and employment status, income and the number of important persons in regular contact. Furthermore, depressive symptoms were negatively associated with age in women, but not men.

In sensitivity analysis, depressive symptoms was replaced by log depressive symptoms to account for the skewness. In terms of significance, linear FE regressions also showed a curvilinear effect of BMI on depressive symptoms in the total sample and in women, but not men.

Moreover, depressive symptoms was considered as a count variable. Thus, FE Poisson regressions and FE negative binomial regression models were computed. Again, both statistical models revealed a curvilinear effect of BMI on depressive symptoms in the total sample and in women, but not men.

In further sensitivity analysis, we additionally controlled for functional health. Changes in functional health were

Table 3 Predictors of depressive symptoms (CES-D) – results of fixed effects regressions (total sample; men; women)

Independent variables	(1) Depressive symptoms	(2) Depressive symptoms	(3) Depressive symptoms	(4) Depressive symptoms - Men	(5) Depressive symptoms - Men	(6) Depressive symptoms - Men	(7) Depressive symptoms - Women	(8) Depressive symptoms - Women	(9) Depressive symptoms - Women
Age	−0.0185	−0.0172	−0.0201	0.00932	0.00943	0.00813	− 0.0504*	−0.0473*	− 0.0501*
	(0.0149)	(0.0150)	(0.0150)	(0.0187)	(0.0187)	(0.0187)	(0.0235)	(0.0235)	(0.0236)
Other marital statuses (Ref.: Married, living together with spouse)	0.480	0.461	0.461	0.133	0.129	0.131	0.904	0.867	0.849
	(0.441)	(0.441)	(0.440)	(0.511)	(0.511)	(0.511)	(0.693)	(0.690)	(0.689)
Retired (Ref.: Working)	−0.364	−0.372	−0.386	−0.306	−0.309	− 0.315	− 0.459	−0.453	− 0.477
	(0.245)	(0.244)	(0.243)	(0.286)	(0.286)	(0.287)	(0.402)	(0.399)	(0.396)
Other: not employed	0.260	0.265	0.263	0.261	0.264	0.271	0.197	0.199	0.173
	(0.285)	(0.284)	(0.283)	(0.372)	(0.372)	(0.371)	(0.422)	(0.420)	(0.418)
Household net equivalent income	−4.92e-06	−1.26e-06	4.66e-06	−3.11e-05	−3.07e-05	−2.92e-05	1.55e-05	2.33e-05	3.37e-05
	(4.47e-05)	(4.44e-05)	(4.39e-05)	(6.36e-05)	(6.37e-05)	(6.38e-05)	(7.20e-05)	(7.17e-05)	(7.05e-05)
Number of important persons in regular contact	−0.0142	−0.0132	−0.0124	−0.00162	−0.00173	−0.000587	−0.0289	− 0.0241	−0.0285
	(0.0228)	(0.0228)	(0.0227)	(0.0279)	(0.0279)	(0.0279)	(0.0365)	(0.0365)	(0.0363)
Self-esteem (Rosenberg scale)	−3.204***	−3.191***	−3.171***	−2.894***	−2.893***	−2.888***	− 3.465***	−3.429***	− 3.399***
	(0.273)	(0.272)	(0.272)	(0.317)	(0.317)	(0.317)	(0.428)	(0.426)	(0.424)
Total number of physical diseases	0.291***	0.288***	0.281***	0.338***	0.337***	0.334***	0.231**	0.231**	0.224**
	(0.0552)	(0.0551)	(0.0549)	(0.0707)	(0.0705)	(0.0702)	(0.0851)	(0.0847)	(0.0843)
BMI	−0.119**	−0.795***	−3.791***	−0.136*	−0.262	−1.291	−0.0963+	−1.204***	−5.766***
	(0.0395)	(0.237)	(0.917)	(0.0561)	(0.257)	(1.288)	(0.0556)	(0.327)	(1.338)
BMI^2		0.0111**	0.107***		0.00206	0.0342		0.0183***	0.167***
		(0.00396)	(0.0275)		(0.00397)	(0.0377)		(0.00554)	(0.0416)
BMI^3			−0.000970***			−0.000319			−0.00154***
			(0.000261)			(0.000346)			(0.000415)
Constant	20.82***	30.60***	60.77***	18.18***	20.03***	30.66*	23.31***	39.04***	84.03***
	(1.728)	(3.800)	(9.927)	(2.240)	(4.400)	(14.19)	(2.552)	(5.252)	(14.07)
R^2	0.045	0.047	0.049	0.050	0.050	0.050	0.045	0.050	0.054
Observations	19,826	19,826	19,826	10,142	10,142	10,142	9684	9684	9684
Number of Individuals	12,793	12,793	12,793	6549	6549	6549	6244	6244	6244

Beta-Coefficients were reported; Cluster-robust standard errors in parentheses; *** $p < 0.001$, ** $p < 0.01$, * $p < 0.05$, + $p < 0.10$; listwise deletion was used. It is worth emphasizing that the Stata command for FE regression analysis include subjects with only one observation in calculating the number of observations since these subjects deliver information about the variance components, the constant, the between R^2, the overall R^2 as well as the correlation between individual effects constant over time and the regressors. However, it does not affect the beta-coefficients and the standard errors

associated with changes in depressive symptoms (β = –.07, $p < .001$, in the total sample and in both sexes). In addition, the nature of the relationship between BMI and depressive symptoms remained virtually the same.

In further analysis, BMI was categorized according to the WHO guidelines. While changes in BMI categories were not associated with changes in depressive symptoms, changes from 'normal weight' to excess weight

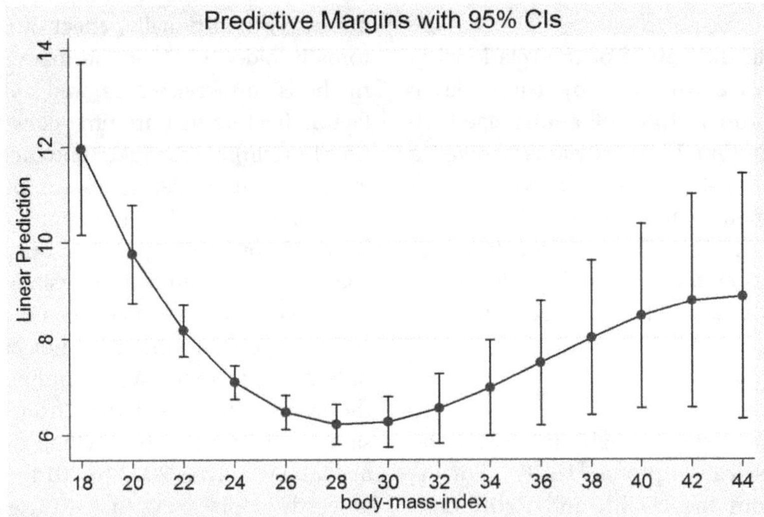

Fig. 1 Relation between depressive symptoms (CES-D) and BMI among women

were positively associated with changes in depressive symptoms in the total sample and in women.

In another model, depressive symptoms were replaced by depression as outcome measure. Consequently, we used conditional fixed effects logistic regressions because we have a binary outcome variable. In this model, FE regressions revealed a curvilinear effect of BMI on depression in the total sample and in women, whereas no association was found in men. With regard to the clinical significance, it is worth noting that in the first model specification where only the linear BMI term was included (beyond the potential confounders), OR for BMI was .931 [95%-CI: .870–997] in the total sample. This means that if an individual increases BMI by one unit, his or her odds of having a depression are multiplied by .93 (ceteris paribus).

In further regression analysis, self-esteem was excluded from our main regression model because it might be on the causal pathway between BMI and depressive symptoms. Compared with our main model findings remained almost the same in terms of significance and effect sizes.

While all self-reported BMI values were used in main analysis, very extreme BMI values (BMI < 15 kg/m^2 and BMI > 55 kg/m^2) were excluded from the FE regression analysis in additional analysis. However, our main results remained virtually the same.

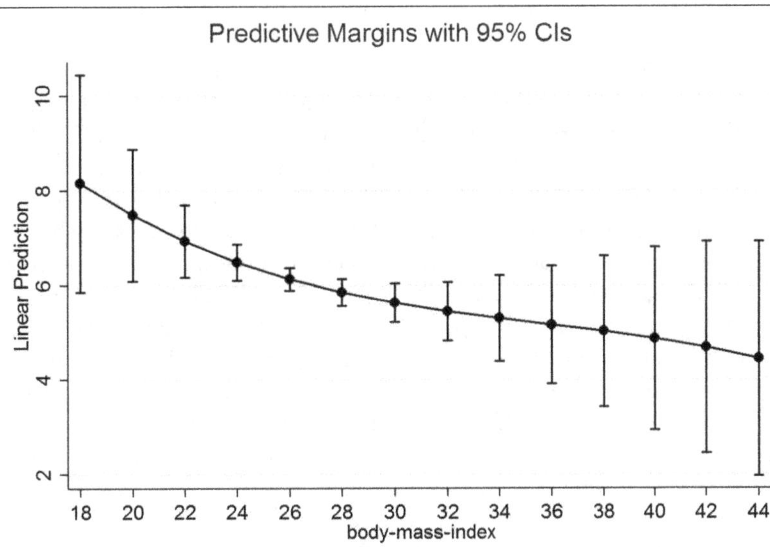

Fig. 2 Relation between depressive symptoms (CES-D) and BMI among men

Discussion

Main findings

We aimed at investigating the nature of the relationship between BMI and depressive symptoms by using a large population-based longitudinal study of adults aged 40 (2002–2011) in Germany. Our FE regressions showed a curvilinear effect of BMI on depressive symptoms in the total sample and in women, but not men, with significant gender differences. Thus, the greater the extreme of BMI (either higher or lower), the greater the risk for depressive symptoms. This effect is likely to be driven by the effect in women.

Previous research

Recent studies found that excess weight increased the risk of subsequent depressive symptoms [15, 17]. For instance, by using data from the Health and Retirement Study (1994 to 2010, 6514 community-dwelling older adults), Xiang and An [15] found that overweight and obesity predicted the onset of depression up to 16 years by using time-dependent Cox proportional hazards model. Moreover, obesity had stronger associations with depression in women. This is also in line with another recent cross-sectional study [45]. A possible explanation for the gender differences is that women have stronger genetic disposition to excess weight and depressed mood [45]. In addition, social factors such as greater peer pressures or reduced career opportunities might explain why the relationship between excess weight and depressive symptoms is stronger in women [45]. Furthermore, by using multilevel random intercept mixed models, Chang et al. [12] found that the odds of elevated depressive symptoms significantly increased as BMI increased over time. Their data were derived from a short run (four years) longitudinal study (1496 participants) taking place in twelve rural communities in Missouri, Arkansas, and Tennessee.

Moreover, Kim et al. [16] examined the association between self-reported BMI and depressive symptoms (CES-D, 10 items) from 2006 to 2010 in older adults aged 45 years and above in South Korea (representative data from the Korean Longitudinal Study of Aging). Using cross-lagged panel models, they found that there is an association between underweight and the development of depressive symptoms. In sum, by using panel data methods, we provide new evidence that the greater the extreme of BMI (either higher or lower), the greater the risk for depressive symptoms in the total sample and in women. Thus, it is likely that this effect is driven by the one in women. Besides, results regarding the control variables such as self-esteem are in accordance with previous studies [22, 46].

Strengths and limitations

Our study is the first study that examined the non-linear (any relationship which is not linear, for example, as BMI increases, the resulting depressive symptoms do not increase proportionally) effect of BMI on depressive symptoms in older adults in Germany. By exploiting panel data methods, unobserved as well as observed time-invariant factors (factors that are time-constant such as sex or country of origin) can be taken into account, leading to consistent estimates under the assumption of strict exogeneity. Reducing the problem of unobserved heterogeneity is a huge advantage compared to cross-sectional studies. More specifically, it is almost impossible to control for differences in genetic dispositions between individuals in large surveys. In FE regressions, one does not have to worry about these differences in time-invariant unobserved factors [39]. Furthermore, data were derived from a large population-based sample of community-dwelling older adults (aged 40 and above). Data from 2002 to 2014 were used. Additionally, it is worth emphasizing that we used a validated measure of depressive symptoms (CES-D).

One limitation is that BMI was self-reported. Hence, the BMI might be biased downwards because individuals tend to underestimate weight and overestimate height [47]. However, as long as this downwards bias is constant within an individual over time, it does not bias linear FE estimates because FE estimates rely exclusively on intraindividual changes over time.

Moreover, we could not distinguish between intentional and unintentional weight loss. Furthermore, due to panel attrition (permanent unit-nonresponse) in the German Ageing Survey [48], our estimates might be biased downwards. Moreover, it might be difficult to generalize findings to, e.g., less educated individuals and individuals with low self-rated health for reasons of sample selection bias. Besides, a simultaneity bias (depressive symptoms affect BMI) cannot be ruled out [49–51]. For example, changes in depressive symptoms could affect the BMI due to a loss of appetite. The simultaneity bias is a typical problem in most cases when observational studies are used. Theoretically, this can be handled by using panel instrumental variable approaches [35]. However, truly exogenous and strong instruments are difficult to identify. Moreover, it rests on some untestable assumptions. As stated by Mouw [52], the researcher has to rely on theoretical justifications. Other available models such as cross-lagged structural equation models have also been criticized for various reasons [39, 52]. Furthermore, other factors such as drugs (antidepressant medications) might play a role in the relationship between BMI and depressive symptoms. However, for reasons of data availability, we were unable to integrate these factors into the model. Nevertheless, we already controlled for numerous important covariates.

Conclusion

Our data indicate that the impact of BMI on depressive symptoms is by no means simple. The current study highlight the importance of comprehensive treatment of depression, which include management of (extreme) weight to manage depressive symptoms. This might also be important since increased depressive symptoms in older age are positively associated with other adverse health outcomes such as functional impairment [53], frailty [54] or admission to nursing home [55].

Abbreviations

BMI: Body Mass Index; CES-D: Center for Epidemiological Studies Depression Scale; DEAS: German Ageing Survey; FE: Fixed effects; ISCED: International Standard Classification of Education; OLS: Ordinary least squares; OR: Odds Ratio; RE: Random effects; SF-36: Short Form-36; WHO: World Health Organization

Authors' contributions

AH, HHK: Design and concept of analyses, preparation of data, statistical analysis and interpretation of data, preparing of the manuscript. Both authors critically reviewed the manuscript, provided significant editing of the article and approved the final manuscript.

Competing interests

The authors declare that they have no competing interests.

References

1. McTigue KM, Hess R, Ziouras J. Obesity in older adults: a systematic review of the evidence for diagnosis and treatment. Obesity. 2006;14(9):1485–97.
2. Rejeski WJ, Marsh AP, Chmelo E, Rejeski JJ. Obesity, intentional weight loss and physical disability in older adults. Obes Rev. 2010;11(9):671–85.
3. Visser M, Langlois J, Guralnik JM, Cauley JA, Kronmal RA, Robbins J, Williamson JD, Harris TB. High body fatness, but not low fat-free mass, predicts disability in older men and women: the cardiovascular health study. Am J Clin Nutr. 1998;68(3):584–90.
4. Lawrence VJ, Kopelman PG. Medical consequences of obesity. Clin Dermatol. 2004;22(4):296–302.
5. Must A, Spadano J, Coakley EH, Field AE, Colditz G, Dietz WH. The disease burden associated with overweight and obesity. JAMA. 1999;282(16):1523–9.
6. Bin Li Z, Yin Ho S, Man Chan W, Sang Ho K, Pik Li M, Leung GM, Hing Lam T. Obesity and depressive symptoms in Chinese elderly. Int J Geriatr Psychiatry. 2004;19(1):68–74.
7. Crisp A, McGuiness B. Jolly fat: relation between obesity and psychoneurosis in general population. Br Med J. 1976;1(6000):7–9.
8. Kittel F, Rustin R, Dramaix M, De Backer G, Kornitzer M. Psycho-socio-biological correlates of moderate overweight in an industrial population. J Psychosom Res. 1978;22(3):145–58.
9. Istvan J, Zavela K, Weidner G. Body weight and psychological distress in NHANES I. Int J Obes Relat Metab Disord. 1992;16(12):999–1003.
10. Roberts RE, Kaplan GA, Shema SJ, Strawbridge WJ. Are the obese at greater risk for depression? Am J Epidemiol. 2000;152(2):163–70.
11. Gunasekara FI, Richardson K, Carter K, Blakely T. Fixed effects analysis of repeated measures data. Int J Epidemiol. 2014;43(1):264–9.
12. Chang JJ, Salas J, Tabet M, Kasper Z, Elder K, Staley H, Brownson RC. Changes in body mass index and the trajectory of depressive symptoms among rural men and women. J Rural Health. 2017;33(2):190–7.
13. Hawkins MA, Miller DK, Stewart JC. A 9-year, bidirectional prospective analysis of depressive symptoms and adiposity: the African American health study. Obesity. 2015;23(1):192–9.
14. Vogelzangs N, Kritchevsky SB, Beekman AT, Brenes GA, Newman AB, Satterfield S, Yaffe K, Harris TB, Penninx BW. Obesity and onset of significant depressive symptoms: results from a prospective community-based cohort study of older men and women. J Clin Psychiatry. 2009;71(4):391–9.
15. Xiang X, An R. Obesity and onset of depression among US middle-aged and older adults. J Psychosom Res. 2015;78(3):242–8.
16. Kim J, Noh J-W, Park J, Kwon YD. Body mass index and depressive symptoms in older adults: a cross-lagged panel analysis. PLoS One. 2014;9(12):e114891.
17. Martin-Rodriguez E, Guillen-Grima F, Aubá E, Martí A, Brugos-Larumbe A. Relationship between body mass index and depression in women: a 7-year prospective cohort study. The APNA study. Eur Psychiatry. 2016;32:55–60.
18. Markowitz S, Friedman MA, Arent SM. Understanding the relation between obesity and depression: causal mechanisms and implications for treatment. Clin Psychol Sci Pract. 2008;15(1):1–20.
19. Geoffroy M-C, Li L, Power C. Depressive symptoms and body mass index: co-morbidity and direction of association in a British birth cohort followed over 50 years. Psychol Med. 2014;44(12):2641–52.
20. Carpenter KM, Hasin DS, Allison DB, Faith MS. Relationships between obesity and DSM-IV major depressive disorder, suicide ideation, and suicide attempts: results from a general population study. Am J Public Health. 2000;90(2):251.
21. Onyike CU, Crum RM, Lee HB, Lyketsos CG, Eaton WW. Is obesity associated with major depression? Results from the third National Health and nutrition examination survey. Am J Epidemiol. 2003;158(12):1139–47.
22. Sachs-Ericsson N, Burns AB, Gordon KH, Eckel LA, Wonderlich SA, Crosby RD, Blazer DG. Body mass index and depressive symptoms in older adults: the moderating roles of race, sex, and socioeconomic status. Am J Geriatr Psychiatry. 2007;15(9):815–25.
23. Chiu HC, Chen CM, Huang CJ, Mau LW. Depressive symptoms, chronic medical conditions and functional status: a comparison of urban and rural elders in Taiwan. Int J Geriatr Psychiatry. 2005;20(7):635–44.
24. Klaus D, Engstler H, Mahne K, Wolff JK, Simonson J, Wurm S, Tesch-Römer C. Cohort profile: the German ageing survey (DEAS). Int J Epidemiol. 2017:1–8.
25. Klaus D, Engstler H. Daten und Methoden des Deutschen Alterssurveys. In: Mahne K, Wolff JK, Simonson J, Tesch-Römer C, editors. Altern im Wandel: Zwei Jahrzehnte Deutscher Alterssurvey (DEAS). Berlin: Springer; 2016. p. 25–42.
26. Pforr K, Blohm M, Blom AG, Erdel B, Felderer B, Fräßdorf M, Hajek K, Helmschrott S, Kleinert C, Koch A. Are incentive effects on response rates and nonresponse bias in large-scale, face-to-face surveys generalizable to Germany? Evidence from ten experiments. Public Opin Q. 2015;79(3):740–68.
27. Ryu E, Couper MP, Marans RW. Survey incentives: cash vs. in-kind; face-to-face vs. mail; response rate vs. nonresponse error. Int J Public Opin Res. 2006;18(1):89–106.
28. Hautzinger M. Die CES-D Skala: Ein Depressionsmessinstrument für Untersuchungen in der Allgemeinbevölkerung [the CES-D scale: a depression-rating scale for research in the general population]. Diagnostica. 1988;34(2):167–73.
29. Radloff LS. The CES-D scale a self-report depression scale for research in the general population. Appl Psychol Meas. 1977;1(3):385–401.
30. Lehr D, Hillert A, Schmitz E, Sosnowsky N. Screening depressiver Störungen mittels Allgemeiner depressions-Skala (ADS-K) und state-trait depressions scales (STDS-T). Eine vergleichende evaluation von cut-off-Werten [assessing depressive disorders using the Center for Epidemiologic Studies-Depression Scale (CES-D) and state-trait depression scales (STDS-T): a comparative analysis of cut-off scores]. Diagnostica. 2008;54(2):61–70.
31. Rosenberg M. Society and the adolescent self-image. Princeton: Princeton University Press; 1965.
32. UNESCO (ed.): International standard classification of education. ISCED 1997, Re-edition edn; 2006.
33. Ware Jr JE, Sherbourne CD. The MOS 36-item short-form health survey (SF-36): I. Conceptual framework and item selection. Med Care. 1992;30(6):473–83.
34. Bullinger M, Kirchberger I. Fragebogen zum Gesundheitszustand. Handanweisung. Göttingen: Hogrefe; 1998.
35. Cameron AC, Trivedi PK. Microeconometrics: methods and applications. New York: Cambridge University Press; 2005.
36. Hajek A, König H-H. Informal caregiving and subjective well-being: evidence of a population-based longitudinal study of older adults in Germany. J Am Med Dir Assoc. 2015;
37. Hajek A, König H-H. The effect of intra-and intergenerational caregiving on subjective well-being–evidence of a population based longitudinal study among older adults in Germany. PLoS One. 2016;11(2):e0148916.
38. Milner A, Krnjacki L, Butterworth P, LaMontagne AD. The role of social support in protecting mental health when employed and unemployed: a longitudinal fixed-effects analysis using 12 annual waves of the HILDA cohort. Soc Sci Med. 2016;153:20–6.
39. Brüderl J, Ludwig V. Fixed-effects panel regression. In: Wolf C, editor. The Sage handbook of regression analysis and causal inference. Los Angeles: SAGE; 2015. p. 327–57.

40. Brüderl J. Kausalanalyse mit Paneldaten. In: Wolf C, Best H, editors. Handbuch der sozialwissenschaftlichen Datenanalyse. Wiesbaden: VS-Verlag; 2010. p. 963–94.
41. Gangl M. Causal inference in sociological research. Annu Rev Sociol. 2010; 36:21–47.
42. Greene WH. Econometric analysis. 7th ed. Boston: Pearson; 2012.
43. Wooldridge JM. Econometric analysis of cross section and panel data. Cambridge: MIT Press; 2010.
44. Drukker D. Re: st: Wrong no. of obs. in xtreg fixed effect option. 2002. https://www.stata.com/statalist/archive/2002-07/msg00311.html.
45. Kodjebacheva G, Kruger DJ, Rybarczyk G, Cupal S. Racial/ethnic and gender differences in the association between depressive symptoms and higher body mass index. Journal of Public Health. 2015;37(3):419–26.
46. Xie B, Chou C, Spruijt-Metz D, Liu C, Xia J, Gong J, Li Y, Johnson C. Effects of perceived peer isolation and social support availability on the relationship between body mass index and depressive symptoms. Int J Obes. 2005;29(9): 1137–43.
47. Gorber SC, Tremblay M, Moher D, Gorber B. A comparison of direct vs. self-report measures for assessing height, weight and body mass index: a systematic review. Obes Rev. 2007;8(4):307–26.
48. Schiel S, Knerr P, Dickmann C, Aust F. Methodenbericht Deutscher Alterssurvey (DEAS): 4. Befragungswelle. Berlin: Panelbefragung; 2011.
49. Luppino FS, de Wit LM, Bouvy PF, Stijnen T, Cuijpers P, Penninx BW, Zitman FG. Overweight, obesity, and depression: a systematic review and meta-analysis of longitudinal studies. Arch Gen Psychiatry. 2010;67(3):220–9.
50. Opel N, Redlich R, Grotegerd D, Dohm K, Heindel W, Kugel H, Arolt V, Dannlowski U. Obesity and major depression: body-mass index (BMI) is associated with a severe course of disease and specific neurostructural alterations. Psychoneuroendocrinology. 2015;51:219–26.
51. Penninx BW, Milaneschi Y, Lamers F, Vogelzangs N. Understanding the somatic consequences of depression: biological mechanisms and the role of depression symptom profile. BMC Med. 2013;11(1):1.
52. Mouw T. Estimating the causal effect of social capital: a review of recent research. Annu Rev Sociol. 2006;32:79–102.
53. Hajek A, König H-H. Longitudinal predictors of functional impairment in older adults in Europe – evidence from the survey of health, ageing and retirement in Europe. PLoS One. 2016;11(1):e0146967.
54. Hajek A, Brettschneider C, Posselt T, Lange C, Mamone S, Wiese B, Weyerer S, Werle J, Fuchs A, Pentzek M, et al. Predictors of frailty in old age–results of a longitudinal study. J Nutr Health Aging. 2016;20(9):952–7.
55. Hajek A, Brettschneider C, Lange C, Posselt T, Wiese B, Steinmann S, Weyerer S, Werle J, Pentzek M, Fuchs A, et al. Longitudinal predictors of institutionalization in old age. PLoS One. 2015;10(12):e0144203.

16

A randomized controlled double-blind clinical trial comparing versus placebo the effect of an edible algal extract (*Ulva Lactuca*) on the component of depression in healthy volunteers with anhedonia

François-André Allaert[1*], Hervé Demais[2] and Pi Nyvall Collén[3]

Abstract

Background: The effects of the seaweed extract were evaluated on the animal model equivalent of depression compared with a control group treated with the carrier (spring water) and a reference group treated with Imipramine and showed significative effect. This clinical trial was intended to confirm in humans the potential efficacy identified in animals. The primary objective was to compare against a placebo the effect of Ulva L.L extract in healthy volunteers whose anhedonia was characterized by a component of depression.

Methods: Single-centre double-blind randomized placebo-controlled clinical trial on parallel arms of two groups of 45 subjects. The study could include men or women aged 18 to 65 years with anhedonia characterized by a Snaith Hamilton Pleasure Scale score (SHAPS) of ≥5 and feeling low morale for at least four weeks characterized by a component of depression evaluated on the Quick Inventory of Depressive Symptomatology – Self Report (QIDS–SR). Evaluation criteria: QIDS-SR; Patient Global Improvement Impression (PGII) and Clinical Global Improvement Impression (CGII).

Results: 86 subjects were included in the trial: 42 in the placebo group and 44 Ulva group. At D84, QIDS-SR significantly decreased more in the Ulva.L.L. group than in the placebo group (p: 0.0389). This difference is essentially linked to an improvement of the sleep disorders (p: 0.0219), of the psychomotor consequences (p: 0.002) and of the nutrition behaviour (p: 0.0694). 90.1% have the feeling of being improved in the Ulva group vs 72.5% in the placebo group (p: 0.0114) and in parallel 90.9% of the practitioners have the feeling that the subject has improved vs 70.8% (p: 0.0214).

Conclusion: This double-blind randomized placebo-controlled trial shows that daily intake for three months of a water-soluble extract of Ulva L.L. continues to significantly improve the component of depression of subjects presenting anhedonia compared with a placebo.

Keywords: Depression, Anhedonia, Seaweed extract

* Correspondence: francois.allaert@groupecen.com
[1]Chair of health claim evaluation EMMAS BSB & CEN Nutriment, 29 rue Sambin, 21000 Dijon, France
Full list of author information is available at the end of the article

Background

Anhedonia, defined as a loss of sensitivity when it comes to feeling pleasure, is observed in various personality disorders but also commonly and to a lesser extent in healthy subjects for whom it is a personality trait [1–7]. It may be attributable to a minor disturbance of the mesocorticolimbic reward system involving serotoininergic and dopaminergic mediators [8–10] that are expressed as ill-being by contrast with the term well-being and characterized notably by a decline in morale with a component of depression. Anhedonia is an isolated symptom and not a psychopathological state unlike depression of which it may a component but which requires the association of numerous other components to meet the DSM V (Diagnostic and statistical Manual of Mental Disorders) definition.

Faced with this symptom, psychotropic substances and especially antidepressants have been and still are used too often in particular because of the danger of addiction and dependence that continued intake may entail [3]. Faced with overconsumption, especially in France, and the need to reduce it (Government scheme for combatting drugs and addictive conduct 2013–2017. La documentation Française) many studies have been directed at research into nutriments or plant extracts that might have a similar action to antidepressants, acting on the same physiological mechanisms, but without inducing pharmacological dependence. They would supposedly provide a solution to the ill-being felt by people experiencing low morale with a component of depression but with no major depressive episode (MDE) as per the DSM V [11], which covers a very large proportion of people to whom antidepressants are still prescribed for want of a satisfactory scientifically-proven alternative.

The seaweed extract tested in this study and developed by OLMIX SA is part of this search for a non-medicinal alternative to combat low morale and its component of depression. Research has isolated a concentrated lyophilized and ground fraction of a water-soluble extract of an edible alga [12] named *Ulva lactuca* Linnaeus and more commonly known as sea lettuce. The extract obtained is rich in oligo-elements (up to 50%) and proteins (10–20%). A pre-clinical study has evaluated the antidepressant effect of the algal extract administered orally as a preventive treatment in three doses (10, 20 and 40 mg/kg/day) in Wistar adult male rats [13]. The effects of the seaweed extract were evaluated on the animal model equivalent of depression compared with a control group treated with the carrier (spring water) and a reference group treated with Imipramine in doses of 10 mg/kg/day. After 15 days of intake of the study products, the results show superior and comparable effects of Imipramine and seaweed extract at 20 and 40 mg/kg/day compared with the control. Moreover, a dose-dependent effect was observed in animals treated with the extract at doses of 10, 20 and 40 mg/kg/day [13]. To confirm in humans the potential efficacy of the product identified in animals, we conducted a randomized controlled double-blind clinical trial on the component of depression in healthy volunteers with anhedonia.

Methods

Study objectives

The primary objective of the trial was to compare against a placebo the effect of the product under test (Ulva L.L) in healthy volunteers whose anhedonia was characterized by a component of depression. The secondary objectives were to compare the repercussion of the anhedonia on work and activities, the investigating doctor's opinion of the change in anhedonia, the subjects' satisfaction with the treatment and tolerance of the product.

Nature of the study

Single-centre double-blind randomized placebo-controlled clinical trial on parallel arms of two groups of 45 subjects. The Ethics committee approval by the French Ethics Committee CPP EST I has been obtained (approval registered under N° 2014/41 ID RCB: 2014-A01019–38) and the consent to participate for all subjects has been obtained by writing from the physician.

Evaluation criteria

The presence and intensity of anhedonia were evaluated on the Snaith-Hamilton Pleasure Scale (SHAPS) [14, 15] and its component of depression by the Quick Inventory of Depressive Symptomatology-Self-Report (QIDS-SR) [16–19] and their repercussion on work and activities by item 7 of the Hamilton Depression Rating Scale (HAM-D) [20]. Subject satisfaction with the treatment was evaluated by the PGII (Patient Global Improvement Impression) and the investigating physician's opinion by the Clinical Global Improvement Impression (CGII) [21].

Course of the study

The trial comprised three visits: a medical enrollment visit on D0, an intermediate visit on D28 and a final visit on D84. A psychologist made a telephone call after 7 days to check there was no sudden change in the subject's depressive state. During the visits, the subject was examined by a doctor and the psychometric tests were administered by a psychologist. Outside the visits, the subject was monitored by a self-reporting questionnaire in the manner described below.

After obtaining informed written consent and validating the inclusion and exclusion criteria, notably the absence of MDE as per DSM V, the investigator enrolled the subject in the trial. The physician described the subject's demographic and general clinical characteristics, the main medical and surgical history and any current treatment if those pathologies were still present, and any previous antidepressant, anxiolytic or neuroleptic treatments. The doctor asked the subject to complete the SHAPS and QIDS –SR questionnaires and item 7 of the HAM-D. The doctor then handed the subject self-evaluation questionnaires explaining how to complete them and the dates at which they were to be completed. The physician gave the patient a batch of the placebo or a batch of *Ulva lactuca* as per the randomization. The doctor told the subject a pyschologist would be in touch after 1 week by telephone to check no DSM V severity criterion had arisen.

The investigating doctor saw the subject again at the four-week intermediate vist and at the final visit at the end of the 12th week of follow-up. The doctor collected the self-questionnaires at these visits and the same items as at the enrollment visit were recorded by the physician for describing how the items had evolved and notably the SHAP scale score, the QIDS–SR and item 7 of the HAM-D. In addition, the physician recorded the subject's satisfaction with the treatment evaluated on the PGII (Patient Global Improvement Impression), reported any undesirable affects and gave his/her own opinion on the efficacy of treatment using the Clinical Global Improvement Impression (CGII).

Selection of the study population

Inclusion criteria

The study could include men or women aged 18 to 65 years with anhedonia characterized by a SHAPS scale score of ≥5 and feeling low morale for at least 4 weeks characterized by a component of depression evaluated on the QIDS–SR.

Exclusion criteria

The study could not include subjects with a major depressive episode as per the DSM V, with a HAM D > 8, already on anxiolytic, antidepressor, neuroleptic or any other medicinal treatment liable to influence mood (e.g. benzodiazepines) in the last 30 days and those who consumed illegal psychotropic substances, with daily alcohol intake of more than three glasses of wine, or having taken in the last 15 days products liable or presented as liable to act on stress, anxiety, mood or mental well-being. Also excluded were people with post-traumatic stress disorder (particularly stressful event, death, death threat, serious injuries, etc.), presenting with unstable or severe comorbidity or psychiatric disorder. In addition, the product under study being a seaweed extract, people with an allergy or intolerance to seafood were excluded.

Treatment

Products under study

The test dose of seaweed extract was 6.45 mg per kg body weight. The selected daily dose was three capsules per day dosed at 130 mg for subjects weighing 50 to 75 kg, four capsules per day for subjects weighing 70 to 90 kg and five capsules per day for subjects weighing 90 to 110 kg. The product was taken in a single daily dose with the evening meal to be swallowed with a glass of water. It is extracted from *Ulva lactuca* by grinding and pressing, pasteurization and ultracentrifugation on ceramic membrane before being concentrated and drying. Then maltodextrine is added and the capsules are filled up with the resulting mixture. Placebo capsules are stricly identical and filled with maltodextrine only.

Prohibited treatments

Any product corresponding to the exclusion criteria was prohibited during the study: food supplements, functional foods, phytotherapy products and any other products liable or presented as liable to act on stress, anxiety or mental well-being other than the study product; anxiolytic, antidepressant, neuroleptic treatment or any medicinal treatment liable to influence mood and anhedonia (e.g. benzodiazepines) during the study. All other treatments than those prohibited were authorized and had to be recorded.

Statistical analyses

Definition of populations

All of the minor and major deviations from the protocol were used to identify the different populations. The efficacy analysis pertains in turn to the intention to treat (ITT) and the per protocol (PP) population. The ITT study was performed on all subject having taken the product at least once and for the primary criterion could be evaluated at one post-enrollment evaluation visit at least (modified ITT). Where evaluation parameter data were missing, the analysis included the last available evaluation by the "Last Observation Carried Forward (LOCF)" technique. The PP evaluation was conducted on volunteers included in the ITT who took the product up to D84 and were seen again at D84, excluding subjects who violated the protocol in any major way. The tolerance analysis pertains to the population including all subjects who took the product under study at least once.

Statistical methods

The quantitative data were described by numbers, means, standard deviations, medians, minima and maxima. The qualitative data were described by their absolute and relative frequency. Means between groups at enrollment were compared using analysis of variance (or by the Kruskal Wallis test if the distributions were not normal distributions). Percentages were compared by the chi-square test (or Fisher's exact test if the conditions for the chi-square test were not satisfied). The quantitative evaluation criteria were compared between the groups at different times by analyses of variance on paired series with two time and treatment factors with interactions between D0 and D84. The evaluation criteria were compared between groups by the chi-square test (or Fisher's exact test if the conditions for applying the chi-square test were not met). Undesirable effects observed were described by their frequency and nature, which were compared by a chi-square test or Fisher's exact test if the conditions for the chi-square test were not met).

Determination of sample size

The computation of sample numbers depended on identifying a 1.4-point difference in scores on the SHAPS scale between the placebo and the Ulva L.L. groups after 12 weeks. According to the calculation made with Nquery software, with a risk alpha = 0.05, power of 80% and a standard deviation of 2,5 [22], the number of subjects to be enrolled was 40 per arm, making 90 subjects in total to allow for lost sight subjects.

Results

Distribution of subjects

A total of 90 subjects were recruited: 45 in the placebo group and 45 in the Ulva L.L. group on enrollment (D0). Three subjects in the placebo group and one subject in the Ulva L.L. group left the study before D28 and could not be evaluated. The ITT analysis relates to 42 subjects in the placebo group and 44 in the Ulva L.L. group. Three subjects present a major deviation in the placebo group, as indicated in Fig. 1, and none in the Ulva L.L. group. The PP analysis relates to 39 subjects in the placebo group versus 44 in the Ulva L.L. group. The tolerance population relates to the 90 subjects who took at least one dose of the study products, 45 in each group (Fig. 1).

Description of subjects at enrollment ($n = 86$)

The 86 subjects included in the ITT study were aged 40.2 ± 13.6 years and nearly two-thirds of them were women (65.1%). Their BMI was 25.2 ± 4.3 kg/m^2 and

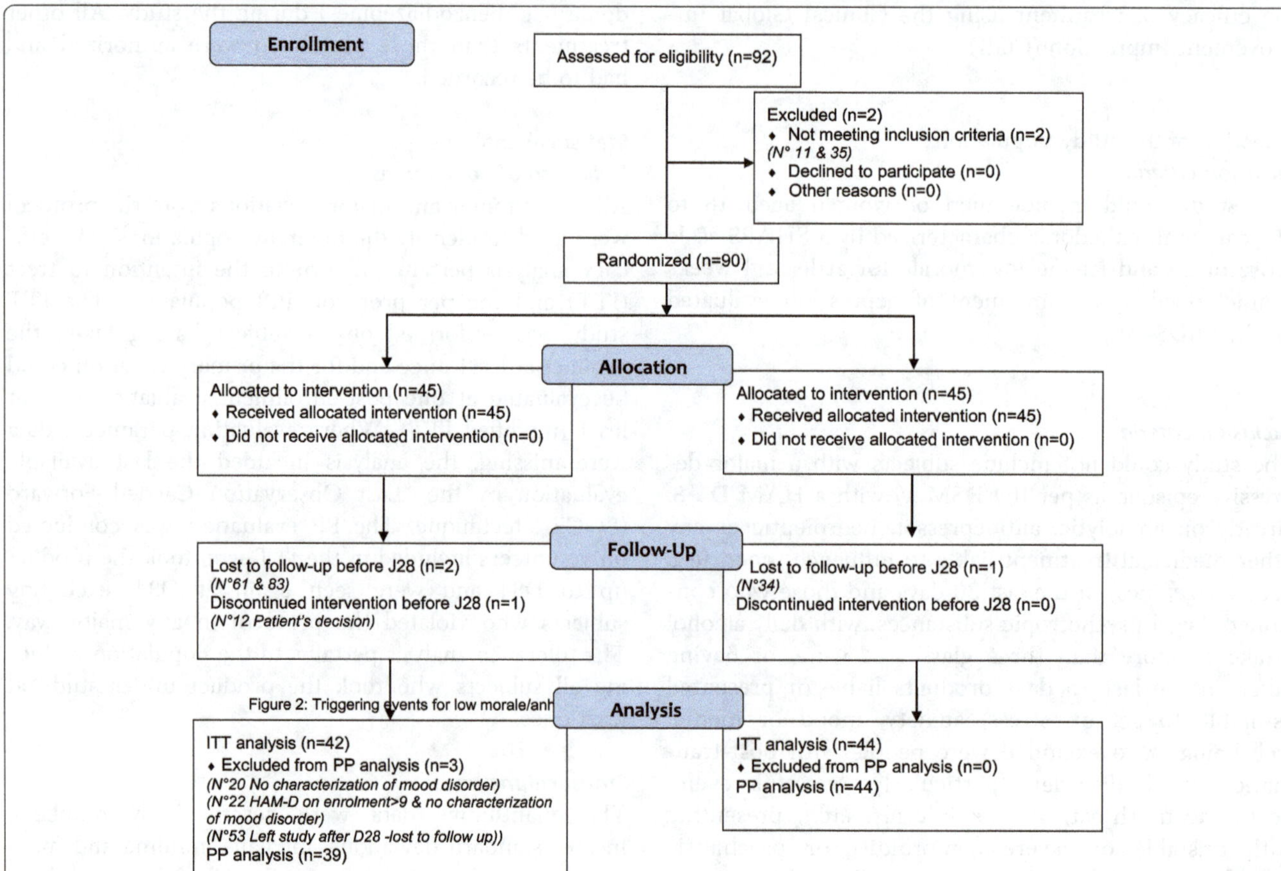

Fig. 1 Distribution of subjects in the study

38.4% were overweight and 11.6% were obese. They had 1.2 ± 1.2 children on average and three-quarters of them (75.6%) lived in urban settings. Most (51.1%) were living alone, being either single (39.5%) or divorced (11.6%). Their level of education was below Bachelor's degree (baccalauréat) for 29.1%, from Bachelor's degree to 2 years in higher education for 39.5% and more than 2 years in higher education for 31.4%. Two-thirds of them (67.6%) had an occupation the nature of which was similar to that of the national population. In terms of lifestyle, 16.2% of subjects had been (8.1%) or still were (8.1%) smokers, 10.5% drank alcohol (9.3% 1 to 3 glasses and 1.2% more than 3 glasses) and 80.8% drank coffee or tea (67.4% from one to three cups and 12.8% more than three cups). It was also recorded that 54.7% engaged in a physical activity (47.7% 1 to 3 times per week and 7.0% more than 3 times per week).

Anhedonia was felt by subjects for 19.9 ± 16.4 weeks on average and was anticipatory anhedonia for 91.8% of subjects and/or consummatory anhedonia for 70.6%. Low morale was also felt for 18.9 ± 14.5 weeks. The low morale was characterized by an unusual aversion to everyday chores for 90.7% of subjects and unusual resignation due to the difficulties of everday life for 30.2%. A triggering event was behind the low morale and anhedonia in nearly two-thirds of subjects (60.5%) essentially in conjunction with problems relating to work (55.8%), children (28.8%), affective relations (15.4%), time of year (15.4%) and financial difficulties (13.5%) (Fig. 2); the same subject could report several sources. 18.6% of the subjects had already experienced on average 1.2 ± 0.5 earlier depressive episodes lasting on average 35.3 ± 38.2 weeks. Subjects' sociodemographic characteristics and anhedonic histories were statistically comparable in the two groups as were their clinical characteristics upon enrollment.

On the Snaith-Hamilton pleasure scale (SHAPS), almost all subjects presented severe anhedonia characterized by a score of more than 5 (92.9% in the placebo group vs 90.9% in the Ulva L.L group and with comparable mean values of 9.0 ± 2.4 vs 9.0 ± 2.4, respectively. The QIDS-SR inventory score of depressive symptoms was 11.2 ± 4.3 in the placebo group vs 12.9 ± 3.9 in the Ulva L.L. group (p: 0.0708) out of a maximum score of 27, reflecting signs of slight to moderate depression. The presence of a component of depression was confirmed by the results of the HAMD Hamilton rating scale for depression with mean values of 6.2 ± 2.0 vs 6.2 ± 1.9 respectively; p: 0.7743.

Comparison of the change in subjects' psychological state

Anhedonia improved significantly ($p < 0.0001$) in both the placebo and Ulva L.L. groups by 4.3 ± 3 points between D0 and D28. This improvement was still ongoing at D84 but more so in the Ulva L.L. group than in the placebo group without, however, being statistically significant: 6.5 ± 2.8 vs 5.6 ± 3.6 (p: 0.1921). This greater improvement in the Ulva L.L. group was also reflected in the frequency of severe anhedonia that persisted in 24.4% of the placebo group subjects versus 13.6% of the Ulva L.L. group subjects but again without being statistically significant (p: 0.2050).

Results for depressive symptoms were, by contrast, far more significant. Analysis of the total QIDS-SR depressive symptoms inventory score showed significant improvements in the placebo and Ulva L.L. groups as from D7 in both goups. These improvements were comparable at D7 (3.5 ± 3.8 vs 3.6 ± 3.7; p: 0.9072) and D28 (4.5 ± 3.7 vs 4.9 ± 3.3; p: 0.6112) but became significantly greater in the Ulva L.L. group than the placebo group by D84 (7.8 ± 3.8 vs 5.9 ± 4; p: 0.0389) (Table 1; Fig. 3).

This greater improvement in the total QIDS-SR depressive symptoms inventory score was accounted for in particular by greater changes in the Ulva L.L. group than in the placebo group for three of its symptomatic dimensions: sleep disturbance, psychomotor change and changes in appetite or weight.

QIDS-SR "Sleep disturbance" improved significantly in the placebo and Ulva L.L. groups but comparably so between the groups at D7 (0.3 ± 0.6 vs 0.5 ± 0.9; p: 0.1623)

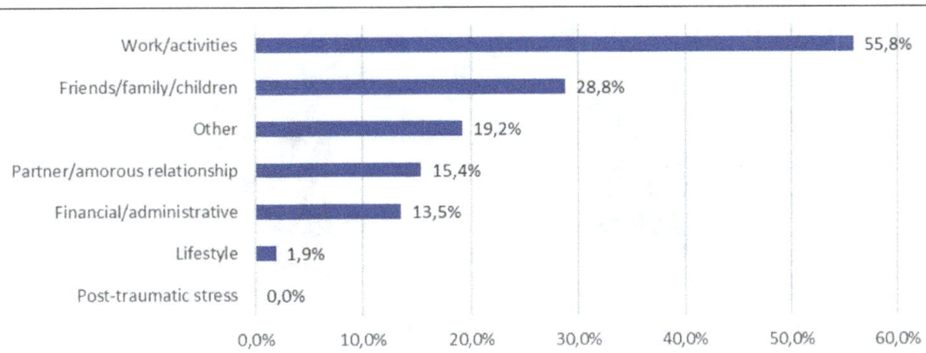

Fig. 2 Triggering events for low morale/anhedonia

Table 1 Comparison of changes in QIDS-SR

Product	D0 m ± SD IC95%:	D7 m ± SD IC95%:	Delta D0/D7 m ± SD IC95%:	D28 m ± SD IC95%:	Delta D0/28 m ± SD IC95%:	D84 m ± SD IC95%:	Delta D0/84 m ± SD IC95%:
Placebo (*n* = 38)	11.2 ± 4.3 [9.8; 12.6]	7.8 ± 3.7 [6.5; 9]	3.5 ± 3.8 [2.2; 4.7]	6.7 ± 4.2 [5.3; 8.1]	4.5 ± 3.7 [4.1; 6.5]	5.3 ± 3.7 [4.1; 6.5]	5.9 ± 4.0 [4.6; 7.2]
Ulva L.L (*n* = 42)	12.9 ± 3.9 [11.7; 14.1]	9.3 ± 4 [8.1; 10.6]	3.6 ± 3.7 [2.4; 4.7]	8.0 ± 3.6 [6.8; 9.1]	4.9 ± 3.3 [3.9; 6]	5.1 ± 2.8 [4.3; 6]	7.8 ± 3.8 [6.6; 9.0]
Anova	*p*-value: 0.0708	*p*-value: 0.0748	*p*-value: 0.9072	*p*-value: 0.1513	*p*-value: 0.6112	*p*-value: 0.8118	*p*-value: 0.0389

and D28 (0.5 ± 1 vs 0.5 ± 0.9; p: 0.1623). However, it remained stable in the placebo group at D84 whereas it continued to improve in the Ulva L.L. group, with the difference between groups reaching the statistically significant level of 0.5 ± 0.9 vs 1.0 ± 1.0; p: 0.0219) (Fig. 4).

"Psychomotor changes" improved significantly in both groups but whereas the changes were comparable at D7 (0.1 ± 0.7 vs 0.3 ± 0.9; p: 0.1684), they diverged significantly by D28. Psychomotor changes remained stable in the placebo group in this interval but continued to improve in the Ulva L.L. group becoming statistically significant (0.1 ± 0.8 vs 0.6 ± 0.9; p: 0.018) and the gap continued to widen at D84 (0.3 ± 0.8 vs 0.9 ± 0.9; p: 0.002) (Fig. 5).

Likewise, whereas the change in appetite and weight improved significantly in the placebo and Ulva L.L. groups comparably at D7 (0.5 ± 1 vs 0.7 ± 1.2; p: 0.3811) and D28 (0.5 ± 1 vs 0.8 ± 1.2; p: 0.1801) this improvement continued in the Ulva L.L. tending to reach the statistically significant level 0.5 ± 0.8 vs 0.9 ± 1.2; p: 0.0694 whereas it remained stable in the placebo group (Fig. 6).

The other symptomatic components of the QUIDS-SR improved significantly but comparably for the two groups whether for mood, concentration and decision-making, self-outlook, involvement in activities or fatigability. Suicidal ideation was too scarcely present in this population of subjects with anhedonia and low morale for their change to be interpreted.

Item 7 of the HAM-D score centred on work improved significantly ($p < 0.01$) in both the placebo and Ulva L.L. groups by 0.4 ± 0.8 points and 0.6 ± 0.9 respectively between D0 and D28 and by 0.7 ± 1 and 0.9 ± 1.1 points by D84 but the higher values recorded in the Ulva L.L. group were not statistically significant.

The percentage of subjects feeling improvement at D28 was higher in the Ulva L.L. group than in the placebo group (65.9% vs 59.5%) which was close to being statistically significant (p: 0.0651) and the difference continued to increase becoming statistically significant by D84 (90.9% vs 72.5%;p: 0.0114) (Fig. 7).

The percentage of subjects that clinicians judged to have improved was comparable in the Ulva L.L. and placebo groups (81.8% vs 75.6%; p: 0.4987) at D28 but the percentage rose signifiantly at D84 in the Ulva L.L. group (90.9% vs 70.7%; p: 0.0092) (Fig. 8).

Evaluation and comparison of tolerance and compliance

Twenty-eight undesirable events occurred in the course of the study concerning a total of 23 volunteers: 9 (20%) in the placebo group and 14 (14.9%) in the Ulva L.L. group (31.1%) (p: 0.2269). These events are essentially respiratory, thoracic and mediastinal affections (42.9%), gastro-intestinal affections (32.1%) and nervous system affections (10.7%) in comparable proportions in both groups. They were slight in 39.3% of cases, moderate in 39.3%, and severe in 21.4% and again in comparable proportions in both groups. Among the undesirable events, it was judged that only three of them for each group could not be excluded. In the placebo group an instance of diarrhoea, increased appetite and abdominal distensions were each deemed to be possibly related to the treatment. In the Ulva L.L. group, an instance of gastroentiritis, increased appetite and abdominal distensions

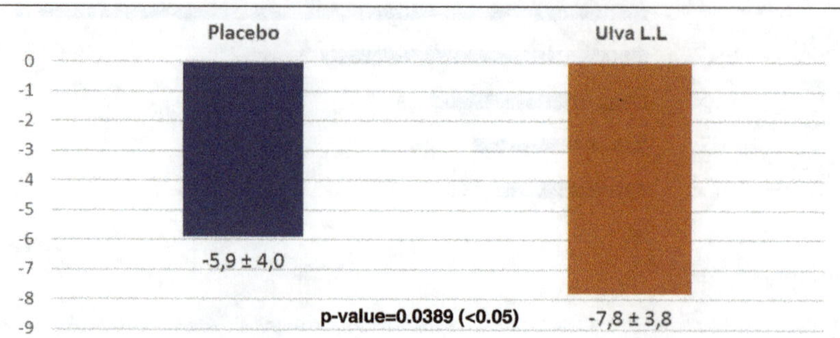

Fig. 3 Change in total QIDS-SR score between D0 and D84 for each treatment

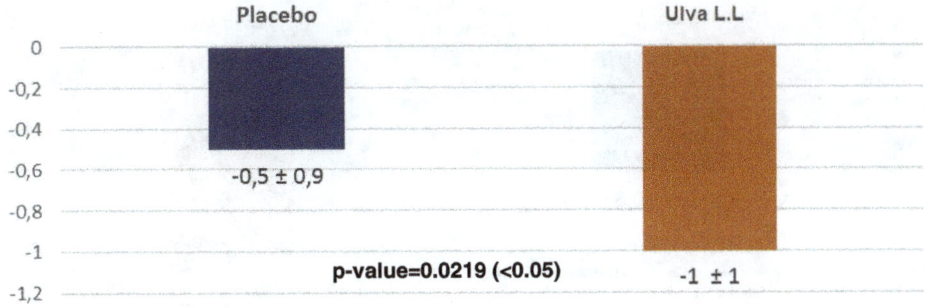

Fig. 4 Changes in the QIDS-SR INSOMNIA/HYPERSOMNIA domain between D0 and D84 for each treatment

were judged to be possibly treatment-related. No serious undesirable event was reported. The compliance was measured by the number of capsules people brought back at the last visit and was good with 96.5% of the subjects having an intake of more than 80% without difference between groups.

Discussion

The major finding of this double-blind randomized control trial is to show the positive effect of the seaweed extract on the component of depression of anhedonic patients measured by the QIDS-SR benchmark despite a substantial placebo effect in the control group. By D84, the total QIDS-SR score. Significantly decreased more in the Ulva.L.L. group than in the placebo group (p: 0.0389). This difference is essentially linked to an improvement of the sleep disorders (p: 0.0219), of the psychomotor consequences (p: 0.002) and of the nutrition behaviour (p: 0.0694).. Some 90.1% of subjects said they felt an improvement with Ulva L.L. versus 72.5% in the placebo group (p: 0.0114) and similarly 90.9% of doctors judged the subjects to have improved versus 70.8% (p: 0.021). It should be pointed out that this effect shows up despite a substantial placebo effect that continued practically until D28 and then declined whereas the depressive symptoms continued to improve in subjects taking the water-soluble extract of Ulva L.L. This gradual improvement perceived by subjects and physicians is consistent with the gradual effect observed in the change in the QIDS-SR total depressive symptom inventory score and three of its subsections. The results attest to the effect of a dietary supplement that requires a relatively long intake period to produce a gradual physiologically significant change and of a placebo whose effect gradually declines with time. The size of the effect is also worth pointing out. In a phase II a trial on the efficacy of a combination of dextromethorphane and quinidine (Q), the observed improvement was -5.9 ± 6.6 [23] and in a trial comparing Quetiapine against a placebo the difference in the QIDS-SR effect was 3.7 [24].

This effect on the component of depression of anhedonia thus seems to be clearly demonstrated and corroborates the results of the preclinical study evaluating the antidepressant effect of the seaweed extracts administered orally in adult male Wistar rats [13]. That study compared the seaweed extract at doses of 10, 20 and 40 mg/kg/day on groups of 12 rats against a control batch treated with the carrier (springwater) and a reference batch treated with Imipramine at doses of 10 mg/kg/day. The primary objective was to determine the efficacy of the extract on depression after 15 days of treatment on the principle of the Behavioural Despair Test (BDT) that is the benchmark for screening substances with an antidepressent effect. The results showed animals treated with Imiparmine and seaweed extract were less resigned than those treated with the placebo.

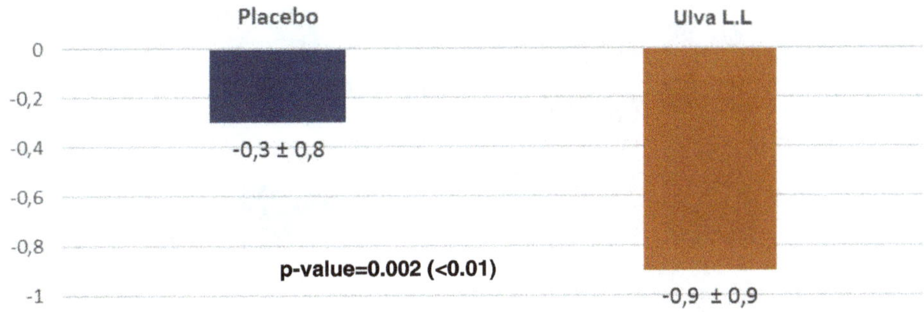

Fig. 5 Changes in the QIDS/SR PSYCHOMOTOR RESTLESS/ SLOW DOWN domain between D0 and D84 for each treatment

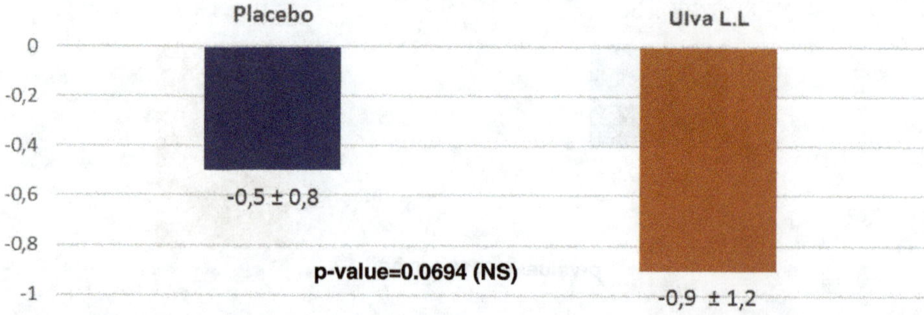

Fig. 6 Changes in the QIDS-SR CHANGE IN APPETITE AND WEIGHT domain between D0 and D84 for each treatment

A dose-dependent effect was observed for the seaweed extract.

Tolerance of the seaweed extracts was good and comparable with that of the placebo. This supports two toxicity studies conducted before the clinical trial: evaluation of acute toxicity and evaluation of sub-chronic toxicity by ingestion [25, 26]. Acute toxicity of the seaweed extract taken orally was evaluated with a single limit dose of 2000 mg/kg in 12 male and female Wistar rats monitored for 15 days. Two experimental series of six rats were studied. No mortality was observed and no abnormal behaviour was observed in the two-experimental series for male and female rats before and 1, 2, 3, 4, 5 and 6 h after administration of the single oral dose until completion of the experiment. No direct or induced significant weight loss was observed [25]. No anomaly of any organ was observed at autopsy. Subchronic toxicity of the seaweed extract was evaluated by oral administration at doses of 250, 500 and 1000 mg/kg/day for 28 days in male and female Wistar rats. No mortality, no abnormal behaviour, no body weight loss, no change in body weight change, no difference in food and water consumption, no opthalmological anomaly, no difference in functional tests and no histopathological anomaly was observed after 28 days of treatment. This good tolerance is an important factor for this product that could be an alternative to benzodiazepines for light to moderate depressive symptoms or at least as first-line treatment so they could be reserved for more severe situations. Further clinical studies must be conducted to confirm this since the registration of products whether as dietary supplements (health claims) or medication (marketing authorization) require at least two convergent clinical trials.

A review of the litterature does not retrieve some similar studies using alga extract. However, it is noticeable that the research of alternative natural products to the benzodiazepines is a growing research way which corresponds to a real patients' and societal need and that clearly appear in the increasing number of published papers presenting good quality randomised clinical trials on that subject in the reference data bases like Pubmed. Among these research, can be mentioned the works of Mosaffa-Jahromi M [27] on the effectiveness of anise oil for Treatment of Mild to Moderate Depression in Patients With Irritable Bowel Syndrome, of Pasalar M [28] on the efficacy of jollab in the treatment of depression in dyspeptic patients, of Anushiravani M [29] comparing the effectiveness of a combined herbal drug based on Echium amoenum with Citalopram in the treatment of Major Depressive Disorder or those of Lopresti AL [30] on a standardised extract from saffron (*Crocus sativus* L.) for the treatment of youth anxiety and depressive symptoms. Unfortunately all these works do not use the same criteria that we used to evaluate the effect on depression and do not target the same profile of depressive patients which do not allow real efficacy comparison.

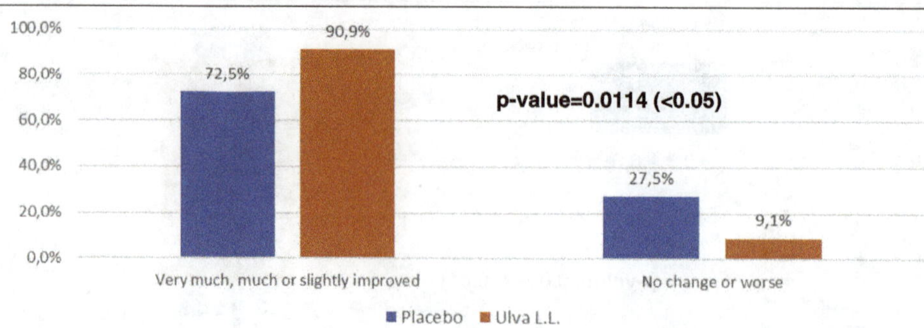

Fig. 7 PGII at D84 for each treatment

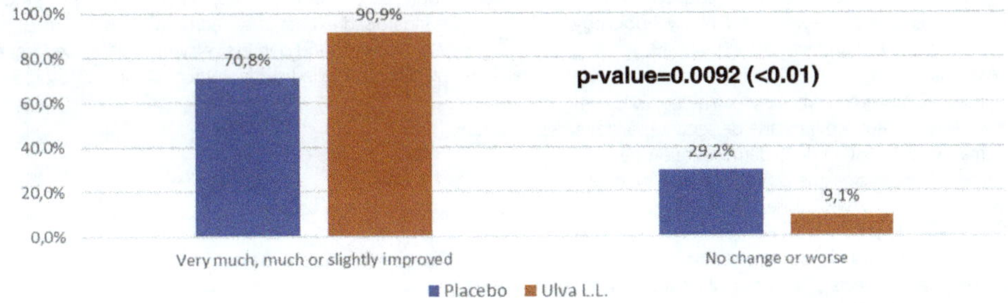

Fig. 8 CGII at D84 for each treatment

The status of the product is another point of discussion. As this pivotal study has demonstrated the action of Ulva L.L. extracts on depressive symptoms in humans, it now remains to be seen whether to continue with it as a dietary supplement with the difficulty of this positioning for depression or to shift towards a plant-based medicinal status for which the product has potential. Identifying the substance contained in the seawaeed extract and the source of the effect would be an added benefit whether for the dietary supplement case or the plant-based medication case, but is not a mandatory requirement.

Conclusion

This double-blind randomized placebo-controlled trial shows that daily intake for 3 months of a water-soluble extract of Ulva L.L. continues to significantly improve the component of depression of subjects presenting anhedonia compared with a placebo. This opens up perspectives for its potential use in everyday clinical care particularly as it would avoid the undesirable effects of medicinal drugs currently used. It is worth underscoring that this effect is shown despite a substantial placebo effect that persisted up to D28 and then diminished whereas the depressive symptoms continued to improve in subjects taking the water-soluble Ulva L.L. extract.

Abbreviations

BDT: Behavioural Despair Test; BMI: Body mass index; CGII: Clinical Global Improvement Impression; CGII: The Clinical Global Improvement Impression; DSM V: Diagnostic and statistical manual of mental disorders) – 5th edition; HAM-D: Hamilton rating scale for depression; ITT: Intention to treat; LOCF: Last Observation Carried Forward; MDE: Major depressive episode; PGII: Patient Global Improvement Impression; PGII: Patient Global Improvement Impression; PP: Per protocol; QIDS-SR: Quick Inventory of Depressive Symptomatology -Self Report; SHAPS: Snaith Hamilton Pleasure Scale

Funding

The authors declare that the clinical investigation center CEN Nutriment has received funding for the data collection and analysis of the data from OLMIX SA.

Authors contributions

FAA has designed the study protocol and has written the article. HD has designed the study protocol and has written the article. PNC has written the article. All authors read and approved the final manuscipt.

Consent for publication

Not applicable

Competing interests

The authors declare that they have no competing interests.

Author details

[1]Chair of health claim evaluation EMMAS BSB & CEN Nutriment, 29 rue Sambin, 21000 Dijon, France. [2]Biovet Conseil, 1 Route du Linès, 56700 Merlevenez, France. [3]Amadéite SAS Pôle biotechnologique du Haut du Bois, 56580 Bréhan, France.

References

1. Agence Française de Sécurité Sanitaire des Produits de Santé, Bon usage des médicaments antidépresseurs dans le traitement des troubles dépressifs et des troubles anxieux de l'adulte. Saint-Denis: Afssaps Octobre 2006. Available on: http://ansm.sante.fr/Dossiers/Traitements-par-antidepresseurs/Traitement-par-antidepresseurs/(offset)/0.
2. Buckner JD, et al. Implications of the DSM's emphasis on sadness and anhedonia in major depressive disorder. Psychiatry Res. 2008;159(1–2):25–30.
3. Agence Française de Sécurité Sanitaire des Produits de Santé. Les troubles du comportement liés à l'utilisation des benzodiazépines et produits apparentés. Mise au point. Saint-Denis: Afssaps; septembre 2001. Disponible sur http://ansm.sante.fr/S-informer/Informations-de-securite-Lettres-aux-professionnels-de-sante/Mise-au-point-sur-les-troubles-du-comportement-lies-a-l-utilisation-des-benzodiazepines-et-produits-apparentes-BZD, dans "Sécurité sanitaire et vigilances".
4. Practice guideline for the treatment of patients with major depressive disorder (revision). American Psychiatric Association. Am J Psychiatry. 2000; 157:1–45.
5. Paykel ES, Hollyman JA, Freeling P, Sedgwick P. Predictors of therapeutic benefit from amitriptyline in mild depression: a general practice placebo-controlled trial. J Affect Disord. 1988;14:83–95.
6. Geddes JR, Freemantle N, Mason J, Eccles MP, Boynton J. Selective serotonin reuptake inhibitors (SSRIs) versus other antidepressants for depression. Cochrane Database Syst Rev. 1999;(4). https://doi.org/10.1002/14651858.CD001851.
7. Loas G. Pierson A. Relation entre anhédonie et attitudes dysfonctionnelles chez le sujet sain : etude chez un groupe de 81 sujects = relationships between anhedonia and dysfunctional attitudes in healthy subject. J De Thérapie Comportementale Et Cognitive 1996, vol. 6, no2, pp. 52–58.
8. Ho N, Sommers M. Anhedonia: a concept analysis. Arch Psychiatr Nurs. 2013;27(3):121–9.
9. Der-Avakian A, Markou A. The neurobiology of anhedonia and other reward-related deficits. Trends Neurosci. 2012;35(1):68–77.

10. Martinotti G, Hatzigiakoumis DS, De Vita O, Clerici M, Petruccelli F, Di Giannantonio M, Janiri L. Anhedonia and reward system: psychobiology, evaluation, and clinical features. Int J Clin Med. 2012;3:697–713.
11. American Psychiatric Association. Diagnostic and statistical manual of mental disorders. 5th ed. Arlington, VA: American Psychiatric Publishing; 2013.
12. Saisine n° 2001-SA-0082. Avis de l'Agence française de sécurité sanitaire des aliments relatif à la demande d'évaluation de la démonstration de l'équivalence en substance d'une microalgue *Odontella aurita* avec des algues autorisées. Available on https://www.anses.fr/fr/system/files/AAAT2001sa0082.pdf. Accessed 13 June 2018.
13. Violle N, Rozan P, Demais H, Collen PN, Bisson JF. Evaluation of the antidepressant- and anxiolytic-like effects of a hydrophilic extract from the green seaweed Ulva sp. in rats. Nutr Neurosci. 2017;21(4):248–56. https://doi.org/10.1080/1028415X.2016.1276704.
14. Snaith RP, et al. A scale for the assessment of hedonic tone the Snaith-Hamilton pleasure scale. Br J Psychiatry. 1995;167(1):99–103.
15. Nakonezny PA, et al. Psychometric evaluation of the Snaith-Hamilton pleasure scale in adult outpatients with major depressive disorder. Int Clin Psychopharmacol. 2010;25(6):328–33.
16. Rush AJ, et al. The 16-item quick inventory of depressive symptomatology (QIDS), clinician rating (QIDS-C), and self-report (QIDS-SR): a psychometric evaluation in patients with chronic major depression. Biol Psychiatry. 2003; 54(5):573–83.
17. Trivedi MH, et al. The inventory of depressive symptomatology, clinician rating (IDS-C) and self-report (IDS-SR), and the quick inventory of depressive symptomatology, clinician rating (QIDS-C) and self-report (QIDS-SR) in public sector patients with mood disorders: a psychometric evaluation. Psychol Med. 2004;34(1):73–82.
18. Carmody TJ, et al. Making clinicians lives easier: guidance on use of the QIDS self-report in place of the MADRS. J Affect Disord. 2006;95(1–3):115–8.
19. Brown ES, et al. The quick inventory of depressive symptomatology-self-report: a psychometric evaluation in patients with asthma and major depressive disorder. Ann Allergy Asthma Immunol. 2008;100(5):433–8.
20. Zimmerman M, Posternak MA, Chelminski I. Is the cutoff to define remission on the Hamilton rating scale for depression too high? J Nerv Ment Dis. 2005;193:170–5.
21. Busner J, Targum SD. The clinical global impressions scale: applying a research tool in clinical practice. Psychiatry (Edgmont). 2007;4:28–37.
22. De Berardis D, Marini S, Serroni N, Rapini G, Iasevoli F, Valchera A, Signorelli M, Aguglia E, Perna G, Salone A, Di Iorio G, Martinotti G, Di Giannantonio M. S-Adenosyl-L-methionine augmentation in patients with stage II treatment-resistant major depressive disorder: an open label, fixed dose, single-blind study. Sci World J. 2013;2013:204649.
23. Murrough JW, Wade E, Sayed S, Ahle G, Kiraly DD, Welch A, Collins KA, Soleimani L, Iosifescu DV, Charney DS. Dextromethorphan/quinidine pharmacotherapy in patients with treatment resistant depression: a proof of concept clinical trial. J Affect Disord. 2017;218:277–83.
24. Li R, Wu R, Ju C, et al. A randomized, placebo-controlled pilot study of quetiapine-XR monotherapy or adjunctive therapy to antidepressant in acute major depressive disorder with current generalized anxiety disorder. Psychopharmacol Bull. 2016;46(1):8–23.
25. Etap lab; study of the acute oral toxicity of a seaweed extract in male and female wistar rats. Study Code: Amadeite/P6-C-0912/Seaweed Extract/Acute Toxicity. Rapport final du 26 février 2013.
26. Etap lab; evaluation of the subchronic toxicity of a seawead extract orally administered at three doses (250, 500 and 1000 mg/kg/day) during 28 days in male and female wistar rats. Study Code: Amadeite/P7-C-0912/Seaweed Extract /28-D Tox; Rapport final du 28 août 2013.
27. Mosaffa-Jahromi M, Tamaddon AM, Afsharypuor S, Salehi A, Seradj SH, Pasalar M, Jafari P, Lankarani KB. Effectiveness of anise oil for treatment of mild to moderate depression in patients with irritable bowel syndrome: A randomized active and placebo-controlled clinical trial. J Evid Based Complementary Altern Med. 2017;22(1):41–6.
28. Pasalar M, Choopani R, Mosaddegh M, Kamalinejad M, Mohagheghzadeh A, Fattahi MR, Zarshenas MM, Jafari P, Lankarani KB. Efficacy of jollab in the treatment of depression in dyspeptic patients: a randomized double-blind controlled trial. J Evid Based Complementary Altern Med. 2015;20(2):104–8.
29. Anushiravani M, Manteghi AA, Taghipur A, Eslami M. Comparing effectiveness of a combined herbal drug based on Echium amoenum with Citalopram in the treatment of Major Depressive Disorder . Curr Drug Discov Technol 2018 Feb 18.
30. Lopresti AL, Drummond PD, Inarejos-García AM, Prodanov M. A standardised extract from saffron (Crocus sativus L.) for the treatment of youth anxiety and depressive symptoms: A randomised, double-blind, placebo-controlled study. J Affect Disord. 2018;232:349–57.

Anaemia and depression before and after birth: a cohort study based on linked population data

Fenglian Xu[1*], Lynette Roberts[2], Colin Binns[3], Elizabeth Sullivan[1] and Caroline S. E. Homer[1]

Abstract

Background: To investigate the rates of hospitalisation for anaemia and depression in women in the six-year period (3 years before and after birth). To compare hospital admissions for depression in women with and without anaemia.

Methods: This is a population-based cohort study. Women's birth records (New South Wales (NSW) Perinatal Data Collection) were linked with NSW Admitted Patients Data Collection records between 1 January 2001 and 31 December 2010, so that hospital admissions for mothers could be traced back for 3 years before birth and followed up 3 years after birth. Setting: NSW Australia. Subjects: all women who gave birth to their first child in NSW between 1 January 2004 and 31 December 2008.

Results: Hospital admissions for both anaemia and depression were increased significantly in the year just before and after birth compared with the years before and after. Women with anaemia were more likely to be admitted to hospital for depression than those without (for principal diagnosis of depression, adjusted OR = 1.62, 95% CI = 1.25–2.11; for all diagnosis of depression, adjusted OR = 2.01, 95% CI = 1.70–2.38).

Conclusions: Depression was associated with anaemia in women before and after birth. This finding highlight the important role of primary care providers in assessing for both anaemia and depressive symptomatology together, given the relationship between the two. Treating or preventing anaemia may help to prevent postnatal depression.

Keywords: Anaemia, Depression, Risk factors, Women, Birth

Background

Depression in the postnatal period is a major health problem [1–3], with adverse outcomes for the mother and baby [4] including bonding [5–8], child's later socio-emotional development [9] academic achievement [10] and risk for psychopathologies [9]. One in every seven or eight women (around 12–16%) will experience depressive symptoms in the post-partum period [11–14], costing the Australian economy $113.86 million annually [13]. We have previously shown that the hospital admission rates for psychiatric disorders increased in the first year after birth significantly between 2001 and 2010 (1.16% in 2001, 2.28% in 2010) [15] in New South Wales (NSW) of Australia. The hospital admission increase was mainly attributed to unipolar depression, adjustment disorders and anxiety disorders [15].

Poor physical health is a risk factor for postnatal depression (PND). A prospective cohort study in1,507 nulliparous women in Melbourne of Australia showed that women with five or more physical health problems had a six-fold increase in the risk of depressive symptoms at 3 months postpartum and a three-fold increase in the risk of subsequent depressive symptoms at 6–12 months postpartum [14]. Women experiencing a greater number of physical health problems may be at an increased risk of postnatal depression.

One of these physical health risk factors is anaemia, a common problem for women (global prevalence of 29%) [16], particularly in pregnancy (global prevalence of 38%) [16] due to additional physiological demands on the mother. A population-based cross-sectional study of

* Correspondence: Fenglian.Xu@uts.edu.au
[1]Faculty of Health, University of Technology Sydney, Ultimo 2007, Australia
Full list of author information is available at the end of the article

all singleton births ($n = 511,938$) in Finland between 2002 and 2010 reported that anaemia is a predictor of depression during pregnancy [17]. A prospective cohort study in Spain ($n = 729$) found that mothers with low levels of the iron marker, ferritin, at 48 h post-partum were 3.73 times more likely to have PND at 32 weeks [18]. Another prospective study in American women found that low concentrations of hemoglobin in mothers at 7 days postpartum correlated with depressive symptoms at 28 days postpartum [19]. However, a study in Chinese mothers found no association between iron levels in pregnancy and 3 days postpartum, with depression scores 24–48 h or 6 weeks after delivery [20].

Given the wide-reaching impact and costs on the individual, parent-child dyad and community, we sought to investigate whether there is an association between anaemia and depression in Australia. These findings could inform public health policy, including highlighting a potential link between preventable physical and mental health problems in the perinatal period. Specifically, we used population-based linked data in Australia to:

1. Describe the rates of hospitalization for anaemia and depression in mothers in the 3 years before and after giving birth.
2. Compare the association of hospital admission of depression in women with and without anaemia.

We hypothesized that anaemia is associated with an increase in hospital admissions for depression.

Methods

Study population and design

This is a population-based cohort study, including all women who gave birth to their first child in New South Wales (NSW) between 1 January 2004 and 31 December 2008. Mothers who had subsequent births in 4 years after the first birth were excluded. Data were linked using the NSW Perinatal Data Collection (PDC) and the NSW Admitted Patients Data Collection (APDC). Women's hospital admissions for anaemia and depressive disorders were identified by APDC records. Mother's birth records were linked with APDC records between 1 January 2001 and 31 December 2010, so that hospital admissions for mothers could be traced back for 3 years before birth and followed up 3 years after birth. The study population and data linkage are detailed in Figs. 1 and 2.

The PDC is a data collection of births of at least 20 weeks gestation or at least 400 g birthweight in NSW of Australia. It includes all births in hospitals (public and private) and home births. The database includes information on maternal characteristics and outcomes of pregnancy, labour and birth. The APDC is a routinely collected census of all hospital separations in NSW hospitals including public, private and psychiatric hospitals and day procedures. It covers all patient hospitalisations and includes information on patient demographics, diagnoses and clinical procedures. The diagnoses for admissions have been coded according to the 10th revision of the International Statistical Classification of Diseases and Related Health Problems, Australian Modification (ICD-10-AM) [21].

Data linkage was carried out by the NSW Department of Health Centre for Health Record Linkage (CHeReL). Each record from PDC and APDC datasets was assigned a Person Project Number to allow records for the same individual to be linked. In the 1000 randomly selected sample of records, the false positive rate of the linkage was 0.3% and false negative < 0.5%.

Diagnosis

The diagnoses in each hospital admission record in APDC data include 55 diagnoses (one principal diagnosis, one stay diagnosis and 53 other diagnoses). Principal diagnosis refers to the one which was chiefly responsible for hospital admissions [22]. The stay diagnosis refers to the one that most influenced the length of stay in hospital [15]. Other diagnosis is an additional diagnosis. It refers to a condition or a complaint coexisting with the principal and stay diagnoses or arising during the hospitalisation [15]. Hospital admission refers to hospitalization (a patient was admitted to hospital for inpatient service). PND refers to the principal diagnoses of depression after birth. Anaemia refers to all diagnoses of anaemia (including principal and non-principal diagnoses). Mothers with anaemia were identified using ICD-10-AM diagnosis codes: (1) D50-D53 [nutritional anaemia]; (2) D55-D59 [haemolytic anaemia], (3) D60-D64 [aplastic and other anaemia] and O99.0 [anaemia complicating pregnancy, childbirth and the puerperium]. Mothers with depressive disorders were identified using ICD-10-AM diagnosis codes: (1) F32-F33 [depressive disorder] and (2) F53 [Mental and behavioural disorders associated with the puerperium]. Only the first hospital admission with the diagnosis of *anaemia* or depressive disorders was used for the analysis of the rate, odds ratio (OR) and adjusted OR.

Statistics

Descriptive statistics were used to summarise the rate and proportion of hospital admissions. The proportion was calculated by women's 1st hospital admissions for the diagnosis of anaemia or depression as nominator and overall hospital admissions as denominator. Logistic regression models were used to estimate the odds ratio (OR) of anaemia on hospitalisation for depression. The dependent variable is the first hospital admission for depression (yes/no) in the study period (3 years before birth and 3 years after the birth). The independent

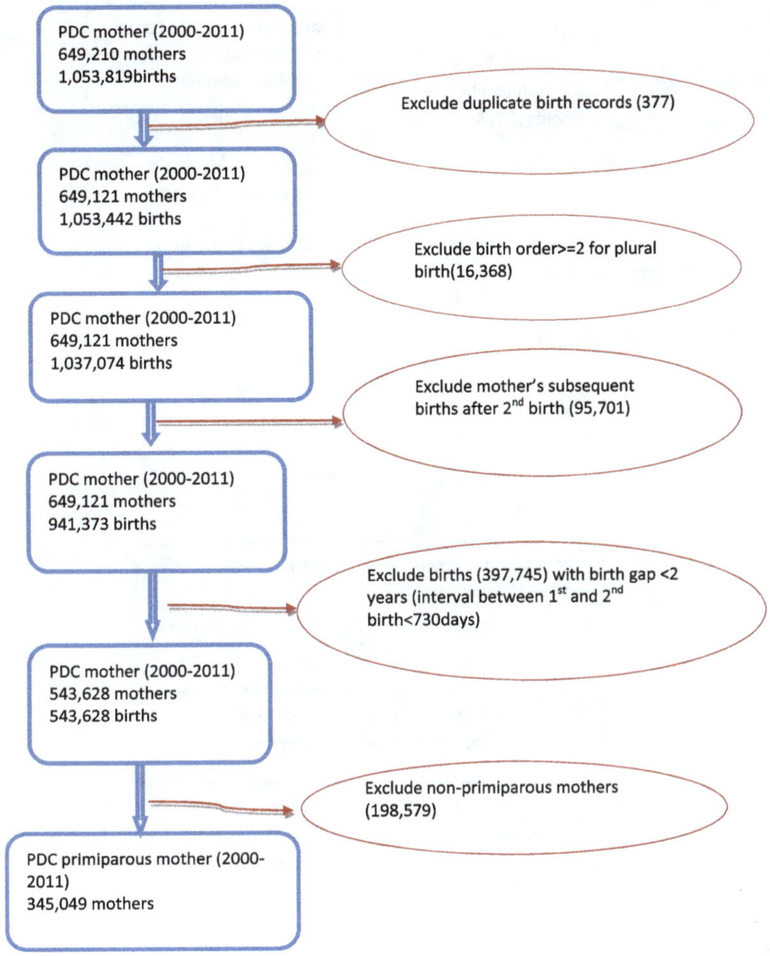

Fig. 1 The study population selection

variable is the first hospital admission for all diagnoses of anaemia in the study period. The adjusted factors for the OR include maternal age, maternal country of birth, maternal diabetes mellitus and hypertension, gestational diabetes, smoking status during pregnancy, remoteness of living area,, method of birth, gestational age, baby's death and place of birth and the Index of Relative Socio-economic Disadvantage Quintile [23]. The analyses were conducted using IBM SPSS (Statistical Package for Social Science) Statistics 20.

Results

Characteristic of the study population and the rate of the first hospital admissions for anaemia are detailed in Table 1. Young women (< 20 years old) were more likely to be admitted to hospital with the diagnosis of anaemia than those aged between 25 and 39 years old. The mothers in disadvantaged group; with maternal diabetes mellitus or hypertension were also more likely to be admitted to hospitals with the diagnosis of anaemia. Mothers with anaemia were more likely to have stillbirth, preterm birth and their babies were more likely to die in neonatal/postnatal period.

There were 236 hospital admissions with principal diagnosis of anaemia and 2569 admissions with all diagnosis of anaemia in the study periods (3 years before birth and 3 years after birth) (Table 2). The admissions with principal diagnosis of anaemia only accounted for 9.19% (236/2569) of the hospital admission for all anaemia diagnoses. That is, more than 90% anaemia was diagnosed as a non-principal diagnoses.

The rates of anaemia in women in the year just before and after giving birth were significantly higher than the 2 years before (the second and third year before birth) and 2 years after (the second and third year after birth) the period, especially for all diagnoses of anaemia (Table 2 and Fig. 3).The hospital admission rate for the principal diagnosis of anaemia was 0.83 per 1000 women (95% CI = 0.63–1.03/1000) in the year just before birth; 0.93 per 1000 women (95% CI = 0.71–1.15/1000) in the year just after birth. The hospital admission rate for all diagnosis of anaemia was 16.06 per 1000

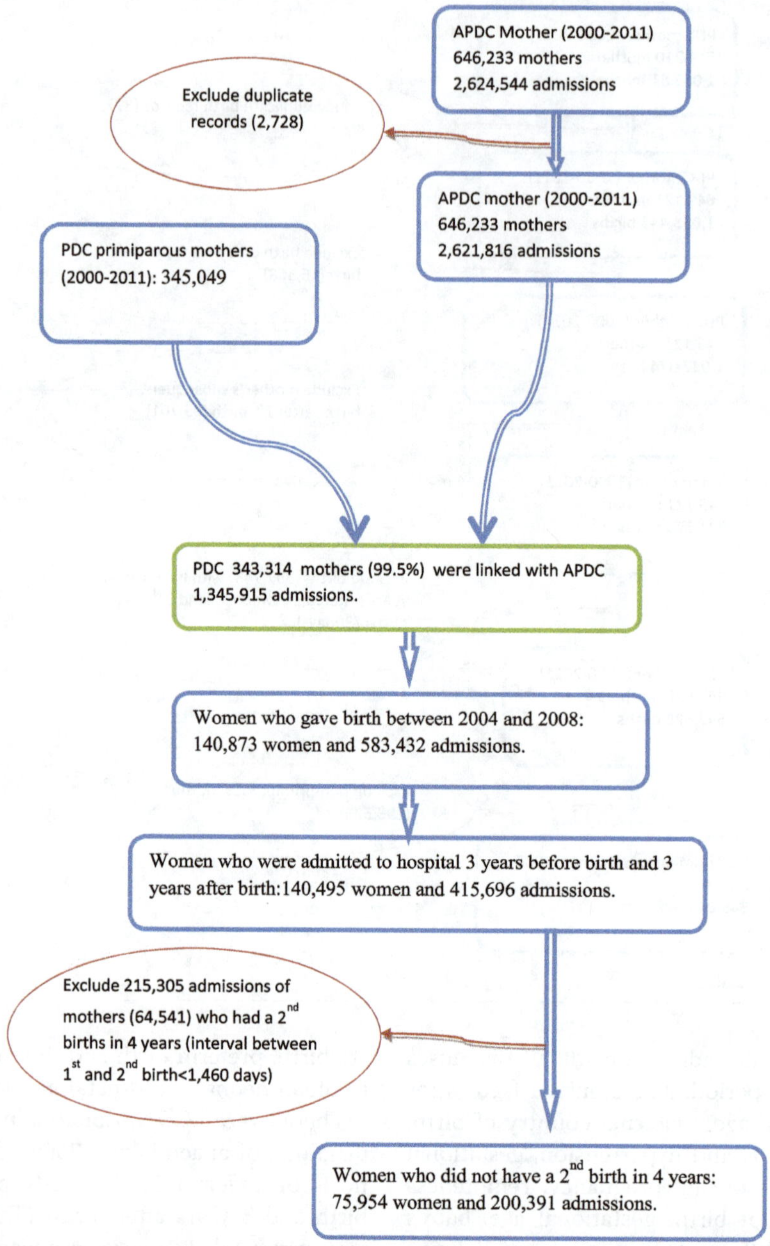

Fig. 2 The data linkage and study population

women (95% CI = 15.17–16.95/1000) in the year just before the birth; 13.15 per 1000 women (95% CI = 12.34–13.96/1000) in the year just after birth (Table 2).

The proportion of women's anaemia in the year just before and after birth were also significantly higher than the 2 years before (the second and third year before birth) and 2 years after (the second and third year after birth) this period for all diagnoses of anaemia (Table 3 and Fig. 3). For the principal diagnosis of anaemia, the proportion in the year just before the birth (0.79/1000 admission, 95% CI = 0.60–0.98) was lower than the third year before birth (2.14/1000 admission, 95% CI = 1.30–2.98) and the third year after birth(2.10/1000 admission, 95% CI = 1.38–2.82); The proportion in the year just before the birth was not significantly different from the second year before birth and the first 2 years after birth.

Figure 4 shows that majority of the anaemia were attributed to anaemia complicating pregnancy, childbirth and the puerperium (38.71% for principal diagnosis and 42.99% for all diagnosis) and nutritional anaemia (35.89% for principal diagnosis and 15.47% for all diagnosis). Haemolytic anaemia accounted for 6.05% for principal diagnosis and 3.94% for all diagnosis of anaemia. Figure 4 also shows that there was more

Table 1 Primiparous mother's characteristic and the 1st hospital admissions for anaemia 2001–2010, Australia

Factor	Value	Mother	Admission for anaemia	Rate (%)	95% CI	
Maternal age*	< 20	6284	262	4.17	3.68	4.66
	20–24	14,350	521	3.63	3.32	3.94
	25–29	19,833	662	3.34	3.09	3.59
	30–34	20,472	644	3.15	2.91	3.39
	35–39	11,479	364	3.17	2.85	3.49
	40+	3529	116	3.29	2.70	3.88
	Total	75,947	2569	3.38	3.25	3.51
Women's country of birth	Australia	48,331	1589	3.29	3.13	3.45
	Other countries	27,623	980	3.55	3.33	3.77
	Total	75,954	2569	3.38	3.25	3.51
Remoteness*	Major cities	53,399	1827	3.42	3.27	3.57
	Inner regional	16,092	497	3.09	2.82	3.36
	Out regional and remote	5252	202	3.85	3.33	4.37
	Total	74,743	2526	3.38	3.25	3.51
Smoking during pregnancy	No	65,899	2224	3.37	3.23	3.51
	Yes	9694	327	3.37	3.01	3.73
	Total	75,593	2551	3.37	3.24	3.50
Index of Relative SE Disadvantage Quintile*	1st quintile least disadvantaged	17,196	487	2.83	2.58	3.08
	2.00	15,490	501	3.23	2.95	3.51
	3.00	14,437	516	3.57	3.27	3.87
	4.00	12,953	455	3.51	3.19	3.83
	5th quintile most disadvantaged	14,667	567	3.87	3.56	4.18
	Total	74,743	2526	3.38	3.25	3.51
Maternal diabetes mellitus*	No	75,488	2543	3.37	3.24	3.50
	Yes	466	26	5.58	3.50	7.66
	Total	75,954	2569	3.38	3.25	3.51
Gestational diabetes	No	72,051	2417	3.35	3.22	3.48
	Yes	3903	152	3.89	3.28	4.50
	Total	75,954	2569	3.38	3.25	3.51
Maternal hypertension*	No	75,175	2529	3.36	3.23	3.49
	Yes	779	40	5.13	3.58	6.68
	Total	75,954	2569	3.38	3.25	3.51
Delivery mode	Vaginal	49,827	1641	3.29	3.13	3.45
	Caesarean section	26,073	928	3.56	3.34	3.78
	Total	75,900	2569	3.38	3.25	3.51
Baby's death*	None	75,401	2526	3.35	3.22	3.48
	Still birth	340	23	6.76	4.09	9.43
	Neonatal/post neonatal death	151	16	10.60	5.69	15.51
	Total	75,892	2565	3.38	3.25	3.51
Gestational age (week)*	< 28	534	39	7.30	5.09	9.51
	28–31	696	50	7.18	5.26	9.10
	32–36	5153	221	4.29	3.74	4.84
	37–41	68,023	2189	3.22	3.09	3.35

Table 1 Primiparous mother's characteristic and the 1st hospital admissions for anaemia 2001–2010, Australia *(Continued)*

Factor	Value	Mother	Admission for anaemia	Rate (%)	95% CI	
	42w+	1540	70	4.55	3.51	5.59
	Total	75,946	2569	3.38	3.25	3.51
Place of birth*	Hospital	74,318	2512	3.38	3.25	3.51
	Birth Centre	1482	46	3.10	2.22	3.98
	Others	145	11	7.59	3.28	11.90
	Total	75,945	2569	3.38	3.25	3.51

SE Socioeconomic
*Significantly associated with the 1st hospital admissions with anaemia by chi square test ($p < 0.05$)

unspecified diagnosis of anaemia in non-principal diagnoses.

Table 4 shows the first hospital admissions for depression before and after birth. Compared with the hospital admissions before birth, the hospital admissions for depression increased significantly in the first and second year after birth. Women in the pregnancy year were less likely to be admitted to hospital compared with the 2 years before pregnancy and 3 years after birth. For principal diagnosis, the first hospital admission rate of depression was 8.94 per 1000 Person Year (PY) (95% CI = 8.27–9.61) in the first year after birth; while the rate of depression was only 0.91/1000PY (95% CI = 0.70–1.12) in the year before birth. For all diagnosis, the rate of depression was 16.02 per 1000 Person Year (PY) (95% CI = 15.12–16.92) in the first year after birth; while the rate of depression was only 6.48/1000PY (95% CI = 5.91–7.05) in the year before birth.

To consider the impact of the increase of overall hospital admissions during pregnancy and perinatal period, the proportion of depression was analysed (Table 5). Similar to the change of rate in Table 4, the proportion of hospital admissions for depression increased significantly in the first and second year after birth. Women's hospital admissions for depression in the year just before birth were the lowest compared with the 2 years before and 3 years after (Table 5 and Fig. 5).

Figure 5 shows that the difference of the proportion and rate of depression for both principal and all diagnosis. The proportions of depression (including both principal and all diagnosis) decreased significantly in the first year before birth compared with the rates of depression.

Table 6 shows the association between anaemia and depression in women. Women with anaemia were more likely to be admitted to hospital for depression (for principal diagnosis of depression, adjusted OR = 1.62, 95% CI = 1.25–2.11) (for all diagnosis of depression, adjusted OR = 2.01, 95% CI = 1.70–2.38) than women without anaemia.

Discussion

This study showed that the hospital admissions for depression increased significantly in the first year after birth compared with those before birth. The increased trend after birth is consistent with our previous study [15] and other studies from other areas [24]. For depression, the proportions (including both principal and all diagnosis) decreased significantly in the year before birth because of the increase of overall hospital admissions.

This study also showed that hospital admissions for anaemia with all diagnosis were significantly increased in the year of pregnancy (16.06 per 1000 women, 95% CI = 15.17–16.95/1000) and the first year after birth (13.15 per 1000 women, 95% CI = 12.34–13.96/1000).

Table 2 The rate of women's 1st hospital admissions with the diagnosis of anaemia before and after birth ($n = 75,954$) 2001–2010, Australia

Period		Principal diagnosis	Rate (/1000)	95% CI		All diagnosis	Rate (/1000)	95% CI	
Before birth	3rd year	25	0.33	0.2	0.46	77	1.01	0.78	1.24
	2nd year	21	0.28	0.16	0.4	88	1.16	0.92	1.4
	1st year	63	0.83	0.63	1.03	1220	16.06	15.17	16.95
After birth	1st year	71	0.93	0.71	1.15	999	13.15	12.34	13.96
	2nd year	23	0.30	0.18	0.42	88	1.16	0.92	1.4
	3rd year	33	0.43	0.28	0.58	97	1.28	1.03	1.53
Total		236	3.11	2.71	3.51	2569	33.82	32.53	35.11

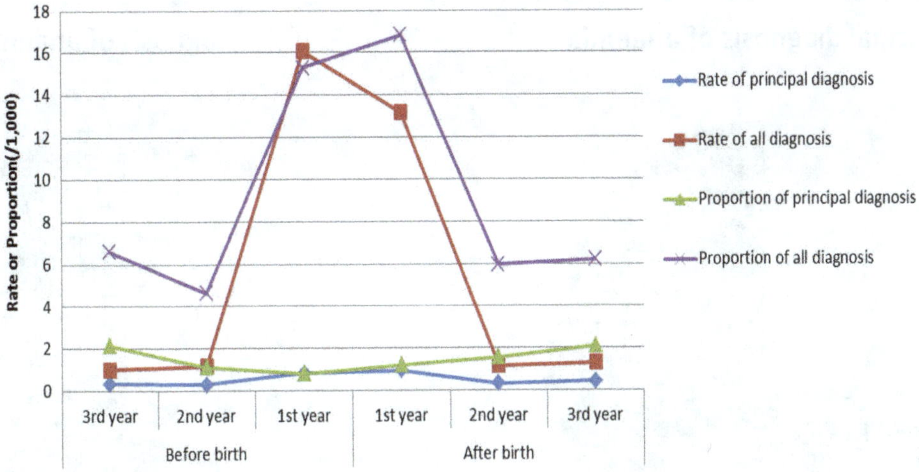

Fig. 3 The rate and proportion of women's hospital admissions for anaemia 2001–2010, Australia

To consider the impact of increased overall hospital admissions before and after birth, the proportion of anaemia was also analyzed. Similar to the hospital admission rate, the proportion of anaemia was also significantly increased in the year of pregnancy and the first after birth. A systematic analysis of population-representative data from 107 countries between 1995 and 2011 showed that global anaemia prevalence was between 29% (95% credibility intervals (CI) = 24–35) and 33% (95% CI = 29–37) in non-pregnant women, 38% (95% CI = 34–43) and 43% (95% CI = 39–47) in pregnant women [16]. In high-income regions (including Australia), anaemia prevalence was between 14% (95% CI = 12–18) and 16% (95% CI = 12–22) in non-pregnant women, 22% (95% CI = 16–29) and 23% (95% CI = 18–30) in pregnant women [16]. The rate of anaemia in NSW women was significantly lower than other areas [16]. This study imply that majority of women with Anaemia were not admitted to hospitals.

Majority of anaemia (91%) was diagnosed as a non-principal diagnosis rather than principal diagnosis, as many women with anaemia were not diagnosed until they were admitted into hospital to give birth or for other medical reasons. Thus the greater the number of hospital admissions for other principal diagnoses, the greater the number of anaemia cases that will be found as an additional diagnosis. In New South Wales, 99.5% women gave birth in hospitals, this provided a good opportunity to identify women with anaemia. To adjust the impact of overall hospital admissions, the proportion of hospital admissions for anaemia (overall hospital admissions as denominator) was calculated.

Women in the pre- and postnatal periods are particularly vulnerable to the effects of iron deficiency on mood through both direct and indirect pathways [25]. Factors such as peripartum blood losses, postpartum haemorrhaging, increased nutritional demands to support fetal developmental and breastfeeding, may cause iron-deficiency [25, 26], which may disrupt the functioning of neurotransmitters which implicated in mood.

This study showed that women with anaemia were more likely to be admitted to hospital for depression than those without. The finding are consistent with the results based on population-based cohort studies from Finland [17] and Spain [18]. Correspondingly, we see an association between iron-deficiency and mood across a

Table 3 The proportion of women's 1st hospital admissions with the diagnosis of anaemia in all hospital admissions 2001–2010, Australia

Period		Hospital admissions	Principal diagnosis	Proportion (/1000)	95% CI		All diagnosis	Proportion (/1000)	95% CI	
Before birth	3rd year	11,671	25	2.14	1.30	2.98	77	6.6	5.13	8.07
	2nd year	18,965	21	1.11	0.64	1.58	88	4.64	3.67	5.61
	1st year	79,903	63	0.79	0.60	0.98	1220	15.27	14.42	16.12
After birth	1st year	59,383	71	1.2	0.92	1.48	999	16.82	15.79	17.85
	2nd year	14,790	23	1.56	0.92	2.20	88	5.95	4.71	7.19
	3rd year	15,679	33	2.1	1.38	2.82	97	6.19	4.96	7.42
Total		200,391	236	1.18	1.03	1.33	2569	12.82	12.33	13.31

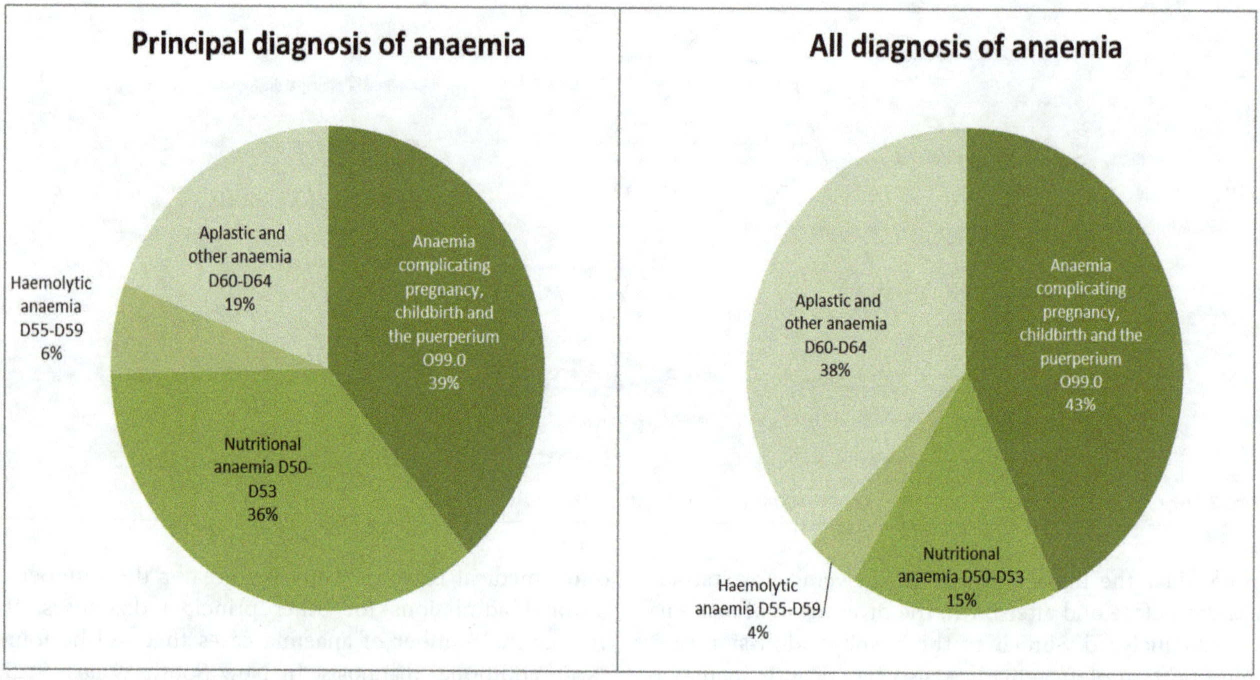

Fig. 4 The percentage of diagnoses of anaemia for women's hospital admissions before and after birth 2001–2010, Australia

range of studies, such as high rates of anaemia in psychiatric patients with chronic depression [2], and conversely, higher rates of depression in people with anaemia [1, 27]. Lever-van Milligen and colleagues found that anaemia status was associated with depression [28].

Potential mechanisms of effect for the relationship between anaemia and depression may associated with the role of iron in mood regulation. Iron contributes to myelination in the brain, as well as the development and functioning of the monamine system, which are key neurotransmitters involved in mood such as serotonin, dopamine and noradrenaline [29, 30]. Iron deficiency alters the signalling, production and metabolism of these monamines, including other key excitatory and inhibitory neurotransmitters such as glutamate and γ-aminobutyric acid respectively, which govern brain activity [29]. Imbalances in the concentration of these neurotransmitters then affect emotion regulation leading to depressed mood and behaviour [31–33]. Research with iron-deficient mothers in Africa found that iron supplementation successfully treated mood and cognitive disturbances [34].

In addition to this proposed direct pathway, iron deficiency and depression may be associated via an indirect, stress-induced inflammatory pathway. The individuals with depression experience chronic psychosocial and physical stressors. The stress lead to an overactive hypothalamic–pituitary–adrenal (HPA) axis, which triggers stress-induced elevated levels of pro-inflammatory cytokines [35–38]. Pro-inflammatory cytokines interfere with the functioning of monamines, resulting in a reduction of available neurotrasmitters [39–42]. This inflammatory response also affects iron metabolism, with depressed patients showing reduced hemoglobin (Hb) levels and red blood cell count relative to controls [43, 44].

Table 4 The 1st Hospital admissions for depressive disorders in 3 years before and after birth 2001–2010, Australia

Period		Mothers (PY)	Principal diagnosis	Rate (/1000PY)	95% CI		Mothers (PY)	All diagnosis	Rate (/1000PY)	95% CI	
Before birth	3rd year	75,954	96	1.26	1.01	1.51	75,954	229	3.01	2.62	3.4
	2nd year	75,858	85	1.12	0.88	1.36	75,725	207	2.73	2.36	3.10
	1st year	75,773	69	0.91	0.70	1.12	75,518	489	6.48	5.91	7.05
After birth	1st year	75,704	677	8.94	8.27	9.61	75,029	1202	16.02	15.12	16.92
	2nd year	75,027	158	2.11	1.78	2.44	73,827	226	3.06	2.66	3.46
	3rd year	74,869	85	1.14	0.90	1.38	73,601	121	1.64	1.35	1.93
Total		453,185	1170	2.58	2.43	2.73	449,654	2474	5.50	5.28	5.72

PY Refers to person year, *CI* Refers to confidence interval

Table 5 The proportion of women's 1st hospital admissions with the diagnosis of depression in all hospital admissions 2001–2010, Australia

Period		Hospital admissions	Principal diagnosis	Rate (/1000PY)	95% CI		All diagnosis	Rate (/1000PY)	95% CI	
Before birth	3rd year	11,671	96	8.23	6.59	9.87	229	19.62	17.1	22.14
	2nd year	18,965	85	4.48	3.53	5.43	207	10.91	9.43	12.39
	1st year	79,903	69	0.86	0.66	1.06	489	6.12	5.58	6.66
After birth	1st year	59,383	677	11.40	10.55	12.25	1202	20.24	19.11	21.37
	2nd year	14,790	158	10.68	9.02	12.34	226	15.28	13.3	17.26
	3rd year	15,679	85	5.42	4.27	6.57	121	7.72	6.35	9.09
	Total	200,391	1170	5.84	5.51	6.17	2474	12.35	11.87	12.83

Strengths and limitations

The strengths of this study include the population-based methodology, and data spanning a 6 year period to offer a richer understanding of mental and physical health in Australian women. Our findings present a baseline period from which to monitor the association between anaemia and depression in Australian women.

These findings also need to be considered within the context of study limitations.

This study shows that, for the principal diagnosis of anaemia, the proportion in the year just before the birth was lower than the third year before birth and the third year after birth. This was because women's hospital admissions increased significantly in the pregnancy year (more than four times than the second and third year before birth and the second and third years after birth), however the absolute hospital admissions were still higher than the 2 years before and the 2 years after the year of birth. This study further showed that the proportion of depression for both principal and all diagnosis decreased significantly in the first year before birth (Fig. 5). This was because of the increase of women's hospital admission in the year of pregnancy. The rates of depression for both principal and all diagnosis were less likely to be impacted by the number of overall admissions because the denominator for the rate analysis was the number of women rather than admissions. For anaemia, the proportion did not decrease as significantly as depression because the number of hospital admissions with the diagnoses of anaemia also increased significantly in the year of pregnancy (Fig. 3).

The 'other anaemia' diagnosis included the cases without clear diagnosis such as unspecified anaemia. As a result, the diagnosis for D60-D64 (aplastic and other anaemia) included relatively more cases. For women before and after birth, unspecified common anaemia such as anaemia complicating pregnancy, childbirth and the puerperium (O99.0) may be included in this group.

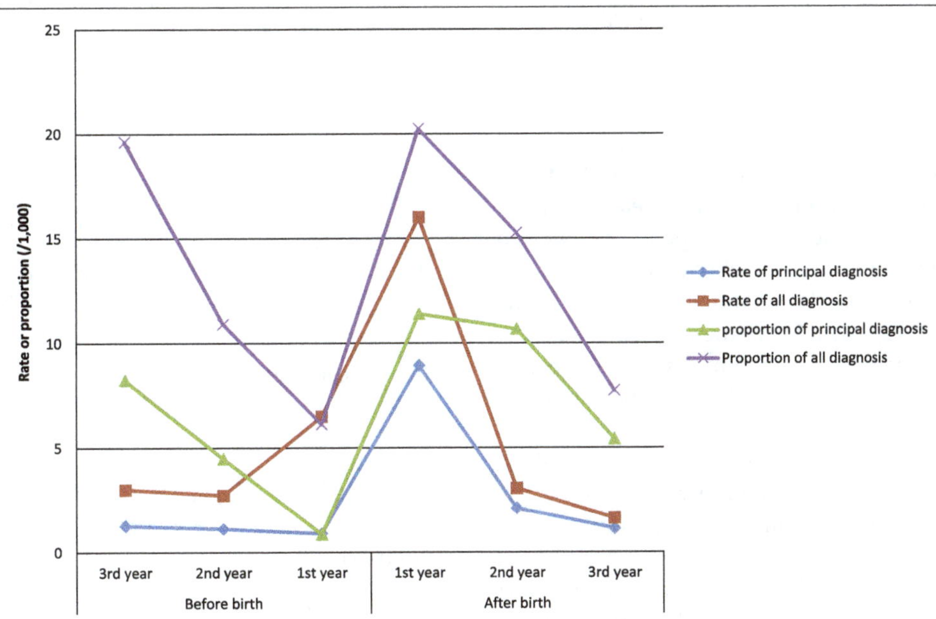

Fig. 5 The rate and proportion of women's hospital admissions for depression 2001–2010, Australia

Table 6 The odds ratios (OR) of hospital admissions for depressive disorders in women with and without anaemia 2001–2010, Australia

Diagnoses of depression	Hospital admissions for anaemia	N	Hospital admissions for depression	Rate (%)	Crude OR	95% CI		Adjusted OR	95% CI	
Principal diagnosis	No	73,385	1109	1.51	1			1		
	Yes	2569	61	2.37	1.59	1.22	2.06	1.62	1.25	2.11
	Total	75,954	1170	1.54						
All diagnosis	No	73,385	2317	3.16	1			1		
	Yes	2569	157	6.11	2.00	1.69	2.36	2.01	1.70	2.38
	Total	75,954	2474	3.26						

The adjusted OR was adjusted for maternal age, maternal country of birth, maternal diabetes mellitus and hypertension, gestational diabetes, smoking status during pregnancy, remoteness of living area, delivery method, gestational age, baby's death, place of birth and a socioeconomic indicator (i.e. the Index of Relative Socio-economic Disadvantage Quintile)

Some researchers mentioned that hospital admissions for PND might be over-enumerated because hospital admission could occur for other medical reasons in the postnatal period [45, 46]. Furthermore, there was discussion over whether PND is a specific disorder distinct from major depressive disorder [47, 48] and maternal fatigue [49]. To minimise the potential overestimation of the rates, we only included the admissions with a 'principal' diagnosis of depressive disorders. On the other hand, the PND rates reported here might be under-estimated rather than over-estimated because hospital admissions would most likely reflect severe cases of PND [50] and majority of women experiencing PND were undetected and un-referred for mental health treatment by their obstetrical providers [51].

Temporal order between anaemia and depression could not be investigated by this study because majority of anaemia were diagnosed later than its occurrence. Majority of anaemia did not be found until women were admitted to hospital for giving birth or other reasons.

Public health recommendations

This is the first population-based study to demonstrate a possible link between anaemia and depression in Australia, and emphasizes the importance and inter-relationship of both mental and physical health in the period before and after birth. Current clinical care practice guidelines recommend psychoeducation on the importance of iron during pregnancy and iron screening for women at risk of anaemia [52], as well as routine screening and monitoring of depressive symptoms [53]. Our findings highlight the important role of primary care providers in assessing for both anaemia and depressive symptomatology together, given the relationship between the two. Knowledge of the psychiatric implications of iron status in the postnatal period is critical given that approximately one-fifth of Australian women are already iron-deficient at the start of pregnancy [54], and PND can also be chronic for a subgroup of women [55].

Conclusion

Anaemia was associated with postnatal depression for women. This finding highlight the important role of primary care providers in assessing for both anaemia and depressive symptomatology together, given the relationship between the two. Treating or preventing anaemia may help to prevent postnatal depression.

Abbreviations

ABS: Australian Bureau of Statistics; ACPCP: Anaemia complicating pregnancy, childbirth and the puerperium O99.0; APDC: Admitted patients data collection; CHeReL: Centre for Health Record Linkage; CI: Confidence interval; HPA: Hypothalamic–pituitary–adrenal axis; MDC: Midwives data collection; NHMRC: The National Health and Medical Research Council; NSW: New South Wales; PDD: Postnatal depressive disorders; PND: Postnatal depression; SNOMED CT: Systematized Nomenclature of Medicine – Clinical Terms

Acknowledgements

We would like to thank data custodians of the Ministry of Health and staff of the Centre for Health Record Linkage (CheReL) for providing the data, providing advice and undertaking data linkage. We acknowledge the families who have contributed their data and professional staff involved in the data collection and management for this study.

Funding

Funding for this study was provided by Chancellor's Postdoctoral Research Fellowship of University of Technology Sydney. 2015–2018.

Authors' contributions

FX analyzed the data, interpreted the results and was involved in manuscript writing. LR contributed to manuscript writing. CH, CB and ES have revised the manuscript. All authors participated in the study design and interpretation of data. All authors read and approved the final manuscript.

Consent for publication

Not applicable.

Competing interests

The authors declare that they have no competing interests.

Author details

[1]Faculty of Health, University of Technology Sydney, Ultimo 2007, Australia. [2]Discipline of Clinical Psychology, Graduate School of Health, University of Technology Sydney, Ultimo 2007, Australia. [3]School of Public Health, Curtin University, Perth, Australia.

References

1. Chen M-H, Su T-P, Chen Y-S, Hsu J-W, Huang K-L, Chang W-H, Chen T-J, Bai Y-M. Association between psychiatric disorders and iron deficiency anemia among children and adolescents: a nationwide population-based study. BMC Psychiatry. 2013;13(1):161.
2. Korkmaz S, Yıldız S, Korucu T, Gundogan B, Sunbul ZE, Korkmaz H, Atmaca M. Frequency of anemia in chronic psychiatry patients. Neuropsychiatr Dis Treat. 2015;11:2737.
3. World Health Organization. Mental health aspects of women's reproductive health : a global review of the literature. Geneva: WHO Library Cataloguing-in-Publication Data; 2009.
4. Dunkel Schetter C, Tanner L. Anxiety, depression and stress in pregnancy: implications for mothers, children, research, and practice. Curr Opin Psychiatry. 2012;25(2):141–8.
5. Muzik M, Bocknek E, Broderick A, Richardson P, Rosenblum K, Thelen K, Seng J. Mother–infant bonding impairment across the first 6 months postpartum: the primacy of psychopathology in women with childhood abuse and neglect histories. Arch Womens Ment Health. 2013;16(1):29–38.
6. O'Higgins M, Roberts I, Glover V, Taylor A. Mother-child bonding at 1 year; associations with symptoms of postnatal depression and bonding in the first few weeks. Arch Womens Ment Health. 2013;16(5):381–9.
7. Beestin L, Hugh-Jones S, Gough B. The impact of maternal postnatal depression on men and their ways of fathering: an interpretative phenomenological analysis. Psychol Health. 2014;29(6):717–35.
8. Letourneau NL, Dennis C-L, Benzies K, Duffett-Leger L, Stewart M, Tryphonopoulos PD, Este D, Watson W. Postpartum depression is a family affair: addressing the impact on mothers, fathers, and children. Issues Ment Health Nurs. 2012;33(7):445–57.
9. Apter-Levy Y, Feldman M, Vakart A, Ebstein RP, Feldman R. Impact of maternal depression across the first 6 years of life on the Child's mental health, social engagement, and empathy: the moderating role of oxytocin. Am J Psychiatr. 2013;170(10):1161–8.
10. Pearson RM, Bornstein MH, Cordero M, Scerif G, Mahedy L, Evans J, Abioye A, Stein A. Maternal perinatal mental health and offspring academic achievement at age 16: the mediating role of childhood executive function. J Child Psychol Psychiatry. 2016;57(4):491-501.
11. Buist AE, Austin M-PV, Hayes BA, Speelman C, Bilszta JL, Gemmill AW, Brooks J, Ellwood D, Milgrom J. Postnatal mental health of women giving birth in Australia 2002–2004: findings from the beyondblue National Postnatal Depression Program. Aust N Z J Psychiatry. 2008;42(1):66–73.
12. Eastwood JG, Phung H, Barnett B. Postnatal depression and socio-demographic risk: factors associated with Edinburgh depression scale scores in a metropolitan area of new South Wales, Australia. Aust N Z J Psychiatry. 2011;45(12):1040–6.
13. PANDA. The cost of perinatal depression in Australia: final report - post and antenatal depression association. Sydney Avenue: Deloitte Access Economics; 2012.
14. Woolhouse H, Gartland D, Perlen S, Donath S, Brown SJ. Physical health after childbirth and maternal depression in the first 12 months post partum: results of an Australian nulliparous pregnancy cohort study. Midwifery. 2014; 30(3):378–84.
15. Xu F, Sullivan EA, Li Z, Burns L, Austin MP, Slade T. The increased trend in mothers' hospital admissions for psychiatric disorders in the first year after birth between 2001 and 2010 in new South Wales, Australia. BMC Womens Health. 2014;14:119.
16. Stevens GA, Finucane MM, De-Regil LM, Paciorek CJ, Flaxman SR, Branca F, Peña-Rosas JP, Bhutta ZA, Ezzati M. Global, regional, and national trends in haemoglobin concentration and prevalence of total and severe anaemia in children and pregnant and non-pregnant women for 1995–2011: a systematic analysis of population-representative data. Lancet Glob Health. 2013;1(1):e16-e25.
17. Räisänen S, Lehto SM, Nielsen HS, Gissler M, Kramer MR, Heinonen S. Risk factors for and perinatal outcomes of major depression during pregnancy: a population-based analysis during 2002–2010 in Finland. BMJ Open. 2014; 4(11):e004883.
18. Albacar G, Sans T, Martín-Santos R, García-Esteve L, Guillamat R, Sanjuan J, Cañellas F, Gratacòs M, Cavalle P, Arija V. An association between plasma ferritin concentrations measured 48h after delivery and postpartum depression. J Affect Disord. 2011;131(1):136–42.
19. Corwin EJ, Murray-Kolb LE, Beard JL. Low hemoglobin level is a risk factor for postpartum depression. J Nutr. 2003;133(12):4139–42.
20. Armony-Sivan R, Shao J, Li M, Zhao G, Zhao Z, Xu G, Zhou M, Zhan J, Bian Y, Ji C. No relationship between maternal iron status and postpartum depression in two samples in China. J Pregnancy. 2012;2012:521431.
21. National Centre for Classification in Health. The international statistical classification of diseases and related health problems, 10th revision, Australian modification (ICD-10-AM). Sydney: National Centre for Classification in Health; 1999.
22. Australian Institute of Health and Welfare. Australian hospital statistics 2008–09. Health services series no. 17. Cat. no. HSE 84. Canberra: AIHW; 2010.
23. Adhikari P. Socio-economic indexes for areas: introduction, use and future directions, vol. 1351.0.55.015. Canberra: Australian Bureau of Statistics; 2006.
24. Almond P. Postnatal depression: a global public health perspective. Perspect Public Health. 2009;129(5):221–7.
25. Milman N. Postpartum anemia I: definition, prevalence, causes, and consequences. Ann Hematol. 2011;90(11):1247–53.
26. Miller JL. Iron deficiency Anemia: a common and curable disease. Cold Spring Harb Perspect Med. 2013;3(7):a011866.
27. Shariatpanaahi MV, Shariatpanaahi ZV, Moshtaaghi M, Shahbaazi S, Abadi A. The relationship between depression and serum ferritin level. Eur J Clin Nutr. 2007;61(4):532–5.
28. Lever-van Milligen BA, Vogelzangs N, Smit JH, Penninx BW. Hemoglobin levels in persons with depressive and/or anxiety disorders. J Psychosom Res. 2014;76(4):317–21.
29. Kim J, Wessling-Resnick M. Iron and mechanisms of emotional behavior. J Nutr Biochem. 2014;25(11):1101–7.
30. Beard JL, Connor JR. Iron status and neural functioning. Annu Rev Nutr. 2003;23(1):41–58.
31. Willner P, Scheel-Krüger J, Belzung C. The neurobiology of depression and antidepressant action. Neurosci Biobehav Rev. 2013;37(10, Part 1):2331–71.
32. Haase J, Brown E. Integrating the monoamine, neurotrophin and cytokine hypotheses of depression—a central role for the serotonin transporter? Pharmacol Ther. 2015;147:1–11.
33. Krishnan V, Nestler EJ. The molecular neurobiology of depression. Nature. 2008;455(7215):894–902.
34. Beard JL, Hendricks MK, Perez EM, Murray-Kolb LE, Berg A, Vernon-Feagans L, Irlam J, Isaacs W, Sive A, Tomlinson M. Maternal iron deficiency anemia affects postpartum emotions and cognition. J Nutr. 2005;135(2):267–72.
35. Maes M, Van de Vyvere J, Vandoolaeghe E, Bril T, Demedts P, Wauters A, Neels H. Alterations in iron metabolism and the erythron in major depression: further evidence for a chronic inflammatory process. J Affect Disord. 1996;40(1–2):23–33.
36. Schiepers OJ, Wichers MC, Maes M. Cytokines and major depression. Prog Neuro-Psychopharmacol Biol Psychiatry. 2005;29(2):201–17.
37. Maes M. Evidence for an immune response in major depression: a review and hypothesis. Prog Neuro-Psychopharmacol Biol Psychiatry. 1995;19(1):11–38.
38. Maes M, Song C, Lin A, De Jongh R, Van Gastel A, Kenis G, Bosmans E, De Meester I, Benoy I, Neels H, et al. The effects of psychological stress on humans: increased production of pro-inflammatory cytokines and Th1-like response in stress-induced anxiety. Cytokine. 1998;10(4):313–8.
39. Young JJ, Bruno D, Pomara N. A review of the relationship between proinflammatory cytokines and major depressive disorder. J Affect Disord. 2014;169:15–20.
40. Miller AH, Maletic V, Raison CL. Inflammation and its discontents: the role of cytokines in the pathophysiology of major depression. Biol Psychiatry. 2009; 65(9):732–41.
41. Leonard BE. The concept of depression as a dysfunction of the immune system. Curr Immunol Rev. 2010;6(3):205–12.
42. Kim Y-K, Na K-S, Myint A-M, Leonard BE. The role of pro-inflammatory cytokines in neuroinflammation, neurogenesis and the neuroendocrine system in major depression. Prog Neuro-Psychopharmacol Biol Psychiatry. 2016;64:277–84.
43. Rybka J, Kędziora-Kornatowska K, Banaś-Leżańska P, Majsterek I, Carvalho LA, Cattaneo A, Anacker C, Kędziora J. Interplay between the pro-oxidant and antioxidant systems and proinflammatory cytokine levels, in relation to iron metabolism and the erythron in depression. Free Radic Biol Med. 2013;63:187–94.
44. Taraz M, Khatami M-R, Gharekhani A, Abdollahi A, Khalili H, Dashti-Khavidaki S. Relationship between a pro-and anti-inflammatory cytokine imbalance and depression in haemodialysis patients. Eur Cytokine Netw. 2012;23(4):179–86.
45. Jones I, Heron J, Blackmore ER, Craddock N. Incidence of hospitalization for postpartum psychotic and bipolar episodes. Arch Gen Psychiatry. 2008; 65(3):356.

46. Matthey S, Ross-Hamid C: The validity of DSM symptoms for depression and anxiety disorders during pregnancy. J Affect Disord. 2011;133(3):546-52.
47. Di Florio A, Meltzer-Brody S. Is postpartum depression a distinct disorder? Curr Psychiatry Rep. 2015;17(10):1–6.
48. Hoertel N, López S, Peyre H, Wall MM, González-Pinto A, Limosin F, Blanco C. Are symptom features of depression during pregnancy, the postpartum period and outside the Peripartum period distinct? Results from a nationally representative sample using item response theory (IRT). Depress Anxiety. 2015;32(2):129–40.
49. Giallo R, Gartland D, Woolhouse H, Brown S. Differentiating maternal fatigue and depressive symptoms at six months and four years post partum: considerations for assessment, diagnosis and intervention. Midwifery. 2015; 31(2):316–22.
50. NICE. Antenatal and postnatal mental health: clinical management and service guidance. 2015.
51. Goodman JH, Tyer-Viola L. Detection, treatment, and referral of perinatal depression and anxiety by obstetrical providers. J Women's Health. 2010; 19(3):477–90.
52. National Blood Authority. The national blood authority's patient blood management guideline: module 5 - obstetrics and maternity. 2015.
53. Beyondblue. Clinical practice guidelines for depression and related disorders – anxiety, bipolar disorder and puerperal psychosis – in the perinatal period. A guideline for primary care health professionals. Melbourne: Beyondblue: The National Depression Initiative; 2011.
54. Khambalia AZ, Collins CE, Roberts CL, Morris JM, Powell KL, Tasevski V, Nassar N. Iron deficiency in early pregnancy using serum ferritin and soluble transferrin receptor concentrations are associated with pregnancy and birth outcomes. Eur J Clin Nutr. 2016;70(3):358–63.
55. Vliegen N, Casalin S, Luyten P. The course of postpartum depression: a review of longitudinal studies. Harv Rev Psychiatry. 2014;22(1):1–22.

18

Self-perceived level of competitiveness, tension, dependency and depression risk in the SUN cohort

Francisca Lahortiga-Ramos[3,4*], Cristian Raquel Unzueta[1], Itziar Zazpe[1,2,4,6], Susana Santiago[1,4], Patricio Molero[3,4], Almudena Sánchez-Villegas[5,6] and Miguel Ángel Martínez-González[2,4,6,7]

Abstract

Background: Emerging evidence suggests a possible etiologic role of certain personality traits (not necessary dysfunctional) in the risk of depression, but the longitudinal long-term available evidence is currently scarce. We longitudinally assessed whether 3 common personality traits (competitiveness, tension and dependency) were associated with the risk of depression after a maximum follow-up of 15 years.

Methods: We assessed 15,604 university graduates free of depression at baseline through a self-administered questionnaire including personality traits. Simple, Likert-type, questions with 11 possible answers ranging from 0 to 10 were used at baseline to assess the 3 personality traits. We compared participants with high scores (7–10) versus those with low scores (0–4). New medical diagnoses of depression during follow-up were used as the outcome.

Results: During a median follow-up of 10.1 y, we prospectively identified 902 new medical diagnoses of depression. The multivariable-adjusted hazard ratios (95% confidence intervals) for depression were 1.85 (1.52–2.24) for participants with higher baseline tension (7–10 versus 0 to 4), P-trend < 0.001; and 1.23 (1.06–1.44) for high versus low baseline dependence levels, P-trend = 0.004. Higher levels of competitiveness were marginally associated with lower risk of depression, with hazard ratio = 0.78 (0.61–1.01), P-trend = 0.105.

Conclusion: A simple scoring system of personality traits shows an independent association with the future occurrence of depression. This finding underscores, with now prospective evidence, the importance of personality traits in the aetiology of depression and can provide a clinically useful tool for gathering valid information about depression-related personality traits.

Keywords: Depression risk, Competitiveness, Tension, Dependency

Background

Depression, is a major global public health problem and is characterized by lowered mood, loss of capacity to experience pleasure, increased sense of worthlessness, fatigue, and concerns about death and suicide [1]. Currently, the estimates are that 350 million people suffer depression [2], and depending on its level of intensity and duration it is a frequent and strong risk factor for suicide. Globally more than 800,000 persons commit suicide every year and suicide has become the first or second cause of mortality among young adults in most Western countries. In the Spanish adult population [3], the prevalence of chronic depression in 2014 was approximately 7.8% (4.8% of men and 10.7% of women). Taking these alarming data into account, depression represents a priority for public health and there is a need to broaden the etiologic research in the field of depression. One of the lines that nowadays is expanding, is the study of the relationship between depression and personality factors or traits (ways of thinking, feeling and behaving), which show heritability and stability across time [4–9].

* Correspondence: flahortiga@unav.es
[3]Department of Psychiatry and Clinical Psychology, University Clinic of Navarra, Pamplona, Navarra, Spain
[4]Navarra Institute for Health Research (IdisNA), Pamplona, Navarra, Spain
Full list of author information is available at the end of the article

Personality traits (especially competitiveness, psychological tension and dependency) are very likely to play a role in the aetiology and development of depression. The hypothesis that depression is linked to personality traits can be traced back to ancient times. Different models have been proposed to explain this association: one model hypothesizes that personality and depression share similar aetiology, but there is not a cause-effect relationship between them. A second model considers that personality does have a truly causal effect on depression onset and progression. Finally, a third model claims that personality and depression have a mutual "pathoplastic" relationship, meaning that each of them can influence the appearance of the other. Previous studies have shown associations between personality factors or specific personality traits and depression risk [10–15]. But these studies followed either cross-sectional designs or had only a short term follow-up. None of them used survival analyses in the long-term nor specifically appraised simultaneously the following 3 traits: dependency, tension and competitiveness in a well-defined cohort. Current evidence mainly suggests that depression is associated with higher levels of neuroticism and lower levels of extraversion, and to some extent, lower levels of agreeableness, measured according to the Five-Factor Model (FFM) [16]. The FFM evaluates five different dimensions of personality, also known as the Big Five personality domains: Neuroticism, Extraversion, Conscientiousness, Openness, and Agreeableness [11], but it does not include dependency, tension or competitiveness.

Only a few studies have aimed to ascertain associations of specific personality traits, such as competitiveness, tension and/or dependency/autonomy with the risk of depression [17–23]. As stated by Costa and McCrae, and also corroborated by Johnson [24], the assessment of the different facets explained in the Big Five Dimensions of the FFM, may lead to conclude that neuroticism includes anxiety, hostility, self-consciousness, impulsiveness, vulnerability, among others. Extraversion incorporates assertiveness, activity level, excitement-seeking, and positive emotions. And Conscientiousness includes competence, self-efficacy, order, dutifulness, achievement-striving, self-discipline, and cautiousness [16, 24]. Thus, it can be inferred that the 3 above-mentioned personality traits (competitiveness, tension, and dependency) represent a new field, though we acknowledged that they are also partly related to these FFM dimensions (conscientiousness, neuroticism and extraversion). Specifically, competitiveness trait is related to conscientiousness, tension trait would be associated with neuroticism, and dependency trait with the negative pole of conscientiousness and extraversion.

To our knowledge, previous studies have focused on analyzing the association between personality constructs or facets, such as extraversion, neuroticism or competitiveness, and depression but not in analyzing the relationship between these 3 specific personality traits (competitiveness, tension, and dependency) and the risk of developing depression in large longitudinal study. Our study aims at filling this existing gap and to investigate the independent association between levels of competitiveness, tension and dependence and the long-term risk of depression in a well-defined cohort of university graduates.

Methods

Participants

The Seguimiento Universidad de Navarra (SUN) project is a cohort study constituted by university alumni from different Spanish universities, and other professionals from different provinces in Spain. The recruitment of participants started in 1999 and is permanently open for new participants. Self-administered baseline (Questionnaire_0; Q_0) and follow-up questionnaires (Q_2-Q_16) are used to assess socio-demographic, diet and clinical characteristics of the subjects. The detailed methodology has been published elsewhere [25]. English version of SUN questionnaires are available in Additional file 1.

Up to December 2016, 22,564 participants had been recruited. Among them, 22,279 who had completed the Q_0 before March 1st of 2014 were considered for the present study (time frame needed for the participants to at least have one follow-up questionnaire completed). We excluded participants who were taking any antidepressant drug or were diagnosed with depression at baseline (n = 2621), and those without incident depression but were under antidepressant medication in any follow-up questionnaire (n = 285). Furthermore, all participants who reported an implausible energy intake (women < 500 kcal or > 3500 kcal, and men < 800 kcal or > 4200 kcal) (n = 1821), those with missing data in questions regarding personality traits (n = 357), and all subjects without at least one follow-up questionnaire completed (n = 1591) were also excluded. The final sample size available for statistical analyses was 15,604.

Exposure assessment

Personality traits items were collected in Q_0 and included the following questions: a) Do you consider yourself a competitive, nonconformist, fighter person, who demands everything of yourself at work and sometimes even more of what you can afford?, b) Do you consider yourself a tense, aggressive, usually feeling overloaded, highly strung person or you think of yourself as a relaxed and calm person, and c) Do you think you have enough resources, preparation and autonomy to solve any problems at work, or do you exclusively depend on others to do it? For each question, 11 possible answers could be chosen by the participant ranging from 0 (more conformist, relaxed or autonomous) to 10 (more competitive, tense or dependent). For the present study, the concepts competitiveness, tension, and dependency will be used to describe the 3 personality traits assessed at baseline (Q_0). Finally, participants were categorized into 3 different groups according to their reported answers in the Q_0: low level (0–4), moderate level (5–6) and high level (7–10).

Outcome assessment

Incidence of depression was assessed through the follow-up questionnaires (Q-2, Q-4, Q-6 and Q-14) with the following question: 'Have you ever been diagnosed with depression by a medical doctor?' All positive answers were considered new cases of depression. This question was previously validated in a subsample of the SUN cohort where 104 participants were also assessed by a Psychiatrist or a Clinical Psychologist through the Structured Clinical Interview for DSM-IV (SCID-I) [26].

The results showed that there were 46 true positives of the 62 self-reported cases of depression (74.2% (95% Confidence Interval (CI) 63.3, 85.1), and 34 true negatives of the 42 non-depressive participants (81.1% (95% CI = 69.1, 92.9).

Covariate assessment

The Q_0 gathered information for many covariates, some of them potentially related to both personality traits and depression. These covariates could be potential confounding factors and we conducted multivariable-adjustments to control for them. Thus, the Q_0 also included a validated 136-item food frequency questionnaire (FFQ) to assess dietary habits. From these data, we calculated the adherence to the Mediterranean diet using the score proposed by Trichopoulou et al. [27]. A physical activity questionnaire (specifically validated in a subsample of the cohort) gathered information on frequency and type of activity. Furthermore, socio-demographic factors, anthropometric measurements, and personal and family clinical history, among other variables were also assessed at baseline. The validity of self-reported weight and body mass index (BMI) as well as the FFQ and physical activity questionnaire have been previously assessed [28–30].

Statistical analysis

To describe baseline characteristics of participants, we used percentages for categorical variables, and mean and standard deviations for quantitative variables.

For each participant we computed person-years of follow-up from the date of returning the Q_0 to the date of depression diagnosis, the date of death or the date of returning the last follow-up questionnaire, whichever came first.

Cox regression models were used to assess the relationship between the 3 categories of each personality trait and the incidence of depression. Hazard ratios (HR) and their 95% CI were calculated for the scores of tension, dependency and competitiveness using the low level as the reference category. For the multiple-adjusted model, the following potential confounders were considered: Model 1 adjusted for age at recruitment (10 groups), sex, total energy intake (continuous variable), Model 2: additionally adjusted for BMI (continuous variable), tobacco consumption (never, former, current smoker < 15 cigarettes per day, and current smoker > 15 cigarettes per day), alcohol consumption (continuous variable), total physical activity per week (continuous variable), average time (hours/day) spent sitting down (continuous variable), Mediterranean diet score (continuous variable), total years of university education (continuous variable), whether the participant was a health professional (yes, no), marital status (single, married, and others), employment status (employed, unemployed/ retired, homemaker and student), baseline prevalence of diabetes (yes, no), prevalence of hypertension (yes, no), prevalence of hypercholesterolemia (yes, no), prevalence of cancer (yes, no). Model 3 additionally adjusted for fast food consumption (continuous variable), trans fatty acid intake (continuous variable), nutritional supplement intake (yes, no), snack consumption between main meals (yes, no), and following a special diet (yes, no). Model 4 additionally adjusted for the 2 other personality traits (low, moderate, high).

We conducted the following sensitivity analyses: 1) after excluding late cases of depression (> 10 y of follow-up), 2) after excluding cancer and cardiovascular disease cases at baseline, 3) subgroup analyses for men and women, 4) subgroup analyses for young and older participants (< 35 y or ≥ 35 y) and, 5) excluding early cases (2 first y).

Tests for linear trend across increasing categories of different personality traits were conducted by assigning the median punctuation within each category and treating this variable as continuous.

All tests were conducted with the statistical program STATA 12.1 and a *P*-value <0.05 was taken as statistically significant.

Results

Baseline characteristics of participants according to their level of competitiveness, tension and dependency are described in Table 1.

During 158,137 person-years of follow-up (mean follow-up: 10.1 y), we documented 902 incident cases of depression. The risks of incident depression during

Table 1 Baseline characteristics according to levels of competitiveness, tension and dependency on a sample of 15,604 participants from the SUN cohort [Mean (standard deviation) or percentage]

	Competitiveness			Tension			Dependency		
	Low (1–4)	Moderate (5–6)	High (7–10)	Low (1–4)	Moderate (5–6)	High (7–10)	Low (1–4)	Moderate (5–6)	High (7–10)
N	1170	3788	10,646	3852	4766	6986	10,407	1653	3544
Sex (% female)	63.3	63.8	57.1	55.9	62.3	58.9	54.1	68.0	58.4
Age (years)	37.3 (11.7)	37.5 (11.8)	37.2 (12.3)	36.5 (12.0)	37.0 (12.2)	37.9 (12.2)	37.4 (11.9)	34.3 (12.4)	38.2 (12.6)
BMI (kg/m^2)	23.6 (3.5)	23.4 (3.5)	23.5 (3.5)	23.8 (3.5)	23.4 (3.4)	23.5 (3.5)	23.5 (3.4)	22.9 (3.2)	23.7 (3.6)
Marital status married (%)	52.6	52.1	50.2	48.9	48.6	53.5	51.8	39.0	53.5
Level of education (years)	4.9 (1.4)	4.9 (1.4)	5.1 (1.6)	5.0 (1.5)	5.0 (1.5)	5.1 (1.6)	5.1 (1.6)	4.8 (1.3)	5.0 (1.5)
Health professionals (%)	56.7	58.0	54.1	57.8	56.1	53.8	55.4	52.6	55.8
Employed (%)	78.2	77.9	78.9	77.7	77.7	79.7	79.9	69.8	78.8
Smoking status (%)									
Ex-smokers	23.2	26.2	24.3	21.0	24.4	26.7	24.8	19.5	26.6
Current smokers	26.1	26.1	23.5	25.0	16.6	15.9	15.9	17.5	16.9
Leisure-time physical activity (MET x h/week)	22.7 (19.1)	25.4 (21.5)	28.3 (25.0)	27.6 (24.8)	27.7 (24.4)	26.5 (22.9)	27.7 (24.3)	24.9 (21.9)	26.7 (23.3)
Sitting (h/day)	5.2 (2.0)	5.1 (2.0)	5.3 (2.1)	5.3 (2.0)	5.2 (2.1)	5.3 (2.1)	5.3 (2.0)	5.4 (2.1)	5.2 (2.0)
Prevalence of diabetes (%)	1.4	1.9	1.8	1.5	1.8	1.9	1.6	1.6	2.2
Prevalence of hypertension (%)	6.1	7.6	8.3	6.8	7.3	9.1	8.1	7.0	8.2
Prevalence of hypercholesterolemia (%)	16.0	16.0	16.7	14.4	15.2	18.4	16.5	14.2	17.4
Prevalence of cancer (%)	3.3	3.4	3.6	3.9	3.1	3.7	3.7	2.7	3.4
Weight gain ≥3 kg in last 5 years (%)	32.1	29.5	29.6	30.5	29.0	30.0	29.6	30.1	30.2
Mediterranean diet score	4.2 (1.8)	4.2 (1.7)	4.3 (1.7)	4.2 (1.7)	4.3 (1.7)	4.2 (1.7)	4.3 (1.7)	4.0 (1.7)	4.2 (1.7)
Dietary attitudes score	6.6 (2.6)	7.0 (2.5)	7.1 (2.5)	6.9 (2.5)	7.1 (2.5)	7.0 (2.5)	7.0 (2.5)	6.9 (2.5)	7.1 (2.5)
Following a special diet (%)	6.9	6.6	8.0	6.9	7.6	8.0	7.5	6.4	8.4
Nutritional supplements (%)	15.5	16.9	18.5	16.2	17.6	19.1	18.0	18.2	17.4
Snacking (%)	40.2	35.7	30.9	32.2	32.1	33.4	31.6	37.9	33.6
Dietary supplements (%)	15.5	16.9	18.5	16.2	17.6	19.1	18.0	18.2	17.4
Total energy intake (kcal/day)	2404 (609)	2335 (618)	2351 (614)	2365 (625)	2339 (608)	2352 (614)	2357 (613)	2369 (619)	2329 (619)
Protein (% E)	17.8 (3.2)	18.0 (3.2)	18.3 (3.3)	18.1 (3.4)	18.3 (3.2)	18.2 (3.3)	18.1 (3.2)	18.0 (3.3)	18.4 (3.3)
Carbohydrates (% E)	43.3 (7.3)	43.4 (7.3)	43.1 (7.3)	43.2 (7.3)	43.3 (7.2)	43.2 (7.4)	43.3 (7.3)	43.2 (7.5)	43.0 (7.3)
Fats (% E)	36.9 (6.7)	36.5 (6.5)	36.6 (6.5)	36.7 (6.5)	36.5 (6.4)	36.6 (6.5)	36.5 (6.4)	37.1 (6.9)	36.5 (6.4)
Cholesterol (mg/day)	422.2 (145.5)	408.9 (147.8)	417.5 (147.9)	417.5 (149.2)	412.5 (144.2)	416.9 (149.3)	414.9 (148.0)	419.9 (143.1)	416.3 (149.2)
Fiber (g/day)	27.5 (11.4)	27.5 (11.8)	27.9 (12.3)	27.6 (12.3)	28.1 (12.1)	27.7 (11.9)	27.9 (12.3)	27.1 (11.4)	27.6 (11.7)
Alcohol (g/day)	6.5 (10.4)	6.8 (10.3)	6.7 (9.9)	6.9 (9.9)	6.5 (9.6)	6.7 (10.4)	6.8 (10.0)	5.5 (9.6)	6.9 (10.4)

follow-up according to baseline levels of each personality trait are shown in Table 2.

No significant association was found between competitiveness and the incidence of depression, with very similar results both in the crude model and in the adjusted models. The adjusted HRs (95% CI) for moderate and high levels of competitiveness as compared to lower level were, respectively, 0.84 (0.64–1.10) and 0.78 (95% CI: 0.61–1.01) in model 4 (P for trend = 0.105).

On the other hand, participants in the moderate and in the high category of tension exhibited a significant direct association with the risk of depression during follow-up as compared to those in the lowest category (HR = 1.32; 95% CI:1.07–1.62 and HR = 1.85; 95% CI:

Table 2 Hazard Ratios and Confidence Intervals (95%) of incident depression according to the level of competitiveness, tension and dependency

	Low (1–4)	Moderate (5–6)	High (7–10)	P for trend
Competitiveness				
N	1170	3788	10,646	
Incidence of depression	72	217	613	
Person/years	12,075	38,901	107,161	
Crude rates	1 (ref)	0.90 (0.69–1.18)	0.92 (0.72–1.17)	0.747
Model 1	1 (ref)	0.90 (0.69–1.17)	0.95 (0.75–1.21)	0.826
Model 2	1 (ref)	0.89 (0.68–1.16)	0.96 (0.75–1.22)	0.721
Model 3	1 (ref)	0.89 (0.68–1.17)	0.95 (0.75–1.22)	0.782
Model 4	1 (ref)	0.84 (0.64–1.10)	0.78 (0.61–1.01)	0.105
Tension				
N	3852	4766	6986	
Incidence of depression	149	238	515	
Person/years	38,793	47,819	71,527	
Crude rates	1 (ref)	1.32 (1.08–1.63)	1.86 (1.55–2.23)	< 0.001
Model 1	1 (ref)	1.29 (1.05–1.58)	1.81 (1.51–2.18)	< 0.001
Model 2	1 (ref)	1.31 (1.07–1.61)	1.83 (1.53–2.20)	< 0.001
Model 3	1 (ref)	1.30 (1.06–1.60)	1.80 (1.50–2.17)	< 0.001
Model 4	1 (ref)	1.32 (1.07–1.62)	1.85 (1.52–2.24)	< 0.001
Dependency				
N	10,407	1653	3544	
Incidence of depression	547	117	238	
Person/years	105,498	17,049	35,592	
Crude rates	1 (ref)	1.36 (1.11–1.67)	1.30 (1.12–1.52)	< 0.001
Model 1	1 (ref)	1.31 (1.07–1.60)	1.30 (1.12–1.52)	< 0.001
Model 2	1 (ref)	1.31 (1.06–1.61)	1.30 (1.12–1.52)	< 0.001
Model 3	1 (ref)	1.30 (1.06–1.59)	1.30 (1.11–1.52)	< 0.001
Model 4	1 (ref)	1.24 (1.01–1.54)	1.23 (1.06–1.44)	0.004

Model 1: Adjusted for age at recruitment (10 groups), sex, total energy intake (continuous variable)
Model 2: Additionally adjusted for BMI (continuous variable), tobacco consumption (never, former, current smoker < 15 cigarettes per day, and current smoker > 15 cigarettes per day), alcohol consumption (continuous variable), total physical activity per week (continuous variable), sedentariness (continuous variable), Mediterranean diet score (continuous variable), total years of college (continuous variable), health professionals (yes, no), marital status (single, married, and others), employment status (employed, unemployed/ retired, homemaker and student), prevalence of diabetes (yes, no), prevalence of hypertension (yes, no), prevalence of hypercholesterolemia (yes, no), prevalence of cancer (yes, no)
Model 3: Additionally adjusted for fast food consumption (continuous variable), trans fatty acids intake (continuous variable), nutritional supplements intake (yes, no), snack consumption between main meals (yes, no), and follows a special diet (yes, no)
Model 4: Additionally adjusted for the other two personality traits according to assessed trait; competitiveness, (low, moderate, high), tension (low, moderate, high), o dependency (low, moderate, high)

1.52–2.24, respectively), P for trend < 0.001 in the fully-adjusted model.

Finally, in multivariate model 4, when we assessed the risk of depression according to categories of dependency, participants in the moderate and high levels presented a 24 and 23% relatively higher risk of developing depression than those in the lowest category (HR = 1.24; 95% CI: 1.01–1.54 and HR = 1.23, respectively; 95% CI: 1.06–1.44). The estimates showed a statistically significant linear trend ($P = 0.004$).

The adjusted HRs for high level of competitiveness, tension and dependency for each standard deviation was 0.95 (0.88–1.02), 1.36 (1.26–1.47) and 1.08 (1.02–1.16) (data not shown).

Finally, we performed several sensitivity analyses. The main results did not change when we excluded late cases of depression (> 10 y of follow-up), after excluding cancer and cardiovascular disease cases at baseline, and when we separately analysed men or women. When we repeated the analyses among young or older participants

(< 35 y or ≥ 35 y) the risk of depression was always higher in participants with higher levels of tension and dependency independently of the age group considered. When early cases were excluded, only tension level was associated with depression (Table 3).

When we assessed the association between each possible answer about the level of competitiveness and the incidence of depression, we found inverse associations after adjusting for several confounders with no significant linear trend (*P* for trend = 0.117) (Fig. 1). In these analyses, we also observed a direct association between a more tense personality (as compared to a more relaxed personality, with *P* for trend< 0.001) and between a more dependent personality ad compared to a more autonomous personality (*P* for trend = 0.007) (Figs. 2 and 3 respectively).

Table 3 Sensitivity analyses. Hazard Ratios and Confidence Intervals (95%) of incident depression according to the level of competitiveness, tension and dependency

	N	Incident depression	Low (1–4)	Moderate (5–6)	High (7–10)	P for trend
Competitiveness						
Main analyses Model 4	15,604	902	1 (ref)	0.84 (0.64–1.10)	0.78 (0.61–1.01)	0.105
Excluding late cases (> 10 y of follow-up)	7319	310	1 (ref)	1.15 (0.72–1.85)	0.96 (0.61–1.53)	0.368
Only men	6367	266	1 (ref)	1.00 (0.58–1.72)	0.86 (0.52–1.43)	0.338
Only women*	9237	636	1 (ref)	0.78 (0.57–1.07)	0.78 (0.58–1.05)	0.311
Age < 35 y	7550	444	1 (ref)	0.65 (0.46–0.92)	0.61 (0.44–0.84)	0.028
Age ≥ 35 y**	8054	458	1 (ref)	1.22 (0.78–1.89)	1.09 (0.71–1.66)	0.714
Excluding cancer and cardiovascular disease prevalent	14,853	857	1 (ref)	0.84 (0.64–1.11)	0.79 (0.61–1.02)	0.111
Excluding early cases (2 first y)	15,354	652	1 (ref)	0.84 (0.62–1.15)	0.76 (0.56–1.02)	0.067
Tension						
Main analyses Model 4	15,604	902	1 (ref)	1.32 (1.07–1.62)	1.85 (1.52–2.24)	< 0.001
Excluding late cases (> 10 y of follow-up)	7319	310	1 (ref)	1.11 (0.79–1.57)	1.42 (1.03–1.96)	0.017
Only men	6367	266	1 (ref)	1.11 (0.75–1.65)	1.88 (1.32–2.66)	< 0.001
Only women¥	9237	636	1 (ref)	1.40 (1.10–1.80)	1.81 (1.43–2.28)	< 0.001
Age < 35 y	7550	444	1 (ref)	1.25 (0.95–1.66)	1.76 (1.36–2.29)	< 0.001
Age ≥ 35 y¥¥	8054	458	1 (ref)	1.47 (1.08–2.00)	2.00 (1.50–2.67)	< 0.001
Excluding cancer and cardiovascular disease prevalent	14,853	857	1 (ref)	1.33 (1.07–1.65)	1.87 (1.53–2.29)	< 0.001
Excluding early cases (2 first y)	15,354	652	1 (ref)	1.36 (1.06–1.73)	1.86 (1.49–2.33)	< 0.001
Dependency						
Main analyses Model 4	15,604	902	1 (ref)	1.24 (1.01–1.54)	1.23 (1.06–1.44)	0.004
Excluding late cases (> 10 y of follow-up)	7319	310	1 (ref)	1.29 (0.89–1.88)	1.42 (1.10–1.84)	0.005
Only men	6367	266	1 (ref)	1.53 (1.02–2.31)	1.32 (1.00–1.74)	0.026
Only women‡	9237	636	1 (ref)	1.15 (0.90–1.47)	1.22 (1.01–1.47)	0.031
Age < 35 y	7550	444	1 (ref)	1.16 (0.88–1.54)	1.06 (0.84–1.33)	0.503
Age ≥ 35 y‡‡	8054	458	1 (ref)	1.36 (0.99–1.87)	1.40 (1.13–1.72)	0.001
Excluding cancer and cardiovascular disease prevalent	14,853	857	1 (ref)	1.30 (1.03–1.59)	1.30 (1.11–1.52)	0.001
Excluding early cases (2 first y)	15,354	652	1 (ref)	1.23 (0.96–1.57)	1.18 (0.98–1.41)	0.052

Model 1: Adjusted for age at recruitment (10 groups), sex, total energy intake (continuous variable)

Model 2: Additionally adjusted for BMI (continuous variable), tobacco consumption (never, former, current smoker < 15 cigarettes per day, and current smoker > 15 cigarettes per day), alcohol consumption (continuous variable), total physical activity per week (continuous variable), sedentariness (continuous variable), Mediterranean diet score (continuous variable), total years of college (continuous variable), health professionals (yes, no), marital status (single, married, and others), employment status (employed, unemployed/ retired, homemaker and student), prevalence of diabetes (yes, no), prevalence of hypertension (yes, no), prevalence of hypercholesterolemia (yes, no), prevalence of cancer (yes, no)

Model 3: Additionally adjusted for fast food consumption (continuous variable), trans fatty acids intake (continuous variable), nutritional supplements intake (yes, no), snack consumption between main meals (yes, no), and follows a special diet (yes, no)

Model 4: Additionally adjusted for the other two personality traits according to assessed trait; competitiveness, (low, moderate, high), tension (low, moderate, high), o dependency (low, moderate, high)

HR estimated with Cox regression and CI of 95%

* p for interaction: 0.821; ** p for interaction: 0.087; ¥ p for interaction: 0.278; ¥¥p for interaction: 0.490; ‡ p for interaction: 0.363; ‡‡ p for interaction: 0.140;

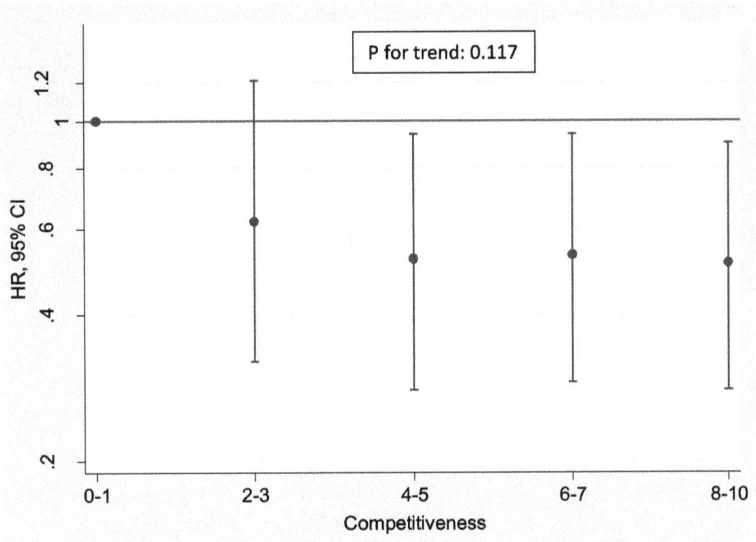

Fig. 1 Hazard Ratios and Confidence Intervals (95%) of incident depression according to the level of competitiveness. Adjusted by age at recruitment (10 groups), sex, total energy intake (continuous variable), BMI (continuous variable), tobacco consumption (never, former, current smoker < 15 cigarettes per day, and current smoker > 15 cigarettes per day), alcohol consumption (continuous variable), total physical activity per week (continuous variable), sedentariness (continuous variable), Mediterranean diet score (continuous variable), total years of college (continuous variable), health professionals (yes, no), marital status (single, married, and others), employment status (employed, unemployed/ retired, homemaker and student), prevalence of diabetes (yes, no), prevalence of hypertension (yes, no), prevalence of hypercholesterolemia (yes, no), prevalence of cancer (yes, no), fast food consumption (continuous variable), trans fatty acids intake (continuous variable), nutritional supplements intake (yes, no), snack consumption between main meals (yes, no), follows a special diet (yes, no), level of tension (low, moderate, high) and level of dependency (low, moderate, high)

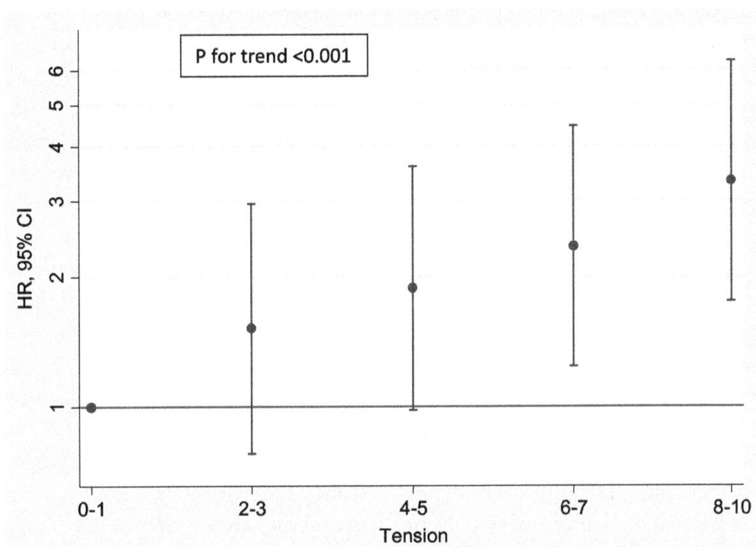

Fig. 2 Hazard Ratios and Confidence Intervals (95%) of incident depression according to the level of tension. Adjusted by age at recruitment (10 groups), sex, total energy intake (continuous variable), BMI (continuous variable), tobacco consumption (never, former, current smoker < 15 cigarettes per day, and current smoker > 15 cigarettes per day), alcohol consumption (continuous variable), total physical activity per week (continuous variable), sedentariness (continuous variable), Mediterranean diet score (continuous variable), total years of college (continuous variable), health professionals (yes, no), marital status (single, married, and others), employment status (employed, unemployed/ retired, homemaker and student), prevalence of diabetes (yes, no), prevalence of hypertension (yes, no), prevalence of hypercholesterolemia (yes, no), prevalence of cancer (yes, no), fast food consumption (continuous variable), trans fatty acids intake (continuous variable), nutritional supplements intake (yes, no), snack consumption between main meals (yes, no), follows a special diet (yes, no), level of competitiveness (low, moderate, high) and level of dependency (low, moderate, high)

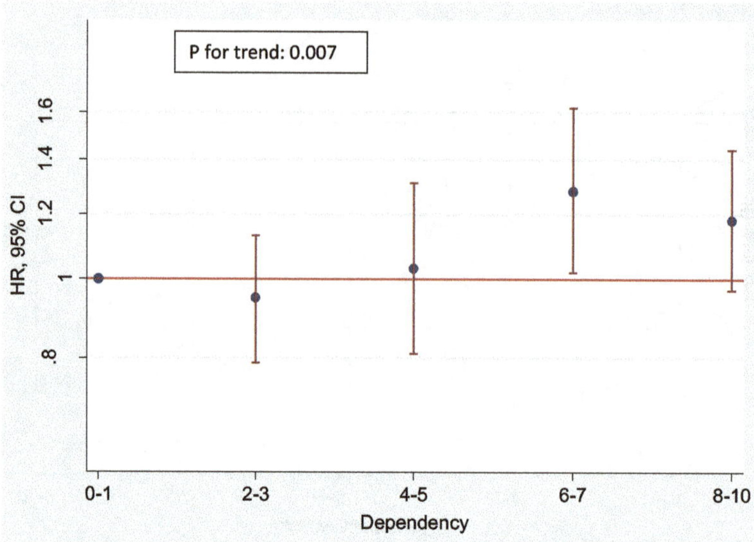

Fig. 3 Hazard Ratios and Confidence Intervals (95%) of incident depression according to the level of dependency. Adjusted by age at recruitment (10 groups), sex, total energy intake (continuous variable), BMI (continuous variable), tobacco consumption (never, former, current smoker < 15 cigarettes per day, and current smoker > 15 cigarettes per day), alcohol consumption (continuous variable), total physical activity per week (continuous variable), sedentariness (continuous variable), Mediterranean diet score (continuous variable), total years of college (continuous variable), health professionals (yes, no), marital status (single, married, and others), employment status (employed, unemployed/ retired, homemaker and student), prevalence of diabetes (yes, no), prevalence of hypertension (yes, no), prevalence of hypercholesterolemia (yes, no), prevalence of cancer (yes, no), fast food consumption (continuous variable), trans fatty acids intake (continuous variable), nutritional supplements intake (yes, no), snack consumption between main meals (yes, no), follows a special diet (yes, no), level of competitiveness (low, moderate, high) and level of tension (low, moderate, high)

Discussion

In this cohort composed of highly educated middle-aged adults, higher levels of self-perceived levels of dependency and tension were significantly associated with a higher risk of incident depression. These traits were assessed with short and simple Likert-type tools at baseline and showed long-term prospective associations with the future risk of depression, representing a novel finding.

However, our findings regarding the association of the personality traits and the risk of developing depression are in line with some previous investigations [15, 21, 22, 31, 32] that reported a higher incidence of depression in subjects who tend to have a more dependent trait.

Additionally, a greater level of psychological tension has been significantly associated with higher rates of depression [18]. Our results are also in line with other studies [14, 24] that have assessed the different facets of the FFM and that have found that higher levels of anxiety (Neuroticism facet), lower positive emotion (Extraversion facet), and lower conventionality (Conscientiousness facet) were prospective predictors of depressive illness.

Several novel methodological characteristics of our prospective study deserve to be underlined. These characteristics include the rigorous control of potential confounding by baseline variables using a comprehensive (Q_0), the elimination of prevalent cases of depression at baseline and the use of statistical methods of survival analyses (Cox regression models) recommended for prospective studies. The design and sensitivity analyses that we conducted support that the identified new cases of depression are in fact new cases of incident depression and mitigate the threat of reverse causality bias. As consequence, the specific personality traits that have been found to have a significant association, are characteristics of personality prior to the onset of the disorder and can be considered to be vulnerability factors that predispose to the future development of depression. While the hypothesis of depression and personality sharing a similar etiology cannot be discarded, our findings seem to be more in line with the model that considers personality as a causal factor for the future development of depression. This is what some authors have described as pre-depressive personality traits. In conjunction with stressful socio-environmental factors, these traits could lead to the development of the depressive symptoms [14, 15, 18].

However, the competitiveness trait only showed a marginal inverse association with depression, that was not statistically significant. This association was more apparent among participants <35 y, which can be explained by the existence of lower requirements at the family and professional level, typical of this age subgroup, but the p for interaction with age was not statistically significant ($p = 0.087$).

We consider that the assessment of these 3 personality traits through 3 short and simple Likert-type questions is a novel contribution that can be useful in many clinical settings. The results obtained in our study suggest that these specific personality traits, as assessed with these simple questions may represent key vulnerability factors to depression onset, and our assessment tool may be an efficient approach for collecting useful information on these traits in clinical evaluations.

Furthermore, the statistical analysis was carried out controlling for lifestyles (diet, physical activity, alcohol and tobacco consumption) and sociodemographic variables that could act as confounder variables for the association between personality and incidence of depression. To our knowledge, there are no other studies conducted with a similar methodology as ours.

We found that participants with moderate or high dependency levels had a greater risk of developing depression compared to the less dependent participants. However, the risk was lower in highly dependent subjects than in the moderately dependent participants. These results contrast with the finding by Eagleton et al. [33] who observed that higher autonomy (or less dependency) was associated with a higher incidence of depressive symptoms. Notwithstanding, another study conducted by Enns et al. [19] showed similar results to our findings and they reported that less autonomous persons, tend to show a greater incidence of depression compared to the individuals with a higher autonomy. Our results for dependency might be modified by the age of the participants (p for interaction = 0.140). Thus, in the subgroup analyses performed, we observed that among older subjects (> 35 y) the relative risk was significant only among older participants. This finding may suggest that it might be the maintenance of this trait in the long term, and the behaviors that derive from it, which increase the vulnerability for developing depression. The tension trait, as defined in our study, coincides largely with the neuroticism factor investigated by different authors, such as Eysenck [34] or Costa and Mcrae, in their model of the Big Five Factors [35] and which have frequently been associated with the presence of depression [36–38].

We acknowledge that the present study has several limitations. First, self-reporting of a clinical diagnosis was used as the criteria to establish depression, but it was previously validated and it is likely to have enough specificity given the high educational background of participants and the fact that more than 50 % of them are health professionals themselves [25]. Moreover, the fact that our participants are highly educated and highly motivated subjects makes unlikely that they may have misreported their correct diagnosis. We think that the optimal procedure to diagnose depression is in fact, the use of a proper general psychiatric interview made by a specialist in psychiatry or clinical psychology. However, the high number of participants in this study made this option less viable. To our knowledge scales that assess depressive symptoms such as the Diagnostic Inventory for Depression or Beck Depression Inventory are often used in most cohort studies as a diagnostic tool. An important limitation of these scales is that cut-off points to define depression status can be arbitrary, which also questions the validity of the diagnosis. Nonetheless, we consider our procedure to be a similar alternative option to assess the incidence of depression with such population size.

Second, the scores for self-perceived personality traits items were derived solely from the response given to three isolated items that report on these traits and not to the application of a standardized complete questionnaire, this may lead to some degree of measurement error. However, our results show as novel contribution that simple and short questions on key personality traits are in fact able to classify participants in categories associated with different risk for the future development of depression.

Dependency trait in our study refers specifically to the workplace, and we acknowledge that excluding other daily life environments is clearly a limitation. The participants that completed the Q_0 were in high proportion young adults, starting their professional career (3592 participants with a mean age inferior to 25 years). We assumed that during this age range, the self- assessment of dependency trait would be better identified in the workplace, instead of other environments more predominant later in life such as the family context. Enns et al. [19] have also assessed the dependency trait in the work environment.

Third, residual confounding is still possible in our study, but we attempted to adjust for the major depression risk factors and other potential confounders to provide utmost validity to our results. Finally, the homogeneity of participants in the SUN cohort (all university graduates) may limit the generalizability of our findings to the general population, although it also increases internal validity because the restriction to university graduates reduces many potential sources of confounding.

Despite these limitations, the strengths of this cohort study are the high retention rate, its prospective design and the large sample of participants highly educated who may be able to provide reliable self-reported data.

Conclusions

In conclusion, self-perceived levels of dependency and tension as personality traits were significantly associated with an increased risk of depression and can be considered as vulnerability factors for future depressive illness development.

Future studies focused on these personality traits are needed to confirm a possible etiologic relationship between these traits and depression.

Abbreviations

CI: Confidence Intervals; HR: Hazard Ratios; Q_0: Baseline Questionnaire; WHO: World Health Organization

Funding

The SUN Project has received funding from the Spanish Government-Instituto de Salud Carlos III, and the European Regional Development Fund (FEDER) (RD 06/0045, CIBER-OBN, Grants PI10/02658, PI10/02293, PI13/00615, PI14/01668, PI14/01798, PI14/01764, and G03/140), the Navarra Regional Government (45/2011, 122/2014), and the University of Navarra. None of the sponsors had any role in the study design, data analysis, or reporting of the results.

Authors' contributions

Conception and Design of the study: MAMG, FL. Analysis and Interpretation of the Data: CRU, IZ, SS, FL, ASV, PM. Writing of the first draft: CRU. Critical revision of the article for important intellectual content and final approval of the article: all authors.

Consent for publication

N/A

Competing interests

The authors declare that they have no competing interests.

Author details

[1]Department of Nutrition, Food Science and Physiology, School of Pharmacy and Nutrition, University of Navarra, Pamplona, Navarra, Spain. [2]Department of Preventive Medicine and Public Health, School of Medicine, University of Navarra, Pamplona, Navarra, Spain. [3]Department of Psychiatry and Clinical Psychology, University Clinic of Navarra, Pamplona, Navarra, Spain. [4]Navarra Institute for Health Research (IdisNA), Pamplona, Navarra, Spain. [5]Nutrition Research Group, Research Institute of Biomedical and Health Sciences, University of Las Palmas de Gran Canaria, Las Palmas de Gran Canaria, Spain. [6]Biomedical Research Center Network on Obesity and Nutrition (CIBERobn) Physiopathology of Obesity and Nutrition, Institute of Health Carlos III, Madrid, Spain. [7]Department of Nutrition, Harvard School of Public Health, Boston, USA.

References

1. Strabridge WJ, Deleger S, Roberts RE, et al. Physical activity reduces the risk of subsequent depression for older adults. Am J Epidemiol. 2002; 156(4):328–34.
2. World Health Organization. DEPRESSION-World prevalence rate. http://www.who.int/es/news-room/fact-sheets/detail/depression. Updated February, 2017. Accessed 1 May 2016.
3. European Commission Eurostat. Chronic Depression-Spain prevalence rate. http://ec.europa.eu/eurostat/statistics-explained/index.php/Mental_health_and_related_issues_statistics. Updated February 21, 2017.
4. Kajonius P, Mac Giolla E. Personality traits across countries: support for similarities rather than differences. PLoS One. 2017;12(6):E0179646.
5. Shi M, Liu L, Yang Y, et al. The mediating role of self-esteem in the relationship between big five personality traits and depressive symptoms among Chinese undergraduate medical students. Pers Individ Dif. 2015;83:55–9.
6. Kövi Z, Odler V, Gacsályi S, et al. Sense of coherence as a mediator between personality and depression. Pers. Individ. Dif. 2017;114:119–24.
7. Tse W, Rochelle T, Cheung J. The relationship between personality, social functioning, and depression: a structural equation modeling analysis. Int J Psychol. 2011;46(3):234–40.
8. Kim S, Kim H, Cho J, et al. Direct and Indirect Effects of Five Factor Personality and Gender on Depressive Symptoms Mediated by Perceived Stress. PLoS One. 2016;11(4):E0154140.
9. Gupta S, Basak P. Depression and type D personality among undergraduate medical students. Indian J Psychiatry. 2013;55(3):287.
10. Noteboom A, Beekman A, Vogelzangs N, et al. Personality and social support as predictors of first and recurrent episodes of depression. J Affect Disord. 2016;15:156–61.
11. Koorevaar A, Comijs H, Dhondt A, et al. Big five personality and depression diagnosis, severity and age of onset in older adults. J Affect Disord. 2013; 151:178–85.
12. Van Dooren F, Verhey F, Pouwer F, et al. Association of Type D personality with increased vulnerability to depression: is there a role for inflammation or endothelial dysfunction? —the Maastricht study. J Affect Disord. 2016; 189:118–25.
13. Gramstad T, Gjestad R, Haver B. Personality traits predict job stress, depression and anxiety among junior physicians. BMC Med Educ. 2013; 13:150.
14. Naragon-Gainey K, Watson D. Consensually defined facets of personality as prospective predictors of change in depression symptoms. ASM. 2014;21: 387–403.
15. Weber K, Giannakopoulos P, Bacchetta J, et al. Personality traits are associated with acute major depression across the age spectrum. Aging Ment Health. 2012;16:472–80.
16. Costa PT, McCrae RR. The NEO-PI/ NEO FFI manual supplement. Odessa, FL: psychological assessment. Resources. 1989;
17. Gilbert P, McEwan K, Bellew R, et al. The dark side of competition: how competitive behaviour and striving to avoid inferiority are linked to depression, anxiety, stress and self-harm. Br J Health Psychol. 2009;82: 123–36.
18. Mattisson C, Bogren M, Horstmann V, et al. Risk factors for depressive disorders in the Lundby cohort-a 50 year prospective clinical follow-up. J Affect Disord. 2009;113:203–15.
19. Enns V, Currie S, Wang J. Professional autonomy and work setting as contributing factors to depression and absenteeism in Canadian nurses. Nurs Outlook. 2015;63:269–77.
20. Eagleton S, Williams A, Merten M. Perceived behavioral autonomy and trajectories of depressive symptoms from adolescence to adulthood. J Child Fam Stud. 2016:198–211.
21. Liu E, Chen W, Tsai L, et al. Interpersonal mechanisms in the relationships between dependency/self-criticism and depressive symptoms in Taiwanese undergraduates: a prospective study. J Soc Clin Psychol. 2012;31:972–1006.
22. Adams P, Abela JR, Auerbach R, et al. Self-criticism, dependency, and stress reactivity: an experience sampling approach to testing blatt and Suroff's theory of personality predispositions to depression in high-risk youth. Personal Soc Psychol Bull. 2009;35:1440–51.
23. Lam DH, Green B, Power MJ, et al. Dependency matching adversities, length of survival and relapse in major depression. J Affect Disord. 1996;37(1–2):81–90.
24. Johnson JA. Measuring thirty facets os the five factor model with a 120-item public domain inventory: Develo'ment of the IPIP-NEO-120. J Res in Personality. 2014;51:78–89.
25. Segui-Gomez M, Cdl F, Vazquez Z, et al. Cohort profile: the 'Seguimiento Universidad de Navarra' (SUN) study. Int J Epidemiol. 2006;35:1417–22.
26. Sanchez-Villegas A, Schlatter J, Ortuno F, et al. Validity of a self-reported diagnosis of depression among participants in a cohort study using the structured clinical interview for DSM-IV (SCID-I). BMC Psychiatry. 2008;8:43.
27. Trichopoulou A, Costacou T, Bamia C, et al. Adherence to a Mediterranean diet and survival in a Greek population. N Engl J Med. 2003;348:2599–608.
28. Bes-Rastrollo M, Pérez Valdivieso JR, Sánchez-Villegas A, et al. Validation of self-declared weight and body mass index of participants from a cohort of university graduates (in spanish). Span J Obes. 2005;3:352–8.
29. Martin-Moreno JM, Boyle P, Gorgojo L, et al. Development and validation of a food frequency questionnaire in Spain. Int J Epidemiol. 1993;22:512–9.

30. Martínez-González MA, López-Fontana C, Varo JJ, et al. Validation of the Spanish version of the physical activity questionnaire used in the Nurses' health study and the health Professionals' follow-up study. Public Health Nutr. 2005;8:920–7.
31. Abela J. The role of self-criticism, dependency, and hassles in the course of depressive illness: a multiwave longitudinal study. Personal Soc Psychol Bull. 2006;32:328–38.
32. Lam DH, Green B, Power MJ, et al. Dependency matching adversities, length of survival and relapse in major depression. J Affect Disord. 1996;37:81–90.
33. Eagleton S, Williams A, Merten M. Perceived behavioral autonomy and trajectories of depressive symptoms from adolescence to adulthood. J Child Fam Stud. 2016;25:198–211.
34. Mitchell R, Kumari V. Hans. Eysenck's interface between the brain and personality: modern evidence on the cognitive neuroscience of personality. Pers. Individ. Dif. 2016;103:74–81.
35. Kraczla M. Personality profiling according to the big five model by P.T. Costa and R. R. McCrae: comparison analysis of managers and specialists. Regional formation and development. Studies. 2017;22(2):77–91.
36. Hakulinen C, Elovainio M, Pulkki-Råback L, et al. Personality and depression symptoms: individual participant meta-analysis of 10 cohort studies. Depress anxiety. 2015;32:461–70.
37. Nemes B, Cozman D. The relevance of personality assessment in estimating the risk of onset and the outcome of major depressive disorder. Clujul Med. 2016;89:212.
38. Jylhä P, Melartin T, Isometsä E. Relationships of neuroticism and extraversion with axis I and II comorbidity among patients with DSM-IV major depressive disorder. J Affec Disord. 2009;114(1–3):110–21.

19

Living with severe perinatal depression: a qualitative study of the experiences of labour migrant and refugee women on the Thai-Myanmar border

Gracia Fellmeth[1,2*], Emma H. Plugge[3], Suphak Nosten[2], May May Oo[2], Mina Fazel[4], Prakaykaew Charunwatthana[5], François Nosten[2,3], Raymond Fitzpatrick[1] and Rose McGready[2,3]

Abstract

Background: Perinatal depression is an important contributor to maternal morbidity and mortality worldwide. Migrant women, particularly those resettling within low- and middle-income settings, are at increased risk of perinatal depression due to multiple stressors experienced before, during and after migration. Evidence on migrant perinatal mental health to date has focused largely on women in high-income destination countries, leaving the voices of displaced women in low-income settings unheard. This study addresses the current evidence gap by exploring the experiences of migrant women living on the Thai-Myanmar border.

Methods: In-depth interviews were conducted with pregnant and post-partum labour migrant and refugee women on the Thai-Myanmar border who had been diagnosed with severe depression. An interview guide covering women's current and past life experiences, social support and the impact of depression on social and occupational functioning was used as a prompt. Thematic analysis was used to identify themes emerging from women's narratives.

Results: Eleven pregnant and post-partum women with severe perinatal depression took part. Participating women provided extensive insight into the many difficult aspects of their lives that they perceived as contributing to their depression status. Predominant themes emerging from women's narratives included difficult relationships with partners, challenging life situations, mechanisms for coping with depression and impressions of mental health care.

Conclusions: Labour migrant and refugee women with severe perinatal depression face a wide range of chronic stressors at the individual, household and community levels that are likely to have both short- and long-term negative effects on their mental well-being and day-to-day functioning. Participating women responded positively to the mental health support they received, and findings provide important insights into how services might further support their needs.

Keywords: Perinatal depression, migrant, refugee, qualitative, pregnancy, post-partum, low- and middle-income

* Correspondence: gracia.fellmeth@dph.ox.ac.uk
[1]Nuffield Department of Population Health, University of Oxford, Old Road Campus, Oxford OX3 7LF, UK
[2]Shoklo Malaria Research Unit, Mahidol-Oxford Tropical Medicine Research Unit, Faculty of Tropical Medicine, Mahidol University, Mae Sot, Tak Province 63110, Thailand
Full list of author information is available at the end of the article

Background

Perinatal depression is one of the commonest morbidities of the perinatal period [1]. Left untreated, depression in pregnancy and the post-partum period can have serious and potentially long-standing consequences for women, their children and families [1, 2]. The burden of perinatal depression is significantly higher in many low- and middle-income countries (LMIC), where exposure to chronic adversity and difficult living conditions is greater and access to adequate mental health services is more limited [3, 4]. Migrant populations are at particularly high risk of perinatal depression due to an array of potential stressors experienced throughout the migration trajectory [5, 6]. Global estimates suggest there are currently over 1 billion migrants worldwide, the majority of whom are labour migrants who move primarily in search of employment opportunities [7, 8]. Despite the majority of global migration occurring within LMIC regions, evidence around the perinatal mental health of migrant women has focused largely on high-income destination settings, and research involving women who have resettled from one low-income setting to another is severely lacking [5, 7, 8].

To date, studies around migrant perinatal mental health have focused on quantifying the prevalence and identifying risk factors. Systematic reviews report pooled estimates of perinatal depression prevalence between 19% [9] and 36.5% [5] among resettled migrant women, though these estimates mask considerable variation between sites. Risk factors include socio-economic disadvantage, low levels of social support and experiences of conflict, exploitation and interpersonal violence [5, 10]. Many of the factors associated with perinatal depression also appear to be context-specific and vary according to culture and setting. For instance, traditional birthing practices such as postpartum confinement and a cultural preference for male infants are associated with postnatal depression in some cultures [11]. Less research has is available which explores in greater depth the lived experiences of migrant women with perinatal depression, particularly among those living in LMIC settings. Given the significant populations involved and the potentially wide-reaching consequences of the condition, there is a need for qualitative work to elicit a greater understanding of the views of affected women in resource-constrained settings. This qualitative study addresses the significant evidence gap by exploring experiences of perinatal depression among refugee and labour migrant women living along the Thai-Myanmar border.

Methods

This qualitative in-depth exploration complements and provides important contextual information for a larger prospective cohort study of perinatal depression, details of which are described elsewhere [12]. In brief, a cohort of 568 refugee and labour migrant women on the Thai-Myanmar border were recruited in the first trimester of pregnancy and followed up until 12 months post-partum. Women's depression status was determined using the *Structured Clinical Interview for the Diagnosis of DSM-IV Disorders* (SCID) [13]. Participating women who experienced major depression during any stage of their pregnancy were eligible for inclusion in this qualitative study.

Setting

This research was conducted in Tak Province, located on the Thai side of the Thai-Myanmar border. Decades of civil conflict in Myanmar have led to large-scale displacement of individuals from Myanmar into Thailand and other neighbouring countries. There are currently an estimated 200,000 labour migrants and an additional 145,000 refugees living along the Thai-Myanmar border [14, 15]. In Tak Province, displaced populations are predominantly of Karen or Burman ethnicity with a small minority of Muslim groups. In this setting, refugees live in established refugee camps on the Thai side of the border where they benefit from housing, food rations and access to health and education services provided by non-governmental and community-based organisations. Labour migrants constitute a separate group who move from Myanmar to rural villages along both sides of the Thai-Myanmar border primarily in search of work in agricultural, service or manufacturing industries. The Shoklo Malaria Research Unit (SMRU) has provided maternity services to displaced communities in this region since 1986. The current study was based at two SMRU antenatal clinics: the first located in Maela refugee camp, the largest camp along the border with an estimated population of 38,000 [16], and the second located in Wang Pha and serving the local rural labour migrant community.

Participants and sampling

Participants were pregnant and post-partum refugee and labour migrant women attending SMRU clinics. The sampling frame consisted of any woman who had participated in the larger cohort study described above and who had been diagnosed with major depressive disorder at any stage during her pregnancy. Eligible women were contacted either by telephone or in person during routine antenatal visits. Efforts were made to contact all eligible women. In an attempt to achieve maximum sampling variation, women from under-represented ethnic, religious and language backgrounds were approached first. Verbal and written descriptions of what the in-depth interview would entail were provided. We explained that participation was entirely voluntary and that participation or non-participation would bear no effect on any aspect of women's care. Women who agreed to take part provided written consent and an interview time and date was arranged. Interviews were conducted at SMRU clinics and whenever possible occurred immediately following women's routine antenatal or postnatal clinic appointments in order to avoid incurring additional travel to and from the clinic. At the end of the interview, participants were offered a small gift (baby clothes and soaps) of an approximate value of GBP £2 as a token of appreciation for their time.

In-depth interviews

In-depth interviews were conducted using an interview guide which covered topics of interest including current and past life experiences, social support and the impact of depression upon social and occupational functioning (Additional file 1). The interview guide was intended to serve as a prompt rather than act as an exhaustive list, and women were encouraged to discuss any other issues they perceived to be relevant to their experiences of depression. Information on participants' age, ethnicity, religion, educational background and migrant status were also collected.

Interviews were conducted by two researchers: an English-speaking physician (GF) and a social scientist fluent in Sgaw Karen, Poe Karen, Burmese and English and highly experienced in interviewing in this setting (SN). Interviews were conducted in private rooms adjacent to the antenatal waiting areas in Sgaw Karen or Burmese, according to each woman's preference. In order to put women at ease, interviews began with general conversation around topics such as where the participant came from, their childhood, their journey to the clinic that day and what they enjoyed doing in their free time. Once a good rapport had been established, the focus moved towards women's experiences of perinatal depression. Participants spoke Burmese or Sgaw Karen, and none spoke English. Questions were asked first in English by GF. The questions were interpeted by by SN into Sgaw Karen or Burmese. Participants' responses were interpreted by SN back into English. As each interview progressed, follow-on questions were asked either in English by GF or directly by SN in the interview language, such that discussions took on the format of three-way conversations rather than two-way questioning-and-answering via an interpreter.

Interviews were audio-recorded using a digital voice recorder. Immediately following the interview, any impressions regarding participants' affect, demeanour and non-verbal communication were noted. Interviews were transcribed directly into English by an experienced transcriber and interpreter. Due to a lack of resources it was not possible to use a two-step process of verbatim transcriptions followed by formal translation of the transcript into English. In order to ensure accuracy, a random selection of transcript excerpts was compared with the original audio recordings. Any ambiguous or unclear language was discussed and clarified. Final versions of the transcripts were imported into *NVivo 11* for analysis [17].

Analysis

A thematic analysis of the data was conducted by one author (GF) using the six consecutive phases described by Braun and Clarke (2006) [18]. First, transcripts were read and re-read until thorough familiarity with each participant's account was achieved. Then, features of note emerging from the data were coded and collated into potential themes and sub-themes. Themes were reviewed and refined until clearly defined themes were established that worked in relation to each of the coded extracts as well as to the entire data set. In order to maximise reliability of the coding and enhance the consistency and quality of data interpretation, a sample of three full interview transcripts was coded independently by a second author (EP) [19]. Themes identified by the two authors were compared and ways in which sub-themes might be grouped together were discussed.

The importance of transparency in qualitative research – including acknowledging researchers' active role in identifying themes and selecting those considered to be of interest – has been highlighted by Braun and Clarke (2006). For our thematic analysis, we adopted an essentialist (or 'realist') approach whereby we report the experiences and lived realities of participants [18]. We do not examine the ways in which such experiences may or may not be the result of discourses operating within the local context [18]. It is also important to acknowledge the potential for researchers to be subject to unconscious biases which may influence data collection and analysis, including how meanings are ascribed to findings. In this study, the interviewers (GF and SN) and data analysts (GF and EP) all have previous experience of working with marginalised populations on the Thai-Myanmar border. One of the interviewers (SN) is of Karen ethnicity and was able to confer a high level of cultural sensitivity to interviews. All three interviewers have experienced life as 'outsiders'; along with their status as mothers they may have held sympathetic leanings towards this population of pregnant migrant women. Nevertheless, detachment and objectivity was maintained as far as possible as a result of none of the researchers being fully immersed within the local culture.

Concurrently with the coding of data, the 'one sheet of paper' (OSOP) method was used. The OSOP method involves reading through each section of qualitative data and noting the different issues raised within coded extracts onto one large sheet of paper. This provides a visual summary of all the issues within a particular code, which might include both anticipated and other, 'emerging' issues

[20]. In our analysis, separate sheets of paper were used for each theme identified in women's narratives. All statements relating to a particular theme were noted, allowing similarities and discrepancies between participants to be highlighted and any examples of unexpected and deviant narratives to be identified. The identification of deviant narratives in particular serves as a means to ensuring that a critical stance is maintained by researchers throughout the analysis [20]. Quotations from women's interview transcripts were used to highlight themes in the presentation of results. Often in qualitative research, such quotes are contextualised by providing a number of key socio-demographic characteristics of the participant. Because of the small number of women interviewed for this study and the sensitive nature of discussions, only a numeric identifier is provided alongside each quote in order to avoid compromising anonymity.

Ethical approval

Ethics approval for this study was granted by the University of Oxford Tropical Research Ethics Committee (OxTREC 28–15), Mahidol University Faculty of Tropical Medicine Ethics Committee (TMEC 15–045) and the Tak Border Community Advisory Board (T-CAB 6/2/2015).

Results

Eleven women with severe perinatal depression participated in in-depth interviews. This final sample represented a convenience sample of women whom we were able to contact and who agreed and were able to attend for an interview. Of a total of twenty eligible women who had been diagnosed with severe perinatal depression within the larger cohort study, thirteen could be contacted. Of these, one declined to be interviewed because she had moved far away from the clinic, and one agreed to participate but did not attend at the arranged interview time. The remaining eleven completed in-depth interviews. Contacting women was considerably easier at Maela refugee camp, as camp residents live within established confines and generally have easier access to the clinic. Labour migrant women – a geographically more mobile group – were comparatively more difficult to contact. As a result, refugee women were over-represented in the final sample. Interviews were carried out between May and July 2016 and ranged in length from 45 min to one and a half hours, with an average duration of just over one hour.

Socio-demographic characteristics of participating women are summarised in Table 1. The majority of participating women were of refugee ($n = 9$), Sgaw Karen ($n = 8$) and Buddhist ($n = 6$) background and most were interviewed in their third trimester of pregnancy (n = 6). The majority of women had been displaced from their homes over six years ago, and only two women had been displaced for a period of less than five years.

Table 1 Characteristics of participants of qualitative study component ($n = 11$)

Characteristics	No. of participants
Age	
20–24 years	2
25–29 years	3
30–34 years	1
35–39 years	3
40–44 years	2
Migration category	
Refugee	9
Labour migrant	2
Ethnicity	
Sgaw Karen	8
Burman	2
Burman Muslim	1
Religion	
Buddhist	6
Christian	4
Muslim	1
Years of education received	
Less than 3 years	4
3 to 6 years	3
7 to 10 years	4
Parity	
1	2
2–4	5
≥5	4
Stage of pregnancy	
2nd trimester	2
3rd trimester	6
Post-partum	3
Duration since migration	
5 years or less	2
6 to 10 years	4
Over 10 years	5

A number of themes and subthemes emerged from in-depth interviews with women. The four main themes were: relationships with partners (encompassing the subthemes of quality of relationships; alcohol use; and interpersonal violence); 'difficult lives' (encompassing the subthemes of past trauma; present challenges; and uncertain futures); coping strategies; and impressions of mental health care.

Relationships with partners

One of the key themes to emerge from in-depth interviews was women's relationships with their partners. When women described relationships with partners, three main subthemes emerged: the quality or nature of their relationships with partners, the use of alcohol among partners and experience of interpersonal violence within their relationships.

Among this group of severely depressed women, a small minority described positive partnership relationships. These women reported that their partners made them feel *"looked after"* and *"cared for"*.

> *"We were in love with each other... Nobody in our family supported us to go to school. We both went to work as daily labourers and supported each other."* (Participant 2)

The majority of women reported being unhappy in their relationships. These women described a perceived lack of attention, empathy and understanding from their partners, resulting in feelings of sadness and frustration. Strained relationships led to feelings of loneliness and isolation, and a sense of having *"nobody to talk to"*.

> *"I felt really sad, so I told my husband about it. But you know what he said? He asked me, 'What happened?' Just this one word he asked. I told him how I feel, but... he said, "You [feel] like this because you are not supporting your family." He never comforts me, only blames [me]."* (Participant 10)

> *"I have no one to talk my worries out of my chest... There is no one who will listen to me patiently. There isn't anyone who will come to me and ask what I am going through. Every worry I feel is kept only inside my chest."* (Participant 5)

Many women blamed negative attributes and behaviours of their husbands for their poor relationships. Men were commonly described as lacking in drive and motivation, and as being unsupportive of women in their roles of caring and household responsibilities, leading to a sense of frustration among women.

> *"He doesn't like to work. If he were a hard worker, there [would] be an income. If you just go and find a job and get hired, it's easy to get an income... But he is too lazy."* (Participant 9)

> *"Once he finishes with his work, he would go and play volleyball and he comes home at 6pm. I have to wait for him for dinner and I would get upset at him... When I get home and there is unfinished housework or an empty water bucket, I have to finish doing the work and fill the water buckets myself."* (Participant 2)

Alcohol use in men was common and invariably associated with negative impacts upon relationships with partners. Frequently, the immediate effects of drunkenness were regarded by women as embarrassing and as bringing shame upon their family.

> *"Each time [my husband] drinks I just want to die. He becomes very loud and it is humiliating."* (Participant 2)

Longer-term implications of alcohol use, including the wasting of household income on alcohol, brought about feelings of stress and *"overthinking"* among women.

> *"I am depressed when he drinks alcohol and then I [start] overthinking. I would cry every time he drank alcohol. I am already preoccupied enough taking care of just one child."* (Participant 2)

> *"He is always getting drunk and looking for trouble... I am very stressed because of him."* (Participant 3)

Women described the negative influence of their husbands' peers on alcohol consumption. Many women felt that their husbands tended to drink more when they were out socialising with friends who might initially offer free drinks, encourage heavy drinking, and tease those men who did not drink.

> *"He sometimes uses drugs and alcohol because his friends make him."*(Participant 5)

> *"His friends made him drink... [They] told him he is afraid of his wife. So, he drank the alcohol to show them that he is not afraid."* (Participant 11)

Poor relationships with partners were also characterised by interpersonal violence, which was reported by almost all the women interviewed and almost always occurred against a background of partners' alcohol use. Women described instances of verbal as well as physical and, to a lesser extent, sexual, abuse. Verbal abuse included *"hurtful words"* and *"accusations"*:

> *"[My husband] says that I am not a good mother and I am hurt by that. When he says that, it hurts me so much that I would cry."* (Participant 2)

"He threatens to cut my throat... He also shouts at me with anger and some abusive words and I feel very frightened and shocked because I just delivered the baby and [the baby] is very young. He has no sense of understanding that at this time women need to keep warm and avoid shocks." (Participant 3)

Physical abuse included being kicked, hit, punched and strangled. Such attacks were commonly severe enough to cause serious injury and require hospitalisation.

"He physically abused me twice. The first time, he did not know I was pregnant. He hit my head with a bamboo stick and he kicked me. The [second] time he already knew that I was pregnant... He was coming home after going to get the wood and I forgot to cook and he got angry and kicked me which left me unconscious." (Participant 7)

"He beat me up and squeezed my neck. That time, my eldest daughter ran [...] to call for help. After the fighting ended, I was not feeling well for four days so I went to the clinic." (Participant 6)

Violence by men was at times directed at their children. When this occurred, women felt a deep sense of shame, helplessness and guilt at being unable to protect their children.

"Sometimes I feel worthless... When my husband shouts at [the children] I think it's all my fault... [Because] I am not good, my children are being scolded and beaten by their step-father. I don't blame my children; I blame myself." (Participant 5)

Sexual violence was reported less frequently. One woman recounted how she had felt pressured into marrying her husband after he kissed her in public – an act deemed to be appropriate only among married couples in this cultural context. This woman described feeling vulnerable as well as *"angry"* at the situation she was placed in, which had left her with no choice other than to marry.

"I was 18 or 19 years old. He was kissing and hugging me in front of people and I was afraid that people will gossip about me so I had to marry him." (Participant 7)

Though less common than male-perpetrated violence, women occasionally acted violently towards their partners. A number of women had spoken out against their partners when they could no longer refrain from doing so.

"I feel so irritated. Right now, I can't just be silent, you know ... I have to speak out to him! I felt great and empty in my chest when I called him a dog!" (Participant 6)

"When I get upset and stressed, I have to speak about it, otherwise I would feel like it was burning inside. I would feel better afterwards." (Participant 2)

Women often laughed while recollecting the occasions when this had occurred, conveying a sense of embarrassment but also of achievement for having stood up for themselves. The act of releasing pent-up anger and frustrations brought a sense of relief and empowerment. Some women had become physically violent towards their partners. Most commonly this was in direct self-defence against husbands' abuse, but at other times it was in reaction to behaviours such as repeated drunkenness which women felt were irritating and unacceptable.

"When [my husband] came back, I told him not to come upstairs... I [made] him stay downstairs until he wasn't drunk anymore... But he came upstairs. I couldn't bear his smell and got angry when he didn't listen. I threw things...at him. If I had not been held back by other people, my husband would have been hit pretty hard... I [insulted] him by calling him: 'Dog! You animal!'... People say that my husband is going to die from the things I throw at him." (Participant 6)

"My husband and I had an argument one day. I said, 'I wish I could kill you and take your heart out;' and I punched him in the eye because I [was] very angry... Since then, he is very terrified of me and apologized [to] me. He said to me: 'My wife, please don't kill me!'" (Participant 7)

"Difficult life"

All women referred in one way or another to their lives being *"hard"*, *"difficult"* or *"tough"*. The concept of a 'difficult life' encompassed three subthemes: past traumas, the multiple challenges of daily life and uncertain futures.

Women's pasts were fraught with hardship:

"If I think about [my childhood] I don't even want to live... There were so many hardships." (Participant 1)

One woman described growing up with an abusive step-father. When he touched her inappropriately, she found herself unable to find support or share her distress.

"He touched me inappropriately... I do not like to sleep with blanket on and whenever he came over to put the blanket on me he would touch my breasts and my lower body part and [when] I opened my eyes he walked away. I was upset with what happened. My mother did not let me report [what my step-father did] to the soldiers, so I did not, so that she would not lose face." (Participant 2)

Death among parents and siblings was common, and many women's childhoods were shaped by the absence of a mother or father. As young children, these women had taken on adult responsibilities such as looking after younger siblings, carrying out household chores and being sent as far as Bangkok to earn an income from a young age.

"After our mother passed away, I had to take on my mother's [role] of taking care of my younger sister and my father." (Participant 5)

"I was sent [to Bangkok] as a house-maid. I was twelve years old at that time." (Participant 10)

"I went to Bangkok with other people. I started working there at nine years old. I did the cleaning and ironing... I was there for one year." (Participant 3)

Many women had not attended school, or attended only intermittently or for brief periods. Often, family finances were insufficient to cover the costs of tuition, uniforms and textbooks. In addition to saving the family money, not enrolling a child in school meant the child was available to help with domestic chores, looking after other family members or potentially earn an additional income for the household.

"I was only able to go to school for the first grade post-kindergarten. My family had to struggle very hard. They could not afford for my school fees easily. I enjoyed school. I [tried] my best when I was in school." (Participant 5)

Conflict and war in Myanmar and the resulting displacement to the Thai border represented, for many, an additional past trauma. The constant threat of violence from Myanmar government army soldiers as well as armed ethnic minority groups was a significant stressor. Women had experienced and witnessed multiple forms of violence, including forced labour, portering and mine-sweeping, land confiscation and killings.

"In my area, the Burmese soldiers came and collected people as their porters. As they were going in and out of our village day and night, we did not dare to go work so that our living conditions started to become unstable and poor." (Participant 8)

Many families had been forced to flee their homes and villages, often very suddenly, taking nothing but *"the one set of clothing on my body"*. Women remembered their arduous journeys to the Thai border in detail even when these events had occurred decades earlier.

"There was an attack in which we had to flee from the Myanmar soldiers. There was an exchange of fire and I had to flee with my two younger siblings. My mother was carrying another sibling and my brother was asked to carry clothes. I carried the cooking pot and some kitchen accessories and some rice... There were many other items which we could not carry." (Participant 2)

"We left because of the civil war. We had to stay in the bunker... Fighting broke out and my mother was three months pregnant at that time. We crossed the border on foot." (Participant 3)

"It probably took about 4-5 days on the way because we had the financial difficultly and my father was not well on our journey. After our mother passed away, I had to take the substitution of my mother's position for taking care of my younger sister and my father. So, we hitchhiked and walked and begged for food." (Participant 5)

Present challenges

Present life challenges were often the result of long-standing poverty and income insecurity. Women worried about not having enough food to feed the family and many were unable to afford school fees.

"Even with our income and monthly ration, we don't have enough for my family. I have to buy one sack of rice once every two months and two sacks of charcoal every month." (Participant 4)

One woman described feeling sad because she could not afford to buy her children small treats. It was common for families to take out loans from friends or informal moneylenders in attempts to make ends meet. Often these loans would set off a downward spiral of mounting debts that women were unable to repay. Many women felt that the responsibility of taking care of the family rested solely upon them, and this created resentment towards partners as well as acting as a constant psychological stressor.

> *"I am the only person providing for the family. I also have to provide for my parents because there is no one else. When I can, I send money to my parents but when I do not earn enough I could not send them any."* (Participant 4)

> *"I work every day... With a bit of money that I...earn at work I have to pay for the babysitter. My father, when he comes around, he asks me for some money to buy alcohol. If I refuse, he starts to become violent and destroys what he sees around. I get some money from my husband but I feel mistrusted by him at the same time. They are putting me under many pressures."* (Participant 3)

Family separation characterised many women's lives. It was common for women to have lost contact with close family members including siblings, parents, former partners and even their own children who had remained behind in Myanmar, left in search of work opportunities or resettled to third countries.

> *"I look after three of my nieces and nephews. Their father was left behind and their mother is having difficulties getting a job so we have to help look after them."* (Participant 2)

> *"The eldest daughter lives with me. The other four children are with my previous husband. He does not care where they go or what happens to them. He lets them go to school but he dislikes them visiting me, so he beats them and makes them stay with his sister. I am uncertain how well they look after my children."* (Participant 8)

Uncertain futures

Among this group of women, most of whom were of refugees (rather than labour migrants), the majority hoped to one day resettle to 'third countries' – a term used to describe high-income destination countries including the United Kingdom, Australia and the USA. However, none of the women had a clear sense of how likely it was for their applications for resettlement to be successful. Those who had not been registered with the refugee camp's UNHCR resettlement scheme expressed doubt as to whether they would ever be allowed to move to another country. But even among those on the resettlement register there was great uncertainty. Some women had been waiting for several years, with no indication of if or when they might move. Others had complicated scenarios whereby only some family members were registered for resettlement, creating difficulties for women faced with the choice of moving to a new country alone or remaining in the camp with their families.

> *"I wish to resettle if I could. I want to go to another country because all my parents and siblings are there. Here, I am not healthy. I am overwhelmed and worried about the future. I wish to go to my parents so that they can also help take care of their grandchildren."* (Participant 5)

Repatriation to Myanmar was not seen as an attractive option due to ongoing conflict and difficult living situations in Myanmar:

> *"I haven't thought about going back to Burma and I don't want to. I will get some land here if I live here. Wars are still breaking out in my old village and we [would] have no place to go."* (Participant 6)

> *"I don't want to go back [to Karen State]. I do not like living there. I would have to work hard if I moved back. It is better to live here."* (Participant 7)

The overarching issue of a "difficult life" encompassing the multiple challenges pervading every aspect of women's lives is summed up by the following two quotes:

> *"My life situation is [similar to] that of the fruit of the Devil's Trumpet: if you swallow it, it will sting you; if you smell it, it will make you dizzy; and if you eat it, it will make you mad. My life is like this: I have no direction I can go, nowhere to run away or escape this trouble. Sometimes I think I want to choose the path of suicide."* (Participant 5)[1]

> *"Everyone has their limit and if the burden is too much then you would no longer be able to tolerate it. There's no need to say it: I have so much burden in this life... Even though I have made a lot of good merit and deeds I have never been lucky. I am carrying this very heavy burden. Sometimes it feels like I cannot take it anymore."* (Participant 7)

Coping mechanisms

Women resorted to a variety of mechanisms to help them cope with symptoms of depression. A number of women sought emotional support from friends, neighbours and work colleagues. One woman received support from her neighbour who could relate to and empathise with her situation.

"She is like a sister and a mother [to me]. Like me, she is also feeling unwell with sadness. When I talk about my problems, she feels sad for me, and I feel the same when she tells me her problems. There is nothing I can do. Besides her, there is no one I could talk to." (Participant 5)

Other women turned to hobbies including weaving, embroidery and gardening as a means of momentary escape. For some, provided a welcome distraction.

"I seem to forget about my worries when I concentrate on work that I enjoy." (Participant 5)

"I forget [my symptoms]...while I am in work. Honestly speaking, I didn't want to come home from there. I wanted to live but there wasn't a room for me. Sometimes, I called my co-worker to ask whether or not I could sleep there because I didn't want to go back." (Participant 10)

For a small number of women, religious activities such as reading the Bible and visiting the church, temple or mosque were perceived as helpful ways of managing symptoms of depression, though more commonly these activities were mentioned in passing rather than being regarded explicitly as coping strategies.

"When I am home, I am not very happy but when I go to church and hear about God's words I feel happy. When I come home, the devil comes to my heart all the time. Whenever my friend invites me to join her to church, I would go but if I refused the invitation and did not go, the devil would come then." (Participant 7)

A couple of women had consulted traditional healers with regards to their symptoms of depression. These women felt that the treatment had helped them to feel more positive and balanced, and given them a more positive perspective on their lives.

"A traditional healer made this necklace for me to protect further bad deeds and evil spirits causing me [to be] unwell. The necklace holds a small piece of scroll that is written in traditional magic words to cast evils away and protect me. While I am wearing this necklace, I mustn't go to places that are unclean and I mustn't eat anything that is unclean." (Participant 5)

"When I felt sad I went to the clinic and had an injection to help with stress. I always pray to lose this symptom of feeling sad when I meet with a good healer because I have been feeling really bad." (Participant 11)

Impressions of mental health care

Counselling offered to women was generally well-received. For many women, counselling provided a rare opportunity to talk about their feelings Women felt it particularly beneficial to speak to the same counsellor regularly over several months, which allowed them to build up rapport and trust. As well as the counselling sessions in themselves, spontaneous conversations that arose with other women while they were waiting for counselling were also helpful.

"This morning, some women were talking about their problems. Sometimes you see that some of them are going through the same problems as [me]. The person I talked to this morning, her husband [gets himself into] trouble...and my husband also steals money... I realise that I am not alone going through the burden of these difficulties, but that there are more people like me." (Participant 6)

Of the eleven women interviewed, all had been offered anti-depressant medication for their severe depression and seven chose to take the medication. Women who took medication reported mixed experiences. Some reported positive experiences: these women found the treatment helpful, describing that it contributed towards an improvement in their symptoms and that they felt "*more active*" and less worried following treatment.

"Since taking the medicine I can sleep well and eat well. I now think less about my worries. I suddenly feel good. I have a good appetite and I can eat well. I also do not worry about my children like before. The thoughts do not stick in my mind for too long." (Participant 8)

"When I take the medicine, I feel better. I feel less tired. It could be other things that have helped me feel better, but personally I think it's because of the medicine. I can laugh...now. Before I took the medicine, I couldn't." (Participant 11)

Others experienced side effects and discontinued taking the medication. Reported side effects included feeling *"uncomfortable"*, *"woozy"* and *"numb"*. One participant felt better when she took the medicine, *"but when I stop taking it the thinking creeps back in"*.

Discussion

This qualitative study was conducted in order to gain a deeper understanding of refugee and labour migrant women's experiences of severe perinatal depression on the Thai-Myanmar border. Participating women provided extensive insight into the many difficult aspects of their lives that they perceived as contributing to their depression status and the coping mechanisms they adopted in order to help them cope with the condition. A complex constellation of overlapping and inter-connected issues shaping women's experiences arose from women's narratives. The concept of a "difficult life" encompassed a variety of on-going but also past social, economic and interpersonal challenges as well as uncertainty regarding the future. Women's lives were to a large extent shaped by past events including difficult childhoods, family separation, conflict and dangerous journeys to the Thai border. As adults, these difficult life circumstances persisted in the form of economic hardship, insecurity, poor support from partners and a lack of certainty around their own futures.

Another central tenet of these women's experiences was difficult relationships with partners, linked closely with partner's alcohol use and interpersonal violence. Strained relationships were common, and men's alcohol consumption formed one of the main frustrations women had with their partners. Alcohol use was regarded as leading to inappropriate behaviour in men, ranging from being unsupportive emotionally and financially to bringing shame on the family through drunken behaviour in public, all with negative impacts upon women's lives. Women were exposed to interpersonal violence in the form of verbal and physical abuse and, to a lesser extent, sexual abuse, and violence was invariably associated with and aggravated by men's alcohol use. The relatively low frequency with which women reported sexual violence is of interest given that the perinatal period has been highlighted as a time of high risk for violence against women [21]. It is possible that women under-disclosed episodes of sexual violence as a result of stigma around this issue or a lack of clarity around definitions of what constitutes sexual abuse [22]. Coping mechanisms included talking to friends and family as well as work, hobbies, religious activities and traditional healing.

The importance of psychosocial factors parallels findings from other settings. Previous research has highlighted the significant contribution of living conditions, interpersonal violence and social support towards perinatal depression among both migrant and non-migrant populations [1, 5, 11, 23]. The inter-association between alcohol use, interpersonal violence and partner relationships has also been reported in other resource-constrained settings, including elsewhere along the Thai-Myanmar border [24–27]. In a previous survey of pregnant women in Maela camp, almost a quarter of women reported high levels of alcohol use by their partners [27]. Similarly, in a different refugee camp on the Thai-Myanmar border, alcohol use and fighting within married couples emerged as predominant stressors [26]. Paralleling the findings of the current study, Meyer et al.'s (2013) respondents attributed relationship discord to multiple, inter-related problems including a lack of income, having nothing to eat, alcohol use and frustrations with general conditions within the refugee camp.

The notion of a 'difficult life' suggests that women in this study represent a particularly vulnerable group as a result of exposure to multiple co-existing and mutually-reinforcing psychosocial challenges. Other studies have reported similar findings. For example, Stewart et al. (2014) found that in Malawi, a lack of support from partners was perceived by pregnant women as a generalised insufficiency of support in their lives, which in turn was associated both with depression and interpersonal violence [28]. Similarly, Fernando et al. (2010), working with conflict-affected Sri Lankan youth, ascribed depression to a "host of enduring stressful conditions of daily life" [29].

Women found therapy in the form of counselling helpful, especially when rapport could be established with the same counsellor over a period of time. The mixed reports with regards to anti-depressant medication suggests more research is required to explore effective and culturally-accepted forms of support within this population. Evidence from other low-income settings has shown the effectiveness of psychosocial interventions delivered by non-specialists and peer supporters [30]. Future work might consider testing such interventions on the Thai-Myanmar border.

It was notable that pregnancy status per se did not feature prominently in women's narratives when, arguably, it might be an important determinant of a woman's emotional state. In this particular context, this could manifest in either a positive manner – for instance, pregnancy and motherhood providing a reason for hope in an otherwise difficult life situation – or in a negative manner – for instance by highlighting and bringing to the forefront of women's minds the on-going challenges they face with little prospect of improvement in the next generation. Within Karen culture, childbearing is considered a fundamental aspect of womanhood: marriages are 'blessed' with having children, and the idea of attributing symptoms of depression on pregnancy may feel inappropriate to women in this context. The lack of explicit mention of pregnancy and motherhood also raises questions around the extent to which experiences of depression among this group of women are in fact tied to pregnancy status, or whether the condition would have occurred regardless. A small number of studies exploring the mental health of women refugees have reported vulnerabilities that are common to all women, regardless of pregnancy status [31, 32]. However, no studies to our knowledge have directly assessed the specific contribution of pregnancy or post-partum status as a contributing factor to mental disorder among migrant or refugee women.

Evidence is also lacking around the experiences of non-migrant Karen and Burmese women's experiences of perinatal mental disorders. Without an in-depth understanding of depression within these cultural groups in their places of origin, it is difficult to attribute the experiences of the women included in this study to their migration histories. Future research should consider the inclusion of non-perinatal women within this migrant community as well as non-migrant women in communities of origin within Myanmar in order to explore the relative contributions of pregnancy status and migration status, respectively.

Limitations and strengths

Findings of this qualitative study are constrained by a number of limitations. Firstly, results are based on a limited number of interviews with a selected group of severely depressed women, and findings may therefore not be generalisable to other women with perinatal depression in this setting. In particular, women interviewed did not reflect the diversity within the migrant community as a whole. Despite attempts to include women from a diverse range of backgrounds, refugee, Sgaw Karen and Buddhist women were over-represented. The small sample size also meant we were unable to provide socio-demographic details of participants alongside their quotes, making it difficult to interpret whether factors such as migration status or cultural background influenced the experiences of these women. A larger and more diverse sample may have enabled differences in experiences of perinatal depression according to factors such as ethnicity, religious background and migrant category to be discerned. However, the small overall number of severely depressed women from which our participants were drawn ($n = 20$) along with the difficulty in contacting many of the women in this highly mobile and hard-to-reach population group limited the ability to select women from a range of backgrounds.

In order to participate, women had to be contactable, willing to participate and available to attend the clinic for interview, introducing the possibility of recruitment and self-selection bias. Importantly, women whom it was not possible to contact may have been the most vulnerable or the most severely depressed. The limited number of participants also meant that data saturation was not achieved, and important factors contributing to experiences of depression may therefore have been missed.

A further limitation relates to language. Interviews were conducted in a combination of English, Karen and Burmese. Compared with English, both Karen and Burmese languages have a limited vocabulary for describing emotional states. It is possible that despite best efforts to minimise losses in translation, inconsistencies across languages or misinterpretation of descriptions of depressive experiences occurred. Furthermore, analyses were conducted in English rather than in the language the participants used, which may have led to subthemes being missed or misplaced.

Finally, though this was beyond the scope of the current study, findings could have been strengthened through the inclusion of women's partners in order to gain the perspective of the men living alongside these women. Further insights could also be gained by including non-depressed women, many of whom might be exposed to the same stressors. These 'control' women may help our understanding of factors contributing to resilience against mental disorders in this setting.

Despite these limitations, this study has a number of strengths. To our knowledge, this qualitative study represents the first in-depth exploration of the experiences of perinatal depression among refugee and labour migrant women in a low-income setting. A number of ethnographic studies of perinatal depression among migrant women exist but all to date have been conducted in high-income settings [33]. A further strength was that one of the interviewers was a trusted member of the migrant community with valuable first-hand understanding of the cultural context, which allowed a strong and trusting rapport with participating women to be established. Finally, analysis was conducted using a rigorous methodological approach. An inter-rater reliability exercise was conducted in which a second author (EP) independently coded three transcripts in order to maximise reliability, while the grouping of sub-themes into themes and the inter-relationship of themes with each other were conducted in consultation and collaboration with the wider team of authors. An explicit acknowledgment of the analytical approach adopted and the inclusion of deviant examples through the OSOP method further helped to ensure that a critical stance was maintained.

Conclusions

This qualitative study explored themes emerging from the narratives of refugee and labour migrant women living with severe perinatal depression on the Thai-Myanmar border. Women provided considerable insight into their lived experiences of depression and linked their symptoms to a wide range of social factors. Participants faced a wide range of chronic stressors at the individual, household and community levels that are likely to have both short- and long-term effects on their mental well-being and day-to-day functioning. Themes included challenging life situations, difficult partnership relationships marked by alcohol use and interpersonal violence and mechanisms for coping with perinatal depression. Severely depressed women responded positively to mental health counselling support, and these interviews have provided important insights into how services might further support these women's needs.

Acknowledgements
We would like to thank the women who participated in in-depth interviews and entrusted us with their stories. Thanks also go to the wider Mental Health Study team Mupawjay Pimanpanarak, Yuwapha Phichitphadungtham, Oh Mu and Kerry Wai along with SMRU doctors Aye Min, Verena Carrara, Mary Ellen Gilder and Bert van Enter for their dedication in ensuring the smooth running of the Mental Health Study.

Funding
The Shoklo Malaria Research Unit (SMRU) is part of the Wellcome Trust Mahidol University Oxford Tropical Medicine Research Program funded by the Wellcome Trust (WT-106698). The funding body had no role in the design, collection, analysis or interpretation of data, nor in the writing or submission of the manuscript for publication.

Authors' contributions
GF, EHP, MF, PC, FN, RF, PC and RM conceptualised the study. GF, EHP, SN, MMO, MF, RF and RM developed the interview topic guide. Data collection was conducted by GF and SN. Data analysis was conducted by GF and EHP. Interpretation of results was conducted by all authors. GF wrote the first draft of the manuscript; all authors contributed to revised versions of the manuscript. All authors read and approved the final manuscript.

Consent for publication
Not applicable.

Competing interests
The authors declare that they have no competing interests.

Author details
[1]Nuffield Department of Population Health, University of Oxford, Old Road Campus, Oxford OX3 7LF, UK. [2]Shoklo Malaria Research Unit, Mahidol-Oxford Tropical Medicine Research Unit, Faculty of Tropical Medicine, Mahidol University, Mae Sot, Tak Province 63110, Thailand. [3]Centre for Tropical Medicine and Global Health, Nuffield Department of Medicine, University of Oxford Peter Medawar Building for Pathogen Research, South Parks Road, Oxford OX2, UK. [4]Department of Psychiatry, University of Oxford, Warneford Hospital, Warneford Lane, Oxford OX3 7JX, UK. [5]Faculty of Tropical Medicine, Mahidol University, 420/6 Ratchawithi Road, Ratchathewi, Bangkok 10400, Thailand.

References

1. Howard LM, Molyneaux E, Dennis CL, Rochat T, Stein A, Milgrom J. Non-psychotic mental disorders in the perinatal period. Lancet. 2014;384(9956): 1775–88.
2. Stein A, Pearson RM, Goodman SH, Rapa E, Rahman A, McCallum M, Howard LM, Pariante CM. Effects of perinatal mental disorders on the fetus and child. Lancet. 2014;384(9956):1800–19.
3. Woody CA, Ferrari AJ, Siskind DJ, Whiteford HA, Harris MG. A systematic review and meta-regression of the prevalence and incidence of perinatal depression. J Affect Disord. 2017;219:86–92.
4. Fisher J, Cabral de Mello M, Patel V, Rahman A, Tran T, Holton S, Holmes W. Prevalence and determinants of common perinatal mental disorders in women in low- and lower-middle-income countries: a systematic review. Bull World Health Organ. 2012;90(2):139g–49g.
5. Fellmeth G, Fazel M, Plugge E. Migration and perinatal mental health in women from low- and middle-income countries: a systematic review and meta-analysis. BJOG. 2017;124(5):742–52.
6. Collins CH, Zimmerman C, Howard LM. Refugee, asylum seeker, immigrant women and postnatal depression: rates and risk factors. Arch Womens Ment Health. 2011;14(1):3–11.
7. IOM. Migrant well-being and development. In: *World Migration Report* 2013. Geneva: International Organization for Migration; 2013.
8. IOM. Migrants and cities: new partnerships to manage mobility. In: *World Migration Report 2015*. Geneva: International Organization for Migration; 2015.
9. Anderson FM, Hatch SL, Comacchio C, Howard LM. Prevalence and risk of mental disorders in the perinatal period among migrant women: a systematic review and meta-analysis. Arch Womens Ment Health. 2017;20(3): 449–62.
10. Shishehgar S, Gholizadeh L, DiGiacomo M, Green A, Davidson PM. Health and socio-cultural experiences of refugee women: an integrative review. J Immigr Minor Health. 2017;19(4):959–73.
11. Norhayati MN, Hazlina NH, Asrenee AR, Emilin WM. Magnitude and risk factors for postpartum symptoms: a literature review. J Affect Disord. 2015; 175:34–52.
12. Fellmeth G, Plugge EH, Carrara V, Fazel M, Oo MM, Phichitphadungtham Y, Pimanpanarak M, Wai NK, Mu O, Charunwatthana P, Nosten F, Fitzpatrick R, McGready R. Migrant perinatal depression study: a prospective cohort study of perinatal depression on the Thai-Myanmar border. BMJ Open. 2018;8(1): e017129.
13. Spitzer RL, Williams JB, Gibbon M, First MB. The structured clinical interview for DSM-III-R (SCID). I: history, rationale, and description. Arch Gen Psychiatry. 1992;49(8):624–9.
14. Dunlop N. Invisible people: stories of migrant labourers in Thailand. Bangkok: Raks Thai Foundation; 2011.
15. Pearson R, Kusakabe K. Thailand's hidden workforce: Burmese migrant women factory workers. London: Zed Books; 2012.
16. The Border Consortium, Annu Rep: *January–December 2015*. 2016.
17. QSR International. NVivo qualitative data analysis software, version 11: QSR International Pty Ltd; 2015.
18. Braun V, Clarke V. Using thematic analysis in psychology. Qual Res Psychol. 2006;3(2):77–101.
19. Pope C And Mays, N, eds. *Qualitative research in health care. Third Edition*. 2006, Blackwell Publishing Ltd: Oxford.
20. Ziebland S, McPherson A. Making sense of qualitative data analysis: an introduction with illustrations from DIPEx (personal experiences of health and illness). Med Educ. 2006;40(5):405–14.
21. Halim N, Beard J, Mesic A, Patel A, Henderson D, Hibberd P. Intimate partner violence during pregnancy and perinatal mental disorders in low and lower middle income countries: a systematic review of literature, 1990-2017. Clin Psychol Rev. 2017;
22. Breckenridge J, Yang T, Poon AWC. Is gender important? Victimisation and perpetration of intimate partner violence in mainland China. Health Soc Care Community. 2018;
23. Gelaye B, Rondon MB, Araya R, Williams MA. Epidemiology of maternal depression, risk factors, and child outcomes in low-income and middle-income countries. Lancet Psychiatry. 2016;3(10):973–82.
24. Connelly CD, Hazen AL, Baker-Ericzen MJ, Landsverk J, Horwitz SM. Is screening for depression in the perinatal period enough? The co-occurrence of depression, substance abuse, and intimate partner violence in culturally diverse pregnant women. J Women's Health (Larchmt). 2013; 22(10):844–52.
25. Falb KL, McCormick MC, Hemenway D, Anfinson K, Silverman JG. Violence against refugee women along the Thai-Burma border. Int J Gynaecol Obstet. 2013;120(3):279–83.
26. Meyer S, Murray LK, Puffer ES, Larsen J, Bolton P. The nature and impact of chronic stressors on refugee children in ban Mai Nai Soi camp, Thailand. Glob Public Health. 2013;8(9):1027–47.
27. Ezard N, Thiptharakun S, Nosten F, Rhodes T, McGready R. Risky alcohol use among reproductive-age men, not women, in Mae La refugee camp, Thailand, 2009. Confl Health. 2012;6(1):7.
28. Stewart RC, Umar E, Tomenson B, Creed F. A cross-sectional study of antenatal depression and associated factors in Malawi. Arch Womens Ment Health. 2014;17(2):145–54.

29. Fernando GA, Miller KE, Berger DE. Growing pains: the impact of disaster-related and daily stressors on the psychological and psychosocial functioning of youth in Sri Lanka. Child Dev. 2010;81(4):1192–210.
30. Patel V. Talking sensibly about depression. PLoS Med. 2017;14(4):e1002257.
31. Seguin M, Lewis R, Amirejibi T, Razmadze M, Makhashvili N, Roberts B. Our flesh is here but our soul stayed there: a qualitative study on resource loss due to war and displacement among internally-displaced women in the republic of Georgia. Soc Sci Med. 2016;150:239–47.
32. Bartolomei L, Eckert R, Pittaway E. "What happens there… follows us here": resettled but still at risk: refugee women and girls in Australia. Refuge. 2014; 30:45–56.
33. Schmied V, Black E, Naidoo N, Dahlen HG, Liamputtong P. Migrant women's experiences, meanings and ways of dealing with postnatal depression: a meta-ethnographic study. PLoS One. 2017;12(3):e0172385.

A systematic review and meta-analysis of epidemiology of depression in people living with HIV in East Africa

Getinet Ayano[1*], Melat Solomon[1] and Mebratu Abraha[2]

Abstract

Background: Depression is the most prevalent psychiatric disorder among people living with HIV (PLWHIV) and is associated with poor quality of life, additional comorbidities, disability, unemployment, poorer therapeutic outcomes and risky behaviors. The present systematic review and meta-analysis aims to systematically summarize empirical evidence and to formulate recommendations for future research.

Methods: We searched PubMed, EMBASE, SCOPUS, and relevant literature for possible studies to include. A qualitative and quantitative analysis was undertaken for this systematic review. Subgroup and sensitivity analysis were performed. Cochran's Q- and the I^2 test were used to assess heterogeneity. The presence of publication bias was evaluated by using Egger's test and visual inspection of the symmetry in funnel plots.

Results: Of 283 titles initially identified, 81 abstracts were eligible for review. Of these, 46 articles qualified for full text review and 19 were retained. In our meta-analysis the pooled prevalence of depression in PLWHIV was 38% (95% CI 29.30-47.54). The pooled prevalence estimates of depression was 49.79% in Ethiopia and 30.88% in Uganda. In addition, the prevalence of depression was 12.40% and 46% as measured by diagnostic and screening instrument respectively. Our qualitative synthesis showed that factors such as having opportunistic infection, perceived stigma, negative life event, WHO clinical staging of disease, hospitalization in the past one month, stressful life events, food insecurity, self-efficacy, missed frequency of clinic visit, frequency of follow-up, older age, low income, urban residence and being government employee were strongly and significantly associated with depression in PLWHIV in east Africa.

Conclusion: The pooled prevalence estimates of prevalence of depression in PLWHIV was 38%. The prevalence estimates of depression in PLWHIV in Ethiopia was significantly higher than Uganda. In addition the prevalence of depression was significantly higher in studies conducted by screening than diagnostic instrument. Routine screening and integrated management of depression into the existing HIV care services is warranted. Validation and use of standard instrument to assess depression in PLWHIV is needed. Moreover, longitudinal and community based studies focusing on incidence and determinates of depression in PLWHIV are recommended.

Keywords: Prevalence, HIV, AIDS, Determinants, Factors, Depression, Systematic review, Meta-analysis, East Africa

* Correspondence: babiget2015@gmail.com
[1]Research and Training Department, Amanuel Mental Specialized Hospital, Addis Ababa, Ethiopia
Full list of author information is available at the end of the article

Background

Depression is the most prevalent psychiatric disorder among people living with HIV (PLWHIV) and is associated with poorer therapeutic outcomes and risky behaviors. Different epidemiological studies have estimated the prevalence of depression in PLWHIVto be between 2.27% and 76.7% [1–20]. In fact, it is one of the leading causes of morbidity and mortality among PLWHIV [21].

In the past decades, studies have determined the prevalence of depression in PLWHIV. However, the overall prevalence rate of depression in PLWHIV remains unclear in east Africa; previous studies reported prevalence rates between 2.7% and 76.7% [1–20]. Several factors may contribute to this wide range of prevalence rates, including: (i) differences between included PLWHIV with respect to the stages of HIV disease, treatment status and CD4 level (ii) the use of different instruments to assess depression with different psychometric properties; and (iii) the use of different criteria to define depression [22].

Depression is the most commonly experienced psychological conditions experienced by PLWHIV and is associated with poor quality of life [23], additional comorbidities [24], disability, and unemployment [25–27]. In addition, depression in PLWHV leads poor social conditions, poor treatment adherence and, poor therapeutic outcomes, and risky behaviors [28–31].

A number of factors can predispose PLWHIV to depression including, having opportunistic infection [9, 10], perceived stigma [2], negative life event [26], having severe WHO clinical stage diseases [2, 9, 10], stressful life events [26], food insecurity [9], older age [17], low income [3] and advanced HIV disease [22].

Evidence shows that east Africa is the region most affected by HIV in the world next to south Africa [32]. However, the there are no systematic review and meta-analysis studies conducted on the epidemiology of depression in PLWHIV in east Africa. Therefore, the main objective of this systematic review and meta-analysis is to summarize the available empirical evidence in east Africa on: [1] the prevalence of depression in people living with HIV (PLWHIV) and [2] the determinants of depressionin PLWHIV and to formulate recommendations for future clinical practice and research.

Methods/design

We conducted extensive search of literature as indicated in the guideline of reporting systematic review and meta-analysis (PRISMA) [32]. Three databases such as PubMed, Embase, and Scopus were consulted for our literature search. We conducted our search in Pubmed using the following terms and keywords: "Epidemiology OR prevalence OR magnitude OR incidence AND depression OR depressive symptoms OR depressive disorder OR depressive AND HIV OR human immunodeficiency virus OR AIDS AND factor OR risk OR risk factor OR determinant AND Ethiopia OR Eritrea OR Kenya OR Uganda OR Tanzania OR Sudan OR Djibouti OR Somalia OR Rwanda OR east Africa". For the other two databases (Embase and Scopus) we employed specific-subjects headings as advised for each databases. In addition, in order to identify other relevant articles we manually searched the reference lists of eligible articles.

Eligibility criteria

Two reviewers (GA and MA) evaluated the relevant articles using their title and abstracts prior to retrieval of full-text articles. The retrieved full-text articles were further screened according to pre-specified inclusion and exclusion criteria. We resolved disagreements by discussing with a third reviewer (MS).

Inclusion criteria

- Design type -Cross sectional and other observational studies
- Study subject– people living with HIV
- Articles published in English language
- Studies which reported magnitude of depression in PLWHIV
- Articles that assessed risk factors of depression in PLWHIV
- Studies done in east Africa

Exclusion criteria

- We excluded commentaries, editorials, letters, reviews, and interventional studies
- Duplicate studies were also excluded

Methods for data extraction and quality assessment

We used standardized data extraction form to extract data from identified studies. The following information were extracted for each included study: The name of the first author, publication date, study design, associated factors, sample size study setting, tools used for assessing outcome, confounders adjusted for, risk estimate (OR) and their 95% confidence interval. Data extraction from source documents was done independently by two investigators. Disagreements were resolved by consensus.

The quality of included studies was evaluated by using a modified version of the Newcastle-Ottawa Scale (NOS) [33]. Sample representativeness and size, comparability between participants, ascertainment of depressive symptoms, and statistical quality were the domains NOS scale uses to assess the quality of each studies. Actual agreement and agreement beyond chance (unweighted Kappa) were used to evaluate the agreement between the two reviewers. We considered the values 0 as poor agreement,

0.01–0.20 as slight agreement, 0.21– 0.40 as fair agreement, 0.41–0.60 = moderate agreement, 0.61– 0.80 as substantial agreement, and 0.81–1.00 as almost perfect agreement [34].

Data synthesis and analysis

Comprehensive meta-analysis software version3 was used for meta-analysis and forest plots that showed combined estimates with 95%CI. The overall pooled prevalence was estimated by random effect meta-analysis [35]. Heterogeneity was evaluated using Q statistic and the I^2statistics [35]. The magnitude of statistical heterogeneity between studies was assessed using I^2 statistic and values of 25, 50 and 75% were considered to represent low, medium and high, respectively [36]. For the data identified as heterogeneous, a random-effects model was used during analysis. When statistical pooling is not possible, non-pooled data was presented in table form. Meta-regression was performed to explore the potential source of heterogeneity.

The instrument used to assess depression and the country where the studies were conducted were used to determine the possible source of heterogeneity between the studies. In addition, we carried out a leave-one-out sensitivity analysis to evaluate the key studies that exert major impact on between-study heterogeneity. Publication bias was assessed by funnel plot and Egger's regression tests

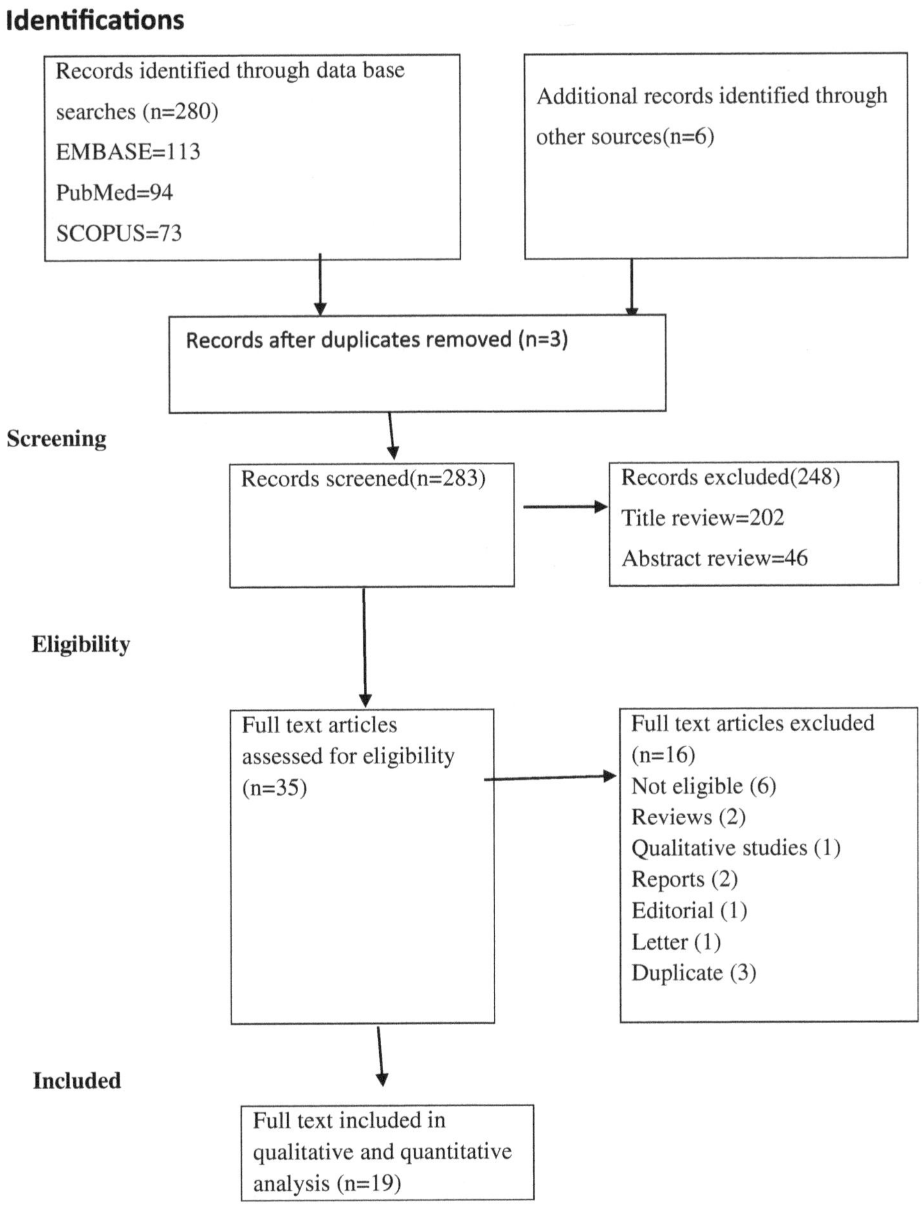

Fig. 1 PRISMA flowchart of review search

Results

Identification of studies

We identified 280 articles in our database search. Our manual search resulted additional six articles. Of these we excluded 205 articles during the review of duplicate and titles as they did not met the inclusion criteria (Fig. 1). In our review of abstracts and keywords we excluded another 46 studies and 19 articles with full-text that met the inclusion criteria were included in our final analysis.

Characteristics of included studies

Among the total of nineteen studies included in our analysis ten of them were done in Uganda [5, 7, 8, 10, 11, 20, 26, 37–39], whereas five of the studies were conducted in Ethiopia [2, 3, 9, 16, 17] and the other studies were conducted in Kenya [18], Tanzania [15], Rwanda [14] and Sudan [40]. The publication year of those studies ranged from 2006 to 2017. All of the included studies used cross-sectional study design. One study used community

Table 1 Distribution of studies on depression in people living with HIV included in qualitative and quantitative analysis based on year, study design, sample size, instrument, country, response rate, study population and prevalence

Author (year) (reference number)	Study design(setting)	Sample size	Tool	Response rate	Country	Sampling	Study population	Outcome (magnitude of depression)
Psaros C. et. al. (2014) [37]	Cross sectional study (institution based)	453	HSC-D	Not reported	Uganda	Used Cohort population sample	adults	38%(*n*=172)
Shumba C, et. al. (2013) [11]	Cross sectional study (Community based study)	732	Self report	Not reported	Uganda	Random sampling (specific technique not reported)	Adults on HAART	59%(*n*=429)
Kinyanda E. et. al. (2017) [5]	Cross sectional study (institution based study)	899	DSM	Not reported	Uganda	Not reported	adults	14%(*n*=126)
Yeneabat T. et. al. (2017) [9]	Cross sectional study (institution)	390	CES-D	Not reported	Ethiopia	Not reported	adults	76.7%(*n*=299)
Kinyanda E. et. al. (2011) [38]	Cross sectional study (institution)	618	DSM-IV	Not reported	Uganda	Not reported	adults	8.1%(*n*=50)
Nakasujja N. et. al. (2010) [39]	Cross sectional study (institution setting)	102	CES-D	Cohort survey	Uganda	Not reported	Adults	53.9%(*n*=55)
Akena D. et. al. (2012) [26]	Cross sectional study (institution setting)	368	PHQ-9	Not reported	Uganda	Simple random sampling	Adults	17.4%(*n*=64)
Hatcher AM. et. al. (2012) [7]	Cross sectional study (institution setting)	270	HSC-D	Not reported	Uganda	Used Cohort population sample	Adults	23.7%(*n*=64)
Cohen MH. et. al. (2009) [14]	Cross sectional study (institution setting)	658	CES-D	Not reported	Rwanda	Used Cohort population sample	Adults	81%(*n*=533)
Musisi S. et. al. (2014) [8]	Cross sectional study (institution setting)	386	PHQ-9	Not reported	Uganda	Used cohort population sample	Adults	30%(n=116)
Tesfaw G. et. al. (2016) [2]	Cross sectional study (institution setting)	417	HADS	100%	Ethiopia	Systematic random sampling	Adults	41.2%(*n*=172)
Elbadawi A. et. al. (2017) [40]	Cross sectional study (institution setting)	362	HADS	Not reported	Sudan	Systematic random sampling	Adults	61.3%(*n*=222)
Eshetu DA. et. al. (2014) [17]	Cross sectional study (institution setting)	416	PHQ-9	Not reported	Ethiopia	Systematic random sampling	Adults	38.94%(*n*=162)
Berhe H. et. al. (2013) [3]	Cross sectional study (institution setting)	269	HAM-D	Not reported	Ethiopia	Not reported	adults	43.9%(*n*=118)
Mohammed M. et. al. (2015) [15]	Cross sectional study (institution setting)	740	PHQ-9	97%	Ethiopia	Systematic random sampling	Adults	45.8%(*n*=339)
MB.ChB.PW (2011) [18]	Cross sectional study (institution setting)	400	BDI	Not reported	Kenya	Systematic random sampling		47.25%(*n*=189)
Marwick KF. et. al. (2010) [15]	Cross sectional study (institution setting)	220	ICD-10	97%	Tanzania	Convenience sampling	Adults	2.7%(*n*=6)
Kahazura FM. et. al. (2006) [20]	Cross sectional study (institution setting)	1017	CES-D	Not reported	Uganda	Used Cohort population sample	Adults	47%(*n*=476)
Mpungu EN. et. al, 2011 [10]	Cross sectional study (institution setting)	500	DSM (MINI)	Not reported	Ugnada	Not clearly indicated	adults	46.4%(232)

Key: *DSM* Diagnostic and Statistical Manual of Mental Disorders, *ICD* International Classification of Disease, *PHQ-9* Patient Health Questionnaire-9, *CES-D* Center for Epidemiologic Studies Depression Scale Revised, *HAM-D* Hamilton Depression Rating Scale, *BDI* Beck's Depression Inventory, *HADS* Hospital Anxiety and Depression Scale, *HSC-D* Hopkins Symptom Checklist for Depression

samples [11] and eighteen studies used samples from institution [2, 3, 5, 7–10, 14–18, 20, 26, 37–40]. Regarding the instrument used, four studies used diagnostic instrument [5, 10, 15, 38], fourteen studies used screening instrument [2, 3, 7–9, 14, 16, 17, 26, 37, 39, 40] and one study used self-report questionnaire to assess depression in PLWHIV [11]. Majority(84.22%) of the studies not reported response rate. Seven studies used random sampling technique, seven used the cohort sample, one study used covenant sampling and four studies not reported the sampling technique (See Table 1).

Quality of included studies

We used a modified version of the Newcastle-Ottawa scale (NOS) scale to evaluate the quality of included studies. The methodological quality was good for all nineteen studies. The risk of selection, measurement and non-response bias was low for all studies. The agreement between reviewers regarding the level of bias was moderate or almost perfect for all studies (Kappa statistic range 0.50-1 (Additional file 1: Table S1).

The results of pooled meta-analysis

Prevalence of depression in people living with HIV (PLWHIV)

Nineteen of the studies provided information regarding the prevalence of depression in PLWHIV in east Africa [1–19] (Table 1). These nineteen studies could be combined to provide the pooled estimates. Based on the results of random-effects method, the pooled prevalence of depression in PLWHIV was 38.00% (95% CI 29.30-47.54) and the heterogeneity was considerable (I^2=98.59%; Q=11276.10, df=18, variance= 0.08, p <0.0001). The forest plots of the prevalence of depression in people living with HIV were shown in Fig. 2.

Subgroup analyses of the prevalence of depression in people living with HIV (PLWHIV)

Subgroup analysis were performed by type of instrument used to assess depression and the country where the studies were conducted as possible source of heterogeneity between the studies as well as to explore the prevalence in each country. For our subgroup analysis based on the country where the studies were conducted, we identified representative data only for Uganda and Ethiopia. For the rest of east African countries (Kenya, Tanzania, Rwanda and Sudan), there is limited data for subgroup analysis.

Of the included studies, ten reported the prevalence of depression in PLWHIV in Uganda [1–4, 6–9, 11, 19, 20]. The pooled prevalence estimates of depression in PLWHIV in Ugandawas30.88% (95% CI 20.84-43.13) (See Table 2).

Study name	Event rate	Lower limit	Upper limit
Mpungu 2011	0.4640	0.4207	0.5079
Psaros 2016	0.3797	0.3361	0.4253
Shumba 2013	0.5861	0.5500	0.6212
Kinyanda 2017	0.1402	0.1190	0.1644
Yeneabat 2017	0.7667	0.7221	0.8060
Kinyanda 2011	0.0809	0.0618	0.1052
Nakajjussa 2016	0.5392	0.4422	0.6333
Akena 2012	0.1739	0.1385	0.2161
Hatcher 2012	0.2370	0.1901	0.2914
Cohen 2009	0.8100	0.7782	0.8382
Musisi 2014	0.3005	0.2568	0.3481
Tesfaw 2016	0.4125	0.3662	0.4604
Elbadawi 2017	0.6133	0.5621	0.6621
Eshetu 2017	0.3894	0.3437	0.4372
Berhe 2015	0.4387	0.3805	0.4986
Mohammed 2015	0.4581	0.4225	0.4942
MB.ChB 2011	0.4725	0.4240	0.5215
Marawik 2010	0.0273	0.0123	0.0594
Kahazura 2006	0.4680	0.4375	0.4988
	0.3800	0.2930	0.4754

Fig. 2 The prevalence of depression in people living with HIV in East Africa: meta-analysis

Table 2 Prevalence of depression in people with HIV in east Africa: Subgroup meta-analysis and heterogeneity analysis

Characteristics	Observation (N)	Prevalence (%)	95% CI	I2	Q	df	*P* value
Geographic location or country							
Uganda	10	30.88	20.84-43.13	98.57%	636.65	9	*P*<0.0001
Ethiopia	5	49.79	37.22-62.38	97.08	136.79	4	*P*<0.0001
Instrument used or tool used							
Diagnostic	4	12.40	4.0-32.80	98.94%	281.77	3	*P*<0.0001
Screening	14	46.00	36.90-55.38	97.96%	638.36	13	*P*<0.0001
Study Setting							
Institution based	18	36.86	27.87-46.86	98.59%	1207.91	17	*P*<0.0001
Sample size							
<400	8	34.20	19.84-52.18	98.32%	416.89	7	*P*<0.0001
>400	11	40.46	29.39-52.60	98.84%	858.66	10	*P*<0.0001
Reference to diagnostic criteria							
DSM/ICD	4	12.40	4.0-32.80	98.94%	281.77	3	*P*<0.0001
PHQ-9	4	32.15	21.58-44.92	96.61%	88.57		*P*<0.0001
HADS	2	51.30	32.20-70.10	96.75%	30.82	1	*P*<0.0001
CES-D	4	66.14	44.34-82.73	98.67%	226.22	3	*P*<0.0001
HSC-D	2	30.50	18.50-46.10	93.51%	14.41	1	*P*<0.0001
Year of publication							
2006-2010	3	33.90	10.17-69.93	99.25%	267.34	2	*P*<0.0001
2011-2013	7	32.03	19.49-47.84	98.52%	406.32	6	*P*<0.0001
2014-2017	9	43.50	31.23-56.69	98.37%	98.37% 489.63	8	*P*<0.0001

Five studies reported the prevalence of depression in PLWHIV in Ethiopia [5, 12, 14–16]. The pooled prevalence of depression in PLWHIV in Ethiopia was 49.79% (95% CI37.22-62.38). (See Table 2). In our analysis the prevalence of depression in PLWHIV in Ethiopia is significantly higher than the prevalent in Uganda (*P*<.00001). For the rest of east African countries, there is limited data for subgroup analysis. We found only one study conducted in each of the other four east African countries such as Kenya [18], Tanzania [15], Rwanda [14] and Sudan [40].

We also performed subgroup analysis based on the instrument used to assess depression. Four studies used diagnostic instrument (DSM or ICD) and [1, 4, 6, 18, 20] and fourteen studies used screening instrument (PHQ-9, HADS, BDI, CES-D, or HSC-D) to assess depression in people living with HIV in east Africa [1, 5, 7–17, 19]. The pooled prevalence of depression in people living with HIV was 12.40% (95% CI 4.0-32.80) and 46% (95% CI 36.90-55.38) for the studies conducted using diagnostic and screening instrument respectively (see Table 2).

Furthermore, we conducted subgroup analysis based on each instrument used to assess depression. The pooled prevalence estimates of depression for the studies conducted using CES-D 66.14% (44.34-82.73) and HADS 51.30% (32.20-70.10) were significantly higher than results of studies conducted using DSM or ICD12.40% (95% CI 4.0-32.80), PHQ-9 32.15% (21.58-44.92), and HSC-D 30.50% (18.50-46.10) (see Table 2).

Finally, we performed subgroup analysis based on the setting where the studies were conducted. The pooled prevalence of depression in people living with HIV in east Africa for institution based studies was 36.86% (95% CI 27.87-46.86) (see Table 2).

Publication bias

The funnel plot and Egger's regression tests (B=-9.17, SE=6.16, P=0.155) provided no evidence of substantial publication bias for the prevalence of depression in PLWHIV in east Africa (Fig. 3).

Sensitivity analysis

For the purpose of further investigating potential source of heterogeneity in the analysis of the prevalence of depression in PLWHIV, we performed leave-one-out sensitivity analysis. Our sensitivity analysis showed that our findings were strong and not dependent on a single study. Our pooled estimated prevalence varied between 35.86(27.53-44.25) and 41.39(32.33-51.07) after deletion of a single study (see Table 3).

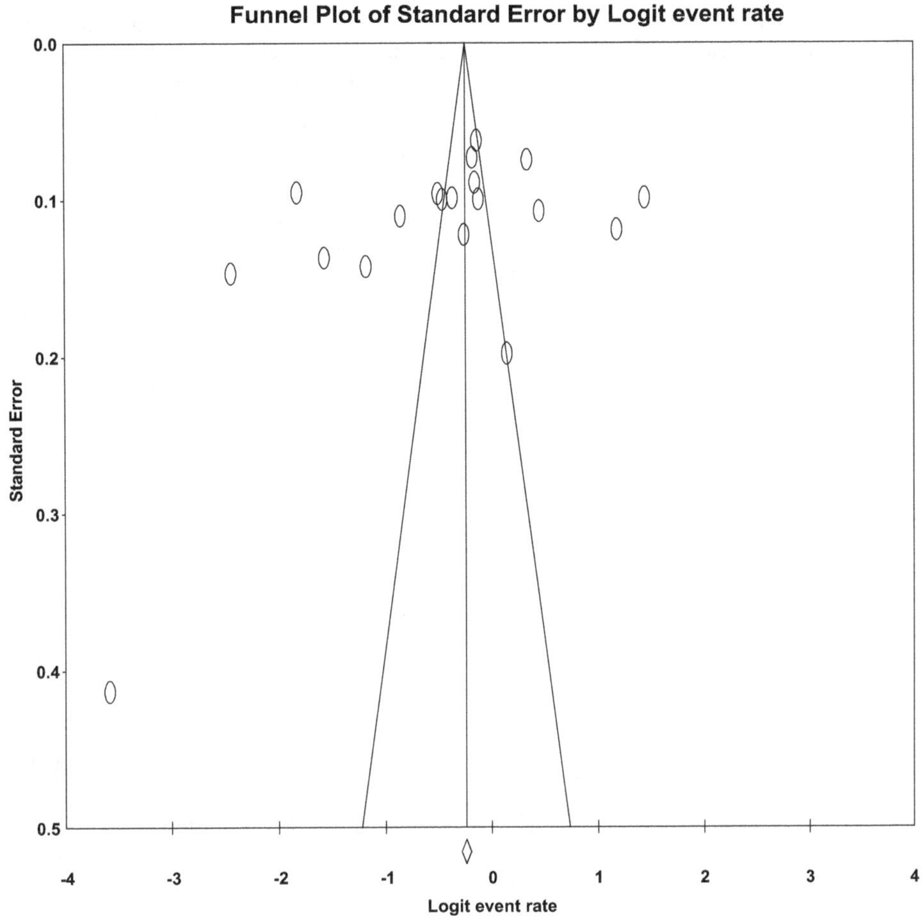

Fig 3 Funnel plot of risk of publication bias for the prevalence of depression in PLWHIV in east Africa

Determinants of depression in people living with HIV

Of 19 included studies, 11 studies that reported factors associated with depression in peoples living with HIV in east Africa were included in the qualitative analysis [2, 3, 5, 7, 9, 10, 16, 17, 20, 26, 38] (See Table 4). Association between WHO clinical staging of disease and depression was observed in three studies [2, 10, 17].

In the current review presence of opportunistic infection [9], perceived stigma [2, 20], negative life event [38], WHO clinical staging of disease [17], hospitalization in the past one month [17], stressful life events [38], food insecurity [9], mean self-efficacy (>80%) [41], missed frequency of clinic visit one to three weeks [16], frequency of follow-up [16], older age (age 60-69) [17], income less than 200 Ethiopian birr [3, 17], urban residence [3] and government employee [3] were strongly and significantly associated with depression in people living with HIV in east Africa (See Table 4).

Discussion

To our knowledge, this is the first systematic review and meta-analysis of depression and determinants in PLWHIV in east Africa. The main aim of the study was identification of epidemiological information on the overall prevalence and common determinants of depression in PLWHIV in the area. It is also believed that the results of this review provide greater precision than the results of the studies individually considered. Nineteen studies that analyzed the prevalence of depression and associated factors in PLWHIV in east Africa were included.

The pooled prevalence estimate of depression in this meta-analysis was found a to be 38% in PLWHIV. The magnitude of depression in PLWHIV differed by the setting and the country where the studies were conducted as well as the type of instrument used to measure depression. When measured by DSM or ICD the estimated pooled prevalence of major depressive disorder appeared to be 12.40 % , but the pooled prevalence of depression was 46% as measured by screening instruments. The magnitude of major depressive disorder in PLWHIV in our meta-analysis is much higher compared with the 4% found in the general population [42].

Table 3 Sensitivity analysis of prevalence for each study being removed at a time: prevalence and 95% confidence interval of depression in people living with HIV in east Africa

Study excluded	Prevalence	95%CI
Mpungu 2011	37.49	28.32–47.66
Psaros 2016	37.96	28.79–48.08
Shumba 2013	36.86	27.87–46.86
Kinyanda 2017	39.90	31.51–48.94
Yeneabat 2017	35.86	27.53–45.14
Kinyanda 2011	40.67	32.13–49.82
Nakajjussa 2016	37.17	28.31–46.99
Akena 2012	39.44	30.52–49.11
Hatcher 2012	38.89	29.88–48.74
Cohen 2009	35.59	27.78–44.25
Musisi 2014	38.45	29.67–48.42
Tesfaw 2016	37.78	28.63–47.89
Elbadawi 2017	36.74	27.90–46.56
Eshetu 2017	37.91	28.76–48.01
Berhe 2015	37.65	28.60–47.65
Mohammed 2015	37.50	28.19–47.84
MB.ChB 2011	37.46	28.36–47.54
Marawik 2010	41.39	32.33–51.07
Kahazura 2006	37.43	27.98–47.95

Key. The analysis is based on random effect model

Our estimated pooled prevalence of depression (38%) was higher than the results of systematic review and meta-analysis studies in sub-Saharan Africa which reported the pooled prevalence estimates of depression was 19% in people living HIV with sub-Saharan Africa [22]. These difference might be due to the socioeconomic and cultural differences of the countries.

In our study the pooled prevalence estimates of depression in PLWHIV in Ethiopia (49.79%) was significantly higher than the pooled prevalence estimates of depression in Uganda(30.88%). The difference might be due to all studies done in Ethiopia used screening instrument to determine depression and based on the pooled prevalence estimate, the prevalence of depression measured by screening instrument(46%) was higher than the prevalence of depression measured by diagnostic instrument (12.40%).

As expected, the magnitude of depression showed a considerable variations depending on the measurement used to determine depression in PLWHIV. The pooled prevalence of depression in PLWHIV was apparently higher in studies conducted using screening instrument than diagnostic instrument. The estimated pooled prevalence of depression in PLWHIV was found to be 66.14% , 51.30%, 12.40%, 32.15% and 30.50% as measured by CES-D, HADS, DSM or ICD, PHQ-9, and HSC-D respectively. The fact that diagnostic instrument give more weights towards the high specificity as compared to screening instrument which gives more emphasis towards high sensitivity might be the main reason for the observed difference. The other possible explanation might be diagnostic instrument uses strict criteria as compared to screening instrument as screening instrument aimed to identify potential indicators for disease or potential disease rather than establishing the presence or absence of disease which is the main purpose of diagnostic instrument. Finally, the possible interpretation for the variation in magnitude of depression among the different screening instrument may be due to difference in the sensitivity and specificity the tools used to screen depression in PLWHIV. The findings support the view that validation and use of standard instrument for screening as well as diagnosis of depression in PLWHIV.

Moreover, in our subgroup analysis of prevalence in PLWHIV by study setting show the pooled prevalence of depression in PLWHIV for the studies conducted institution-based setting was 36.86%. This results are lower than unpooled results of depression in community setting which reported magnitude of depression 59%. (see Tables 1 and 2). The fact that the community based study included in this review used self report of depression and all institution based studies used standard diagnostic or screening instrument to assess depression might be the possible reason for the observed difference in magnitude of depression in clinical and community based settings. In addition, the community based study is only one study so the observed result might be highly biased as it is self-report. The study suggest replication of studies in community samples to strengthen our finding as well as understanding of the precise estimates of depression in PLWHIV.

Concerning associated factors, Our qualitative synthesis showed that factors such as having opportunistic infection, perceived stigma, negative life event, WHO clinical staging of disease, hospitalization in the past one month, stressful life events, food insecurity, self-efficacy, missed frequency of clinic visit, frequency of follow-up, older age, low income, urban residence and being government employee were strongly and significantly associated with depression in people living with HIV in east Africa.

Difference between studies

The variation between the studies included in our systematic review and meta-analysis led to high level of heterogeneity in our analysis. The possible contributing factors for the variance in prevalence rates of depression in PLWHIV in east Africa includes the instrument used to measure depression, the study setting and populations. We conducted leave-one-out sensitivity analysis for the purpose of further investigating potential source of heterogeneity in the analysis of the prevalence of depression in PLWHIV. Our

Table 4 Characteristics of factors associated with depression in people living with HIV east Africa by their odds ratio, confidence interval strength of association, author and year

Factors	Odds ratio (AOR)	95% Confidence interval	Strength of association	Adjusted for	Author, year
Past history of mania	2.73	1.16–6.40	Moderate, negative	Gender, age, educational status, income, social support, self-efficacy, cognitive impairment, current alcohol use, current alcohol use disorder, duration of ART, CD4 count, WHO clinical staging of HIV disease, tuberculosis	Mpungu, 2011
Mean self efficacy score > 89%	0.61	0.41–0.90	Strong, negative	Gender, age, educational status, income, social support, mania, cognitive impairment, current alcohol use, current alcohol use disorder, duration of ART, CD4 count, WHO clinical staging of HIV disease, tuberculosis	Mpungu, 2011
WHO clinical staging of HIV disease	1.88	1.24–2.44	Moderate, positive	Gender, age, educational status, income, social support, mania, self-efficacy, cognitive impairment, current alcohol use, current alcohol use disorder, duration of ART, CD4 count, mania, tuberculosis	Mpungu, 2011
Tuberculosis	2.37	1.20–4.66	Moderate, positive	Gender, age, educational status, income, social support, mania, self-efficacy, cognitive impairment, current alcohol use, current alcohol use disorder, duration of ART, CD4 count, mania, WHO clinical staging of HIV disease	Mpungu, 2011
Age group 40–49	0.95	0.92–0.98	Strong, negative	AIDS stigma, CD4 counts, sex	Akena, 2012
AIDS stigma	1.65	1.20–1.26	Moderate, positive	Age, CD4 counts, sex	Akena, 2012
CD4 count	0.43	0.20–0.91	Moderate, negative	Age, AIDS stigma, sex	Akena, 2012
Not have enough food security	2.89	1.40–5.98	Moderate, positive	Distance from HIV clinic, When knew HIV status, On ART, social support, negative life events, stress score index	Kinyanda. 2011
Negative life event score 6–10	4.89	1.83–10.06	Strong, positive	Distance from HIV clinic, When knew HIV status, On ART, social support, food security, stress score index	Kinyanda. 2011
Negative life event score 6–11+	16.67	7.01–39.66	Strong, positive	Distance from HIV clinic, When knew HIV status, On ART, social support, food security, stress score index	Kinyanda. 2011
Stress score index> 10	7.18	2.65–19.47	Strong, positive	Distance from HIV clinic, When knew HIV status, On ART, social support, food security, negative life event	Kinyanda. 2011
Food insecurity	3.83	1.58–9.32	Strong, positive	Sex, age educational status, marital status, occupation, residence, number of dependent children, access to food aids, practice of agriculture, ownership of livestock, CD4 level, OIs	Yeneabat, 2017
Presence of OIs	5.20	1.34–20.16	Strong, negative	Sex, age educational status, marital status, occupation, residence, number of dependent children, access to food aids, practice of agriculture, ownership of livestock, CD4 level, food insecurity	Yeneabat, 2017
HIV stage three	2.80	1.50–5.21	Moderate, positive	Age, educational status, marital status, residence, CD4 level, perceived stigma, medication adherence, social support	Tesfaw, 2016
Perceived stigma	3.60	2.23–5.80	Strong, positive	Age, educational status, marital status, residence, CD4 level, HIV stage, medication adherence, socia; support	Tesfaw, 2016
Medication adherence	1.61	1.02–2.55	Moderate, positive	Age, educational status, marital status, residence, CD4 level, HIV stage, social support	Tesfaw, 2016
Social support	2.02	1.25–3.27	Moderate, positive	Age, educational status, marital status, residence, CD4 level, HIV stage, medication adherence	Tesfaw, 2016

Table 4 Characteristics of factors associated with depression in people living with HIV east Africa by their odds ratio, confidence interval strength of association, author and year *(Continued)*

Factors	Odds ratio (AOR)	95% Confidence interval	Strength of association	Adjusted for	Author, year
Married	0.01	0.01–0.07	Weak, positive	Sexual relationship power scale, age, educational status, heavy drinking, tobacco use, WHO HIV stage, CD4 count, previously treated with ART	Hatcher, 2012
Resilience score	1.28	1.12–1.45	Weak, positive	Study site, age, sex, stigma score, childhood trauma score, negative coping score, negative life event experience	Kinyanda, 2017
Stigma score	1.37	1.08–1.73	Weak, positive	Study site, age, sex, resilience childhood trauma score, negative coping score, negative life event experience	Kinyanda, 2017
Childhood trauma score	1.25	1.02–1.55	Weak, positive	Study site, age, sex, resilience stigma score, negative coping score, negative life event experience	Kinyanda, 2017
Negative scoping score	1.50	1.17–1.92	Moderate, positive	Study site, age, sex, resilience stigma score, childhood trauma, negative life event experience	Kinyanda, 2017
Negative life experience score	1.81	1.46–2.25	Moderate, positive	Study site, age, sex, resilience stigma score, childhood trauma, *negative scoring score*	Kinyanda, 2017
Male sex	1.633	1.138–2.342	Moderate, positive	Marital status,income, verbal stigma, missed frequency of clinic visit, frequency of clinic visit/month	Mohammed, 2016
Monthly income<500eth.birr	1.924	1.159,3.195	Moderate, positive	Marital status, sex,, verbal stigma, missed frequency of clinic visit, frequency of clinic visit/month	Mohammed, 2016
Had verbal stigma	2.705	1.445,5.063	Moderate, positive	Marital status, sex,, verbal stigma, missed frequency of clinic visit, frequency of clinic visit/month	Mohammed, 2016
Missed frequency of clinic visit past one,two and three weeks	4.35 4.56 and 3.75 respectively	2.20–8.59, 2.42–8.58 and 1.39–9.93 respectively	Strong, positive	Marital status, sex,, verbal stigma, frequency of clinic visit/month	Mohammed, 2016
Once, twice and three times frequency of clinic visit/month	19.033, 13.784 and 22.729	2.095–172.878, 1.430–132.871, and 2.450–210.873 respectively	Strong, positive	Marital status, sex,, verbal stigma, verbal stigma, missed frequency of clinic visit	Mohammed, 2016
Female sex	2.071	1.077–3.985	Moderate, positive	Age, income, HIV stage, hospitalization in past one month, felt stigmatized	Eshetu 2015
Age 30–39	2.761	1.165–6.540	Moderate, positive	Sex, Income, HIV stage, hospitalization in past one month, felt stigmatized	Eshetu 2015
Age 50–59	2.596	1.49–9.94	Moderate, positive	Sex, Income, HIV stage, hospitalization in past one month, felt stigmatized	Eshetu 2015
Age 60–69	19.645	4.02–95.99	Strong, positive	Sex, Income, HIV stage, hospitalization in past one month, felt stigmatized	Eshetu 2015
Income < 200 Birr	3.917	1.559, 9.845	Strong, positive	Age,Sex, HIV stage, hospitalization in past one month, felt stigmatized	Eshetu 2015
Income201–400 Birr	2.796	1.139–6.865	Moderate, positive	Age, Sex, HIV stage, hospitalization in past one month, felt stigmatized	Eshetu 2015
Income 401–700 Birr	2.590	1.058–6.340	Moderate, positive	Age, Sex, HIV stage, hospitalization in past one month, felt stigmatized	Eshetu 2015
HIVStage III	2.317	1.108–4.85	Moderate, positive	Age, Sex, income hospitalization in past one month, felt stigmatized	Eshetu 2015
HIV Stage Iv	8.769	1.93–39.87	Strong, positive	Age, Sex, income hospitalization in past one month, felt stigmatized	Eshetu 2015
Hospitalized in the past one Month	15.26	1.463–159.22	Strong, positive	Age, Sex, income month, felt stigmatized, HIVStage	Eshetu 2015

Table 4 Characteristics of factors associated with depression in people living with HIV east Africa by their odds ratio, confidence interval strength of association, author and year *(Continued)*

Factors	Odds ratio (AOR)	95% Confidence interval	Strength of association	Adjusted for	Author, year
Felt stigmatized	3.597	1.86–6.95	Strong, positive	Age, Sex, income month,, HIVStage, hospitalized in the past one Month	Eshetu 2015
Age > 50 years	1.93	1.09–3.42	Moderate, positive	Religion, education, marital status, sex, source of income, CD4 level, HIVStage, number of living children	Kaharuza, 2006
Pensions as source of income	1.81	1.24–2.66	Moderate, positive	Religion, education, marital status, sex, CD4 level, HIVStage, number of living children, age	Kaharuza, 2006
Primary education	1.69	1.12–2.52	Moderate, positive	Religion, marital status, sex, CD4 level, HIVStage, number of living children, age, source of income	Kaharuza, 2006
CD4 count 50–99	2.02	1.22–3.36	Moderate, positive	Religion, marital status, sex, education, HIVStage, number of living children, age, source of income	Kaharuza, 2006
CD4 count < 50	2.34	1.39–3.93	Moderate, positive	Religion, education, marital status, sex, HIVStage, number of living children, age, source of income	Kaharuza, 2006
Urban residence	3.19	1.50–6.65	Strong, positive	Sex, marital status, income, educational status, occupation, CD4 level	Berhe, 2013
Income < 200 ETB	4.43	1.35–14.58	Strong, positive	Sex, residence, marital status,, educational status, occupation, CD4 level	Berhe, 2013
Unemployed	2.74	1.34–5.57	Moderate, positive	Sex, residence, marital status, educational status, CD4 level	Berhe, 2013
Government employee	3.56	1.73–7.30	Strong, positive	Sex, residence, marital status, educational status, CD4 level	Berhe, 2013

sensitivity analysis showed that our findings were strong and not dependent on a single study.

Strength and limitations

The strength of the study includes the use of predefined search strategy in order to reduce reviewers bias as well as performing data extraction and quality assessment by two independent reviewers to minimize the possible reviewer bias. The other strength is performing sensitivity and subgroup analysis based on study setting, instrument used, and country of study to identify the small study effect and the risk of heterogeneity. Finally, evaluating the quality of the studies included in analysis and based on the results from the assessment of the study quality the methodological quality was generally good. Nevertheless, the study has some limitations: first, small number of studies were included in our subgroup analysis which reduce the precision of the estimate; second, apparent heterogeneity was identified among the studies; due to inconsistent adjustment and inclusion of factors determining depression in PLWHIV we done only qualitative analysis for associated factors of depression.

Conclusion

Our study found that the pooled prevalence estimate of depression in PLWHIV was 38% (95% CI 29.30-47.54). In our study the pooled prevalence estimates of depression in PLWHIV in Ethiopia was significantly higher than the pooled prevalence estimates of depression in Uganda. In addition the prevalence of depression was significantly higher in studies conducted by using screening as compared to diagnostic instrument. The study also resulted in a significant variation in prevalence of depression based on the instrument used. These findings have several implications for clinical practice and research. Based on this finding routine screening and integrated management of mental health condition into the existing HIV care services is warranted in east Africa. Validation and use of standard instrument to assess depression in PLWHIV is needed. In addition longitudinal and community based studies focusing on incidence and determinates of depression in PLWHIV are recommended. Attention need to be given for those people who have opportunistic infection, older age, advanced HIV stage, experienced stressful life events,who have perceived stigma and those who are on ART to prevent risk of non-adherence and treatment resistance and further to improve the quality PLWHIV.

Abbreviations

BDI: Beck's Depression Inventory; CES-D: Center for Epidemiologic Studies Depression Scale Revised; DSM: Diagnostic and Statistical Manual of Mental Disorders; HADS: Hospital Anxiety and Depression Scale; HAM-D: Hamilton Depression Rating Scale; HIV: Human Immunodeficiency Virus; HSC-D: Hopkins Symptom Checklist for Depression; ICD: International Classification of Disease; PHQ-9: Patient Health Questionnaire-9,; PLWHIV: people living with Human Immunodeficiency Virus

Authors' contributions

The author (GA) performed the search, data extraction, analyses and draft and approval of final manuscript. MA performed data extraction, quality assessment and approved final manuscript. MS participated in discussion and consensus and approved the final manuscript.

Consent for publication

N/A.

Competing interests

The authors declare that they have no competing interests.

Author details

[1]Research and Training Department, Amanuel Mental Specialized Hospital, Addis Ababa, Ethiopia. [2]Department of Psychiatry, Paulo's millennium medical college, Addis Ababa, Ethiopia.

References

1. Feuillet P, Lert F, Tron L, Aubriere C, Spire B, Dray-Spira R. Prevalence of and factors associated with depression among people living with HIV in France. Hiv Medicine. 2017;18(6):383–94.
2. Tesfaw G, Ayano G, Awoke T, Assefa D, Birhanu Z, Miheretie G, et al. Prevalence and correlates of depression and anxiety among patients with HIV on-follow up at Alert Hospital, Addis Ababa. Ethiopia. BMC psychiatry. 2016;16(1):368.
3. Berhe H, Bayray A. Prevalence of depression and associated factors among people living with HIV/AIDS in tigray, North Ethiopia: A cross sectional hospital based study. International Journal of Pharmaceutical Sciences and Research. 2013;4(2):761–71.
4. Kinyanda E, Kuteesa M, Scholten F, Mugisha J, Baisley K, Seeley J. Risk of major depressive disorder among older persons living in HIV-endemic central and southwestern Uganda. AIDS care. 2016;28(12):1516–21.
5. Kinyanda E, Nakasujja N, Levin J, Birabwa H, Mpango R, Grosskurth H, et al. Major depressive disorder and suicidality in early HIV infection and its association with risk factors and negative outcomes as seen in semi-urban and rural Uganda. Journal of affective disorders. 2017;212:117–27.
6. Peterson K, Togun T, Klis S, Menten J, Colebunders R. Depression and posttraumatic stress disorder among HIV-infected Gambians on antiretroviral therapy. AIDS Patient Care STDs. 2012;26(10):589–96.
7. Hatcher AM, Tsai AC, Kumbakumba E, Dworkin SL, Hunt PW, Martin JN, et al. Sexual relationship power and depression among HIV-infected women in Rural Uganda. PloS one. 2012;7(12):e49821.
8. Musisi S, Wagner GJ, Ghosh-Dastidar B, Nakasujja N, Dickens A, Okello E. Depression and sexual risk behaviour among clients about to start HIV antiretroviral therapy in Uganda. International journal of STD & AIDS. 2014;25(2):130–7.
9. Yeneabat T, Bedaso A, Amare T. Factors associated with depressive symptoms in people living with HIV attending antiretroviral clinic at Fitche Zonal Hospital, Central Ethiopia: Cross-sectional study conducted in 2012. Neuropsychiatric Disease and Treatment. 2017;13:2125–31.
10. Nanni MG, Caruso R, Mitchell AJ, Meggiolaro E, Grassi L. Depression in HIV infected patients: a review. Curr Psychiatry Rep. 2015;17(1):530.
11. Shumba C, Atukunda R, Imakit R, Memiah P. Prevalence of depressive symptoms amongst highly active antiretroviral therapy (HAART) patients in AIDSrelief Uganda. Journal of Public Health in Africa. 2013;4(2):84–7.
12. Niu L, Luo D, Liu Y, Silenzio VMB, Xiao S. The Mental Health of People Living with HIV in China, 1998–2014: A Systematic Review. PLOS ONE. 2016;11(4):e0153489.
13. Wang T, Fu H, Kaminga AC, Li Z, Guo G, Chen L, et al. Prevalence of depression or depressive symptoms among people living with HIV/AIDS in China: a systematic review and meta-analysis. BMC Psychiatry. 2018;18(1):160.
14. Cohen MH, Fabri M, Cai X, Shi Q, Hoover DR, Binagwaho A, et al. Prevalence and predictors of posttraumatic stress disorder and depression in HIV-infected and at-risk Rwandan women. Journal of women's health (2002). 2009;18(11):1783–91.
15. Marwick KF, Kaaya SF. Prevalence of depression and anxiety disorders in HIV-positive outpatients in rural Tanzania. AIDS care. 2010;22(4):415–9.
16. Mohammed M, Mengistie B, Dessie Y, Godana W. Prevalence of depression and associated factors among HIV patients seeking treatments in ART clinics at Harar Town. Eastern Ethiopia. J AIDS Clin Res. 2015;6(474):2.
17. Eshetu DA, Meseret S, Kebede MA, Techane GN, Gizachew KD, Tegegne MT, et al. Prevalence of depression and associated factors among HIV/AIDS Patients attending ART Clinic at Debrebirhan referral hospital, North Showa, Amhara Region, Ethiopia. Clin Psychiatry. 2015;1(1):1–7.
18. Ng'ang'a PW. Mathai M. and Obondo A. Prevalence of anxiety and depression among hiv/aids patients attending the comprehensive care centre (ccc), Kenyatta national hospital (knh). Grey literature. 2011.
19. Belete A, Andaregie G, Tareke M, Birhan T, Azale T. Prevalence of anxiety and associated factors among people living HIV/AIDS at debretabor general hospital anti retro viral clinic Debretabor, Amhara, Ethiopia, 2014. American Journal of Psychiatry and Neuroscience. 2014;2(6):109–14.
20. Kaharuza FM, Bunnell R, Moss S, Purcell DW, Bikaako-Kajura W, Wamai N, et al. Depression and CD4 cell count among persons with HIV infection in Uganda. AIDS and behavior. 2006;10(4 Suppl):S105–11.
21. Global, regional, and national incidence, prevalence, and years lived with disability for 310 diseases and injuries, 1990-2015: a systematic analysis for the Global Burden of Disease Study 2015. Lancet. 2016; 388(10053):1545-602.
22. Bernard C, Dabis F, de Rekeneire N. Prevalence and factors associated with depression in people living with HIV in sub-Saharan Africa: A systematic review and meta-analysis. PloS one. 2017;12(8):e0181960.
23. Adewuya AO, Afolabi MO, Ola BA, Ogundele OA, Ajibare AO, Oladipo BF, et al. Relationship between depression and quality of life in persons with HIV infection in Nigeria. The International Journal of Psychiatry in Medicine. 2008;38(1):43–51.
24. Nakimuli-Mpungu E, Musisi S, Katabira E, Nachega J, Bass J. Prevalence and factors associated with depressive disorders in an HIV+ rural patient population in southern Uganda. Journal of affective disorders. 2011;135(1):160–7.
25. Olley BO, Seedat S, Stein DJ. Persistence of psychiatric disorders in a cohort of HIV/AIDS patients in South Africa: a 6-month follow-up study. Journal of psychosomatic research. 2006;61(4):479–84.
26. Akena D, Musisi S, Joska J, Stein DJ. The association between aids related stigma and major depressive disorder among HIV-positive individuals in Uganda. PloS one. 2012;7(11):e48671.
27. Olley B, Seedat S, Nei D, Stein D. Predictors of major depression in recently diagnosed patients with HIV/AIDS in South Africa. AIDS patient care and STDs. 2004;18(8):481–7.
28. Sin NL, DiMatteo MR. Depression treatment enhances adherence to antiretroviral therapy: a meta-analysis. Annals of Behavioral Medicine. 2014; 47(3):259–69.
29. Gonzalez JS, Batchelder AW, Psaros C, Safren SA. Depression and HIV/AIDS treatment nonadherence: a review and meta-analysis. Journal of acquired immune deficiency syndromes (1999). 2011;58(2):181–7.
30. Hartzell JD, Janke IE, Weintrob AC. Impact of depression on HIV outcomes in the HAART era. Journal of Antimicrobial Chemotherapy. 2008;62(2):246–55.
31. Asangbeh SL, Sobngwi JL, Ekali GL, Eyoum C, Msellati P. Predictors of depression among patients on art in a rural health district in North West Cameroon. AIDS care. 2016;28(2):205–8.
32. Reviews UoYCf, Dissemination. Systematic reviews: CRD's guidance for undertaking reviews in health care. University of York: Centre for Reviews & Dissemination; 2009.
33. Stang A. Critical evaluation of the Newcastle-Ottawa scale for the assessment of the quality of nonrandomized studies in meta-analyses. European journal of epidemiology. 2010;25(9):603–5.
34. Landis JR, Koch GG. The measurement of observer agreement for categorical data. Biometrics. 1977;33:159–74.
35. Borenstein M, Hedges LV, Higgins J, Rothstein HR. A basic introduction to fixed-effect and random-effects models for meta-analysis. Research synthesis methods. 2010;1(2):97–111.
36. Higgins JP, Thompson SG, Deeks JJ, Altman DG. Measuring inconsistency in meta-analyses. BMJ: British Medical Journal. 2003;327(7414):557.
37. Psaros C, Haberer JE, Boum Y II, Tsai AC, Martin JN, Hunt PW, et al. The Factor Structure and Presentation of Depression Among HIV-Positive Adults in Uganda. AIDS and behavior. 2014;19(1):27–33.
38. Kinyanda E, Hoskins S, Nakku J, Nawaz S, Patel V. Prevalence and risk factors of major depressive disorder in HIV/AIDS as seen in semi-urban Entebbe district. Uganda. BMC psychiatry. 2011;11:205.
39. Nakasujja N, Skolasky RL, Musisi S, Allebeck P, Robertson K, Ronald A, et al. Depression symptoms and cognitive function among individuals with advanced HIV infection initiating HAART in Uganda. BMC psychiatry. 2010;10:44.

40. Elbadawi A, Mirghani H. Depression among HIV/AIDS Sudanese patients: a cross-sectional analytic study. The Pan African medical journal. 2017;26:43.
41. Nakimuli-Mpungu E, Mojtabai R, Alexandre PK, Musisi S, Katabira E, Nachega JB, et al. Lifetime depressive disorders and adherence to anti-retroviral therapy in HIV-infected Ugandan adults: A case-control study. Journal of affective disorders. 2013;145(2):221–6.
42. Waraich P, Goldner EM, Somers JM, Hsu L. Prevalence and incidence studies of mood disorders: a systematic review of the literature. Canadian journal of psychiatry Revue canadienne de psychiatrie. 2004;49(2):124–38.

Plasma nesfatin-1 level is associated with severity of depression in Chinese depressive patients

Min-Min Xiao[1,2], Jiang-Bo Li[3], Lan-Lan Jiang[2], Hui Shao[2] and Bao-Long Wang[1*]

Abstract

Background: Nesfatin-1 plays a role in the regulation of emotional states like depression. The aim of this study was to investigate the plasma nesfatin-1levels in Chinese patients with depression and healthy subjects, and to determine the possible association between the plasma nesfatin-1 level and the severity of depression.

Methods: A total of 103 depressive patients and 32 healthy subjects were assessed. According to HAMD-17scores, 51, 18, and 34 patients were enrolled in the mild depression, moderate depression, and severe depression groups, respectively. Plasma nesfatin-1 levels were determined by the ELISA method. Differences between groups were compared and associations between plasma nesfatin-1 and other variables were analyzed.

Results: The plasma nesfatin-1 was significantly positively correlated with HAMD-17 score ($r = 0.651$). Compared with healthy controls (8.11 ± 3.31 ng/mL), the plasma nesfatin-1 level significantly increased in patients with mild depression (11.17 ± 3.58 ng/mL), with moderate depression (16.33 ± 8.78 ng/mL), and with severe depression (27.65 ± 8.26 ng/mL) respectively. Plasma nesfatin-1 level (Odds ratio [OR] = 1.269) was an independent indicator for severe depression by multivariate logistic regression analysis.

Conclusion: The plasma nesfatin-1 level is positively correlated with the severity of depression. Plasma nesfatin-1 level may be a potential indicator for depression severity.

Keywords: Plasma nesfatin-1, Depression, Severity

Background

Depression is a state of low mood and demotivated condition that affects a person's feelings, cognition, and behaviors. Major depressive disorder is the most common of serious psychiatric disorders and is recognized to be a high risk factor of suicide [1]. Thus, evaluating the severity of depression is crucial for treatment [2]. In patients diagnosed with depression, Hamilton Rating Scale for depression (HAMD) is a widely used, standardized, clinician administered questionnaire to assess and rate the severity of depression. However, there are no commonly accepted depression biomarkers to improve diagnostic accuracy or to evaluate severity ratings [3]. Although the cellular and molecular mechanisms underlying the pathophysiology of depression are not been fully elucidated, there have been increasing interests in associations between depression and changes in various biochemical pathways, including inflammatory, neurotrophic and hypothalamic-pituitary-adrenal (HPA) axis alterations [4, 5].

* Correspondence: wbl196555@163.com
[1]Clinical Laboratory, Affiliated Provincial Hospital of Anhui Medical University, 17 Lujiang Road, Hefei 230001, Anhui, China
Full list of author information is available at the end of the article

Nesfatin-1, a newly discovered hormone, was derived from nucleobindin-2 (NUCB2). Some previous studies have reported that nesfatin-1 played a role in integrating feeding, glucose homeostasis, and energy expenditure [6, 7]. Furthermore, the nesfatin-1 role in the regulation of emotional states including anxiety and stress was also be found [8]. The plasma level and mRNA expression of nesfatin-1 were increased by acute stress in rats [9]. In fact, nesfatin-1 can activate the HPA axis, the hyperactivity of which is proposed to be among the causal factors for triggering depressive episodes [10]. Because of the dysfunction of the HPA axes, with the important role of nesfatin-1 in the pathophysiology of depression [11], we hypothesized that the plasma nesfatin-1 level may be associated with depression severity. Thus, the aim of this study was to investigate the levels of plasma nesfatin-1 in Chinese patients with depression and healthy subjects, and to determine the possible association between the plasma nesfatin-1 level and the severity of depression.

Methods

Study population

All subjects in the depressive group were recruited from the outpatient department of psychological consultation and treatment center, the Second People's Hospital of Wuhu City from January 2016 to April 2017. The inclusion criteria were the following: a) HAMD-17scores > 7; b) meeting diagnostic criteria for depression according to the Diagnostic and Statistical Manual for Psychiatric Disorders-Fourth Version. The exclusion criteria were the following: a) unstable psychiatric features; b) currently suffering from a severe medical condition; c) currently pregnant or lactating; d) presence of comorbid psychotic disorder, psychotic symptoms, psychoactive substance dependency or abuse, personality disorder, or mental retardation; e) received psychotropic medication within 2 weeks; f) had a history of bariatric surgery or any gastric disease; g) diagnosed of diabetes mellitus; h) FT3, FT4 or TSH was abnormal.

All subjects in the control group were recruited from the annual health examination of the Second People's Hospital of Wuhu City. The inclusion criteria were the following: a) no mental disorders after being evaluated by psychiatrists; b) no family history of mental disorders and no history of taking psychiatric drugs; c) HAMD-17 scores ≤7. Exclusion criteria were the following: a) history of stroke or central nervous system disease; b) pregnant or lactating women.

The protocol was approved by the Ethical Committee of the Second People's Hospital of Wuhu City. All subjects signed written informed consent in accordance with the Declaration of Helsinki.

Measurements

The body mass index (BMI) of all participants were calculated. All blood samples from a forearm vein were collected in the morning following one night of fasting by 5-mL tubes containing EDTA. All plasma samples were obtained after centrifugation (3000×g for 5 min at 4 °C) and stored at − 80 °C until the time of assay.

The level of plasma nesfatin-1 was measured by ELISA kit from USCN Life Science Instruments (Wuhan, China) according to the manufacturer's instructions. Thyroid Stimulating Hormone (TSH), free triiodothyronine (FT3), and free thyroxine (FT4) were assayed using an automatic electrochemistry luminescence immunoassay system (Roche Cobas E601, Mannheim, Germany). Fasting plasma glucose (FBG), triglycerides (TG), total cholesterol (TC), low-density lipoprotein cholesterol (LDL-C), and high-density lipoprotein cholesterol (HDL-C) were measured by an automatic analyzer (Beckman AU5800, Tokyo, Japan) according to the standard techniques.

17-item Hamilton Depression Rating Scale(HAMD-17) was examined for all subjects [12]. The severity of depressive symptom was classified by the following severity range for HAMD-17 score: mild depression (8–17), moderate depression (18–24), and severe depression (> 24) [13].

Statistical analysis

Distributions of data were tested for normality using the Shapiro-Wilk test. The continuous variables were presented as mean ± standard deviation and were analyzed with the one-way ANOVA. The Chi-squared test was employed for percentages of variables. Relationships between plasma nesfatin-1 and other variables were analyzed by Spearman correlation analysis and the independent relationships were determined by multivariate linear regression analysis. A multivariate logistic regression analysis was performed to validate the risk factors of depression severity. The receiver operating characteristic (ROC) curve analysis was used to determine the cut-off value of plasma nesfatin-1. Statistical analysis

Table 1 Comparison of mean values (or ratios) of study variables in depressive group and control group

Variables	Depressive group (n = 103)	Control group (n = 32)	P value
Age (years)	53.3 ± 9.9	51.8 ± 9.5	0.447
Gender (female/male)	59/44	20/12	0.601[a]
Duration of depression (years)	7.4 ± 4.9	–	
BMI (kg/m^2)	22.49 ± 3.25	22.32 ± 2.45	0.782
HAMD-17 score	19.2 ± 8.4	4.2 ± 0.9	**< 0.001**
FBG (mmol/L)	6.10 ± 1.25	4.86 ± 0.49	**< 0.001**
TG (mmol/L)	1.78 ± 1.22	1.21 ± 0.54	**0.012**
TC (mmol/L)	4.61 ± 1.14	4.57 ± 0.92	0.845
HDL-C (mmol/L)	1.23 ± 0.51	1.64 ± 0.47	**< 0.001**
LDL-C (mmol/L)	2.51 ± 0.83	2.39 ± 0.79	0.509
TSH (mIU/L)	2.81 ± 0.79	2.40 ± 0.61	**0.009**
FT3 (pmol/L)	4.55 ± 0.56	4.49 ± 0.58	0.615
FT4 (pmol/L)	12.22 ± 1.54	12.56 ± 1.68	0.847
Nesfatin-1 (ng/mL)	17.52 ± 9.79	8.11 ± 3.31	**< 0.001**

[a]Calculated by Chi-squared test

was performed using the SPSS 13.0 software package, and R version 3.3.2 (http:///www.r-project.org/). Furthermore, *P*-values (two-sided) < 0.05 were considered to be statistically significant.

Results

The study population was composed of 103 depressive patients (44 male, 59 female) and 32 healthy individuals (12 male, 20 female). Demographic variables and biochemical values of depressive group and control group are shown in Table 1. Differences between the groups were not statistically significant in terms of age, gender and BMI. Compared with the healthy controls, depressive patients had higher FBG, higher TG, higher TSH, and lower HDL-C (all $P < 0.05$). The mean plasma nesfatin-1 level in the depressive patients was 17.52 ± 9. 79 ng/mL, whereas it was 8.11 ± 3.31 ng/mL in the healthy controls. Difference of mean plasma nesfatin-1 level between groups was statistically significant ($P < 0.001$, Table 1). The mean HAMD-17 scores were statistically higher in patients with depression than that in the control group (19.2 ± 8.4 in depressive group vs. 4.2 ± 0.9 in control group, $P < 0.001$).

By Spearman correlation analysis, the plasma nesfatin-1 level was significantly correlated with age ($r = -0.287$, $P = 0.003$), duration of depression ($r = 0.302$, $P = 0.002$), BMI ($r = -0.305$, $P = 0.002$), FBG ($r = -0.287$, $P = 0.003$), TC ($r = 0.254$, $P = 0.010$), HDL-C ($r = 0.232$, $P = 0.019$), TSH ($r = 0.350$, $P < 0.001$), and HAMD-17 score ($r = 0.651$, $P < 0.001$, Fig. 1) in the depressive patients.

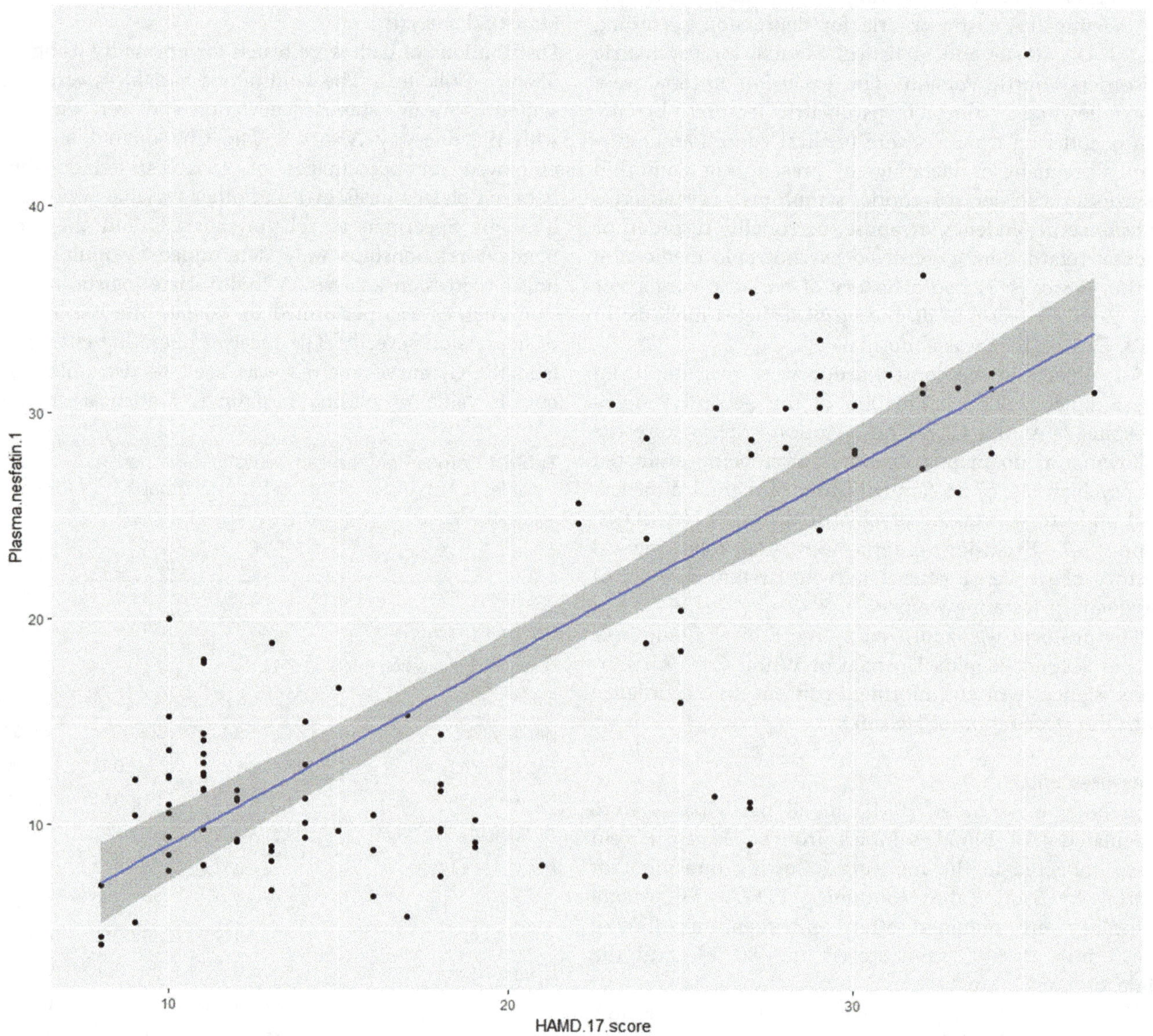

Fig. 1 Correlation between plasma nesfatin-1 levels and HAMD-17 scores (Linear Regression)

Table 2 Multivariate linear regression analysis between plasma nesfatin-1 (dependent variable) and clinical characteristics (independent variables)

	β (95%confidence interval)	SE	*P* value
Age	−0.120 (− 0.238 to − 0.002)	0.059	**0.047**
Gender	0.459 (−1.981 to 2.900)	1.228	0.709
Duration of depression	0.507 (0.301 to 0.752)	0.114	**< 0.001**
BMI	0.174 (−0.226 to 0.574)	0.201	0.389
HAMD-17 score	0.715 (0.550 to 0880)	0.083	**< 0.001**
FBG	−0.886 (−1.842 to 0.070)	0.481	0.069
TG	0.583 (−0.309 to1.476)	0.449	0.198
TC	0.965 (−0.262 to 2.192)	0.617	0.122
HDL-C	1.957 (−0.454 to 4.368)	1.213	0.110
LDL-C	−1.336 (−3.097 to 0.425)	0.886	0.135
TSH	2.173 (0.718 to3.629)	0.732	**0.004**
FT3	−0.718 (−2.677 to 1.242)	0.986	0.469
FT4	−0.360 (−1.095 to 0.374)	0.370	0.332

Multivariate linear regression analysis showed that plasma nesfatin-1 level was negatively associated with age, whereas that was positively associated with duration of depression, HAMD-17score, and TSH (Table 2).

The level of plasma nesfatin-1 in females (n = 59) was significantly higher than that in males (n = 44) (19.37 ± 10.05 vs. 15.04 ± 8.96, P = 0.023). Among 103 depressive patients, 51 patients (49.5%) had mild depression, 18 patients (17.5%) had moderate depression, and 34 patients (33.0%) had severe depression respectively. Figure 2 shows that a significant increased trend of the plasma nesfatin-1 level among mild depressive patients (11.17 ± 3.58 ng/mL) compared to moderate depressive patients (16.33 ± 8. 78 ng/mL) (P = 0.005), and moderate depressive patients compared to severe depressive patients (27. 65 ± 8.26 ng/mL) (P < 0.001).

By multivariate logistic regression analysis, BMI (OR = 0.671, P = 0.017), plasma nesfatin-1 (OR = 1.269, P = 0. 001) were the independent indicators for severe depression in the depressive patients (Fig. 3). Based on the ROC curve analysis, plasma nesfatin-1 cut-off point of 20.25 ng/mL showed 82.4% sensitivity and 91.3% specificity, and with the Area Under Curve (AUC) 0.903 (95% CI 0.835–0.971) was the optimal cut-off point for identification of severe depression (Fig. 4).

Discussion

Recently, nesfatin-1 has been implicated in the regulation of anxiety and depression in humans [14, 15]. In this study, the plasma nesfatin-1 levels were measured in depressive patients and healthy controls in China. According to our results, the plasma nesfatin-1 level was significantly increased in depressive patients, most notably in patients with severe depression, compared to healthy controls. Our finding is in agreement with the previous report [16].

There are some studies suggesting that serum nesfatin-1 levels were significantly lower in patients with type 2 diabetes mellitus compared to healthy subjects

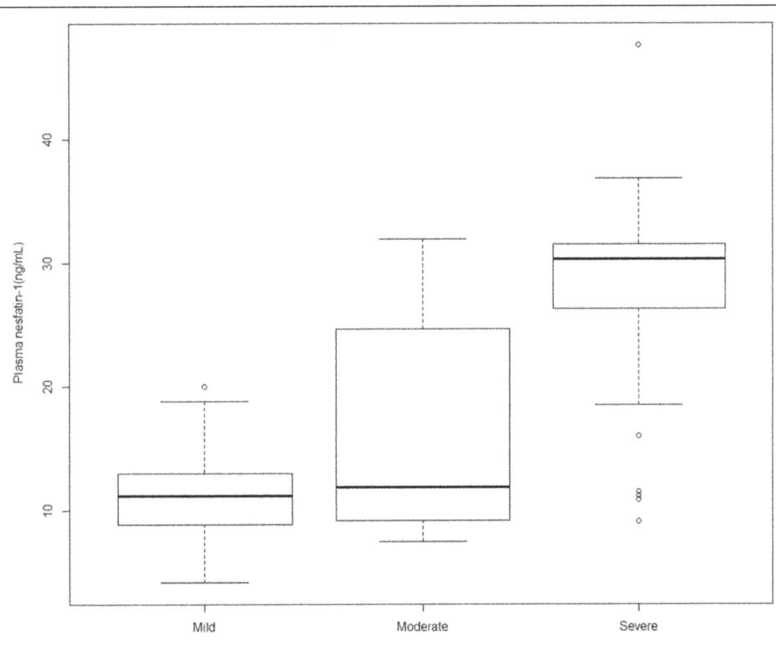

Fig. 2 Plasma nesfatin-1 (mean ± SD) in the mild depression group, the moderate depression group, and the severe depression group

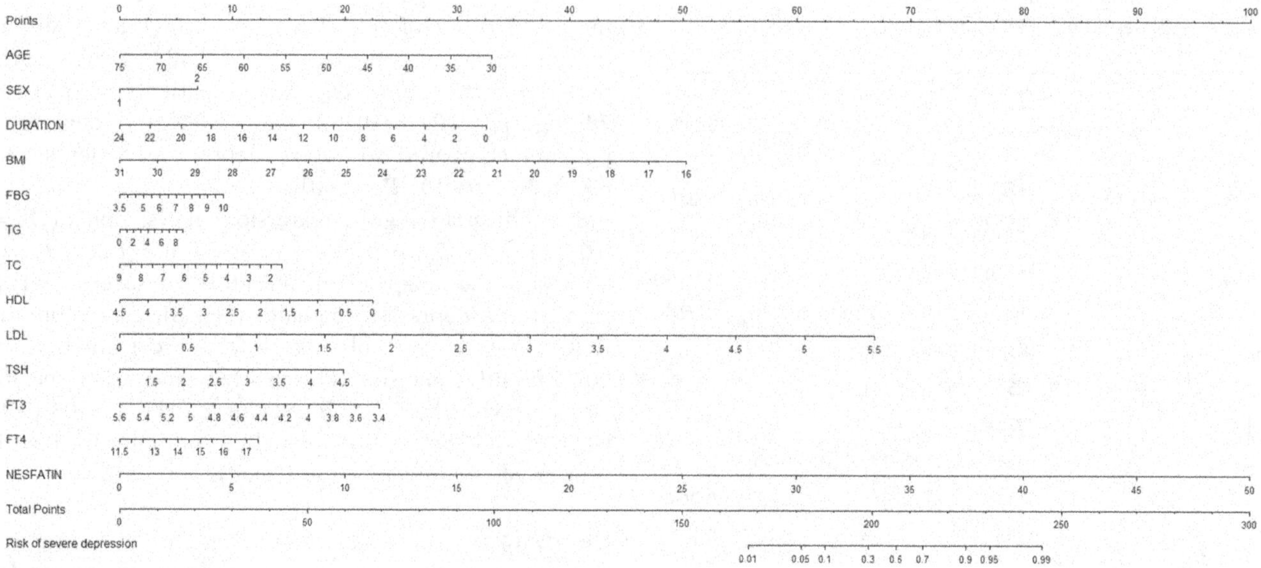

Fig. 3 Risk factors of severe depression nomogram. (Code of sex [1: male, 2: female]) (To use the nomogram, an individual patient's value is located on each variable axis, and a line is drawn upward to determine the number of points received for each variable value. The sum of these numbers is located on the Total Points axis, and a line is drawn downward to the Risk of severe depression axes to determine the severe depression risk)

[17, 18]. Considering the effect of high blood sugar on nesfatin-1 level, we excluded patients with diabetes mellitus in our study. A positive correlation between plasma nesfatin-1and HDL-C in the depressive patients was observed in present study, and this relationship had been previously reported by Li et al. [19] in the diabetic patients. However, the mechanism and physiological significance of this relationship is unclear. Some studies indicate that thyroid dysfunction is associate with the mood disorders and particularly with depression [20, 21]. The symptomatic of depression could be improved through the levothyroxine replacement therapy [22]. In

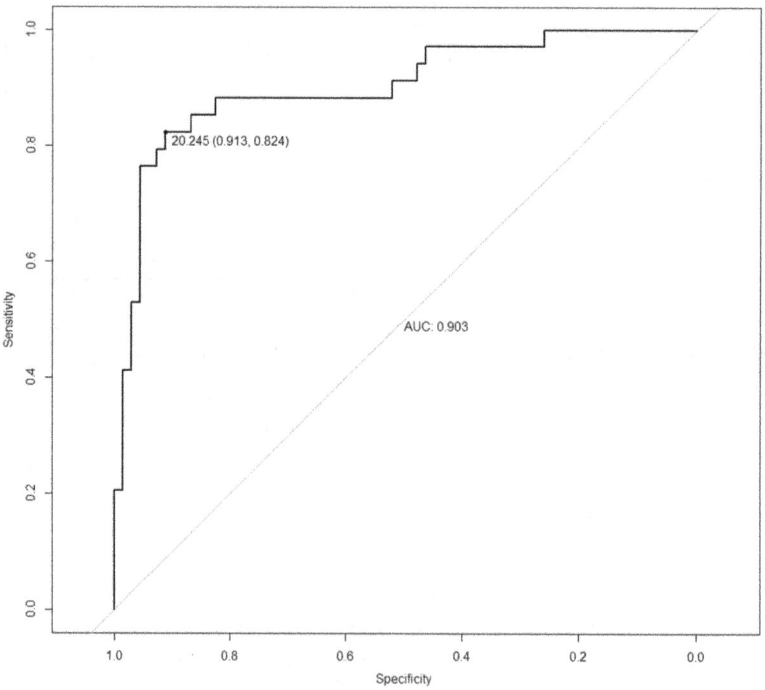

Fig. 4 Receiver operating characteristic (ROC) curve of plasma nesfatin-1 in identification of the patients with severe depression

addition, the relationship between nesfatin-1 and thyroid function had been reported in previous literature [23]. Thus, the patients with abnormal TSH, FT3 and FT4 were excluded in our study. We also observed a statistically significant association between TSH and plasma nesfatin-1 by multivariate linear regression analysis.

In the present study, plasma nesfatin-1 was significantly correlated with HAMD-17 score, furthermore, we observed the level of plasma nesfatin-1 increased gradually from mild depression to moderate depression, and from moderate depression to severe depression. This increased trend suggests that plasma nesfatin-1 is associated with severity of depression. Multivariate logistic regression analysis identified that plasma nesfatin-1 was an indicator for severe depression in our study population. In addition, the patients with severe depression could be identified with a sensitivity of 82.4% at specificity of 91.3% by plasma nesfatin-1 (cut-off value = 20.25 ng/mL). Therefore, the plasma nesfatin-1 level may be considered as a biomarker to identify Chinese patients who have severe depression.

Several limitations in this study should also be acknowledged. First, all subjects were collected from a single hospital. Second, the future studies are needed to identify the role of plasma nesfatin-1 in the progression of depression. Additionally, although all drugs had been discontinued at least 2 weeks before measurement of plasma nesfatin-1, the long-term effects of previous drugs on plasma nesfatin-1 remains unknown.

Conclusions

The level of plasma nesfatin-1 was positively correlated with depression severity. Plasma nesfatin-1 level may be a potential indicator for depression severity. Multicentric and longitudinal studies are clearly required to validate an association between plasma nesfatin-1 level and depression severity.

Acknowledgements

We thank the patientsand controls who participated in this study. We thank Pr. Gang Feng for technical assistance.

Funding

This research was supported by the National High Technology Research and Development Program 863 (2014AA022304). The funding bodies did not participate in the design of the study, the collection of data, analysis of data, interpretation of data or in writing the manuscript.

Authors' contributions

MMX, JBL, and BLW designed the study; MMX, JBL, LLJ, and HS performed the study and collected data; MMX, JBL, LLJ, and BLW analysed data; MMX and BLW wrote the paper. All authors read and approved the final manuscript.

Consent for publication

Not applicable.

Competing interests

The authors declare that they have no competing interests.

Author details

[1]Clinical Laboratory, Affiliated Provincial Hospital of Anhui Medical University, 17 Lujiang Road, Hefei 230001, Anhui, China. [2]Clinical Laboratory, The Second People's Hospital of Wuhu City, Wuhu 241001, Anhui, China. [3]Department of Clinical Psychiatry, The Second People's Hospital of Wuhu City, Wuhu 241001, Anhui, China.

References

1. Mogi T, Toda H, Yoshino A. Clinical characteristics of patients with diagnostic uncertainty of major depressive disorder. Asian J Psychiatr. 2017; 30:159–62.
2. Setoyama D, Kato TA, Hashimoto R, Kunugi H, Hattori K, Hayakawa K, et al. Plasma metabolites predict severity of depression and suicidal ideation in psychiatric patients-a multicenter pilot analysis. PLoS One. 2016;11: e0165267.
3. Huang TL, Lin CC. Advances in biomarkers of major depressive disorder. Adv Clin Chem. 2015;68:177–204.
4. Cenik B, Cenik C, Snyder MP, Brown ES. Plasma sterols and depressive symptom severity in a population-based cohort. PLoS One. 2017;12: e0184382.
5. Lamers F, Milaneschi Y, de Jonge P, Giltay EJ, Penninx BWJH. Metabolic and inflammatory markers: associations with individual depressive symptoms. Psychol Med. 2017; doi: https://doi.org/10.1017/S0033291717002483.
6. Aydin S. Role of NUCB2/nesfatin-1 as a possible biomarker. Curr Pharm Des. 2013;19:6986–92.
7. Çelik F, Belviranli M, Okudan N. Circulating levels of leptin, nesfatin-1 and kisspeptin in postmenopausal obese women. Arch Physiol Biochem. 2016; 122:195–9.
8. Emmerzaal TL, Kozicz T. Nesfatin-1; implication in stress and stress-associated anxiety and depression. Curr Pharm Des. 2013;19:6941–8.
9. Xu YY, Ge JF, Qin G, Peng YN, Zhang CF, Liu XR, et al. Acute, but not chronic, stress increased the plasma concentration and hypothalamic mRNA expression of NUCB2/nesfatin-1 in rats. Neuropeptides. 2015;54:47–53.
10. Könczöl K, Bodnár I, Zelena D, Pintér O, Papp RS, Palkovits M, et al. Nesfatin-1/NUCB2 may participate in the activation of the hypothalamic-pituitary-adrenal axis in rats. Neurochem Int. 2010;57:189–97.
11. Ge JF, Xu YY, Qin G, Peng YN, Zhang CF, Liu XR, et al. Depression-like behavior induced by Nesfatin-1 in rats: involvement of increased immune activation and imbalance of synaptic vesicle proteins. Front Neurosci. 2015;9:429.
12. Geng LY, Qian FY, Qian JF, Zhang ZJ. The combination of plasma glutamate and physical impairment after acute stroke as a potential indicator for the early-onset post-stroke depression. J Psychosom Res. 2017;96:35–41.
13. Liu Z, Zhu Z, Zhao J, Ren W, Cai Y, Wang Q, et al. Malondialdehyde: a novel predictive biomarker for post-stroke depression. J Affect Disord. 2017; 220:95–101.
14. Bez Y, Ari M, Ozturk OH, Oktar S, Can Y, Sogut S. Plasma Nesfatin-1 level may be associated with disease severity in patients with panic disorder. Psychopharmacology. 2010;20:288–92.
15. Bez Y, Ari M, Ozturk OH, Oktar S, Can Y. Increased plasma Nesfatin-1 levels in patients with obsessive compulsive disorder. Psychopharmacology. 2012;22:5–9.
16. Ari M, Ozturk OH, Bez Y, Oktar S, Erduran D. High plasma nesfatin-1 level in patients with major depressive disorder. Prog Neuro-Psychopharmacol Biol Psychiatry. 2011;35:497–500.
17. Ding S, Qu W, Dang S, Xie X, Xu J, Wang Y, et al. Serum nesfatin-1 is reduced in type 2 diabetes mellitus patients with peripheral arterial disease. Med Sci Monit. 2015;21:987–91.

18. Algul S, Ozkan Y, Ozcelik O. Serum nesfatin-1 levels in patients with different glucose tolerance levels. Physiol Res. 2016;65:979–85.
19. Li QC, Wang HY, Chen X, Guan HZ, Jiang ZY. Fasting plasma levels of nesfatin-1 in patients with type 1 and type 2 diabetes mellitus and the nutrient-related fluctuation of nesfatin-1 level in normal humans. Regul Pept. 2010;159:72–7.
20. Delitala AP, Terracciano A, Fiorillo E, Orrù V, Schlessinger D, Cucca F. Depressive symptoms, thyroid hormone and autoimmunity in a population-based cohort from Sardinia. J Affect Disord. 2016;191:82–7.
21. Talaei A, Rafee N, Rafei F, Chehrei A. TSH cut off point based on depression in hypothyroid patients. BMC Psychiatry. 2017;17:327.
22. Yu J, Tian AJ, Yuan X, Cheng XX. Subclinical hypothyroidism after ^{131}I-treatment of Graves' disease: a risk factor for depression? PLoS One. 2016; 11:e0154846.
23. Liu F, Yang Q, Gao N, Liu F, Chen S. Decreased plasma nesfatin-1 level is related to the thyroid dysfunction in patients with type 2 diabetes mellitus. J Diabetes Res. 2014;2014:128014.

22

Characteristics of patients with depression initiating or switching antidepressant treatment: baseline analyses of the PERFORM cohort study

Josep Maria Haro[1], François-Xavier Lamy[2,7], Bengt Jönsson[3], Martin Knapp[4], Mélanie Brignone[2], Hugo Caillou[5,8], Ylana Chalem[2,9], Lene Hammer-Helmich[6*], Benoît Rive[2,10] and Delphine Saragoussi[2]

Abstract

Background: Patients who require a switch in their antidepressant therapy may have different clinical profiles and treatment needs compared with patients initiating or maintaining a first-line antidepressant therapy.

Methods: The Prospective Epidemiological Research on Functioning Outcomes Related to Major depressive disorder (MDD) (PERFORM) study was a 2-year observational cohort study in outpatients with MDD in five European countries. Enrolled patients were either initiating or undergoing the first switch to an antidepressant monotherapy. Baseline data on patients' clinical status, functioning, productivity, quality of life and medical-resource use were compared in a cross-sectional baseline analysis.

Results: A total of 1402 patients were enrolled, of whom 1159 (82.7%) provided analysable baseline data. The majority (78.7%) of the analysable population were initiating antidepressant treatment and most (83.6%) were enrolled and followed up by general practitioners. Compared with patients initiating antidepressants, those switching antidepressants (21.3%) tended to have more severe depressive symptoms, greater anxiety, worse health-related quality of life, greater functional impairment, greater medical-resource use and had a different medical history. Limitations included an over-representation of switches due to lack of efficacy among patients who were switching treatment, as patients were selected based on presence of depressive symptoms.

Conclusions: Patients with MDD who are switching treatment for the first time have a different profile and different depression-associated health needs compared with those initiating treatment. Therapeutic management should therefore be adapted for patients who switch.

Keywords: Depression, Drug switching, Observational study, Baseline survey

Background

Pharmacological therapies are commonly used in the management of patients with depression; however, a significant proportion of patients do not respond to an adequate trial of the first antidepressant prescribed in a depressive episode [1–3]. The Sequenced Treatment Alternatives to Relieve Depression (STAR*D) trial reported that up to 37% of patients initiating antidepressant treatment in clinical practice achieved remission with first-line treatment [2, 4]. Change of treatment is thus a frequent therapeutic action in patients with depression who do not respond to their initial treatment. Treatment guidelines recommend a range of pharmacotherapeutic approaches for patients who need a treatment change from their first-line treatment, including treatment switch (changing to a different antidepressant), combination therapy (adding a second antidepressant) and augmentation (adding an agent that is not generally considered an anti-depressant, e.g. an antipsychotic) [5–8]. Switching therapy

* Correspondence: LEEM@lundbeck.com
[6]H. Lundbeck A/S, Ottiliavej 9, 2500 Valby, Denmark
Full list of author information is available at the end of the article

tends to be recommended if a patient experiences an inadequate response and/or tolerability problems, whereas combination and augmentation strategies would be used for patients who had experienced a partial response to the initial therapy but had residual symptoms and had not experienced tolerability problems [9]. Several studies have found that switching is a common choice in clinical practice for patients requiring second-line treatment, including those with an inadequate response to first-line antidepressant therapy [10–13]. Clinical evidence supports switching antidepressants in such patients [14, 15].

In considering a switch from first-line treatment, guidelines recommend taking into account whether the patient has experienced adverse effects and patient preference [5, 8]. However, some studies have shown that, in clinical practice, patients who switch antidepressants may have a very different clinical profile compared with those who do not switch treatment. An observational study based on data from the General Practice Research Database (GPRD; now known as the Clinical Practice Research Datalink) in the UK found that patients who switched antidepressants tended to have a more severe psychiatric profile compared with those who maintained their initial therapy [12]. In addition, differences in the degree of resolution for symptoms of occupational impairment have been noted between patients responding to first-line treatment and those responding to second-line treatment [16]. Such findings suggest that patients who require a switch in their antidepressant therapy may benefit from a more detailed clinical assessment of their illness and a specific management approach, distinct from that taken with patients who are initiating or maintaining a first-line antidepressant therapy.

The Prospective Epidemiological Research on Functioning Outcomes Related to Major depressive disorder (MDD) (PERFORM) study was designed to better understand the course of a depressive episode and its impact on patient functioning over a 2-year period in patients with MDD in clinical practice in five European countries. The study recruited patients with a diagnosis of MDD who were either initiating antidepressant monotherapy or who were switching antidepressant monotherapy for the first time. The aim of the cross-sectional baseline analyses presented in this paper was to describe the characteristics of patients who were initiating or switching antidepressant monotherapy when entering the PERFORM study and to compare their depression-related clinical profile, daily functioning, health-related quality of life and resource use.

Methods

Study design and patients

The PERFORM study is a 2-year observational cohort study in outpatients with MDD enrolled by either a primary care physician or a psychiatrist at 194 sites in five European countries (France, Germany, Spain, Sweden and the UK). In each country the study sites were selected to reflect the national proportions of these clinicians treating patients with depression. At enrolment, eligible patients were aged 18–65 years, had a current diagnosis of MDD according to the Diagnostic and Statistical Manual of Mental Disorders IV Text Revision (DSM-IV-TR), and were either initiating antidepressant monotherapy or were undergoing their first switch of antidepressant. Patients were excluded if they had schizophrenia or other psychotic disorders; bipolar disorder; substance dependence; dementia or other neurodegenerative disease significantly affecting cognitive functioning; or a mood disorder due to a general medical condition or substances. Patients receiving a combination of different antidepressant treatments at the time of the initial consultation were also excluded.

The physician's choice of the drug used to treat each patient was based on clinical judgement alone and was not influenced by the decision to enter the study. All patients enrolled in the study provided written informed consent. The necessary ethical approvals were obtained for each study site before study initiation. The study was registered at ClinicalTrials.gov: NCT01427439 on 26 August 2011.

Baseline characteristics

Patient characteristics recorded at baseline included demographic information; the characteristics of the current episode of depression and – for patients switching antidepressants – the main reason for switching, according to the physician; history of depression; and the presence of mental health disorders other than depression, and of any functional syndromes.

Clinical profile at baseline was assessed by all patients using the 9-item Patient Health Questionnaire (PHQ-9) [17] and by all participating investigators using the Clinical Global Impressions–Severity of illness scale (CGI-S) [18]. The Montgomery–Åsberg Depression Rating Scale (MADRS) [19] was also administered when recruitment was conducted in the specialized sector and patients were evaluated by psychiatrists. The PHQ-9 scores were used to categorize the severity of symptoms as "minimal" (score 0–4), "mild" (score 5–9), "moderate" (score 10–14), "moderately severe" (score 15–19) or "severe" (score 20–27) for analysis. The CGI-S responses were analysed by the category assigned by the physician on a 7-point scale ranging from 1 = not ill, to 7 = extremely ill. The MADRS responses were analysed by total score.

Daily functioning and quality of life were assessed using self-administered instruments. Functioning was evaluated using the Sheehan Disability Scale (SDS) [20] including three dimensions (work, social and family functioning). The "activity impairment" dimension of the

Work Productivity and Activity Impairment questionnaire (WPAI) was also applied in order to evaluate functioning [21]. The other dimensions of the WPAI are not presented as they aim to measure productivity and are relevant only to the subpopulation in employment. The Arizona Sexual Experience Scale (ASEX; five items, each scored from 1 to 6) [22] was used to assess sexual functioning. Patients were categorized as having sexual dysfunction if their total ASEX score was ≥19 or their score was ≥5 for one item or ≥ 4 for at least three items. Patient-reported outcomes were also used to assess health-related quality of life using the physical and mental health dimensions of the Medical Outcomes Study Short-Form (12-item) Health Survey (SF-12) [23] and the EuroQol 5-Dimensions questionnaire (EQ-5D; in UK patients only) [24]. Utility scores were derived from the EQ-5D scales by applying UK tariffs [25].

Resource use during the 12 weeks before baseline was assessed by physician reporting of physician visits, hospitalizations and periods of sick leave. Resource-use data were reported for patients who had experienced a depressive episode of at least 8 weeks' duration as: per cent of patients reporting at least one visit (physician or other healthcare professional) or 1 day of hospitalization or sick leave over the recall period; number of visits (physician or other healthcare professional) or days of hospitalization or sick leave for patients with at least one visit or day of the corresponding resource item; and overall number of visits (physician or other healthcare professional) or days of hospitalization or sick leave. The restriction of this analysis to patients with a minimum depressive-episode duration of 8 weeks was applied to allow an appropriate comparison between the two treatment groups, given the between-group difference in duration of the current depressive episode.

Data analysis

Patients included in the analysable dataset were those who met the study selection criteria and completed a baseline assessment form as well as at least one post-baseline assessment or outcome questionnaire. Summary statistics (mean, standard deviation, median, minimum and maximum) were calculated for continuous variables, and numbers and percentages were calculated for categorical variables. Analyses were performed for both groups of patients: those switching and those initiating treatment. Differences between these groups were investigated using either Student's t test for quantitative variables or chi-squared test (or Fisher's exact test where appropriate) for qualitative variables. All analyses were univariate as the aim was to describe the characteristics of the study populations rather than to explain or identify any associations. Statistical significance was assumed at $p < 0.05$. Statistical analyses were performed using SAS® statistical software, Version 9.2 (SAS Institute, Cary, NC, USA).

Results

Subjects

A total of 1895 patients were screened, 1402 of whom were enrolled in the study. The first patient was screened on 25 February 2011 and the last patient completed the study on 19 February 2015. The most frequent reason for non-enrolment of screened patients (n = 493) was patient's decision (n = 203; 41.2%). Of those who were enrolled, 1159 (82.7%) provided analysable data. Patients who were enrolled but not included in the analysable population (n = 243) were excluded because they violated at least one of the inclusion and/or exclusion criteria at baseline (n = 167) or they had not completed a post-baseline case report form or at least one post-baseline questionnaire in the predefined timeframe (n = 101, including 76 who met the inclusion criteria at baseline). The majority of patients were enrolled and followed up by general practitioners (n = 969; 83.6%). Overall the analysable population had a mean age of approximately 44 years, and the majority (n = 848; 73.2%) were female (Table 1). Included patients were from the UK (n = 341; 29.4%), France (n = 339; 29.2%), Spain (n = 270; 23.3%), Germany (n = 164; 14.2%) and Sweden (n = 45; 3.9%).

At baseline 910 (78.7%) patients were initiating antidepressant treatment and 247 (21.3%) were switching antidepressant for the first time; the treatment status of two patients was unknown. The main causes of switching (recorded for 216 patients) were lack of efficacy (167; 77.3%), adverse events (n = 20; 9.3%), patient's decision (n = 15; 6.9%) and lack of compliance (n = 7; 3.2%). Compared with patients who were initiating antidepressants, approximately twice as many patients in the analysable population who were switching antidepressants were being treated by psychiatrists at the time of enrolment (n = 124 vs 66, respectively; $P < 0.001$; Table 2).

There were statistically significant demographic differences between the two patient groups: compared with patients who were initiating treatment, those who were switching were significantly older (P = 0.012) and more likely to be widowed or divorced/separated (Table 1). Patients who were initiating antidepressant treatment were more likely to be educated to university degree level and were more likely to be in paid employment or self-employed compared with patients who were switching antidepressant treatment (Table 1).

Clinical profile

With regard to their current episode of depression, the duration of the episode – classified in time categories – differed significantly ($P < 0.001$) between the two patient groups. Greater proportions of patients who were switching antidepressants than those initiating treatment had been experiencing the current episode of depression

Table 1 Patient characteristics at baseline

Characteristic	Switching (*n* = 247)[a]	Initiating (*n* = 910)[a]	*P*-value: switching vs initiating	Total (*n* = 1159)[b]
Age, mean ± SD (years)	46.0 ± 11.7	43.8 ± 12.0	**0.012**	44.3 ± 12.0
Female (%)	76.1	72.5	0.259	73.2
Marital status (%)			**0.021**	
Single	20.6	21.9		21.6
Married/couple	54.7	59.6		58.5
Divorced/separated	18.6	16.2		16.7
Widowed	6.1	2.4		3.2
Education (%)			**< 0.001**	
No degree or diploma	8.1	3.5		4.5
Elementary school	32.8	22.1		24.4
High school	31.6	38.4		36.9
Non-university degree	13.0	14.3		14.0
University degree	14.6	21.8		20.2
Work status (%)				
Paid employment or self-employed	59.5	68.8	**0.006**	66.8
Unemployed	20.2	17.1	0.259	17.8

Abbreviation: SD standard deviation
P-values in bold indicate statistically significant differences
[a]Number of patients included in the between-group comparison; information regarding whether the patient was initiating or switching treatment was missing for two patients
[b]Total number of patients providing data

for more than 8 weeks (Table 2). In addition, a significantly higher proportion of patients who were switching treatment were experiencing symptoms of anxiety ($P < 0.001$); among patients with anxiety, those who were switching were significantly more likely to be treated with anxiolytics ($P = 0.004$).

Severity of illness, as rated by the patient using the PHQ-9, indicated little clinical difference between the treatment groups. Although the between-group difference in mean scores reached statistical significance ($P = 0.014$), the mean score was only marginally higher for patients switching antidepressants versus those initiating treatment (Table 2). Conversely, the difference in distribution by category of severity did not reach statistical significance ($P = 0.084$), despite a greater proportion of patients who switched treatment ranking their illness as severe (PHQ-9 score 20–27) compared with those initiating antidepressant treatment (Fig. 1).

The severity of the current depressive episode, as measured by the mean physician-assigned CGI-S score, was significantly higher in patients who were switching antidepressants compared with those initiating the treatment ($P < 0.001$) (Table 2). The profile of disease severity differed significantly in the two populations ($P < 0.001$), with a greater proportion of patients in the switching group rated as markedly, severely or extremely ill (48.4% versus 36.2% in the initiating group) (Fig. 2).

Compared with patients initiating antidepressant monotherapy, significantly greater proportions of patients switching antidepressants had experienced a previous episode of depression at any time ($P < 0.001$; Table 2).

No significant differences were seen with regard to the presence of comorbid mental disorders, but differences were noted for comorbid physical disorders: significantly higher proportions of patients who were switching had a diagnosis of a chronic pain ($P < 0.001$) or fibromyalgia ($P < 0.001$) compared with those initiating treatment (Table 2).

Functioning and health-related quality of life

With regard to functioning as assessed by the SDS, the mean total SDS score was significantly higher – indicating greater functional impairment – in patients who were switching compared with those initiating antidepressants ($P = 0.004$) (Table 2). Furthermore, the individual SDS domain scores were also significantly higher in patients who were switching (each $P < 0.05$) (Table 2). The WPAI dimension of overall activity impairment showed a significant between-group difference, with a significantly higher mean score, i.e. worse impairment, in the group switching than in the group initiating antidepressants ($P = 0.002$; Table 2). The mean total ASEX sexual-function score was statistically significantly higher in the group switching than in the group initiating antidepressants ($P = 0.031$), although the numerical difference was small (Table 2).

Table 2 Medical profile, functioning and quality of life at baseline

	Switching (*n* analysed)[a]	Initiating (*n* analysed)[a]	*P*-value: switching vs initiating	Total[b] (*n*)
Characteristics of current depressive episode				
Treating physician (% of patient group)	(247)	(910)	**< 0.001**	(1159)
General practitioner	73.3	86.4		83.6
Psychiatrist	26.7	13.6		16.4
Duration of episode (%)[c]	(247)	(910)	**< 0.001**	(1157)
< 1 week	0.4	1.9		1.6
1–2 weeks	2.8	6.7		5.9
2–4 weeks	14.6	23.2		21.3
4–8 weeks	17.4	20.4		19.8
> 8 weeks	64.8	47.8		51.4
Significant symptoms of anxiety (%)[d]	74.5 (247)	59.3 (910)	**< 0.001**	62.6 (1158)
Symptoms treated with anxiolytics (%)	53.1 (130)	38.6 (376)	**0.004**	42.2 (507)
Questionnaire scores, mean ± SD				
PHQ-9	18.4 ± 5.3 (198)	17.4 ± 5.3 (740)	**0.014**	17.6 ± 5.3 (940)
CGI-S	4.4 ± 1.0 (246)	4.1 ± 1.0 (908)	**< 0.001**	4.2 ± 1.0 (1155)
MADRS[e]	32.5 ± 7.1 (66)	32.9 ± 7.2 (124)	0.724	32.7 ± 7.1 (190)
SDS				
Total score	20.6 ± 6.6 (147)	18.9 ± 6.7 (601)	**0.004**	19.2 ± 6.8 (750)
Work/school disruption	6.7 ± 2.7 (150)	6.1 ± 2.8 (614)	**0.020**	6.3 ± 2.8 (766)
Social life/leisure activities' disruption	7.0 ± 2.4 (179)	6.4 ± 2.5 (704)	**0.003**	6.6 ± 2.5 (885)
Family life/home duties' disruption	7.0 ± 2.4 (179)	6.4 ± 2.5 (701)	**0.001**	6.5 ± 2.5 (882)
WPAI[f]	66.0 ± 23.5 (194)	59.9 ± 24.9 (740)	**0.002**	61.1 ± 24.8 (936)
ASEX				
Total score	22.2 ± 5.8 (169)	21.2 ± 5.7 (623)	**0.031**	21.4 ± 5.7 (793)
Sexual dysfunction (%)	84.6 (188)	80.3 (695)	0.182	81.1 (884)
SF-12	(190)	(720)		(912)
PCS	40.6 ± 11.4	46.4 ± 12.0	**< 0.001**	45.2 ± 12.1
MCS	26.8 ± 9.0	26.4 ± 9.2	0.598	26.5 ± 9.2
EQ-5D utility score[g]	0.5 ± 0.3 (48)	0.6 ± 0.3 (227)	**0.044**	0.5 ± 0.3 (276)
Other current illnesses				
Mental-health disorders other than depression (%)	(247)	(910)		(1159)
Alcohol abuse or dependence	1.6	3.0	0.245	2.7
Other abuse disorders	1.2	1.3	1.000	1.3
Somatoform disorders	10.5	7.0	0.069	7.9
Eating disorders (anorexia, bulimia)	10.5	7.5	0.119	8.1
Other	0.0	0.8	0.357	0.6
Functional syndromes (%)	(247)	(910)		(1159)
Chronic pain	23.9	14.7	**< 0.001**	16.7
Chronic fatigue	17.0	15.9	0.685	16.1
Fibromyalgia	13.0	5.2	**< 0.001**	6.8
Premenstrual syndrome	4.9	3.1	0.174	3.5
Sleep disorders	29.1	27.9	0.701	28.2
Other	2.4	2.9	0.716	2.8

Table 2 Medical profile, functioning and quality of life at baseline *(Continued)*

	Switching (*n* analysed)[a]	Initiating (*n* analysed)[a]	*P*-value: switching vs initiating	Total[b] (*n*)
Previous depressive episodes				
History of depression (%)				
Previous episode	72.0 (246)	52.4 (910)	**< 0.001**	56.6 (1157)
Episode within previous 12 months if previous episode	33.9 (177)	22.4 (477)	**0.003**	25.5 (655)
Antidepressant treatment if previous episode	91.0 (177)	77.1 (476)	**< 0.001**	80.9 (654)
Previous hospitalization for depression	15.3 (177)	6.5 (477)	**< 0.001**	8.9 (655)
Remission of previous episode	72.3 (177)	87.2 (477)	**< 0.001**	83.2 (655)
Previous suicide attempt	18.1 (177)	11.3 (477)	**0.023**	13.1 (655)

Abbreviations: ASEX Arizona Sexual Experience Scale, *CGI-S* Clinical Global Improvement Severity scale, *EQ-5D* EuroQol 5-Dimensions questionnaire, *MADRS* Montgomery–Åsberg Depression Rating Scale, *MCS* mental component summary, *PCS* physical component summary, *PHQ-9* 9-item Patient Health Questionnaire, *SD* standard deviation, *SDS* Sheehan Disability Scale, *SF-12* Medical Outcomes Study Short-Form (12-item) Health Survey, *WPAI* Work Productivity and Activity Impairment questionnaire

P-values in bold indicate statistically significant differences

[a]Number of patients included in the between-group comparison; information regarding whether the patient was initiating or switching treatment was missing for two patients

[b]Total number of patients providing data

[c]Physicians' response

[d]The percentages refer to patients "probably" or "definitely" presenting clinically significant symptoms of anxiety according to physician; the *P*-value indicates the between-group comparison taking into account all five categories ("definitely", "probably", "probably not", "definitely not" and "don't know")

[e]Assessment used by psychiatrists only

[f]Activity impairment due to problem

[g]UK sample population only

The SF-12 mean physical component summary (PCS) score was significantly lower (indicating worse physical functioning) in the switching compared with the initiating group ($P < 0.001$); however the mean mental component summary (MCS) score did not differ between groups (Table 2).

Resource use

Resource use within the 12 weeks before the baseline visit by patients with a depressive episode of greater than 8 weeks' duration is summarized in Table 3. Compared with patients who initiated antidepressant medication, a statistically significantly greater proportion of patients who were switching antidepressants made at least one visit to any physician in the previous 12 weeks (88.0% vs 96.2%; $P = 0.003$). Patients who were switching antidepressants had more physician visits than patients initiating treatment in the same period (Table 3).

In terms of the type of physician visited, patients who were switching were also significantly more likely than those initiating treatment to have visited a psychiatrist ($P = 0.001$) or psychotherapist/counselling ($P = 0.047$) in the previous 12 weeks. A significantly greater proportion of patients switching antidepressants than those initiating treatment had taken at least one period of sick leave in the previous 12 weeks ($P = 0.033$).

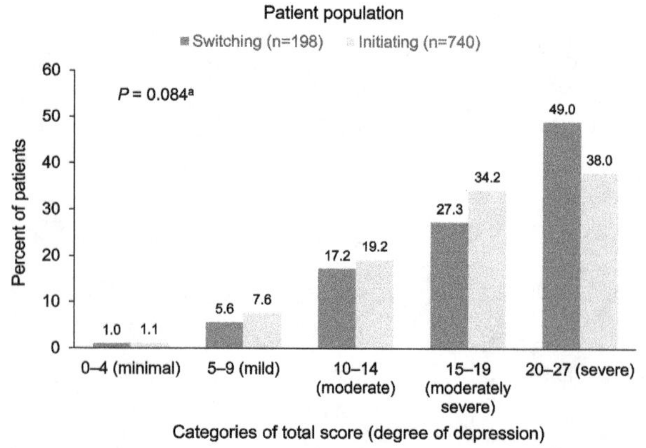

Fig. 1 Distribution of PHQ-9 score categories at baseline, by treatment status. [a]The between-group comparison of the categorical data was conducted using a chi-squared test. *Abbreviations: AD* antidepressant, *PHQ-9,* 9-item Patient Health Questionnaire

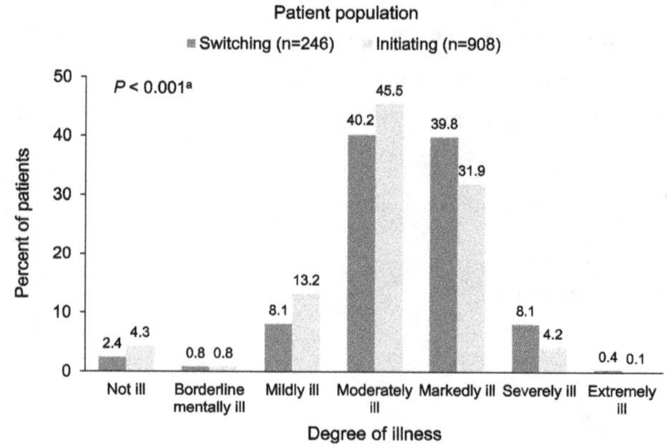

Fig. 2 Distribution of CGI-S score categories at baseline by treatment status. [a]The between-group comparison of the categorical data was conducted using Fisher's exact test. *Abbreviations: AD* antidepressant, *CGI-S* Clinical Global Improvement Severity scale

Table 3 Resource use for patients with a depressive episode of more than 8 weeks' duration[a]

Resource use in the past 12 weeks	Percent of patients (*n* analysed)[b]		*P*-value: switching vs initiating	Percent of patients overall (*n*)[c]
	Switching	Initiating		
No. of physician visits	(157)	(432)	**< 0.001**	(589)
0	3.8	12.0		9.8
1	10.8	22.5		19.4
2	11.5	17.6		16.0
3	17.2	13.2		14.3
≥ 4	56.7	34.5		40.4
Unknown	0	0.2		0.2
General practitioner (any cause)[d]	91.2 (160)	82.8 (435)	**0.010**	85.0 (595)
Psychiatrist[d]	27.5 (160)	15.9 (435)	**0.001**	19.0 (595)
Psychotherapist/counselling[d]	19.4 (160)	12.9 (435)	**0.047**	14.6 (595)
Other specialist[d]	26.2 (160)	19.1 (435)	**0.057**	21.0 (595)
Hospitalization	3.8 (160)	2.1 (435)	0.248	2.5 (595)
Sick leave	90.5 (63)	78.0 (141)	**0.033**	81.9 (204)

P-values in bold indicate statistically significant differences
[a] $n = 595$ patients in total: $n = 160$ switching and $n = 435$ initiating antidepressant therapy
[b] Number of patients included in between-group comparison
[c] Total number of patients providing data
[d] Patients ($n = 8$–20 in total for each resource) for whom the information was reported as 'unknown' by the physician were included in the analysis as having used the resource

Discussion

The objective of this paper was to describe and compare the baseline characteristics of patients with MDD who initiated versus switched antidepressant treatment for the first time at inclusion in the PERFORM study. Overall, the baseline characteristics indicate significant differences between patients who are initiating and those who are switching antidepressants (i.e. undergoing first- and second-line monotherapy, respectively) in the course of a depressive episode. Compared with patients initiating antidepressants, those switching antidepressants tended to have more severe depressive symptoms, greater anxiety, worse health-related quality of life and greater functional impairment; be more likely to experience chronic pain and fibromyalgia; have a different socioeconomic and medical-history background; and use more health-care resources.

Switching antidepressants is likely to be a common approach in clinical practice [10–13]. This is particularly the case in patients who fail to achieve an adequate response with an initial antidepressant [10, 13]. For example, in a retrospective cohort study of medical records of patients with depression in Spain, 43% of those with an inadequate response to first-line antidepressant treatment were switched to another antidepressant [13]. A high proportion of patients in clinical trials and clinical practice do not respond adequately to first-line treatment [2, 4, 26–32]. Switching antidepressants has been demonstrated to be effective in a number of clinical studies, with remission rates of up to 42% achieved in patients who previously failed to achieve remission [14, 15, 33]. While current guidelines recommend switching antidepressants if a patient who has adhered to the prescribed treatment regimen fails to achieve a satisfactory response to initial antidepressant treatment [5, 8], they do not generally recommend a specific assessment of severity, functioning or other aspects of the patient's depressive episode when considering switching to second-line therapy.

The observation in the current study that the patients switching antidepressants were reporting more severe depressive symptoms than those initiating antidepressants is of particular note, given that the patients switching treatment had been receiving antidepressant treatment for some time. The patients who switched treatment may have been even more severely depressed when they initiated treatment. Although the mean between-group differences in depression severity scores were not large, they were consistent across patient (PHQ-9) and physician (CGI-S) reports.

Approximately 77% of patients who switched in the present study did so because of lack of efficacy. However, in other studies lower proportions of patients have cited this as the reason: a previous longitudinal naturalistic study found that 41% of patients with depression who switched within 4 weeks of initiating treatment said it was due lack of efficacy [34]. The relatively high proportion noted in the current study may in part be due to selection bias as discussed below.

Differences in the profile of the current depressive episode and in the history of psychiatric illness have previously been noted between patients who switch to second-line treatment and those who maintain first-line treatment [12]. In a study using historical cohort data from the UK's GPRD, patients who switched antidepressant had more severe depression, were more likely to have concomitant anxiety disorders and were more likely to have experienced a previous episode of depression than those maintaining treatment [12]. The present study augments such findings by providing a more detailed clinical profile of switching and non-switching populations.

The results of the present analysis also suggest that patients who fail to respond adequately to first-line treatment may experience more severe functional impairment. In a cohort study Trivedi and colleagues [16] found that although patients who responded to first-line antidepressant treatment experienced improvements in work productivity in parallel with reductions in the severity of depressive symptoms, patients receiving second-line treatment (i.e. those who switched or received augmented treatment) did not experience such improvements when they responded to treatment.

Compared with maintaining treatment, switching has also been found to be associated with worse health-related quality-of-life outcomes in a longitudinal study of inpatients with MDD [35]. In the present study, the mean SF-12 PCS score in the group switching antidepressants was considerably lower than might be expected in the general population [23, 36, 37], which may also reflect the frequency of chronic pain and fibromyalgia in the study group. As would be expected, the mean MCS scores were far lower than in the general population (attributed a score of 50 ± 10.0 in a US general population and 48.9 ± 9.2 in a Greek general population) [23, 36, 37]. The mean MCS scores were similar in the two patient groups in the current study. This is surprising given the overall more severe depressive clinical profile in the group switching antidepressants; however, this may reflect the improved sensitivity expected from a disease-specific (PHQ-9) versus a generic instrument (SF-12).

In addition to factors such as those discussed above, there are a multitude of other aspects of a patient's life that influence their recovery from MDD, including life events and personal circumstances. In the present study patients who switched medication had a longer duration of illness, were older, were more likely to be widowed or divorced, had lower levels of educational achievement and were more likely to be unemployed than patients initiating treatment. While it is possible to speculate on the role of such factors in patients' response to treatment and recovery from MDD, their contribution is difficult to gauge. Social disadvantage, greater depression severity and anxiety have previously been linked to reduced likelihood of achieving remission after switching to second-line therapy in patients with MDD [38].

Previous studies have demonstrated increased healthcare resource use by patients who switch therapy compared with those who maintain their initial antidepressant therapy [13, 39, 40]. For example, using data from a US medical and pharmacy claims database, Schultz and Joish [39] found that patients with MDD who switched therapy incurred statistically significantly more depression-related ambulatory, emergency-room and inpatient visits than those who maintained their antidepressant therapy, leading to almost double the depression-related costs. The greater resource use observed in patients who switch would be anticipated, given their requirement for treatment before switching.

Depression-associated functional impairment and reductions in health-related quality of life have previously been shown to be linked to the severity of the illness [41, 42]. Some functional comorbidities, such as chronic pain and fibromyalgia – which were significantly more prevalent in the group switching antidepressants in the present study – may influence health-related quality of life independently of depressive symptoms and may contribute to greater severity of depression and functional impairment [43–46]. Indeed, there is evidence of complex interrelationships between depression and pain [47, 48]. The greater prevalence of anxiety in the group switching antidepressants may also contribute to the greater severity of depression seen in this group [49].

As in other therapeutic areas, with greater understanding of the underlying pathophysiology of depression and of the mechanisms of action of antidepressants, there is the potential for personalized treatment, such that patients with particular depressive symptoms or features may be prescribed specific pharmacotherapies [50]. Careful consideration of the patient's full profile with the aim of optimizing antidepressant treatment as early as possible is warranted in light of observations that the risk of treatment failure increases with the number of lines of treatment required [2].

Strengths and limitations

The strengths of this study include the large sample size and its international scope. In addition, this is one of the first studies in which the collected baseline data comprise such a wealth of naturalistic information, including detailed individual medical histories and both physician- and patient-reported information on the current depressive episode, as well as functional, quality-of-life and resource-use data. The study population had the expected demographic characteristics of patients with depression: as previously reported in other observational studies, the majority of patients with depression were women, and the mean age of the population was approximately 45 years [11, 51, 52]. Although the categorization of depression severity using patient-reported outcome in the majority of patients in the present study (rather than by scales more frequently used in clinical trials) may be perceived as a limitation of the study, this approach is increasingly recognised as appropriate and may be considered a study strength. Greater focus on patient-reported outcomes reflects the general move towards increased patient involvement in treatment decisions, and awareness of the limitations of the more 'traditional' clinical symptom-based measures in assessing recovery from mental illness in a way that is meaningful to patients [53–56]. In PERFORM a validated questionnaire, based on DSM-IV diagnostic criteria (PHQ-9) [17] was used to evaluate patient-reported depression, and the severity levels revealed by physician assessment using the CGI-S support the findings of the patient-reported assessment that patients switching antidepressants had more severe depression.

We acknowledge a number of study limitations. Patients were selected on the basis of having symptoms of depression, resulting in an over-representation in the switching population of patients switching treatment due to lack of efficacy (i.e. inadequate response to the previous antidepressant) compared with other reasons. The difference in depression severity between the two study populations may therefore be greater than would be seen in clinical practice; however, as drug-related adverse effects (the next most common reason for switching) may affect functioning and quality of life to a similar degree as a lack of efficacy, the potential bias towards selecting patients with more severe depression in the switching group may not have an effect on the findings. The study comprised outpatients only, potentially excluding some of the most severely affected patients. These criteria may have led to the study population of patients switching treatment having less severe depression than would be encountered in patients switching treatment in clinical practice, however, in Europe the vast majority of patients with MDD are treated in the outpatient setting [1, 57]. The study also excluded patients treated with combination or augmentation therapies. However, guidelines currently applied in Europe recommend initiating treatment with antidepressant monotherapy, with a switch to a different monotherapy in the event that an inadequate response is achieved with the initial therapy [8]. It would therefore be anticipated that in clinical practice few patients would receive a combination of antidepressants or antidepressant therapy augmented with another agent as either first- or second-line therapy. Because of these criteria, the outcomes may be more applicable to patients in the early rather than later period of their depressive episode. A degree of recall bias may also have occurred, which would have resulted in more extensive retrospective reporting of medical issues and resource use by the patients switching treatment. However, such patients would genuinely have experienced more clinical encounters as they had been treated for depression in the preceding weeks; as the recall period was restricted to 12 weeks, the potential for recall bias is low. Analyses of the MADRS and EQ-5D data were based on small sample numbers as these tools were only used in specific settings. This limits the statistical power of these analyses to detect between-group differences. However, the reasonably good response rate for other assessments of depression severity and quality of life – despite the fact that completion of the self-administered instruments was on an entirely voluntary basis – permitted reliable comparisons for these characteristics.

Conclusions

In conclusion, the results of this analysis suggest that patients with depression who are switching treatment have different profiles and depression-associated health needs and should be managed differently from patients who are initiating treatment. In such cases the physician should consider the severity of depression and other aspects of the patient's illness, such as daily functioning and anxiety, in order to select the optimal second-line treatment.

Abbreviations

ASEX: Arizona Sexual Experience Scale; CGI-S: Clinical Global Impressions–Severity of illness scale; DSM-IV-TR: Diagnostic and Statistical Manual of Mental Disorders IV Text Revision; EQ-5D: EuroQol 5-Dimensions questionnaire; GPRD: General Practice Research Database; MADRS: Montgomery–Åsberg Depression Rating Scale; MCS: Mental component summary; MDD: Major depressive disorder; PCS: Physical component summary; PERFORM: Prospective Epidemiological Research on Functioning Outcomes Related to Major depressive disorder; PHQ-9: 9-item Patient Health Questionnaire; SDS: Sheehan Disability Scale; SF-12: Medical Outcomes Study Short-Form (12-item) Health Survey; STAR*D: Sequenced Treatment Alternatives to Relieve Depression; WPAI: Work Productivity and Activity Impairment questionnaire

Acknowledgements

The authors thank Julien Chollet (Lundbeck) for his scientific and operational contribution to the study and MAPI Registrat for the logistical management of the study. The authors would also like to express their gratitude to all the physicians and patients who kindly provided data for the study.
Editorial support in the development of the paper was provided by Dr. Julie Ponting of Anthemis Consulting Ltd, funded by Lundbeck SAS.

Funding

This study was funded by Lundbeck SAS. Lundbeck personnel were involved in the study design; in the collection and interpretation of data; in the writing of the report; and in the decision to submit the article for publication.

Authors' contributions

JMH, BJ, MK, DS and BR designed the study. HC conducted the analyses. All authors interpreted the results, contributed to the development of the article and approved the final article.

Consent for publication

Not applicable.

Competing interests

JMH has received honoraria for participating in advisory boards for Eli Lilly and Co, Roche, Lundbeck and Otsuka. F-XL was employed by Lundbeck SAS at the time the study was conducted and the data presented in this paper were analysed. BJ has received honoraria for being an advisor to Lundbeck. MK has received consultancy funding from Lundbeck and Takeda, and has received research funding from Lundbeck. MB, BR and DS were employed by Lundbeck SAS at the time of the study concept, analysis and reporting. At the time the study was conducted and the data presented in this paper analysed HC was an employee of Inferential, a provider of biostatistical consulting services working with pharmaceutical companies including Lundbeck. YC was employed by Lundbeck SAS at time of the study concept and analysis. LH-H is a full-time employee of H. Lundbeck A/S.

Author details

[1]Parc Sanitari Sant Joan de Deu, Universitat de Barcelona, CIBERSAM, C/ Doctor Antoni Pujadas 42, 08830 Sant Boi de Llobregat, Barcelona, Spain. [2]Lundbeck SAS, 37-45 Quai du Président Roosevelt, 92445 Issy-les-Moulineaux, France. [3]Department of Economics, Stockholm School of Economics, Sveavägen 65, 113 83 Stockholm, Sweden. [4]Personal Social Services Research Unit, Cowdray House, London School of Economics and Political Science, Houghton Street, London WC2A 2AE, UK. [5]Inferential, 35 rue Godot de Mauroy, 75009 Paris, France. [6]H. Lundbeck A/S, Ottiliavej 9, 2500 Valby, Denmark. [7]Present address: Merck KGaA, Darmstadt, Germany. [8]Present address: Capionis, Bordeaux, France. [9]Present address: Pierre Fabre SA, Boulogne, France. [10]Present address: Janssen, Issy-les-Moulineaux, France.

References

1. National Collaborating Centre for Mental Health. Depression: The NICE guideline on the treatment and management of depression in adults (updated edition). 2010. https://www.ncbi.nlm.nih.gov/pubmedhealth/PMH0016605/pdf/PubMedHealth_PMH0016605.pdf. Accessed 24 Jan 2017.
2. Rush AJ, Trivedi MH, Wisniewski SR, Nierenberg AA, Stewart JW, Warden D, et al. Acute and longer-term outcomes in depressed outpatients requiring one or several treatment steps: a STAR*D report. Am J Psychiatry. 2006; 163(11):1905–17.
3. Souery D, Amsterdam J, De Montigny C, Lecrubier Y, Montgomery S, Lipp O, et al. Treatment resistant depression: methodological overview and operational criteria. Eur Neuropsychopharmacol. 1999;9(1–2):83–91.
4. Trivedi MH, Rush AJ, Wisniewski SR, Nierenberg AA, Warden D, Ritz L, et al.; STAR*D study team. Evaluation of outcomes with citalopram for depression using measurement-based care in STAR*D: implications for clinical practice. Am J Psychiatry 2006;163(1):28–40.
5. American Psychiatric Association. Practice guideline for the treatment of patients with major depressive disorder. Third edition. 2010. http://psychiatryonline.org/pb/assets/raw/sitewide/practice_guidelines/guidelines/mdd.pdf. Accessed 24 Jan 2017.
6. Bauer M, Pfennig A, Severus E, Whybrow PC, Angst J, Möller HJ. World Federation of Societies of biological psychiatry (WFSBP) guidelines for biological treatment of unipolar depressive disorders, part 1: update 2013 on the acute and continuation treatment of unipolar depressive disorders. World J Biol Psychiatry. 2013;14(5):334–85.
7. Möller HJ, Bitter I, Bobes J, Fountoulakis K, Höschl C, Kasper S. European Psychiatric Association. Position statement of the European Psychiatric Association (EPA) on the value of antidepressants in the treatment of unipolar depression. Eur Psychiatry. 2012;27(2):114–28.
8. National Institute for Health and Clinical Excellence. NICE clinical guideline 90. Depression in adults: recognition and management. 2009. https://www.nice.org.uk/guidance/cg90/resources/depression-in-adults-recognition-and-management-975742636741. Accessed 24 Jan 2017.
9. Rubo J, Macpherson H, Young A. Atypical antipsychotics and other therapeutic options for treatment of resistant major depressive disorder. Pharmaceuticals. 2010;3:3522–42.
10. Garcia-Toro M, Medina E, Galan JL, Gonzalez MA, Maurino J. Treatment patterns in major depressive disorder after an inadequate response to first-line antidepressant treatment. BMC Psychiatry. 2012;12:143.
11. Lamy FX, Chollet J, Clay E, Brignone M, Rive B, Saragoussi D. Pharmacotherapeutic strategies for patients treated for depression in UK primary care: a database analysis. Curr Med Res Opin. 2015;31(4):795–807.
12. Saragoussi D, Chollet J, Bineau S, Chalem Y, Milea D. Antidepressant switching patterns in the treatment of major depressive disorder: a General Practice Research Database (GPRD) study. Int J Clin Pract. 2012;66(11):1079–87.
13. Sicras-Mainar A, Maurino J, Cordero L, Blanca-Tamayo M, Navarro-Artieda R. Assessment of pharmacological strategies for management of major depressive disorder and their costs after an inadequate response to first-line antidepressant treatment in primary care. Ann General Psychiatry. 2012;11(1):22.
14. Papakostas GI, Fava M, Thase ME. Treatment of SSRI-resistant depression: a meta-analysis comparing within- versus across-class switches. Biol Psychiatry. 2008;63(7):699–704.
15. Papakostas GI. Managing partial response or nonresponse: switching, augmentation, and combination strategies for major depressive disorder. J Clin Psychiatry. 2009;70(Suppl 6):16–25.
16. Trivedi MH, Morris DW, Wisniewski SR, Lesser I, Nierenberg AA, Daly E, et al. Increase in work productivity of depressed individuals with improvement in depressive symptom severity. Am J Psychiatry. 2013;170(6):633–41.
17. Kroenke K, Spitzer RL, Williams JB. The PHQ-9: validity of a brief depression severity measure. J Gen Intern Med. 2001;16(9):606–13.
18. Guy W. Clinical global impressions. ECDEU assessment manual for psychopharmacology. Rockville: National Institute of Mental Health; 1976.
19. Montgomery SA, Asberg M. A new depression scale designed to be sensitive to change. Br J Psychiatry. 1979;134:382–9.
20. Sheehan DV, Harnett-Sheehan K, Raj BA. The measurement of disability. Int Clin Psychopharmacol. 1996;11(Suppl 3):89–95.
21. Reilly MC, Zbrozek AS, Dukes EM. The validity and reproducibility of a work productivity and activity impairment instrument. Pharmacoeconomics. 1993; 4(5):353–65.
22. McGahuey CA, Gelenberg AJ, Laukes CA, Moreno FA, Delgado PL, McKnight KM, et al. The Arizona sexual experience scale (ASEX): reliability and validity. J Sex Marital Ther. 2000;26(1):25–40.
23. Ware J Jr, Kosinski M, Keller SD. A 12-item short-form health survey: construction of scales and preliminary tests of reliability and validity. Med Care. 1996;34(3):220–33.
24. EuroQol Group. EuroQol – a new facility for the measurement of health-related quality of life. Health Policy. 1990;16(3):199–208.
25. Dolan P, Gudex C, Kind P, Williams A. A social tariff for EuroQol: results from a UK population survey. Discussion paper 138. York: University of York; September 1995. http://www.york.ac.uk/che/pdf/DP138.pdf. Accessed 24 Jan 2017.
26. Kennedy SH, Andersen HF, Thase ME. Escitalopram in the treatment of major depressive disorder: a meta-analysis. Curr Med Res Opin. 2009;25(1):161–75.
27. Machado M, Einarson TR. Comparison of SSRIs and SNRIs in major depressive disorder: a meta-analysis of head-to-head randomized clinical trials. J Clin Pharm Ther. 2013;35(2):177–88.
28. Santaguida PL, MacQueen G, Keshavarz H, Levine M, Beyene J, Raina P. Treatment for depression after unsatisfactory response to SSRIs. AHRQ publication no.12-EHC050-EF. Rockville: Agency for Healthcare Research and Quality; 2012.
29. Simon GE, Revicki D, Heiligenstein J, Grothaus L, VonKorff M, Katon WJ, et al. Recovery from depression, work productivity, and health care costs among primary care patients. Gen Hosp Psychiatry. 2000;22(3):153–62.
30. Thase ME, Entsuah AR, Rudolph RL. Remission rates during treatment with venlafaxine or selective serotonin reuptake inhibitors. Br J Psychiatry. 2001; 178:234–41.
31. Thase ME, Pritchett YL, Ossanna MJ, Swindle RW, Xu J, Detke MJ. Efficacy of duloxetine and selective serotonin reuptake inhibitors: comparisons as assessed by remission rates in patients with major depressive disorder. J Clin Psychopharmacol. 2007;27(6):672–6.
32. Vergouwen AC, Burger H, Koerselman F, Verheij TJ. Initial rate of improvement in relation to remission of major depressive disorder in primary care. Prim Care Companion J Clin Psychiatry. 2007;9(5):364–6.
33. Rush AJ, Trivedi MH, Wisniewski SR, Stewart JW, Nierenberg AA, Thase ME, et al.; STAR*D Study Team. Bupropion-SR, sertraline, or venlafaxine-XR after failure of SSRIs for depression. N Engl J Med. 2006;354(12):1231–42.

34. Lenderking W, Samp J, Hanlon J, Hsieh R, Revicki DA, Akhras KS. Adherence, switching and discontinuation during the 12 weeks following antidepressant initiation in patients with depressive disorder: results of a prospective longitudinal study. Value Health. 2013;16(7):A550.
35. Köhler S, Unger T, Hoffmann S, Mackert A, Ross B, Fydrich T. The relationship of health-related quality of life and treatment outcome during inpatient treatment of depression. Qual Life Res. 2015;24(3):641–9.
36. Kontodimopoulos N, Pappa E, Niakas D, Tountas Y. Validity of SF-12 summary scores in a Greek general population. Health Qual Life Outcomes. 2007;5:55.
37. Ware J, Kosinski M, Keller SK. SF-36® physical and mental health summary scales: a user's manual. Boston: The Health Institute; 1994.
38. Rush AJ, Wisniewski SR, Warden D, Luther JF, Davis LL, Fava M, et al. Selecting among second-step antidepressant medication monotherapies: predictive value of clinical, demographic, or first-step treatment features. Arch Gen Psychiatry. 2008;65(8):870–80.
39. Schultz J, Joish V. Costs associated with changes in antidepressant treatment in a managed care population with major depressive disorder. Psychiatr Serv. 2009;60(12):1604–11.
40. Sheffield RE, Lo Sasso AT, Young CH, Way K. Selective serotonin reuptake inhibitor usage patterns as risk factors for hospitalization. Admin Policy Ment Health. 2002;30(2):121–39.
41. Beck A, Crain AL, Solberg LI, Unützer J, Glasgow RE, Maciosek MV, et al. Severity of depression and magnitude of productivity loss. Ann Fam Med. 2011;9(4):305–11.
42. Sapin C, Fantino B, Nowicki ML, Kind P. Usefulness of EQ-5D in assessing health status in primary care patients with major depressive disorder. Health Qual Life Outcomes. 2004;2:20.
43. Elliott TE, Renier CM, Palcher JA. Chronic pain, depression, and quality of life: correlations and predictive value of the SF-36. Pain Med. 2003;4(4):331–9.
44. Jiao J, Vincent A, Cha SS, Luedtke CA, Oh TH. Relation of age with symptom severity and quality of life in patients with fibromyalgia. Mayo Clin Proc. 2014;89(2):199–206.
45. Novick D, Montgomery W, Kadziola Z, Moneta V, Peng X, Brugnoli R, Haro JM. Do concomitant pain symptoms in patients with major depression affect quality of life even when taking into account baseline depression severity? Patient Prefer Adherence. 2013;7:463–70.
46. Soriano-Maldonado A, Amris K, Ortega FB, Segura-Jiménez V, Estévez-López F, Álvarez-Gallardo IC, et al. Association of different levels of depressive symptoms with symptomatology, overall disease severity, and quality of life in women with fibromyalgia. Qual Life Res. 2015;24(12):2951–7.
47. Castillo RC, Wegener ST, Heins SE, Haythornthwaite JA, Mackenzie EJ, Bosse MJ; LEAP study group. Longitudinal relationships between anxiety, depression, and pain: results from a two-year cohort study of lower extremity trauma patients. Pain. 2013;154(12):2860–6.
48. Means-Christensen AJ, Roy-Byrne PP, Sherbourne CD, Craske MG, Stein MB. Relationships among pain, anxiety, and depression in primary care. Depress Anxiety. 2008;25(7):593–600.
49. Fava M, Rush AJ, Alpert JE, Carmin CN, Balasubramani GK, Wisniewski SR, et al. What clinical and symptom features and comorbid disorders characterize outpatients with anxious major depressive disorder: a replication and extension. Can J Psychiatr. 2006;51(13):823–35.
50. Saltiel PF, Silvershein DI. Major depressive disorder: mechanism-based prescribing for personalized medicine. Neuropsychiatr Dis Treat. 2015;11: 875–88.
51. Boyd A, Van de Velde S, Vilagut G, de Graaf R, O'Neill S, Florescu S, et al. Gender differences in mental disorders and suicidality in Europe: results from a large cross-sectional population-based study. J Affect Disord. 2015; 173:245–54.
52. Trivedi MH, Rush AJ, Wisniewski SR, Warden D, McKinney W, Downing M. Factors associated with health-related quality of life among outpatients with major depressive disorder: a STAR*D report. J Clin Psychiatry. 2006; 67(2):185–95.
53. Andresen R, Caputi P, Oades LG. Do clinical outcome measures assess consumer-defined recovery? Psychiatry Res. 2010;177(3):309–17.
54. IsHak WW, Mirocha J, Pi S, Tobia G, Becker B, Peselow ED, Cohen RM. Patient-reported outcomes before and after treatment of major depressive disorder. Dialogues Clin Neurosci. 2014;16(2):171–83.
55. Slade M, Longden E. Empirical evidence about recovery and mental health. BMC Psychiatry. 2015;15:285. https://doi.org/10.1186/s12888-015-0678-4.
56. Oliveira-Maia AJ, Mendonça C, Pessoa MJ, Camacho M, Gago J. The mental health recovery measure can be used to assess aspects of both customer-based and service-based recovery in the context of severe mental illness. Front Psychol. 2016;7:1679.
57. Kovess-Masfety V, Alonso J, Brugha TS, Angermeyer MC, Haro JM, Sevilla-Dedieu C; ESEMeD/MHEDEA 2000 investigators. Differences in lifetime use of services for mental health problems in six European countries. Psychiatr Serv. 2007;58(2):213–20.

23

Anxiety and its predictive value for pain and regular analgesic intake after lumbar disc surgery

Rita Laufenberg-Feldmann[1*], Bernd Kappis[1], Rafael J. A. Cámara[2] and Marion Ferner[1]

Abstract

Background: Ongoing pain after surgery is a major problem and influences recovery and the quality of life of the patient. Associations between anxiety and their impact on postoperative pain after herniated disc surgery have been reported, but the results are inconsistent. The aim of the present longitudinal study was to evaluate the predictive value of preoperative anxiety for postoperative ongoing pain and prolonged analgesic intake after herniated disc surgery.

Methods: 106 patients with lumbar disc herniation were evaluated in the study. Anxiety was measured with the Generalized Anxiety Disorder 7-Item Scale (GAD-7) before surgery. Pain intensity was assessed on a numeric rating scale (NRS) at baseline, 6-weeks and 6-months after surgery. Regression analysis was performed to identify independent predictors of pain and regular utilization of analgesics up to 6 months after surgery while controlling for confounding variables.

Results: 42.5% of the patients were rated as anxiety cases (sum scores GAD-7 > 5), mean scores of anxiety showed mild to moderate symptom severity, and 43% suffered from chronic pain before surgery. Six months after surgery, 55.6% of the patients indicated pain levels of 4/10 (NRS) or higher and about 40% still took pain medication on a regular basis, regardless of their preoperative classification as anxiety-case (37.7% and 41.5%). The preoperative pain level was statistically significant for ongoing postsurgical pain in all four analyses ($p < 0.001$). With binary logistic regression analyses, preoperative pain intensity, but neither demographic factors nor preoperative anxiety, was identified as predictor for postoperative pain and need for analgesic medication up to 6 months after lumbar disc surgery.

Conclusion: We found no evidence for the presence of anxiety before disc surgery being a prognostic factor for ongoing pain and regular postoperative intake of analgesics. Only preoperative pain intensity was predictive for increased pain and continued need for analgesic medication up to 6 months after lumbar disc surgery.

Keywords: Lumbar, Spine surgery, Anxiety, Postoperative pain, Prediction, Analgesics, Opioids

* Correspondence: rita.laufenberg@unimedizin-mainz.de
[1]Department of Anesthesiology, University Medical Center of the Johannes Gutenberg University Mainz, Langenbeckstrasse 1, D-55131 Mainz, Germany
Full list of author information is available at the end of the article

Background

Low back pain is a common medical condition, often recurring, and a major cause for sick leave and activity limitation [1]. In most cases no specific patho-anatomical correlates are found [2]. Among the specific causes for low back pain disc herniation is most common, with prevalence rates from 1% to 5% [3, 4]. Ninety percent of patients with acute lumbar back pain recover with conservative treatment [5] including physiotherapy, back exercises, manual therapy and analgesic medication. Absolute indications for surgery are rare and include neurological deficit causing weakness of functionally important muscles or cauda equina syndrome. Usually, surgical indication for nucleotomy due to herniated disc is chosen if persistent radicular pain and neurological deficits do not improve after conservative treatment [6, 7]. Percutaneous nucleotomy is one of the most frequent lumbar spine operations. Nevertheless the long-term benefit of a surgical intervention regarding pain reduction, improvement of functionality and return to work is often not superior to non-surgical approaches, as demonstrated in several studies [6–10]. The analysis of predictors contributing to good postoperative outcomes is crucial.

Associations between psychological factors such as anxiety and depression and musculoskeletal disorders and their impact on postoperative results after herniated disc surgery have been reported [11–13]. In a prior study we found that 19% of patients experienced preoperative anxiety [14]. It seems plausible that anxiety may contribute to worse patient-reported outcomes such as ongoing post-operative pain and intake of analgesics. However, the results of the only two longitudinal studies on the topic are inconsistent [15, 16]. The evidence on possible associations between preoperative anxiety and postoperative analgesic intake is even poorer.

The aim of the present longitudinal study was to investigate the role of preoperative anxiety as a potential influencing factor for postoperative ongoing pain and predictor for prolonged analgesic intake after herniated disc surgery.

Methods

This single center cohort study was conducted at the Department of Anesthesiology of the University Medical Center of the Johannes Gutenberg University Mainz, Germany. Data were extracted from a data set evaluating the influence of psychological variables on pain-related outcome after major neurological (spine), orthopaedic (hip or knee) or urological surgery (Mainz Outcome Predictor Study). Ethical approval for this study [Ethical Committee N° 837.519.11 (8061)] was provided on 3rd January 2012 by the Regional Ethics Committee of Rhineland-Palatinate, Mainz, Germany. The study was registered in clinicaltrials.gov (Identifier: NCT01488617) before patient enrolment. All patients gave their written informed consent.

Data of 143 patients undergoing spine surgery were evaluated (see CONSORT diagram, Fig. 1). For this subgroup analysis we identified 106 patients undergoing surgery due to lumbar disc herniation (percutaneous endoscopic lumbar discectomy) between January 2012 and August 2013. Inclusion criteria were herniated disc with neurological deficit as determined by clinical and radiological examination and a diagnosis according to the International Classification of Diseases (ICD-10) M51. Patients were aged ≥18 years, could read and understand German language and were capable to complete questionnaires.

The study included three time points for data collection: Baseline (= 1 day prior to surgery), 6-weeks after surgery, and 6-months after surgery. At baseline, all patients provided demographic, anxiety, clinical, and pain data. Pain data were additionally collected 6-weeks and 6-months after surgery and data on analgesic intake 6-months after surgery. Demographic data included age, gender, marital status, and education level. Clinical data included body mass index (BMI), physical status, and duration of surgery.

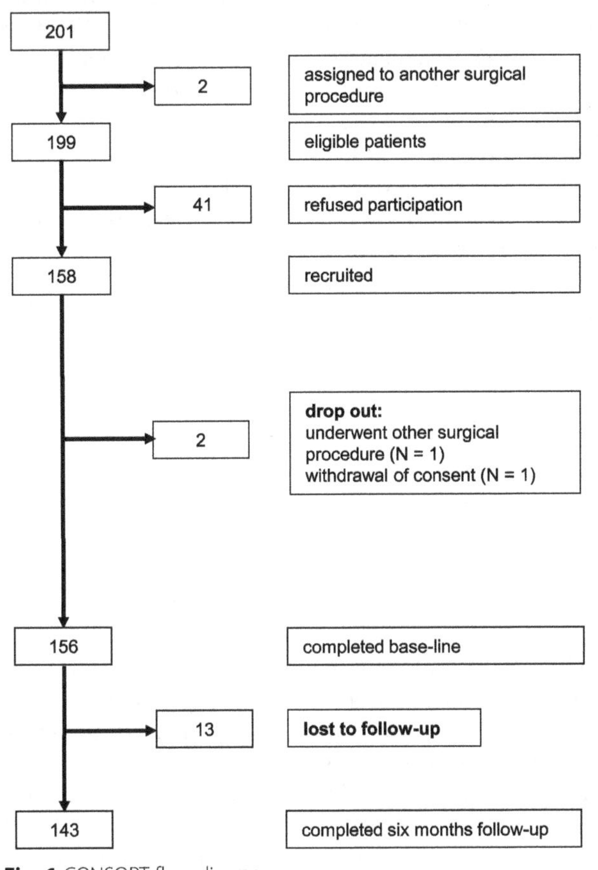

Fig. 1 CONSORT flow diagram

Demographic data were collected with a questionnaire. Anxiety was assessed with the Generalized Anxiety Disorder 7-Item Scale GAD-7 (see Additional file 1) [17]. Physical status was measured with the American Society of Anesthesiologists physical status classification system (ASA), which ranges from I (normal healthy person) to VI (declared brain-dead patient) [18].

Preoperative pain duration for more than 6 months was defined as chronic pain as specified in the German pain questionnaire [19]. Pain during movement has more clinical impact after surgery of the musculoskeletal system than pain at rest with regard to assess mobilization and long-term outcome after surgery [20], thus patients were asked to indicate pain intensity during movement or stress, e.g. during mobilization or coughing. Pain intensity during movement, also called "dynamic pain" [21], was assessed on a numerical rating scale at baseline (NRS, 0–10 integers with 0 = no pain and 10 = worst possible pain) and at follow-up. Postoperative pain ratings > 3/10 were defined as clinically relevant. Pain and analgesics data at follow-up were collected by letter and by structured telephone interviews. If no questionnaire was returned to the study center, patients were called by telephone and asked to rate their pain intensity using a numerical rating scale.

To assess anxiety, the GAD-7 is a brief, validated, and freely available self-administered patient questionnaire. It is used as a screening tool and severity measure for generalized anxiety disorder, referring to specific criteria of a Generalized Anxiety Disorder according to DSM-IV [22]. As the GAD-7 focuses on the assessment of moods, cognitions, or behaviors (e.g. feeling afraid or nervous, inability to control worrying, and restlessness), it is an appropriate measure for a global assessment of anxiety [23]. Items apply for the last 2 weeks and are scored from 0 (not at all) to 3 (nearly every day). Sum scores range from 0 to 21, reflecting the severity of the symptoms. Scores of ≥5, ≥10, and ≥15 represent mild, moderate, and severe anxiety symptom levels, respectively [22].

Statistical analysis

Demographic, anxiety, clinical, pain, and analgesics data were described as absolute (N) and relative frequencies (%) for categorical parameters and means and SD for continuous parameters. Pain was additionally described by one bar chart per measurement time point.

The association between preoperative anxiety (independent variable) and postoperative pain intensity during movement (dependent variable) was analyzed graphically and in four linear regression models.

Graphical analysis included medians and interquartile ranges by presence versus absence of preoperative anxiety on the GAD-7 [17]. Participants scoring > 5 were defined as "anxiety cases". Four regression models of postoperative pain by preoperative anxiety were performed for binary and continuous anxiety and for each follow-up time point (6-weeks and 6-months postoperatively). Continuous anxiety was z-transformed in order to obtain the number of 0–10 pain rating points per standard deviation of preoperative anxiety. All models were adjusted for age, BMI, sex, preoperative pain, and presence versus absence of chronic pain.

The association between preoperative anxiety (independent variable) and 6-months postoperative analgesic intake (dependent variable) was analyzed graphically and in two binary logistic regression models. Graphical analysis included bar charts of analgesic consumption by presence versus absence of preoperative anxiety as defined above. One regression model of postoperative analgesic intake by preoperative anxiety was performed for binary and for continuous anxiety, respectively. Transformations of continuous anxiety and adjustment for potential confounders were performed as described above.

All analyses were performed using IBM SPSS Statistics for Windows, Version 22 (Released 2013. IBM SPSS Statistics for Windows, Armonk, NY: IBM Corp.). *P*-values < 0.05 were considered statistically significant.

Results

Patients

Start of enrolment of patients was in January 2012. Of 199 eligible patients, 156 patients underwent spine surgery (see CONSORT diagram, Fig. 1). Thereof 106 patients (67.5%) were identified with discectomy due to lumbar herniated disc and completed the follow-up questionnaire 6-months after surgery.

Demographic, anxiety and clinical baseline data

At baseline, the mean age of the 106 participants was 58.8 years (±16.5), and 51 (48.1%) were female (Table 1). With a mean GAD-7 score of 5.0 (95% CI: 4.3 to 5.8), 45 (42.5%) of the patients were rated as "anxiety cases" (Table 1).

Pain at baseline and follow-up

Less than half of the patients ($N = 43$, 43.0%) suffered from chronic pain prior to surgery, which was defined as pain lasting for at least 6 months. Generally, patients' mean pain ratings before surgery were higher than postoperatively. Mean NRS scores preoperatively were 6.8 (SD 2.6), and decreased to 2.9 (SD 2.4) 6-weeks after surgery. After 6 months, the mean NRS score was 3.7 (SD 2.7). While only five patients (4.7%) reported absence of preoperative movement pain, 23 patients (21.7%) indicated to be pain-free during movement after 6-weeks and 21 patients (19.8%) after 6-months (Fig. 2).

Table 1 Demographic and clinical data at baseline

Number	106
Mean age (standard deviation)	58.8 (16.5)
95% confidence interval of age	55.7–62.0
Range of age	24.4–86.9
Number of females (%)	51 (48.1)
Without partnership[a] (%)	31 (30.7)
Educational level [b]	
Number of "low" [b] (%), up to 9 school years	48 (49.0)
Number of "medium" [b] (%), 10 school years	26 (26.5)
Number of "high" [b] (%),12 or more school years	24 (24.5)
Mean preoperative anxiety [c] (standard deviation)	5.0 (3.8)
Number of anxiety cases [c] (N, %)	45 (42.5)
Mild anxiety (GAD-7 score 6–9) (N, %)	35 (33.0)
Moderate anxiety (GAD-7 score 10–14) (N, %)	7 (6.6)
Severe anxiety (GAD-7 score > =15) (N, %)	3 (2.8)
Mean body mass index (standard deviation)	27.9 (4.4)
Preoperative ASA (American Society of Anesthesiologists physical status classification system)	
ASA 1 (%)	9 (8.5)
ASA 2 (%)	51 (48.1)
ASA 3 (%)	45 (42.5)
ASA 4 (%)	1 (0.9)
Mean duration of surgery in minutes (standard deviation)	117 (53)
95% confidence interval of duration of surgery	107–127
Range of duration of surgery	40–299

[a] 101 non-missing values;
[b] 98 non-missing values;
[c] Generalized Anxiety Disorder 7-Item Scale: > 5 = anxiety case

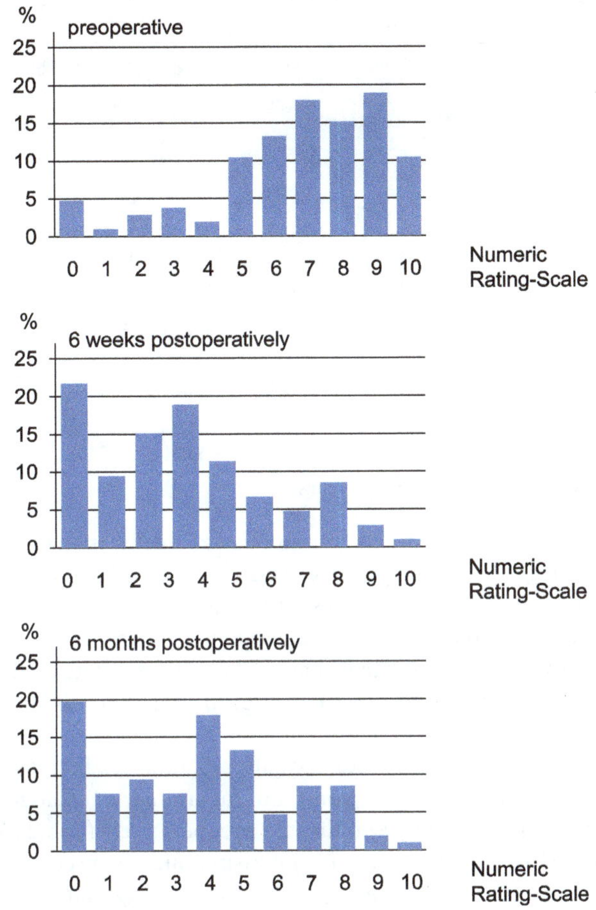

Fig. 2 Pain distribution before, 6 weeks after, and 6 months after surgery

Analgesics at follow-up

6-weeks after surgery, data concerning pain medication were obtained from 101 patients. 40 (39.6%) of the patients reported a regular use of pain medication, 10 (9.9%) still took opioids. At 6-months 37 patients (39.4%) reported to take pain medication on a regular basis, and 9 (9.6%) took opioids, respectively ($N = 94$ patients).

Association between preoperative anxiety and postoperative pain

Postoperative pain scores of patients with and without preoperative anxiety were compared. In both groups the pain levels decreased at 6-weeks after surgery, and slightly increased at 6-months. Pain ratings for patients with and without anxiety did not differ at any of the three time points (Fig. 3).

Regression analyses were performed to evaluate the influence of preoperative anxiety on postoperative pain at 6-weeks and 6-months. First, the presence or absence of preoperative anxiety was the main independent variable (see Table 2). In addition, the extent of preoperative

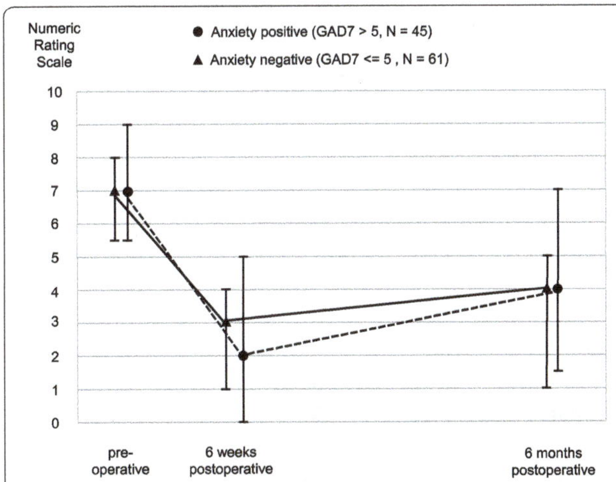

Fig. 3 Pain distribution (medians and interquartile ranges) by presence versus absence of preoperative anxiety on the Generalized Anxiety Disorder 7-Item Scale: > 5 = anxiety cases

Table 2 Pain after 6 weeks and 6 months by presence versus absence of preoperative anxiety (n = 100)

	Pain increase at 6-weeks.		Pain increase at 6-months.	
	NRS Points (95% confidence interval)	*P* value	NRS Points (95% confidence interval)	*P* value
Preoperative anxiety (yes/no)	–.30 (–1.22–.63)	.52	.42 (–.63–1.46)	.43
Age (years)	–.02 (–.04–.01)	.31	.00 (–.03–.03)	.98
BMI (points)	–.06 (–.16–.05)	.29	.13 (.01–.25)	.04*
Sex (male)	–.22 (– 1.15–.71)	.64	–.46 (– 1.51–.59)	.39
Preoperative pain (points)	.36 (.18–.54)	.00*	.36 (.16–.56)	.00*
Chronic pain (yes/no [a])	.88 (–.08–1.85)	.07	.55 (–.54–1.63)	.32
Intercept	3.04 (–.56–6.64)	.10	– 1.96 (–6.02–2.10)	.34

[a] Preoperative pain duration > 6 months

anxiety (GAD-7 score as continuous variable) was analysed with regard to postoperative pain at the two time points (Table 3). In none of these four analyses preoperative anxiety was found to predict postoperative pain.

However, preoperative pain levels were statistically significant for ongoing postsurgical pain in all four analyses ($p < 0.001$).

Postoperative pain intensity after 6 months increases by 0.3–0.4 points per point on the numeric analogue pain rating scale (NRS) indicated preoperatively (Table 3). Therefore preoperative pain intensity, but not preoperative anxiety has a predictive value for ongoing pain up to 6 months after surgery.

Association between anxiety and postoperative analgesic intake

After 6 months, about 40% of the patients still took pain medication on a regular basis, regardless of preoperative classification as an anxiety-case (37.7% and 41.5%, Fig. 4). Preoperative anxiety showed no correlation with postoperative

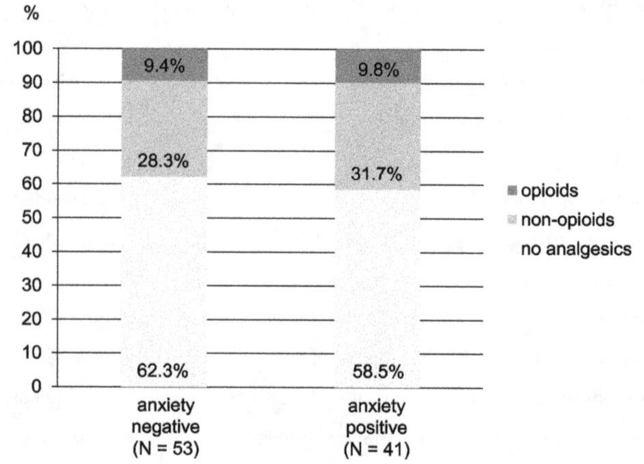

Fig. 4 6-months postoperative analgesic consumption by presence versus absence of preoperative anxiety on the Generalized Anxiety Disorder 7-Item Scale: > 5 = anxiety cases

analgesic intake. Patients with or without preoperative anxiety do not differ with regard to postoperative intake of analgesics (Table 4, part A). Also, the level of preoperative anxiety was not predictive for postoperative analgesic consumption (Table 4, part B).

Table 3 Pain after 6 weeks and 6 months by one standard deviation (SD) of preoperative anxiety (*n* = 100)

	Pain increase at 6-weeks.		Pain increase at 6-months.	
	NRS Points (95% confidence interval)	*P* value	NRS Points (95% confidence interval)	*P* value
Preoperative anxiety (SD)	–.12 (–.60–.37)	.64	.19 (–.36–.74)	.50
Age (years)	–.01 (–.04–.01)	.32	.00 (–.03–.03)	.99
BMI (points)	–.06 (–.16–.05)	.30	.12 (.00–.24)	.04*
Sex (male)	–.22 (– 1.16–.73)	.65	–.48 (– 1.54–.59)	.38
Preoperative pain (points)	.36 (.18–.55)	.00*	.36 (.15–.56)	.00*
Chronic pain (yes/no [a])	.86 (–.10–1.82)	.08	.58 (–.50–1.66)	.29
Intercept	2.85 (–.75–6.45)	.12	– 1.68 (– 5.74–2.38)	.41

[a] Preoperative pain duration > 6 months

Table 4 Binary logistic regression analyses of 6-months postoperative analgesics consumption by preoperative anxiety

A. Analgesics consumption by presence versus absence of preoperative anxiety [a] (*n* = 90)		
	Odds ratio of analgesics consumption (95% confidence interval)	*P* value
Preoperative anxiety (yes/no [a])	1.03 (.38–2.78)	.96
Age (years)	1.01 (.98–1.04)	.66
BMI (points)	1.12 (1.00–1.26)	.06
Sex (male)	.93 (.35–2.50)	.89
Preoperative pain intensity	1.47 (1.13–1.89)	.00*
Chronic pain (yes/no [b])	1.10 (.39–3.12)	.85
Intercept	.00 (–)	.00
B. Analgesics consumption by one standard deviation (SD) of preoperative anxiety (n = 90)		
	Odds ratio of analgesics consumption (95% confidence interval)	
Preoperative anxiety (one SD)	.79 (.45–1.40)	.42
Age (years)	1.01 (.95–1.04)	.72
BMI (points)	1.11 (.99–1.25)	.07
Sex (male)	1.00 (.37–2.73)	1.00
Preoperative pain intensity	1.50 (1.15–1.96)	.00*
Chronic pain (yes/no [b])	1.15 (.40–3.27)	.79
Intercept	.00 (–)	.00

[a] Generalized Anxiety Disorder 7-Item Scale: > 5 = preoperative anxiety: yes
[b] Preoperative pain duration > 6 months

Discussion

The aim of this study was to investigate the role of preoperative anxiety as a potential influencing factor for postoperative ongoing pain and predictor for prolonged analgesic intake after lumbar herniated disc surgery. We found that preoperative pain intensity was the only predictor for persistence of pain and need for analgesics up to 6-months after surgery.

Among socio-demographic variables, BMI, but not age or sex, was also predictive for ongoing pain 6-months after lumbar disc surgery, but not for the intake of analgesics. Anxiety, assessed with the GAD-7 questionnaire, had no predictive value, neither for pain nor for analgesic consumption.

The role of psychological factors such as anxiety, depression or catastrophizing for the outcome of patients (e.g. persistent pain, return to work etc.) undergoing herniated disc surgery is considered as relevant, as shown in several review articles [12, 13, 24]. In a systematic review using different measures for preoperative anxiety and catastrophizing, these psychological factors were shown to play a role (odds ratio of 1.55 to 2.10) in the development of chronic postsurgical pain [24]. In a previous study, we identified nearly 20% of patients with preoperative anxiety [14]. So far, the association between preoperative anxiety and postoperative pain intensity has been outlined in only two prospective studies with different results [15, 16]. In one study evaluating the role of trait anxiety on persistent radicular pain after lumbar disc herniation surgery, patients identified with trait anxiety had significantly higher postoperative VAS (visual analog scale) pain scores until 12 months after surgery ($p < .0001$) [15]. However, the other study found only a minor association between preoperative anxiety and ongoing postoperative pain 3 months after lumbar discectomy (Spearman's rho = .18, $p > 0.2$) in a small sample of 53 patients [16].

Although we identified a considerable percentage of patients experiencing anxiety (GAD-7 > 5, corresponding to 42.5% of the patients), the presence of anxiety prior to surgery does not represent a valid prognostic factor for persistent pain and analgesic intake 6 weeks or 6 months after nucleotomy due to herniated lumbar disc.

These conflicting results may be due to small sample sizes in all three studies, including ours, differences in socio-demographic patient characteristics, duration of follow-up and instruments to measure preoperative anxiety. Questionnaires to assess anxiety differ with regards to their sensitivity and specificity to measure state or trait anxiety. Compared to other self-assessment instruments such as APAIS [25] or STAI [26], the GAD-7 is applicable to measure anxiety independent of contextual factors, but as a short questionnaire it is suitable also in a preoperative situation.

Our results also suggest that a higher BMI is predictive for increased postoperative pain 6-months after lumbar disc surgery. However, in two retrospective cohort studies of patients undergoing lumbar spine surgery, obesity was associated with higher complication rates, but body mass index did not have an effect on the pain-related clinical outcome [27, 28]. Different results may be due to the longer follow-up period in both cited studies. Possibly the healing process is longer in obese patients, so that is takes more time until they are pain-free after lumbar spine surgery.

While we found no influence of demographic factors such as female gender and younger age as risk factors for persistent postoperative pain, their effect was inconsistent in other studies [29, 30]. In a recent Swedish register study, it was demonstrated that elderly patients appeared to have worse postoperative outcomes after lumbar disc herniation surgery than young and middle-aged patients. The authors postulated that these patients were referred to surgery with inferior clinical status, and thus improve less postoperatively [31]. Among the elderly patients with lumbar disc herniation, women reported inferior outcome compared to males [32].

In the present study we could demonstrate that preoperative pain was the strongest predictor for persistent postoperative pain. Although the majority of our patients indicated a decrease in pain of about 3 points on a NRS after surgery, the benefit was significantly lower in patients with a higher preoperative pain level. The fact that stronger preoperative pain is associated with increased postsurgical pain is supported in a review article by Kehlet et al. [33].

Prediction of the severity of early postoperative pain with a combined scoring system, based on age, sex, type of surgery, extent of preoperative pain, and level of anxiety has been proposed by Kalkman et al. [34]. However this approach has not been validated in larger studies for specific procedures and does not fit for chronic postoperative pain. Due to a complicated mathematical model it is not applicable for decision-making in clinical routine. Nevertheless, the assessment of risk factors including psychosocial factors can contribute to predict the individual risk for the development of chronic postsurgical pain and helps clinicians in the decision making for surgical treatment of chronic low back pain [35].

Despite overall pain reduction in the entire sample 6-months after surgery more than half of the patients (55.6%) still reported pain levels above 4/10 NRS 6 months postoperatively. Furthermore, we found that 30% of all patients still reported the intake of non-opioid analgesics 6 months after surgery, and additional 10% even indicated the intake of opioids. These aspects show that the analysis of factors contributing to the development and the persistence of pain symptoms to weigh up the potential benefit of a surgical intervention against a conservative therapeutic approach should be considered before decision-making for surgery. In addition, it is important to identify and treat psychological comorbidities related to the genesis of ongoing pain. A better identification of patients at risk to develop chronic postoperative pain would be helpful to find preventive approaches, including e.g. preemptive multimodal analgesia or psychological therapeutic attempts, e.g. behavior therapy.

The major limitation of the present study is lack of power for the secondary outcome (analgesics), while the power was sufficient for the primary outcome (pain). Thus, the large association between preoperative anxiety and medication use at follow-up was not statistically significant. A further limitation is the lack of information on pain-related patient disability beyond 6-months of follow-up, as well as an associated interference with daily life activities and work. A longer follow-up period would have been helpful to better adjust for clinical risk factors of postoperative pain and to assess their impact on disability and return to work.

Conclusions

In conclusion, in patients with nucleotomy due to lumbar disc herniation the intensity of the preoperative pain was identified as an influencing factor for the persistence of postoperative pain up to 6 months after surgery. The influence of preoperative anxiety, measured with the GAD-7, on postoperative pain and analgesic intake during the first 6-months after disc surgery could not be confirmed in this relatively small sample of patients. Considering the number of patients without benefit in terms of long-lasting pain relief after disc surgery, further research on psychological prognostic factors is needed.

Abbreviations

APAIS: The Amsterdam Preoperative Anxiety and Information Scale; ASA-grade: American society of Anesthesiologists grade; BMI: Body Mass Index; CONSORT: Consolidated Standards of Reporting Trials; DSM: Diagnostic and Statistical Manual of Mental Disorders; GAD-7: Generalized Anxiety Disorder 7-Item Scale; NRS: Numeric Rating Scale; STAI: State Trait Anxiety Inventory

Acknowledgements

Assistance with the study: We would like to thank all patients who participated in the Mainz Outcome Predictor Study. Special thanks go to Susanne Mauff for her discreet and accurate study coordination, Peter Straub for his affectionate patient care and diligent study assistance, and Hans-Jürgen Baldering for his patience and efforts to resolve all IT problems. Without their commitment, the study would never have been completed.

Funding

Not applicable

Authors' contributions

RL, BK, RC and MF were in charge and contributed to all stages of the present study. RL, BK and MF were responsible for the original data collection. RC contributed to interpreting the data and writing the final manuscript. RL, BK, RC and MF contributed to reviewing the accuracy of the data and writing the final manuscript. All authors read and approved the final manuscript.

Consent for publication

Not applicable.

Competing interests

The authors declare that they have no competing interests.

Author details

[1]Department of Anesthesiology, University Medical Center of the Johannes Gutenberg University Mainz, Langenbeckstrasse 1, D-55131 Mainz, Germany. [2]Institute for Medical Biostatistics, Epidemiology and Informatics (IMBEI), University Medical Center of the Johannes Gutenberg University Mainz, Mainz, Germany.

References

1. Lidgren L. The bone and joint decade 2000-2010. Bull World Health Organ. 2003;81:629.
2. Maher C, Underwood M, Buchbinder R. Non-specific low back pain. Lancet. 2017;389:736–47.
3. Jordan J, Konstantinou K, O'Dowd J. Herniated lumbar disc. BMJ Clin Evid. 2009;2009
4. Casser HR, Seddigh S, Rauschmann M. Acute Lumbar Back Pain. Dtsch Arztebl Int. 2016;113:223–34.
5. Gibson JN, Waddell G. Surgical interventions for lumbar disc prolapse: updated Cochrane review. Spine (Phila Pa 1976). 2007;32:1735–47.
6. Peul WC, van Houwelingen HC, van den Hout WB, Brand R, Eekhof JA, Tans JT, Thomeer RT, Koes BW, Leiden-The Hague Spine Intervention Prognostic Study G. Surgery versus prolonged conservative treatment for sciatica. N Engl J Med. 2007;356:2245–56.
7. Weinstein JN, Tosteson TD, Lurie JD, Tosteson AN, Hanscom B, Skinner JS, Abdu WA, Hilibrand AS, Boden SD, Deyo RA. Surgical vs nonoperative treatment for lumbar disk herniation: the spine patient outcomes research trial (SPORT): a randomized trial. JAMA. 2006;296:2441–50.
8. Kerr D, Zhao W, Lurie JD. What are long-term predictors of outcomes for lumbar disc herniation? A randomized and observational study. Clin Orthop Relat Res. 2014;473:1920–30.
9. Lequin MB, Verbaan D, Jacobs WCH, et al. Surgery versus prolonged conservative treatment for sciatica: 5-year results of a randomised controlled trial. BMJ Open 2013;3:e002534. https://doi.org/10.1136/bmjopen-2012-002534.
10. Gugliotta M, da Costa BR, Dabis E, Theiler R, Juni P, Reichenbach S, Landolt H, Hasler P. Surgical versus conservative treatment for lumbar disc herniation: a prospective cohort study. BMJ Open. 2016;6:e012938.
11. Junge A, Dvorak J, Ahrens S. Predictors of bad and good outcomes of lumbar disc surgery. A prospective clinical study with recommendations for screening to avoid bad outcomes. Spine (Phila Pa 1976). 1995;20:460–8.
12. Zieger M, Schwarz R, König HH, Härter M, Riedel-Heller SG. Depression and anxiety in patients undergoing herniated disc surgery: relevant but Underresearched – a systematic review. Cen Eur Neurosurg. 2010;71:26–34.
13. Dorow M, Lobner M, Stein J, Konnopka A, Meisel HJ, Gunther L, Meixensberger J, Stengler K, Konig HH, Riedel-Heller SG. Risk factors for postoperative pain intensity in patients undergoing lumbar disc surgery: a systematic review. PLoS One. 2017;12:e0170303.
14. Laufenberg-Feldmann R, Kappis B. Assessing preoperative anxiety using a questionnaire and clinical rating: a prospective observational study. Eur J Anaesthesiol. 2013;30:758–63.
15. D'Angelo C, Mirijello A, Ferrulli A, Leggio L, Berardi A, Icolaro N, Miceli A, D'Angelo V, Gasbarrini G, Addolorato G. Role of trait anxiety in persistent radicular pain after surgery for lumbar disc herniation: a 1-year longitudinal study. Neurosurgery. 2010;67:265–71.
16. Hegarty D, Shorten G. Multivariate prognostic modeling of persistent pain following lumbar discectomy. Pain Physician. 2012;15:421–34.
17. Lowe B, Decker O, Muller S, Brahler E, Schellberg D, Herzog W, Herzberg PY. Validation and standardization of the generalized anxiety disorder screener (GAD-7) in the general population. Med Care. 2008;46:266–74.
18. Asa Physical Status Classification System [www.asahq.org/resources/clinical-information/asa-physical-status-classification-system].
19. Nagel B, Gerbershagen HU, Lindena G, Pfingsten M. Development and

evaluation of the multidimensional German pain questionnaire. Schmerz. 2002;16:263–70.
20. Stubhaug A, Breivik H. Prevention and treatment of hyperalgesia and persistent pain after surgery. In: Breivik H, Shipley M, editors. Pain best practice and research compendium. London: Elsevier; 2007. p. 281–8.
21. Breivik H, Borchgrevink PC, Allen SM, Rosseland LA, Romundstad L, Hals EK, Kvarstein G, Stubhaug A. Assessment of pain. Br J Anaesth. 2008;101:17–24.
22. Spitzer RL, Kroenke K, Williams JB, Lowe B. A brief measure for assessing generalized anxiety disorder: the GAD-7. Arch Intern Med. 2006;166:1092–7.
23. Rose M, Devine J. Assessment of patient-reported symptoms of anxiety. Dialogues Clin Neurosci. 2014;16:197–211.
24. Theunissen M, Peters ML, Bruce J, Gramke HF, Marcus MA. Preoperative anxiety and catastrophizing: a systematic review and meta-analysis of the association with chronic postsurgical pain. Clin J Pain. 2012;28:819–41.
25. Moerman N, van Dam FS, Muller MJ, Oosting H. The Amsterdam preoperative anxiety and information scale (APAIS). Anesth Analg. 1996;82:445–51.
26. Spielberger CD, Gorsuch RL, Lushene R, Vagg PR, Jacobs GA. Manual for the state-trait anxiety inventory. Palo Alto: Consulting Psychologists Press; 1983.
27. Rihn JA, Radcliff K, Hilibrand AS, Anderson DT, Zhao W, Lurie J, Vaccaro AR, Freedman MK, Albert TJ, Weinstein JN. Does obesity affect outcomes of treatment for lumbar stenosis and degenerative spondylolisthesis? Analysis of the spine patient outcomes research trial (SPORT). Spine (Phila Pa 1976). 2012;37:1933–46.
28. Onyekwelu I, Glassman SD, Asher AL, Shaffrey CI, Mummaneni PV, Carreon LY. Impact of obesity on complications and outcomes: a comparison of fusion and nonfusion lumbar spine surgery. J Neurosurg Spine. 2017;26:158–62.
29. Kinjo S, Sands LP, Lim E, Paul S, Leung JM. Prediction of postoperative pain using path analysis in older patients. J Anesth. 2012;26:1–8.
30. Rosseland LA, Stubhaug A. Gender is a confounding factor in pain trials: women report more pain than men after arthroscopic surgery. Pain. 2004; 112:248–53.
31. Stromqvist F, Stromqvist B, Jonsson B, Karlsson MK. The outcome of lumbar disc herniation surgery is worse in old adults than in young adults. Acta Orthop. 2016;87:516–21.
32. Stromqvist F, Stromqvist B, Jonsson B, Karlsson MK. Gender differences in the surgical treatment of lumbar disc herniation in elderly. Eur Spine J. 2016;25:3528–35.
33. Kehlet H, Jensen TS, Woolf CJ. Persistent postsurgical pain: risk factors and prevention. Lancet. 2006;367:1618–25.
34. Kalkman CJ, Visser K, Moen J, Bonsel GJ, Grobbee DE, Moons KG. Preoperative prediction of severe postoperative pain. Pain. 2003;105:415–23.
35. Schug SA, Bruce J. Risk stratification for the development of chronic postsurgical pain. Pain Rep. 2017;2:e627.

Attentional bias modification in reducing test anxiety vulnerability

Wenpeng Cai[1†], Yu Pan[2†], Huangyangzi Chai[3], Yi Cui[1], Jin Yan[1], Wei Dong[1*] and Guanghui Deng[1*]

Abstract

Background: A tendency to selectively process a threat to positive information may be involved in the etiology of anxiety disorders. The aim of this study is to examine whether attentional bias modification (ABM) can be used to modify high test-anxiety individuals' attention to emotional information and whether this change is related to anxiety vulnerability.

Methods: Seventy-seven undergraduates were included: 28 individuals received a 5-day modified dot probe task as ABM training, 29 individuals received a 5-day classic dot probe task as placebo, and 20 individuals did not receive an intervention between the two test sections. In addition to the measure of biased attention, salivary α-amylase (sAA) and the visual analogue scale of anxiety were assessed as emotional reactivity to stress.

Results: A repeated measurement of variance analysis and paired sample *t*-test indicated that the ABM group showed a significant change in attentional bias scores after the 5-day training, whereas there were no changes in the attentional bias scores in the placebo or waiting list groups. Importantly, anxiety vulnerability with attention to threats was significantly decreased in the training group.

Conclusions: These results suggest that attentional bias toward threat stimuli may play an important role in anxiety vulnerability. The attentional bias modification away from the threat is effective for the individuals preparing for an exam.

Keywords: Test anxiety, Anxiety vulnerability, Attentional bias modification, Salivary amylase, Behavioral training, Dot probe, eStroop

Background

In general, anxious individuals preferentially allocate their attention towards threatening information in the environment over non-threatening stimuli, a pattern that is not detected in non-anxious individuals [1]. A range of evidence has suggested that this attentional bias may play an important role in the development and maintenance of anxiety and fear [2, 3].

Studies in non-anxious populations indicate that systematic training to attend to threats can increase susceptibility to stress [4, 5]. Moreover, several researchers have managed to reduce the attentional bias in anxious individuals using computerized attention tasks in which participants are trained to avoid the threat [6–8]. A modified dot-probe task was used in these studies. Two stimuli, including one threatening stimulus and one neutral stimulus, are typically involved and simultaneously presented. Following the removal of the stimuli, a target probe appears in the location previously occupied by one of the stimuli. Participants are instructed to determine the orientation of the dots by pressing one of two pre-specified buttons as soon as possible. The probes are

* Correspondence: sophiedongwei@163.com; bfbedu@126.com
†Equal contributors
[1]Faculty of Psychology and Mental Health, Second Military Medical University, Xiangyin Road 800, Shanghai 200433, China
Full list of author information is available at the end of the article

more likely to appear in the location of the non-threatening stimulus, referred to as an attentional bias modification (ABM), which has been demonstrated to reduce anxiety and stress responsiveness at a medium effect size (d = 0.61) in a meta-analysis by Hakamata et al. [9]. However, more recent meta-analyses have failed to yield consistent findings regarding the beneficial effects of ABM on symptoms [10–13], and the effect sizes may be smaller than previously reported [10].

In contrast to a specific psychiatric disorder, test anxiety (TA) refers to "the set of phenomenological, physiological, and behavioral responses that accompany concern about the possible negative consequences or failure on an exam or similar evaluative situation" [14]. According to Zeidner, test anxiety is a combination of three facets: cognitive, physiological, and behavioral [15]. Cognitive symptoms include self-deprecating thoughts, expectations of failure, low self-esteem, and other off-task thoughts that detract attention from the task at hand. Physiological (i.e., emotional) symptoms may consist of an increased heart rate, perspiration, stomachaches, headaches, or other somatic symptoms that occur in response to evaluative situations. Finally, behavioral symptoms may include numerous observable behaviors, such as looking around the room, fidgeting, or chewing fingernails and pencils [16]. Many studies suggest TA contributes to impaired performances on examinations [17, 18]. This may be because individuals with TA are more likely to experience state anxiety across situations, which impedes focus and concentration in preparation for and during the examination. According to Lynn [19], individuals with high TA did not show longer response latencies to incongruent trials of words that denoted test anxiety or threat and were more likely to avoid threatening words rather than attend to them. However, additional research has suggested highly test anxious individuals exhibited an attentional bias to threat information [20, 21]. In this case, the effect of ABM on test anxiety individuals appears to be an interesting and valuable topic. Regrettably, few studies have addressed this issue. First, Dandeneau and Baldwin aimed to train a positive cognitive habit that would buffer against social and performance threats, thus making students less vulnerable and more resilient to rejection. Interestingly, participants in the ABM condition reported less interfering thoughts of being rejected when completing the anagrams task and an overall higher state self-esteem after having been rejected and experiencing failure [22]. McNally et al. subsequently reported reductions in self-report, behavioral, and physiological measures of speech anxiety using ABM [23]. Similarly, Hullu et at assessed the efficacy of a 10-week internet-delivered Cognitive Bias Modification with a focus on modifying both attentional and interpretive biases as a cost and time-efficient strategy to reduce social and test anxiety [24]. Moreover, self-reported social and test anxiety generally decreased from the pre-test to two-year follow-up.

Voogd's research [25] is the first randomized controlled trial to assess the dot-probe and visual search training effects with up to one-year of follow-up. Three hundred forty adolescents were randomly assigned to dot-probe (DP) training, visual searching (VS) training, or placebo; the VS training was effective in reducing attentional bias in contrast to the DP training. As a result of the nature of online training, however, there were substantial drop-out rates and a lack of supervision. Therefore, a more optimal standard lab study is required to replicate the effect of ABM on test anxiety individuals. To explore the effect of ABM on test anxiety individuals, the current study recruited the participants preparing the College English Test 6 (CET-6). The CET-6 is a national English exam held twice per year in China. If college students fail to pass it, it results in substantial troubles for achieving their final degree and seeking jobs after graduation. In this case, majority of the candidates who are preparing for CET-6 must experience test anxiety.

Furthermore, there are several common limitations in previous ABM studies. First, the same behavioral paradigm was used in both the pre–/post-training and training tasks [26–28], which made it difficult to ensure whether the AB had been altered or it was only a result of a practice effect. Furthermore, several studies have indicated a relatively poor reliability of the dot-probe task [10, 13]. Many widely accepted paradigms have been used to assess attentional bias, such as the visual-probe task, emotion Stroop task, spatial-cueing task and visual-search task. Therefore, different AB paradigms were implemented in the pre–/post-training and training tasks in the following study. Second, several previous studies lacked a placebo training condition [27, 29]; thus, the direct effects of training towards threat could not be examined between different groups. Moreover, several studies have indicated that the control condition had a similar effect in reducing the AB or anxious symptoms as ABM [23, 30, 31]. Therefore, a no-training waiting list group was included in the current study to control for the placebo effects, positive expectations and demand effects.

Additionally, it has been widely accepted that salivary α-amylase (sAA), an oral cavity enzyme, is a powerful tool to indicate stress-reactive bodily changes, particularly the autonomic nervous system (ANS) [32]. This enzyme is rapidly increased in response to physiological and psychosocial stress [33–36]. The secretion of salivary amylase is directly stimulated by innervation followed by hormonal regulation in response to changes in serum noradrenalin levels. Therefore, the salivary gland acts more quickly and sensitively responds to psychological stress [37]. Compared with traditional stress makers, such as cortisol and catecholamines, salivary amylase has the advantages of noninvasiveness, a more significant increase, and a rapid response [35, 38]. Given the potential individual variability in responding to the same stressful condition, sAA were measured and integrated with the changes in attentional bias before and after the attentional bias modification.

Based on the previously reviewed literature, we aimed to determine whether attentional bias modification can be used to modify high test-anxiety individuals' attention to emotional information and whether this change is related to emotional vulnerability, such as sAA reactivity. In addition to the placebo group, a waiting list group was employed to examine the direct effects of training.

Methods

Study design overview

The design included repeated-measures across two assessment times (pre-training and post-training). The pre-post assessment included physiological (salivary amylase), psychological (anxiety), and behavioral (attentional bias scores) indicators.

Participant recruitment and allocation

G*Power 3.1.9.2 (Heinrich-Heine-Universität, Düsseldorf, Germany) was used to determine the sample size. For an effect size of 0.4, an alpha probability of 0.05 and a beta probability of 0.8, the sample size required to detect a statistically significant difference is 20 participants per group. Given the loss of samples, ten additional individuals are required in the two intervention groups. Therefore, 80 participants were recruited from a medical university via advertisements placed in various settings (e.g., canteen, dormitory, and classroom building). During an initial phone and Internet instant message tool screen, the participants were told that the researchers were testing a new computer program designed to help individuals, who were preparing for the following CET-6, reduce test anxiety and develop healthy mental habits; moreover, the entire procedure, including the completion of the psychological scales and collection of saliva and computer behavioral data, would last one week. The Test Anxiety Scale (TAS) was used to assess test anxiety [39], and the Depression Anxiety Stress Scales (DASS) were used to assess the individuals' depression, anxiety and stress states [40]. According to the CONSORT guidelines, the participants were randomly assigned to three groups (a: ABM group, b: placebo group and c: waiting list group) through the use of a computer-based random assignment program with a 3:3:2 allocation ratio. After the first day when they provided the baseline data, the participants were informed via e-mails regarding their assigned group (A, B or C) and the following programs. WC assigned the participants to an intervention based on a random allocation sequence in opaque, sealed, and stapled envelopes. The participants remained blind to the treatment hypotheses and the content of the other treatment groups. Moreover, the treatment allocation was concealed from the outcome assessor HC. As depicted in Fig. 1, three participants were excluded from the analysis for the following reasons: participant quit halfway through the study (n = 2), and there were too many incorrect responses during the eStroop task (n = 1). Thus, the final sample consisted of 77 undergraduates (57 males, 20 females), aged 18–25 years (M = 21.00, SD = 1.556). All participants were right-handed and reported normal color vision and normal or corrected-to-normal visual acuity.

Procedure

Figure 2 describes the sequence of events used in the procedure. After obtaining consent, the participants were instructed to rate their current anxiety using the visual analogue scale (VAS). A 10 cm line was divided into 10 equal partitions with the terminal labels "relaxed" and "anxious". The participants circled the mark on the scale that most accurately reflected their current mood state. Scores ranged from 1 to 10, in which higher scores reflected a more anxious mood.

Salivary samples were subsequently collected using the hand-held monitor of sAA (Salivary Amylase Monitor, Nipro Co. Ltd., Japan), which was developed by analytical chemists Yamaguchi and colleagues. It had been reported to accurately and rapidly (within two min) assess individuals' sAA levels associated with SAM activity [41]. The participants were instructed to rinse their mouths and wipe out all water. The collecting paper was then directly inserted into the oral cavity, and approximately 20–30 ml of saliva were collected from under the tongue over a period of 25 to 30 s. The reflectance 30 s after the initial time was automatically measured by this optical device. Thus, the measurement of the sAA level was completed in approximately two minutes. Salivary amylase measures were assessed four times in total (before and after the eStroop task in the pre- and post-training sections).

Besides, another central thesis in current study is that such attentional bias modification could serve to change individuals' emotional vulnerability, resulting in a differential tendency to display elevated levels of anxiety mood state and sAA reactivity in response to a given stressor. To address this hypothesis, sAA reactivity and anxiety vulnerability were assessed for each eStroop task (i.e., pre-training and post-training). Scores were calculated by subtracting the pre-task state from the post-task state. For example, the pre-training sAA reactivity score

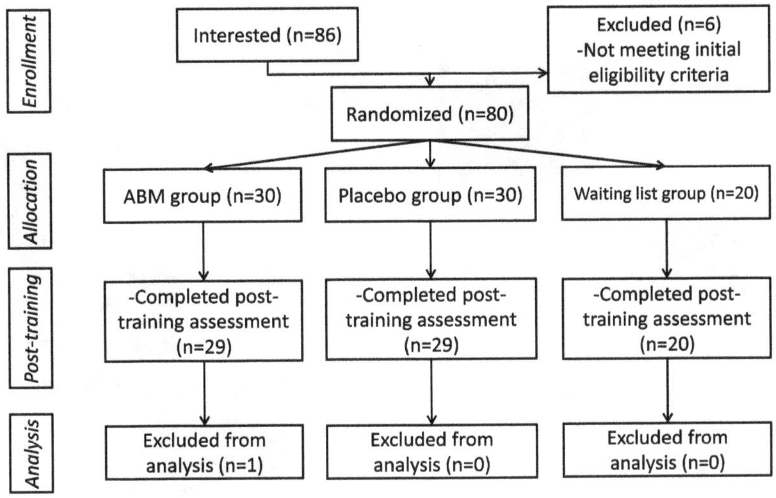

Fig. 1 Flowchart depicting passage of participants

for the first eStroop task was calculated by subtracting the salivary amylase before the first eStroop task (sAA_{1-1}) from the salivary amylase after the first eStroop task (sAA_{1-2}). Similarly, anxiety vulnerability prior to ABM was calculated by subtracting the anxiety visual analogue scales administered before the first eStroop task (VAS_{1-1}) from the anxiety visual analogue scales administered after the first eStroop task (VAS_{1-2}). The vulnerability scores after ABM used the salivary amylase and anxiety visual analogue scales from before and after the post-training eStroop task.

The participants completed behavioral tasks in a sound-attenuated psychology laboratory setting at a distance of approximately 60 cm from a 20-in LCD screen. Emotional Stroop tasks were used to assess the participants' attentional bias in the first and last days, whereas dot probe tasks were used as attentional bias modification in the middle five training days. The ABM and placebo groups are instructed to perform the training between 12:00 p.m. and 9:30 p.m. every training day in the same laboratory.

eStroop

One hundred twenty-eight emotional words, including 32 threat, 32 positive and 64 neutral words (Appendix A) were selected. The neutral words originated from the

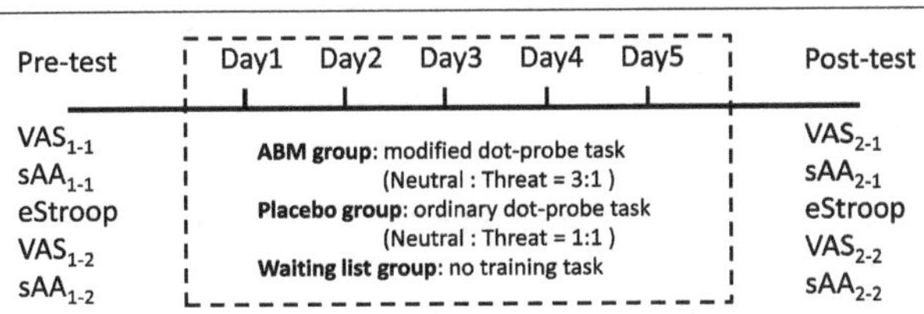

Fig. 2 Repeated-measures study procedure

Chinese Affective Words System (CAWS), which was developed by the Psychology Institute of the Chinese Academy of Science [42]. In their study, 64 undergraduate students were instructed to rate the valence level, arousal level and dominance level for their word list using a 9-point Likert scale, which established the final CAWS. Similarly, the threat and positive words were exam-related and were rated by 30 undergraduates prior to the experience. In the current study, threat words ($Valence_{M \pm SD}$ = 3.04 ± 0.94), positive words ($Valence_{M \pm SD}$ = 7.80 ± 0.53), and neutral words ($Valence_{M \pm SD}$ = 5.49 ± 0.17) were presented in one of four colors (blue, yellow, red or green).

The current task was similar to that used by Taake et al. [43], which was divided into two different types of experimental blocks (threat/positive). In the Threat block, threat words and neutral words were randomly intermixed, with equal probability. The positive words and neutral words were in the Positive Block. Moreover, the emotional words were individually matched to neutral words for the frequency of use and length within each block. Two Threat and two Positive Blocks were run in the current task, and each block comprised 32 stimuli. The order of presentation was counterbalanced across participants. Each trial consisted of a white fixation cross against a black background for 500 ms, followed by the stimulus for 300 ms. The inter-stimuli interval randomly varied between 600 ms and 1000 ms (Fig. 3). The participants were instructed to maintain central fixation and discriminate the word color as quickly as possible by pressing the appropriate button ("S" for blue, "F" for yellow, "J" for red, and "L" for green), while ignoring the word meaning. Data were not collected until the participants performed more than 16 practice trials and the correct rate reached 75%. In current study, the eStroop

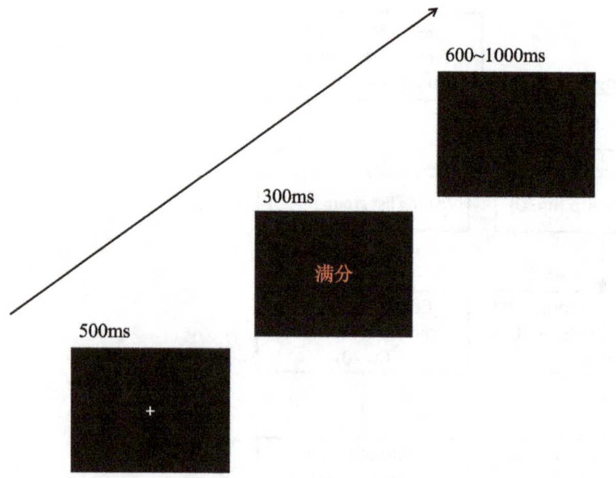

Fig. 3 Sequence of events in the eStroop task

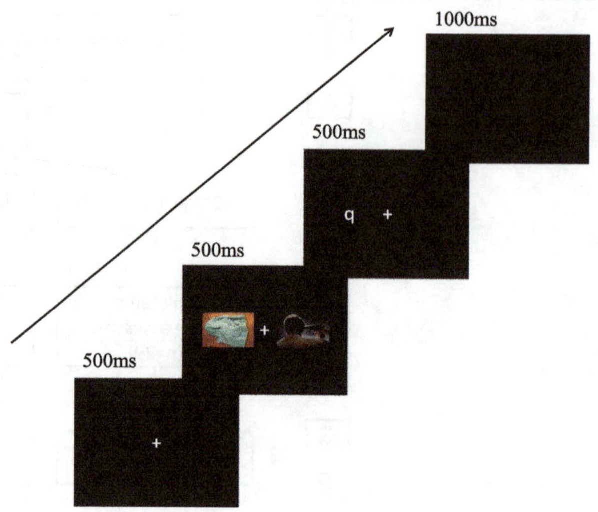

Fig. 4 Sequence of events in the dot-probe task

task was used both as a measure of attentional bias and as a stress induction.

Dot probe task

Sixty threat and 60 neutral images were selected from the International Affective Picture System (IAPS) [44]. The neutral images included household objects, plants and neutral animals, whereas the threat images included natural catastrophes, dirty environments and aggressive animals. The dot-probe task consisted of 3 blocks, each of which included 120 trials. Following a 500 ms presentation of a fixation cross at the center of the screen, a pair of Threat-Neutral images was presented for 500 ms. The images were presented with equal distance to the right and left of the fixation cross (16.5 cm center-to-center). Following the removal of the images, a target display appeared for 500 ms, after which the screen went blank. The target display was the letter *p* or letter *q* and appeared at a distance of 8.5 cm to the left or right of the fixation at the location of the center of the left or right image (Fig. 4). The participants were instructed to determine the word by pressing one of two specified buttons. A new trial was initiated 1000 ms after target offset. The participants in the ABM group were presented with trials in which targets most likely replaced neutral images (75%). The participants in the placebo group were exposed to trials in which targets were equally likely to replace threat images. For both conditions, the neutral image was equally likely to appear on the left or right, and the target was equally likely to comprise the letter p or q. These variables were randomly mixed in presentation. Moreover, the participants in the waiting list group did not receive a task during these five days.

Data analysis

The primary index of the training effect was derived by assessing the change in salivary amylase and visual analogue scales of anxiety over the 5-day training or placebo tasks. The changes in the response time of the eStroop were of specific interest. Only the reaction from correct hits was used in the following analysis. Moreover, RTs <300 ms or >1200 ms were excluded. We compared the pre- and post- training/placebo attentional bias scores (mean RT for Threat block – mean RT for Positive block). Positive bias values reflected attention towards threat, whereas threat values reflected the avoidance of threat.

The demographic variables were compared among the groups using analysis of variance (ANOVA) for continuous data and chi-square tests for categorical data. Attentional bias scores were subjected to 2 × 3 repeated measurement of variance analysis with time (pre-training, post-training) as a within subject factor and training condition (ABM, placebo, blank) as a between subject factor. In addition, changes in the salivary amylase and visual analogue scales of anxiety were assessed via univariate analysis. Pearson correlation was computed to explore the relationship between attentional bias toward threat and anxiety vulnerability.

Results

Clinical and demographic variables

The demographic characteristics of the participant groups are summarized in Table 1. There were no significant differences among the groups in the clinical or demographic variables, which indicates that randomization was successful.

Change in attentional bias measured with eStroop task

Table 2 presents the mean RTs of pre-training and post-training for the emotional (threat/positive/neutral) words in the threat and positive blocks for the ABM, placebo and waiting list groups. There was a nonsignificant difference between the groups on the attentional bias scores prior to the 5-day training ($F(2, 74) = 0.006$, $p = 0.994$, $\eta^2 < 0.01$). A 2 (Test: pre-training, post-training) * 3 (Group: ABM, placebo, blank) repeated measurement of variance analysis was conducted on the attentional bias scores, with Group as a between-subject factor and Test as a within-subject factor. There were no test differences, $F(1, 74) = 0.072$, $p = 0.789$, $\eta^2 < 0.01$. However, there was a group difference, $F(2, 74) = 3.426$, $p = 0.038$, $\eta^2 = 0.145$. Moreover, the interaction of test and group was significant, $F(2,74) = 3.323$, $p = 0.042$, $\eta^2 = 0.082$. Exploratory analyses were conducted via paired sample t-tests to examine group changes in attentional bias. As indicated in Fig. 5, the ABM group showed a significant change in the attentional bias scores after the 5-day training (2.73 ± 58.198 vs. -26.96 ± 46.549, respectively, $t(27) = 2.077$, $p = 0.047$, Cohen' d = 0.392), whereas there were no changes in the attentional bias scores in the placebo group (1.59 ± 56.327 vs. 10.14 ± 71.737, respectively, $t(28) = -0.493$, $p = 0.626$, Cohen' d = −0.09) or the waiting list group (3.30 ± 46.182 vs. 32.08 ± 53.001, respectively, $t(19) = -1.862$, $p = 0.078$, Cohen' d = −0.416). It meant the attentional bias towards threat information could be altered by the attentional bias modification. The individuals after ABM training tended to have less attention on threats than before, but the other two groups remained unchanged.

Effects of attentional bias modification on salivary amylase

Table 3 presents the mean sAA and sAA reactivity in the pre- and post- training sections. Changes in salivary amylase were initially tested as a function of the ABM procedure. Our dependent variables were the sAA values assessed directly after the training procedure (sAA_{2-1}), and our covariates were the sAA values assessed at the beginning of the session (sAA_{1-1}). After controlling for the pre-training sAA values, there were no group differences following the training ($F(2,73) = 1.947$, $p = 0.15$, $\eta^2 = 0.051$).

The sAA reactivity to stress was computed using sAA_{1-2}-sAA_{1-1} and sAA_{2-2}-sAA_{2-1}. When controlling for the pre-training vulnerability, no significant vulnerability changes were identified ($F(2,73) = 0.567$, $p = 0.57$, $\eta^2 = 0.015$).

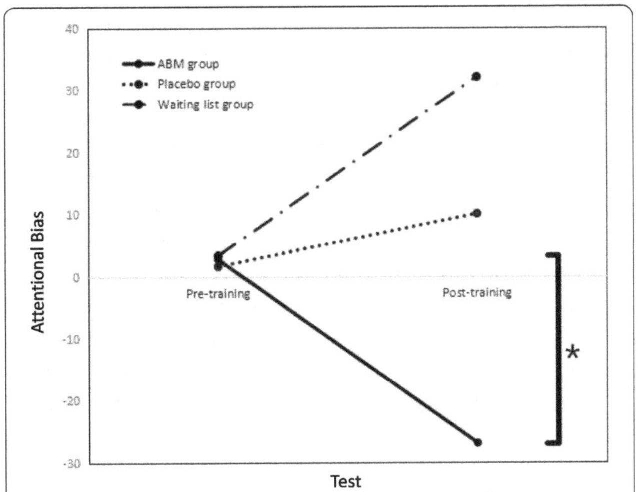

Fig. 5 Attentional bias for the pre- and post- training

Effects of attentional bias modification on anxious mood

Table 4 presents the mean VAS and anxiety vulnerability in the pre- and post- training sections. Similarly, changes in the visual analogue scale of anxiety were tested. Our dependent variables were the VAS values assessed directly after the training procedure (VAS_{2-1}), and our covariates were the VAS values assessed at the beginning of the session (VAS_{1-1}). After controlling for the pre-training VAS values, there were no group differences following the training ($F(2,73) = 1.193$, $p = 0.309$, $\eta^2 = 0.032$).

The anxiety vulnerability to stress was computed using VAS_{1-2}-VAS_{1-1} and VAS_{2-2}-VAS_{2-1}. When controlling for the pre-training vulnerability, a trend group difference in the anxiety vulnerability was identified ($F(2,73) = 2.765$, $p = 0.07$, $\eta^2 = 0.07$). To further examine this finding, pairwise comparisons were conducted, which suggested that individuals in the ABM group showed lower anxiety vulnerability to stress than individuals in the placebo group, $t = -0.905$, $p = 0.026$, Cohen' d = −0.527.

We further assessed whether this anxiety vulnerability following training or placebo as a function was associated with changes in the attentional bias scores. A significant correlation between changes in anxiety vulnerability (post-training vulnerability minus pre-training vulnerability) and changes in the attentional bias score emerged only in the ABM group ($r = 0.391$, $p = 0.040$) and not in the placebo group ($r = 0.194$, $p = 0.314$) or the waiting list group ($r = 0.122$, $p = 0.609$).

Discussion

Previous studies have indicated that attentional bias modification using a modified dot-probe task could influence cognitive styles and anxiety levels [2, 6, 8]; however, the effect of ABM on anxiety disorders has remained inconclusive, particularly with recent meta-analysis findings of dismissive appraisal as a viable clinical intervention [11, 13]. The current study aimed to determine whether ABM could alter the cognitive functions of attention processing in non-clinical (test anxiety) individuals and investigate the degree to which ABM reduces anxiety vulnerability.

The behavioral findings suggested that attentional bias toward threat information significantly decreased after the 5-day training away from the threat. The dot-probe task with a left-right orientation was used in the current study, which has been shown to be more effective than a top-down orientation [13]. In contrast to previous studies, the eStroop task used in the current study may indicate an automatic preferential allocation of attention resources to threat rather than task-related information. The attentional bias score can be assessed as the level of emotional stimulus content ability in interfering with the color naming, which causes a delayed reaction time compared with positive and threat words [45]. This modified Stroop paradigm was created to be task-wise unrelated to the training (dot-probe task), which was helpful to investigate how cognitive styles were influenced by attention training. Thus, the participants in the ABM group showed a significant reduction in attentional bias. They started to pay more attention to the positive words than the threat words after the 5-day training. In contrast, the participants in the placebo and waiting list groups tended to allocate their attention toward threatening stimuli with the approaching exam. These findings from the eStroop task may also be equally attributed to a bias in attentional engagement with or disengagement from the content of the threat stimuli [46]. After training, the participants in the ABM group showed an improved ability to shift attention from the meanings of negative words to task-related color naming, whereas an impaired disengagement account for attentional bias appeared in the placebo and waiting list groups.

Interestingly, the current findings linked attentional bias toward threat and anxiety vulnerability. The randomized block design effectively indicated that there were no differences among the three groups in anxiety, depression and stress prior to the training. After the 5-day attentional bias modification, the anxiety vulnerability with the attention to threats significantly decreased, which was not detected in the placebo and waiting list groups. These findings were consistent with previous studies [2, 4]. In both Eldar's and Mathews' studies, participants trained to attend to threat subsequently reported increased anxiety. These results suggested attentional bias toward threat information was implicated in the development of anxiety. The ABM could modify individuals' attention processes and further influenced the reduction in anxiety vulnerability during a stress task.

Few researchers have directly explored the effects of attentional bias training on physiological markers of stress; however, preliminary results have been promising. According to the classical cognitive load theory, higher cognitive loads cause psychophysiological stress, as attention requires cognitive selection, and this effort elicits autonomic arousal [47]. Dandeneau et al. [48] reported basal cortisol was diminished after modified visual search training. Baert et al. [49] determined the indices of Heart Rate Variability (HRV) improved stress recovery by attention training via the dot probe. Moreover, Pilgrim et al. [50] showed attentional training elicits a paradoxical increase in cortisol and sAA reactivity. However, there were no significant changes in the salivary cortisol level after the 5-day training in the current study. One reason may be the lack of a well-validated psychosocial stressor. Emotional Stroop was not a novel task for the participants and failed to induce high cognitive loads and psychophysiological responses. Therefore, the sAA activity tended to decrease after the 5-day training in all three groups. Thus, a standardized task (e.g., Trier Social Stress Test [51]) is necessary in future studies.

Moreover, several recent studies have indicated a noncontingency-based training ABM task can be as anxiolytic as the typical contingency-based ABM training task [23, 52, 53]. Based on this finding, a waiting list group was included in the current study to control for potential placebo effects, positive expectations and demand effects. Consequently, there were no significant differences between the groups in anxious mood and physiological indicators, which is consistent with previous studies. Participants in the placebo group failed to improve their attentional bias, and the attentional bias scores of individuals in the waiting list group tended to increase (p = 0.07) at the post-training section. These findings suggested that the participants who received no training (or placebo training) started to develop negative cognitive processing with the approaching exam. These findings provided initial evidence that repeated concreteness training, not placebo, may have positive effects on attentional bias and naturally occurring symptoms in a test anxiety sample.

There are several limitations in the current study. First, limited participants were included in the waiting list group, which made it difficult to interpret the marginal significance. Practically, compared with the waiting list group, it is advised to set a group which trained individuals to attend to threat in the following studies. Thus, three types of dot-probe tasks should be included to investigate the effect of attentional bias modification on individuals' attention processing. In addition, images from the International Affective Picture System rather than exam related images were used in the dot probe task. In most cases, it is exam-related information that induces the candidate's negative feelings [54]. Therefore, it is suggested that standardized exam related images be used in future research. In this case, it may be more effective to modify high TA individual's AB from negative exam-related information to positive exam-related one. Finally, there may be laboratory effects in this research. Previous studies have indicated larger effect sizes for anxiety symptoms at post-training in laboratory settings

[13, 55]. Therefore, practical indices (e.g., test scores, sleep quality) appear equally critical. For example, exam performance has been shown to be improved by expressive writing [56, 57] and may improve high test anxiety individuals' biology exam scores regarding writing about their thoughts about the upcoming exam. These issues indicate the need for systematic follow-up studies with a specific focus on practical indices on the eve of or exam day.

Conclusions

In summary, the current study demonstrates that attentional bias modification away from a threat is effective for individuals preparing for an exam, and anxiety vulnerability can be modified by this simple cognitive intervention with the dot probe, which has been shown to alter attentional bias. Future studies in this area should investigate the effects of attentional bias modification on individuals' performance on exam day, as well as the effects on cognitive processing over time.

Abbreviations

ABM: Attentional Bias Modification; ANOVA: Analysis of Variance; CAWS: Chinese Affective Words System; CET-6: College English Test 6; DASS: Depression Anxiety Stress Scales; DP: Dot Probe; HRV: Heart Rate Variability; IAPS: International Affective Picture System; RT: Reaction Time; sAA: Salivary Amylase; TA: Test Anxiety; TAS: Test Anxiety Scale; VAS: Visual Analogue Scale; VS: Visual Searching

Acknowledgements

We thank all participants for volunteering in this study and provide our sincere gratitude to Prof. Libo Geng (Jiangsu Normal University) and Jiaming Ding (Peking University) for their support at different stages of the design and implementation of the study. We would also like to thank our adorable students, Yingnan Ge, Kaixuan Ma, Jinchun Li, Zhuangzhuang Wei, and Yue Yang, for their careful data collection.

Funding

This work was funded by the Major Program of the "12th Five-Year Plan" for Medical Development of PLA (14CXZ002), the General Program of the "12th Five-Year Plan" for Medical Development of PLA (CWS12J015), the Second Military Medical University 2016 Annual PhD Innovative Research Fund (20152049), and financial support from the China Scholarship Council (201603170127), the Military Medical Program of Second Military Medical University (2014JS20) and the Shanghai Municipal Commission of Health and Family Planning (2013Y168). The funders had no role in study design, data collection and analysis, or writing the manuscript.

Authors' contributions

WC and YP conceived the study, prepared the protocol and developed the training programs. WC and YC conducted the day-to-day study in the lab. HC developed the analysis plan and performed the statistical analyses. WC and WD were major contributors in writing the manuscript. JY and GD contributed to the development of the idea and revising the manuscript. WD and GD were responsible for staff management and overall coordination of the study. All authors have read and approved the final manuscript.

Consent for publication

Not applicable.

Competing interests

The authors declare that they have no competing interest.

Author details

[1]Faculty of Psychology and Mental Health, Second Military Medical University, Xiangyin Road 800, Shanghai 200433, China. [2]Department of Medical Psychology, General Hospital of PLA, Beijing 100853, China. [3]Department of Engineering and Information, Nanjing City Vocational College, Nanjing 210038, China.

References

1. Bar-Haim Y, Lamy D, Pergamin L, Bakermans-Kranenburg MJ, Van Ijzendoorn MH. Threat-related attentional bias in anxious and nonanxious individuals: a meta-analytic study. Psychol Bull. 2007;133(1):1–24.
2. Mathews A, MacLeod C. Induced processing biases have causal effects on anxiety. Cognit Emot. 2002;16(3):331–54.
3. Mogg K, Bradley BP. Anxiety and attention to threat: cognitive mechanisms and treatment with attention bias modification. Behav Res Ther. 2016;87:76–108.
4. Eldar S, Ricon T, Bar-Haim Y. Plasticity in attention: implications for stress response in children. Behav Res Ther. 2008;46(4):450–61.
5. MacLeod C, Rutherford E, Campbell L, Ebsworthy G, Holker L: Selective attention and emotional vulnerability: assessing the causal basis of their association through the experimental manipulation of attentional bias. J Abnorm Psychol 2002, 111(1):107–123.
6. Amir N, Beard C, Burns M, Bomyea J. Attention modification program in individuals with generalized anxiety disorder. J Abnorm Psychol. 2009; 118(1):28–33.
7. Hazen RA, Vasey MW, Schmidt NB. Attentional retraining: a randomized clinical trial for pathological worry. J Psychiatr Res. 2009;43(6):627–33.
8. Schmidt NB, Richey JA, Buckner JD, Timpano KR. Attention training for generalized social anxiety disorder. J Abnorm Psychol. 2009;118(1):5–14.
9. Hakamata Y, Lissek S, Bar-Haim Y, Britton JC, Fox NA, Leibenluft E, Ernst M, Pine DS. Attention bias modification treatment: a meta-analysis toward the establishment of novel treatment for anxiety. Biol Psychiatry. 2010;68(11): 982–90.
10. Hallion LS, Ruscio AM. A meta-analysis of the effect of cognitive bias modification on anxiety and depression. Psychol Bull. 2011;137(6):940–58.
11. Mogoaşe C, David D, Koster EH. Clinical efficacy of attentional bias modification procedures: an updated meta-analysis. J Clin Psychol. 2014; 70(12):1133–57.
12. Cristea IA, Kok RN, Cuijpers P. Efficacy of cognitive bias modification interventions in anxiety and depression: meta-analysis. Br J Psychiatry. 2015; 206(1):7–16.
13. Heeren A, Mogoaşe C, Philippot P, McNally RJ. Attention bias modification for social anxiety: a systematic review and meta-analysis. Clin Psychol Rev. 2015;40:76–90.
14. Zeidner M: Test anxiety in educational contexts: concepts, findings. Emotion in Education 2007, 165:50011–50013.
15. Zeidner M. Test anxiety: the state of the art: Springer Science & Business. Media. 1998;
16. Harris MT: Psychological and environmental predictors of test anxiety: a structural equation model. 2016.
17. Cassady JC, Johnson RE. Cognitive test anxiety and academic performance. Contemp Educ Psychol. 2002;27(2):270–95.
18. Putwain DW, Aveyard B: Is perceived control a critical factor in understanding the negative relationship between cognitive test anxiety and examination performance? 2016.
19. Ryzewicz L. Behavioral manifestations of worry in test anxiety and intolerance of uncertainty: a laboratory investigation of attention bias with a university population. The Brooklyn Center: Long Island University; 2008.
20. Putwain DW, Langdale HC, Woods KA, Nicholson LJ. Developing and piloting a dot-probe measure of attentional bias for test anxiety. Learn Individ Differ. 2011;21(4):478–82.
21. Liu Y, Zhang W, Zhou R. Cognitive and neural basis of attentional bias in test anxiety students. Psychological Exploration. 2015;35(3):233–8.
22. Dandeneau SD, Baldwin MW. The buffering effects of rejection-inhibiting attentional training on social and performance threat among adult students. Contemp Educ Psychol. 2009;34(1):42–50.
23. McNally RJ, Enock PM, Tsai C, Tousian M. Attention bias modification for reducing speech anxiety. Behav Res Ther. 2013;51(12):882–8.

24. de Hullu E, Sportel BE, Nauta MH, de Jong PJ. Cognitive bias modification and CBT as early interventions for adolescent social and test anxiety: two-year follow-up of a randomized controlled trial. J Behav Ther Exp Psychiatry. 2017;55:81–9.
25. De Voogd E, Wiers R, Prins P, de Jong P, Boendermaker W, Zwitser R, Salemink E. Online attentional bias modification training targeting anxiety and depression in unselected adolescents: short-and long-term effects of a randomized controlled trial. Behav Res Ther. 2016;87:11–22.
26. Sportel BE, de Hullu E, de Jong PJ, Nauta MH. Cognitive bias modification versus CBT in reducing adolescent social anxiety: a randomized controlled trial. PLoS One. 2013;8(5):e64355.
27. Browning M, Holmes EA, Murphy SE, Goodwin GM, Harmer CJ. Lateral prefrontal cortex mediates the cognitive modification of attentional bias. Biol Psychiatry. 2010;67(10):919–25.
28. Eldar S, Bar-Haim Y. Neural plasticity in response to attention training in anxiety. Psychol Med. 2010;40(04):667–77.
29. O'Toole L, Dennis TA. Attention training and the threat bias: an ERP study. Brain Cogn. 2012;78(1):63–73.
30. Boettcher J, Berger T, Renneberg B. Internet-based attention training for social anxiety: a randomized controlled trial. Cogn Ther Res. 2012;36(5):522–36.
31. Carlbring P, Apelstrand M, Sehlin H, Amir N, Rousseau A, Hofmann SG, Andersson G. Internet-delivered attention bias modification training in individuals with social anxiety disorder-a double blind randomized controlled trial. BMC psychiatry. 2012;12(1):66.
32. Nater UM, Rohleder N. Salivary alpha-amylase as a non-invasive biomarker for the sympathetic nervous system: current state of research. Psychoneuroendocrinology. 2009;34(4):486–96.
33. Almela M, Hidalgo V, Villada C, van der Meij L, Espín L, Gómez-amor J, Salvador A. Salivary alpha-amylase response to acute psychosocial stress: the impact of age. Biol Psychol. 2011;87(3):421–9.
34. Nater UM, Rohleder N, Gaab J, Berger S, Jud A, Kirschbaum C, Ehlert U. Human salivary alpha-amylase reactivity in a psychosocial stress paradigm. Int J Psychophysiol. 2005;55(3):333–42.
35. Nater UM, La Marca R, Florin L, Moses A, Langhans W, Koller MM, Ehlert U. Stress-induced changes in human salivary alpha-amylase activity—associations with adrenergic activity. Psychoneuroendocrinology. 2006;31(1):49–58.
36. Rohleder N, Nater UM, Wolf JM, Ehlert U, Kirschbaum C. Psychosocial stress-induced activation of salivary alpha-amylase: an indicator of sympathetic activity? Ann N Y Acad Sci. 2004;1032(1):258–63.
37. Yamaguchi M, Kanemori T, Kanemaru M, Takai N, Mizuno Y, Yoshida H. Performance evaluation of salivary amylase activity monitor. Biosens Bioelectron. 2004;20(3):491–7.
38. Takai N, Yamaguchi M, Aragaki T, Eto K, Uchihashi K, Nishikawa Y. Effect of psychological stress on the salivary cortisol and amylase levels in healthy young adults. Arch Oral Biol. 2004;49(12):963–8.
39. Sarason IG. The test anxiety scale: concept and research. In: DTIC Document. 1977;
40. Henry JD, Crawford JR. The short-form version of the depression anxiety stress scales (DASS-21): construct validity and normative data in a large non-clinical sample. Br J Clin Psychol. 2005;44(2):227–39.
41. Yamaguchi M, Deguchi M, Wakasugi J, Ono S, Takai N, Higashi T, Mizuno Y. Hand-held monitor of sympathetic nervous system using salivary amylase activity and its validation by driver fatigue assessment. Biosens Bioelectron. 2006;21(7):1007–14.
42. Wang Y, Zhou L, Luo Y. The pilot establishment and evaluation of Chinese affective words system. Chin Ment Health J. 2008;22(8):608–12.
43. Taake I, Jaspers-Fayer F, Liotti M. Early frontal responses elicited by physical threat words in an emotional Stroop task: modulation by anxiety sensitivity. Biol Psychol. 2009;81(1):48–57.
44. Lang P, Bradley M, Cuthbert B: Technical Report A-6, International Affective Picture System (IAPS): Digitized Photographs, Instruction Manual and Affective Ratings. In.: Gainesville, FL.: University of Florida; 2005.
45. Wentura D, Rothermund K, Bak P. Automatic vigilance: the attention-grabbing power of approach-and avoidance-related social information. J Pers Soc Psychol. 2000;78(6):1024–37.
46. Clarke PJ, MacLeod C, Guastella AJ. Assessing the role of spatial engagement and disengagement of attention in anxiety-linked attentional bias: a critique of current paradigms and suggestions for future research directions. Anxiety, Stress & Coping. 2013;26(1):1–19.
47. Posner MI. Psychobiology of attention. Handbook of Psychobiology. 1975:441–80.
48. Dandeneau SD, Baldwin MW, Baccus JR, Sakellaropoulo M, Pruessner JC. Cutting stress off at the pass: reducing vigilance and responsiveness to social threat by manipulating attention. J Pers Soc Psychol. 2007;93(4):651.
49. Baert S, Casier A, De Raedt R. The effects of attentional training on physiological stress recovery after induced social threat. Anxiety, Stress & Coping. 2012;25(4):365–79.
50. Pilgrim K, Ellenbogen MA, Paquin K. The impact of attentional training on the salivary cortisol and alpha amylase response to psychosocial stress: importance of attentional control. Psychoneuroendocrinology. 2014;44:88–99.
51. Kirschbaum C, Pirke K-M, Hellhammer DH. The 'trier social stress test'–a tool for investigating psychobiological stress responses in a laboratory setting. Neuropsychobiology. 1993;28(1–2):76–81.
52. Heeren A, Coussement C, McNally RJ. Untangling attention bias modification from emotion: a double-blind randomized experiment with individuals with social anxiety disorder. J Behav Ther Exp Psychiatry. 2016;50:61–7.
53. Heeren A, Baeken C, Vanderhasselt M-A, Philippot P, De Raedt R. Impact of anodal and cathodal transcranial direct current stimulation over the left dorsolateral prefrontal cortex during attention bias modification: an eye-tracking study. PLoS One. 2015;10(4):e0124182.
54. Smith CA, Ellsworth PC. Patterns of appraisal and emotion related to taking an exam. J Pers Soc Psychol. 1987;52(3):475.
55. Kuckertz JM, Gildebrant E, Liliequist B, Karlström P, Väppling C, Bodlund O, Stenlund T, Hofmann SG, Andersson G, Amir N. Moderation and mediation of the effect of attention training in social anxiety disorder. Behav Res Ther. 2014;53:30–40.
56. Ramirez G, Beilock SL. Writing about testing worries boosts exam performance in the classroom. Science. 2011;331(6014):211–3.
57. Zhang X, Zhou J, Zhang H, Dong Y, Zhou R. The effect of expressive writing on high test-anxious college students' CET-6 scores. s. 2015;3:92–6.

Permissions

All chapters in this book were first published in PSYCHIATRY, by BioMed Central; hereby published with permission under the Creative Commons Attribution License or equivalent. Every chapter published in this book has been scrutinized by our experts. Their significance has been extensively debated. The topics covered herein carry significant findings which will fuel the growth of the discipline. They may even be implemented as practical applications or may be referred to as a beginning point for another development.

The contributors of this book come from diverse backgrounds, making this book a truly international effort. This book will bring forth new frontiers with its revolutionizing research information and detailed analysis of the nascent developments around the world.

We would like to thank all the contributing authors for lending their expertise to make the book truly unique. They have played a crucial role in the development of this book. Without their invaluable contributions this book wouldn't have been possible. They have made vital efforts to compile up to date information on the varied aspects of this subject to make this book a valuable addition to the collection of many professionals and students.

This book was conceptualized with the vision of imparting up-to-date information and advanced data in this field. To ensure the same, a matchless editorial board was set up. Every individual on the board went through rigorous rounds of assessment to prove their worth. After which they invested a large part of their time researching and compiling the most relevant data for our readers.

The editorial board has been involved in producing this book since its inception. They have spent rigorous hours researching and exploring the diverse topics which have resulted in the successful publishing of this book. They have passed on their knowledge of decades through this book. To expedite this challenging task, the publisher supported the team at every step. A small team of assistant editors was also appointed to further simplify the editing procedure and attain best results for the readers.

Apart from the editorial board, the designing team has also invested a significant amount of their time in understanding the subject and creating the most relevant covers. They scrutinized every image to scout for the most suitable representation of the subject and create an appropriate cover for the book.

The publishing team has been an ardent support to the editorial, designing and production team. Their endless efforts to recruit the best for this project, has resulted in the accomplishment of this book. They are a veteran in the field of academics and their pool of knowledge is as vast as their experience in printing. Their expertise and guidance has proved useful at every step. Their uncompromising quality standards have made this book an exceptional effort. Their encouragement from time to time has been an inspiration for everyone.

The publisher and the editorial board hope that this book will prove to be a valuable piece of knowledge for researchers, students, practitioners and scholars across the globe.

List of Contributors

Hawkar Ibrahim
Department of Psychology, Clinical Psychology and Psychotherapy, Bielefeld University, Bielefeld, Germany
Vivo international, Konstanz, Germany
Department of Clinical Psychology, Koya University, Koya, Kurdistan Region of Iraq, Iraq

Verena Ertl, Claudia Catani and Frank Neuner
Department of Psychology, Clinical Psychology and Psychotherapy, Bielefeld University, Bielefeld, Germany
Vivo international, Konstanz, Germany

Azad Ali Ismail
Department of Psychology, Clinical Psychology and Psychotherapy, Bielefeld University, Bielefeld, Germany
Department of Clinical Psychology, Koya University, Koya, Kurdistan Region of Iraq, Iraq

Rafael J. A. Cámara
Institute for Medical Biostatistics, Epidemiology and Informatics (IMBEI), University Medical Center of the Johannes Gutenberg University Mainz, Mainz, Germany

Josep Maria Haro
Parc Sanitari Sant Joan de Deu, Universitat de Barcelona, CIBERSAM, C/ Doctor Antoni Pujadas 42, 08830 Sant Boi de Llobregat, Barcelona, Spain

Delphine Saragoussi and Mélanie Brignone
Lundbeck SAS, 37-45 Quai du Président Roosevelt, 92445 Issy-les-Moulineaux, France

François-Xavier Lamy
Lundbeck SAS, 37-45 Quai du Président Roosevelt, 92445 Issy-les-Moulineaux, France
Merck KGaA, Darmstadt, Germany

Ylana Chalem
Lundbeck SAS, 37-45 Quai du Président Roosevelt, 92445 Issy-les-Moulineaux, France
Pierre Fabre SA, Boulogne, France

Benoît Rive
Lundbeck SAS, 37-45 Quai du Président Roosevelt, 92445 Issy-les-Moulineaux, France
Janssen, Issy-les-Moulineaux, France

Bengt Jönsson
Department of Economics, Stockholm School of Economics, Sveavägen 65, 113 83 Stockholm, Sweden

Martin Knapp
Personal Social Services Research Unit, Cowdray House, London School of Economics and Political Science, Houghton Street, London WC2A 2AE, UK

Hugo Caillou
Inferential, 35 rue Godot de Mauroy, 75009 Paris, France
Capionis, Bordeaux, France

Lene Hammer-Helmich
H. Lundbeck A/S, Ottiliavej 9, 2500 Valby, Denmark

Ruth Evers
Talmor, Andreas Bonnstraat 20hs, 1091AZ Amsterdam, The Netherlands

Lea M. Dijksman
Department of Research and Epidemiology, OLVG, 1090 HM Amsterdam, The Netherlands
Department of Research and Epidemiology, St. Antoniusziekenhuis, 3430EM Nieuwegein, The Netherlands

Bao-Long Wang
Clinical Laboratory, Affiliated Provincial Hospital of Anhui Medical University, 17 Lujiang Road, Hefei 230001, Anhui, China

Min-Min Xiao
Clinical Laboratory, Affiliated Provincial Hospital of Anhui Medical University, 17 Lujiang Road, Hefei 230001, Anhui, China
Clinical Laboratory, The Second People's Hospital of Wuhu City, Wuhu 241001, Anhui, China

Lan-Lan Jiang and Hui Shao
Clinical Laboratory, The Second People's Hospital of Wuhu City, Wuhu 241001, Anhui, China

Jiang-Bo Li
Department of Clinical Psychiatry, The Second People's Hospital of Wuhu City, Wuhu 241001, Anhui, China

Naser Morina, Ulrich Schnyder and Richard Klaghofer
Department of Consultation-Liaison-Psychiatry and Psychosomatic Medicine, University Hospital, University of Zurich, Culmannstrasse 8, 8091 Zurich, Switzerland

Julia Müller
Psychiatric Services Thurgau, 8596 Münsterlingen, Switzerland
Paracelsus Medical University, Salzburg, Austria

Chantal Martin-Soelch
Division of Clinical and Health Psychology, Department of Psychology, University of Fribourg, 1700 Fribourg, Switzerland

Shan Lv, Zan Wang and Hang Jin
Department of Neurology, The First Hospital of Jilin University, Xinmin Street 71#, Chang Chun 130021, China

Zhen-Ni Guo and Yi Yang
Department of Neurology, The First Hospital of Jilin University, Xinmin Street 71#, Chang Chun 130021, China
Clinical Trail and Research Center for Stroke, Department of Neurology, The First Hospital of Jilin University, Chang Chun, China

Xin Sun
Clinical Trail and Research Center for Stroke, Department of Neurology, The First Hospital of Jilin University, Chang Chun, China

Jia Liu and Quanli Qiu
Shenzhen Institutes of Advanced Technology, Chinese Academy of Sciences, Xueyuan Avenue, Shenzhen University Town, Shenzhen, China

Bailee L. Malivoire, Todd A. Girard and Candice M. Monson
Department of Psychology, Ryerson University, 350 Victoria St, Toronto, ON M5B 2K3, Canada

Ronak Patel
Department of Clinical Health Psychology, University of Manitoba, Winnipeg, MB, Canada

Aljohara A. Alhassan, Ethar M. Alqadhib and Nada W. Taha
College of Rehabilitation and Health Sciences, Princess Noura Bint Abdulrahman University, Riyadh, Saudi Arabia

Raneem A. Alahmari
King Abdullah International Medical Research Center, King Saud bin Abdulaziz University for Health Sciences, College of Applied Medical Sciences, Echography Cardiovascular Technology, Ministry of National Guard - Health Affairs, Riyadh, Saudi Arabia

Mahmoud Salam and Adel F. Almutairi
King Abdullah International Medical Research Center, King Saud bin Abdulaziz University for Health Sciences, Science and Technology Unit, Ministry of National Guard - Health Affairs, Riyadh 11426, Saudi Arabia

André Hajek and Hans-Helmut König
Department of Health Economics and Health Services Research, Hamburg Center for Health Economics, University Medical Center Hamburg-Eppendorf, Hamburg, Germany

François-André Allaert
Chair of health claim evaluation EMMAS BSB & CEN Nutriment, 29 rue Sambin, 21000 Dijon, France

Hervé Demais
Biovet Conseil, 1 Route du Linès, 56700 Merlevenez, France

Pi Nyvall Collén
Amadéite SAS Pôle biotechnologique du Haut du Bois, 56580 Bréhan, France

Fenglian Xu, Elizabeth Sullivan and Caroline S. E. Homer
Faculty of Health, University of Technology Sydney, Ultimo 2007, Australia

Lynette Roberts
Discipline of Clinical Psychology, Graduate School of Health, University of Technology Sydney, Ultimo 2007, Australia

Colin Binns
School of Public Health, Curtin University, Perth, Australia

Cristian Raquel Unzueta
Department of Nutrition, Food Science and Physiology, School of Pharmacy and Nutrition, University of Navarra, Pamplona, Navarra, Spain

Susana Santiago
Department of Nutrition, Food Science and Physiology, School of Pharmacy and Nutrition, University of Navarra, Pamplona, Navarra, Spain
Navarra Institute for Health Research (IdisNA), Pamplona, Navarra, Spain

Itziar Zazpe
Department of Nutrition, Food Science and Physiology, School of Pharmacy and Nutrition, University of Navarra, Pamplona, Navarra, Spain
Department of Preventive Medicine and Public Health, School of Medicine, University of Navarra, Pamplona, Navarra, Spain
Navarra Institute for Health Research (IdisNA), Pamplona, Navarra, Spain
Biomedical Research Center Network on Obesity and Nutrition (CIBERobn) Physiopathology of Obesity and Nutrition, Institute of Health Carlos III, Madrid, Spain

Miguel Ángel Martínez-González
Department of Preventive Medicine and Public Health, School of Medicine, University of Navarra, Pamplona, Navarra, Spain
Navarra Institute for Health Research (IdisNA), Pamplona, Navarra, Spain
Biomedical Research Center Network on Obesity and Nutrition (CIBERobn) Physiopathology of Obesity and Nutrition, Institute of Health Carlos III, Madrid, Spain
Department of Nutrition, Harvard School of Public Health, Boston, USA

Francisca Lahortiga-Ramos and Patricio Molero
Department of Psychiatry and Clinical Psychology, University Clinic of Navarra, Pamplona, Navarra, Spain
Navarra Institute for Health Research (IdisNA), Pamplona, Navarra, Spain

Almudena Sánchez-Villegas
Nutrition Research Group, Research Institute of Biomedical and Health Sciences, University of Las Palmas de Gran Canaria, Las Palmas de Gran Canaria, Spain
Biomedical Research Center Network on Obesity and Nutrition (CIBERobn) Physiopathology of Obesity and Nutrition, Institute of Health Carlos III, Madrid, Spain

Raymond Fitzpatrick
Nuffield Department of Population Health, University of Oxford, Old Road Campus, Oxford OX3 7LF, UK

Gracia Fellmeth
Nuffield Department of Population Health, University of Oxford, Old Road Campus, Oxford OX3 7LF, UK
Shoklo Malaria Research Unit, Mahidol-Oxford Tropical Medicine Research Unit, Faculty of Tropical Medicine, Mahidol University, Mae Sot, Tak Province 63110, Thailand

Suphak Nosten and May May Oo
Shoklo Malaria Research Unit, Mahidol-Oxford Tropical Medicine Research Unit, Faculty of Tropical Medicine, Mahidol University, Mae Sot, Tak Province 63110, Thailand

François Nosten and Rose McGready
Shoklo Malaria Research Unit, Mahidol-Oxford Tropical Medicine Research Unit, Faculty of Tropical Medicine, Mahidol University, Mae Sot, Tak Province 63110, Thailand
Centre for Tropical Medicine and Global Health, Nuffield Department of Medicine, University of Oxford Peter Medawar Building for Pathogen Research, South Parks Road, Oxford OX2, UK

Emma H. Plugge
Centre for Tropical Medicine and Global Health, Nuffield Department of Medicine, University of Oxford Peter Medawar Building for Pathogen Research, South Parks Road, Oxford OX2, UK

Mina Fazel
Department of Psychiatry, University of Oxford, Warneford Hospital, Warneford Lane, Oxford OX3 7JX, UK

Prakaykaew Charunwatthana
Faculty of Tropical Medicine, Mahidol University, 420/6 Ratchawithi Road, Ratchathewi, Bangkok 10400, Thailand

Getinet Ayano and Melat Solomon
Research and Training Department, Amanuel Mental Specialized Hospital, Addis Ababa, Ethiopia

Mebratu Abraha
Department of Psychiatry, Paulo's millennium medical college, Addis Ababa, Ethiopia

Rita Laufenberg-Feldmann, Bernd Kappis and Marion Ferner
Department of Anesthesiology, University Medical Center of the Johannes Gutenberg University Mainz, Langenbeckstrasse 1, D-55131 Mainz, Germany

Melanie A. M. Baas and Maria G. van Pampus
Department of Obstetrics and Gynecology, OLVG, 1090 HM Amsterdam, The Netherlands

Karel W. F. Scheepstra
Department of Obstetrics and Gynecology, OLVG, 1090 HM Amsterdam, The Netherlands
Department of Psychiatry, Academic Medical Center, 1100 DD Amsterdam, The Netherlands

Claire A. I. Stramrood
Department of Obstetrics and Gynecology, University Medical Center Utrecht, 3508GA Utrecht, The Netherlands

Dilys Lam
Cancer & Disease Epigenetics, Murdoch Children's Research Institute, Royal Children's Hospital, Parkville, VIC, Australia

Richard Saffery
Cancer & Disease Epigenetics, Murdoch Children's Research Institute, Royal Children's Hospital, Parkville, VIC, Australia
Department of Paediatrics, University of Melbourne, Parkville, VIC, Australia

Joanne Ryan
Cancer & Disease Epigenetics, Murdoch Children's Research Institute, Royal Children's Hospital, Parkville, VIC, Australia
Department of Paediatrics, University of Melbourne, Parkville, VIC, Australia
INSERM, Univ Montpellier, Neuropsychiatry: Epidemiological and Clinical Research, Montpellier, France
Department of Epidemiology and Preventive Medicine, Monash University, Level 5, The Alfred Centre, 99 Commercial Road, Melbourne 3004, Australia

Marie-Laure Ancelin
INSERM, Univ Montpellier, Neuropsychiatry: Epidemiological and Clinical Research, Montpellier, France

Karen Ritchie
INSERM, Univ Montpellier, Neuropsychiatry: Epidemiological and Clinical Research, Montpellier, France
Centre for Clinical Brain Sciences, University of Edinburgh, Edinburgh, UK

Rosanne Freak-Poli
Department of Epidemiology and Preventive Medicine, Monash University, Level 5, The Alfred Centre, 99 Commercial Road, Melbourne 3004, Australia

Saman Maroufizadeh, Mostafa Hosseini and Abbas Rahimi Foroushani
Department of Epidemiology and Biostatistics, School of Public Health, Tehran University of Medical Sciences, Tehran, Iran

Reza Omani-Samani and Payam Amini
Department of Epidemiology and Reproductive Health, Reproductive Epidemiology Research Center, Royan Institute for Reproductive Biomedicine, ACECR, Tehran, Iran

Masanori Nagamine and Kunio Shimizu
Division of Behavioral Science, National Defense Medical College Research Institute, 3-2 Namiki, Tokorozawa, Saitama 359-8513, Japan

Jun Shigemura, Masaaki Tanichi, Taku Saito, Hiroyuki Toda and Aihide Yoshino
Department of Psychiatry, School of Medicine, National Defense Medical College, 3-2 Namiki, Tokorozawa, Saitama, Japan

Toshimichi Fujiwara and Fumiko Waki
Japan Ground Self-Defense Force Medical School, 1-2-24, Ikejiri, Setagaya-ku, Tokyo, Japan

Josephine Akpalu and Ernest Yorke
Department of Medicine & Therapeutics, School of Medicine & Dentistry, University of Ghana, Accra, Ghana

Joana Ainuson-Quampah
Department of Dietetics, School of Biomedical and Allied Health Sciences, University of Ghana, Accra, Ghana

Williams Balogun
College of Medicine, University of Ibadan, Ibadan, Nigeria

Kwame Yeboah
Department of Physiology, School of Biomedical and Allied Health Sciences, University of Ghana, Accra, Ghana

Steve Kyende Mutiso, Alfred Murage and Abraham Mwaniki Mukaindo
Department of Obstetrics and Gynaecology, Aga Khan University hospital, Nairobi, Kenya

Kingsley E. Agho
Translational Health Research Institute, School of Medicine, Western Sydney University, Campbelltown Campus, Penrith, NSW 2571, Australia

Felix Akpojene Ogbo and Andrew Page
Translational Health Research Institute, School of Medicine, Western Sydney University, Campbelltown Campus, Penrith, NSW 2571, Australia
Ingham Institute for Applied Medical Research, University of New South Wales, 1 Campbell Street, Liverpool, NSW 2170, Australia

John Eastwood
Ingham Institute for Applied Medical Research, University of New South Wales, 1 Campbell Street, Liverpool, NSW 2170, Australia
School of Women's and Children's Health, University of New South Wales, Kensington, Sydney, NSW 2052, Australia
Menzies Centre for Health Policy, Charles Perkins Centre, School of Public Health, Sydney University, Sydney, NSW 2006, Australia
School of Public Health, Griffith University, Gold Coast, QLD 4222, Australia
Department of Community Paediatrics, Sydney Local Health District, Croydon Community Health Centre, 24 Liverpool Rd, Croydon, NSW 2132, Australia

Alexandra Hendry
Ingham Institute for Applied Medical Research, University of New South Wales, 1 Campbell Street, Liverpool, NSW 2170, Australia
National Centre for Immunisation Research and Surveillance, The Children's Hospital at Westmead, Westmead, NSW 2145, Australia

Bin Jalaludin
Ingham Institute for Applied Medical Research, University of New South Wales, 1 Campbell Street, Liverpool, NSW 2170, Australia
Healthy People and Places Unit, South Western Sydney Local Health District, Liverpool, NSW, Australia

Bryanne Barnett
St John of God Health Care, Blacktown, NSW, Australia

Hanna E. Schwendemann and Eva Maria Bitzer
Pädagogische Hochschule Freiburg/University of Education, Kunzenweg 21, 79117 Freiburg, Germany

Heidi Kuttler
Cooptima, Talweg 44, 79540 Lörrach, Germany

Thomas Mößle
State Police College Baden-Württemberg, Sturmbühlstraße 250, 78054 Villingen-Schwenningen, Germany

Adam Cooper
Deployment Health Research Department, Naval Health Research Center, 140 Sylvester Road, San Diego, CA 92106-3521, USA

Richard F. Armenta and Cynthia A. LeardMann
Deployment Health Research Department, Naval Health Research Center, 140 Sylvester Road, San Diego, CA 92106-3521, USA
The Henry M. Jackson Foundation for the Advancement of Military Medicine, Inc, Bethesda, MD, USA

Toni Rush
Department of Family Medicine and Public Health, La Jolla, University of California, San Diego, School of Medicine, San Diego, CA, USA

Jeffrey Millegan
Directorate of Mental Health, Naval Medical Center San Diego, San Diego, CA, USA

Charles W. Hoge
Walter Reed Army Institute of Research, Silver Spring, MD, USA

Wenpeng Cai, Yi Cui, Jin Yan, Wei Dong and Guanghui Deng
Faculty of Psychology and Mental Health, Second Military Medical University, Xiangyin Road 800, Shanghai 200433, China

Yu Pan
Department of Medical Psychology, General Hospital of PLA, Beijing 100853, China

Huangyangzi Chai
Department of Engineering and Information, Nanjing City Vocational College, Nanjing 210038, China

Index

www.ingramcontent.com/pod-product-compliance
Lightning Source LLC
LaVergne TN
LVHW080709210926
848485LV00003B/438